Frommer's®

Poland

2nd Edition

by Mark Baker &
Kit F. Chung

John Wiley & Sons Canada, Ltd.

Published by:
JOHN WILEY & SONS CANADA, LTD.
6045 Freemont Blvd.
Mississauga, ON L5R 4J3

ISBN 978-0-470-68160-2 (paper); 978-0-470-96425-5 (eMobi); 978-0-470-96424-8 (ePDF)

Editor: Gene Shannon
Developmental Editor: Melissa Klurman
Production Editor: Pauline Ricablanca
Editorial Assistant: Katie Wolsley
Cartographer: Lohnes+Wright
Production by Wiley Indianapolis Composition Services
Front cover photo: Morskie Oko lake, Tatra Mountains © Jan Wlodarczyk / Alamy Images
Back cover photo: The Old Square in Poznan © Jan Wlodarczyk / Alamy Images

For information on our other products and services or to obtain technical support, please contact our Customer Care Department within the U.S. at 877/762-2974, outside the U.S. at 317/572-3993 or fax 317/572-4002.

Wiley also publishes its books in a variety of electronic formats. Some content that appears in print may not be available in electronic formats.

Manufactured in the United States of America

1 2 3 4 5 RRD 15 14 13 12 11

CONTENTS

5 WARSAW 64

6 ŁÓDŹ & SOUTH-CENTRAL POLAND 99

7 KRAKÓW, ZAKOPANE & THE TATRA MOUNTAINS 120

8 LUBLIN & SOUTHEASTERN POLAND 167

9 WROCŁAW & LOWER SILESIA 189

10 CENTRAL & NORTHWEST POLAND 212

11 GDAŃSK & THE BALTIC COAST 234

12 NORTHEAST POLAND 268

APPENDIX A: FAST FACTS & USEFUL WEBSITES 291

APPENDIX B: USEFUL TERMS & PHRASES 297

Index 303

LIST OF MAPS

HOW TO CONTACT US

In researching this book, we discovered many wonderful places—hotels, restaurants, shops, and more. We're sure you'll find others. Please tell us about them, so we can share the information with your fellow travelers in upcoming editions. If you were disappointed with a recommendation, we'd love to know that, too. Please write to:

Frommer's Poland, 2nd Edition
John Wiley & Sons Canada, Ltd. • 6045 Freemont Blvd. • Mississauga, ON L5R 4J3

AN ADDITIONAL NOTE

Please be advised that travel information is subject to change at any time—and this is especially true of prices. We therefore suggest that you write or call ahead for confirmation when making your travel plans. The authors, editors, and publisher cannot be held responsible for the experiences of readers while traveling. Your safety is important to us, however, so we encourage you to stay alert and be aware of your surroundings. Keep a close eye on cameras, purses, and wallets, all favorite targets of thieves and pickpockets.

ABOUT THE AUTHORS

Journalist, photographer, and freelance writer **Mark Baker** has had a deep interest in Central Europe since receiving a degree in International Affairs at Columbia University in the 1980s. He currently lives in Prague, Czech Republic, but is a frequent visitor to, and a big fan of, Poland. In addition to writing guide books, he is a contributor to *The Wall Street Journal Europe* and *National Geographic Traveler,* among other publications.

Kit F. Chung is a Malaysian-born freelance writer who has been based in Warsaw since 2001. Poland is her first encounter with a former "Iron Curtain" country. Decoding her adopted home has been made fun and easy by Poles who tolerate her incessant inquisitive questions on anything and everything Polish. Kit contributes regularly to local and international publications on all things Polish, covering food and travel (naturally) as well as people, culture, art and designs.

FROMMER'S STAR RATINGS, ICONS & ABBREVIATIONS

Every hotel, restaurant, and attraction listing in this guide has been ranked for quality, value, service, amenities, and special features using a **star-rating system.** In country, state, and regional guides, we also rate towns and regions to help you narrow down your choices and budget your time accordingly. Hotels and restaurants are rated on a scale of zero (recommended) to three stars (exceptional). Attractions, shopping, nightlife, towns, and regions are rated according to the following scale: zero stars (recommended), one star (highly recommended), two stars (very highly recommended), and three stars (must-see).

In addition to the star-rating system, we also use **four feature icons** that point you to the great deals, in-the-know advice, and unique experiences that separate travelers from tourists. Throughout the book, look for:

special finds—those places only insiders know about

fun facts—details that make travelers more informed and their trips more fun

kids—best bets for kids and advice for the whole family

special moments—those experiences that memories are made of

The following **abbreviations** are used for credit cards:

AE	American Express	**DISC**	Discover	**V**	Visa
DC	Diners Club	**MC**	MasterCard		

TRAVEL RESOURCES AT FROMMERS.COM

Frommer's travel resources don't end with this guide. Frommer's website, **www.frommers.com**, has travel information on more than 4,000 destinations. We update features regularly, giving you access to the most current trip-planning information and the best airfare, lodging, and car-rental bargains. You can also listen to podcasts, connect with other Frommers.com members through our active-reader forums, share your travel photos, read blogs from guidebook editors and fellow travelers, and much more.

THE BEST OF POLAND

1

Nowhere in Europe does history feel as alive and contemporary as it does in Poland, a country that's a virtual living history museum. Whether, like me, you're a budding World War II buff with a healthy dose of curiosity about the Communist period or your interests stretch further back in time to the duchies and kingdoms of the Middle Ages, there's riveting history here for every interest. It's an inspiring destination, as well. Cities such as Warsaw, Gdańsk, and Wrocław were flattened in World War II; now, they've been restored to their former beauty and are brimming with culture and energy. The country's medieval capital, Kraków, is easily Prague's equal for architectural splendor, and maybe a notch above when it comes to concerts, museums, and Jewish heritage (just don't tell the Czechs).

There's also an undeniable "off the beaten track" appeal to Poland. Poles have long known about their country's treasures, but for the rest of us, the country is still largely *terra incognita*. That's changing slowly, but for the time being, that means the lines into the attractions are a bit less crushing and the welcomes here that much more genuine than you might find in better-known destinations.

THE best TRAVEL EXPERIENCES

- **Sip Your Coffee on Kraków's Main Square:** Superlatives don't do justice to Kraków's main square, the Rynek Główny. It's said to be Central Europe's largest town square and is reputed to have the most bars and cafes per square meter than any other place in the world. Even if that's not the case, it's still one of the most jaw-droppingly beautiful public spaces you'll find in Poland and the perfect spot to enjoy a cup of coffee or a glass of beer, and watch the world go by. Don't forget to listen for the bugler on top of St. Mary's Church at the top of the hour. See p. 126.
- **Reflect on History at the Auschwitz-Birkenau Concentration Camp** (Oświęcim): The word "best" is clearly a misnomer here, yet a visit to the Nazi wartime extermination camp that came to define the Holocaust is one of the most deeply affecting and moving experiences you will have anywhere. Give yourself several hours to take in both camps

(just a couple of miles apart). Auschwitz is undeniably horrible, but it is at Birkenau where you really grasp the scale of the tragedy. See p. 152.

- **Shop for Souvenirs along Gdańsk's Długa Street:** As you stroll Gdańsk's main pedestrian thoroughfare, it's hard to believe this stunning port city was reduced to rubble in World War II, so historically sensitive was the reconstruction. Amberphiles will think they died and went to heaven. It's not surprising when you consider that the Baltic Sea (where amber comes from) is just a block away. Still, the quality and choice is overwhelming. There's even an amber museum if the shops don't have what you're looking for. See p. 249.
- **Look for Bison in Białowieża** (Białowieża National Park): Better put this under your "Most Unexpected Travel Experiences." Who would have imagined that part of Poland's eastern border with Belarus is primeval forest that's home to Europe's largest surviving bison herd? Both children and adults alike will enjoy touring the pristine national park. See p. 289.
- **Visit a Wooden "Peace" Church** (Jawor and Świdnica): Few visitors to Poland have heard of these two massive 17th-century wooden Protestant churches in southwest Poland. Congregations had to build the churches from wood because of strictures on Protestant worship at the time by the Catholic Habsburg rulers. The churches' size, grace, and stunning beauty all testify to the builders' faith and their remarkable engineering skills. See p. 201.
- **See the Miraculous Icon of the "Black Madonna"** (Częstochowa): The first Pauline monks started coming to the Jasna Góra Monastery in the 14th century. Over the years, it evolved into Catholic Poland's most important pilgrimage destination and place of worship, drawing millions of Poles and other people from around the world every year. Authorship of the miraculous Black Madonna icon is traditionally attributed to Luke, and the painting is said to have made its way here through the centuries from the Holy Lands, to Constantinople (now Istanbul), to the Ukrainian city of Belz, and finally to Częstochowa in 1382. The monastery allows the painting to be viewed for only a few hours each day, and getting a glimpse of it among the throngs is not unlike trying to see the *Mona Lisa* at the Louvre. Still, it's worth the effort. See p. 109.
- **Take in Some Socialist Realist Architecture** (Warsaw, Kraków, and Katowice): Poles loathe it, but the architecture built during the Communist period is worth seeking out, if only for its downright wackiness. Some of the "finest" buildings include Warsaw's Palace of Culture and the housing development of Pl. Konstytucja, the Nowa Huta housing project near Kraków, and the "Spodek" in Katowice.

THE best HOTEL SPLURGES

- **Podewils** (Gdańsk): Boutique hotels with genuine Old World flair, run by a crew with Jeeves' touch for pampering guests, are few and far between in Poland. Podewils is one of these rarities. You'll feel like the personal guest of an aristocratic pal. See p. 245.
- **Hotel Carska** (Białowieża National Park): A hotel fit for a tsar—in this case, Russia's Tsar Nicholas II. A must for fans of unusual hotel design, this hotel/restaurant occupies a refurbished railway station that was built to welcome the tsar and his family in the 19th century. The waiting room has been converted into an upscale restaurant, but you may not want to ever leave your room. See p. 289.

- **Palac Bonerowski** (Kraków): One of Kraków's most recent entries in the five-star category is a stunner: a sensitively restored 13th-century town house just off the main square. Many period elements, including original stonework and carvings, have been preserved in the spacious rooms. See p. 140.
- **Jaczno Lodge** (Suwałki Landscape Park): This lovely cluster of stone-and-timber houses is hemmed in by woods and the pristine water of Lake Jaczno. The owners are architects who have meticulously designed every space, from the luxurious rooms to the rose bushes and fruit trees in the garden. See p. 280.
- **Hotel Monopol** (Wrocław): The hotel where Marlene Dietrich once stayed has undergone a thorough renovation. Purists might lament the loss of the old Art Nouveau interiors, but the sleek ultra-modern rooms will certainly appeal to lovers of cutting-edge contemporary design. This is the only hotel we've seen with its own in-house high-end wine-and-cheese shop. See p. 195.
- **Pałac Paulinum** (Jelenia Góra): This elegant 19th-century *palais* was originally the home of a Silesian textile baron; now, it's a stunningly renovated luxury hotel but, thankfully, still without the ultra-luxury price tag. See p. 207.
- **Lalala Arthotel** (Sopot): Several imaginative and eccentric rooms designed by photographers and artists are on offer here. The owners have a deft touch for making you feel right at home. See p. 254.
- **Andel's** (Łódź): Trendy, gleaming high-end luxury hotel carved out of one of the city's abandoned textile mills. This is a must visit for fans of *Dwell* and *Wallpaper* magazines to see what can be done with a warehouse made of blackened mortar and with loads and loads of vision (and cash). See p. 105.

THE best HOTEL BARGAINS

- **Hotel Karmel** (Kraków): This lovely family-run inn, tucked away on a quiet street in the former Jewish quarter of Kazimierz, is a total surprise. From the warm and smiling receptionist at the front desk to the parquet flooring and the crisp linens on the beds, everything about this place says quality. See p. 142.
- **Premiere Classe** (Warsaw): This French-run chain came up with the novel idea of offering clean, modern rooms the size of a cubicle for a fraction of the price of other hotels. Sure, the rooms are microscopic, but the beds are big and comfortable, the bathrooms are clean, and the hotel location is just a couple of tram stops from the main sights. See p. 75.
- **Castle Inn** (Warsaw): A restored 16th-century inn that's clean, priced to please, and has a wacky, theatrical side, to boot. The effects are created by bold colors and an eclectic blend of antique and modern furnishings. See p. 73.
- **Pensjonat Szarotka** (Zakopane): This quirky 1930s mountain chalet is the perfect place to try to tap into Zakopane's funky, artistic past. The squeaky stairways, the cozy little reading room with a fireplace, and the evocative black-and-white photos on the wall will remind you of your grandmother's house. See p. 160.
- **U Pana Cogito** (Kraków): One of the best hotel bargains in Kraków is a remodeled former rectory about 15 minutes by foot from the city center. The modern rooms don't have loads of personality, but they are spotlessly clean and quiet. See p. 143.
- **Wenecki** (Częstochowa): A bargain hotel offering inviting, even beautiful, rooms with hardwood floors and big comfortable beds. The reception is welcoming, and the overall effect is actually much nicer and more comfortable than the most expensive hotels in town. See p. 111.

- **Angelo** (Katowice): Plan to arrive on the weekend to slip in under 100€ a night for a posh and arty room that would cost at least twice that anywhere else. Everything is brand new, from the splashy interiors to the big flat-screen TVs. See p. 115.
- **Liburnia** (Cieszyn): A cross between a business hotel and a boutique at prices you'd expect to pay at a pension. The mattresses are thick and comfortable, and the cotton-thread count in the sheets is well above the average at this price point. The in-house Italian restaurant is one of the best places in town to eat. See p. 119.
- **Hotel Savoy** (Łódź): A likeably rundown, turn-of-the-20th-century hotel that feels perfectly in sync with Łódź's "seen better days" aesthetic. Don't expect a charming boutique; this is a pure time-warp property (the kind of hotel that might appear in a noir detective novel). If you've got a bit more to spend, try the tonier **Grand Hotel** around the corner—all of the Old World charm, but without the creaky floors and antiquated plumbing. See p. 106.
- **Tourist Information Office** (Tarnów): The Tarnów city tourist information office rents out the rooms above the office at some of the cheapest rates you'll find in the whole country. See p. 163.
- **Pensjonat Sioło Budy** (Białowieża National Park): This is homestead living for those wanting a taste of rural life without forsaking clean toilets, hot showers, and espresso. The owners, folk-history enthusiasts, have fashioned four traditional chalets around a garden of apple trees, flowers, ferns, and fluttering butterflies. See p. 290.
- **Oberża Pod Psem** (Mazury): Get a taste of Mazurian village life at this charming cottage. The owners are conservationists and champions of folk culture who salvaged the century-old wooden buildings here to open up a restaurant, a folk museum, and an inn. See p. 276.
- **Kamienica Gotyk** (Gdańsk): Ordinarily, you'd expect to part with a fortune to enjoy the hotel's setting in Gdańsk's oldest house and on its loveliest street. Breakfast on the petite patio in the shadows of St. Mary's Church adds to the sense of history. Book well in advance. See p. 246.
- **Vincent Pensjonat** (Kazimierz Dolny): An enchanting, family-run pension, situated about 5 minutes from the center of town. See p. 188.

THE best LOCAL DINING

- **Piwnica Świdnicka** (Wrocław): At first glance, this pub looks like a classic tourist trap; but it's actually an excellent traditional Polish restaurant serving big plates of classic dishes. See p. 198.
- **U Kucharzy** (Warsaw): It's perhaps an ironic comment on Polish cooking that one of the capital's best restaurants—it received a Michelin "Bib Gourmand"—is actually in a hotel kitchen. If you're a kitchen voyeur, book a table in front of the mega-burners to watch the chefs prepare Polish mainstays up close and personal. See p. 77.
- **Alfredo** (Szklarska Poręba): Proof that in Poland you can never judge a restaurant by its cover. If so, you'd never dream of stopping at this tiny mom-and-pop, and you'd end up missing some excellent home-style Polish cooking. See p. 208.
- **Pawłowicz** (Warsaw): A take-out-only, hole-in-the-wall operation that draws a constant flow of customers looking for the city's best doughnuts (*pączki*) and pastries at bargain prices. You'll find branches in Sopot and Wrocław. See p. 79.

- **Bolków Hotel Restaurant** (Bolków/Jawor): The restaurant at the tiny Bolków Hotel specializes in home cooking done well, including big plates of roasted meats served with mounds of mashed potatoes. The desserts are homemade, and the throwback atmosphere to the 1920s is fun and inviting. See p. 203.
- **Ciągoty i Tęsknoty** (Łódź): Perched between two ghastly apartment blocks, this small, unassuming restaurant is an oasis of '50s jazz and fresh flowers. The menu is perched somewhere between home cooking and haute cuisine, with salads, pierogi, and pasta dishes, and some seriously good entrees. Take a taxi to get there or risk never finding it. See p. 107.
- **Wierzynek** (Kraków): This esteemed eatery has played host to visiting dignitaries, celebs, and heads of state since way back in 1364. The cuisine is an imaginative take on traditional Polish cooking, with an emphasis on local treats such as wild boar, quail, and venison. See p. 144.
- **Dawno Temu Na Kazimierzu (Once Upon a Time in Kazimierz)** (Kraków-Kazimierz): Finally, a Jewish-themed restaurant in Kazimierz that doesn't feel like a kitschy tourist trap. The interior is relaxed and intimate, and the food is great. See p. 146.
- **La Rotisserie** (Warsaw): For those in the know, this is one of the capital's most inviting splurge options. It helps to be a foodie to know some of the terms on the menu, but everything is great, so just point to an item and relax. For great value, try the five-course Sunday "linner" (a word play on "lunch" and "dinner"). See p. 76.
- **Hacjenda** (Poznań): This is rumored to be the best place in Poland to try *czernina,* a soup made from duck's blood and bits of offal. They also do a good roast duck, if blood soup isn't on your list of must-tries. See p. 222.
- **Jurta** (Kruszyniany): A breath away from the Belarusian border, you can dig into hearty Tatar cuisine made by descendents of the original Mongol invaders. Try the donuts; they'd outmatch Krispy Kreme's any day of the week. See p. 285.
- **Kawiarnia Naleśnikarnia** (Jelenia Góra): What a surprise to find this excellent *creperie*—with fantastic concoctions of chocolate, nuts, and whipped cream—right on Jelenia Góra's handsome town square. See p. 208.
- **Fantasmagoria** (Katowice): Easily the best restaurant in town, and possibly all of this part of Poland. Excellent and inventive home-style cooking that takes equal inspiration from Ukrainian and eastern Polish classics, mixed with more modern notions of using local ingredients and a fresh presentation. See p. 116.
- **Ogródek Pod Jabłoniami** (Augustów): A casual, family-friendly restaurant set alongside the Augustów canal in an apple orchard. You won't find any airs or themes here, just owners Paweł and Sylwia, who want you to leave with good culinary memories of the local fish and traditional soup and meat dishes. See p. 281.
- **Knajpa U Fryzjera** (Kazimierz Dolny): Wacky Jewish-themed tavern restaurant with hearty dishes featuring roast meats and stews. The atmosphere is festive, with lots of alcohol to accompany the excellent cooking. In nice weather, grab a table out back and drink long into the night. See p. 188.
- **Maszoperia** (Hel Peninsula): A simple fish restaurant where all they need for you to have an "I've never had fish this good!" experience is a frying pan and a little butter to fry the fish in. The setting is nothing more than a high-end fish shack stuffed with fishermen's tools. See p. 258.

- **Muzealna** (Zamość): Handsome and memorable restaurant set in three brick Renaissance cellars that look like they've just stepped out of the 16th century. The traditional Polish cooking is superb. See p. 184.

THE best PLACES TO GET PIEROGI

- **Leniwa** (Toruń): Leniwa means "lazy," but the genial folks here are anything but in making some of the best pierogi in the country. The various types of sweet and savory dumplings come with bargain-basement prices. It's popular with locals, so be prepared to wait. See p. 232.
- **Pierogarnia na Bednarskiej** (Warsaw): Not far from the Royal Castle, a lovely cobblestone lane leads to this vaulted-ceilinged chamber. The menu has all the usual suspects and a bunch of hard-to-find varieties. See p. 79.
- **Pierogarnia U Dzika** (Gdańsk): Pierogi used to be widely dismissed as dowdy peasant food, but no longer. At this is upscale *pierogarnia*—literally, pierogi restaurant—they're all the rage. The menu includes the usual fillings, plus a few inventive variants such as Pierogi "Wileński," stuffed with a delicious buckwheat and bacon combo. See p. 248.
- **Pierożki U Vincenta** (Kraków): This tiny and inviting pierogi joint in Kazimierz serves every style of pierogi imaginable. The house special, "Vincent," is stuffed with minced meat and spicy lentils, and served with fried onions and bits of bacon. Other concoctions include Moroccan-inspired couscous pierogi and "Górale" (highlander) pierogi stuffed with sheep's cheese. See p. 147.
- **Domowy Przysmaki** (Kraków): An informal lunch counter, with excellent pierogi (try the fruit-filled varieties). It's just a few minutes' walk from the main square and has the best-value lunch for miles around. See p. 147.

THE best SOUVENIRS

- **Amber** (Gdańsk): What is it about this ossified pine-tar resin that's so mesmerizing? Gdańsk grew wealthy over the centuries on the amber trade, and the demand today is as strong as ever. Gdańsk, on the Baltic (the source of amber), is the traditional home of the stuff, but you'll find amber at shops all around the country. Just be careful to buy the genuine article—fakes abound. See p. 249.
- **Salt from the Wieliczka Salt Mine** (Kraków): This might be the most famous salt mine in the world. For years, salt was to Kraków as amber was to Gdańsk: the goose that laid golden eggs, and kept laying and laying. Salt is not nearly so important for Kraków these days, but the resplendent Wieliczka Salt Mine is a reminder of how valuable a commodity salt once was. See p. 149.
- **Bison Grass from Białowieża** (Białowieża National Park): This is an especially long, fragrant grass that grows near the Białowieża National Forest. Despite the name, the bison don't actually graze on it. You'll find a blade of bison grass in every bottle of Żubrówka Vodka, which might be the most practical way to buy (or consume) it. You can even make your own "bison grass" vodka by referring to the instructions on the package the grass is sold in. See p. 286.

- **Household Items from the Communist Era** (Warsaw and Poznań): Poles tend to shun the retro tea services, ashtrays, and glassware of the Soviet period; however, that doesn't mean they don't have real kitsch value. Skip the upscale antique shops and try looking at flea markets such as Koło in Warsaw and the Antique Market at Stara Rzeźnia in Poznań. See p. 93 and 218.
- **Gingerbread** (Toruń): Toruń is the country's gingerbread capital, and Toruń gingerbread is sold all around the country. The gingerbread comes in all shapes and sizes, and usually is sold well wrapped for the long trip home. See p. 230.
- **Smoked Sheep's Cheese** (Giant Mountains/Zakopane): The closer you get to the mountains, the more likely you are to see mountain people lined up along the road to sell their little rounds of smoked sheep's cheese called *oscypek.* It's considered a delicacy, and the recipe goes back some 500 years. Buy several different types to see which ones you like best. The salty cheese goes especially well with beer. See p. 162.
- **Vodka:** Poland is known for the high quality of its vodka. Among the most popular brands, Belvedere and Chopin are considered the best. In addition, you'll find a range of unusual vodkas, including Żubrówka, slightly greenish due to a long blade of bison grass in every bottle, and Miodówka, honey-flavored and easy to drink in large quantities. See p. 28.

THE best COMMUNIST-ERA EXPERIENCES

- **Visit the Palace of Culture and Science** (Warsaw): Warsaw's landmark Socialist-Realist palace is the granddaddy of all Communist architectural icons. Universally loathed, yet at the same time thoroughly riveting, you won't be able to take your eyes off it. Tour the museums inside or take an elevator ride to the top to look out over Warsaw. Part of the fun are the ever-present guards, ready to bark *nie dotykać* (do not touch!) the moment you get close to any of the exhibits. See p. 84.
- **Check in at the Jantar Hotel** (Hel Peninsula): Back in the day, job perks often came in the form of time off at resorts like this one, set up by the government for their very best employees. Hotel Jantar was originally conceived for military personnel out for a bit of R&R, but now it's open to civilians, as well. Happily, the original decor and "spirit" remain intact. Definitely a close-up of "the way we were." See p. 258.
- **Eat at a Milk Bar:** Every visitor to Poland eventually has to have his or her "milk bar" experience. A milk bar—the milk refers to the fact that no alcohol is served—has no direct American or Western European equivalent. "Cafeteria" sounds too sterile, and "greasy spoon," well, too greasy. But that's the idea, at any rate: heaping steam tables of mostly meatless Polish specialties that you line up for and then point to. Not bad tasting and can be a good value, but bring your phrase book since milk-bar staff tend to speak Polish and only Polish.
- **See a Concert at the Spodek** (Katowice): Katowice's retro-futuristic "Flying Saucer" building may be the coolest rock concert venue ever built. It's the city's best representative of the "Brussels Expo '58" style of design inspired by 1950s-era science and science fiction that influenced so many architects behind the Iron Curtain at the time. Performers like Robbie Williams, Pearl Jam, and Sir Elton John have played here. See p. 114.

THE best WAYS TO ACT LIKE A LOCAL

- **Drink Beer from a Straw:** This inexplicable practice is especially popular among women, but occasionally you'll see Polish guys doing it, as well. The idea is to sweeten the beer first with fruit juice, usually raspberry, and then sip the mixture like a cocktail. Watch out for the consequences, though. Polish beer is unusually strong, and drinking through a straw only heightens the effect of the alcohol.
- **Line up for Ice Cream:** Poles are loony for *lody* (ice cream). Part of the attraction comes from Communist days, when ice cream was one of the few pleasures accessible to most people. Part of the attraction is also, well, because it's ice cream and it tastes really good. Each city has its own ice cream stand of choice. The best strategy is to scout around and see where the longest lines are.
- **Eat Sushi:** That doesn't sound Polish at all, yet the country is currently experiencing sushi mania, and some seriously good sushi joints are springing up all over. The Poles' love affair with fish is understandable. After all, Poland is right on the Baltic Sea, and dishes such as herring have been part of the local cuisine for centuries. For some of the best sushi in the country, try the Sakana Sushi Bar in Wrocław or Edo Sushi Bar in Kazimierz. See p. 197 and p. 144.
- **Feed Breadcrumbs to the Pigeons:** You'll see the young and old alike at nearly every big square in every Polish town tossing breadcrumbs to flocks of pigeons. And they are the bane of city officials around the country trying to fight the onslaught of unwanted fowl. The problem is so serious that officials in Kraków even considered dynamiting the birds. But as the old saying goes—if you can't beat them, might as well join them.
- **Go Mushroom-Picking:** Mushroom-picking is a popular autumn pastime for all Poles. The best strategy for success is to get up early to scour the forest floors for the fungus of choice, usually chanterelle, porcini, and milk caps. One caveat: Don't try this if you're not experienced at sorting out the edible from the poisonous varieties. If you're staying in the countryside, simply ask your host to arrange a mushroom hunt for you. Most likely, they will have an aunt or cousin who knows the best place to land a bagful of mushrooms for your morning omelet.
- **Go Shopping at a Farmer's Market:** Most Polish cities will have a central market filled with goodies such as fresh fruits and vegetables, cheeses, breads, and meats. Often, these will also have a little pierogi stand for a quick bite. They're the perfect one-stop shop for a picnic lunch. Check out the Hala Mirowska in Warsaw or the Hala Targowa in Wrocław. See p. 93 and p. 249.
- **Have a Kebab:** In recent years, Poles have developed an insatiable appetite for anything vaguely Middle Eastern. Truth be told, the quality of the street-stand kebabs is only average at best, but the mood is always festive, and you get to rub shoulders with all walks of Polish life—students, business folks, the homeless, and late-night clubbers. In Kraków, you'll get the same local feeling by indulging in a *zapiekanka,* a toasted baguette slathered with cheese, ham, and ketchup, and baked in a hot oven. Find the best of these is at Plac Nowy in Kazimierz. See p. 132.

THE best DIAMONDS IN THE ROUGH

- **Łódź:** On the outside, Poland's second-largest city (pronounced "Woodge") appears cold and gray, a former industrial powerhouse that has gone through some tough times and looks it. But the more you find out about the place, the more fascinating it gets: the center of Poland's film industry, an enormous prewar Jewish population, the biggest shopping mall in Europe, an active culture calendar, and a great art museum. The list goes on. See p. 100.
- **Kazimierz** (Kraków): Next to Kraków's glamorous Old Town, Kazimierz, the city's former Jewish ghetto, looks positively derelict. And that appears to be its secret charm. What else could explain Kazimierz's increasing popularity among Kraków's ultra-cool and arty set? After admiring the handsome buildings of the Old Town, come out here to party and let your hair down—and see what really makes Kraków tick. See p. 132.
- **Tarnów:** The small city of Tarnów, east of Kraków, came late to the tourism party but is making up for lost time with the friendliest tourist information office in the country, as well as some decent museums and the occasional blockbuster exhibition. If Kraków's crowded streets get a little too much to bear, head to Tarnów for a respite before it too becomes too popular for its own good. One nice surprise is a Western-style horse-riding ranch in the vicinity that's happy to set up greenhorns for the day. See p. 162.
- **Katowice:** Cool in the way that Cleveland is cool or, in the U.K., maybe the way Glasgow or Manchester is cool. This big industrial city's charms are hard to pin down, but there is definitely something there. Maybe it's the retro-futuristic flying-saucer building—the Spodek—or all of the other Communist-era architecture around. Or the fact that it feels authentic, and there are absolutely no other tourists around. The wags at the local office of *Katowice, In Your Pocket* have tried to carve out a kind of anti-cool image for the city, calling it a needed antidote to overly prettified and touristed Kraków. See p. 112.
- **Nowa Huta** (Kraków): It's hard to make a Socialist-era housing project next to a steel mill sound like something you might want to see on your vacation. But this planned 1950s community is undeniably chic. Architecture and urban planning buffs will be drawn to the plans and designs of housing designed especially for the workers' state. Irony of ironies, they even named the main square after union-busting, anti-Communist U.S. President Ronald Reagan. See p. 135.
- **Praga District** (Warsaw): Not too many years ago, Warsaw's rough-and-tumble Praga district, on the other side of the Vistula River from the heart of the city, used to be a no-go zone. The low rents, though, attracted the artistic crowd, and now it's emerging into the capital's coolest neighborhood. Don't expect anything quite like Kazimierz in Kraków yet, but several good restaurants and clubs are up and running, and the future promises to bring more. See p. 89.

THE best OUTDOOR ACTIVITIES

- **Hiking in the Tatras** (Zakopane): Zakopane is the jumping-off point for hundreds of miles of gorgeous hiking trails. You can try one of the 2,000m (6,562-ft.) assaults on the peaks or a more leisurely stroll along breathtaking valleys carved out by tiny mountain streams. For more ambitious climbers, plan a whole-day outing to cross the peaks into Slovakia in summer. See p. 157.
- **Biking in the Giant Mountains** (Szklarska Poręba): Szklarska Poręba has evolved into the mountain-biking capital of southern Poland. More than a dozen trails, catering to all skill levels, fan out from the town in every direction. Some of the trails are all-day affairs, while others are shorter and oriented more toward recreational cyclists or families with children. Pick up a free cycling map from the tourist information office. See p. 206.
- **Rafting the Dunajec River** (near Zakopane): The Dunajec River marks the country's southeastern border with Slovakia. It winds through a picturesque gorge in the Pieniny Mountains east of the Tatras that makes it absolutely perfect for rafting. The season runs from April through October, and on a sunny afternoon, this can be a fabulous day out, especially for kids. It's less whitewater rafting and more of a slow, gentle float down the river on group rafts manned by Górale mountain men kitted out in their traditional folk garb. The boating center on the Polish side is at Sromowce Kąty, not far from Zakopane. See p. 158.
- **Kayaking in Northeastern Poland** (Mazury and Augustów): Rivers and canals crisscross the lake districts of northeastern Poland, allowing you to drift from marshland to woodland, with plenty of bird-watching in between. You can paddle for 1 day or 7; there are plenty of routes—rated from kid-friendly to daredevil—to choose from. See p. 274 and p. 277.
- **Downhill Skiing** (Giant Mountains and Tatras): Poland is not the first country that comes to mind when you think of skiing in Europe. But in the south of the country, in the mountainous areas near the Czech Republic and Slovakia, there are several excellent ski resorts and some very good downhill runs. The country's longest ski run is at Szklarska Poręba in the Giant Mountains. The most popular resort is Zakopane in the Tatras. Both have good infrastructures with lifts and ski rentals. See p. 206 and p. 158.
- **Swimming in the Baltic** (Hel Peninsula and Łeba): A beach holiday in Poland? It doesn't seem possible, yet thousands of people flock to the resorts around Sopot in the summer to dip their toes (quite literally, given the temperature of the water) in the Baltic Sea. There are miles of sandy beaches, and the water is clean and refreshing. Pity that the surf temp rarely rises to above tolerable, but that's really part of the charm. See p. 256.

THE best MUSEUMS

- **Museum of the Warsaw Uprising** (Warsaw): When you're done walking through the exhibitions and watching the startling documentaries filmed during the fighting in 1944 on display here, you'll understand a lot more about the Poles' resolve to preserve their nation. Just the photos alone of Warsaw's total destruction will leave you in awe that this city still exists at all. See p. 86.

- **Museum of Zakopane Style** (Zakopane): This low-key museum is dedicated to the fine woodworking craft of the early Zakopane architects of the late 19th and early 20th centuries. No stunning, high-tech visuals, just beautifully carved furnishings and a wonderful aesthetic feel. They took the lowly log cabin and made it a palace. See p. 157.
- **Galicia Jewish Museum** (Kraków-Kazimierz): The main exhibition here features contemporary and often beautiful photographs of important Jewish sites throughout southern Poland taken by the late British photographer Chris Schwarz. Schwarz spent 12 years traveling throughout Poland using photography as a way of trying to preserve the country's rapidly disappearing Jewish heritage. The effect here works beautifully. See p. 133.
- **Czartoryski Museum** (Kraków): Members of the noble Czartoryski family were gifted art collectors, and this collection is one of the finest in central Europe. Two international masterpieces are on display: Leonardo da Vinci's *Lady with an Ermine* and Rembrandt's *Landscape with the Good Samaritan*. See p. 129.
- **Gingerbread Museum** (Toruń): The town of Toruń is famous for two things: the birthplace of Copernicus and gingerbread cookies. At this privately owned museum, you not only learn the secret ingredients of great gingerbread, but also get to make your own. Good fun and great for kids. See p. 230.
- **Roads to Freedom Exhibition** (Gdańsk): An inspiring and sobering history lesson of the anti-Communist struggle in Poland. The mock-up of a typical empty grocery store in late 1970s, grainy news reels, interactive displays, and documentary films keenly capture the atmosphere of the times. See p. 240.
- **Łódź Art Museum:** A must for fans of modern art, the collection includes works by Marc Chagall and Max Ernst. Skip the bottom floors and head straight for the museum's prize pieces on the upper levels, including several of Stanislaw Witkacy's amazing society sketches from the 1920s. See p. 104.
- **Amber Museum** (Gdańsk): A must for all fans of the beautiful ossified pine resin that helped make Gdańsk wealthy. On six floors of exhibits, you'll learn everything you'll ever need to know about amber; if you're thinking of buying some amber while you're in Gdańsk, you might want to stop here first for an educational primer. See p. 238.
- **Museum of Cinematography** (Łódź): International film fans will want to stop here to pay tribute to Poland's panoply of great directors, including Roman Polański, Andrzej Wajda, and Krzysztof Kieslowski, all of whom studied and worked in Łódź. See p. 105.
- **Ethnographic Museum** (Tarnów): A rare and fascinating exhibition on the history and culture of Europe's Roma (Gypsy) population, it traces the emergence of the Roma from parts of modern-day India some 1,000 years ago to their arrival in Europe and subsequent (mostly tragic) history. See p. 164.
- **Chopin Museum** (Warsaw): The city where Chopin was raised wants to tell you everything there is to know about the composer. The museum was recently thoroughly revamped to deliver Chopin stories and melodies via high-tech media. See p. 83.
- **Museum of Icons** (Supraśl): This is the most extensive collection of Orthodox icons in Poland. The exhibits are thoughtfully laid out to give you a full picture of the history of the Orthodox faith. See p. 283.
- **Pharmacy Museum** (Kraków): One of the biggest and best old-style pharmacy museums in this part of the world, with fascinating exhibits of potions, leeches, and concoctions that show just how far modern medicine has come. See p. 130.

THE best CASTLES & CHURCHES

- **Wawel** (Kraków): Poland's pride and joy, and the country's number-one tourist attraction, the original castle dates from around the 10th century, when the area was first chosen as the seat of Polish kings. For more than 5 centuries, the castle stood as the home of Polish royalty. See p. 131.
- **Malbork Castle:** This castle, a UNESCO World Heritage Site and the biggest brick castle in the world, is silent testimony to the power and influence the Teutonic Knights once had in this part of Poland. See p. 262.
- **Książ Castle** (Wałbrzych): The 400-room Książ Castle is the biggest castle in Lower Silesia. It was originally laid out in the 13th century by members of the early Polish nobility but was refurbished and rebuilt several times down through the centuries, resulting in today's baroque-Renaissance-rococo-neoclassical mishmash. See p. 200.
- **St. Mary's Basilica** (Kraków): Kraków is a city of churches, and this is its signature house of worship, right on the main square. The elaborately carved 15th-century wooden altarpiece is the biggest of its kind in Europe. The rest of the interior is similarly impressive, but the highlight of the church is not on the inside, it's the forlorn bugler in the high tower, playing his hourly dirge. See p. 130.
- **Zamość Synagogue** (Zamość): An unexpected and beautiful reminder of the size and vitality of the pre–World War II Jewish community in Zamość. Nearly every southern Polish city had a sizable Jewish community before the war, but very few synagogues of this quality have survived. See p. 183.
- **St. Mary's Church** (Gdańsk): This enormous red-brick church is reputedly the largest of its kind in the world. Its nave and 31 chapels can hold more than 20,000 people. The church endeared itself to the people of Gdańsk in the years after the imposition of martial law in 1981, when members of the Solidarity trade union sheltered here. See p. 242.
- **St. Elizabeth Church** (Wrocław): Wrocław was so thoroughly rebuilt following World War II that it's only in the city's solemn red-brick churches, like this one on the northwest corner of the main square, that you really see something of prewar Breslau (and witness the surviving scars of the war). See p. 193.
- **Kłodzko Fortress:** This fortress has played an important strategic role for centuries, straddling the traditional borderland first between the Polish and Bohemian kingdoms, and then later Prussia and Austria. The present massive structure dates from the middle of the 18th century. Napoleon, early on, shattered the fortress's illusion of invincibility by capturing the structure in 1807. During World War II, the Nazis used the fortress to hold political prisoners. Today, it is the region's leading tourist attraction for the labyrinth of underground tunnels once used for troop mustering, hiding, and escape, if necessary. See p. 210.

POLAND IN DEPTH

2

Poland suddenly finds itself on everyone's hot list for European travel. That's right, Poland—the land of cabbage, potatoes, and vodka—which not all that long ago was still trapped behind the Iron Curtain with its own bleak images of strikes and tanks. All of that seems a world away these days. Poland has gone on a more than 20-year renovation project since the Communist government fell in 1989. The hotels and restaurants have had long-overdue makeovers, the buildings and squares have been spruced up, and Poland these days is very much open for business.

And while the cabbage and vodka are still great, there are lots of other good reasons to visit. For some, a trip to Poland is an opportunity to reconnect with their Polish roots, a chance to sample some of their grandmother's kielbasa and pierogi in their natural setting. Others are attracted to the unique beauty of cities such as Kraków, which has rightfully joined Prague and Budapest as part of the trinity of must-sees in central Europe.

Still others are drawn by Poland's dramatic and often tragic history. The horrors of World War II, followed by decades of Communist rule, have etched painful and moving memories throughout this land. No country, with the possible exception of Russia, suffered as much as Poland during World War II. Millions of Poles, and nearly the entire prewar Jewish population of more than 3 million, were killed in fighting or in the concentration camps. The deeply affecting and sobering experience of seeing the extermination camps at Auschwitz and Birkenau, near Kraków, will last a lifetime. Nearly equally moving are the stories of the Łódź and Warsaw Jewish ghettos, or the tragic story of the Warsaw uprising of 1944, when the city's residents rose up courageously, but futilely, against their Nazi oppressors.

There are plenty of triumphant moments from history, as well. In Warsaw, which was 85% destroyed during World War II, the entire Old Town has been rebuilt brick by brick in an emotional show of a city reclaiming its identity from the rubble. In Gdańsk, you can visit the shipyards where Lech Wałęsa and his Solidarity trade union first rose to power to oppose Poland's Communist government in 1980. It was the rise of Solidarity that helped to bring down Communism in Poland and arguably sparked the anti-Communist revolutions that swept through all of Eastern Europe in 1989.

And there is plenty of natural beauty here, as well. In the south of the country, below Kraków, rise the majestic High Tatras, one of Europe's

Euro Cup 2012: Soccer Comes to Poland

In summer 2012, both Poland and Ukraine will co-host the UEFA Euro 2012 football (soccer) championship—the biggest event in soccer after the FIFA World Cup. Participating teams are drawn from around Europe in a series of qualifying matches in the run-up to the tournament, which kicks off June 8, 2012, in Warsaw. The final will be held in the Ukrainian capital, Kyiv, on July 1.

If you're a soccer fan, these 3 short weeks are certain to be the closest thing to heaven on Earth as tens of thousands of like-minded fans from around the globe descend on the country in droves for games in Gdańsk, Poznań, Wrocław, and Warsaw. High hotel prices, fully booked restaurants, and packed train cars are just part of the "fun;" a small price to pay if you're a soccer fanatic and want to take part in the party. On the other hand, if you've got only a passing interest in the game, you might consider planning your trip to avoid the tournament, though Polish officials have made a point of saying there will be sufficient accommodation for all.

Tickets for the Polish matches go on sale in spring 2011. For more information and schedules, consult the UEFA website: www.uefa.com/uefaeuro2012.

most starkly beautiful alpine ranges. To the north, the Baltic Sea coast, with its pristine beaches, stretches for miles. The little-traveled northeast is covered with lakes that run to the borderlands with Lithuania and Belarus. In the east of the country, you'll find patches of some of Europe's last-remaining primeval forest and a small herd of the indigenous bison that once covered large parts of the European continent.

POLAND TODAY

Poland these days finds itself a bit like a gangly adolescent on the world stage. With a population of around 40 million people, Poland is by far the biggest of the mainly former Communist countries that joined the European Union in 2004, and it has slowly grown into a kind of regional leader, though the region in question, Eastern Europe, can seldom agree on anything. It's also one of the biggest EU member states overall, just below the most-populous countries of Germany, France, and Britain, but on par with mid-sized countries like Spain. After 40 years of Communist rule, and with just a few short years to hone its Western diplomatic skills, you'd expect a few blunders, and Poland has made its share. But it's also shown itself willing to oppose bigger states to protect its own interests. It went up against Germany a couple of years ago when the Germans wanted to make a separate natural gas deal with Russia and cut Poland out of the picture. It's also gone up against France several times, most vocally to get France to open up its labor market to Polish workers. And it defied the EU as a whole on several occasions, famously siding with the U.S. in the Iraq war, over French objections, and agreeing to host part of a U.S. anti-missile battery aimed at defending the U.S. and Europe against rockets fired from Iran. That project was later cancelled by the administration of U.S. President Barack Obama, but Poland's decision to back the U.S. cemented the country's reputation as arguably the strongest U.S. ally on the European continent.

Domestic Politics

Poland suffered a tremendous setback in April 2010 when a tragic plane crash in Russia took the lives of Polish President Lech Kaczyński, his wife, and more than 90 other Polish leaders and dignitaries. The officials were on their way to commemorate the anniversary of the slaughter of thousands of Polish military officers by the Soviet Union at Katyń in 1940. The fatal crash, not far from the Katyń site, was painfully reminiscent of that original tragedy, cementing forever in Poles' minds the view of Katyń as "that cursed place."

If there's a bright side to such an epic tragedy, it might be in the way the plane crash served to pull Poles together from all points of the political spectrum. While there was considerable controversy over the decision to bury the right-wing Kaczyński and his wife at Kraków's fabled Wawel Castle, there was also a palpable feeling of a shared national tragedy and the need to work together to heal divisions. Given Poland's fragmented politics, it's hard to say how long this warm, fuzzy feeling will last, but it's fair to point out that Poland survived the crash, and the loss of staggering number of leaders and politicians, without skipping a beat, and that's a considerable achievement.

As with many of the new Eastern European democracies in the years following the fall of Communism in 1989, Poland has lurched rightward and leftward over the years without really establishing any firm political framework.

In the immediate aftermath of the fall of Communism, the country was led by former Solidarity leader Lech Wałęsa. Wałęsa's presidency was marked by back-biting, infighting, and a splintering of the party system to such an extent that governing proved practically impossible. Voters then surprisingly opted for a former Communist, Aleksander Kwaśniewski. Kwaśniewski's rule brought unexpected stability and political progress, though in time gave way to the right-wing government of the late Lech Kaczyński and renewed bickering. In July 2010, Polish voters elected center-right candidate Bronisław Komorowski to succeed Kaczyński as president in an election widely praised for showing the country's growing political maturity.

Economy

Luckily for Poles, this lack of political stability has not seemed to harm economic development. Indeed, even as the global economic crisis was bearing down on Europe in 2009 and 2010, the Polish economy continued to buck the trend. Whereas most national economies in Europe went into a recession in 2009, Poland actually experienced modest growth that year and the economy expanded again in 2010. Poland's currency, the złoty, has declined modestly in value with respect to the U.S. dollar but, as we were going to press, had managed to avoid the precipitous drop of the EU's common currency, the euro (and Polish efforts to adapt the euro have been put on the back burner for several years to come).

The rising economy continues a trend that began some 2 decades ago as Poland began to pull itself out of an economic collapse caused by a catastrophic World War and 4 decades of incompetent Communist rule. Communism bequeathed to Poland some of the European continent's lowest living standards. Now, young Poles can realistically look forward to a time in their lifetimes when wages and living standards begin to approximate Western Europe.

To be sure, in spite of the economic progress over the past 20 years, you'll still run across many depressed areas—particularly in industrial cities such as Łódź and in large parts of Warsaw itself. You'll also see greater numbers than you might expect of homeless people, public drunks, beggars, and those who have simply fallen through the cracks. Not everyone has benefited equally from the country's rapid transformation to a democratic political system and a free-market economy. Industrial workers, particularly those over the age of 50, for whom adapting to the changes proved more difficult, have been hardest hit.

Young people, too, have found it difficult to cope with ever-rising living costs on very low wages. Many have left the country for places like the U.K. and Ireland, where they can earn more tending bar than they can working as young professionals at home.

But it's important to put this into perspective. Just 20 years ago, Poland was literally falling apart. The country was $30 billion in debt to international lenders. The air was unbreathable, particularly in Kraków, downwind from the enormous steel mill complex at Nowa Huta. It wasn't unusual for Poles to spend hours standing in line simply to buy a piece of fruit or a bottle of imported shampoo. And membership in the European Union was unthinkable. Worst of all, perhaps, was the feeling of utter hopelessness, as if it were somehow Poland's fate to end up on the wrong side of history every time. That's been replaced by something better and infectious: a cautious optimism that maybe this time around the good times are here to stay.

Contact with Poles

In your travels, you'll find that Poles are generally highly educated and cultured, with a firm grasp of their country's long and rich tradition in literature, poetry, performing arts, and film. The strong role of culture in everyday life is not surprising given the country's tragic history. For the 125 years, until 1918, that Poland ceased to exist as a country, it was this shared culture that held the people together. In modern times, it was a common cultural heritage that helped Poles weather the Nazi and Soviet occupations, and endure 40 years of Communist rule after World War II.

You'll sense, too, a strong feeling of national pride. Poles are proud of their history. They're proud of their resistance, however futile, to the Nazi invasion in 1939 and of the tragic Warsaw uprising in 1944. And they're proud of their country's leading role in ending Communism in the 1980s. Today, this pride extends to Poland's membership in the European Union. Americans are likely to feel particularly welcome. Poland's ties to the United States go back all the way to Tadeusz Kościuszko and the Revolutionary War. Poles proudly cite Chicago as the second-biggest Polish city in the world after Warsaw (even though these days more young Poles are emigrating to Ireland and the U.K. than to the U.S.). Just about everyone has a cousin, uncle, or grandparent who lives or used to live in one of the 50 states.

LOOKING BACK AT POLAND

Nowhere in Europe will you feel recent history more strongly than in Poland. The country's unenviable physical position through the ages—between Germany in the west and Russia to the east, and without defensible natural borders—has meant Polish history has been one long struggle for survival. It all reads like a giant novel. And, indeed, American author James A. Michener did write a giant novel in 1981 called *Poland,* chronicling the trials and tribulations of three Polish families over 8 centuries (see "Books," later in this chapter). He hardly had to make up a single word.

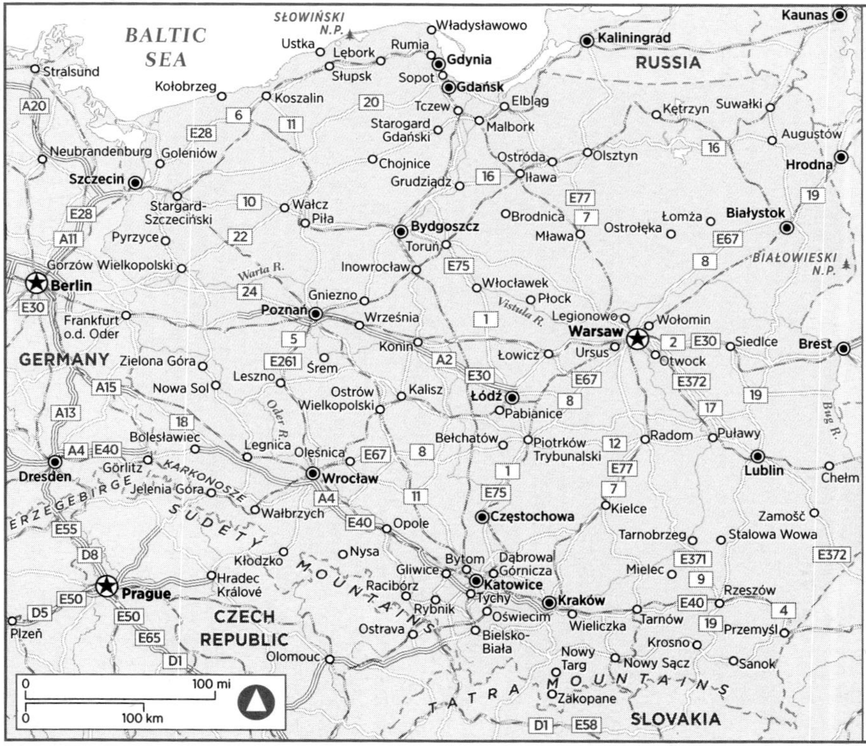

Looking Back at Poland

966: Duke Mieszko I, in Poznań, agrees to be baptized, making Christianity Poland's official religion and creating what would become the modern Polish state.

February 19, 1473: Polish astronomer Nicolaus Copernicus is born in the city of Toruń.

July 1, 1569: At a signing ceremony in Lublin, the kingdoms of Poland and Lithuania agree to merge, creating for a time Europe's largest country.

1596: Poland's capital is shifted from Kraków to Warsaw following the union with Lithuania and the enormous expansion of Polish territory.

March 1, 1810: Polish composer Frédéric Chopin is born in the village of Żelazowa Wola in what was then the Duchy of Warsaw.

1899: Rail workers extend the line south to the Tatra resort of Zakopane, paving the way for the town to emerge as the cultural center of Polish art and architecture.

September 1, 1939: World War II begins as Nazi Germany fires on Polish forces at Westerplatte, across from Gdańsk harbor.

July 20, 1944: German army officer Claus Schenk Graf von Stauffenberg fails in his attempt to assassinate Adolf Hitler at Hitler's command bunker in the former East Prussia.

January 27, 1945: The Soviet Red Army liberates the Auschwitz concentration camp, finding the remains of thousands dead and just around 7,500 survivors.

October 16, 1978: The Vatican elevates Kraków cardinal Karol Wojtyła as pope, becoming John Paul II.

August 31, 1980: The "Gdańsk Accords" are signed in the port city between Poland's Communist regime and the Solidarity trade union led by Lech Wałęsa, legitimizing Eastern Europe's first non-Communist labor union and paving the way for the end of Communism nine years later.

The Early Polish Kings

The Poles first established themselves in the areas to the west of Warsaw around the turn of the 1st millennium, descendants of migrant Slav tribes that came to Eastern Europe around A.D. 700–A.D. 800. The first documented Polish dynasty was the Piast dynasty, and the country's first ruler was Duke Mieszko I, who ruled from Poznań's Ostrów Tumski (see p. 194). It was Mieszko who made the decision to be baptized in 966, making Christianity Poland's official religion and setting the tone for what would remain to this day one of Europe's most deeply Christian and Catholic countries. Though it had its ups and downs, the way that any medieval kingdom would, Poland in the early centuries of its existence was one of Europe's most successful countries. From its capital in Kraków, it prospered under first the Piast and later the Jagiellon dynasties, stretching at one point from the Baltic in the north to the Hungarian kingdom in the south. It was also known as a comparatively tolerant kingdom, and it was at this time that Poland became known as a sanctuary for Jews. In 1410, the Polish king, allied with Lithuania, successfully fought off a challenge by a wayward order of crusaders, the Teutonic Knights, at the battle of Grünwald in one of the great epic battles of the late Middle Ages. The knights had originally been brought to Poland from the Holy Lands to try to subdue the pagan Prussians. The problem was that they had gotten too big for their own britches and had to be put down: The Teutonic Knights' castle at Malbork (p. 262) is testament to their boundless ambition.

The seat of government was moved from Kraków to Warsaw in the 16th century after a formal political union with Lithuania greatly expanded Poland's territory. The union was signed in 1569 in the city of Lublin (p. 168) and still bears the name "Union of Lublin." To this day, it's probably the most exciting thing to ever happen to Poland's eastern metropolis.

In the 17th century, the Poles are generally credited with saving Europe in another epic battle, this one against the Ottoman Turks. Commander Jan Sobieski saved the day for Christian Europe, repelling the Turks at the gates of Vienna in 1683.

The Rise of Rivals & the Polish Partitions

From this point, Polish history runs mostly downhill. A series of wars, first with Sweden and later with Russia, sapped the monarchy's energy and money. Complicated voting rules in Poland's early parliament, the Sejm, completely paralyzed the government. At the same time, both Prussia and tsarist Russia began their long-term rises as great powers. The result was that at the end of the 18th century, Poland was divided up like a pie, with big pieces going to both Prussia and Russia, and a smaller piece in the south going to Habsburg, Austria. This is known in history textbooks as the Polish partitions. For some 125 years, until the end of World War I, Poland disappeared from the map of Europe.

During the 19th century, various Polish heroes tried valiantly—and fruitlessly—to win back the country's independence. Polish patriots of the time threw in their lot with Napoleon, who was storming Europe and promising to recreate the Polish state. In fact, Napoleon did reconstitute part of old Poland in the Duchy of Warsaw in 1807, but his eventual defeat in Russia meant that Poland was divided again, losing vast tracts of territory to tsarist Russia in the east. In spite of the disappearance of the Polish state, Polish language and culture managed to survive. Kraków, at this point, reestablished itself as the center of Polish culture. It was located deep in the Austrian part of Poland, which—compared to the Russian- and Prussian-controlled zones, at least—was a bastion of freedom and free expression.

Local Wisdom: Napoleon & the Poles

At the turn of the 19th century, the French leader Napoleon and Polish patriots trying to reestablish their country formed a kind of marriage of convenience. The Poles needed Napoleon to defeat the Russians, and Napoleon needed the Poles, well, for the very same thing. In the end, it all came to naught as Napoleon was rebuffed at the gates of Moscow. Nevertheless, Napoleon grew quite respectful of the abilities of Polish fighters, once saying famously: "800 Poles equal 8,000 enemy soldiers."

World War I & Polish Independence

Independent Poland was restored in 1918 after the defeat of Austria-Hungary and Germany in World War I. Indeed, Point 13 of U.S. President Woodrow Wilson's famed "14 Points," which set the terms for the surrender of Germany, called directly for the reconstitution of Poland:

An independent Polish state should be erected which should include the territories inhabited by indisputably Polish populations, which should be assured a free and secure access to the sea, and whose political and economic independence and territorial integrity should be guaranteed by international covenant.

The initial years for the independent Polish state were rocky. The first order of business was to fend off attack by the Soviet Union in the Polish–Soviet war of 1919–1921. Polish forces, led by Marshal Józef Piłsudski, succeeded in repelling the Red Army at the 1920 Battle of Warsaw, called the "Miracle on the Vistula." Victory, though, could not guarantee the success of Poland's fledgling democracy, and in 1926, amid rampant hyperinflation, Piłsudski came to power in a military coup. Piłsudski guided the Poles until his death in 1935, and is widely credited with preserving the Polish state under difficult times. Though in effect a dictator, he is fondly remembered and buried with the Polish kings (and now the late president Lech Kaczyński) at Kraków's Wawel Castle (p. 131).

World War II & the Holocaust

If the interwar years were hard, World War II was Poland's worst nightmare come to life. Nazi Germany fired the first shot of the war at Polish forces garrisoned near Gdańsk harbor on September 1, 1939. Soviet Russia, under terms of a nonaggression pact with Germany, then seized the eastern part of the country a few weeks later. In June 1941, the Nazis violated their nonaggression pact and declared war on Russia, initially pushing the Soviet Red Army out of Poland and deep into Russian territory. In the ensuing battle between Fascism and Communism, Poland was literally caught in the middle. Nearly a quarter of all Poles died in the war, including some 3 million Polish Jews.

For Poles, the most poignant memories of the war include the 1940 massacre of Polish army officers by Soviet forces at the Katyń forest. For years, the Soviets denied they had carried out the mass killing, instead blaming the Nazis. Only after the fall of the Soviet Union was the historical record made clear. The story of the massacre was later made into a blockbuster movie by director Andrzej Wajda (*Katyń;* see "Film," below). Poles also recall the ultimately futile uprising of 1944, when the residents of

Warsaw rose up against the Nazis. The Soviet Red Army was closing in on German positions from the East, and the Poles expected the Soviets to join in the fight. Instead, the Red Army chose to watch the fighting from across the Vistula River. The Poles scored some initial successes, but the Germans ultimately prevailed and retaliated ruthlessly. Hitler ordered that Warsaw be destroyed, building by building.

The war itself was bad enough, but the Nazis used Polish soil for the worst of their plans to exterminate Europe's Jewish population and to reduce the Polish and Russian residents to slaves. The Nazis established extermination camps around the country. The most famous of these were at Auschwitz-Birkenau (p. 153) and Treblinka (p. 91), but smaller or less-well-known extermination camps were established in all parts of the country. In addition, the Nazis set up huge ghettos to forcibly hold Poland's once-enormous Jewish population before they could be sent to the camps. Today, you can tour several of the death camps, as well as walk around the former ghettos at Warsaw (p. 86), Łódź (p. 103), Kraków-Kazimierz (p. 132), and Lublin (p. 172), among others. Though these types of Holocaust visits sound depressing, they will likely constitute the most moving memories you bring home from your trip to Poland.

Though ethnic Poles were generally spared the organized genocide of the Holocaust, they too suffered greatly under the Nazis. Countless numbers of Polish POWs, resisters, and ordinary citizens, as well as thousands of Russian POWs, died at Auschwitz and at the other camps alongside Jewish Poles.

The destruction of Poland's physical property during the war is hard to exaggerate. Take Warsaw as an example. Following the 1944 failed Warsaw uprising, the Nazis ordered Poland's once-handsome capital razed to the ground. The buildings were dynamited one by one in order of their importance. By the end of the war, 85% of the city lay in ruins. The numbers are similar for other large cities. Gdańsk was nearly totally destroyed. Wrocław (the former German city of Breslau) was a smoking ash heap.

The Communist Period & the Rise of Solidarity

Poland was reconstituted at the end of the war, but with radically different borders. Bowing to Soviet leader Josef Stalin's demands, the U.S. and U.K. ceded vast tracts of formerly Polish territory in the east to the Soviet Union. In turn, the new Poland was compensated with former German territory in the west. The Polish borders were shifted some 200km (124 miles) westward. The ethnic German population was expelled and replaced by Poles transferred from the east of the country.

But the end of the war brought little relief. Poland fell on the Soviet side of the Iron Curtain, and though Communism as an ideology held little appeal for most Poles, a series of Soviet-backed Communist governments uneasily led the country for the next 4 decades, until 1989.

Local Voices: Josef Stalin on Bringing Communism to Poland

Former Soviet dictator Josef Stalin was under no illusions when it came to the problems of establishing Communism in a staunchly conservative and Catholic country like Poland. He once famously quipped that imposing Communism on Poland was like "putting a saddle on a cow."

Important Historical Events

- 966: Duke Mieszko I, in Poznań, agrees to be baptized, making Christianity Poland's official religion and creating what would become the modern Polish state.
- February 19, 1473: Polish astronomer Nicolaus Copernicus is born in the city of Toruń.
- July 1, 1569: At a signing ceremony in Lublin, the kingdoms of Poland and Lithuania agree to merge, creating Europe's largest country at the time.
- 1596: Poland's capital is shifted from Kraków to Warsaw following the union with Lithuania and the enormous expansion of Polish territory.
- March 1, 1810: Polish composer Frédéric Chopin is born in the village of Żelazowa Wola in what was then the Duchy of Warsaw.
- 1894: Stanisław Witkiewicz finishes the giant wooden Willa Koliba in Zakopane, the first building to use the groundbreaking "Zakopane style" of architecture.
- 1899: Rail workers extend the line south to the Tatra resort of Zakopane, paving the way for the town to emerge as the cultural center of Polish art and architecture.
- November 11, 1918: Poland regains its independence after 125 years, with Warsaw to be the country's new capital.
- September 1, 1939: World War II begins as Nazi Germany fires on Polish forces at Westerplatte, across from Gdańsk harbor.
- July 20, 1944: German army officer Claus Schenk Graf von Stauffenberg fails in his attempt to assassinate Adolf Hitler at Hitler's command bunker (the Wolf's Lair) in the former East Prussia.
- January 27, 1945: The Soviet Red Army liberates the Auschwitz concentration camp, finding the remains of thousands dead and just around 7,500 survivors.
- October 16, 1978: The Vatican elevates Kraków cardinal Karol Woytyła to pope, anointing him Pope John Paul II.
- August 31, 1980: The "Gdańsk Accords" are signed in the port city between Poland's Communist regime and the Solidarity trade union led by Lech Wałęsa, legitimizing Eastern Europe's first non-Communist labor union and paving the way for the end of Communism 9 years later.
- May 1, 2004: Poland fulfills its long-term foreign-policy goal of joining the European Union with celebrations in the capital, Warsaw, and around the country.

The government managed to maintain order through massive borrowing on international financial markets, but mismanagement of the economy led to one crisis after another, including bloody riots in 1970 that killed more than 40 people and shocked the country and the world.

In the end, it was the desire for higher living standards—perhaps even more than a desire for political freedom—that led to the creation of the Solidarity trade union and the genesis of the anti-Communist movement. Solidarity began at the shipyards in Gdańsk, but eventually spread to the rest of the country. The union's breakthrough came in 1980, under the leadership of the young, charismatic Lech Wałęsa. The Polish government had been forced to raise food prices in the summer of 1980, sparking nationwide protests and strikes. The workers of the Lenin Shipyard in Gdańsk (p. 235) called a strike and refused to back down, ultimately forcing the government to recognize Solidarity as a free and independent trade union, the first of its kind in Eastern Europe. The strike led to the August 1980 Gdańsk Accords and the first step in what would be Poland's decade-long struggle to break the bonds of Communism. The low point came a year later, as the Communist authorities—pushed by their Soviet overlords—were forced to declare martial law in December 1981 to prevent a complete loss of control. Thousands of people were arrested and some 100 died in the crackdown.

In 1978, at around the same time that all this was happening, the Catholic Church had elevated another charismatic Pole, a cardinal from Kraków named Karol Woytyła, to be pope. If Solidarity provided the organizational framework for Poles to resist, Pope John Paul, through his visits and sermons, provided the moral inspiration.

In early 1989, the Poles held their first semi-free election—a landmark vote that bolstered anti-Communist activists across Eastern Europe. By the end of that epic year, Poland, and the entire Eastern bloc, was free.

The Period Since 1989

The period since 1989 has been hugely chaotic, but the result has been the creation of a stable, democratic Polish state that's a member of both NATO and the European Union. Each of the former Soviet satellite states chose a different path toward democratization and creation of a free market, and Poland's contribution in this regard has accurately been called "shock therapy." Designed by Poland's finance minister at the time, Leszek Balcerowicz, shock therapy essentially meant allowing wages and prices to float freely and indebted Communist companies to go bankrupt. Understandably, it caused massive disruption in the economy, and millions lost their jobs. The jury is still out on whether shock therapy was good or bad, but it's generally credited with promoting high rates of growth, albeit at a high social cost. Politically, however, the country stagnated. Lech Wałęsa's early stint as president (1990–95) proved to be disastrous—he was a much better labor leader than national leader—and since then, Poland has lurched left and right without finding a stable middle. The high point of the post-Communist period came in 2004, when Poland, along with seven other formerly Communist states, joined the European Union.

POLAND IN POPULAR CULTURE: FILM, BOOKS, AND MUSIC

Poland is well-known for its contribution to international cinema, having spawned a generation of world-renowned directors in the immediate aftermath of World War II. Poland's contribution to world literature—at least, to English-language readers—is limited by what's available in translation, but the Communist period was particularly rich, and the country has at least two internationally renowned poets to its credit. In music, at least in classical music, the name Chopin rises above all others. Wherever you travel in Poland, you can be certain you won't be far from a Chopin concert.

Film

Poland's greatest contribution to popular culture, arguably, is in film. No fewer than three of the world's great postwar directors are Polish and learned their craft at the country's school of cinematography in Łódź: Roman Polański, Krzysztof Kieslowski, and Andrzej Wajda. Łódź, incidentally, has the country's only museum devoted to cinematography, and film buffs should certainly seek it out.

Of the three, Polański is probably the best-known abroad (though Kieslowski rates a close second), both for his films and his tragic and stormy personal life, including living through the brutal murder of his pregnant wife, Sharon Tate, in 1969 by members of the Charles Manson gang and by a conviction in the U.S. in 1977 for allegedly having sexual relations with a 13-year-old girl. Polański's films are best known for having a dark and sinister feel. His breakout film was 1962's *Knife in the Water,* made in Poland, concerning a murderous *ménage à trois.* It was received coolly by Poland's Communist authorities but was a big international hit, securing him a filmmaking future in Great Britain and later the United States. In Britain, Polański collaborated with French actress Catherine Deneuve to make the thriller *Repulsion.* Once in the U.S., in the late 1960s, he scored a series of blockbusters, including *Rosemary's Baby* (1968) with Mia Farrow and *Chinatown* (1974) with Faye Dunaway and Jack Nicholson. Later hits included *Frantic* (1987), starring Harrison Ford, and 2002's critically acclaimed *The Pianist,* with Adrien Brody in the lead role of Warsaw Jewish ghetto survivor Władysław Szpilman. That movie earned Polański an Oscar for Best Director.

Krzysztof Kieslowski is best known abroad for his *Three Colors* movies: *Blue* (1993), *White* (1994), and *Red* (1994). Kieslowski made the films—based on the French virtues of liberty, equality, and fraternity—after he had moved to France. However, he had already earned a formidable reputation in Poland for his ironic Socialist Realist movies of the 1970s and '80s, the best of which is probably *Camera Buff* (1979). He's also the director of the critically acclaimed *Decalogue* (1988) series (10 movies based on the 10 commandments), and the art-house favorite *The Double Life of Veronique* (1991).

Andrzej Wajda may be less well known to those outside Poland, but within the country, he's widely considered the most important director to emerge after World War II. He earned his reputation in the 1950s, with unsparing movies about World War II, including the tragic *Ashes and Diamonds* (1957). Two films depicting the abysmal quality of life in Soviet-dominated Poland—1976's *Man of Marble* and 1981's *Man of Iron*—won Wajda widespread international critical acclaim. Now in his 80s, he's still going strong, and 2007's premiere of *Katyń,* about the mass execution of Polish officers in the Katyń forest by the Soviets in 1940, was Poland's biggest film event in years.

MOVIES ABOUT POLAND

In addition to movies made by Poles, there are countless movies about Poland, usually focused on World War II or the Holocaust. The best known of these is Steven Spielberg's 1993 epic *Schindler's List.* The movie depicts the efforts of German industrialist Oskar Schindler to shield his Jewish factory workers from deportation to the concentration camps and his subsequent actions that saved 1,000 people from a certain death at Auschwitz. Much of the movie was filmed in and around Kraków's former Jewish quarter of Kazimierz, and Schindler's factory, now a museum, is still standing (see p. 134). Janusz Kamiński, Spielberg's Polish cameraman for *Schindler's List* and then later for *Saving Private Ryan,* won Oscars for both films.

Another outstanding movie that features wartime Poland is 1982's *Sophie's Choice,* starring Meryl Streep and based on the William Styron novel of the same name. In the movie, Streep plays a Polish immigrant and Auschwitz survivor living in Brooklyn who finds it impossible to escape the world she left behind, and the horrific choice she had to make.

It's also worth noting that American cult filmmaker David Lynch reportedly has a love affair with Poland's film capital, Łódź. His ultra-creepy film *Inland Empire* was apparently inspired by a visit to the city.

Books

Polish literature, with few exceptions, remains largely unknown to people outside the country, due mainly to publishers' reluctance to invest in translating the books into English rather than to a lack of literary merit. Poland, in fact, has four Nobel Prize winners for literature: Henryk Sienkiewicz (1905), the author of *Quo Vadis;* Władysław Reymont (1924), a now-forgotten journalist who won the prize for the book *Chłopi (Peasants);* and poets Czesław Miłosz (1980) and Wisława Szymborska (1996) (see "Poetry" below). There are also two Jewish Nobel prize laureates who it could be argued have some connection to Poland: Shmuel Yosef Agnon (1966) and I. B. Singer (1978). You might even make a case for a seventh Nobel by including German writer Günter Grass, who was born and raised in Gdańsk when the city was part of Germany and known as Danzig.

For Poles, the most fruitful period in literature came during the two world wars, when writers such as Witold Gombrowicz and Stanisław Ignacy Witkiewicz shocked polite society with novels involving previously taboo themes like homosexuality and illicit drugs. Gombrowicz's *Pornografia* and Witkiewicz's *Insatiability* are both available in English translation and are difficult but worthwhile reads.

THE COMMUNIST PERIOD

The post–World War II period proved to be a surprisingly productive time in Polish literature as writers reacted to the war and life under Communism. Penguin publishers' highly influential 1980s series "Writers from the Other Europe," edited by American writer Philip Roth, introduced several of the most talented Eastern Bloc writers to an international audience (you can still find many of these books on bookstore shelves or on the Internet). Writers in the series from Poland include Bruno Schulz (*Street of Crocodiles* and *Sanatorium Under the Sign of the Hourglass*), Jerzy Andrzejewski (*Ashes and Diamonds*), Tadeusz Borowski (*This Way for the Gas, Ladies and Gentlemen;* see "Holocaust Literature," below), and Tadeusz Konwicki (*A Dreambook for Our Time* and *The Polish Complex*). Though Schulz was included in the collection, he wrote mostly about Jewish life in interwar Poland and during World War II.

Arguably the biggest book (at least, in the United States and Western Europe) to come out of Poland in the postwar period was Jerzy Kosinski's *The Painted Bird,* which provoked a firestorm when it was published in 1965. The book tells the story of a young Jewish or Roma orphan (it's not made clear in the text) who wanders from village to village during World War II, experiencing the anti-Semitism, violence, and frank perversions of the Polish peasantry at the time. The book was banned in Poland on publication but wowed Western critics in the 1960s. It's since lost some of its luster amid controversy that Kosinski greatly embellished the stories and in fact profited from the book's association with Holocaust literature, but it still makes for a gripping read.

OTHER WRITERS

Aside from literature, Polish writers are well known in other genres. Fans of science fiction will no doubt know the name Stanisław Lem, the late author of the 1961 classic *Solaris* and dozens of other titles.

The late journalist Ryszard Kapuściński carved out an immense reputation as a travel writer, focusing particularly on accounts in the developing world. His best-known work remains *Another Day of Life* (1976), about the collapse of Portuguese colonialism in Angola.

American writer Alan Furst, though not a Pole, has written several fun and worthwhile spy and noir novels set in World War II Poland or involving Polish characters. His best is probably 1995's *The Polish Officer.* In 2008, he published the thriller *The Spies of Warsaw.*

For a Polish page-turner that will have you thumbing through 8 centuries of Polish history in the course of a long afternoon, try James Michener's epic *Poland* (1981). The novel traces the tortured histories of three families through some 8 centuries of war and upheaval. It's a surprisingly gripping read and Michener, as usual, manages to bring to life what might in the hands of another writer be just a dry, historical account.

HOLOCAUST LITERATURE

There's no shortage of great books written about the Holocaust, and bringing a few titles along with you can greatly enhance your experience as you visit former Nazi concentration camps and wartime Jewish ghettos. There are several excellent accounts written by survivors of the camps, but two of the best include Italian writer Primo Levi's *Survival in Auschwitz,* an unvarnished account of Levi's arrival at Auschwitz's Monowitz camp in 1944 and what happened to him after he got there, and Rudolf Vrba's *Escape from Auschwitz: I Cannot Forgive,* the true account of one of the few men to have escaped from Auschwitz and lived to tell the tale: Vrba and a fellow Slovak managed to escape from Auschwitz's Birkenau camp in 1944. This book tells the incredible story of how they did it and how they later tried to tell the world about the Holocaust but found that few were willing to listen.

Tadeusz Borowski's *This Way for the Gas, Ladies and Gentlemen* tells the Auschwitz story from a different perspective. Borowski was a Polish political prisoner at Auschwitz and worked in the coveted "Kanada" brigade which was responsible for cleaning up and storing possessions of new arrivals as they entered the camp (meaning they always had enough food to eat). Far from the one-dimensional portraits of the victims of some accounts, Borowski paints a disturbing and unsparing picture of desperate prisoners willing to do anything it took—including collaborating with their captors—in order to survive. (Borowski ended up committing suicide after the war.)

Commandant of Auschwitz: The Autobiography of Rudolf Hoess tells the story of Auschwitz's camp commander in his own words. Hoess, a member of the SS, wrote his autobiography in 1946 after being captured by Allied troops at the end of the war. It's chilling for its coldness and lack of regret. Hoess was hanged by Polish authorities in 1947 at Auschwitz, not far from one of the crematoria he helped to build.

In terms of better trying to understand the Nazis' extermination plans, an excellent if somewhat academic read is Christopher R. Browning's *The Origins of the Final Solution.* Laurence Rees's remarkable *Auschwitz: A New History* covers much the same ground but interweaves dozens of first-person accounts and makes for an absorbing experience.

POETRY

Poland has produced two Nobel Prize–winning poets: Czesław Miłosz (1980) and Wisława Szymborska (1996). Miłosz, who died in 2004, spent much of his life as a professor of Slavic literature at the University of California at Berkeley. Aside from

"For Where Thy Treasure Is, There Will Thy Heart Be Also"

Though Chopin spent much of his life in France, his heart—quite literally—belongs to Poland. Shortly before his death, as the story goes, Chopin asked that his heart be moved to the country of his birth. Complying with his wishes, doctors removed the composer's heart after he died, and it was taken to Warsaw by his sister. The heart is preserved in a pillar of the Holy Cross Church *(Kościół Świętego Krzyża)* on Warsaw's Krakówskie Przedmieście, beneath the inscription taken from the Bible, Matthew 6, verse 21 (the title of this box). Chopin's heart is still there. It was removed briefly during the fighting in World War II, and then restored to the church after it was rebuilt.

numerous volumes of poetry, Miłosz is the author the highly regarded "The Captive Mind" (1953), a long and absorbing essay that attempts to describe intellectuals' acceptance of Stalinism at the end of World War II. Szymborska is a Kraków-based poet and essayist, known for short, witty, and humorous poems on life's ironies.

Music

Though Poland has a rich musical tradition going back centuries, it's probably best known for two contributions: the polka and Frédéric Chopin.

Crediting Poland with the polka is actually a common error, probably because of the similarity of the names. Though the polka is as popular in Poland as anywhere else in Central Europe, it actually comes from Bohemia, in the modern-day Czech Republic.

Poles have a more legitimate claim on Chopin, though another country, France, is involved there too. Though Chopin was born in the village of Żelazowa Wola, not far from Warsaw, to a Polish mother, his father was French, and the composer spent much of his short life in Paris (and even for a time became a French citizen). To bolster the French claim, he also had a stormy affair with French intellectual George Sand (female).

Chopin is generally regarded as one of the foremost composers of the 19th-century Romantic Movement. His music is still wildly popular in Poland, and wherever you travel in the country, you're certain to be able to catch a Chopin concert somewhere nearby. Poles say that no matter where they are in the world, when they hear a Chopin piece, such as "Polonaise" Op. 53, they are immediately transported back to the Polish countryside. Chopin is most famous for his études, compositions written mainly to help students learn their instruments, but which have become concert pieces in their own right. His best-known piece of music is probably his "Funeral March" (Piano Sonata no. 2), which nearly everyone will recognize after just a few bars (imagine the somber tones they play on a cartoon when someone has to walk the plank).

Chopin died in Paris at the age of 39 of chronic lung failure brought on by tuberculosis. He is buried at Paris's fabled Père Lachaise Cemetery—everything except his heart, of course, which was carted off to Warsaw shortly after his death and sealed in a pillar at the Holy Cross Church (*Kościół Świętego Krzyża;* see p. 83).

EATING & DRINKING IN POLAND

Polish food has a hearty, homemade feel, and when it's done well, it can be delicious. It's similar to other Central European national cuisines in that it's centered on main courses of mostly meat dishes and features plenty of hearty soups and sides of potatoes and grains. Game dishes, such as venison, boar, and duck, play a more prominent role here than in the United States or Western Europe. Poles also have a mania for mushrooms, the best being those picked in the forest that morning.

Visitors to Poland will be happy to see that traditional **pierogi** are still going strong. These hand-rolled dumplings are stuffed with everything from potato and cottage cheese to cabbage, from ground meat to even plums or strawberries in season. Pierogi are traditionally prepared by boiling in water, though they can also be baked or fried. Pierogi with savory fillings, such as cheese and meat, are traditionally topped with fried onions or bacon bits; fruit pierogi are best eaten with butter or cream.

Pierogi have lots to recommend them. For one thing, they're often the cheapest item on the menu, making them tailor-made budget food. They are also extremely flexible, and can be eaten as a snack or as a main course, for lunch or dinner. They also make a great option for vegetarians; just be sure to tell them to hold the bacon bits they sometimes pour on top. Pierogi prepared "Ruskie" style are meatless, stuffed with potatoes and cottage cheese.

Placki, potato pancakes, are nearly as ubiquitous and delicious as pierogi, and are often cooked with mushrooms or smoked meat.

Traditional Meal

Polish meals generally begin with an appetizer, which can be either cold *(przekąski zimne)* or warm *(przekąski gorące)*. Among the former, herring (*śledź*), usually served in a sour cream sauce and piled with chopped onions, is invariably a good choice. Other popular cold starters include stuffed fish or pâté *(pasztet)*. Hot starters can include pierogi or a piece of homemade sausage *(kiełbasa)*.

Soups *(zupy)* are a mainstay of a Polish meal. *Żurek* is a filling, sourish rye broth, seasoned with dill and usually served with sausage and egg. *Barszcz* is based on red beets, but it isn't exactly "borscht." In Poland, it's usually served as a broth, often with a little pastry on the side. *Bigos,* often called "hunter's stew" on English menus, is another national mania and is made from sauerkraut and smoked meat, and often flavored with caraway seeds or juniper berries. Every Polish grandmother has her own version, and local lore says the homemade variety tastes best on the seventh reheating!

Main courses are less original and often revolve around chicken, pork, or beef, though game (usually venison or boar) and fish (pike and trout) are also common. Sides *(dodatki)* usually involve some form of potato, fried or boiled, or sometimes fried potato dumplings. More creative sides include buckwheat groats *(kasza)* or mashed beets, the latter sometimes flavored with apple. Common desserts include fruit pierogi; apple pie *(szarlotka);* the ubiquitous ice cream *(lody);* and pancakes, sometimes filled with cottage cheese and served with fruit sauce.

Breakfast is taken early and is often no more than a cup of tea or instant coffee, and a bread roll. Hotels usually lay on the traditional buffet-style breakfast centered on cold cuts, cheeses, yogurts, and cereals, but this is more than what Poles normally eat in the morning. Lunches are served late, around 1 or 2pm, and restaurants don't usually get rolling until about 1pm. Dinner starts around 7pm and can run until 9 or 10pm, though restaurants often claim to stay open "until the last customer." Some actually do stay open late, but many kitchens start closing down after 10pm, so get there early to avoid disappointment.

Fast Food

Poles are big snackers, and the latest mania is for Middle Eastern and Greek snack foods such as chicken and meat shawarma and kebabs. You'll find dozens of stands and windows serving some variation of a sandwich based on shaved meat, tomatoes, onions, and plenty of mayo. Pizza is also ubiquitous, and no self-respecting Polish city or town would be complete without at least half a dozen pizza restaurants of varying quality. Look also for *zapiekanki*—foot-long, open-faced baguettes, topped with sauce and cheese and then baked. It's known affectionately as "Polish pizza."

In addition to the "mom and pop" places, the big international fast food chains have made inroads. The big players in Poland are McDonald's and KFC, and you'll invariably find one or the other (often both) in city centers and train stations. Polish domestic chains are also becoming more common. The best known is probably Sphinx, which seems to have an outlet in every city in the country. The specialty is fairly mediocre Middle Eastern–style food, served in a smoke-free, family-friendly atmosphere. It's easy to criticize the chains, but they can be a lifesaver if you're looking for something fast and reliable.

Vodka & Beer

While Poles may be best known for their vodka, it is in fact beer that's the national drink. You'll find the major beer brands—Okocim, Lech, Tyskie, and Żywiec—just about everywhere. There's little difference among the majors, and they are all pretty good, though Tyskie appears to be the most popular. Men take theirs straight up. Women frequently sweeten their beer with fruit syrup (raspberry is the most common) and drink it through a straw. Among the most popular vodkas, Belvedere and Chopin are considered top-shelf, though imported vodkas are increasingly squeezing out the local brands. In addition, you'll find a range of flavored vodkas, including highly popular cherry. Żubrówka is slightly greenish, owing to the long blade of bison grass in every bottle. Miodówka, honey-flavored and easy to drink, is worth a try. Wine is much less common, and nearly always imported.

PLANNING YOUR TRIP TO POLAND

Visiting Poland has never been easier. Travelers from the U.S. and the European Union, including the U.K., don't require visas or need to take any particular health or safety precautions. Indeed, Poland is a member of the "Schengen Zone" (EU-speak for the European Union's common border area), and if you're arriving from a bordering EU member state (Germany, Czech Republic, Slovakia, Lithuania), you're unlikely even to have to show a passport or ID card at the border.

As far as packing goes, your suitcase or backpack will look pretty much the same as for any other U.S. or European continental destination with four distinct seasons (bearing in mind that a Polish winter might be colder than what you're used to). If you forget anything, rest assured that, just like at home, there's likely to be a shopping mall or drugstore down the street where you can find a suitable substitute.

More challenging might be deciding where to spend your time. Poland is relatively large as European countries go, and road and rail connections still leave a lot to be desired. That means you'll have to pick and choose your target destinations carefully, leaving plenty of extra time for getting from here to there. A week in Poland, for example, would leave a comfortable amount of time for seeing Warsaw and the northern half of the country or seeing Kraków and the southern half, but unless you plan on flying from city to city, it would not leave enough time to do it all.

Another factor to consider is what you plan to do. Poland is an active destination; depending on what you interests are, you might want to bring golf clubs, hiking boots, or even skis. Whatever is in the cards, don't forget comfortable walking shoes. Although there's great public transportation within the cities, you're going to do a lot of walking wherever you go.

For additional help in planning your trip and for more on-the-ground resources in Poland, please turn to "Fast Facts," on p. 291.

WHEN TO GO

Poland's climate has four distinct seasons and is characterized by hot summers and dark, cold winters. Unless you're heading to the Tatras to ski, avoid travel from January to March. Many of the attractions are closed for the season, and the cold and snow make getting around difficult. Note that Kraków and Zakopane are both popular Christmas and New Year's destinations, and hotel prices rise accordingly. Summer brings good weather but more crowds as Poles take to the roads on their summer holidays. September and October are ideal, with fewer crowds and usually reliably good weather.

Warsaw Average Monthly Temperatures (°F/°C) & Precipitation (mm/in.)

	JAN	FEB	MAR	APR	MAY	JUNE	JULY	AUG	SEPT	OCT	NOV	DEC
AVG. HIGH (°F/°C)	32/0	32/0	43/6	53/12	68/20	73/23	75/24	73/23	66/19	55/13	43/6	35/2
AVG. LOW (°F/°C	21/-6	21/-6	28/-2	37/3	48/9	53/12	59/15	57/14	50/10	41/5	34/1	27/-3
PREC. (MM/IN.)	27/1.1	32/1.3	27/1.1	37/1.5	46/1.8	69/2.7	96/3.8	65/2.6	43/1.7	38/1.5	31/1.2	44/1.7

Poland Calendar of Events

The calendar is filled with festivals of all kinds; the most popular are connected to religious dates or Poland's folk or cultural traditions. The annual Marian pilgrimages culminate in August at the Jasna Góra shrine in Częstochowa for the Feast of the Assumption on August 15. Warsaw, Kraków, Wrocław, and Poznań all host various jazz and classical music festivals throughout the year. Check with local tourist information offices when you arrive to see what's going on during the time you're there. For an exhaustive list of events beyond those listed here, check http://events.frommers.com, where you'll find a searchable, up-to-the-minute roster of what's happening in cities all over the world.

FEBRUARY

Shanties: International Sailors' Song Festival, Kraków. A true anomaly for a landlocked city, each February, Kraków hosts this international festival dedicated to maritime and sailors' songs (think nautical poetry and ballads). Events are held around town. Call ✆ **12/423-22-36** or visit **www.shanties.pl.**

APRIL

Cracovia Marathon, Kraków. Kraków's marathon draws well over 1,000 runners each spring. Call ✆ **12/616-63-00** or visit **www.cracoviamaraton.pl.**

Ludwig van Beethoven Festival, Warsaw. Though this Easter festival bears Beethoven's name, it's not just about him. The program features a variety of classical composers. The festival unfolds over 2 weeks, timed to coincide with the Easter holidays. Concerts are held around town. Call ✆ **22/331-91-91** or visit **www.beethoven.org.pl.**

MAY

Film Music Festival, Kraków. Three days of concerts dedicated to music composed for the silver screen. Composers join audiences for concerts accompanying film showings at various venues. Call ✆ **12/424-96-50** or visit **www.fmf.fm.**

Floriański Fair, Warsaw. This popular street fair takes place across the river in Warsaw's gritty but lively district of Praga. The highlight is a street market bustling with antiques, crafts, and foods. On the card are live bands and local celebs. For details, visit **http://en.praga-pn.waw.pl.**

International Book Fair, Warsaw. A strong line-up of international writers and publishers attend this event held at the Stalin-era Palace of Culture & Science. Call ✆ **22/509-86-00** or check out **www.bookfair.pl.**

Juwenalia, Kraków. A fun fair dedicated to the city's thousands of students. In a tradition dating back to the Middle Ages, the mayor gives the students the keys to the city. Lots of concerts, parades, and shows. Lots of alcohol, too. Call ✆ **12/633-35-38** or visit **http://juwenalia.krakow.pl.**

Night of Museums, Warsaw. For one night each May, the city's museums, galleries, and other art institutions stay open late into the night. Part of the fun is visiting the exhibits, but mostly, it's a late-night street party. For more information, visit **http://noc-muzeow.pl.**

JUNE

Fair Hetmański, Zamość. Lots of fun if you're into handicrafts and Renaissance culture; events are held on the city's large market square. Lots of music and food, and plenty of things to buy. Early June.

Jewish Culture Festival, Kraków. Over the past decade, this festival of Jewish culture, music, dance, and film has evolved into one of the city's premier events. Most of the action takes place in Kraków's historic Jewish district, Kazimierz. Synagogues, cafes, and outdoor venues celebrate the richness of Jewish culture. Street musicians play klezmer tunes, and everyone ends up dancing. Book well in advance; the festival draws thousands. Call ✆ **12/431-15-17** or visit **www.jewishfestival.pl.**

Malta International Theater Festival, Poznań. A week of street theater and events draws tens of thousands of people to the country's biggest festival dedicated to the dramatic arts. Visit **www.malta-festival.pl.**

Selector Festival, Kraków. Fans of dance, trance, electronic, and techno arrive by the thousands for 2 days of gigs from top bands and DJs. Visit **www.selectorfestival.pl.**

Sonisphere, Warsaw. A festival of rock and metal music held in the Warsaw suburb of Lotnisko Bemowo. Past acts include Metallica, Slayer, Anthrax, and Megadeth. Visit **http://pl.sonispherefestivals.com.**

Warsaw Chamber Opera Mozart Festival. Reputedly the only company in the world to present all of Mozart's stage works every year. Call ✆ **22/831-22-40.**

Wianki & Free Music Festival, Kraków. This pagan-era fertility festival features maidens floating garlands *(wianki)* down the river to predict when they'll be married (and to whom), as well as top Polish and international music acts. After the concerts, crowds head to the city's bars and clubs. Call ✆ **12/424-96-50** or visit **www.wianki.krakow.pl.**

JULY

Chopiniana, Warsaw. Concerts, theater, film, and ballet performances dedicated to the composer whom the capital claims as its own. Performances take place in venues connected to the composer's life. Call ✆ **22/620-39-62** or visit **www.mckis.waw.pl.**

Crossroads Traditional Music Festival, Kraków. This annual music festival fills the streets of Kraków with folk music from the nearby Tatra Mountains. Many concerts take place in Kraków's Market Square (Rynek Glówny), with musicians mixing traditional folk with genres such as jazz. Call ✆ **12/424-96-50** or visit **www.rozstaje.pl.**

International Street Arts Festival, Warsaw. Warsaw's biggest outdoor festival of music and dramatic arts, with performances in 20 or so of the city's most popular spots. Visit **www.sztukaulicy.pl.**

International Street & Open-Air Theaters Festival, Gdańsk. The streets of Gdańsk come alive each July for the annual FETA festival, which features jugglers, mimes, stilt walkers, dancers, and storytellers from around the world. Call ✆) **58/557-42-47** or visit **www.feta.pl.**

St Dominic's Fair, Gdańsk. Lively 3-week street fair of arts and crafts in Gdańsk's Old Town that goes back some 750 years. Most events take place in Długi Targ, one of the city's nicest areas. Call ✆ **58/554-92-00** or visit **www.mtgsa.com.pl.**

StreetArt International Festival of Street Theater, Kraków. Kraków's main market square plays host to magicians, jugglers, and puppeteers in one of the oldest medieval-style festivals in Central Europe. Call ✆ **12/623-73-00** or visit **http://teatrkto.pl.**

Summer Jazz Days, Warsaw. One of the continent's leading jazz festivals, drawing international stars and emerging names to the Palace of Culture and Science. The program includes a concert of avant-garde jazz and free open air performances in Warsaw's Plac Zamkowy. Call ✆ **22/620-50-72** or visit **www.adamiakjazz.pl.**

AUGUST

Chopin and His Europe International Music Festival, Warsaw. Inaugurated in 2005, "Chopin and His Europe" not surprisingly celebrates the life and work of Fryderyk Chopin. A number of venues across Warsaw, including the city's Philharmonic Hall, host concerts. Call ✆ **22/441-61-17** or check out **http://en.chopin.nifc.pl/festival.**

Coke Live Music Festival, Kraków. Festival of indie and pop music held over 2 days and three stages at the airfield of Kraków's Aviation Museum. There's space to pitch a tent, as well as bathroom facilities and food stalls. The festival traditionally lures some of the biggest names in popular music. Visit **www.livefestival.pl.**

Feast of the Assumption, Częstochowa. Draws tens of thousands of pilgrims annually to the Jasna Góra monastery. If you're planning to visit during this period, be sure to book your accommodation far in advance. August 15.

Gdańsk Shakespeare Festival. Both Polish and international theater companies come to the Baltic shoreline to host traditional and experimental versions of Shakespeare's plays. There are also concerts and a parade. Call ✆ **58/300-01-70** or visit the festival website at **www.shakespearefestival.pl.**

International Mime Art Festival, Warsaw. Mimes. Love 'em or hate 'em, the Polish capital hosts Europe's largest mime fest. Theater companies from across Europe and the world take part. Call ✆ **22/632-03-60** or visit **www.mime.pl.**

Music in Old Kraków. A 17-day event filled with classical concerts and recitals at venues around the city. Visit **www.muzykaw starymkrakowie.eu.**

Singer's Jewish Culture Festival, Warsaw. This popular festival hosts exhibitions, films, music, and theater performances relating to the history of Warsaw's Jewish community. Events are held around Plac Grzybowski. Call ✆ **22/850-56-56** or visit **http://festiwalsingera.pl.**

International Highlanders' Folk Festival, Zakopane. One of the oldest and biggest folk events in Poland. Highlanders from all over the world congregate in Zakopane to celebrate their customs through regional costumes, music, and dance. Call ✆ **18/206-69-50** or visit **www.mffzg.pl.**

SEPTEMBER

Autumn Contemporary Music Festival, Warsaw. This acclaimed festival presents contemporary classical music from around the world. Concerts are held at the National Philharmonic Hall and other city venues. Call ✆ **22/635-92-38** or visit **http://warszawska-jesien.art.pl.**

Cross Culture Festival, Warsaw. Musicians gather at the Palace of Culture and Science for a week-long series of concerts celebrating world music in all its diversity. Films and workshops are also included on the program. Call ✆ **22/849-32-86** or visit **www.estrada.com.pl/46.**

Festival of Four Cultures, Łódź. This popular music, culture, and film festival celebrates the city's traditional point at the crossroads of four cultures: Polish, German, Jewish, and Russian. Call ✆ **42/636-38-21** or visit **http://en.4kultury.pl.**

Wratislavia Cantans, Wrocław. The annual Wratislavia Cantans celebrates sacred choral music. If it sounds boring, it's anything but. The quality of the performances is outstanding, and the atmosphere is nothing short of riveting. Call ✆ **71/330-52-10** or visit **www.wratislaviacantans.pl.**

OCTOBER

International Film Festival, Warsaw. One of Europe's leading international film festivals offers a great chance to see dozens of films you might never see anywhere else. Visit **www.wff.pl.**

Rawa Blues Festival, Katowice. Reputedly the world's largest indoor blues festival, it takes place in Katowice's futuristic Spodek concert hall. Visit **www.rawablues.com.**

NOVEMBER

All Souls' Jazz Festival, Kraków. Poland's oldest jazz festival takes place every year around All Souls' Day (Nov 2). Musicians from around the world perform in bars, churches, and other venues across town. Visit **www.krakowskiezaduszkijazzowe.xt.pl.**

Jazz Jamboree, Warsaw. For more than 50 years, the Jazz Jamboree has been bringing jazz to the Polish capital. Concerts are held in various venues, including Teatr Polski. Call ✆ **22/827-39-26** or visit **www.jazz-jamboree.pl.**

Jazz Jantar Festival, Gdańsk. The Żak Club in Gdańsk is the traditional host of the annual Jazz Jantar Festival of improvised music. The event showcases experimental compositions and lots of blues. Call ✆ **58/344-05-73** or visit **http://jazzjantar.pl.**

St. Martin's Day, Poznań. November 11 is a day of pageantry, featuring St Martin himself riding on a white horse accompanied by jugglers, clowns, stilt walkers, and lots of hangers-on. There are parades and festivities until well into the night, as well as the traditional eating of the St. Martin crescent-shaped buns, tasty croissants you can find around town. Visit **www.poznan.pl.**

DECEMBER

New Year's Eve, Kraków. New Year's Eve brings thousands of revelers to Kraków's main square to celebrate with fireworks and live music. Large screens help the crowds see all the action onstage. This website can help guide you to the festivities **www.wownight.eu.**

Christmas Market, Warsaw. Poland's capital comes alive during Christmas. The center of the action is the beautifully restored Old Town, with market stalls, filled with gifts and holiday food. In Zamkowy (Castle) Square, the Christmas tree is lit at night.

What to Pack

Poland is a modern European country, and there are no special packing needs. Rest assured that anything you might forget at home is fairly easily obtainable once you arrive. A couple of items which might come in handy include a good mosquito repellent if you're planning on traveling in the summer (plus lotion to take the itch out of the bites) and an eye mask, since many hotels and pensions for some reason lack heavy curtains to block out the early morning sunshine. Bring along sturdy and comfortable walking shoes, since you're going to be using them a lot. If your itinerary includes any special activities like cycling or skiing, you might consider lugging your own gear. The quality of rental equipment has gone up in recent years, but it's probably not what you're used to at home.

ENTRY REQUIREMENTS

Passports & Visas

All visitors to Poland are required to hold a passport that is valid for at least 6 months beyond the date of entry into the country. Passport holders from the U.S., Canada, and Australia can enter Poland without a visa and stay for 90 days. Passport holders from EU member countries, including the U.K., do not need a visa. Poland is a member of the EU's "Schengen" common border zone, meaning that—in theory, at least—if you are arriving from another EU country, you will not be asked to show a passport. Note that you are still obliged to carry your passport with you and show it if requested. Citizens of other countries should check in with the Polish Ministry of Foreign Affairs website (www.msz.gov.pl) to see whether they are required to have a visa and for any specific instructions necessary for obtaining it.

Customs

Travelers from outside the European Union, including the U.S., Canada, Australia, and New Zealand, are permitted to bring with them into Poland duty-free: 200 cigarettes, 50 cigars, or 250g (8¾ oz.) of pipe tobacco, 2L (68 oz.) of wine, and 1L (34 oz.) of spirits. For travelers coming from within the EU, at least in theory, the duty-free limit is 800 cigarettes, 200 cigars, or 1kg (2¼ lb.) of pipe tobacco, 110L (29 gal.) of beer, 90L (24 gal.) of wine, and 10L (2¾ gal.) of spirits. There are no limits on what

Destination Poland: Pre-Departure Checklist

- Is your passport valid for at least 6 months after the end of your trip?
- Do you have the address and phone number of your country's embassy or consulate with you?
- Did you notify your credit card issuers that you would be traveling to, and using your cards in, Poland?
- Do you have your credit card/ATM four-digit PIN?
- If you purchased traveler's checks, have you recorded the check numbers and stored the documentation separately from the checks?
- Did you bring ID cards that might entitle you to discounts, such as AAA, AARP, and student IDs?
- Did you leave a copy of your itinerary with someone at home?

you can take out of Poland, but special restrictions apply on exports of certain cultural items, including works of art created before 1950.

What You Can Take Home

For information on what you're allowed to bring home, contact one of the following agencies:

U.S. Citizens: U.S. Customs & Border Protection (CBP), 1300 Pennsylvania Ave., NW, Washington, DC 20229 (✆ **877/287-8667;** www.cbp.gov).

Canadian Citizens: Canada Border Services Agency, Ottawa, Ontario, K1A 0L8 (✆ **800/461-9999** in Canada or 204/983-3500; www.cbsa-asfc.gc.ca).

U.K. Citizens: HM Customs & Excise, Crownhill Court, Tailyour Road, Plymouth, PL6 5BZ (✆ **845/010-9000;** www.hmce.gov.uk).

Australian Citizens: Australian Customs Service, Customs House, 5 Constitution Ave., Canberra City, ACT 2601 (✆ **1300/363-263;** www.customs.gov.au).

New Zealand Citizens: New Zealand Customs, The Customhouse, 17–21 Whitmore St., P.O. Box 2218, Wellington, 6140 (✆ **04/473-6099** or 0800/428-786; www.customs.govt.nz).

Medical Requirements

There are no unusual health concerns for visiting Poland, and visitors are not required to get any special inoculations or show medical documents to enter the country. Medical and hospital standards are generally high. Though there are pharmacies everywhere, you should consider bringing along extra supplies of any prescription drugs you are taking. Tap water is drinkable, but you may want to avoid drinking from taps in old buildings since the pipes may be rusty. Bottled water is widely available.

GETTING THERE & GETTING AROUND

Getting to Poland

BY PLANE

Warsaw's Frederic Chopin airport (WAW) is the major air gateway into Poland, with extensive connections throughout Europe and some nonstop flights to North America. Warsaw is well served by the major European flag carriers, including Poland's

Sample Driving Times between Major Cities

The times here are only approximate and depend very much on weather and traffic conditions. In general, Polish roads are busy, and it's best to travel at off-peak hours.

- Prague to Wrocław: 3 to 4 hours
- Prague to Kraków: 7 to 8 hours
- Kraków to Wrocław: 3 to 4 hours
- Kraków to Warsaw: 3 to 4 hours
- Kraków to Zakopane: 2 hours
- Łódź to Warsaw: 3 hours
- Warsaw to Gdańsk: 5 to 6 hours
- Poznań to Warsaw: 3 hours
- Lublin to Warsaw: 3 hours

LOT, British Airways, Czech Airlines (CSA), Air France, KLM, and Lufthansa, as well as a growing number of budget carriers. See Warsaw's "Getting There" (p. 65) for more details. Kraków's Jan Paweł II Airport (KRK) is the country's second-most-important airport and is also easy to reach from nearly any large city in Europe and includes at least one nonstop to North America. The advent of low-cost budget carriers in Europe in recent years has opened up several other major cities to regular and convenient air travel, including Łódź (LCJ), Poznań (POZ), Wrocław (WRO), and Gdańsk (GDN).

IMMIGRATION & CUSTOMS CLEARANCE Immigrations and customs clearance is relatively straightforward and shouldn't take too long. Incoming passengers will be divided into two groups for passport control: "EU" and "All Others," the latter being where travelers from the U.S., Canada, Australia, and New Zealand must go. Customs is a breeze. If you're an ordinary traveler with nothing to declare, simply sail through the green-marked line (if you need to declare something, you'll have to go through the red line). You'll rarely even be asked to open your suitcase.

GETTING INTO TOWN FROM THE AIRPORT Depending on where you fly into, you'll usually have the option of taking a taxi, shuttle bus, or public bus into town. Kraków airport is even served by an express train that takes you to the center of town. For specific airport arrival information, see Warsaw's "Getting There" (p. 65) or Kraków's "Getting There" (p. 122).

BY CAR

Poland is easily accessible by car, and Polish highways are well integrated into the larger EU highway grid. If entering from an EU country (Germany, Czech Republic, Slovakia, or Lithuania), you no longer have to stop to show a passport. Standard border controls are still in effect if traveling to or from Ukraine, Belarus, or the Russian Federation.

Car rental agencies are ubiquitous in Poland and include most of the major international agencies, such as Hertz, as well as locally owned companies. Spot rental rates can be high—much higher than in the United States. It's often cheaper to rent in advance over the Internet. Rentals will usually include the legally required third-party liability insurance but will not include things like vehicle theft or damage. Be sure to ask what is covered. Most cars will have standard transmissions, but some agencies may offer cars with automatic transmission at a much higher price. The minimum age to rent a car is usually 21, though it can be higher at some agencies.

Before setting off, be sure to buy a good Polish road atlas (the excellent *Polska Atlas Samochodowy* is available at large service stations). Better yet, car satellite navigation systems, such as Garmin, have become very popular in the past few years. If you have one and plan on driving during your trip, certainly consider bringing it along with you. Make sure that you have the proper maps installed. Most GPS systems include Poland in their "European maps," but be sure to check. If you don't have a sat-nav system but are renting a car, ask the rental agency to include one with the car. A functioning satellite navigation system will spare you hours of frustration behind the wheel.

BY TRAIN

Poland is easy to get to by train. The Polish national rail network, PKP (www.pkp.pl), is well integrated into the Europe-wide rail system. Poznań and Warsaw lie on the main east–west line running from Berlin to Moscow. Kraków is easily accessible from Prague, Vienna, and points south, though many connections will require you to change trains at Katowice.

BY BUS

International bus travel has become less popular in recent years due to the arrival of the budget air carriers, which often match bus ticket prices but get you there much more quickly. Nevertheless, the Polish national bus carrier works in cooperation with the trans-European carrier Eurolines, and large Polish cities are easy to reach by bus.

Getting around Poland

BY PLANE

The Polish national carrier **LOT** (**© 801/703-703;** www.lot.com) offers regularly scheduled flights between major Polish cities, including Warsaw, Kraków, and Gdańsk.

BY CAR

Car travel offers maximum flexibility, but driving in Poland can be a slow and highly frustrating experience. Most Polish highways—even those connecting major cities—are of the narrow, two-lane variety and are usually clogged with trucks, buses, tractors, and even occasionally horse-drawn carts. For most stretches, plan on at least 2 hours' driving time per 100km (62 miles) distance. And drive defensively. Polish drivers have an abysmal record when it comes to per capita accidents and fatalities.

Poland follows normal continental rules of the road, with priority given to cars on roundabouts and vehicles coming from the right at unmarked intersections. Note that drivers are required to keep their headlights on at all times. The speed limit on (the few) four-lane freeways is 130kmph (81 mph). This drops to 90kmph (56 mph) on two-lane highways outside urban areas, and 50kmph (31 mph) or slower in built-up areas. Speed checks are common. Random sobriety checks are also frequent. The blood/alcohol limit is 0.02%—approximately one beer.

BY TRAIN

The Polish state railroad, **PKP** (www.pkp.pl), has improved its service in recent years, and train travel is usually the quickest and best way to move between big cities or to cover long distances. PKP maintains a useful online timetable (but be sure to use Polish spellings for city names) at www.rozklad-pkp.pl.

The best trains are the intercity (IC) trains, which link nearly all the country's biggest cities. You'll see IC trains marked in red on timetables; these are more expensive than regular trains and require an obligatory seat reservation. Next best are express trains (Ex), which also require a reservation. Avoid other types of trains for longer distances.

You can buy tickets at stations or directly from the conductor on the train, though you'll have to pay a surcharge of 8 zł. Fares are relatively low by Western standards. A second-class ticket from Kraków to Warsaw, for example, costs about 90 zł. For overnight trips, you can usually book a couchette in a six-bunk car or a sleeper in a three-bunk car. Sleepers run about 120 zł. Be sure to book these in advance.

BY BUS

Poland is well served by myriad public and private bus companies that go everywhere, from the biggest cities to the smallest towns. Prices and journey times are often comparable to the trains, and buses can be a highly useful alternative if you can't find a convenient train connection. In fact, within specific regions, buses are often better than trains for getting to outlying cities and towns. From Kraków, for example, buses are much quicker and cheaper than trains for the popular day trip to Zakopane. The tourist information office can usually help you figure out the best way of getting from one place to another, or whether the train or bus is a quicker or cheaper alternative.

With some notable exceptions (including Lublin and Katowice), in most cities, you'll usually find the main bus station located just next to the train station. Buy tickets in advance from ticket windows at stations or directly from the driver. Watch to have exact change on hand since drivers may not have enough cash to deal with large bills. Try to arrive at the station well before your bus is scheduled to leave. Lines at bus platforms start forming early, and the best seats go to those who get there first.

BY PUBLIC TRANSPORTATION

Most Polish cities have excellent public transportation systems consisting of buses, trams, trolley buses, and in Warsaw, a small metro. See separate city listings for public transportation details. Though each city's system differs slightly, the overall idea is the same. Buy single-ride tickets from tobacconists and news agents for about 2.50 zł per ride, validate the ticket in machines on entering the tram or bus, and keep the ticket until you get off. Once you've mastered public transportation, you'll find there's rarely any need to take a taxi.

ON FOOT

You'll likely spend a lot of time walking. Since cars and taxis are often barred from the centers of large cities and public transportation can get you only so close to where you need to go, walking is often the only alternative. Buy comfortable shoes and break them in before you arrive; you're going to use them.

BY BIKE

Poland is relatively flat, and depending how much time you have and what kind of shape you're in, you could conceivably cycle around the entire country. There are plenty of cycling trails that crisscross the country. Check out the organization **Bicycles for Poland** (www.rowery.org.pl) for some rules of the road and ideas on good routes. Cycling in cities is not recommended. Though some cities, like Kraków, do have specially marked bike lanes, traffic is heavy, and the lanes are not that well maintained.

MONEY & COSTS

THE VALUE OF THE POLISH ZŁOTY VS. OTHER POPULAR CURRENCIES

Zł	US$	Can$	UK£	Euro (€)	Aus$	NZ$
1	$.31	C$.32	£.20	€.25	A$.35	NZ$.43

Frommer's lists exact prices in the local currency. The currency conversions quoted above were correct at press time. However, rates fluctuate, so before departing consult a currency exchange website such as **www.oanda.com/convert/classic** to check up-to-the-minute rates.

The main unit of currency is the złoty (zł), which is divided (in theory) into 100 groszy (gr). Bills come in denominations of 10 zł, 20 zł, 50 zł, 100 zł, and 200 zł. The most useful coins are the 5 zł, 2 zł, and 1 zł. You'll also see less-useful coins of 50 gr, 10 gr, 2 gr, and rarely, 1 gr. At press time, $1 equaled about 3.20 zł.

Though Poland is a member of the European Union, the euro does not circulate in Poland and cannot be used for making purchases. The government recently committed itself to adopting the euro at some point in the future, but that date is still considered to be fairly far off. For convenience's sake, some hotels will quote their rates in euros and accept euros as payment, but in general, it's best to carry local currency.

Poland is not as cheap a destination as it was a few years ago, but it remains generally less expensive than Western Europe. Prices for everyday travel expenses, such as food and drink, hotels, and museum admissions, are substantially less than they would be in Paris or London. The exceptions are rental cars, five-star hotels, and imported clothing and other imported luxury goods, for which prices are as high here as anywhere else.

You can change money at nearly any bank or exchange office, identified in Polish as a *kantor*. You'll see these privately run exchanges everywhere, but be sure to shop around for the best rates and fees, since these differ from office to office.

WHAT THINGS COST IN POLAND	ZŁ
Taxi from the airport	60
Double room, moderate	250
Double room, inexpensive	180
3-course dinner without wine	45
Bottle of decent beer	7
Bottle of Coca-Cola	7
Good cup of coffee	8
Tram or bus ticket	2.50
Gallon (4L) of gasoline	18
Admission to a museum (adult)	7
Admission to national park	5

You'll get a decent, no-hassle exchange rate simply by using your credit or debit card at a bank ATM. In large cities and towns, you'll see an ATM on nearly every block. Before you leave home, be sure to alert your bank or credit card company that you will be traveling abroad. The bank or card company could block your card if security personnel see unusual charges coming through (such as purchases coming from Poland if you don't usually travel here). Also, make sure your card has a four-digit PIN code, since some Polish ATMs cannot take longer codes.

Credit cards are gaining in popularity and are now almost universally accepted at hotels and expensive restaurants. The most popular cards are American Express, Diners Club, MasterCard, and Visa. Travelers' checks can still be cashed at large banks but are almost more of a hassle than they are worth since they aren't usually accepted at shops, hotels, or restaurants.

HEALTH

A trip to Poland poses no unusual health concerns, aside from the bromides of not overindulging in food and, especially, drink, and looking both ways before you cross the streets (especially for trams). Still, there are a few things to keep in mind.

General Availability of Health Care

Polish health care is generally good and of high standard. Hospitals and doctors' offices may look shabby on the outside, but they are acceptably clean and well maintained. Polish dentists have a reputation around Europe for high-quality work and are usually much cheaper than their American or U.K. counterparts. Travelers do not require any specific shots before a trip to Poland, and aside from vaccinations against tick-bite encephalitis if you plan on doing a lot of hiking or sleeping in the open (see below), none are advised.

Poland has relaxed its rules for selling over-the-counter medications, and you can now usually find things like aspirin, cold medicines, cough syrup, and the like at convenience stores and large service stations. Still, it's best to bring along extra aspirin or Tylenol (or whatever you're used to) so as to minimize time looking around if you need to buy some. Pharmacies also sell common over-the-counter remedies, as well as all prescription drugs, but bring along extra doses of prescription medications since the local pharmacist may not recognize your doctor's prescription.

Common Ailments

DIETARY RED FLAGS Meat is a staple of Polish cooking, and vegetarians will have to pre-plan to avoid seeing it show up on their plate. Even seemingly "safe" options such as pierogi "Ruskie" style (stuffed with potato and cheese) may come covered in bacon drippings. (See "Vegetarian Travel," below.)

BUGS & OTHER WILDLIFE CONCERNS Mosquitoes are rampant in Poland, particularly in forested areas and near lakes and rivers, and can be a major nuisance. Be sure to pack strong mosquito repellant and some after-bite cream to reduce itching and swelling when you are inevitably bitten. Most pharmacies stock these if you forget to bring them.

Tick-bite encephalitis is also a problem, and you're strongly advised to get vaccinated if you plan on spending a lot of time hiking and/or sleeping in woods and fields. Always check your body thoroughly for ticks at the end of a long day of hiking and be sure to seek medical attention if you're concerned. Poisonous snakes and spiders are rare and not usually a problem.

RESPIRATORY ILLNESSES Polish air quality is improving, though during winter, you may encounter short periods of poor air quality, particularly in the industrial areas around Katowice and Kraków. Residents are usually advised to stay inside on bad air days.

SUN/ELEMENTS/EXTREME WEATHER EXPOSURE The sun is a constant danger, so be sure to pack plenty of sunscreen. Choose a higher SPF if you plan to spend a day on the beach or skiing in the mountains. Also, don't forget to bring along a hat, sunglasses, a long-sleeved shirt, and good sunscreen on summer mountain hikes, where you may be exposed to the sun for hours at a time.

What to Do If You Get Sick Away from Home

Polish medical care is good; rest assured that if something bad does happen on your vacation, you'll receive adequate care. In an emergency, immediately call ✆ **112** (general emergency) or ✆ **999** (ambulance). Most operators are trained to understand at least a little bit of English. Slowly try to explain the problem and your location, and an ambulance will come as quickly as possible to take you to the nearest hospital. Be sure to take along your passport, as well as some means of payment (cash or credit card).

Though Poles have universal medical coverage, foreign visitors are obliged to cover the total costs of any medical care they get in Poland. It's worth checking before you arrive whether your health insurance will cover you while you are abroad and, if not, how to supplement your insurance to get international coverage. Usually, you will have to pay any hospital fees out of pocket and then try to reclaim the costs later through your insurance. Retain all of the hospital paperwork, since you can never be sure what the insurance company might ask for.

Canadians should check with their provincial health plan offices or contact **Health Canada** (✆ **866/225-0709;** www.hc-sc.gc.ca) to find out the extent of their coverage and what documentation and receipts they must take home in case they are treated abroad.

Travelers from the U.K. should carry their European Health Insurance Card (EHIC), which covers emergency treatment.

In addition to the publicly financed health system, Poland has several excellent private medical clinics. These often offer higher standards and more personalized care, though they are usually more expensive. Additionally, they may be familiar with your insurance company and be able to bill directly. In Warsaw, the **LIM Medical Center** (Al. Jerozolimskie 65/79; ✆ **22/458-70-00;** www.cmlim.pl) is centrally located in the Marriott complex and staffs a full range of English-speaking doctors and specialists. For other cities, check with your hotel or the local tourist information office. We list additional **emergency numbers** in "Fast Facts," p. 292.

SAFETY

Poland is a relatively safe country, and travelers should not have any major safety or security concerns. The biggest potential threat is likely to be crime. Petty theft, pickpocketing, and car break-ins remain a problem. Watch your wallets and purses in crowded areas, particularly areas frequented by tourists. Always park your car in a well-lit area and use hotel or guarded parking lots in urban areas. Never leave valuables in the car or packages in plain view, as this may invite a break-in. Bike theft is rife. Never leave a bike unattended for more than a few minutes (even if it is securely locked) and always store it inside overnight. Hotels will often have a special area for storing bikes; otherwise, simply take it with you to your room.

Though robberies and violent crime are rare, it's best to avoid seedy areas at night (such as Warsaw's Praga neighborhood or parts of Łódź, or around train stations in any city). This is particularly strong advice for single women travelers, though in most other instances, women shouldn't encounter difficulties in Poland.

Polish police and law-enforcement agencies are invariably friendly and helpful to tourists, but they take a dim view toward public drunkenness. If you're out drinking, it's best to keep it down and keep your cool, otherwise you might find yourself spending a night in the drunk tank.

Drugs of any kind, including marijuana, are strictly illegal, and anti-drug laws are rigorously enforced. If you're caught with illegal drugs, you're best advised to contact your local embassy or consulate immediately, though you're unlikely to find much sympathy there or among law-enforcement agencies.

Prostitution is legal, though it's unregulated and potentially high-risk. While you probably won't see prostitutes standing on street corners in big cities, you may occasionally see them along highways, offering their services to passing truckers and other motorists. The "bars" you see along highways are often little more than brothels for truckers. You'll also find plenty of nightclubs, strip joints, escort agencies, and massage parlors around. Many of these are more or less legitimate businesses, but some are fronts for prostitution or organized crime. If you choose to patronize one of these places, minimize your risk by taking only small sums of money with you and leaving your credit cards back at the hotel. Maintain a high state of awareness and be prepared to leave at the slightest sign that something's not right.

While Poland is ethnically and racially homogenous, travelers from other countries and of different races are not likely to encounter overt discrimination. Homosexuality is publicly frowned upon, but openly gay travelers are not likely to experience specific problems. Gay couples are advised to avoid open displays of affection, though it's unlikely anything bad would happen.

Remember to be respectful around churches, particularly during masses. Make sure to wear appropriate dress. The rules aren't too strict on this, but in practice, women should cover their shoulders and avoid too-short skirts; men should wear long pants. Both sexes should wear shoes. Also, be sure to heed any prohibitions against making noise or taking photos, videos, or using flash photography.

Finally, be sure to donate something, however small, at the entrance if the church is not taking an admission fee. Many churches wouldn't be able to survive without visitor donations.

SPECIALIZED TRAVEL RESOURCES

Travelers with Disabilities

Sadly, Poland is decades behind the United States and many other countries in making its buildings and sidewalks more easily accessible to people in wheelchairs or with disabilities. The only exceptions are likely to be newly built hotels, which will usually have at least one room set aside for wheelchair access. The leading Polish group promoting the elimination of architectural barriers in Poland is **Integracja** (✆ **22/530-65-70;** www.integracja.org).

For more on organizations that offer resources to disabled travelers, go to www.frommers.com/planning.

Gay & Lesbian Travelers

Poland is not particularly gay-friendly, and the country's center-right government has recently spoken out against granting homosexuals legal rights or even discussing homosexuality in the public schools. That said, gays and lesbians visiting Poland are not likely to encounter overt discrimination or have trouble booking rooms. There are active gay populations in both Warsaw and Kraków, and several gay-friendly bars and clubs. **GayGuide.net** (http://warsaw.gayguide.net) publishes a useful list of gay clubs in the capital.

For more gay and lesbian travel resources, visit www.frommers.com/planning.

Senior Travel

Senior citizens can qualify for a 50% discount on Polish rail tickets if they buy a PKP Senior Citizen ID *(Legitymacja Seniora)*. The card costs 75 zł and is available to anyone over 60 (bring along a passport-sized photo). Museums will often grant senior discounts to anyone over 65. Try showing your passport or an AARP card.

For more information and resources on travel for seniors, see www.frommers.com/planning.

Family Travel

Poland is not particularly well suited to traveling with small children. Distances between cities are relatively far, and kid-friendly sights are few. To make things worse, museum exhibits tend to be static rather than interactive (on the plus side, many museums do not charge admission for children 5 and under). It pays to read up a bit in order to entertain the kids with tidbits of historic tales. Among Polish cities, Toruń (see p. 228) is compact and easy to manage, with tales like the Teutonic Knights and Copernicus, and rewards like a trip to the Gingerbread Museum to keep children motivated. Malbork Castle (see p. 262) will certainly set a benchmark for kids in sizing up any castle they are likely to see in the future. For real interactive family fun, try kayaking in Mazury and Suwałki (see p. 274), or rafting down the Dunajec river (see p. 158).

To locate accommodations, restaurants, and attractions that are particularly kid-friendly, refer to the "Kids" icon throughout this guide. For a list of more family-friendly travel resources, visit www.frommers.com/planning.

Women Travelers

Solo women travelers will face no extraordinary safety or security issues in Poland. Women should avoid walking alone in unsavory areas at night, but at most other times, there are no special dangers.

For general travel resources for women, go to www.frommers.com/planning.

Student Travel

Polish organizations frequently offer considerable discounts for students and young people. Check out the International Student Travel Confederation (ISTC) website (www.istc.org) for comprehensive travel services information and details on how to get an International Student Identity Card (ISIC), which qualifies students for substantial savings on rail passes, plane tickets, entrance fees, and more. It also provides students with basic health and life insurance, and a 24-hour helpline. The card is valid for a maximum of 18 months. You can apply for the card online or in person at **STA Travel** (✆ **800/781-4040** in North America, ✆ **132-782** in Australia, or ✆ **0871/2-300-040** in the U.K.; www.statravel.com), the biggest student travel agency in the world; check out the website to locate STA Travel offices worldwide.

If you're no longer a student but are still under 26, you can get an International Youth Travel Card (IYTC) from the same people that entitles you to some discounts. **Travel CUTS** (✆ **800/592-2887;** www2.travelcuts.com) offers similar services for both Canadians and U.S. residents. Irish students may prefer to turn to **USIT** (✆ **01/602-1904;** www.usit.ie), an Irish-based specialist in student, youth, and independent travel.

Single Travelers

Single travelers will encounter no specific problems in Poland. Most hotels set aside at least a few rooms for single occupancy, though prices are often nearly as high as for double occupancy. Single diners at restaurants may have to work a little harder to get a waiter's attention but face no unique difficulties.

For more information on traveling single, go to www.frommers.com/planning.

Vegetarian Travel

Polish food, built as it is around pork and game, is not particularly vegetarian-friendly, though there are plenty of meatless items on menus that you can build a meal around. Pierogi "Ruskie," for example, are stuffed with potato and cheese, but be sure to ask them to hold the bacon bits they sometimes throw on top. Other popular meatless pierogi fillings include cabbage and wild mushroom.

Green Way (www.greenway.pl) is an inexpensive and excellent chain of vegetarian restaurants with branches around the country, including in Warsaw, Kraków, Katowice, Gdańsk, Poznań, and Łódź.

For more vegetarian-friendly travel resources, go to www.frommers.com/planning.

RESPONSIBLE TOURISM

Poland has taken enormous steps in the past 2 decades to clean up its environment and to undo the decades of environmental degradation experienced under Communism. The Communist authorities placed a primacy on heavy industries like shipbuilding and steel production, spoiling parts of the Baltic seacoast, soiling rivers, and laying waste to thousands of square miles in the area of Upper Silesia, around Katowice. So enamored were they of glorifying the industrial proletariat that they even built an enormous steel mill complex, Nowa Huta, on the doorsteps of Kraków. The point there seems to have been to try to win over the bourgeois Cracovians to the Communist cause, but the result was exactly the opposite. The acrid smoke and acid rain coated buildings and damaged centuries-old monuments and statuary, not to mention the devastating impact on human health.

The good news is that all that belongs to the past. Nearly from the start of the collapse of Communism in 1989, Polish authorities have taken steps to reduce the environmental impact of heavy industries. The Nowa Huta complex is now a shadow of its former self, and many of the smelters, coking plants, and mills in the surrounding region have been shuttered or cleaned up. You might still catch the sharp whiff of a nearby steel mill on your travels (particularly in Upper Silesia), but nothing remotely like it was just 20 years ago.

Part of the impetus for change has been Poland's entry into the European Union and new legal restraints placed on emissions of greenhouse gases and particle pollution. Part, too, is simply the rising living standards and a new appreciation among the population for clean rivers and healthy forests. Poles, at heart, are inveterate hikers, bikers, and kayakers, and that awareness is only likely to grow.

That doesn't mean there are not problem areas. The rise in incomes has brought with it unique challenges. Car-ownership rates are now at an all-time high, and whereas modern cars burn much more cleanly than those old "Polski Fiat" clunkers favored under Communism (and which you still see motoring around occasionally), the sheer increase in cars on the road has mitigated some of the progress in combating air pollution. Prosperity, too, has led to significant land-use challenges. While population levels in Poland's big cities have leveled off, each year, thousands of people move to the fringes of big cities in new suburban developments. Cities like Warsaw and Kraków are now ringed by the single-family housing and shopping/office complexes familiar to anyone in the U.S. and Western Europe. That may be fine for the people who live there, but the result annually is a huge loss of open land and increased pressure on the country's creaking road network.

As a short-term visitor to the country, your environmental impact is likely to be small. Still, there are steps you can take to reinforce the country's growing green awareness. If you're just planning on hitting the big cities, for example, there's no need to drive your own car. Poland's train and bus networks are comprehensive, and the time you save driving will be minimal. Also, plan to incorporate into your itinerary activities like hiking, biking, and canoeing that reinforce this trend and put money into the hands of operators who promote it. Even the minimal fee (5 zł) you pay to enter one of the country's national parks goes some way toward protecting these lands for future generations.

Animal-Rights Issues

Animal-rights issues are making slow progress in Poland, a largely agrarian country that still depends on animals, in some cases, for farm labor. Some may take issue with the horse-drawn carriages that line up along Kraków's main square, the Rynek Główny, where the horses stand in the hot sun and occasionally suffer the whips of their masters.

For information on animal-friendly issues throughout the world, visit Tread Lightly (www.treadlightly.org).

General Resources for Green Travel

The following websites provide valuable wide-ranging information on sustainable travel:

- **Responsible Travel** (www.responsibletravel.com) is a great source of sustainable travel ideas; the site is run by a spokesperson for ethical tourism in the travel industry. **Sustainable Travel International** (www.sustainabletravelinternational.org) promotes ethical tourism practices and manages an extensive directory of sustainable properties and tour operators around the world.
- In the U.K., **Tourism Concern** (www.tourismconcern.org.uk) works to reduce social and environmental problems connected to tourism. The **Association of**

Independent Tour Operators (**AITO;** www.aito.co.uk) is a group of specialist operators leading the field in making holidays sustainable.

- **Carbonfund** (www.carbonfund.org), **TerraPass** (www.terrapass.org), and **Cool Climate** (http://coolclimate.berkeley.edu) provide info on "carbon offsetting," or offsetting the greenhouse gas emitted during flights.
- **Greenhotels** (www.greenhotels.com) recommends green-rated member hotels around the world that fulfill the company's stringent environmental requirements. **Environmentally Friendly Hotels** (www.environmentallyfriendlyhotels.com) offers more green accommodation ratings. The **Hotel Association of Canada** (www.hacgreenhotels.com) has a Green Key Eco-Rating Program, which audits the environmental performance of Canadian hotels, motels, and resorts.
- **Volunteer International** (www.volunteerinternational.org) has a list of questions to help you determine the intentions and the nature of a volunteer program. For general info on volunteer travel, visit **www.volunteerabroad.org** and **www.idealist.org**.

SPECIAL INTEREST & ESCORTED TRIPS

Several international travel agencies offer travel packages that focus exclusively on Poland or offer Polish destinations as part of a "Central European" or "Eastern European" tour. A few of the best are described below.

U.S.–based **Kensington Tours** (300 Delaware Ave., Suite 1704, Wilmington, DE 19801; ✆ **888/903-2001;** Fax 866/613-7599; www.kensingtontours.com) offers a signature "Eight Days in Poland" tour that starts in Gdańsk and makes its way across the country to Warsaw and Kraków.

U.S. operator **Tauck's** (✆ **800/788-7885;** www.tauck.com) 2-week Eastern European and Poland tour includes Kraków, Auschwitz, and a private Chopin recital in Warsaw on a regional getaway that includes stops in Budapest, Vienna, and Prague. Tauck also offers a 5-day, 4-night extension package to lengthen your stay in Poland.

The Polish operator **Almatur-Opole** (Ozimska 26/2, 45-058 Opole; ✆ **77/423-28-48;** Fax 77/423-28-40; www.excitingpoland.com) offers several highly rated Polish packages, including "Poland in One Week," the "Pearls of Northern Poland," and "Polish-Jewish Heritage."

For more information on package tours and for tips on booking your trip, see www.frommers.com/planning.

Academic Trips & Language Classes

Jagiellonian University in Kraków offers 3-, 4-, and 6-week Polish language and culture courses during the summer months at both the beginner and intermediate levels. The courses are administered through the **Kosciuszko Foundation** in New York (15 E. 65th St., New York, NY 10065; ✆ **212/734-2130;** www.thekf.org). Fees start at around $2,750 and include dormitory accommodation and weekend sightseeing trips.

Adventure & Wellness Trips

Poland's relatively flat terrain makes for ideal cycling country. Several operators offer trips of 1- or 2-week duration. Fees normally include bike and helmet rentals and guides, as well as accommodation and at least some meals. U.K.-based **Cycling Holidays Poland** (✆ **44/1536-738-038;** www.cyclingpoland.com) offers three separate 7-day tours that focus on the country's UNESCO World Heritage Sites, the Baltic coast, and the Mazurian Lakes district. Tours are offered on both road and mountain bikes. Poland also has thousands of kilometers of navigable waterways and a thriving canoeing and kayaking scene. Dozens of companies can help organize short or relatively long canoeing trips, depending on the need. **Canoe Kayak Poland** (www.canoekayakpoland.com) offers made-to-order canoe trips, can arrange for boat and equipment hire, and will provide guides.

Food & Wine Trips

Poland's culinary reputation is on the rise, having been named recently to several "top new cuisine" lists. **Poland Culinary Vacations** (1020 Durham Ave., Bozeman, MT 59718; ✆ **888/703-8130** or 406/522-7711; www.polandculinaryvacations.com) offers a series of 1-week trips specializing in regional cooking, including the "Flavors of Lower Silesia." The owner, Malgorzata Rose, was born in Wrocław, and though she's relocated to the U.S., she retains a passion for the cooking she grew up on.

Jewish Heritage Tours

For centuries, Poland was the center of Jewish life in Europe. The best way to uncover this history is through a knowledgeable guided tour. There are many reputable tour groups offering these kinds of services, and the tourist information offices in Łódź, Lublin, and Kraków can suggest local guides and tour operators. U.S.-based Polish Jewish Heritage (✆ 800/354-8320; www.polandjewishheritagetours.com) offers a standard 9-day tour package during the summer months starting at around $2,200 per person, as well as allowing for guided DIY tours, depending on what you want to see. Rates include meals, entrance fees, and accommodation.

Volunteer & Working Trips

Harvard University's **WorldTeach** (79 John F. Kennedy St., P.O. Box 122, Cambridge, MA 02138; ✆ **617/495-5527;** www.worldteach.org) operates a Polish program that is open to volunteers of almost any age and nationality. WorldTeach provides a thorough cultural immersion where volunteers teach elementary- to high school–age youth conversational English skills and American culture. Prior teaching experience is not required, though the application process is lengthy. Placements are in both rural and urban settings for 8 weeks during the summer.

STAYING CONNECTED

Telephones

Poland's country code is 48. To dial Poland from abroad, dial the international access code (011 in the U.S.), plus 48 and the local Poland area code. The area code for Warsaw, for example, is 22, so a call from the U.S. to Warsaw would begin 011-48-22, plus the local number. To call long distance within Poland, dial the city's area code, plus the number. To dial a number in Warsaw from another city in Poland, for example, you would dial 22, plus the local number. To dial abroad from within Poland, dial 00 and then the country code and area code to where you are calling. The country code for the U.S. and Canada is 1, meaning that a call to the U.S. from Poland would begin 00-1, plus the area code and local number.

Cellphones

Polish cellphones operate on a GSM band of 900/1800MHz. This is the same standard in use throughout Europe but different from the one used in the United States. U.S. mobiles will work here, provided they are tri-band phones (not all phones are tri-band) and that you've contacted your service provider to allow for international roaming. Keep calls to a minimum, however, since roaming charges can be steep.

U.K. mobiles should work without any problem, provided that you've contacted your service provider to activate international roaming (the same precautions about steep prices apply to U.K. mobiles).

One way of avoiding international roaming charges is to purchase a pay-as-you-go SIM card for your cellphone and a pre-paid calling card. This provides you with a local number and allows you to make calls and send text messages at local rates. All the major local telephone operators offer this service.

Voice over Internet Protocol (VoIP)

If you have Web access while traveling, consider a broadband-based telephone service (in technical terms, Voice over Internet protocol, or VoIP) such as **Skype** (www.skype.com) or **Vonage** (www.vonage.com), which allows you to make free international calls from your laptop or in a cybercafe. Neither service requires the people you're calling to also have that service (though there are fees if they do not). Check the websites for details.

Internet & E-Mail

WITH YOUR OWN COMPUTER OR SMARTPHONE

Nearly every hotel from a two-star property on up will offer some kind of in-room Internet access. Most often these days, this will be wireless, though occasionally it will be a LAN (dataport) connection. If the hotel offers LAN connections, they usually also loan out Ethernet cables for guests to use during their stay. Check with the reception desk. If having a good in-room Internet connection is important to you, make this clear when you register for your room. Wi-Fi signal strength drops off considerably the farther your room is from the router. Though the hotel may generally offer Wi-Fi, some rooms may not be close enough to make this practical.

Also, be sure to ask before you check in whether the Internet is working that day. The hotel may advertise in-room Internet access knowing full well the Internet is on the blink and is not likely to be fixed anytime soon.

Even if your hotel doesn't offer in-room Internet, there are usually lots of options for logging on with your own laptop. A surprising number of cafes, restaurants, and bars now offer free Wi-Fi to customers with a purchase. You may have to finagle a bit with the password (particularly if it uses Polish letters), but you'll normally be able to get it to work. Look for Costa Coffee outlets (www.costacoffee.com), which—in addition to having excellent coffee—also usually offer reliable, free Wi-Fi connections.

To locate Wi-Fi hotspots in Poland (and around the world), go to www.jiwire.com; its Hotspot Finder holds the world's largest directory of public wireless hotspots.

WITHOUT YOUR OWN COMPUTER OR SMARTPHONE

Many hotels will have a public computer or a business center for guests to use. If your hotel doesn't and you just want to check e-mail, it's sometimes worth asking at the reception desk whether you can use the hotel's computer for a few minutes. The answer is likely to be yes if it's a small place and the reception desk is not busy at the time.

Your hotel receptionist will certainly know the location of the nearest Internet cafe. The number of Internet cafes has stagnated in recent years as more and more people have gotten their own home computers, but most towns and cities will have at least a couple of cyber hangouts, usually stuffed to the gills with teens playing video games. Internet cafes have reasonable rates and charge around 6 zł per hour.

For help locating cybercafes and other establishments where you can go for Internet access, see "Internet Access," in Fast Facts (p. 293).

TIPS ON ACCOMMODATIONS

Decent hotels in Poland tend to be expensive. This is particularly true in large cities like Warsaw and Kraków. The past decade has seen a boom in hotel construction, but most of that has come in the high and high-middle ends of the market in order to cater to the growing amount of business travel to Poland. That means rates will probably be higher than you expect. On the plus side, however, this dependence on business travelers means that hotels often reduce rates on the weekends to fill beds; it never hurts to ask if the rate they are quoting is the best one available. Rates are often also lower if you pre-book over a hotel's website or use hotel booking sites or aggregators like Expedia.com.

Popular Polish Hotel Chains

Many international hotel chains, including InterContinental, Sheraton, Best Western, Marriott, and Radisson, own or operate at least one property in Poland. The following companies maintain chains in Poland with properties around the country:

- **Campanile** (✆ **331/64-62-59-70**; www.campanile.com.pl): French-owned chain that runs hotels under the Kyriad Prestige, Campanile, and Premiere Classe brands. The mid-market Campanile hotels are particularly good value, invariably cheerful, clean, and well-run.
- **Likus** (✆ **48/12-636-62-10**; www.hotel.com.pl): This local luxury group has several five-star hotels in Kraków, including the Copernicus, as well as five-star properties in Wrocław (Hotel Monopol), Katowice (Hotel Monopol), and Łódź (Grand). If you've got the money, you'll find no finer lodging in the country.
- **Orbis** (✆ **801/606-606**; www.orbis.pl): The former state-owned Polish hotel operator Orbis has hooked up with a French group and now operates hotels under the Novotel, Mercure, IBIS, and Etap brands. Novotels and Mercures tend to be up-market (and occasionally overpriced) affairs, while IBIS hotels are short on personality but big on value. Etap hotels can also be great—priced like youth hostels, but much cleaner and quieter.
- **Qubus** (✆ **71/782-87-65**; www.qubus.pl): A relatively young Polish chain that aims for the upscale business traveler and has properties in major cities around the country. Qubus hotels invariably have a high standard and are an excellent choice.
- **Vienna International** (www.vi-hotels.com): Features hip new properties like Andel's and Angelo in Kraków, Łódź, and Katowice, among other locations.

"Standard double rooms" are usually understood to mean twin beds; rooms with queen-size beds are often classified as "deluxe" and cost more. Most places now have nonsmoking accommodations, and a growing number of hotels are now mostly or entirely smoke-free.

If you're traveling by car, hotels outside of urban areas usually offer parking for free or for a nominal fee (around 10 zł). Within urban areas, such as Warsaw and Kraków, however, hotels sometimes use parking fees as a profit center and charge through the nose. Before agreeing to plunk down as much as 100 zł a night for parking at a four- or five-star hotel, it's worth checking to see if there's metered street parking out front or a municipal parking garage nearby for a fraction of the fee. The Sheraton Hotel in Kraków, for example, charges 100 zł per night to park in its underground garage, but right next door is the perfectly safe Kraków municipal garage that charges 30 zł a night.

In addition to hotels and pensions *(pensjonaty),* there's no shortage of people offering private accommodations in their homes or flats. This is more common in heavily touristed areas away from larger cities—in places like Zakopane, for example. Look for the signs saying *wolny pokój* (free room) or *noclegi* (lodging) hanging from a house. Prices are lower than hotels, but standards vary considerably. Always take a look at the room first before accepting.

For tips on surfing for hotel deals online, visit www.frommers.com/planning.

SUGGESTED POLAND ITINERARIES

4

Poland is a deceptively large country, so it's best to scale down your geographic ambitions from the outset. One week in Poland is ideal if your goal is to get in two big cities—say, Warsaw and Kraków—and a little bit in between. For anything more comprehensive, give yourself 10 days or, ideally, 2 weeks.

The problem isn't so much Poland's size, but the transportation infrastructure. Train travel in Poland continues to improve, and an express train can now get you from Warsaw to Kraków in around 3 hours, but most trains still move aggravatingly slowly, and you can literally spend a whole day on the train going from, say, Kraków to Gdańsk or from Lublin to Wrocław. Bus travel is similar; buses can travel only as fast as the roads allow. That said, buses are often a better bet than trains for travel within regions and along selected city-to-city routes.

And then there are the roads. Poland's antiquated network of two-lane highways is the butt of national jokes and a real bottleneck to the country's economic growth. The country has launched a massive road-building effort funded by the European Union, but for the foreseeable future (certainly the lifetime of this book), be prepared to put up with huge traffic jams, crowded and impassable roads, and frustrating detours that always seem to pop up just as you approach your destination. As a rule of thumb, figure on 2 hours of car travel for every 100km (62 miles). One notable exception is the excellent A4 superhighway (*autobahn* might be a more apt term, given the speeds people drive), linking Kraków with the German border in the west and passing through Katowice and Wrocław along the way. The EU's involvement has a darkly comic dimension. Invariably, when you see a sign saying something like "This road brought to you by the European Union," expect to find traffic backed up for miles in both directions ("This traffic jam brought to you by the EU," might be more appropriate). Even with the hassles and inconveniences, car travel might still be the best way to explore smaller towns and off-the-beaten-track destinations otherwise accessible only by sporadic bus service.

Depending on the length of your stay, there are several ways you could focus your itinerary to get the most out of your trip. One logical choice is to divide the country into north and south, including Warsaw in both, but making Gdańsk (north) or Kraków (south) the focal point of your travel.

Another way would be to focus on a particular interest—World War II or Jewish heritage, for example—or on an activity such as hiking, biking, boating, or, yes, even sunbathing on the beach.

POLAND IN 1 WEEK

There's no way to cover the entire country in just 1 week, so this itinerary is divided into two itineraries for you to choose between, depending on how you want to spend your time: Warsaw plus Kraków and southern Poland; or Warsaw plus Gdańsk and northern Poland.

Southern Poland Itinerary: Warsaw & South

Days 1 & 2: Warsaw

Get settled in and, if you've got the energy, try to arrange for an organized city tour by bus in the afternoon. Warsaw is sprawling, and even if you're not an "organized tour" type of person, this is one place where a bus tour makes sense. Spend the second day with a more leisurely stroll of the Old Town, admiring the "old" look of the place, even though it's barely 30 years old. Warsaw's Old Town was totally destroyed in World War II and rebuilt brick by brick. Don't pass up the chance to see the Museum of the Warsaw Uprising ★★★, which will help you to understand that spirit of the city. If it's a nice day, try to get out to Łazienki Park ★★. On Sunday, you might even catch the weekly open-air Chopin concert. For a more intense immersion, touch-screen through the multimedia presentations at the revamped Chopin Museum ★★.

Days 3 & 4: Kraków

Drive or take the train to Kraków—either way, it will take about 3 to 4 hours. Give yourself plenty of time to enjoy Poland's most popular travel destination. Dedicate at least 1 full day to the Old Town and the Wawel Castle area, including the castle Cathedral ★★★, whose crypt is filled with tombs of Polish kings. Leave another full day for Kazimierz and the sights of the former Jewish quarter.

Day 5: Kraków Daytrip—Auschwitz or Wieliczka

The former Nazi extermination camp at Auschwitz-Birkenau ★★★ lies about 90 minutes west of Kraków by car; alternatively, you can go by train or bus, or book one of several Auschwitz day tours through the tourist information office. It's a must, particularly if you've never had the chance to visit a Holocaust site in the past. Plan to sleep back in Kraków; after a day of touring the camps, you'll want to come back to a place full of life. If you're traveling with small children and looking for a more suitable day trip, try the Wieliczka Salt Mines ★★★, easily reachable from Kraków by bus or train, or via a guided tour booked through the Kraków tourist information office.

Day 6: Zakopane

If you've got time and energy for more travel, hit the bus and head down to the Tatra resort of Zakopane. If you get an early enough start, you'll have enough time for a bit of a mountain walk; otherwise, you'll have to content yourself with a stroll around town and maybe a cable-car ride to the top of one of the peaks.

Poland in 1 Week

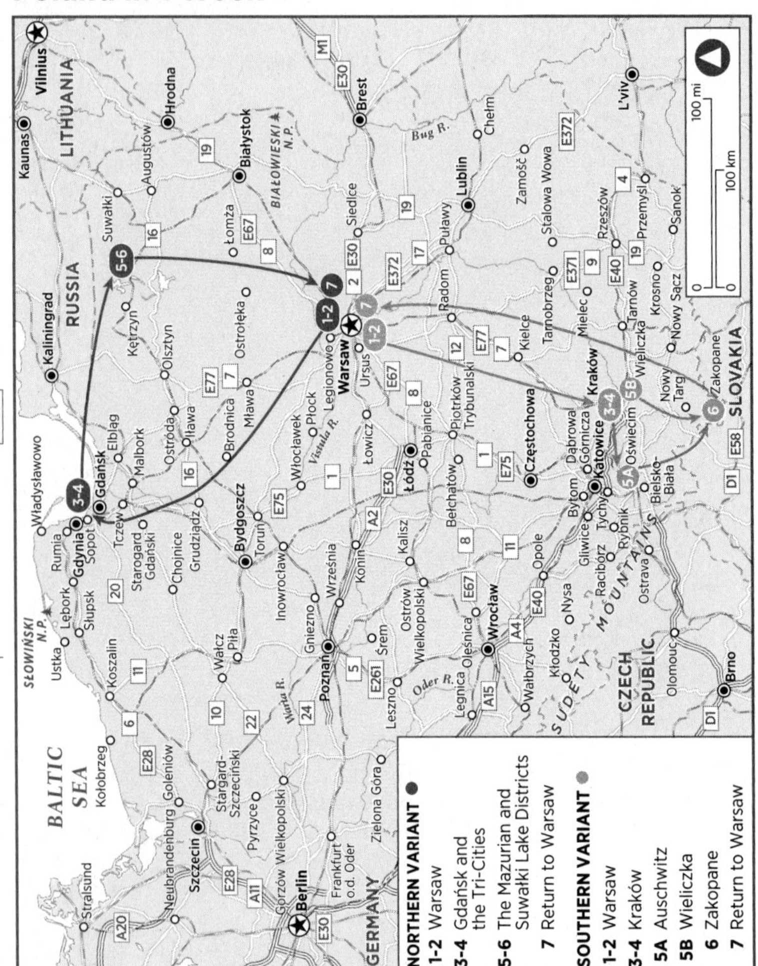

For an offbeat, old-style villa that really captures old Zakopane, book a room at the Pensjonat Szarotka ★★.

Day 7: Return to Warsaw

If you're leaving from Zakopane, take the bus back to Kraków and the train back to Warsaw. Leave at least 2 hours for the journey to Kraków and 3 to 4 more for the trip back to Warsaw.

Northern Poland Itinerary: Warsaw & North

Days 1 & 2: Warsaw

See the "Southern Poland Itinerary: Warsaw & South" tour, above.

Days 3 & 4: Gdańsk & the Tri-Cities

This Baltic Sea port is one of the real highlights of any trip to Poland: a beautifully restored city, rich with history and natural beauty. Don't miss stunning ul. Długa, Gdańsk's main shopping thoroughfare; also take in the Amber Museum ★★ and a walk along the pier. To understand why Gdańsk natives are so proud of their political past, visit the Roads to Freedom ★★★ exhibition. For a change of scene, track down the giant murals in Zaspa ★★, a housing estate from the Communist era. If the weather is warm, be sure too to spend some time on the beach and greet the sunset from Sopot's long and lively pier; after sunset, Sopot comes alive with drinking and dancing spots.

Days 5 & 6: The Mazurian & Suwałki Lake Districts

Head south and east to visit a nature-lover's paradise: The Mazurian Lake district. This area is famous in Poland for its ample sailing and kayaking opportunities. While you're in the area, stop in at the Wolf's Lair ★★, the site of the 1944 assassination attempt on Hitler's life made by his own officers (an episode explored in the 2008 Tom Cruise movie *Valkyrie*). In the Suwałki Landscape Park, try getting a room at the Jaczno Lodge ★★★, a lovely cluster of stone and timber houses hemmed in by woods and the pristine water of Lake Jaczno.

Day 7: Return to Warsaw

Catch the train or bus back to the capital. Depending on where you start from, the trip back could take the better part of a day. If you're driving, allow time to hit plenty of traffic on your way into Warsaw.

POLAND IN 2 WEEKS

In 2 weeks, you can cover a lot of ground, even in Poland. While you'll still have to pick and choose, you'll at least have a chance to relax at the major sites and hit some out-of-the-way places. One way to approach Poland in 2 weeks would be to simply combine the two 1-week tours, above, using one of your weeks for the south of the country and the second week for the north. The tour below is a modified version of this, heading to Gdańsk first after Warsaw and then moving around Poland in a clockwise circle. It could also be done quite easily by going to Kraków first after Warsaw and moving, again, clockwise.

Days 1 & 2: Warsaw

See the "Poland in 1 Week" tour, above.

Days 3 & 4: Gdańsk & the Tri-Cities

The first stop after Warsaw is the Baltic port city. Stroll the Old Town, hit the beaches, and try to get out for a day on the Hel peninsula ★★, where restaurants offer the fresh catch of the day. You may opt to spend an extra day in Gdańsk (especially in hot weather) and skip the day at Malbork (see below). Alternatively, you can keep heading west to Słowiński National Park and its amazing and enormous sand dunes.

Poland in 2 Weeks

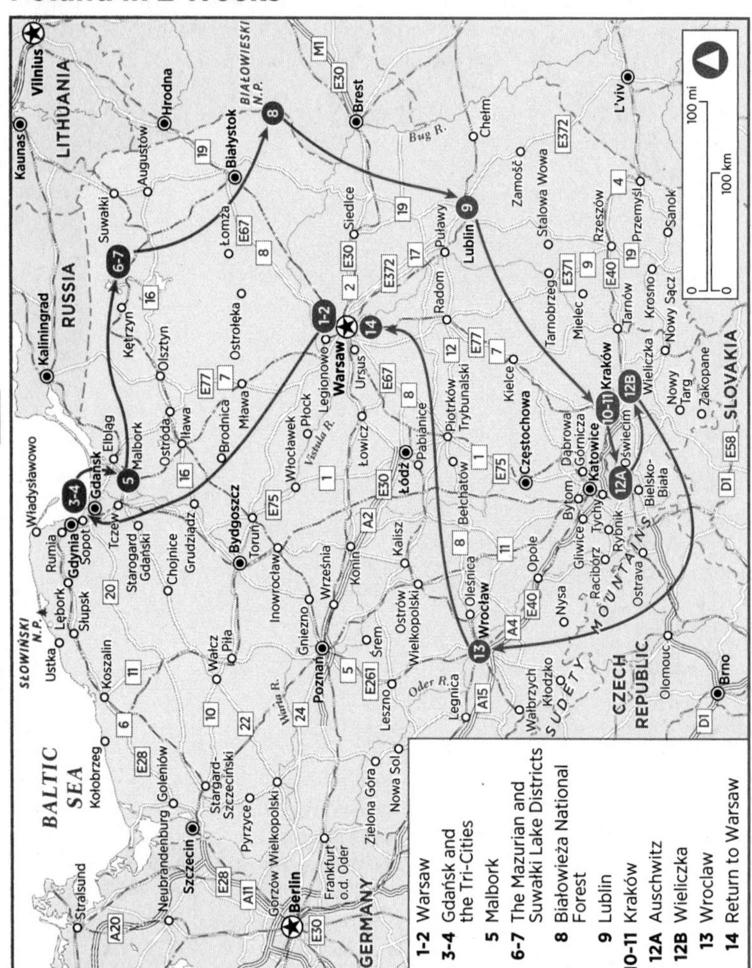

Day 5: Malbork

If you've got the time, don't pass up the chance to see the enormous Teutonic Knights' castle at Malbork ★★★. You can use Gdańsk as your base or treat Malbork as a stopover en route to the Mazurian Lakes. The knights once schemed to control the rich Baltic amber trade, but ultimately, their ambition did them in. This massive castle is silent testimony to the size of those ambitions. If you're looking to give your feet a rest, hop on a one-of-a-kind in Europe boat-and-rail ride on the Elbląg-Ostróda Canal.

Days 6 & 7: The Mazurian & Suwałki Lake Districts

See the "Poland in 1 Week" tour, above. If the weather is good, you may want to add an extra day canoeing and skip the trip to the Białowieża National Forest or Lublin (see below).

Day 8: Białowieża National Forest ★★★

Now for something completely unexpected: Who would have thought that Poland would have some of Europe's last primeval forest, untouched by man over the centuries? Hire a guide and take a long walk through the woods, admiring the old growth and the interaction of flora and fauna (but don't forget your mosquito repellant—some interactions with nature are better than others). At Białowieża, the Hotel Carska ★★ was literally built for a tsar—specifically, Russia's Tsar Nicholas II. A real splurge and a must for fans of unusual hotel design.

Day 9: Lublin

Continue south to the city of Lublin, with its great hotels and restaurants, and big-city diversions that you may have been missing when you were at the lakes and Białowieża. Be sure to walk through the Old Town, chock full of pubs and restaurants, and home to lively open-air concerts in summer. Lublin has a clutch of great hotels and some of the best restaurants in this part of Poland. If you aren't going to Auschwitz but would like to visit a Holocaust site, the infamous Majdanek ★★★ camp is just a short bus ride from the center of town.

Days 10 & 11: Kraków

See the "Poland in 1 Week" tour, above.

Day 12: Kraków Daytrip—Auschwitz or Wieliczka

See the "Poland in 1 Week" tour, above.

Day 13: Wrocław

Wrocław is Poland's hidden gem. Find a place to stay—if you're up for a bit of a splurge, try the classy Qubus ★★—and then head for the Rynek and a traditional Polish dinner at the Piwnica Świdnicka ★★ pub. Walk along the river and unwind from your long trip around the country. If you're up for a night of carousing, try the strip of bars along Kiełbaśnicza.

Day 14: Return to Warsaw

See the "Poland in 1 Week" tour, above.

POLAND FOR FAMILIES

Poland isn't the easiest of destinations for families with children. Walking with younger children can prove strenuous, and even older kids may not have an appreciation of the historic sites. It doesn't help that most of the museums are of the old-school variety, more static than interactive. However, there are a number of unique spots that are captivating for kids of all ages.

Poland for Families

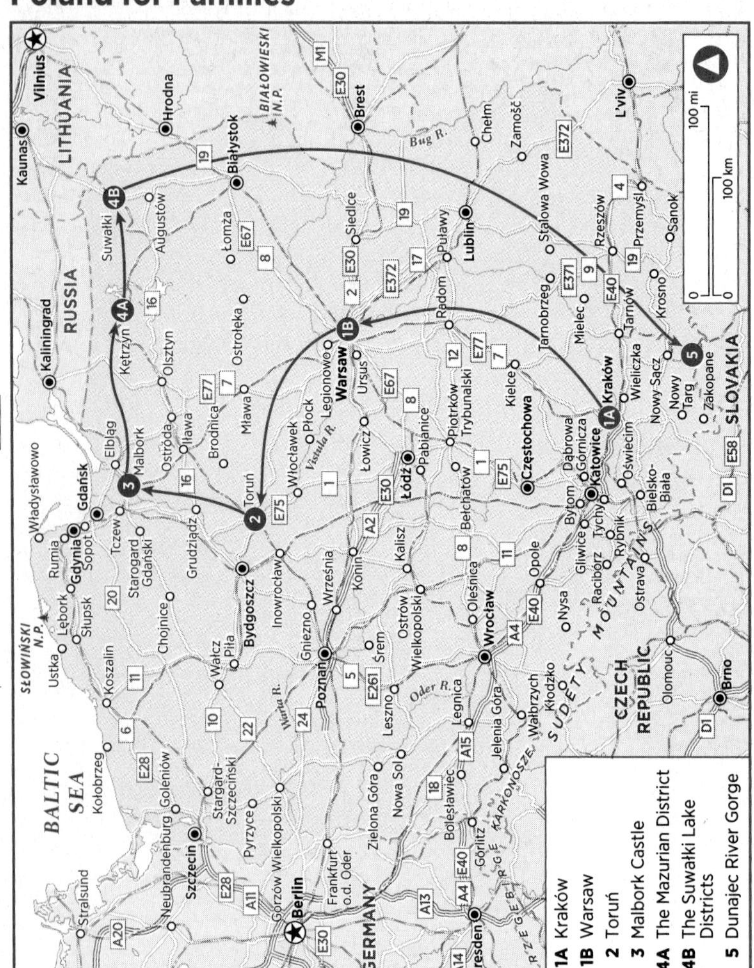

Day 1: Kraków/Warsaw

Krakow is definitely the most kid-friendly of Poland's big cities. The Old Town Square is a natural draw, not to mention the city's zoo, with its big collection of exotic hippos, and the country's largest water park. In recent years, Warsaw, too, has become increasingly aware of the needs of junior travelers. The Chopin Museum ★★ has a kid's section that just might spark an interest in classical music. Across the river, the Warsaw Zoo has a collection of European bison (sparing you the journey all the way to Białowieża National Forest).

Day 2: Toruń

The central Polish city of Toruń is compact and easy to manage, and is laced with tales about the Teutonic Knights and Copernicus, and rewards such as gingerbread to keep the kids motivated. Be sure to visit the Gingerbread Museum, where you get to not only look at the confections, but make them and eat them, too.

Day 3: Malbork Castle ★★★

The massive former Teutonic Knights' castle at Malbork will certainly set the benchmark for children when sizing up other castles in the future. Tales of the knights will likely keep them enthralled longer than other sites, as well. In summer, the castle hosts reenactments of historical battles, where meticulous attention is paid to costumes, hairstyles, weaponry, and horsemanship. "Magic Malbork," held in August, has dazzling acrobats and fireworks.

Day 4: The Mazurian & Suwałki Lake Districts

If the kids are suffering from overexposure to "Old Towns," try a day of kayaking in Mazury and Suwałki. The Krutynia route in Mazury, and the lower section of the Czarna Hańcza route, are an easy and enjoyable introduction to rafting.

Day 5: Rafting Down the Dunajec

In the south of the country, take the kids for a great day of rafting down the Dunajec. See the "5-Day Outdoor Vacation in Poland" tour, below.

5-DAY FOCUS ON JEWISH HERITAGE

Five days is barely enough time to begin to scratch the surface of Poland's immense and important Jewish history. This tour assumes you're beginning in Warsaw and includes a stop in the industrial city of Łódź, which was made wealthy by Jewish industrialists in the 19th and 20th centuries, as well as stops in Kraków's former Jewish quarter, Kazimierz, and at the Nazi extermination camps of Auschwitz and Birkenau. The eastern city of Lublin is not included in this tour, though there are numerous Jewish heritage sites there that are worth visiting.

Day 1: Warsaw

Arrive in Warsaw and find your feet. Spend the afternoon walking Warsaw's former Jewish ghetto, taking in sites such as the Monument to the Ghetto Heroes, which recalls the heroic Jewish uprising in 1943, and a concrete-bunker-type memorial at the "Umschlagplatz." The Jewish Cemetery ★★ is a poignant reminder of the lost Jewish heritage. Time might be tight, but it's possible to make it out to Treblinka ★★, an extermination camp 100km (62 miles) outside the city, where most of Warsaw's Jews perished.

Day 2: Łódź

Get an early start and drive or take the train to the former industrial powerhouse of Łódź. Before World War II, Łódź's Jewish population numbered more than

A 5-Day Focus on Jewish Heritage

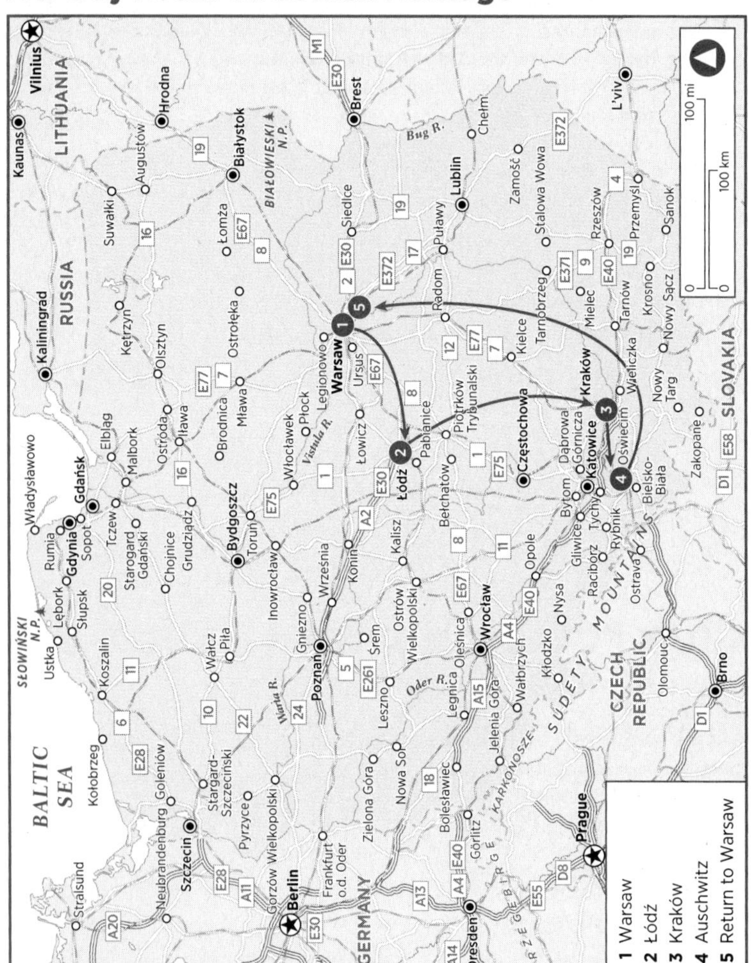

200,000—the largest concentration of Jews in Europe after Warsaw. Today, just a handful remain. The Jewish sites here, however, are some of the best in the country. A tour of the former wartime ghetto is an absolute must, as is a stop at the former Jewish cemetery and the Radegast train station, where trains to the concentration camps left from. Be sure, too, to stop by the History of Łódź Museum, housed in the former residence of Jewish industrialist par excellence, Izrael Kalmanowicz Poznański. Have dinner at Anatewka ★★, an informal Jewish-themed restaurant.

Days 3 & 4: Kraków & Auschwitz

From Łódź, take the bus to Kraków, once one of the most important centers of Jewish life and scholarship in Europe. Save plenty of time for an enthralling walking tour of Kazimierz and the adjoining wartime ghetto of Podgórze across the river. Try to get a room in Kazimierz and experience its new lease on life in the evening as one of Poland's liveliest clubbing districts. For dinner, book a table at Dawno Temu Na Kazimierzu ★★★, a great mix of excellent food and just enough kitsch to keep it interesting. On your second day, plan an all-day trip to visit the Auschwitz-Birkenau concentration camps ★★★. Spend the night back in Kraków.

Day 5: Return to Warsaw

The trip to Warsaw will take around 3 hours by train, leaving you a little time left in the morning to explore Kraków's Old Town and Wawel Castle ★★★ if you haven't already seen it. Alternatively, return to Warsaw as early as possible for a trip to Tykocin ★, 170km (106 miles) east of Warsaw, to see a 17th-century synagogue and its sensitively restored interior.

5-DAY SCENIC DRIVE THROUGH POLAND

There are plenty of scenic road trips through Poland. This particular trip focuses on the Giant Mountains and the province of Lower Silesia, south of Wrocław. But the lakes north of Warsaw and the coastal areas to the west of Gdańsk are all spectacular; even if they're just seen from the car window.

Day 1: Wrocław

The capital of Lower Silesia makes a good base for starting this exploration of Poland's scenic southwest. Once you've had a chance to walk around Wrocław's Old Town square, the Rynek, take the train, bus, or your own wheels to the nearby city of Wałbrzych, home to one of Poland's most spectacular castles, Książ Castle ★★. Wrocław is also a great base for exploring Poland's two wooden "Peace" churches, one at Świdnica ★★ and the other at Jawor ★★. Plan on spending the night at one of Książ Castle's very nice hotels or (if you are driving) at the Bolków Hotel ★ near Jawor, with its excellent restaurant ★★★.

Day 2: Jelenia Góra

The regional capital of Jelenia Góra is a natural stopping off point for exploring Karkonosze National Park and Poland's Giant Mountains. But before heading for the hills, stop to admire the town's nearly perfect baroque town square and be sure, too, to have a nut-and-chocolate pancake at the little cafe Kawiarnia Naleśnikarnia ★ on the square. There's a museum here to help you bone up on your Karkonosze history before venturing onward. Spend the night at the Pałac Paulinum ★★, a renovated villa deep in the forest that surrounds the town.

A 5-Day Scenic Drive through Poland

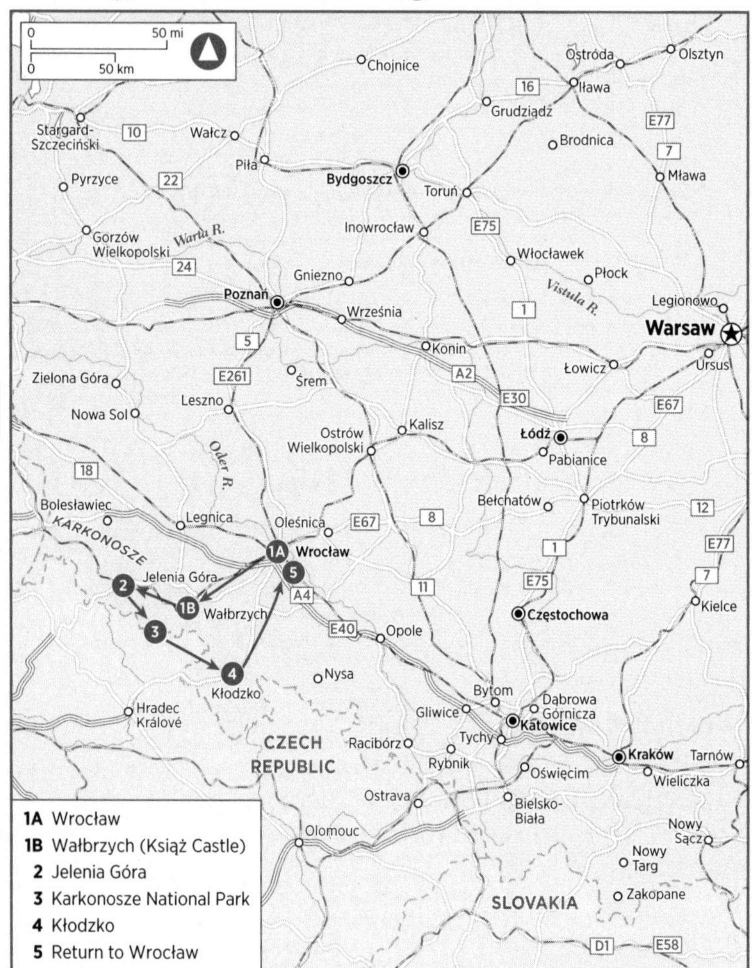

Day 3: Karkonosze National Park

Get an early start and head for one of the park's main resorts of Szklarska Poręba or Karpacz. Both are more or less the same: Ramshackle collections of old mountain lodges, hotels, cafes, ticky-tacky gift shops, and plenty of bike- and ski-rental outlets. The drive along the main road between the two towns is absolutely jaw-dropping, cutting through tiny mountain villages, green fields, and here and there, rocky peaks. The drive is fun, but if you've got the time and energy, try one of Szklarska Poręba's mountain bike trails. Around a dozen trails fan out from the town, catering to all levels of ability. You may want to extend your visit here and skip the trip to Kłodzko (below).

Day 4: Kłodzko

Get another early start and begin the journey east to the town of Kłodzko. A trip here feels like a journey back in time; not long ago the towns and villages along the route were part of Germany, and the area retains a strong Teutonic feel. Kłodzko itself feels like one of the most remote towns in Poland, stuck in the center of a sliver of land that extends deep into the Czech Republic. Don't miss a tour of the Kłodzko fortress and, if you have time, check out the picturesque village of Międzygórze, another Alpine village on the lip of the mountains. Book a room or at least have a meal at the Hotel Korona ★, a good value hotel/motel on the edge of Kłodzko.

Day 5: Back to Wrocław

The drive back to Wrocław is a straight shot north on the E67 highway about 120km (75 miles), or an easy bus ride. Leave about 2 to 3 hours for the journey. On the other hand, if you've got more time, keep pushing east toward Zakopane and the Tatras and more mountain splendor (see below).

5-DAY OUTDOOR VACATION IN POLAND

In Poland, an "outdoor" vacation invariably boils down to either mountains or seashore. That means having to choose between the Baltic Sea and Mazurian Lakes far in the north, or the Giant Mountains and the Tatras far to the south. Unless you've got lots of time to travel, you'll have to make the same choice, too. Below are two 5-day itineraries, depending on whether you're a "seashore" or a "mountain" person.

Seashore Itinerary

Days 1 & 2: Gdańsk & the Tri-Cities

This is the center of Poland's beach scene, and a surprisingly lively beach scene it is. Most of the best beaches are in Sopot or on the Hel Peninsula, reachable by boat from Gdańsk. You'll find all the usual beach diversions in Sopot, including a long pier, a "boardwalk"—actually a sidewalk—that runs for miles on both sides of the pier, and a late-night disco scene. If you're traveling in July or August and you get a patch of hot weather, this is where you'll find a good percentage of the Polish population.

Days 3 & 4: The Mazurian & Suwałki Lake Districts

From Gdańsk, make your way over to the Mazurian lakes for some long-distance canoeing. See "Poland in 1 Week," earlier in this chapter.

Day 5: Białowieża National Forest

From the lakes, head south and east to the Belarusian border for some unspoiled forest and gorgeous hiking territory. See "Poland in 2 Weeks," earlier in this chapter.

A 5-Day Outdoor Vacation in Poland

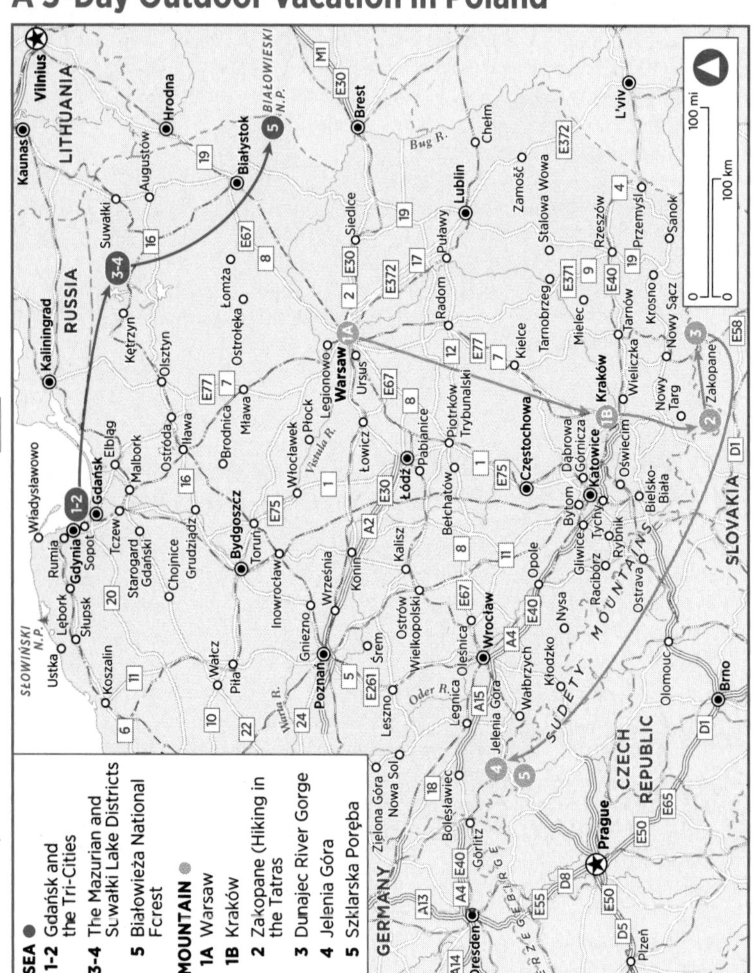

Mountain Itinerary

Day 1: Warsaw or Kraków to Zakopane

Depending on your base, make your way to the Tatra resort of Zakopane, one of the country's most popular hiking centers in summer and a leading ski resort in winter. In summer, pick up some hiking maps once you hit town and plot your assault on the peaks. There are hundreds of kilometers of marked trails for all skill levels. Check our hiking suggestions (p. 157) or consult the tourist information office for some ideas.

Day 2: Hiking in the Tatras ★★★

Hit the mountains early and remember to wear sturdy shoes and bring plenty of water, sunscreen, a rain slicker, sunglasses, a bite to eat, and a map. The trails may be well marked, but believe us, you're going to need the map anyway. With luck, you'll get a clear, sunny day, but remember to start heading back down the hill the moment it starts to look like afternoon showers.

Day 3: Boating Down the Dunajec ★★

After an exhausting hike, take it easy today with a relaxing float down the scenic Dunajec River. Several travel agencies in Zakopane book rafting trips down the Dunajec. Each raft holds around a dozen people, and the guides are decked out in mountain garb. The float takes a couple of hours, and you have the option of walking back to the parking lot or renting and riding bikes. It's a great day out and perfect for kids.

Day 4: Travel to the Giant Mountains

There's no easy way to get from the Tatras to the Giant Mountains in the southwest. The easiest is to drive down the A4 highway from Kraków to Wrocław (3–4 hr.) or, alternatively, take a bus. From Wrocław, make your way by car or bus to one of the Giant Mountain resorts or the regional capital of Jelenia Góra. Plan on traveling most of the day. Reward yourself with an excellent Polish meal at Metafora ★★ in Szklarska Poręba.

Day 5: Cycling in the Giant Mountains ★★

Find your way to the resort town of Szklarska Poręba for a day of heaven in the open air. Stop by the tourist information office to pick up some cycling maps and good advice on rentals and trails. Szklarska Poręba has cast itself as southern Poland's biking capital, and some of the best mountain trails in the country—including plenty for novice riders and families—are here. Some of the most rewarding and longest trails dip into the Czech side of the mountains, but be sure not to go overboard on your first ride. These are mountains, and you'll have to work hard uphill for every easy downhill (but it's worth it).

WARSAW

by Kit F. Chung

Poland's capital city, not often included on tourist itineraries, deserves a fresh look. While it may not be a place you'll fall in love with instantly, there's an energetic spirit of rebirth here that's immediately contagious. Get to know the city, and you could very well develop a soft spot for it. Visiting Warsaw is about seeing a capital city getting back on its feet time and time again after military and ideological occupations. With some 85% of the city demolished in World War II, nearly everything you see, including the charming and very "old" looking Old Town (Stare Miasto), has been around only for a few decades. The Old Town was so faithfully rebuilt that it earned a place on the UNESCO list of World Cultural Heritage Sites. Much of the city center was propped up by the workers' power philosophy of Communism, creating the Eastern Bloc look of imposing Socialist Realism structures and sculptures, as well as dreary and drab housing blocks. In the post-Communism years, modern skyscrapers—both beautiful and ugly—jostle for space in the city's skyline. The riverfront is also being developed. The changes are every bit as dramatic on the cultural front. New clubs, theaters, museums, performance spaces, and restaurants have opened their doors, and Warsaw feels like it's in a hurry to make up for time lost in the Communist years.

5

To understand this city, a visit to the **Warsaw Uprising Museum** is a must. The museum gives a full-blown account of the single event in World War II that was largely accountable for the scarred cityscape. And as you trace the former Jewish quarter, you'll sense the void left by a community that made up one-third of the city's population before the war. Top on most sightseeing agendas are the **Old Town,** the **Royal Route,** and the sprawling **Łazienki Park.** While these enclaves of beauty and history are well deserving of your time, recently, more attention has been shifting to the leftover relics of Communism as the younger generation comes to accept the quirks of that era as part of the city's heritage. Also gaining limelight is the rundown district of Praga—relatively undamaged during the war, it has some of the oldest original buildings in the city. It is also the site of one of the most modern stadiums in the country: the National Stadium is currently being constructed to host the opening match of the Euro Cup Football Championship in 2012.

You'll want to budget at least 2 days to get the most out of Warsaw's diverse daytime and after-dark activities.

ESSENTIALS

Getting There

BY PLANE Warsaw's **Okęcie Airport** (Żwirki i Wigury 1; ✆ **22/650-42-20;** www.lotnisko-chopina.pl), sometimes called by its formal name, Fryderyk Chopin Airport, is 10km (6¼ miles) from the city center. Most major international carriers land at, and take off from, the new Terminal 2. The older Terminal 1 is still in use for domestic flights. Terminal 2 is well served by a tourist information office, automated teller machines, car rental booths, and kiosks for tram and bus tickets. By bus or taxi, it takes approximately 20 to 30 minutes to get to the city center. During the day, take bus no. 175; in the evening, bus no. N32. Tickets cost 2.80 zł. Taxis, operated by SAWA, Merc, and MPT, make the run to the center for around 40 zł. Watch out for unlicensed drivers; there are fewer of them these days, but they still manage to nab unwary travelers, charging three to four times the going rate. Another alternative is the shared or private transfers operated by **Warsaw Shuttle** (✆ **500/012-838;** www.warsawshuttle.com), which charges 9.90 zł per person. You can pre-book your ride on their website.

BY TRAIN Major international and domestic trains arrive and depart from Warsaw's **Central Station (Warszawa Centralna;** Al. Jerozolimskie 54; ✆ **197-57;** www.pkp.pl), located in the heart of the city in Śródmieście (just across the street from the Marriott Hotel). Centralna is, to put it mildly, confusing. It's a vast 1970s concrete jungle, filled with underground passageways that seemingly lead nowhere and misleadingly marked stairways that will have you coming and going, and getting no place at all. Fortunately, the officials at Polish Rail have cleaned up the station. Centralna is well served by tramlines and buses; the only trick is finding which stairway to use to locate the tram going in the direction you want to travel. Taxis stationed here are expensive; it's cheaper to call for an independent taxi (see "Getting Around," below).

BY BUS Warsaw's main **bus station (Dworzec Autobusowy Warszawa Zachodnia;** Al. Jerozolimskie 144; ✆ **703/403-330;** www.pksbilety.pl) is situated in the city center, about 1km (½ mile) to the west of the Centralna train station. The station handles all of the bus traffic to and from Western Europe, as well as most major Polish routes. The station is well served by tram, bus, or taxi to anywhere in the city. Buses no. 127 and 130, and night buses no. N35 and N85, run to the Centralna train station. Journey time is about 15 minutes. A 2-zł ticket, valid for 20 minutes, will suffice. Validate your ticket upon boarding.

BY CAR As Poland's capital city, all roads lead to Warsaw. You'll have no problem finding your way here. You may be surprised, though, by how long it takes to get here, and once you're here, by the sheer volume of traffic. After you've found your hotel, stow the car and use public transportation and taxis.

Visitor Information

The Warsaw city authorities (✆ **194-31** or 22/474-11-42; www.warsawtour.pl) maintain a helpful network of tourist information agencies at entry points to the city, including the airport, central train station, and the Old Town. All are open daily; operating hours are as follows: **Warszawa Centralna Train Station,** May to September 8am to 9pm, October to April 8am to 7pm; **Fryderyk Chopin Airport,** May to September 8am to 9pm, October to April 8am to 7pm; **Rynek Starego Miasta 19/21/21A** (Old Town), May to September 9am to 9pm, October to April 9am to

7pm. **MUFA Warsaw Tourist Information Center** (Zamkowy 1/3; © **22/635-18-81;** www.wcit.waw.pl) is privately run, therefore it also sells tour packages, and is located at the square outside the Royal Castle in the Old Town. It's open weekdays 9am to 6pm, Saturday 10am to 6pm, and Sunday 11am to 6pm.

You can pick up walking-tour itineraries such as *Warsaw City Breaks* and *Jewish Warsaw* at any tourist office. You'll almost always find an English speaker on hand to help with general directions and hotel advice, and provide maps and brochures. If you're planning to use public transportation, get the free ZTM (www.ztm.waw.pl) map of tram and bus routes. Warsaw is blessed with a number of English-language publications that include cultural listings, restaurant reviews, and general information. Look out particularly for the comprehensive bi-monthly *Warsaw, in Your Pocket* (5 zł) and the monthly *Warsaw Insider* (9.90 zł), both are free of charge in most hotels.

City Layout

Warsaw is cut in two by the Vistula River (Wisła), but nearly all the interesting things to see and do lie on the river's western side. The heart of the city, and where you'll find most of the hotels, restaurants, and nightlife, is the central district known as Śródmieście. With its huge avenues and acres of space between buildings, it's not particularly pedestrian-friendly. But trams scoot down the rails at an impressive speed and can whisk you around in a few minutes. The center of Śródmieście is the intersection of Al. Jerozolimskie (Jerusalem Ave.) and Marszałkowska Street. The Old Town (Stare Miasto) lies about 1km (½ mile) to the north. The best way to find it on foot is to follow the "Royal Route," which intersects with Al. Jerozolimskie. The Royal Route was the journey taken by Polish royalty to travel from the Royal Castle in the Old Town to the Wilanów Palace in the south. This stretch passes along Krakowskie Przedmieście, Nowy Świat, Plac Trzech Krzyży, and Al. Ujazdowskie. To the south of Jerozolimskie, along the Al. Ujazdowskie, beginning at Plac Trzech Krzyży, you'll find Warsaw's embassy district and some of the city's swankiest shops, cafes, restaurants, and nightclubs. Farther to the south lie the enormous residential districts of Mokotów and Ursynów, the bedrooms for half of the city's 2 million people. Across the Vistula from the Old Town is the up-and-coming district of Praga. This area has long been one of the poorest districts in Warsaw but is starting to see something of a revival, primarily led by artists attracted by Praga's rock-bottom rents. The new National Stadium for the UEFA Euro Cup 2012 is also located here and is expected to be up and running in June 2011.

GETTING AROUND

ON FOOT Warsaw is a big city, so walking is an option only within specific areas, such as the Old Town or in Śródmieście. For longer distances, you'll want to use public transportation or taxis.

BY TRAM Trams trundle down Warsaw's enormous avenues regularly from about 4:30am to 11pm and are the best means for covering large distances quickly and cheaply. The tram network will look highly confusing at first, but once you have learned the names of major roads and intersections, you'll get the hang of it. You can also get the free map of the tram and bus routes (www.ztm.waw.pl) from the tourist information centers. Warsaw Transport Authority (© **22/194-84**) has public transportation information and usually has English-speaking operators.

Tickets costs 2.80 zł per ride, and you can buy them from Ruch kiosks around town or almost any place near a tram stop that sells newspapers and cigarettes. You can also

DIY Sightseeing: Hop-on-Hop-off

You can easily see the top sights in town using public transportation. Bus no. **180** runs daily from the Powązki Cemetery to Wilanów and passes by the Old Town and Royal Route in its 1-hour north–south traverse. Weekends from July to August, **Tram T,** a restored historical tram, is a loop service starting from pl. Narutowicza. It trundles into Praga and passes through places like the Socialist Realism housing project pl. Konstytucji. For both options, a day ticket is all you need.

look out for the new ticket machines that have been installed at selected points. You may have a hard time finding a place to buy a ticket in the evening, so buy several during the day and stock up. You can also buy reasonably priced long-term tickets: for 1 day (9 zł), 3 days (16 zł), and 1 week (32 zł). The **Warsaw Tourist Card** (www.warsawtour.pl), issued by the Warsaw City authorities, is available at various places, including tourist information centers. It gives access to public transportation, and free or discounted rates for attractions, restaurants, and hotels. A 24-hour card costs 35 zł; a 3-day card is 65 zł.

BY BUS Buses supplement the tram network and run pretty much the same hours and use the same ticketing and information system. The bus layout is even more confusing than the trams, so get specific directions to your destination.

BY METRO Warsaw has a small subway (metro) system, and most likely, you won't use it. There's only one functioning line, and it connects the center of town to the districts in the north and south of the city. A much-needed east–west line is under construction, but it won't be ready till late 2013. Tickets are the same as for the buses and trams, and must be validated before boarding the train.

BY TAXI Taxis are a cheap and reliable way of getting from point A to point B. The meter starts at 6 zł. The rates vary depending on the company. Expect to pay about 25 zł for in-town destinations. Dishonest drivers have been a problem in the past, but the situation is improving. Nevertheless, **use only clearly marked cabs** and always make sure the driver has switched on the meter. It is also common to book by phone, even when there's a taxi rank nearby. Most of the time, there are English-speaking operators who can help you. Good choices include **Merc Taxi** (✆ **22/677-77-77**), Super Taxi (✆ **196-22**), and MPT (✆ **191-91**).

BY BIKE Cycling in the city is getting more common, but it's still viewed by many as a suicidal undertaking. The bike rental shop **Wygodny Rower** (Stawki 19; ✆ **888/498-498;** www.wygodnyrower.pl) is open weekdays from 11am to 7pm and on Saturday from 10am to 3pm. The **Oki Doki Hostel** (see "Where to Stay," below) also has bikes for rent.

[FastFACTS] WARSAW

American Express The office (Chłodna 51; (✆ **22/581-51-00**) is open weekdays 9am to 7pm and Saturday 10am to 3pm.

Business Hours Stores and offices are generally open Monday to Friday 9am to 6pm. Banks are open Monday to Friday 9am to 4pm. Some larger stores have limited Saturday hours, usually 9am to noon. Museums and other tourist attractions are often closed on Mondays.

Camera Repair **Adam Bieniek** (Al. Jerozolimskie 113/115; ✆ **22/629-99-59**) can handle repair work for most camera models. The shop is on the second floor, and the staircase is by the kebab stall. It's open on weekdays from 9am to 6pm.

Car Rental At the airport, you'll find global chains such as **Avis** (✆ **22/650-48-72;** www.avis.pl), **Budget** (✆ **22/650-40-62;** www.budget.pl), and **Hertz** (✆ **22/650-28-96;** www.hertz.com.pl). **Joka** (Okopowa 47; ✆ **22/636-63-93;** www.joka.com.pl) offers cars with GPS. For luxury cars, contact **LimoInvest** (Piłsudskiego 11, Józefów; ✆ **722/233-355** or 22/252-07-25; www.limoinvest.pl).

Currency Exchange Most banks and some hotels have currency exchange counters. The airport and train station also have *kantor* (currency exchange) booths, but you'll find better rates in the city's malls and streets. A 24-hour *kantor* is at Piękna 11 (✆ **22/625-14-25**).

Doctors & Dentists The **LIM Medical Center** (al. Jerozolimskie 65/79; ✆ **22/458-70-00;** www.cmlim.pl) has several facilities in the city. A centrally located option is in the Marriott Hotel tower and staffs a full range of English-speaking doctors and specialists. For dentists, the **Austria-Dent-Center** (Żelazna 54; ✆ **022/654-21-16;** www.austriadent.pl) is highly recommended.

Drugstores Independent *"apteka"* are everywhere. **Apteka Grabowskiego** (Al. Jerozolimskie 54; ✆ **22/825-69-86**), at the Central Station, is open 24 hours. So is **Apteka Beata** at Al. Solidarności 149 (entrance from Al. Jana Pawła; ✆ **22/620-08-18**). **Super Pharm** is a chain found in most malls.

Embassies **U.S.:** Al. Ujazdowskie 29/31, ✆ **22/625-14-01; Canada:** Matejki 1/5, ✆ **22/584-31-00; U.K.:** Kawalerii 12, ✆ **22/311-00-00.**

Emergencies In an emergency, dial the following numbers: police ✆ **997,** fire ✆ **998,** ambulance ✆ **999.** The general emergency number if using a cellphone is ✆ **112.**

Internet Access If you have a laptop, Wi-Fi access is complimentary in many cafes and restaurants. Nearly all hotels either have Wi-Fi or Internet terminals. Internet cafes around town charge about 6 zł per hour. **Arena 2** at pl. Konstytucji 5 (✆ **22/629-07-76**) is a smoke-free 24-hour facility. At the centrally located British Council (Al. Jerozolimskie 59; ✆ **22/695-59-00;** www.britishcouncil.org), there are three terminals that you can use at no charge. The British Council is open weekdays from 8:30am to 9pm and on Saturdays from 8:30am to 1:30pm.

Laundry Laundry chains with same-day service, such as **5 à Sec** (www.5asec.pl), can be found in most malls, including Złote Tarasy and Arkadia.

Maps City and regional maps are widely available in bookshops, roadside kiosks, and petrol stations. One of the most popular brands is **Copernicus.**

Newspapers & Magazines Local news in English is carried in the ***Warsaw Voice,*** available in bookshops such as Empik and the American Bookstore (see "Shopping," later in this chapter). The ***Warsaw Business Journal*** is a weekly publication on market news. The ***New Poland Express*** is a weekly electronic publication you can subscribe to on www.newpolandexpress.pl.

Post Offices The **Central Post Office** is at Świętokrzyska 31/33 (✆ **22/505-33-29;** www.poczta-polska.pl), and it is open 24 hours. There is also a post office at the Central Station on the ground floor.

Safety Violent crime is relatively rare, but theft is a serious problem. Don't leave valuables in cars overnight. Watch your pockets and purses carefully. If you're traveling with a bike, don't leave it outside unattended (even if it's firmly locked). Many hotels and pensions will allow you to take your bicycle in with you to your room.

Telephones & Fax

The area code for Warsaw is 22. To call long distance within Poland, dial the area code, plus the number. When dialing the 5-digit information lines (including for taxis), drop the 22 prefix if you are calling from a Polish landline. However, to call from a Polish cellphone, the 22 prefix is required.

WHERE TO STAY

Global chains like the **Radisson Blu Centrum** (Grzybowska 24; ✆ **22/321-88-88;** www.radissonblu.com), **Sheraton** (ul. Prusa 2; ✆ **22/450-61-00;** www.sheraton.com.pl), and **Westin** (Jana Pawła II 21; ✆ **22/450-88-44;** www.westin.com.pl) are all centrally located. These high-end places thrive on business travel and can be quite expensive, especially in April, May, September, and October. The good news is that once the business community goes home, including weekends, many hotels slash rates by as much as 40%. Note that some hotels in Warsaw quote their prices in euros only.

Very Expensive

InterContinental Hotel ★ Just about all the luxury and professionalism you'd expect from the InterContinental chain can be found in this postmodern glass skyscraper. Its next-door neighbor is the iconic Palace of Culture; if you can't keep your eyes off this piece of Socialist Realism even when you're freshening up, ask for room no. 11 on any floor where bathrooms have windows looking out to the Palace. The pool on the 43rd floor has views of the city. The breakfast buffet is one of the few in the city catering to a wide palate, including Asian options like miso soup and nori salad. The hotel nabbed Polish celebrity chef Karol Okrasa to run **Platter,** their new fine dining restaurant.

Emilii Plater 49. ✆ **22/328-88-88.** Fax 22/328-88-89. www.warsaw.intercontinental.com. 404 units. 120€ double. AE, DC, MC, V. Parking 100 zł. **Amenities:** 3 restaurants; bar; cafe; lounge; concierge; club floor; health club; indoor pool; room service; sauna; Wi-Fi (in lounge, free). *In room:* A/C, TV, hair dryer, Internet, minibar.

Le Méridien Bristol ★ Regarded as Warsaw's most prestigious address, the Bristol is the custodian of quintessential Old World charm. The sensitively restored Art Nouveau building is part of the city's architectural heritage. Through the years, Picasso, Jackie Onassis, Queen Elizabeth II, and Bob Dylan have been among the luminaries who graced the premises. The ornate period details, location on the Royal Route, and history are compelling reasons for checking in. But for the asking price, they could update the well-trampled carpet, clean up the random bits of chipping paint, and liven up the somber gray marble bathrooms. If you're a history buff, you'll want to stay in the Paderewski Suite, named after the former prime minister of Poland who was also a world-class composer.

Krakowskie Przedmieście 42/44. ✆ **22/551-10-00.** Fax 22/625-25-77. www.lemeridien.com/warsaw. 204 units. 550 zł–1,130 zł double; 7,800 zł suite. AE, DC, MC, V. Limited free parking. **Amenities:** 2 restaurants; bar; cafe; concierge; executive floor; health club; pool; room service; sauna. *In room:* A/C, plasma TV, fax (in business rooms), hair dryer, Internet, minibar.

Mamaison Hotel Le Regina Warsaw ★★ Converted from a restored 18th-century palace, this boutique hotel is tucked in the serenely quiet far end of the New Town. All rooms have a slightly different configuration, but have the same sleek

Warsaw

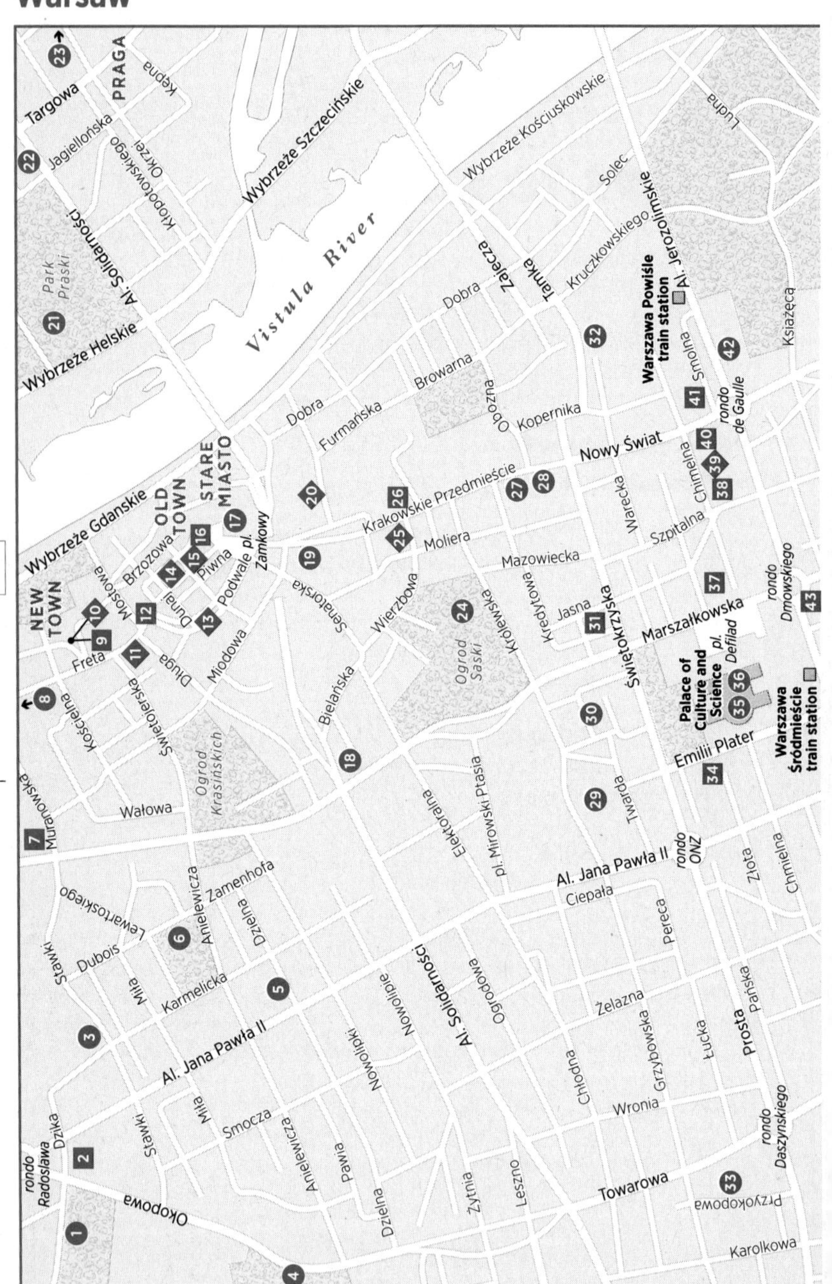
PRAGA
Targowa
Jagiellońska
Kępna
Okrzei
Kłopotowskiego
Park Praski
Al. Solidarności
Wybrzeże Helskie
Wybrzeże Szczecińskie
Wybrzeże Kościuszkowskie
Vistula River
Ludna
Solec
Al. Jerozolimskie
Warszawa Powiśle train station
Kruczkowskiego
Tamka
Zajęcza
Dobra
Browarna
Furmańska
Oboźna
Kopernika
Nowy Świat
Smolna
rondo de Gaulle
Książęca
Wybrzeże Gdanskie
OLD TOWN
STARE MIASTO
NEW TOWN
Brzozowa
Mostowa
Piwna
Dunaj
Podwale
pl. Zamkowy
Krakowskie Przedmieście
Moliera
Mazowiecka
Warecka
Chmielna
Szpitalna
Freta
Długa
Miodowa
Senatorska
Wierzbowa
Ogród Saski
Królewska
Kredytowa
Jasna
Świętokrzyska
Marszałkowska
pl. Defilad
rondo Dmowskiego
Palace of Culture and Science
Warszawa Śródmieście train station
Emilii Plater
Kościelna
Świętojerska
Muranowska
Wałowa
Ogród Krasińskich
Bielańska
Elektoralna
pl. Mirowski Ptasia
Twarda
rondo ONZ
Al. Jana Pawła II
Ciepła
Złota
Chmielna
Zamenhofa
Anielewicza
Dzielna
Lewartowskiego
Dubois
Stawki
Miła
Karmelicka
Nowolipie
Nowolipki
Al. Solidarności
Ogrodowa
Żelazna
Pereca
Chłodna
Grzybowska
Łucka
Prosta
Pańska
Wronia
Smocza
Dzika
rondo Radosława
Okopowa
Anielewicza
Pawia
Dzielna
Żytnia
Leszno
Towarowa
Przykopowa
rondo Daszyńskiego
Karolkowa
1 2 3 4 5 6 7 8 9 10 11 12 13 14 15 16 17 18 19 20 21 22 23 24 25 26 27 28 29 30 31 32 33 34 35 36 37 38 39 40 41 42 43

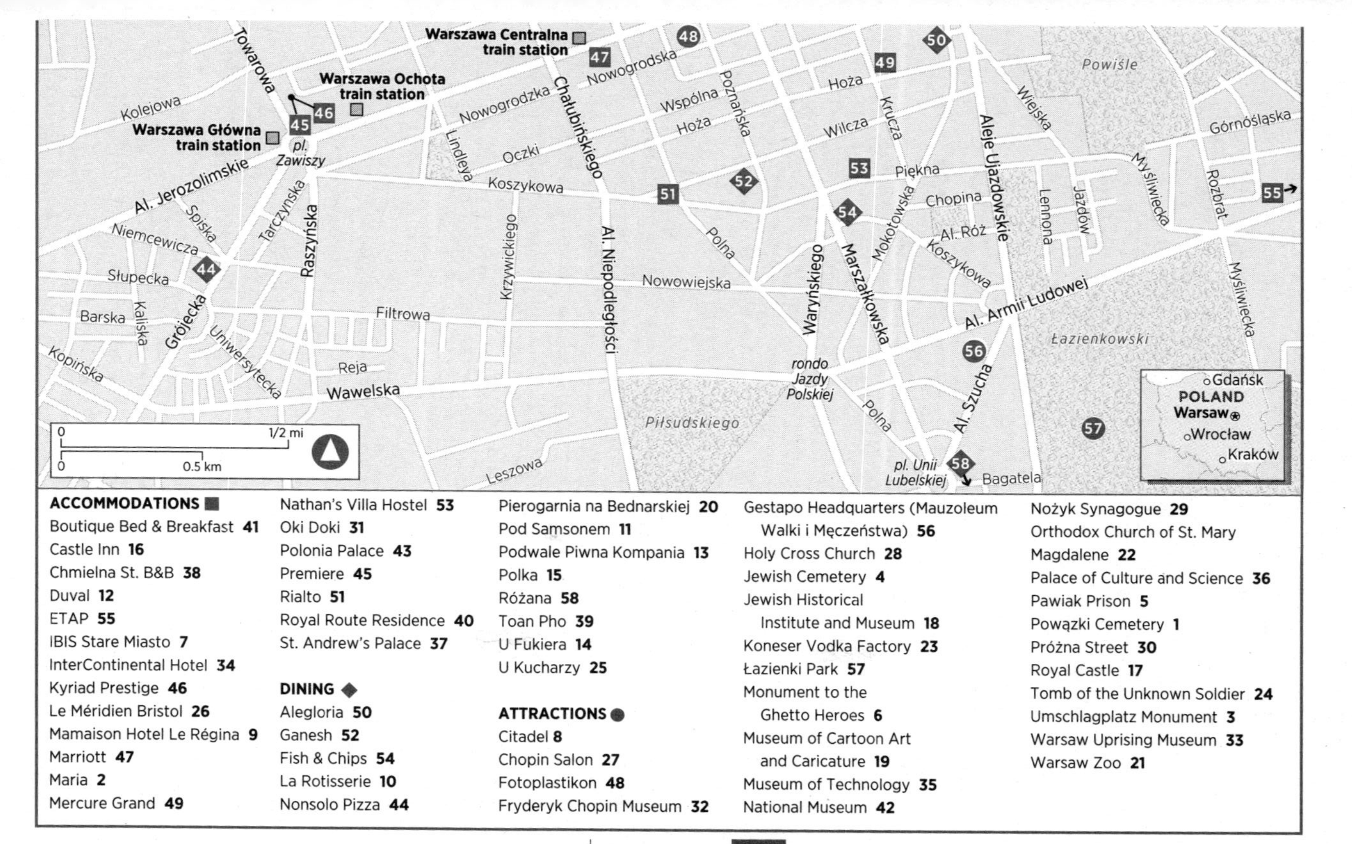
Warszawa Centralna train station
Warszawa Ochota train station
Warszawa Główna train station
Towarowa
Kolejowa
pl. Zawiszy
Al. Jerozolimskie
Nowogrodzka
Chałubińskiego
Lindleya
Oczki
Koszykowa
Wspólna
Hoża
Poznańska
Krucza
Wilcza
Piękna
Chopina
Al. Róż
Mokotowska
Aleje Ujazdowskie
Wiejska
Lennona
Jazdów
Myśliwiecka
Rozbrat
Górnośląska
Powiśle
Spiska
Niemcewicza
Tarczyńska
Raszyńska
Słupecka
Barska
Kaliska
Grójecka
Uniwersytecka
Kopińska
Filtrowa
Reja
Wawelska
Krzywickiego
Al. Niepodległości
Nowowiejska
Polna
Waryńskiego
Marszałkowska
Koszykowa
Al. Armii Ludowej
rondo Jazdy Polskiej
Al. Szucha
pl. Unii Lubelskiej
Bagatela
Łazienkowski
Piłsudskiego
Leszowa
0 1/2 mi
0 0.5 km
Gdańsk
POLAND
Warsaw
Wrocław
Kraków
ACCOMMODATIONS
Boutique Bed & Breakfast 41
Castle Inn 16
Chmielna St. B&B 38
Duval 12
ETAP 55
IBIS Stare Miasto 7
InterContinental Hotel 34
Kyriad Prestige 46
Le Méridien Bristol 26
Mamaison Hotel Le Régina 9
Marriott 47
Maria 2
Mercure Grand 49
Nathan's Villa Hostel 53
Oki Doki 31
Polonia Palace 43
Premiere 45
Rialto 51
Royal Route Residence 40
St. Andrew's Palace 37
DINING
Alegloria 50
Ganesh 52
Fish & Chips 54
La Rotisserie 10
Nonsolo Pizza 44
Pierogarnia na Bednarskiej 20
Pod Samsonem 11
Podwale Piwna Kompania 13
Polka 15
Różana 58
Toan Pho 39
U Fukiera 14
U Kucharzy 25
ATTRACTIONS
Citadel 8
Chopin Salon 27
Fotoplastikon 48
Fryderyk Chopin Museum 32
Gestapo Headquarters (Mauzoleum Walki i Męczeństwa) 56
Holy Cross Church 28
Jewish Cemetery 4
Jewish Historical Institute and Museum 18
Koneser Vodka Factory 23
Łazienki Park 57
Monument to the Ghetto Heroes 6
Museum of Cartoon Art and Caricature 19
Museum of Technology 35
National Museum 42
Nożyk Synagogue 29
Orthodox Church of St. Mary Magdalene 22
Palace of Culture and Science 36
Pawiak Prison 5
Powązki Cemetery 1
Próżna Street 30
Royal Castle 17
Tomb of the Unknown Soldier 24
Umschlagplatz Monument 3
Warsaw Uprising Museum 33
Warsaw Zoo 21

furnishings in shades of brown and champagne. Hand-painted frescos act as headboards or accents on creamy walls. The Zebra room stands out with a different color scheme. Two rooms on the ground floor have access to a sun-kissed private patio, and several rooms on the top floor have private rooftop terraces. Staff here is some of the best-trained in town. Rooms are modestly sized; if you want more space, look into the full-service apartments of their associated property, **Residence Diana** (Chmielna 13A; ✆ **22/505-91-00;** http://mamaison.com/warsaw-diana.html), which has similar upscale minimalistic decor in a prime location in the city center.

Kościelna 12. ✆ **22/531-60-00.** Fax 22/531-60-01. http://mamaison.com/warsaw-leregina-hotel.html. 61 units. 179€–229€ double. AE, DC, MC, V. Valet parking 100 zł. **Amenities:** Restaurant (p. 76); bar; lounge; babysitting; gym; indoor pool; room service; sauna. *In room:* A/C, plasma TV w/pay movies, hair dryer, minibar, Wi-Fi (free).

Expensive

Marriott ★ Of the big chains in town, this one offers arguably the best location and the best value. Previous guests include former U.S. President George W. Bush. Directly opposite the Central Station and the Palace of Culture, it's popular with business travelers; the lobby has all the hubbub of a busy airport. The hotel completed major refurbishment works, and the results are visible in the luxurious and comfortable bedding, new carpets, and updated bathrooms. If you like bathrooms with a view, ask for a corner room.

Al. Jerozolimskie 65/79. ✆ **22/630-63-06.** Fax 22/830-03-11. www.marriott.com/wawpl. 518 units. 285 zł–700 zł double. AE, DC, MC, V. Parking 135 zł. **Amenities:** 4 restaurants; 3 cafes; bar; concierge; health club; indoor pool; room service; spa. *In room:* A/C, plasma TV, hair dryer, minibar, Wi-Fi.

Mercure Grand ★★ A hotel from Communist times that has been transformed by a thorough overhaul. What remains from the past are the Social Realism facade and the marble-and-granite staircase. Everything else is brand new, including the service-oriented crew. The room count was reduced from 355 to just under 300 rooms, creating larger spaces, all with the comforts of a high-end hotel. Bathrooms have heated floors, and most feature showers with glass walls between the bathroom and bedroom (privacy curtains available)—great for exhibitionists. The location is ideal: Some of the city's best restaurants, cafes, and shops are within walking distance.

Krucza 28. ✆ **22/583-21-00.** Fax 22/583-21-21. www.mercure.com. 299 units. 270 zł–500 zł double. AE, DC, MC, V. Parking 60 zł. **Amenities:** Restaurant; bar; health center; room service; sauna; Wi-Fi (free). *In room:* A/C, plasma TV, hair dryer, Internet, minibar.

Polonia Palace ★★ Built in 1913, the building survived the war and recently underwent 2 years of a thorough top-to-bottom spruce up. The result is a winning merge of Old World charm and plush contemporary appeal. Two blocks away from the Marriott, it also has views of the Palace of Culture, but it is right by the crossroads of two major arteries. Step beyond the busy streets and the grand facade, however, and it's all peace and quiet inside. Watch for excellent weekend deals that reduce prices by as much as 40%.

Al. Jerozolimskie 45. ✆ **22/318-28-00.** Fax 22/318-28-01. www.poloniapalace.com. 206 units. 85€–235€ double. AE, DC, MC, V. Parking 45 zł. **Amenities:** Restaurant; bar; health center; room service. *In room:* A/C, TV, hair dryer, Internet, Wi-Fi (free; in business-level rooms).

Rialto ★★ A high-style boutique hotel for those who demand original Thonet chairs and William Morris furniture. The inspiration here is Art Deco, using a mix of authentic and reproduction furnishings. The meticulous attention to detail is reflected by touches like Honeywell's retro air-conditioning control panels. And the bathrooms—reminiscent of the Great Gatsby's heyday—are an antidote for those jaded by modern minimalism. The only small detraction is the lack of a garden/patio. But the location, a 10-minute walk from pl. Konstytucji, is atmospheric. From the sixth-floor gym, and some rooms, you can see neighborhood buildings with pockmarked walls, left by bullets from the Warsaw Uprising.

Wilcza 73. ✆ **22/584-87-00.** Fax 22/584-87-01. www.rialto.pl. 44 units. 280 zł–800 zł double. AE, DC, MC, V. Valet parking 100 zł. **Amenities:** Restaurant; lounge; bar; gym; room service; Russian sauna; steam rooms. *In room:* A/C, plasma TV w/movies, CD/DVD player, hair dryer, minibar.

Moderate

Boutique Bed & Breakfast ★★ A unique B&B in the city center aiming to create the best small-hotel experience in the city. Located in a prewar town house, each of the high-ceilinged rooms is decorated differently, but the emphasis is on top-quality traditional furniture and Art Deco highlights. It has a decidedly prewar ambience of a well-to-do family. Five studio apartments are in a separate building across the street. If Jarek, the owner, is in town, you'll find him at breakfast, waxing enthusiastically about his hometown while you enjoy a fine organic spread. They also organize music festivals, and the dining room and hallway double as galleries for young Polish artists.

Smolna 14/7. ✆ **22/829-48-01.** www.bedandbreakfast.pl. 10 units. 280 zł–420 zł double. DC, MC, V. Public parking. *In room:* TV, fridge (in some), hair dryer, kitchen (in some), Wi-Fi (free).

Castle Inn ★★ Occupying a restored 16th-century building in the Old Town opposite the Royal Castle, the inn is well-priced, spick-and-span, and has a bit of a theatrical feel, to boot. Unique room adornments range from the hearts and spades in the "Alice in Wonderland" room to an 800kg (1,764-pound) four-poster bed in the "Maharaja" room to blown-up cartoons in the "Comic" sanctum. The effects are created by bold colors, plus an eclectic blend of antique and modern furnishings. Deluxe rooms have supersized bathrooms complete with claw-foot tubs. It's quiet, in general, but there are complimentary earplugs for you to filter out the 6am castle bell peals or the evening music from the concerts in the castle. The management is professional, having graduated from Oki Doki (see below). Everything promises to be a memorable stay. ***Note:*** No elevators.

Świętojańska 2 (entrance from pl. Zamkowy). ✆ **22/425-01-00.** Fax 22/635-04-25. www.castleinn.pl. 22 units. 230 zł–340 zł double. MC, V. **Amenities:** Room service. *In room:* Plasma TV, hair dryer, minibar, Wi-Fi (free).

Duval ★ Along the lane merging the Old Town and the New Town are these four individually furnished, new-feeling apartments. The themes are loosely based on "Japanese," "Glass," "Polish," and "Retro." The Japanese room has the most natural light. Two rooms look out to a courtyard and the others to Nowomiejska Street. This section of the Old Town hushes up after dark, so you'll have a quiet sleep. There are no stoves for you to whip up a meal, but restaurants of all price brackets are within walking distance. ***Note:*** No elevators.

Nowomiejska 10. ✆ **22/849-70-24.** Fax 22/831-91-04. www.duval.net.pl. 4 units. 70€–100€ apt. AE, MC, V. Street parking. **Amenities:** Restaurant; cafe. *In room:* TV, fridge, hair dryer, kitchenette, Wi-Fi (free).

IBIS Stare Miasto ★★ Sometimes, the IBIS hotel chain is a real lifesaver. The philosophy of a clean, modern, stripped-down business hotel at tourist rates is especially welcome in a city like Warsaw, where every other place seems to assume that

Expense Account is footing the bill. The rooms and public areas are stark, in keeping with the IBIS philosophy, but you won't find a nicer room at this price so close to the Old Town (a 5-min. walk). Another alternative is **IBIS Warszawa Centrum** (Al. Solidarności 165; ✆ **22/530-30-00**), located near a tram stop, just a 10-minute hop to Old Town. For comparable standards at lower rates, **IBIS Ostrobramska** (Ostrobramska 36; ✆ **22/515-78-00**) is in the heartlands of Praga.

Muranowska 2. ✆ **22/310-10-00.** Fax 22/310-10-10. www.ibishotel.com. 333 units. Weekdays 269 zł double; weekends 199 zł double. AE, MC, V. Underground parking 45 zł. **Amenities:** Restaurant; bar. *In room:* A/C, TV, Wi-Fi.

Kyriad Prestige ★★ This hotel is owned by the same chain as the Premiere Classe (see below), but the philosophy here is to offer top-end business services at moderate prices. Travelers accustomed to four-star luxuries can save substantial cash over the likes of the Marriott. The neighborhood is on the gray side, but a nearby tram can get you to the center in about 5 minutes. The rooms are large and comfortably furnished in contemporary styles. **Campanile** (Towarowa 2; ✆ **22/582-72-00**), run by the same folks, is next door in the same complex. Their rooms are just as comfortable but smaller and the furnishings simpler to go with the lower price tag. The Kyriad also offers rooms for travelers with mobility issues.

Towarowa 2. ✆ **22/582-75-00.** Fax 22/582-75-01. www.kyriadprestige.com.pl. 144 units. Sun–Thurs 399 zł double; Fri & Sat 309 zł double. AE, DC, MC, V. Parking 50 zł. **Amenities:** Restaurant; bar; health club; limited room service. *In room:* A/C, TV, hair dryer, minibar, Wi-Fi (free).

Maria ★ Arguably the best of the smaller, family-run hotels in town. The rooms are on the austere side of modern, but several have hardwood floors and tend to be more attractive and more comfortable. Rooms at the back, peering at McDonald's, are quieter. The restaurant is old-fashioned but cheerful, and the staff couldn't be more welcoming. The in-town location is convenient to get to the sights, especially to the former Jewish ghetto. The Old Town is about a 20-minute walk.

Jana Pawła II 71. ✆ **22/838-40-62.** Fax 22/838-38-40. www.hotelmaria.pl. 24 units. Weekdays 380 zł double; weekends 280 zł double. AE, DC, MC, V. Free parking. **Amenities:** Restaurant; bar; limited room service. *In room:* A/C, TV, hair dryer, Wi-Fi (free).

Royal Route Residence These comfortable, full-service apartments are located on the trendy Nowy Świat and Chmielna streets. The apartments come in various sizes; some have two bedrooms, a spacious living room, and good-size kitchen, while others are only big enough for a double bed and a closet-size kitchen. The furnishing is mainly sourced from IKEA. Most guests are long-term business travelers. The **Old Town Apartments,** owned by the same company, offer 25 apartments scattered in various buildings in the Old Town. Although these rooms are modern, the standards are not as high as at the Royal Route Residence.

Nowy Świat 29/3 (entrance from Nowy Świat 27). ✆ **22/692-84-95.** Fax 22/826-52-09. www.apartmentsapart.com. 16 units. 120€ apt for 4. AE, DC, MC, V. Limited parking 18 zł. *In room:* Fully equipped kitchen; Wi-Fi (free).

St. Andrew's Palace ★★ A palace it isn't, but the size of the suites is palatial. You get a whole lot more breathing space here, compared to other rooms in the same price range and location. Each unit has a separate living room and bedroom, and the bathrooms are recently renovated. In line with its name, the style is conservative chic. The roomy kitchen is ideal for self-catering, but you have plenty of cafes and restaurants frequented by locals at your doorstep. This being in the city center, you'll have to ask for a room facing the courtyard to have silent nights.

Chmielna 30. ✆ **22/826-46-40.** Fax 22/826-96-35. www.residencestandrews.pl. 24 units. 99€ double. AE, MC, V. **Amenities:** Cafe. *In room:* A/C, TV, DVD player, fax, hair dryer, Internet (free), fully-equipped kitchen.

Inexpensive

Chmielna St. B&B ★ The property is executed in a vibrant, contemporary style with an ensemble of designer works and flea-market finds. Most rooms are just big enough to fit in a poster bed, but the en suite rooms have more leg space. Like your fellow-guests, you'll oscillate towards the cozy living room to socialize. Being located along a central, trendy street, it all looks perfect; the only drawback is the stairs. You have to plod up two flights to get in, and before that, you pick the keys up at the reception (the given address) that is 200m (656 ft.) away and perched on the third floor of a high-ceilinged no-elevator building. Note that this is actually a "B w/o B" (bed without breakfast).

Nowy Świat 27. ✆ **22/745-36-60.** Fax 22/622-55-01. www.nws-hostel.pl. 7 units. 174 zł double w/ shared bathroom; 220 zł double. AE, MC, V. **Amenities:** Wi-Fi (free). *In room:* TV.

Etap ★ The budget cousin of IBIS (see above) has the same dependable concept: cheap, clean, and modern. Pared-down means the basin and shower cubicle are next to the beds, but a sturdy door separates the toilet. To spare yourself the clatter from the busy road, request a room facing the courtyard. Etap is on the quiet side of town near the river and an uphill workout to get to the happening places. Buses 171 and 155 from nearby Rozbrat Street will get you to the center.

Zagórna 1. ✆ **22/745-36-60.** Fax 22/622-55-01. www.orbisonline.pl. 176 units. 139 zł–169 zł double. AE, MC, V. Parking 18 zł. *In room:* A/C, TV, Wi-Fi.

Nathan's Villa Hostel ★ The owner of the Nathan's hostel in Kraków uses the same popular formula here: combining some of the amenities of a decent hotel with the sociability of a hostel. Several private double rooms are on offer, so you don't have to sleep *en groupe*. The dorms, which sleep 4 to 12, are neat and clean. Free laundry is one of several perks that you wouldn't normally expect. The fully equipped kitchen, cleaned three times daily, is a great place to swap travel tales with your hostel-mates. The location is central but still quiet enough for you to catch 40 winks.

Piękna 24/26. ✆ **22/622-29-46.** Fax 22/622-29-46. www.nathansvilla.com. 13 units. 36 zł–70 zł dorm bed; 160 zł–180 zł double w/shared bathroom; 175 zł–190 zł double. DC, MC, V. **Amenities:** Wi-Fi (free).

Oki Doki ★★ Opened by backpackers (with a penchant for art and antiques) for backpackers, this is not your typical hostel where the central location is the only frill. Located in a reconstructed prewar building, each of the high-ceilinged rooms is in a different theme, from "Mexico" to "the Communist Dorm." The kitchen has recently been expanded. The bar's happy hour, from 7 to 8pm, claims to have the cheapest beer in town. The front desk's tips on getting the best out of Warsaw are more creative than at the city's tourist information centers. ***Note:*** No elevators.

Pl Dąbrowskiego 3. ✆ **22/826-51-12.** Fax 22/826-83-57. www.okidoki.pl. 82 units. 34 zł–70 zł dorm bed; 140 zł–175 zł double w/shared bathroom; 175 zł–220 zł double. MC, V. Street parking. **Amenities:** Bike rental; Wi-Fi (free). *In room:* TV.

Premiere Classe ★ The theory behind this French hotel chain is to offer spotless, modern rooms with absolutely no frills at cut-rate prices. It's found a real niche in Warsaw, where decent, affordable rooms in the center are in short supply. The rooms themselves are microscopic—we've seen Winnebagos with bigger bathrooms—but they're very clean and comfortable. The breakfast buffet is rather miserable; the cafes on al. Jerozolimskie can be your salvation.

Towarowa 2. ✆ **22/624-08-00.** Fax 22/620-26-29. www.premiereclasse.com.pl. 126 units. 189 zł double. AE, DC, MC, V. Parking 50 zł. **Amenities:** Bar; Wi-Fi (free). *In room:* TV.

WHERE TO DINE

While in Warsaw, take the chance to branch out to non-Polish cuisine. After you get to the smaller towns, it's mainly Polish or Italian staples. The budget Vietnamese-Chinese eateries here are deft with the sizzling hotplates. As for Indian, the no-frills joints do just as good a job, if not better, than their up-market cousins. And you'll no doubt notice the sushi rage. Locals tend to avoid eating in the Old Town Square due to the inflated price tag. But you don't have to wander far from the square to find reasonably priced meals. And the New Town (Nowe Miasto) is also strewn with eating options. Most restaurants, even the formal ones, welcome kids.

Very Expensive & Expensive

AleGloria ★★ MODERN POLISH AleGloria's decor takes Polish folk art as the underlining motif but updates it with a magical wand to create a cheerful, fairytale feel. Get the waiter to give you a tour of the strawberry, crystal, and hunting rooms and point out the Malczewski reproductions. The menu, saturated with posh noshes like lobster, foie gras, and truffles, shares the same spirit as the decor: a Polish repertoire with flights of fancy whipped in. The "carp ribbons" are fillets twirled to mimic *faworki,* a traditional festive treat. The herring *tartare* with nuts and ginger may sound odd but tastes heavenly. Most dishes pair fruits with meat, like roasted figs with pork tenderloin. Save room for the Pavlova with strawberry sauce, which can be shared by two. The top-notch service wraps up an evening that will leave you reminiscing about AleGloria for quite a while.

Plac Trzech Krzyży 3. ✆ **22/584-70-80.** www.alegloria.pl. Reservations recommended. Main courses 54 zł–104 zł. Daily 11am–11pm.

La Rotisserie ★★★ INTERNATIONAL Although it's one of the best fine-dining experiences in Poland, the restaurant of Le Régina's boutique hotel (see earlier in this chapter) has largely stayed under the mainstream radar. However, it's the splurge option of those in the know. Chef Paweł Oszczyk stands among the country's top talents. His short menu changes regularly, but the ragout of scallops with pine nuts is a permanent feature due to popular demand. The wine list also changes to keep pace with the menu. Weather permitting, meals can be eaten in the secluded courtyard. The upscale setting is one of understated elegance, and the mood is approachable and relaxed; it's great for an intimate dinner. For the value deal, try the Sunday Linner (a play on words fusing "lunch" and "dinner"). From 1 to 6pm, 175 zł gets you a five-course tasting menu and two glasses of wine.

Kościelna 12. ✆ **22/531-60-00.** http://mamaison.com/warsaw-leregina-hotel.html. Reservations recommended. Main courses 79 zł–96 zł. AE, DC, MC, V. Daily 6:30am–11pm.

Różana ★★ POLISH Slightly out of the way, but worth the taxi ride to get to this double-story villa that has all the refined touches of aristocratic country manors. The compact menu, in the same vein, is "noble" food. Calves' brains on toast are a traditional morsel that has become a rare find. Familiar fillers come in forms of roast duck, baked salmon, and braised pork tenderloin brought to your table by deft and confident waiters. You'll be sharing space with the Expense Account people, treating themselves to caviar and pancakes with crayfish and bantering up the noise level and thus chipping away the romantic ambience. If you don't feel like having a full meal, it's a treat just to have their coffee and meringue cakes in the dreamy private garden.

Chocimska 7. ✆ **22/848-12-25.** www.restauracjatradycja.pl. Reservations required. Main courses 26 zł–79 zł. AE, DC, MC, V. Daily noon–midnight.

U Fukiera ★ POLISH A Warsaw institution and one of the fanciest spots for a meal in the city, served in an overwrought but undeniably romantic space in the Old Town's main square. The guest list reads like an international Who's Who, for this used to be *the* place to wine and dine visiting dignitaries. These days, with rampant competition, it has to do more to stay on the top of the game. The menu doesn't razzle and dazzle you with recherché items, but instead takes everyday Polish classics like *żurek, kołduny,* and pork and delivers them in sheer perfection. It does a fabulous *nożki* (jellied pork trotters). If you're a petite eater, two can share the generous main course portions so as to leave space for the tempting desserts. Despite the romantic accents, U Fukiera is more suited for groups, rather than a party of two. The competent service is at times a bit stiff and somber.

Rynek Starego Miasto 27. ✆ **22/831-10-13.** www.ufukiera.pl. Reservations recommended. Main courses 41 zł–99 zł. AE, DC, MC, V. Daily noon–11pm.

U Kucharzy ★★ POLISH "At the Chefs" you eat in the kitchen of the former Europejski Hotel, spruced up to look at once Spartan and luxurious. The chefs come to your table and serve you straight to your plate from their cast-iron pots and skillets; they'll even slice and dice your steak *tartare* in front of you. Book a table in front of the mega-burners to watch the men-in-uniform prepare Polish mainstays such as roast boar and venison. These "front row" seats have become so popular that you almost rub elbows with other diners. Other tables are quieter, but you miss out on the kitchen buzz that generates the fun and magical experience of dining here. Although the staff fusses over guests, service is not the most efficient. The owner, who bears a passing resemblance to Van Gogh, often hobnobs with the diners, making everyone feel like a special guest. The whole package helped it earn a coveted Michelin Bib Gourmand in 2010.

Ossolińskich 7. ✆ **22/826-79-36.** www.gessler.pl. Reservations recommended. Main courses 40 zł–80 zł. AE, DC, MC, V. Daily noon–midnight.

Moderate

Ganesh ★★ INDIAN Warsaw can very well bid to be the Central & European Capital of Indian cuisine with Ganesh being one of the city's best representatives. The smart-casual ambience works for the full spectrum of diners, from dates to business chow-downs. Their top sellers are chicken *tikka masala* and *dahi gosht* (mutton in yogurt sauce) that have plenty of sauces to be sopped up with *naan.* Also available are Indian translations of South East Asian dishes like Singapore fried rice.

Wilcza 50/52. ✆ **22/623-02-66.** www.ganesh.pl. Reservations recommended. Main courses 18 zł–45 zł. AE, MC, V. Daily 8:30am–midnight.

Nonsolo Pizza ★ ITALIAN These pizzas, made in a wood-fired oven, are the real deal and some of the best in town. The newer and larger location has a bland, modern decor, but that's offset by the merry buzz of locals breaking bread here. The house specialty is the "Nonsolo" pizza, topped with tomato, mozzarella, ham, mushrooms, and garlic. If you're in the mood for pasta, try the fettuccine *arrabiata* (spicy tomato sauce). In the evenings, you may have to wait for a table.

Grójecka 28/30. ✆ **22/824-12-73.** www.nonsolo.pl. Reservations recommended. Pizza 17 zł–32 zł; pasta 14 zł–30 zł. MC, V. Daily noon–11pm. Tram: 7, 9, 25.

Biting into the Past

For a glimpse of the dining scene during the Communist era, a visit to a milk bar is a must. **Bar Mleczny Prasowy** (Marszałkowska 10/16; ✆ 22/628-44-27) is particularly quaint and the place to go if you have time to visit only one. The coffee is awful, but where else can you get scrambled eggs for 3.50 zł at 7am on a weekday? Go soon; these old diner-like digs are dwindling fast in a gentrifying city. Also dying are the likes of **Lotos** (Belwederska 2; ✆ 22/841-13-01; www.restauracjalotos.pl), located to the south of the Łazienki Park. This type of "elegant" restaurant was originally limited to bigwigs and those who had scrimped and saved for a special occasion. At Lotos, the clock is stuck in the '80s, from the cloakroom to the dinner clientele, who all sport a bottle of vodka to accompany the traditional Polish food. Service, happily, has moved on and is quite friendly.

Pod Samsonem JEWISH/POLISH With a strategic location in the New Town coupled with easy-to-stomach prices, the tables here are snapped up by tourists and locals alike. Most items on the menu are routine Polish, but they do a good Jewish-style cold appetizer of jellied carp. It's one of oldest restaurants in the city, and it still hasn't shaken off the habit of charging 1 zł for the use of the restrooms. A young set of servers have replaced the original surly ones, but the speed in which the dishes come out of the kitchen is still erratic.

Freta 3/5. ✆ **22/831-17-88.** www.podsamsonem.pl. Reservations recommended. Main courses 18 zł–35 zł. DC, MC, V. Daily 10am–11pm.

Podwale Piwna Kompania ★★ EUROPEAN The good-value-for-money meat platters keep this Bavarian/Czech-inspired beer hall constantly abuzz with merry locals and visitors. It's ideal for groups; tables for two are squeezed into leftover corners or along corridors. The most popular order is the chunky stump of *golonka* (pork knuckles), weighing at least a kilo. Mind you, the crispy crust is very salty and will leave you parched long after the meal is over. The menu also offers Polish staples like *bigos* (hunter's stew), pierogi, and blood sausage. If you want something a bit lighter, a hearty *żurek* soup supplemented with the complimentary breadbasket and cream cheese will fill you up. *Nalewka* (fruit-infused vodka) comes with the bill gratis. **U Szwejka** (pl. Konstytucji 1; ✆ **22/339-17-10;** www.uszwejka.pl) is the city-center cousin with the same successful partnership of meat and beer.

Podwale 25. ✆ **22/635-63-14.** www.podwale25.pl. Reservations recommended. Main courses 21 zł–49 zł. DC, MC, V. Mon–Fri 11am–1am; Sat & Sun noon–1am.

Polka ★ ☺ POLISH The busy bee behind many of the city's fancy restaurants has lent her name to an "economy" edition of the Magda Gessler empire. It still feels quite luxurious here; the food quality has not been compromised, but portions are downsized. Take care when ordering the sides, which are charged separately and can bump up the final bill. The "*wuzetka*" chocolate cake, said to be named after a major road in Warsaw, is justly popular.

Świętojańska 2. ✆ **22/635-35-35.** www.restauracjapolka.pl. Reservations recommended. Main courses 18 zł–65 zł. AE, DC, MC, V. Daily noon–11pm.

Inexpensive

Fish & Chips ★ BRITISH Should you find yourself pining for flavors of the U.K., get your quick fix at this takeaway shop that has a couple of seats for dine-in customers. The fish and chubby, twice-cooked chips can be had with mushy peas and curry sauce. For dessert, the genial chef (English-speaking, naturally) will convince you that a deep-fried Mars Bar is a winner. There are also salt and vinegar chips and an assortment of British candy and beverages for the road.

Koszykowa 30. ✆ **692/240-804.** www.fishandchips.pl. Main courses 17 zł–23 zł. MC, V. Mon–Fri 10am–10pm; Sat 11am–10pm; Sun 11am–7pm.

Pierogarnia na Bednarskiej ★★ POLISH Not far from the Royal Castle, a lovely cobblestone lane leads you to this vaulted-ceiling chamber. The interior says monastic simplicity, but the collective mealtime chatter and clatter of cutlery can be an inner-peace breaker. However, it's still the place the locals go for a dependably satisfying pierogi fix. A self-service setup, it has the usual parade of sweet and savory varieties, with plenty of consideration given to vegetarians. If you can't decide what to have, share the mixed platters and add a cup of their equally reliable *żurek* soup.

Bednarska 28/30. ✆ **22/828-03-92.** www.pierogarnianabednarskiej.pl. Main courses 13 zł. No credit cards. Daily 11am–9pm.

Toan Pho ★★ VIETNAMESE Pho in Poland doesn't get better than the beef soup with noodles here. Authentic, too, is the chaotic self-service system where the staff hollers out the name of the dish when it's ready. Somehow, no matter how packed the place is, everyone gets what they've ordered, and there are no dissatisfied

SWEET spots

- **Batida** (Krakowskie Przedmieście 11; ✆ **22/826-44-74**) has a dessert selection that includes tangy lemon meringue tarts and Warsaw's best French pastry. Another outlet is on pl. Konstytucji (✆ **22/621-53-15**).
- **Blikle** (Nowy Świat 35; ✆ **22/826-45-68**) has been in business since 1869 and is famous for its *pączki* (donuts).
- **Pawłowicz** ★★ (Chmielna 13; no phone) is a take-out-only, hole-in-the-wall operation catering to a constant queue looking for fresh, made-on-site donuts and sweet bread for only about 2 zł a pop.
- **Słodki Słony** ★ (Mokotowska 45; ✆ **22/622-49-34**) serves fancy, mouth-watering cakes in a Laura Ashley–esque rustic milieu.
- **Smaki Warszawy** ★ (Żurawia 47/49; ✆ **22/621-82-68**) is the place for pretty parcels of "pepper and vanilla" and *kajmak* (Polish toffee) tarts.
- **To Lubię** (Freta 10; ✆ **22/635-90-23**) is a smoke-free cafe converted from a belfry in the New Town. Tuck in to hot chocolate and homemade desserts like pumpkin cake, and then pick up some cookies for the road.
- **Wedel** ★★★ (Szpitalna 8; ✆ **022/827-29-16**) "chocolate drinking house" has become a nationwide franchise, but the original store is still *the* place to lap up Old World charm. A must-do.
- **Wróble** (Noakowskiego 10; ✆ **22/825-55-29**) has been baking standard Polish sweet snacks since 1921. It's low-key and offers an inexpensive selection.

voices. The short menu is in Vietnamese decoded into Polish, but they have an English version tucked away at the counter.

Chmielna 5/6. ✆ **888/147-307.** Main courses 14 zł–15 zł. No credit cards. Mon–Fri 9:30am–11pm; Sat & Sun 10am–10pm.

EXPLORING WARSAW

Warsaw is a large city, so plan your exploration to utilize trams or taxis to move between areas. A good place to start a walking tour of the city is the **Old Town (Stare Miasto)** and the adjacent **New Town (Nowe Miasto)**. Just as the Old Town isn't old (but reconstructed), the New Town isn't new but a settlement dating back to the 15th century. Aside from churches and museums, the New Town has scores of lovely cafes and restaurants. In the same itinerary, you can also bundle in part of the **Royal Route.** As you stroll along the swanky, cafe-lined streets of **Krakowskie Przedmieście** and **Nowy Świat,** bear in mind that these streets once saw intense fighting during World War II and were rebuilt from rubble after the war. Much of Krakowskie Przedmieście is dominated by Warsaw University, and the streets are often filled with students. Set aside half a day for tracing the remnants of Jewish Warsaw. And if time permits, the streets of Praga are definitely worth half a day's time, as well.

In addition to the major sights listed below, there are small museums to suit every interest, including one dedicated to Polish Romantic poet **Adam Mickiewicz** (Rynek Starego Miasta 20; ✆ **22/831-40-61;** www.muzeumliteratury.pl); one to the Nobel Prize–winning scientist **Maria Skłodowksa-Curie** (Freta 16; ✆ **22/831-80-92;** http://muzeum.if.pw.edu.pl); and one to the horrific **Katyń** massacre, in which an entire generation of Polish army officers—some 20,000 in all—were shot and killed by the Soviet Red Army in the Katyń woods (Powsińska 13; ✆ **22/687-72-44;** www.muzeumwp.pl). The newly open riverfront **Copernicus Science Center** (Wybrzeże Kościuszkowskie 20; ✆ **22/596-41-00;** www.kopernik.org.pl) is an interactive museum with plenty of hands-on fun for kids and adults.

Top Attractions

OLD TOWN & ROYAL ROUTE

The beautiful baroque and Renaissance-style burghers' houses of the Old Town would be remarkable in their own right for their period detailing, but what makes these buildings truly astounding is that they're only a few decades old. As one of the main centers of the 1944 Warsaw Uprising (see "The Warsaw Uprising," later in this chapter), the Old Town bore the brunt of German reprisal attacks, and the entire area, save for one building, was blown to bits at the end of 1944. After the war, to reclaim their heritage, the Polish people launched an enormous project to rebuild the Old Town exactly as it was, brick by brick. Many of the original architectural sketches were destroyed in the war, so the town was rebuilt from paintings, photographs, drawings, and people's memories. The reconstruction was so authentic that UNESCO in 1980 listed the Old Town as a World Heritage Site. Today, the Old Town is given over mostly to touts and tourists, but still rewards a couple of hours of strolling.

Museum of Cartoon Art and Caricature ★ Hidden in a back alley off the Royal Route, this low-profile museum displays the creative and witty doodles of Polish cartoonists on just about any subject under the sun. There are only two small rooms and no permanent collection. Each themed exhibit is on display for about 4 months, and they usually provide a lighthearted contrast to the more serious topics in the other museums in the city. Well worth the 15-minute stopover.

History in Brief

Warsaw started life as a relatively small river town in the 14th century, but within a century, it had become the capital city of the Duchy of Mazovia, ruling over small fiefdoms in central Poland. The city's fortunes steadily improved in the 16th century after the duchy was incorporated into the Polish crown and Poland formed a union with Lithuania. The union greatly expanded the amount of territory under Polish influence. In 1596, King Sigismund III moved the capital to Warsaw from Kraków. The city remembers his efforts with the King Sigismund's Column outside the Royal Castle. The Polish partitions at the end of the 18th century relegated Warsaw to the status of a provincial town for the next 125 years. Initially, the Prussians ruled the city, but in 1815, the Congress of Vienna placed tsarist Russia in firm control. Despite the occupation, Warsaw thrived in the 19th century as a western outpost of the Russian empire. Finally, in 1918, after Germany's defeat and Russia's collapse in World War I, Warsaw was reconstituted as the capital of newly independent Poland. The brief period of optimism ended when Nazis occupied the city in 1939 and held it for nearly the entire course of the war. The occupation was brutal. Warsaw lost almost its entire Jewish population (see "Exploring Jewish Warsaw," later in this chapter). The August 1944 Warsaw Uprising (see "The Warsaw Uprising," later in this chapter) is another significant turning point that still haunts the city. By the end of the war, 85% of Warsaw lay in ruins, and two out of every three residents—nearly 900,000 people—had died or were missing. The postwar years were bleak ones. Reconstruction was in the hands of Socialist-inspired planners (see "Socialist Realism," below). One notable exception is the Old Town. Warsaw residents overwhelmingly chose to reconstruct exactly what they had lost. It's a moving story of reclaiming identity from history, and the results are phenomenal, even earning it a place on the UNESCO list of World Heritage Sites.

Kozia 11. ✆ **22/827-88-95.** www.muzeumkarykatury.pl. 5 zł adults, 3 zł children & seniors; Sat free admission. Tues–Sun 11am–6pm.

Royal Castle (Zamek Królewski) ★★ The original residence of Polish kings and later the seat of the Polish parliament, the 14th-century castle was completely destroyed in the Warsaw uprising and its aftermath. What you see today is a painstaking reconstruction that was finished only in 1984. The main "Castle Tour" takes you through the regal apartments of Poland's last monarch, King Stanisław August Poniatowski, and to the Canaletto room, where the famed cityscapes of Warsaw by the Italian painter Bernardo Bellotto hang. These paintings, and others not on display, were of extreme value in rebuilding the Old Town from scratch after the war. It is also a magical experience to attend the classical music concerts held in the castle's courtyard and Great Ballroom. The concerts usually start at 6pm. The repertoire is on the Castle's website, and concert tickets can be bought at the Castle's information desk an hour before the start of the concert.

Pl. Zamkowy 4. ✆ **22/355-53-38** or 22/355-51-78 (to book guides). www.zamek-krolewski.pl. 22 zł adults, 14 zł children & seniors; Sun free admission. Guided tour in English 100 zł; audio guide 15 zł. May–Sept Mon–Sat 10am–5pm, Sun 11am–5pm; Oct–Apr Tues–Sat 9:50am–3pm, Sun 10:50am–3pm.

The Citadel (Cytadela) ★ A mid-19th-century brick fortress that was commissioned by Russian Tsar Nicholas I following the 1830 November Uprising. The sprawling fortress, along Vistula River, is located off the beaten track on the north side of New Town. Most of the compound is now used by the Polish military. The section opened to the public is the grounds of the Museum Pavilion-X, formerly the prison for Polish insurgents. Stenciled on the wall by the cell entrances are names of famous inmates, such as Józef Piłsudski, the man credited with regaining Poland's independence in 1918. The exhibits include farewell letters to loved ones. There is hardly any information in English, but the brooding paintings relay the oppressive mood of the times. The Gate of Execution (Brama Straceń) was the site where Polish patriots were publicly executed.

Skazańców 25 (entrance from Wybrzeże Gdyńskie, corner of Czujna St. or Brama Straceń). ✆ **22/839-12-68.** www.muzeumniepodleglosci.art.pl. Free admission. Wed–Sun 9am–4pm. Bus: 118. On foot: 25 min from the New Town Square; go north on Zakroczymska St. & turn right at Krajewskiego St. to get to Wybrzeże Gdyńskie.

Tomb of the Unknown Soldier Located in the Saxon Garden (Ogród Saski), the three arches of a colonnade are the remains of the Saxon Palace, destroyed in World War II. There are plans to eventually rebuild the palace. The monument honors the soldiers who perished in World War I, the subsequent Polish-Soviet Wars, and World War II. The main ceremonial changing of the guards is at noon on Sunday. At other times, there is an hourly small-scale guard change.

Pl. Piłsudskiego.

Łazienki Park ★★ The 76 hectares (188 acres) classicist-style "Royal Baths" along the Royal Route is where the city's residents go for a stroll in good weather. Established in the 17th century, the park got its moniker from a bathhouse located here. King Stanisław Poniatowski, the last king of Poland, acquired the property in 1764. No matter which entrance you take, the footpaths will lead you to the neoclassical **Palace on the Water** (Agrykoli 1; ✆ **22/506-01-01;** www.lazienki-krolewskie.pl), a royal summer residence and now a museum where you can view the king's private chambers and opulent baroque-style ballrooms. Or it's great just to spend time in the park and coax "Basia" (Barbara; the local pet name for squirrels) into nipping walnuts from your hands. Try to catch the piano recitals, held from May to September, in the rose garden, where a larger-than-life sculpture of Chopin is the centerpiece. The 45-minute free recitals are held Sunday at noon and 4pm. It's a great place to slow down, but keep off the grass.

Al. Ujazdowskie. Łazienki Park: Free admission; daily dawn–dusk. Palace on the Water: 12 zł adults; Tues–Sun 9am–4pm. Bus: 180.

EXPLORING THE CITY CENTER

Fotoplastikon ★★ Fotoplastikon, or stereoscopy, is an invention of the mid-19th century and the precursor of movies. Through these lenses, you see 3D images of anything from the streets of prewar Warsaw, where the shops' signs are in Russian, to the postwar construction of the Palace of Culture. With more than 3,000 images in its archives, the show changes monthly. Since the Warsaw Uprising Museum took over the operation, the selection leans on visuals from the autumn 1944 insurgency. However, there are thematic exhibitions allowing you to time travel to the *fin de siècle* epoch of Paris, Beijing, and Moscow. A stop here takes about 20 minutes; a great way to make a quick journey into the past.

Al. Jerozolimskie 51. ✆ **22/629-60-78.** www.fotoplastikonwarszawski.pl. 4 zł adults. Wed–Mon 10am–6pm.

Chopin, Our Chopin

Even classical music fans are blissfully unaware of Chopin's Polish roots. Born to a French father and a Polish mother, Fryderyk Chopin (1810–49) is Poland's most famous composer. The capital city, in particular, is very possessive of this talent since Warsaw was where he spent his formative years. In November 1830, Chopin left to perform in Vienna, not knowing that he would never again return to Poland. Later that month, the November Uprising against the Russians broke out, and Chopin sought refuge in Paris, which became his base for the rest of his short life. However, Chopin left his heart in Warsaw, in the literal as well as the emotional sense. As was his wish, upon his death, his heart was sealed in an urn and returned to Warsaw. The urn is in the **Holy Cross Church** (Krakowskie Przedmieście 3; ✆ **022/556-88-20;** www.swkrzyz.pl). Don't miss the **Chopin Monument** and Sunday piano recitals in **Łazienki Park** (see above). Chopin's birthplace in **Żelazowa Wola** (see later in this chapter) is the pilgrimage point for fans worldwide. The **Chopin Museum** ★ (see below), totally revamped for the 200th anniversary of the composer's birth in 2010, gives you a high-tech delivery of Chopin's biography. Also as part of the bicentennial birthday bash, 15 **"Chopin Benches"** were installed, mostly along the Royal Route, at places that can claim "Chopin was here." At the touch of a button, the bench dispenses melodies. Follow the inscribed instructions, and you can upload Chopin tunes, photos, and trivia onto your mobile phone. A more conventional memorial to the composer is the modest **Chopin Salon** (Salonik Chopina; Krakowskie Przedmieście 5; ✆ **22/320-02-75**), the living room used by the family when they were residing in Warsaw. It has a copy of the piano Chopin played on. The salon is poorly signposted: You'll find it through the second door on the left side of the courtyard. The room is on the second floor. There are also tour operators that dish out Chopin's Warsaw excursions (see "Organized Tours," later in this chapter).

Gestapo Headquarters (Mauzoleum Walki i Męczeństwa) Currently the home of the Ministry of Education, from 1939 to 1945, this was the one place in town you absolutely did not want to visit. A small museum in the building's lower reaches holds the cells and interrogation rooms that are nearly untouched from how they were at the end of the war. The displays paint a vivid picture of the torture and killing that went on here—and the lengths to which the Nazis went to break the Polish opposition. Children under 14 are not admitted.

Szucha 25. ✆ **22/629-49-19.** www.muzeumniepodleglosci.art.pl. Free admission. Wed 9am–5pm; Thurs & Sat 9am–4pm; Fri 10am–5pm; Sun 10am–4pm.

Fryderyk Chopin Museum (Muzeum Fryderyka Chopina) ★ Reopened in 2010, on the 200 anniversary of Chopin's birth, the four flours of Ostrogoski Palace are fitted with hi-tech gadgets and soft ambient light to deliver a Zen-like experience of the life and work of Poland's most famous composer. Although tangible Chopin paraphernalia is limited to notes, a lock of hair, cufflinks, a death mask, and a copy of Chopin's salon in Paris, what it excels at is the encyclopedic audio repository of Chopin's output. In the basement level, the "listening booths" and e-books let you "browse" through the music at your own pace. In the other halls, via touch-screens activated by a micro-chipped ticket, are audio-visual presentations on topics from

Live in the Park

Music spills out from the **Fryderyk Chopin University of Music** (Okólnik 2; ✆ **22/827-72-41,** ext. 235; www.chopin.edu.pl) into the park at the rear of the building. Join locals who sit on the benches to enjoy pieces played by visiting international pianists rehearsing for competitions or students delivering their practical exams. Every Sunday at 5pm, the university hosts free (indoor) concerts.

Chopin's early education and his family to his travels in Europe and the women who influenced him, such as George Sand. You can tailor these narrations, available in eight languages, to your attention span, graded as "children," "long," or "short." Other displays include the last piano used by Chopin. Only about 70 visitors are allowed in hourly; to avoid being told to come back later, pre-book your tickets online. Opposite the museum entrance, you'll find a cafe and a gift shop that sells, among routine t-shirts and mugs, a cast of Chopin's left hand.

Okólnik 1. ✆ **22/441-62-51.** www.chopin.museum. 22 zł adults, 13 zł children & seniors; 62 zł families. Tues free admission. 5 zł refundable deposit for micro-chip ticket. Daily noon–9pm.

Museum of Technology (Muzeum Techniki) ★ Don't come expecting to see cutting-edge technology and hands-on interactive exhibits. Instead, there's a sprawling collection of dated technology, from bicycles with wooden wheels to the first transistor differential analyzer built in 1959—it's really more of a History of Technology Museum, and therein lies the quirky fun of the place. Fans of retro designs will enjoy the home appliances and motorbike sections. Even the items not meant as exhibits, such as the dustbins, the lamps, and the cafe, are steeped in Socialist-era design. Adding to the throw-back-to-Communism experience is the posse of "guards" ever ready to bark *nie dotykać* (do not touch!) should your nose hover too close to the artifacts. It's a time capsule of sorts that you shouldn't miss.

Pl. Defilad 1 (Palace of Culture). ✆ **22/656-67-47.** www.muzeum-techniki.waw.pl. 10 zł adults; 5 zł children & seniors. Apr–Oct Tues–Fri 9am–5pm, Sat & Sun 10am–5pm; Nov–Mar Tues–Fri 8:30am–4:30pm, Sat & Sun 10am–5pm.

National Museum (Muzeum Narodowe) ★ This 1930s oversized bunker houses a collection ranging from archaeology to early Christian art and 15th-century Flemish paintings. The star attraction from the Polish masters is the Jan Matejko collection. Look for *Stańczyk* (1862), depicting a 16th-century court jester mulling over the grave content of a letter while behind him the royal household partied on in oblivion. And don't miss *The Battle of Grünwald* (1878), another of Matejko's masterpieces chronicling the Teutonic Knights' downfall in 1410. The postwar section covers painting and sculptures glorifying the workers' utopia. Well worth a stopover, even if you have only an hour to spare.

Al. Jerozolimskie 3. ✆ **22/621-10-31.** www.mnw.art.pl. Temporary & permanent exhibitions 17 zł adults, permanent exhibition only 12 zł adults; Sat free admission to permanent exhibition. Tues 10am–5pm; Wed & Thurs 10am–4pm; Fri noon–9pm; Sat & Sun noon–6pm.

Palace of Culture and Science (Palac Kultury i Nauki) ★ Warsaw's landmark tower is a building many residents would like to see knocked down. The 1950s Socialist-Realist wedding cake was commissioned by Josef Stalin as "a gift from the

Soviet people." The symbolic intention was clear from the start: Stalin was marking his turf, and Poland was part of the Eastern Bloc. After the fall of Communism, there were heated talks of pulling it down. However, public attitudes toward the "palace" have softened somewhat. You can ride to the top—30 stories—for a fine view over the city (but let's be honest here—30 stories isn't really *that* dramatic). The building continues in its role as a cultural and trade venue. One way of seeing some of the grand halls, Socialist-Realist reliefs, and wacky chandeliers is to buy a ticket to a trade fair (anything from books to pet food) being held during your visit or go to one of the many museums housed within. Better still, catch a concert at the **Congress Hall** (**Sala Kongresowa;** see "After Dark," later in this chapter), the venue where the Rolling Stones had their first concert behind the Iron Curtain in 1967.

Pl. Defilad 1. ✆ **22/656-76-00.** www.pkin.pl. Viewing terrace 20 zł adults. Daily 9am–8pm.

Pawiak Prison ★ Another frightening reminder of the horrific times of World War II. Something like 100,000 prisoners passed through the gates here during the years of the Nazi occupation, when the prison was run by the Gestapo. Among the prisoners were political activists, members of the clergy, university professors, or simply anyone suspected of opposing the Germans. Very few of the people imprisoned here got out alive. Most were sent to extermination camps, while around 40,000 people were actually executed on the grounds. Children under 14 are not admitted.

Dzielna 24/26. ✆ **22/831-92-89.** www.muzeumniepodleglosci.art.pl. Free admission. Wed 9am–5pm; Thurs & Sat 9am–4pm; Fri 10am–5pm; Sun 10am–4pm.

Powązki Cemetery ★★ Established in 1790, it is one of the oldest cemeteries in Warsaw. The 43-hectare (106-acre) ground is filled with ornate and grand tombs, topped with elaborate sculptures from the 18th and 19th centuries. A mausoleum holds the ashes of those who perished in concentration camps, and the "Avenue of Merit" has

Socialist Realism

In the postwar years, Poland was cut off from Marshall Plan aid, and the bulk of the reconstruction funds initially came from the Soviet Union. With 85% of the city in ruins, the Soviet-inspired planners could start from scratch. They knocked down prewar tenement houses that had survived the war to make way for the wide avenues you see today, and then stacked the roads with drab Socialist-Realist–style offices and apartment blocks. To be fair, some of these buildings aren't so awful. The unmissable **Palace of Culture and Science** is the granddaddy of them all. **Pl. Konstytucji,** the focal point of the MDM (Marszałkowska Housing Estate), has impressive Socialist reliefs of miners, farmhands, and the women's workforce. The KFC at the northeast corner gives an ironic juxtaposition of Socialism vs. Capitalism. From the square, stretching along **Marszałkowska Street** all the way south to **pl. Unii Lubelskiej,** are some handsome postwar buildings. Make a detour to the **Ministry of Agriculture** (Wspólna 30) to witness how classic Greek colonnades were incorporated into the extravagance of workers' power. At the crossing of al. Jerozolimskie and Nowy Świat is the **former headquarters of the Communist Party.** After the fall of Communism, it housed the Warsaw Stock Exchange from 1991 to 2000. Now, you'll find luxury boutiques occupying the ground level. For Communism tours, see "Organized Tours," below.

> **Sign of Resistance**
>
> **You'll soon notice the symbol of a "P" fused to a "W" on monuments and buildings in Warsaw and all over Poland. "PW" stands for "Polska Walczy" (Poland Fights) and represented the Polish Resistance Army during World War II. It also stands for "Powstanie Warszawskie" (Warsaw Uprising; see below).**

the tombs of famous citizens. Among those buried here are Nobel Prize winner Władysław Reymont and the second President of the Republic of Poland, Stanisław Wojciechowski. At all times of the year, the cemetery is well-kept, but on All Saints' Day (Nov 1), the traditional day for Poles to visit cemeteries, the compound is ablaze with candlelight and filled with visitors until way past midnight. The Jewish Cemetery (see below) is within walking distance from the Powązki Cemetery and can be covered in one visit.

Powązkowska 14. Free admission. Daily dawn–dusk. Bus: 180.

Warsaw Uprising Museum (Muzeum Powstania Warszawskiego) ★★ Within the walls of this museum lies the answer to why Warsaw is nowhere as pretty as Kraków. And, some say, to understand Poland's political stance on the world stage, a visit here is a must. The majestic red-brick building is a spruced-up former tramway power station. Along the self-guided path, historical posters, flyers, photos, newsreels, radio broadcasts, and replicas give a blow-by-blow account of the social-political events prior to, during, and after the autumn 1944 uprising against the Nazis. The replicas include an impressive life-sized B-24 plane and the underground sewage tunnels used by the insurgents. The occupiers hit back hard, taking a toll on lives and the city's architectural heritage. All the details can be information overload for newcomers to Polish history. If so, rest your feet in the museum's cafe, created to resemble cafes from the interwar period, right down to the cakes and music. This award-winning museum doubles as a memorial. In an adjacent park, a wall is inscribed with the names of over 6,000 casualties. There is a chapel for those in need of quiet contemplation. With advanced booking, guides in almost every European language are available. However, even without knowing a word of Polish, you can manage on your own. Free babysitting is available on Sundays, and there's also a children's museum area. This museum is one of the most interactive and visitor-friendly in Poland.

Grzybowska 79. ✆ **22/539-79-05.** www.1944.pl. 7 zł adults, 5 zł children & seniors; Sun free admission. June 28 to Aug Mon & Wed–Fri 10am–6pm, Sat & Sun 10am–8pm; off-season Mon, Wed & Fri–Sun 8am–6pm, Thurs 10am–6pm. Tram: 22.

EXPLORING JEWISH WARSAW

Before World War II, the Jewish community in Warsaw stood at about 350,000. That was almost one-third of the city's population and the second-largest Jewish community outside of New York. Toward the end of 1940, the Nazis herded the city's entire Jewish population, as well as around 100,000 Jews from elsewhere in Poland, into a small ghetto area west of the Old Town. Walls went up, and an elaborate system of gates and staircases was built to allow Jews to move within the ghetto, but no one was permitted to enter or leave. The first deportations and mass killings began at the end of 1941. In the 1943 Ghetto Uprising (not to be confused with the 1944 Warsaw Uprising), the Jews heroically rose up against their oppressors. The uprising was quickly put down, and what remained of the ghetto was liquidated.

In postwar reconstruction, the area was planted with cheap housing blocks. The **Monument to the Ghetto Heroes** (**Pomnik Bohaterów Getta;** ul. Zamenhofa, near the crossing with ul. Anielewicza) is amid these Communist-era buildings. Opposite the monument, work is underway to build the **Museum of the History of Polish Jews** (www.jewishmuseum.org.pl), scheduled to open in 2012. To the west of the monument is the **Willy Brandt Statue** (Skwer Willy Brandta), erected to commemorate the visit of Chancellor Willy Brandt in December 1970 when the German head of state knelt in front of the Ghetto Heroes' monument.

To see surviving samples of the derelict 19th-century tenement houses riddled with bullets, head to **Próżna Street ★★** in the former Jewish ghetto. At the courtyard of **no. 55 Sienna St.,** you'll find a fragment of a ghetto wall and a simple plaque. Long narrow metal plaques have been installed on pavements to mark the places where some of the ghetto walls stood. You'll find these plaques at the crossing of Żelazna and Chłodna streets, and also at the crossing of Żelazna Street and Solidarności Avenue.

Today, hardly any of the Jewish culture remains. But in recent years, there has been a growing interest in the lost heritage. The **Jewish Theater** (see "The Performing Arts," later in this chapter) presents a repertoire of Jewish cultural plays and musical performances. Check the website of the **Shalom Foundation** (Pl. Grzybowski 12/16; ✆ **22/620-30-36;** www.shalom.org.pl) for the schedule of the annual **Festival of Singer's Warsaw,** which can be in any week from August to October. A wider range of Jewish cuisine is slowly showing up on the city's tables. Leading the way is the **Tel Aviv Café** (Poznańska 11; ✆ **22/621-11-28;** www.tel-aviv.pl). It has good soups and a lavish Sunday breakfast.

The Warsaw Uprising

On August 1, 1944, at precisely 5pm, the commander of the Polish insurgent Home Army, loyal to Poland's government-in-exile based in London, called for a general uprising throughout Nazi-occupied Warsaw. The Nazis were in retreat on all sides, having suffered reversals on the western fronts, in France and Italy, and in the East, at the hands of the Soviet Red Army. By the end of July that year, the Red Army had moved to within the city limits of Warsaw and was camped on the eastern bank of the Vistula in the district of Praga. With the combined forces of the Home Army and the Red Army, it seemed the right moment to drive the Germans out and liberate Warsaw. Alas, it was not to be. The first few happy days of the uprising saw the Polish insurgents capture pockets of the city, including the Old Town and adjacent districts. But the Nazis resisted fiercely, and the Red Army, with its own agenda, never stepped in to help. The resistance lasted weeks before Polish commanders were forced to capitulate in the face of rapidly escalating civilian casualties. The uprising so infuriated Hitler that he ordered the complete annihilation of the city. In the weeks following the uprising, Warsaw's buildings were listed in terms of their cultural significance and dynamited one by one. Some 85% of the city was eventually destroyed. The **Monument to the Warsaw Uprising** (pl. Krasińskich 1), in the New Town, commemorates the thousands of residents who died in the fighting.

The Pianist's Warsaw

Roman Polański's Oscar-winning film *The Pianist* (2002) recounts life in Warsaw during World War II through the eyes of Władysław Szpilman, an accomplished pianist and composer and one of the Warsaw ghetto's best-known survivors. Adrien Brody starred as the protagonist in the production that garnered three Oscars and numerous international awards. Based on Szpilman's autobiography, the film shows the horrific conditions of life within the perimeters of the ghetto, one of the largest of the Jewish ghettos in Poland during the war. The concrete-bunker style **Umschlagplatz Monument** (Stawki 10, near the corner with Dzika St.) marks the place where the Jews boarded cattle wagons to the Treblinka extermination camp (see below). Although Szpilman narrowly escaped deportation to Treblinka here, this scene for the movie was filmed in a military compound in the outskirts of the city. To capture the mood of war-torn Warsaw, part of the filming took place in Praga (see below), with its scores of dilapidated prewar buildings. After the war, Szpilman returned to his job at the Polish Radio. He passed away in July 2000 and is buried in the **Powązki Cemetery** (see above).

Most of the city's tourist agencies have tours of Jewish Warsaw (see "Organized Tours," below). For a self-guided tour, pick up the *Jewish Warsaw* walking itinerary designed by the Warsaw Tourist Office.

Jewish Historical Institute and Museum (Żydowski Instytut Historyczny) ★ A must for anyone tracing the history of Jews in Poland. Brace yourself for the emotional impact from the photos and news reels chronicling the dire conditions of life within the ghetto walls. On the second level of the museum, there is a small segment of religious and secular Jewish art, some dating to the late 19th century. Between the levels, you'll find the mock-up of a synagogue. The institute's library has a repository of Jewish-related documents, books, and journals. It's a game of hide-and-seek to locate this museum: It's hidden from view by a glass-fronted modern office tower. This modern tower was once the site of the Great Synagogue, the largest temple in Warsaw, which was blown up in the aftermath of the May 1943 Ghetto Uprising.

Tłomackie 3/5. ✆ **22/827-92-21.** www.jhi.pl. 10 zł adults, 5 zł children & seniors; guided tours 130 zł. Mon–Wed & Fri 9am–4pm; Thurs 11am–6pm; Sun 10am–6pm.

Jewish Cemetery (Cmentarz Żydowski) ★★ Established in 1806, it holds more than 150,000 tombs on 34 hectares (83 acres), making it one of the largest Jewish cemeteries in Europe. Ludwik Zamenhof, the creator of the Esperanto language, was among those buried here. Although the site was relatively unscathed during the war, many of the headstones are now barely legible or crumbling, and the grounds are overgrown. It is a poignant "memorial" and not to be missed.

Okopowa 49/51. ✆ **22/838-26-22.** www.beisolam.jewish.org.pl. 8 zł adults. Mon–Thurs 10am–5pm; Fri 9am–1pm; Sun 9am–4pm. Bus: 180.

Nożyk Synagogue (Synagoga Nożyków) This is the only synagogue in Warsaw to survive World War II. Named after its founders, it opened its doors to worshipers in 1902. The facade is in neo-Romanesque style, and the interior can hold up to

600 people. It is closed to tourists during prayers and special events. Access to the synagogue is not via the front door, but from the far end. Admission includes a guide, but you must call in advance to reserve one, and there are no guides on Sunday.

Twarda 6. ✆ **22/620-43-24.** www.warszawa.jewish.org.pl. 6 zł adults. Mon–Fri 9am–6pm; Sun 11am–7pm.

EXPLORING PRAGA

Praga, on the right bank of the river, is often regarded as Warsaw's poor cousin and the haunt of criminals. The district wasn't damaged much during World War II but fell into disrepair in the postwar years. The streets, lined with derelict, plaster-bared, prewar tenement blocks, served as the set for Roman Polański's *The Pianist*. Recently, however, Praga has been enjoying a slow rejuvenation as artists and businesses move in, searching for cheaper real estate. As the location for the new **National Stadium** (see "Outdoor Activities," below), more projects are underway to raise Praga's profile. Though the district is no longer off-limits, care should still be taken when visiting, especially when flashing cameras or camcorders. It's advisable not to wander about alone after sunset. Most explorations of the area are centered along **Targowa** (see "Shopping," below) and **Ząbkowska** streets. Across the street from the Orthodox Church (see below) is the **Soviet War Memorial** commemorating the soldiers who "liberated" Warsaw in 1945. For an in-depth look into the area, stop by the **To Tu** agency (see "Organized Tours," below), opposite the Koneser Vodka Factory, for local maps and tips from Praga-enthusiasts.

Koneser Vodka Factory (Wytwórnia Wódek Koneser) ★ Listed on the Polish Architectural Heritage list (a protected status that prohibits tearing down a building), this red-brick complex was built in 1895 specifically to supply 1L (34 oz.) of vodka per day to the 120,000 Russian soldiers based at this outpost. Aside from its own labels, the plant also had contracts with brands like Finlandia. Production halted in 2007, and the facility is gradually being transformed into a cultural center. It leases space to shops, art galleries (see "Shopping," below), a theater, and a restaurant. You're free to kick about the forlorn grounds and the storage area now used as exhibition halls. To access the bottling section, book a day in advance (see "Organized Tours," below) for a weekday tour that includes vodka sampling and snacks of cold cuts and bread.

Ząbkowska 27/31. ✆ **22/670-01-56.** www.monopolpraski.pl. Free admission. Daily 8am–7pm.

Orthodox Church of St. Mary Magdalene (Cerkiew Św. Marii Magdaleny) Built in the 1860s to serve Russians arriving from St. Petersburg at the nearby Wileńska train station, the golden chapel retains its original Byzantine portraits. The impressive building sports five onion domes and is in Russo-Byzantine style. It is one of the two Orthodox churches that survived demolition in the 1920s.

Al. Solidarności 52. ✆ **22/619-84-67.** Free admission. Tues–Fri 11am–4pm; Sun 1–4pm. Tram: 4.

Warsaw Zoo ☺ Dating from 1928, the 40-hectare (99-acre) compound is home to more than 280 species of animals from all corners of the globe. The most famous inhabitants are the bears, who look jaded from years of being the zoo's live advertisement in a concrete enclosure by the busy Solidarności Road. If you're not going to northeastern Poland, this is the place to see the European bison.

Ratuszowa 1/3. ✆ **22/619-40-41.** www.zoo.waw.pl. 16 zł adults; 11 zł children & seniors; free for children 3 & under. Daily 9am–7pm. Tram: 4, 13.

Outdoor Activities

GOLF **First Warsaw Golf & Country Club** (Golfowa 44, Rajszew; ✆ **22/782-45-55;** www.warsawgolf.pl), located 29km (18 miles) from the city, is an 18-hole facility, complete with a driving range, equipment rental, and English-speaking staff.

PLAYGROUNDS Warsaw has woefully few attractions targeted at kids, but the saving grace is there's always a playground at hand. In and around the Old Town, the swings and slides are in the **Saxon Garden** (Ogród Saski, near the Tomb of the Unknown Soldier) and in **Krasińkich Garden** (near the Monument to the Warsaw Uprising). Along the Royal Route, the play area in **Ujazdowski Park** (al. Ujazdowskie) is often crowded. There's also a sandy play corner in the southern section of **Łazienki Park.** In the Żoliborz district in the north, **Park S. Żeromskiego** (pl. Wilsona) has a large playground, and the nearby **Kalimba i Kofifi** cafe and shop (see "Shopping," below) is very family-friendly. One of the largest rumble-and-tumble terrains is the **Jordanowski Garden** (at the corner of al. Niepodległości and Odyńca St.) in the Mokotów district; the nearest subway station is Racławicka.

SPECTATOR SPORTS The new **National Stadium** (Al. Księcia J. Poniatowskiego 1; www.stadionnarodowy.org.pl) is located on the right bank of the river in the Praga district. It's scheduled to be completed by June 2011, in time to host the opening match of the UEFA Euro Cup 2012 football (soccer) championship. Cultural events will also be held here.

Organized Tours

GUIDED TOURS You can hire guides fluent in almost any language from the tourist information offices. The going rate is about 500 zł for 4 hours, with every subsequent hour an additional 100 zł. It's best to call a day ahead to book.

Most tourist agencies have city tours and day excursions to Żelazowa Wola, Kraków, Auschwitz, the Wieliczka Salt Mines, Gdańsk, and Malbork. **Mazurkas Travel** (Wojska Polskiego 27; ✆ **22/389-41-82;** www.mazurkas.com.pl) offers several different daily city tours and will pick up guests from most hotels. They cover the essentials like the Old Town, the Royal Route, Jewish points of interest, and the Łazienki Park in about 3 hours, charging 120 zł adults, 60 zł children 3 to 12. ***Note:*** The pickups from hotel to hotel can add an extra hour. For customized explorations of Warsaw and environs, contact **StayPoland ★** (Miła 2; ✆ **22/351-22-44** or 22/351-22-22; www.staypoland.com), which can move you around in minibuses, cars, or limousines. Specializing in sightseeing or clubbing with chauffeur-driven new BMW and Mercedes limousines is **LimoInvest** (see "Fast Facts," earlier in this chapter).

The **City Sightseeing** (✆ **793/973-356;** www.city-sightseeing.pl) bus is a hop-on, hop-off open-top double-decker equipped with audio guides. It loops around the city, starting at 10am opposite the Central Station. You can buy tickets (60 zł for 24 hours, 80 zł for 48 hours) from the driver. In winter, they operate only on weekends.

SPECIALTY TOURS One of the most interesting ways to connect the Warsaw you see today with the Warsaw that was lost in World War II is to play **Enigma Warsaw ★★**, a 3- to 4-hour outdoor quiz-cracking game designed by **StayPoland** (Miła 2; ✆ **22/351-22-22;** www.enigmawarsaw.com). Supplied with a map of the capital in 1939 and a set of clues, you hunt for streets and buildings that no longer exist. Be sure to book in advance for this unusual outing.

Chopin's Warsaw is a standard package you can find at most agencies. It takes you to the Chopin-Was-Here points and usually concludes with an evening piano recital in the Palace on the Water in the Łazienki Park.

Adventure Warsaw (© **606/225-525;** www.adventurewarsaw.com) ferries you around in a Nysa 522, a retro van designed in Poland in the '60s, for a tour of Communist Warsaw. The 169-zł–per–person price tag also gets you a vodka-tasting and lunch in a milk bar. Book a day ahead.

ToTu Praskie Buiro Przewodnicke (Ząbkowska 36; © **22/670-01-56;** www.totu.travel.pl) is an NGO promoting the Praga district. They provide guides to the Koneser Vodka Factory and rent bicycles. It's best to call before popping in, as they don't abide strictly by the operating hours.

The **Night Guides ★** (© **501/226-939;** www.night-guides.com) specialize in dusk-to-dawn pub-and-club crawls, tailored to your personal preferences. They even have a special program for those with limited mobility.

Outside the City Center

While in the vicinity of the Wilanów Palace, pop in to the **Poster Museum** (**Muzeum Plakatu ★**; Potockiego 10/16; © **22/842-48-48;** www.postermuseum.pl), which has an impressive collection of more than 55,000 posters mostly of Polish works, but also from around the globe. Poland's poster art can be traced back to the late 19th century. The gallery is open on Monday noon to 4pm, Tuesday to Sunday 10am to 4pm.

Wilanów Palace Poles are rightfully proud of this baroque-era palace built to honor King Jan Sobieski. Although it's not as grand as some other sites in the country, it also isn't a reconstructed building, and that counts for a lot in a city so ravaged in World War II. The 45-hectare (111-acre) property sports a palace with no fewer than 60 rooms, most stuffed with royal memorabilia and portraits of Polish monarchs and heavyweights. Some rooms, like the Etruscan Room, display oddities such as vases dating from the 4th century B.C. The palace can be seen only with a guided tour. Take the hourly Polish tour if you're not particularly interested in all the details of all the portraits; otherwise, gets the audio guide (10 zł) or book an English tour (80 zł) in advance. It's best to visit in good weather so that you can also explore the park, which comprises a neo-Renaissance rose garden, a split-level baroque garden, an English landscaped park, a Chinese-English park, and a lake. ***Note:*** In summer, the Sunday free tickets to the palace are all snapped up as early as 1pm.

Potockiego 10/16. © **22/842-81-01.** www.wilanow-palac.art.pl. Palace 20 zł adults, Sun free admission; park 5 zł adults, Thurs free admission. Palace Mid-may to mid-Sept Mon, Wed & Sat 9:30am–6:30pm; Tues, Thurs & Fri 9:30am–4:30pm; Sun 10:30am–6:30pm. Mid-Sept to mid-May Mon & Wed-Sat 9:30am–4:30pm; Sun 10:30am–4:30pm. Last entry to palace 1½ hr. before closing. Park daily 9am–dusk. Bus: 180.

Day Trips from Warsaw

Treblinka ★★ From July 1942 to August 1943, an estimated 850,000 people, mainly those of Jewish descent, perished in the Treblinka II extermination camp and the Treblinka I labor camp. It's the second largest of such Nazi camps, after Auschwitz. Unlike Auschwitz, Treblinka is often described as "not much to see" since much of it was razed by the Nazis. The whole site now operates under the name of the **Museum of Fighting and Martyrdom** (Muzeum Walki i Męczeństwa). By the information office, you'll find the visitors' books filled with touching messages in all languages, including English, Yiddish, and Spanish. The memorial standing in Treblinka II consists of hauntingly silent islets of jagged stones and boulders, a symbolic cremation pit, and a stretch of symbolic railway track. Surrounded by pinewoods and in the middle of nowhere, the impact is surreal and powerfully poignant. Another 10-minute walk takes you to Treblinka I and another execution site.

Strictly speaking, Treblinka is in Northeastern Poland. From Warsaw, by car, it should take about 2 hours, but factor in another hour for ongoing road work. There are regular trains from Warsaw to Małkinia, taking about 90 minutes. It's 8km (5 miles) to Treblinka from the Małkinia station. Your options are a 1½-hour walk or the 30-to-40-minute taxi ride. A round trip by taxi is about 150 zł to 200 zł, depending on how long the driver waits for you at Treblinka. Most visitors spend 1 to 2 hours here.

Kosów Lacki. ✆ **25/781-16-58.** www.muzeum-treblinka.pl. 2 zł adults. Daily sunrise–sunset.

Żelazowa Wola A petite manor annex and park whose claim to fame is being Chopin's birthplace, thus a key pilgrimage point for Chopin fans. It is one of three places in Poland (the other two are in Kraków) listed in Patricia Schultz's *1,000 Places to See Before You Die.* Even though the property was given a facelift for the 200th anniversary celebration of Chopin's birth in 2010, that is still a debatable accolade. Looted in World War II, the interior has no original fixtures. The family portraits are reproductions of the ones on display at the Chopin Salon in Warsaw. The Chopin memorabilia is sparse, and the 7-hectare (17-acre) park is nothing sensational. Having said all that, the property truly sparkles during the Sunday piano recitals, when you can bask in the sunshine while listening to renditions of Chopin's *polonaise* and *mazurkas* by international pianists.

Żelazowa Wola is 55km (34 miles) west of Warsaw. The route sees heavy traffic, resulting in a longish travel time of about 1½ hours. In season, the **Chopin Museum** (see earlier in this chapter) runs daily buses to Żelazowa Wola. From Monday to Thursday, the bus leaves at noon from the Chopin Museum and gets you back to Warsaw at about 5:30pm. From Friday to Sunday, the departure time is 10am, and the return leg reaches Warsaw at about 3:30pm; bus fares are 30 zł. Seats are limited, so book early. Adjacent to the park, there is a branch of the **Polka Restaurant** (✆ **46/863-21-68**), where you can also listen to the live concerts while digging into fairly priced Polish meals.

Żelazowa Wola 15. ✆ **46/863-33-00.** Museum & park 23 zł adults, 14 zł children & seniors; park only 7 zł adults, 4 zł children & seniors; concerts 30 zł indoors, outdoors free admission. Museum May–Sept Tues–Sun 9am–7pm, Oct & Apr Tues–Sun 9am–6pm, Nov–Mar Tues–Sun 9am–5pm. Park May–Sept daily 9am–7pm, Oct & Apr daily 9am–6pm, Nov–Mar daily 9am–5pm. Concerts May–Sept Sun noon & 3pm.

SHOPPING

Warsaw is not an obvious shopping haven, but it has a blend of familiar malls, quirky old-style bazaars, and plenty of creative local crafts to sate your shopping appetite. Those looking for global heavyweights like Boss, Escada, and Trussardi will find them in the trendy enclave of **Plac Trzech Krzyży** and the malls around the city. Along nearby **Mokotowska Street,** there are interesting small boutiques. In the past, **Nowy Świat** and **Chmielna streets** were the places for luxury goods; today, there are several antiques and design shops here, but cafes and restaurants have taken up most of the floor space.

Most shops in the city are open Monday through Friday 11am to 7pm, Saturday 10am to 2pm. Malls are open Monday through Saturday 10am to 10pm, Sunday 10am to 8pm.

Shopping Malls

The hippest mall in town is the new **Złote Tarasy** (Złota 59; ✆ **22/222-22-00;** www.zlotetarasy.pl). It's also well stocked with restaurants—including a branch of the Hard Rock Café—and cafes. Even if you're not after retail therapy, pop in to see the perspective of the city from beneath the wavy, glass domes. **Arkadia** (Jana Pawła II 82; ✆ **22/323-67-67;** www.arkadia.com.pl) and **Galeria Mokotów** (Wołoska 12; ✆ **022/541-41-41;** www.galeriamokotow.com.pl) are two larger malls outside the city center.

Outdoor & Street Markets

For time-traveling to the past, hop across the eastern bank to the legendary 105-year-old **Russian Bazaar** (**Bazar Różyckiego;** entrances from Targowa and Ząbkowska sts.; ✆ **22/619-86-42;** www.br.waw.pl) in Praga. During the Communist days, the rows of wooden stalls were the prime source for foreign goods such as Coca-Cola, jeans, and radios. It is a shadow of its former self but still musters up some life on Saturdays. Don't confuse this bazaar with the **Russian Market (Dziesięciolecia Stadium)**—the outdoor market infamous for counterfeit Tommy Hilfiger, pirated DVDs, and pick-pockets—which has been shut down to make room for the new National Stadium.

Hala Mirowska ★★ One of the oldest food markets in the center of Warsaw; though it's not quite as spectacular as Barcelona's La Boqueria, it buzzes with life and clues you in on the feeding habits of typical Poles. Within the ochre brick walls, the warren of stalls sells everything from beetroot and blood sausage to pig's head. Walk around to the outside wall, and you'll find traders proffering honey, pickled mushrooms, and German chocolates from the backs of their beat-up cars. Pl. Mirowski 1 (main entrance from Al. Jana Pawła II). No phone. Tram: 17.

Koło Bazaar (Bazar Na Kole) ★★ An open-air antiques bazaar that's a history museum of sorts: You can rummage through Socialist-era tableware, obsolete surgical equipment, fur coats, period furniture, and somewhat morbid World War II paraphernalia. Few traders here speak English. Come with a local, and you might pick up a six-piece set of silver cutlery for a reasonable 100 zł. On your own, traders will flog made-yesterday-in-China Ming vases for an indecent 250 zł. Saturday early mornings are best for bargains. By afternoon, some goods have changed hands several times among the traders, and each such transaction sees a price mark-up. Sunday at around 1pm is also good for bargains, when the traders are keen to offload their stock. It opens on weekends from dawn to early afternoon. Obozowa 99. No phone. Tram: 13.

The Goods A to Z

ANTIQUES & ART

To take art objects (including jewelry) out of Poland, you'll need legal paperwork for items that are older than 55 years or produced by an artist who is no longer living.

Desa Unicum The biggest auction house and gallery in Poland, with several branches, including one in the Old Town Square. The English-speaking staff can advise you on the art and antique market scene, but they do not assist with the legal paperwork required for exports. Marszałkowska 34/50. ✆ **22/584-95-35.** www.desa.pl.

Farbiarnia na Pięknej A noted gallery for contemporary art; it showcases Polish works. Piękna 28/34. ✆ **22/621-72-35.** www.galeriafarbiarnia.pl.

Galeria Autorska Andrzeja Mleczki The store of Polish caricaturist Andrzej Mleczko is stocked with socio-political humor cartoons in the form of reprints, calendars, mugs, postcards, and T-shirts. Original sketches can be purchased, too. Marszałkowska 140. ✆ **22/829-57-60.** www.mleczko.pl.

Galeria Sztuki Katarzyny Napiórkowskiej Another well-regarded gallery for Polish contemporary art. It has several outlets, including one in the Old Town. Świętokrzyska 32. ✆ **022/652-11-77.** www.napiorkowska.pl.

Galeria Plakatu ★ An impressive collection of Polish posters, the most eye-catching of which are the Communist-era works in the "Political and Propaganda" and Solidarity Movement sections. Rynek Starego Miasta 23. ✆ **22/831-93-06.** www.poster.com.pl.

Ostoya Not much English is spoken in this art and antique store, but the friendly staff will assist you with the export paperwork. They also hold regular auctions. Freta 25. ✆ **22/635-55-78.** www.aukcjeostoya.pl.

Sygnatura Located in the compound of the Koneser Vodka Factory, this spot showcases paintings and photos by a Polish pair. Ząbkowska 27/31. ✆ **506/032-207.** www.sygnatura.art.pl.

Yours Gallery ★ Enthralling documentary and artistic snapshots by Polish and international photographers. Krakowskie Przedmieście 33. ✆ **22/890-95-00.** www.yoursgallery.pl.

BOOKS & CDS

American Bookstore This English-language chain, with a central location, as well as outlets in the malls, has a range of Polish authors in translation and books on the Holocaust, World War II, the Warsaw Uprising, and other Poland-centric topics. Nowy Świat 61. ✆ **22/827-48-52.** www.americanbookstore.pl.

Empik This major national chain is good for maps, coffee-table books of Poland, and international newspapers. Nowy Świat 15/17. ✆ **22/551-33-99.** www.empik.com.

Sawart A small store near the Grand Theater with plenty to offer for classical music lovers, including music scores published by Edition Peters and Chopin recordings by labels like Decca and Deutsche Grammophon. Moliera 8. ✆ **22/826-23-78.** www.sawart.com.pl.

CERAMICS, GLASS & POTTERY

Banasik A sizeable two-story store stacked with Polish and European tableware. Representing the host nation are names like Bolesławic, Włocławek, and Krosno. If needed, the store will bubble wrap items for you. Piękna 28/34. ✆ **22/621-83-37.** www.dhbanasik.pl.

Bolesławiec Company Store A warehouse-style store with an extensive choice of Bolesławiec stoneware, from mugs to casserole dishes, in prints ranging from the classic blue-and-white peacock to special edition stars-and-stripes. Prosta 2/14. ✆ **22/624-84-08.** www.ceramicboleslawiec.com.pl.

CRAFTS, LINENS & SOUVENIRS

Abonda Gallery ★ Enjoy the rustic ambience as you peruse the embroidered linen, pottery, lamps, and jewelry on display here, all handmade by Polish craftsmen based on traditional design. Śniadeckich 12/16. ✆ **22/628-89-95.** www.abonda.com.pl.

Bracia Łopieńscy ★ A humble workshop with an impressive history behind it. Since 1862, the Łopieński family has produced a number of the bronze monuments in Poland. You may not need a monument, but take a look at the pitchers, sugar bowls, lamps, and small sculptures handmade from four generations of expertise. Poznańska 24. ✆ **22/629-20-45.** www.b.lopienscy.webpark.pl.

Brush Workshop (Pracownia Pędzli i Szczotek) ★ Such shops are a rarity these days. It's brushes galore, from common hairbrushes and shaving brushes to unusual face brushes, mostly handmade from natural bristles. The owner learned the craft from his brush-maker grandfather. Poznańska 26. ✆ **22/621-76-56.** www.khaja.pl.

Cepelia Goods in this nationwide chain are slightly overpriced but handy for last-minute souvenir shopping since most of the traditional Polish crafts—from ceramics to sculptures, jewelry to paintings—are under one roof. Pl. Konstytucji 5. ✆ **22/621-26-18.** www.cepelia.pl.

Galeria Lnu A pokey shop offering table cloths, napkins, bedding, tunics, and other items, all made from linen. There are also bundles of fabric to choose from, should you opt for custom-made tablecloths. Senatorska 20. ✆ **22/827-54-18.** www.galerialnu.pl.

Magazyn Praga ★ A creative and quirky repository of fashion, home accessories and furniture, electronics, and paintings by young Polish talents in a warehouse located in the old Koneser Vodka Factory. Ząbkowska 27/31. ✆ **22/670-11-85.** www.magazynpraga.pl.

Manufaktura Królewska ★ A unique tapestry workshop inside a converted greenhouse at Łazienki Park (next to the Belvedere Restaurant). The tapestries, tablecloths, and scarves are hand-woven with tradition wooden looms using linen, silk, or wool threads. Agrykoli 1. ✆ **519/795-493.**

FASHION

Andrzej Jedynak If fur coats and hats are your thing, you'll find a wide selection of made-in-Poland designs here. Al. Jerozolimskie 23. ✆ **22/628-62-56.** www.andrzejjedynak.pl.

Maciej Zień A young Polish talent who dresses the A-list of Polish celebrities. Get sized up for bespoke layers or pick from the ready-to-wear for men and women. The boutique is located in a mall on the right bank of the river. Ostrobramska 75C. ✆ **22/611-73-73.** www.zien.pl.

FOOD & DRINKS

Chopin Luxury Alcohol bottles are stacked from floor to ceiling here. Among the bottles are more than 20 types of vodka, mostly made from potato or rye. Goldwasser, vodka with gold flakes, is also available. Złota 59 (Złote Tarasy). ✆ **22/222-01-03.**

Krakowski Kredens Stacked full with Polish larder staples such as jams and pickles in pretty jars. The most portable item is the *krówki* (similar to fudge) in a tin box. Nowy Świat 22. ✆ **22/826-40-01.**

Wedel Although it is now owned by the Japanese Lotte Group, Wedel (founded in 1851) is still very much a Polish icon. The circular *torcik* (chocolate-coated wafer) is an instantly recognizable Polish treat. Szpitalna 8. ✆ **22/827-29-16.** www.wedelpijalnie.pl.

JEWELRY

W. Kruk ★ Poland's best-known family-run jeweler was founded in 1840. The fourth-generation owners take pride in using local material, designers, and craftsmen. You'll find amber, but look out for the *krzemień pasiasty* series, which is made from banded flint found only in the Sandomierz area of southern Poland. Pl. Konstytucji 6. ✆ **661/980-576.** http://wkruk.pl.

LEATHER

Wittchen A Polish high-end brand known for its handbags, it also produces shoes, jackets, gloves, belts, and other leathery accessories. You can also find them in most malls. Marszałkowska 72. ✆ **22/349-23-70.** www.wittchen.com.

TABLEWARE

Platerland The shop carries silver and silver-plated tableware and cutlery made by Hefra, a Polish brand known for its ornate, period designs. You'll find chafing dishes, water pitchers, trays, candelabras, and all the trimmings for a formal dining table. Jana Pawła II 43A. ✆ **22/624-26-23.** www.platerland.pl.

Szlif A small shop with a long tradition of carrying cutlery and knives produced by Grelach, a renowned Polish brand. Książęca 6. ✆ **22/621-75-00.**

TOYS

Kalimba i Kofifi A cafe-cum-shop noted for its unique toys designed by the owner. Mierosławskiego 19. ✆ **22/839-75-60.** www.kalimba.pl.

AFTER DARK

The Performing Arts

The city's opera and classical music offerings are some of the best in the country, and the availability of relatively cheap tickets means the performances are accessible to just about anyone. Aside from the box office, you can also buy tickets at most Empik stores (see "Shopping," above) or online at www.ebilet.pl.

CLASSICAL MUSIC The **Filharmonia Narodowa** is the home of the National Philharmonic (Jasna 5; ✆ **22/551-71-30;** www.filharmonia.pl). The box office is located at Sienkiewicza 10 and is open Monday to Saturday 10am to 2pm and 3 to 7pm. They are closed from June to mid-August. Tickets are from 15 zł to 90 zł. Arrive just before show time to get cheaper last-minute tickets.

OPERA The grand opera venue is the **Teatr Wielki** (Grand Theater; pl. Teatralny 1; ✆ **22/826-50-19;** www.teatrwielki.pl). Here, you'll find everything from the Italian classics (its production of *Madame Butterfly* is very well-received) to bolder works featuring Polish avant-garde composers. The box office is open Monday to Friday 9am to 7pm, Saturday and Sunday 10am to 7pm. The **Warsaw Chamber of Opera** (Solidarności 76B; ✆ **22/831-22-40;** www.operakameralna.pl) stages performances in several venues around town, including the Great Ballroom of the Royal Castle. The box office is open weekdays from 9am to 6pm, and on weekends an hour before the performance starts.

VENUES The **Museum of Modern Art** at the **Ujazdowski Castle** (Jazdów 2; ✆ **22/628-12-71;** www.csw.art.pl) not only holds exhibitions, but also has concerts of contemporary music and screenings of indie films. **Congress Hall** (**Sala Kongresowa ★★**; pl. Defilad 1, entrance from E. Plater; ✆ **22/656-72-99;** www.kongresowa.pl), in the Palace of Culture, is an atmospheric rotund concert hall used by a range of stars, from the Rolling Stones to Goran Bregovic. The box office, by entrance C, is open on weekdays 11am to 6pm and on weekends 11am to 3pm. The **Jewish Theater** (**Teatr Żydowski;** pl. Grzybowski 12/16; ✆ **22/850-56-56;** www.teatr-zydowski.art.pl) has cultural productions in Yiddish. The box office is open Monday to Friday 11am to 2pm and 3 to 6pm, Saturday 12:30 to 7pm, and Sunday 2:30 to 6pm. **Klub Stodoła** (Batorego 10; ✆ **22/825-60-31;** www.stodola.pl) is the

Warsaw University of Technology's student concert hall. Aside from local performers, it also brings in renowned international rock bands and artists.

The Bar & Wine Bar Scene

BrowArmia ★ A lively pub-cum-restaurant with the capacity to seat more than 200 people. The microbrewery dispenses 10 types of light and dark concoctions, including cherry beer. The best views of the copper vats and giant tubes are in the subterranean level. Królewska 1. ✆ **22/826-54-55.** www.browarmia.pl.

Champions Sports Bar ★ An American-style sports bar, run by the Marriott, offering hearty burgers and ribs, and beer by the pitcher. It gets filled up by expats and sports fans catching the live telecasts on the big-screen TVs. Al. Jerozolimskie 65/79. ✆ **22/630-51-19.**

Lolek A BBQ pit and pub under giant marquees in the middle of the Pole Mokotowskie Park, it is swarmed by youngish residents, especially on nights when there's live music or sports on the big screens. Rokitnicka 20 (Pole Mokotowskie Park). ✆ **22/825-62-02.** www.lolekpub.pl.

Mielżyński Wine Bar ★★★ Absolutely peerless in Warsaw, it's a wine bar with bistro fare and a shop attached. Converted from a disused lace factory, the chic industrial-warehouse mood works well for the buffed and glossed society clientele. Book a table in advance or risk a 2-hour wait. Burakowska 5/7. ✆ **22/636-87-09.** www.mielzynski.pl.

Panorama Bar ★ A dual-level bar with stunning night views of the city from the 40th floor of the Marriott. Every last Wednesday of the month is ladies' night, with free sparkling wine from 6 to 8pm. Al. Jerozolimskie 65/79. ✆ **22/630-74-35.**

Pewex ★ Pewex stores, in the bad old days, were state-run hard-currency stores, where imported goods—everything from "Lee Cooper" jeans to "Fa" shampoo—were priced in dollars and available only to the lucky few. This Pewex is filled with kitschy '70s memorabilia and lots of good-natured irony. It's located in a labyrinth of quirky bars with inexpensive beer and therefore a good place to begin the pub-crawling. Nowy Świat 22/28. ✆ **22/826-54-81.**

Warsaw Tortilla Factory ★ Since it's take-over by an Irish owner, the strength here has shifted from burritos and fajitas to beer, cocktails, sports on widescreen TVs, live music, and chain smoking. The atmosphere is casual, and the clientele is mostly young professionals and expats. Wilcza 46. ✆ **22/621-86-22.** www.warsawtortillafactory.pl.

The Club Scene

Most of the action is still in the central part of the city, though some of the trendier places are pioneering areas farther afield, like the still-dingy but cool district of Praga. The pace is fairly lethargic on weekday nights but goes into overdrive on weekends. Most places are open Tuesday to Thursday until midnight. On Friday and Saturday, it's party till you drop at dawn. Drinks on average cost 20 zł. Some clubs have covers ranging from 5 zł to 30 zł. There's also the somewhat sexist practice of letting in women for free and charging the men. The door policy (or "door selection," in local lingo) is quirky.

Balsam ★ Out of way in the Mokotów district, this plain but atmospheric place was once a military fort and now is the hideout of those in the know who don't care for glitz and kitsch. Racławicka 99. ✆ **22/898-28-24.** www.balsam.net.pl.

Café Kulturalna Not really a cafe or a typical club, either, this bar in the Palace of Culture is happening on most nights of the week. With imperialist-style decor and occasional live jazz concerts, it hits the spot for those who are not fans of typical clubs. Pl. Defilad 1. ✆ **22/656-62-81.** www.kulturalna.pl.

Enklawa A two-story club staffed by female bartenders, dispensing a varied range of commercial music. Tuesday is ladies' night, with an occasional stripper thrown in. Mazowiecka 12. ✆ **22/827-31-51.** www.enklawa.com.

The Eve This is basically the Platinium Club with a different name and address, but the same management in door policy and the same kind of clientele on a look-cool-and-happening jaunt. Pl. Piłsudskiego 9. ✆ **604/145-462.** www.theeve.pl.

Fabryka Trzciny ★ Funky performance art space in a rundown old factory in Praga. There's no regular program, and the opening hours are spotty, but Friday and Saturday nights usually offer some interesting DJs or live music. Otwocka 14. ✆ **22/619-05-13.** www.fabrykatrzciny.pl.

Klubo Kawiarnia A Communist-themed club that's difficult to locate and equally difficult to get into. But once you're in, the kitschy props are good for a laugh and the electro/house music good for all-night dancing. Czackiego 8 (at the corner of Świętokrzyska St.). No phone. www.klubokawiarnia.pl.

Obiekt Znaleziony ★ Eclectic, rough-and-ready minimalism in sprawling Gothic-like subterranean chambers of the Zachęta National Gallery. Popular with a young crowd. Małachowskiego 3. ✆ **22/828-05-84.** www.obiektznaleziony.pl.

Platinium Club The top dog in the capital's glitzy night scene; dress up, or you won't be let in to play show-off with the expat regulars, business travelers, and well-heeled Poles. Fredry 6. ✆ **22/596-46-66.** www.platiniumclub.pl.

Tygmont Low-key in terms of decor, but the best venue for live jazz, with both veterans and rookies taking the stage nightly. Mazowiecka 6/8. ✆ **22/823-34-09.** www.tygmont.com.pl.

Gay & Lesbian

In July 2010, Warsaw became the first city from the former Iron Curtain states to host the EuroPride festival. It was seen as a step forward in tolerance and equal rights, but the city still has a long way to go before the gay and lesbian way of life becomes as open as in Western European cities.

Delikatesy It isn't a gay club, but a gay-friendly locale that's good for a coffee, drink, and meal. Most of the guests will be discussing art, music, and films. Marszałkowska 8. ✆ **22/480-80-18.** www.delikatesytr.blog.pl.

Queer Located in the Old Town, it's frequented by a youngish crowd with generous resources for looking smart. Rynek Starego Miasta 1/3. ✆ **22/635-57-40.** www.queer.com.pl.

Rasko One of the least snobbish gay clubs where you can watch drag-queen shows and karaoke contests. It's more of a warm-up point for an evening out and empties out at around 10pm. Burakowska 12. ✆ **22/838-01-30.** www.klubrasko.pl.

Toro A two-level dance club where the basement is for men only. They bring in shows and striptease acts from abroad. Marszałkowska 3/5 (entrance from Emila Zoli St.). ✆ **22/825-60-14.** www.toro.waw.pl.

Utopia Finicky door policy grants entry only to those with super hot (or super cool) clothing and war paint, but charm the doorman and he might relent. The dance floor is small, but the DJs and live acts never fail to deliver great music. Jasna 1. ✆ **22/827-15-40.** www.utopiaclub.eu.

ŁÓDŹ & SOUTH-CENTRAL POLAND

6

by Mark Baker

The big swath of territory that lies southwest of Warsaw and between the popular cities of Wrocław and Kraków is mostly, unfortunately, unvisited by visitors to Poland. Łódź (pronounced *woodge*), Poland's second-largest city, is a 19th-century boom town that, like parts of the industrial Midwest of the United States or the Midlands in the U.K., fell on hard times in the modern era and has had to reinvent itself. The results, so far, have been mostly positive, but the city hasn't quite yet broken into the top tier of tourist destinations.

Farther south, the Upper Silesian heartland (not to be confused with Lower Silesia near Wrocław) has long been Poland's main industrialized region. The smokestack-laden megalopolis centered on Katowice and including the cities of Bytom and Gliwice is home to some 3 million people but largely devoid of traditional tourist sites.

Still, there are several good reasons you may want to schedule a stop in either Łódź or Katowice (or both). Łódź—sometimes called HollyŁódź (pronounced *Hollywoodge)*—is home to Poland's famed film industry and was the early stomping ground for Poland's trilogy of world-leading film directors: Andrzej Wajda, Krzysztof Kieslowski, and Roman Polański. It was also the site of Poland's second-largest wartime Jewish ghetto, after Warsaw, and parts of the former ghetto still look very much as they did during World War II. If you're interested in Jewish or Holocaust history, you can walk the former streets and take in the story of the Łódź ghetto at your own pace. It's deeply moving in a way that more highly polished memorials or museums often are not.

Katowice is an important transportation hub, lying on the main rail line between Prague and Kraków, and the highway between Wrocław and Kraków. It's got some great restaurants and some offbeat attractions that can feel like a much-needed antidote to sometimes overly touristy Kraków.

The pilgrimage city of Częstochowa is arguably the region's only genuine must-see. The **Jasna Góra Monastery,** home to the fabled painting of the "Black Madonna," has drawn believers and miracle-seekers for centuries, and retains an aura of hushed holiness into the modern age. History buffs may want to push farther south to the city of Cieszyn, which straddles the border between Poland and the Czech Republic. This once-independent duchy in the Middle Ages proved a sore point between Poland and then-Czechoslovakia in the run-up to World War II, when Poland forcibly annexed territory on both sides of the border just as Adolf Hitler was making his own Czech land grab. Polish-Czech relations are much improved since then, and you can leisurely stroll both sides of the border by crossing a small footbridge over the charming Olza River.

ŁÓDŹ

Poland's second-largest city has traditionally been called the "Manchester of Poland," a reference to its rise in the 19th century as an industrial powerhouse, and to the vast textile mills that employed tens of thousands of workers at the turn of the 20th century. For Americans, the hulking relics and depressed building stock of a bygone era may bring to mind parts of Detroit or Cleveland. Still, there's an energy and vitality here that many Polish cities lack, and if you're passing by, Łódź merits at least a day of exploration. The city can be visited as a long daytrip from Warsaw, but it's better approached as a destination in its own right. The prospect of some excellent restaurants and a couple of nice hotels sweetens the deal.

Łódź is relatively young as Polish cities go. It came into its own only in the mid-19th century, when German and later Jewish industrialists built large textile mills to exploit access to the vast Russian and Chinese markets to the east. Unlike Kraków or Wrocław, you'll search in vain here for a large market square, a *rynek,* surrounded by gabled baroque and Renaissance houses. Instead, you'll find—amid the tenements and badly neglected housing stock—fine examples of the sumptuous neo-baroque and neoclassical mansions and town palaces favored by the wealthy 19th-century bourgeoisie.

By the start of the 20th century, Łódź had grown from a village just a few decades earlier to a city of more than 300,000 people, and its factories, mansions, and civic institutions were among the finest in the country. It was a magnet for poor Poles from around the country, but above all, it attracted Jews, drawn here by the relatively tolerant social climate and economic opportunity. At its height, the Jewish community numbered some 230,000 people, around a third of the city's pre–World War II population of around 700,000 people.

But if the city's economic rise was rapid, its decline was precipitous, as well. At the end of World War I, with the establishment of independent Poland, the city lost its privileged access to the Russian and Far Eastern markets. World War II, and the Nazi occupation, was an unmitigated disaster. While many of the buildings survived the war intact, nearly the entire Jewish population was wiped out—first herded into a massive ghetto north of the city center, and then shipped off, train by train, to the death camps at Chełmno and Auschwitz-Birkenau. For decades after the war, the story of the "Litzmannstadt" ghetto, as the Nazis called it, was little known outside of Poland. Now, Jewish groups from around the world are getting the word out. You can tour much of the former ghetto, as well as visit the Jewish cemetery, the largest of its kind in Europe.

The Communist period brought more ruin to the city. The once-profitable mills were run into the ground by inept state ownership. The city was blighted by some of

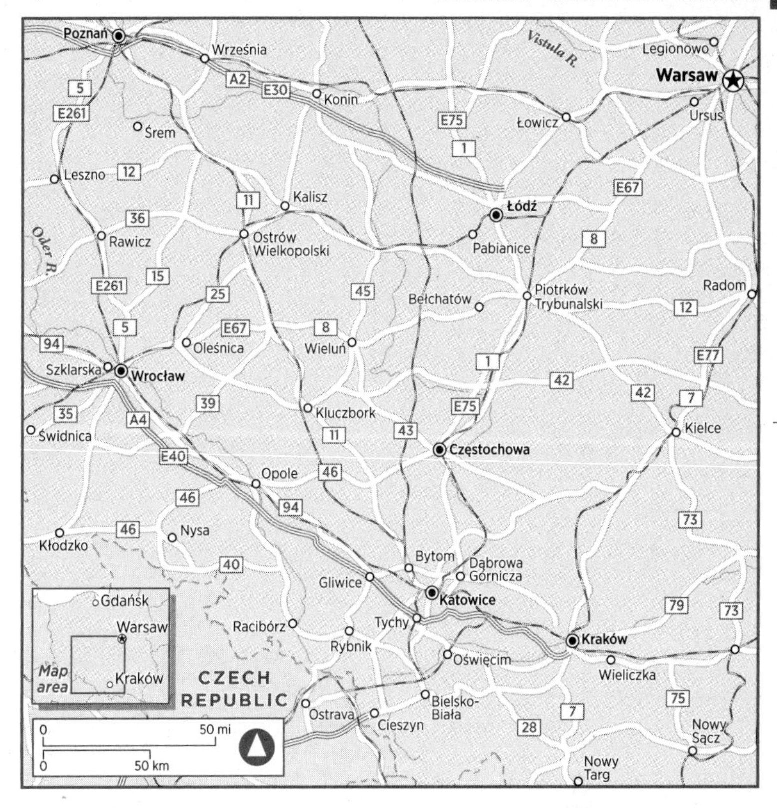

the most insensitive Communist-era planning to ever come off the drawing board. The period since 1989 has seen a massive effort to transform the bleak postindustrial cityscape into a lively cultural center. And that effort is partially succeeding. The heart of the transformation is the city's main drag, **Piotrkowska,** a nearly 4km-long (2½-mile) pedestrian strip lined with restaurants, cafes, bars, clubs, and shops. By day, it's a place to stroll, window-shop, and have an open-air coffee. By night, it's arguably Poland's most intense street party, filled with raucous revelers swilling beer as club music blares from behind nearly every door. Just to the north of the city center, the huge complex of former textile mills has now been transformed into Europe's biggest shopping and entertainment complex, **Manufaktura.**

Łódź also boasts one of Poland's best museums of modern art and a clutch of other interesting museums, many housed in the mansions of the old industrial elite. For fans of international film, Łódź is home to the Poland's most highly regarded film school and the country's only Museum of Cinematography. Legendary Polish film directors Andrzej Wajda, Krzysztof Kieslowski, and Roman Polański, among others, all learned their craft here.

Essentials

GETTING THERE

BY PLANE Łódź's **Władysław Reymont Airport** (Gen. Stanisława Maczka 35; ✆ **42/688-84-14;** www.airport.lodz.pl) is small, though several budget carriers, including Ryanair, fly here from various cities in the U.K. and continental Europe. The airport is a 15-minute drive southwest of the city center. On arriving, take bus no. 55 to get to the main street, Piotrkowska. A ticket for the 30-minute bus ride costs 2.40 zł. A taxi into town will run about 40 zł.

BY TRAIN Most trains, including the Warsaw express trains, arrive and depart from the main station: **Fabryczna** (pl. Salacińskiego 1; ✆ **42/194-36;** www.pkp.pl). Fabryczna is a 10-minute walk from the center of town. A taxi to the center will cost about 10 zł. Some trains also arrive at and depart from suburban **Kaliska station** (ul. Unii Lubelskiej 3/5; ✆ **42/194-36**) or **Widzew station** (Słozbowa 8; ✆ **42/194-36**), so be sure to check your ticket.

BY BUS The main bus station (pl. Salacińskiego 1; ✆ **42/631-97-06;** www.pks.lodz.pl) is situated just behind Fabryczna train station, about a 10-minute walk from the center of town or a 10-zł cab ride. Łódź has excellent bus connections to all of Poland's major cities and is a central hub for buses throughout the south-central Polish region.

BY CAR Łódź lies at the geographic center of Poland and at the crossroads of several major highways, including the main E75 highway that runs from Gdańsk to the Czech border. Figure on about a 3-hour drive from Warsaw and Wrocław, and about 4 hours south from Gdańsk. Once in Łódź, paid street parking during working hours will cost 1 zł for the first hour and 2 zł for every hour after that.

VISITOR INFORMATION

The city of Łódź **Tourist Information Center** (Piotrkowska 87; ✆ **42/638-59-55;** www.cityoflodz.pl) is one-stop shopping for all you'll ever need to know. Here, you'll find helpful pamphlets for negotiating the city: *Łódź Tourist Attractions* and the *Łódź City Guide*, as well as the essential *Jewish Landmarks in Łódź*. The latter includes a (long) self-guided walking tour of the Łódź (Litzmannstadt) ghetto. The staff maintains a complete list of hotels and can help arrange transportation and restaurant reservations. Inside the Tourist Information Center, you'll also find the **Łódź Airport Travel Agency** (Piotrkowska 87; ✆ **42/638-59-80;** www.airporttravel.lodz.pl), which can help arrange flights in and out of Poland, as well as around the country.

CITY LAYOUT

Łódź is a sprawling city situated on a loose grid based around the long pedestrian thoroughfare Piotrkowska. Łódź doesn't have a traditional town center, though the intersection of Piotrkowska and the giant avenue Piłsudskiego, near the Ibis Hotel (see "Where to Stay," below), is usually considered the center. Most of the better places to eat, as well as the main tourist sites and the Manufaktura shopping center, lie on or within easy walking distance of Piotrkowska.

GETTING AROUND

Distances are vast in Łódź, so depending on where you stay, you may find yourself mixing walking with taking trams, taxis, and the occasional pedicab.

ON FOOT The city's main boulevard, Piotrkowska, is largely closed to car traffic, so walking (or taking a pedicab) is the only way of getting down this street. It's around

4km (2½ miles), end to end, and takes about 45 minutes to walk its length. Walking is also the best way to see the former Jewish ghetto. Elsewhere, going on foot is not much fun. The distances are too long, and there's not much to see along the way.

BY PEDICAB/RICKSHAW Pedicabs whisk you from one end of Piotrkowska to the other in about 10 minutes for about 5 zł with tip. Rates tend to go up sharply for destinations away from Piotrkowska; in these cases, be sure to negotiate the fare in advance.

BY TRAM/BUS Łódź has an excellent public transportation system of buses and trams. Tickets cost 2.40 zł for a standard 30-minute trip and are available from newsagents.

BY TAXI Taxis are cheap and plentiful. Figure on fares of 15 zł to 20 zł around town. Reputable firms include **Merc Radio Taxi** (✆ **42/650-50-50**) and **MPT Taxi** (✆ **42/191-91**).

BY BIKE Łódź is flat as a pancake, and car-free Piotrkowska is fun to cycle—but rentals are few and far between; your best bet is to consult with the tourist information office.

Top Attractions

To get your bearings, start out at one end of Piotrkowska (it doesn't matter which) and walk to the other end. Piotrkowska is where it all happens in Łódź. Meander down the various side streets. You'll find houses and buildings in all states of repair and disrepair. It's an urban-rehabber's dream, and someday, this all might be trendy shops and boutiques. In addition to the numerous pubs, restaurants, and coffee bars, Piotrkowska is lined up and down with turn-of-the-last-century neo-this, neo-that architectural gems. The house at no. 78 marks the birthplace of renowned pianist Artur Rubinstein, the city's most famous local son.

The former textile mills, now the **Manufaktura** shopping mall, as well as the History of Łódź Museum and the former Jewish ghetto, lie to the north of the city center, beyond the terminus of Piotrkowska at the Plac Wolności, identified by the statue of Polish national hero Tadeusz Kościuszko at the center. At the other end of Piotrkowska is the highly recommended Cinematography Museum, situated in another sumptuous former industrialist's mansion.

The Łódź Ghetto (Litzmannstadt) ★★ If one of your reasons for visiting Poland is to trace Jewish heritage, then you'll certainly want to explore what remains of the Łódź ghetto (often called by its German name, *Litzmannstadt*), once the second-biggest urban concentration of Jews in Europe after the Warsaw ghetto. But be forewarned: Although spending time here is highly worthwhile, not all of the former ghetto survived World War II, and some of the area has been rebuilt with mostly prefab Communist housing blocks and shops. Much of the walking tour of the ghetto consists of weaving through drab and depressed streets, looking for hard-to-find memorial plaques and trying to imagine what life must have been like during what was a much different era.

The Litzmannstadt ghetto is one of the saddest and least-well-known stories of the war. The Germans first formed the ghetto in 1940, after invading Poland and incorporating the Łódź area into the German Reich. In all, some 200,000 Jews from Łódź and around Europe were moved here to live in cramped, appalling conditions. Next to the Jewish ghetto, the Nazis formed a second camp for several thousand Gypsies (Roma) brought here from Austria's Burgenland province. High fences and a system of heavily guarded steps and pathways allowed the detainees to move between various parts of the ghetto, but prevented anyone from entering or leaving. For a time, the ghetto functioned as a quasi-normal city, with the Jews more or less allowed to administer their own affairs in exchange for forced labor that contributed to the Nazi war effort. In 1944, with the coming of the end of the war, the Nazis stepped up their extermination campaign and began regular large-scale transports to death camps at Chełmno and Auschwitz. By the end of the war, there were just a handful of survivors left.

Begin the tour by picking up a copy of the brochure *Jewish Landmarks in Łódź,* available at the tourist information office on Piotrkowska (you can also find an abridged version of the tour in the publication *Łódź In Your Pocket,* usually available at large hotel reception desks). The walk starts north of the city center at the **Bałucki Rynek,** once the city's main market and the site of the German administration of the ghetto. You can find it by walking north along Piotrkowska, crossing the Plac Wolności, and continuing on through the park. From here the trail snakes along about 10km (6¼ miles), ending at the **Jewish Cemetery (Cmentarz Żydowski) ★★**, the largest of its kind in Europe, and the **Radegast ★★** train station, from where the transports to the extermination camps departed. (If you want to skip the trail, you can go directly to the cemetery and the Radegast station.) The cemetery is open Sunday to Friday and has a small exhibition of photographs of Jewish life in Łódź and the ghetto. The Radegast station (about a 15-min. walk north of the Jewish cemetery) has been restored to its appearance during the war, with three Deutsche Reichsbahn transport railcars ominously left standing on the tracks, the doors wide open.

After the war, a scattering of Jews returned to the city to try to rebuild a fraction of what they lost. Today, the Jewish population numbers just a few hundred from a pre–World War II population of nearly a quarter million.

Jewish Cemetery (Cmentarz Żydowski): ul. Bracka (entrance on ul. Zmienna). Free admission. Sun–Fri 10am–4pm.

Aquarium ★ ☺ An interesting diversion and a treat for kids if you're in town on a rainy day, Łódź's aquarium is situated in the Manufaktura shopping complex (see "Shopping," below). There are around 30 big tanks holding everything from Polish river and sea fish to more exotic species like piranhas and stingrays.

Drewnowska 58. ✆ **42/632-89-15.** www.manufaktura.com. 9 zł adults, 6 zł children. Daily 9am–9pm.

City of Łódź Museum ★★ If you're intrigued by the industrial history of the city and want to know more, this is where to come. Information about textiles, the history of the city's barons, a bit about Artur Rubinstein, and even background on Jewish Łódź, is all housed in the sumptuous neo-baroque palace of Łódź industrialist par excellence, Izrael Kalmanowicz Poznański.

Ogrodowa 15. ✆ **42/654-03-23.** www.poznanskipalace.muzeum-lodz.pl. 8 zł adults. Mon 10am–2pm; Tues & Thurs 10am–4pm; Wed 2–6pm; Sat & Sun 11am–4pm.

Łódź Art Museum (Muzeum Sztuki w Łódźi) ★★ A must for fans of modern art, from the functionalist, constructivist 1920s to the abstract 1950s and pop-art, op-art 1960s. The collection includes works by Marc Chagall and Max Ernst, as well as the best Polish artists of their generations. The museum recently opened an annex called "ms2" at the Manufaktura complex (see "Shopping," below), where push-the-envelope experimental exhibitions are mounted using the museum's original collection. The new space also houses a gift shop and a coffee shop. Both are definitely worth a visit.

Museum: Więckowskiego 36; ✆ **42/633-97-90;** www.msl.org.pl; 8 zł adults; Tues-Sun noon-7pm. ms2: Ogrodowa 19; ✆ **42/634-39-48;** 12 zł adults; Tues 10am-6pm, Wed-Sun noon-8pm.

Museum of Cinematography ★★ If you're a fan of international film, you'll want to stop by to pay tribute to Poland's panoply of great directors, including Roman Polański, Andrzej Wajda, and Krzysztof Kieslowski, all of whom studied and worked in Łódź. The museum's annual rotating exhibitions highlight the work of one of the directors, including stills and posters from the films and various memorabilia, though it should be said there's not much English commentary. The museum is housed in the former residence of one of the city's great capitalist barons, Karol Scheibler, and part of the fun is just poking around this incredible neo-baroque mansion.

Pl. Zwycięstwa 1. ✆ **42/674-09-57.** www.kinomuzeum.pl. 8 zł adults. Tues 10am–5pm; Wed & Fri-Sun 9am–4pm; Thurs 11am–6pm.

Radogoszcz Prison ★★ This former wartime Nazi detention and torture center for political prisoners today holds fascinating exhibitions on Łódź during the German occupation, as well as photos and displays of the Litzmannstadt ghetto. In 1945, the fleeing Nazis torched the prison ahead of the advance of the Soviet Red Army, killing some 1,500 inmates; only 30 or so survived.

Zgierska 147. ✆ **42/655-36-66.** www.muzeumtradycji.pl. 8 zł adults. Tues & Thurs 10am–6pm; Wed & Fri 9am–4pm; Sat & Sun 10am–3pm.

Shopping

Łódź offers one of the most unusual shopping opportunities in Poland and possibly all of Europe. In an effort to revitalize the city, the former textile mills have been converted into an enormous shopping mall and entertainment facility, **Manufaktura** (Jana Karskiego 5; ✆ **42/664-92-60;** www.manufaktura.com; daily 10am–9pm), complete with a 15-screen multiplex theater, a luxury hotel, a climbing wall, Europe's longest fountain at 300m (984 ft.), an aquarium, and an on-site sandpit for beach volleyball. The 19th-century red-brick factory architecture is stunning, and the restoration work a model for similar reconstruction efforts around the country. If you're a fan of urban rehab or just want to spend the day at the mall, stop by and take a look.

Where to Stay

The better hotels are clustered around the center at Piotrkowska, but the area can get noisy at night. Ask for a room away from the main street. Rates are generally high for what's offered, but many hotels offer steep discounts on weekends.

VERY EXPENSIVE

Andel's ★★★ If your budget allows, definitely stay at this stunningly renovated modern hotel carved out of the former textile mills in the Manufaktura shopping complex. The stylish contemporary furnishings meshed with the cavernous spaces and exposed brick of the former factory combine for an eye-opening aesthetic that will have you snapping photos of everything from your room to the gargantuan hotel lobby. There's a big enclosed swimming pool on the roof and state-of-the-art fitness and conference facilities, not to mention the enormous shopping mall and entertainment complex next door.

Ogrodowa 17. ✆ **42/279-10-00.** Fax 42/279-10-01. www.andelslodz.com. 278 units. 400 zł double. AE, DC, MC, V. Parking (paid). **Amenities:** Restaurant; exercise room; indoor pool; room service; sauna. *In room:* A/C, TV, DVD/CD player, hair dryer, minibar, Wi-Fi (free).

EXPENSIVE

Grand Hotel ★★ This turn-of-the-20th-century grande dame of a hotel was in the midst of a major renovation as this book went to press, after being purchased by the luxury Likus chain that manages the Hotel Copernicus in Kraków and the Monopol in Wrocław, among other five-star properties. The marble-clad lobby and dining areas, filled with priceless Art Nouveau details, had already been considerably spruced up, but the rooms were still somewhat of a disappointment. This will all change by 2012, when the renovation is finished. Expect eye-opening contemporary style, a state-of-the-art fitness center, and room prices in the 500-zł-to-700-zł-a-night range. The location is also a major plus, right at the heart of the pedestrian zone.

Piotrkowska 72. ✆ **42/633-99-20.** Fax 42/633-78-76. www.grandlodz.pl. 161 units. 390 zł double. AE, DC, MC, V. Parking (paid). **Amenities:** Restaurant; exercise room; room service; sauna. *In room:* A/C, TV, hair dryer, Internet (free), minibar.

MODERATE

Campanile ★★ A French chain that aims for the high-middle market and delivers with well-designed, clean, stylish rooms and a professional, hospitable staff. It's similar to the IBIS (see below) down the street, but a step up in quality. Good location, just a couple of tram stops from Piotrkowska (or a 15-minute walk). There's a decent on-site restaurant and an excellent breakfast buffet (not included in the room price).

Piłsudskiego 11. ✆ **42/664-26-00.** Fax 42/664-26-01. www.campanile.com. 104 units. 270 zł double. AE, DC, MC, V. Parking (paid). **Amenities:** Restaurant; limited room service. *In room:* A/C, TV, hair dryer, Internet (free), minibar.

INEXPENSIVE

Hotel Savoy ★ This shabby but likeable turn-of-the-20th-century hotel will appeal to those who prefer the atmosphere of historic hotels but can't justify the higher price of the much-nicer Grand (see above) across the street. The Savoy feels smaller and more intimate than the Grand, though it's far inferior. Many of the older period elements have been stripped away through countless, often thoughtless, renovations. That said, several rooms on the second and fourth floors have been spruced up recently and are not half bad. Room 407 is a cute double, while 409 is a bright minisuite with twin beds. For fans of Austrian writer Josef Roth, this is the "Hotel Savoy" of his quirky novel of the same name.

Traugutta 6. ✆ **42/632-93-60.** Fax 42/632-93-68. www.centrumhotele.pl. 70 units. 240 zł double. AE, DC, MC, V. Metered street parking. **Amenities:** Restaurant; limited room service. *In room:* A/C (in some), TV, hair dryer.

IBIS ★ Similar to the Campanile (see above) and a good option, whether you're here for business or pleasure. This modern hotel offers relatively rare local amenities like full conference facilities, in-room Internet access, and a dedicated business center. It's also a good choice in midsummer, since it's one of a handful of hotels in town with in-room air-conditioning. Big weekend discounts.

Piłsudskiego 11. ✆ **42/638-67-00.** Fax 42/638-67-77. www.ibishotel.com. 208 units. 180 zł double. AE, DC, MC, V. Parking (paid). **Amenities:** Restaurant; limited room service. *In room:* A/C, TV, hair dryer, Internet, minibar.

Where to Dine

You'll find most restaurants, including the big Polish chains such as Sphinx and Sioux, grouped along Piotrkowska. But stay clear of the big chains and try one of the local places listed below.

VERY EXPENSIVE

Anatewka ★★ JEWISH Fun, informal Jewish-themed restaurant; the kind of place where the chef comes out halfway through the meal to pour you a shot of kosher vodka on the house. The two tiny, crowded dining rooms feel more like the parlor of an old Jewish aunt, with overstuffed chairs and walls crammed with bric-a-brac. A fiddler, while not quite on the roof, plays some nights from a little perch just below the ceiling. The food is very good. The signature "Duck Rubenstein" comes served in a tart sauce of cherries, seasoned with clove.

Ul. 6 Sierpnia 2/4. ✆ **42/630-36-35.** Main courses 30 zł–50 zł. AE, DC, MC, V. Daily noon–11pm.

EXPENSIVE

Ciągoty i Tęsknoty ★★★ 🎁 INTERNATIONAL Don't despair as your taxi heads out of town past row after row of falling-down, Socialist-era housing projects. You're heading to one of the best meals in Łódź. Perched between two ghastly apartment blocks is a little oasis of '50s jazz and fresh flowers. The menu is perched somewhere between home cooking and haute cuisine, with salads, pierogi, pasta dishes, and some seriously good mains centered on pork, chicken, and boiled beef. The tagliatelle with brie and fresh tomatoes is a creative vegetarian option. It's about 3km (1¾ miles) from the center of town but well worth the taxi fare (15 zł) to get there.

Wojska Polskiego 144a. ✆ **42/650-87-94.** Main courses 20 zł–40 zł. AE, DC, MC, V. Mon–Fri noon–10pm; Sat & Sun 1–10pm.

MODERATE

Varoska ★ HUNGARIAN What could be better—or weirder—than having an authentic Hungarian stew or a chicken paprika while sitting in the geographic center of Poland? If your taste buds need re-awakening after all of those pierogi, this spicy Hungarian cooking, built around hot red peppers, might be just the ticket. The Hungarian potato pancake is a great and filling mix of pork goulash, sour cream, and snips of red pepper wrapped up in a fresh-baked potato pancake. The service is friendly, and the atmosphere somewhere between homey and intimate.

Traugutta 4. ✆ **42/632-45-46.** Main courses 20 zł–30 zł. No credit cards. Daily noon–10pm.

Ganesh ★★ INDIAN Polish food is good, but sometimes you need a change of pace. This is excellent Indian cuisine, prepared here informally in an open kitchen. The menu lists the usual mix of curry and tandoori dishes, with fresh *naan* bread and delicious *lassi* drinks. Tell the server if you'd like your food on the spicy side, or it could turn out bland. The restaurant is small, so book ahead to be on the safe side. There's now a second location at Piotrkowska 55, in case you can't get a seat.

Piotrkowska 69 (in the passageway). ✆ **42/632-23-20.** Reservations suggested. Main courses 15 zł–30 zł. No credit cards. Daily noon–10pm.

INEXPENSIVE

Presto ITALIAN Much better than the average Polish pizzeria, the doughy pies here are topped with a slightly sweetish red sauce and cooked in a traditional wood-fired oven. The menu includes the usual suspects, but pizza "San Francisco" breaks new ground with banana, pineapple, and curry sauce. A more reliable choice might be "Sparare," with bacon, mushrooms, and onions. Also on offer are a good range of salads and pasta dishes. It's especially popular on Friday and Saturday nights because of its location in a little passageway just off Łódź's main pedestrian walk. Service can be slow, so plan on a long evening.

Piotrkowska 67 (in the passageway). ✆ **42/630-88-83.** Main courses 15 zł–22 zł. No credit cards. Daily noon–10pm.

After Dark

Łódź has a lively cultural calendar jammed with art and film festivals. Check with the tourist information office to see if something big is happening while you are there. The highlight is November's "Camerimage" (www.pluscamerimage.pl) international film festival. The "Four Cultures" festival (www.4kultury.pl) in September celebrates the city's Polish, Jewish, German, and Russian roots.

CAFES, PUBS & CLUBS

Łódź is a shot-and-a-beer town in the best sense of the term, and if you're looking for a spot to drink, carouse, and club, you needn't go any farther than Piotrkowska: 4km (2½ miles) of restaurants, cafes, and bars that open early and close late. One reliable suggestion is **Łódź Kaliska** (Piotrkowska 102; ✆ **42/630-69-55**), a rowdy bar and club filled with inventive photography on the walls and packed with university students and other revelers. **Jazzga Jazz Club** (Piotrkowska 17; ✆ **42/630-27-44**), through a passageway and up some metal stairs, is a lively bar and music club with frequent live rock acts but, it should be noted, rarely jazz. **Art & Caffe** (Piotrkowska 83; ✆ **694/512-511**), in a little passage off the main street, is a relaxing, welcoming spot for coffee and has the added benefit of a reliable, free Wi-Fi connection.

CZĘSTOCHOWA

The south-central city of Częstochowa (say *chen-stow-hoe-vah*) provides an unremarkable setting for one of the country's leading attractions for visitors, particularly devout Catholics: the **Jasna Góra Monastery** (sometimes called the Pauline Monastery). For Catholics, Częstochowa occupies a rung on par with Lourdes in France, and just below the Vatican itself. Every year, millions of pilgrims come here to see the monastery's miracle-working pride and joy: an icon of Mary holding the infant Jesus, known as the *Miraculous Painting of Our Lady* (usually shortened to the "Black Madonna"). Not surprisingly, negotiating the crowds and actually getting close enough to see the painting is no small feat (comparable on some days to seeing the *Mona Lisa* at the Louvre in Paris). The best strategy for seeing the painting is to plan an overnight stop and get an early start. The painting is open to the public throughout the morning, but then revealed only once an hour during the afternoon. Aside from the monastery, there's not much else to do in town. Nevertheless, the town center, built around an enormous pedestrian boulevard, the Aleja Najświętszej Maryi Panny (often shortened to Al. NMP), is a pleasant enough place to pass the time, with plenty of cafes to grab a coffee or piece of cake and a number of surprisingly good restaurants.

Essentials

GETTING THERE

BY TRAIN Częstochowa lies on main train lines, with hourly train service to Katowice and several fast connections a day to Wrocław, Warsaw, and Kraków. The train station, the **Dworzec PKP** (Al. Wolności 21/23; ✆ **34/376-14-00**), is situated in the center of town, about 2 blocks off of the Al. NMP and about 25 minutes on foot to the Jasna Góra monastery.

BY BUS The main bus station, the **Dworzec PKS** (Al. Wolności 45; ✆ **34/379-11-49**), is about 183m (600 ft.) beyond the train station, about 10 minutes walk to the center of town, and 25 to 30 minutes on foot to the Jasna Góra monastery. It's a big bus station with regular bus service to most regional towns and cities, as well as longer-haul service to Łódź, Wrocław, Warsaw, and Kraków.

BY CAR Częstochowa is easy to reach by car. From Kraków, take the E40 west to Katowice and then the E75 north to Częstochowa; from Warsaw, first follow the E67 south out of town, then the E75 to Częstochowa.

VISITOR INFORMATION

Częstochowa's helpful **City Information Center** is located in the center of town (Al. Najświętszej Maryi Panny 65; ✆ **34/368-22-50;** www.czestochowa.pl). This office tends to have more information in English on the town and the Jasna Góra monastery than the smaller **Jasna Góra Information Center** located in the monastery itself (Kordeckiego 2; ✆ **34/365-38-88**). If you plan on doing a thorough tour of the monastery, consider renting audio headphones from the Jasna Góra info center (15 zł), which takes you on a long but helpful tour of the monastery and its many rooms and chapels.

GETTING AROUND

The Jasna Góra Monastery is situated just off Aleja Najświętszej Maryi Panny, about a 15-minute walk from the tourist information center. Unless you're staying far from the center, you'll be able to walk everywhere you want to go.

ON FOOT The monastery lies atop a smallish hill, so you'll have to climb a little. Otherwise, Częstochowa is mostly flat and easy to negotiate.

BY BUS Częstochowa has a good public bus and tram system, but you'll probably never have to use it. Tickets (2.50 zł per ride) are available from news agents.

BY TAXI Taxis are easy to find and relatively cheap. Use only cabs that are clearly marked.

Top Attractions

Though there are a few attractions in Częstochowa itself, including a city museum and a match museum (the kind you light), the overwhelming number of visitors come here to see the Jasna Góra Monastery and, more particularly, the painting of the Black Madonna. Even if you intend to see some of the city's other sights, be sure to get to the monastery first since it's hard to predict in advance how crowded it will be.

Jasna Góra Monastery ★★★ Even if it weren't for the icon of the Black Madonna, the fabled Jasna Góra Monastery (sometimes called the Pauline Monastery) would still be an impressive sight. The first Pauline monks starting coming here from the territory of modern-day Hungary in the 14th century, and over the years, the monastery was gradually built up and fortified. On several occasions throughout the centuries, the monastery successfully fought off attacks from Swedish and Austrian invaders (attributed in large part to what are believed to be the powers of the Black Madonna), before succumbing for a time to the forces of tsarist Russia. Even today, the monastery retains the appearance of a fortress.

The layout is confusing for first-time visitors. The best approach is to visit the small Jasna Góra Information Center (see "Visitor Information," above) within the monastery for an orientation map and an optional audio headset (if you want to take a complete tour of the buildings). The main entrance to the Cathedral and the chapels, including the Chapel of the Holy Virgin Mary where the Black Madonna is displayed, is just to the right of the information center. The Cathedral is dazzling, with each room and chapel meticulously decorated in a mix of Gothic, Renaissance, and baroque styles. Particularly impressive is the 46m-long (151-ft.) basilica. The mood throughout is hushed and holy, and even non-believers will be touched by a feeling of something sacred. The crowds will naturally lead you to the icon of the Black Madonna. The icon's setting, the ornate Chapel of the Holy Virgin Mary, is in Gothic style, including a richly carved wooden altar of the crucifix from 1400, but has been given a rich baroque overlay. The Black Madonna painting resembles a Byzantine icon and depicts the Virgin Mary holding the infant Jesus. Authorship of the painting is traditionally attributed to Luke, and the painting is said to have made its way here through the centuries from the Holy Lands to Constantinople (now Istanbul), to the Ukrainian city Belz, and finally to Częstochowa in 1382. The painting was partially damaged by Hussite (Protestant) fighters in the 15th century, but this doesn't appear to have diminished its miraculous appeal. The icon is open to the public throughout the morning hours, but a protective screen is lowered at noon, and then it's displayed just once an hour throughout the afternoon. Get there early in the morning to maximize your chances of seeing it. You're free to tour the monastery at will, taking in the various chapels, as well as the museum of the 600th anniversary, the Bastion of St. Roch (where Lech Wałęsa's Nobel Peace Prize is displayed), the Tower (at 106m/348 ft.—516 steps—one of the highest in the country), and the Treasury, where the most valuable votive offerings to the Black Madonna are exhibited.

Kordeckiego 2. © **34/377-77-77** (for monastery) or 34/365-38-88 (for tourist information). www.jasnagora.pl. Free admission. Monastery & chapels daily 5am–9:30pm; treasury, 600th anniversary museum & Bastion of St. Roch daily 9am–5pm; tower daily 8am–4pm.

Match Production Museum ★ ☺ Poles know Częstochowa for two things: the holy icon of the Black Madonna and wooden matches for lighting pipes and stoves. This is a mildly diverting rainy-day event, where you get to see how matches were once made using steam technology from the 19th century. The factory is still in use today.

Ogrodowa 68. © **34/365-12-10.** www.zapalki.pl. 7 zł adults. Mon–Fri 8am–1pm.

Częstochowa Museum A nice overview of the history of the city and region, with more information on the monastery, as well as collections of old coins, medals, paintings, and coats of arms. The main collection is situated here in the Old Town Hall, but various other exhibitions related to the main museum are scattered around the city.

Al. NMP 45a (Old Town Hall). © **34/360-56-31.** www.muzeumczestochowa.pl. 5 zł adults. Tues–Sun 9:30am–5:30pm (11am–5pm in winter).

Where to Stay

Częstochowa gets millions of visitors every year, so be sure to book well in advance and try to avoid travel on major Catholic holidays, especially the Feast of the Assumption on August 15, when something like 500,000 people crowd into town for the festivities.

Mercure Patria ★★ Sadly, this is the only hotel in Czestochowa that we can whole-heartedly recommend, given the paucity of decent hotels in town. The local representative of the Mercure chain boasts smart, well-appointed rooms done out in a clean, contemporary style that have in-room (paid) Internet and air-conditioning. The location is excellent: a 10-minute walk to the monastery and within easy walking distance of other main sights in town.

Ks. J. Popiełuszki 2. ✆ **34/360-31-00.** Fax 34/360-32-00. www.accorhotels.com. 102 units. 320 zł double. AE, DC, MC, V. Parking (paid). **Amenities:** Restaurant. *In room:* A/C, TV, hair dryer, Internet.

Sekwana Sekwana is the kind of hotel that will do in a pinch but that's really good for only a night. On the plus side, it's cheap and within easy walking distance of the Jasna Góra monastery. There's in-room Wi-Fi and free parking, and several good restaurants nearby. On the minus side, the rooms can be stiflingly hot in summer and freezing in winter, and the beds and hallways all have a worn-out feel. The in-house French restaurant is decent, but the morning breakfast (10 zł extra per person) is only basic: bread, butter, cheese, and a cup of instant coffee.

Wieluńska 24. ✆ **34/324-89-54.** Fax 34/324-63-67. www.sekwana.pl. 20 units. 130 zł double. AE, DC, MC, V. Parking (paid). **Amenities:** Restaurant. *In room:* TV, hair dryer, Wi-Fi (free).

Wenecki ★★ A better choice than the similarly priced Sekwana, Wenecki offers warmly colored, even beautiful rooms with hardwood floors and big comfortable beds for the same rack rate. Each room is slightly different, so ask to see a couple before choosing. Your room rate includes free guarded parking and in-room Internet. The breakfast (not included) is excellent. The only drawback is location: It's on the opposite end of town from the monastery, meaning you'll have to walk 20 minutes or take the bus.

Berka Joselewicza 12. ✆ **34/324-33-03.** Fax 34/324-28-07. www.hotelwenecki.pl. 33 units. 140 zł double. AE, DC, MC, V. Parking (paid). **Amenities:** Restaurant. *In room:* TV, hair dryer, Internet (free).

Where to Dine

Most of the better restaurants are clustered along a side street just next to the Jasna Góra monastery, close to the Hotel Sekwana, so if you're staying there, you need only step outside your hotel door to find good Polish food, decent Greek, and even acceptably good pizza. The main boulevard that connects the Jasna Góra monastery to the center of town, the Al. NMP, is lined with cafes and restaurants that cater to the thousands of pilgrims that come here every year.

Cafe Skrzynka ★ CAFE This stylish cafe serves excellent Lavazza espressos, with ample nonsmoking spaces. It has good cakes, including excellent cheesecake, plus small entrees and salads that make for a perfect light lunch. To find it, walk along the main boulevard, Aleja Najświętszej Maryi Panny, away from the monastery about 450m (1,476 ft.), and then turn left. If this place is filled up, you can grab a quick coffee at the stylish **Red Café** around the corner (Dąbrowskiego 3; ✆ **34/368-08-00**).

Dąbrowskiego 1. ✆ **34/324-30-98.** www.cafeskrzynka.pl. Main courses 15 zł–25 zł. AE, DC, MC, V. Daily 9am–10pm.

Diavolo ☺ ITALIAN/MEXICAN This family-friendly pizzeria is conveniently located near the Jasna Góra monastery. Kids will like the interior, done up as something between an Italian trattoria and a Mexican theme park. A giant cactus is engraved into the ceiling, reflecting the restaurant's dabbling in (only so-so) Mexican food. The pizzas are sized sensibly as S, M, and XL, with the "small" at 24cm (9½ in.) across—big enough to satisfy most appetites. The staff is friendly, and the place doubles as a neighborhood bar in the evenings, making it one of the few places around to have an after-dinner drink.

Wieluńska 17. ✆ **34/361-00-07.** www.restauracjadiavolo.pl. Main courses 15 zł–25 zł. MC, V. Daily noon–11pm.

Obiady Domowe ★ POLISH You'll find decent Polish cooking—including *bigos*, pork cutlets, and pierogi—at reasonable prices at this informal, family-oriented spot on Czestochowa's former market square, the Stary Rynek. The square itself has been undergoing a slow renovation for several years now but is still slightly seedy, and Obiady Domowe is really only an option if you happen to be staying at the Wenecki Hotel (see "Where to Stay," above) or another place nearby.

Stary Rynek 13. ✆ **34/362-01-01.** Main courses 20 zł–30 zł. MC, V. Daily noon–11pm.

Pireus ★ GREEK This upscale Greek restaurant is near the Hotel Sekwana and just down the street from the Jasna Góra monastery. Excellent and authentic Greek dishes—including a delicious lemon chicken soup, Greek salad, and favorites like moussaka—combined with friendly service make this a good stop for lunch or dinner.

Wieluńska 12. ✆ **34/368-06-80.** www.restauracja-pireus.com.pl. Main courses 25 zł–50 zł. AE, DC, MC, V. Daily noon–11pm.

KATOWICE

Upper Silesia's industrial metropolis attracts lots of business travelers but relatively few tourists. The reasons are obvious once you exit the train station or drive into town. It's an undeniably homely city; the historical center was ravaged by insensitive post–World War II planning that left hulking modernist structures standing next to dilapidated historical buildings. You'll look in vain for that touristic mainstay of Polish towns: a handsome square, ringed with shops and cafes. Katowice (pronounced *kaht-oh-veet-seh*) was born in the 19th-century Industrial Age and thrived on mining and heavy industry (which continues to this day).

That doesn't mean, however, it's not interesting in its own way, and the local wags at the offices of *Katowice, In Your Pocket* have even crafted a kind of wacky, anti-tourist image for the city: "If you want pealing cathedral bells and horse-drawn carriages . . . check out Kraków instead. If, however, you want to explore a completely bizarre, unexplored, and some would say unexplainable, corner of Poland, then you've hit the bulls-eye."

Even if you don't choose to come here, there's a good chance you'll pass through anyway. Katowice lies on the main rail line that connects Prague with Kraków, so it sits astride the modern-day Central European equivalent of the Silk Road. It's also on the main A4 superhighway, making it an easy car jog from Kraków or Wrocław. If you've got a couple hours to kill between trains or need to squeeze in an overnight stop, there's enough to see and do to make a stop here worthwhile.

Essentials

GETTING THERE

BY PLANE **Katowice International Airport** (Wolności 90; ✆ **32/392-72-00;** www.katowice-airport.com) is located 35km (22 miles) northeast of Katowice near the village of Pyrzowice. The small airport has two terminals, with most services for incoming visitors, including a small tourist information office, situated in terminal A. You have two options for getting into town. A special airport shuttle bus leaves every hour and costs 20 zł to 25 zł per person each way (buy tickets directly from the driver). The bus drops you at Katowice's train station (some buses include a stop at the Novotel hotel; ask the driver). Catch the bus here for getting to the airport, as well. The second option, a taxi, costs around 120 zł to destinations in the center, but be careful to use only clearly marked taxis.

BY TRAIN Most trains arrive and depart from Katowice's central station **Katowice Dworzec Kolejowy** (Pl. Szewczyka 1; ✆ **32/710-14-00;** www.pkp.pl). The station is conveniently located in the middle of the city, with hotels, restaurants, and sights just a short walk away. Departures to Kraków are frequent, and the journey takes 90 minutes. There are also four trains daily to Oświęcim (Auschwitz). The trip takes about an hour, meaning it's possible to go out and back in a day. The only hitch is that to do this, you'll have to catch the first train out, which leaves at 6:58am. Katowice is also well served by international trains, with regular daily service to Vienna, Prague, Budapest, and Bratislava, among other major cities.

BY BUS Katowice's bus station, **Dworzec Autobusowy Katowice** (Skargi 1; ✆ **32/253-83-14;** www.pkskatowice.internetdsl.pl), isn't much of a station, more of a drop-off and pick-up point. Bus destinations are displayed on the front end of the bus above the driver. In most cases, simply signal the bus to stop and buy the ticket from the driver.

BY CAR Katowice lies at the center of Poland's best superhighway, the A4, connecting Wrocław in the west with Kraków in the southeast. Kraków is about a 1 hour drive, and Wrocław 2 to 3 hours by car.

VISITOR INFORMATION

Despite not drawing many tourists, Katowice does have a useful, centrally located **tourist information office** (Rynek 13; ✆ **32/259-38-08;** www.katowice.eu; Mon–Fri 9am–6pm, Sat 9am–4pm). The office doesn't book rooms, but it's a one-stop source for maps and info about eating, what to see, and what's going on in town.

GETTING AROUND

Katowice is a large city, but just about everything you'll want to see or do is situated in the compact city center. Walking is usually the best option.

ON FOOT Much of the immediate area around the central train station is a pedestrian zone, with lots of shops, bars, and restaurants (including maybe the city's only decent coffee at Costa Coffee; see "Where to Dine," below) situated along Stawowa.

BY TRAM/BUS As you would expect from a Polish city of this size, Katowice has an excellent public transportation system of buses and trams: **Katowice Public Transport Company** (✆ **32/743-84-46;** www.kzkgop.com.pl). Tickets cost 2.40 zł for a standard trip within the center and are available from newsagents.

BY TAXI Taxis are easy to find and relatively cheap. The meter starts at 5 zł and heads north from there. Use only well-known companies. Two reputable firms are **Hallo Taxi** (✆ **32/196-27**) and **Radio Taxi** (✆ **32/191-91**).

Top Attractions

In the past 100 years or so, Katowice—a relatively prosperous industrial city without a very long history—has served as a kind of laboratory for modern architects working in whatever style was in fashion at the time. The city has two undeniable architectural masterpieces, one from the crazy retro-futuristic 1960s and the other from the more staid, functional 1930s. Other modern styles abound: everything from pieces of Art Nouveau to Art Deco, from postwar Socialist–Realist to the sort of kitschy "Communist" style that came to dominate much of Polish design in the 1960s and '70s. Just take a walk and look around.

Spodek ★ This eye-opening concert venue is called the "Flying Saucer"—it really does look like Martians have landed in the middle of Katowice. It's the city's best representative of the "Brussels Expo '58" style of design inspired by 1950s-era science and science fiction that influenced so many architects behind the Iron Curtain at the time. Though the building was designed in the 1950s, delays and safety concerns postponed the opening until 1971. Today, it hosts exhibitions, sporting events, and big-time rock concerts, drawing performers such as Robbie Williams, Pearl Jam, and Sir Elton John, among others.

Al. Korfantego 35. ✆ **32/258-32-61.** www.spodek.com.pl. Open to visitors only during exhibitions & performances.

Cloud Scraper (Drapacz Chmur) This early skyscraper dates from the golden years between world wars I and II, when modern architecture, particularly that unadorned style known as *Bauhaus,* was all the rage. When it was finished in 1934, it was the tallest building in the country, measuring 60m (197 ft.) in height. Now, it's often overlooked but a must for fans of functionalist architecture.

Żwirki i Wigury 15. Not open to the public.

Katowice Historical Museum (Muzeum Historii Katowic) ★ A much-better-than-average museum dedicated to Katowice's tumultuous history, first under Prussian rule, then Polish, then German, then under Soviet domination—when Katowice for a time was called "Stalinogrod" (Stalin's city)—and today. Unfortunately, most of the commentary is in Polish only, but the exhibits are straightforward enough to make the point.

Szafranka 9. ✆ **32/256-18-10.** www.mhk.katowice.pl. 6 zł adults. Tues–Thurs 10am–3pm; Fri 10am–5:30pm; Sat & Sun 11am–2pm.

Where to Stay

Katowice attracts an abundance of business travelers; hence, prices tend to be higher than the facilities might otherwise warrant, and getting a room is much harder on a weekday than a weekend. On the flip side, however, hotels almost always discount heavily on weekends. The Katowice (see below) is a Communist-era mega hotel, but because of its size, you can almost always count on getting a room.

VERY EXPENSIVE

Monopol ★★★ It's hard to imagine a more appealing urban hotel than this luxury property in the center of Katowice, and if you've got the money to spend, it's certainly worth booking an overnight stay to break up the train journey between Kraków and Prague. The Likus Group, which owns the Monopol in Wrocław and the Grand in Łódź among other five-star properties, has spared no expense here, including the sleek 1920s-style lobby, the atrium restaurant, a lush fitness and wellness center, and the elegant rooms with hardwood floors and marble baths (that you may find yourself photographing for the folks back home). The location is superb, within easy walking distance of the train station and the center of town. The Italian restaurant under the atrium is one of the city's best restaurants.

Dworcowa 5. ✆ **32/782-82-82.** Fax 32/782-82-83. www.hotel.com.pl/monopol. 114 units. 600 zł double. AE, DC, MC, V. Parking (paid). **Amenities:** Restaurant; concierge; exercise room; room service; sauna. *In room:* A/C, TV, hair dryer, Internet (free), minibar.

EXPENSIVE

Angelo ★★ This upscale business hotel opened in 2010 and may represent the city's best value for quality lodging. The rooms are on the smallish side but are decorated with high-quality, colorful furnishings and have high-thread-count cottons, LCD TVs, and lots of extras. The multilingual staff is polite and helpful, and while the hotel is aimed at the corporate segment, prices drop to around 250 zł per double on weekends, meaning you don't need an expense account to stay here. There's a small fitness room and plenty of parking. The location is a bit outside the center but an easy 10 minutes on foot to anything you're likely to want to see.

Sokolska 24. ✆ **32/783-81-00.** Fax 32/783-81-03. www.vi-hotels.com. 203 units. Weekdays 340 zł double; weekends 250 zł double. AE, DC, MC, V. Parking (paid). **Amenities:** Restaurant; concierge; exercise room; room service; sauna. *In room:* A/C, TV, hair dryer, Internet (free), minibar.

Novotel ★ Novotel hotels are known for good quality yet unexciting lodging, and Katowice's local representative is no exception. On the plus side, the rooms are well laid out, clean, and comfortable, and the reception staff speaks English and will go out of their way to help. There's a small pool and fitness center, and the lobby restaurant is very good. The negatives include expensive on-site parking at 65 zł (though you can park more cheaply in the Etap lot next door) and a remote location that puts it a good 15 minutes walk to the center.

Al. Rozdzienskiego 16. ✆ **32/200-44-44.** Fax 32/200-44-11. www.novotel.com. 300 units. 280 zł double. AE, DC, MC, V. Parking 65 zł. **Amenities:** Restaurant; exercise room; pool; room service; sauna. *In room:* A/C, TV, hair dryer, Internet (free), minibar.

MODERATE

Hotel Katowice An abomination of a hotel in almost every respect. Its 1970s Communist-era panel construction features threadbare floors and paper-thin walls. It's the kind of place where the chambermaids are banging—not knocking—at the door at 7am to clean the rooms. Still, in overpriced Katowice, it's a decent value for the money, and the central location is excellent. The large size means it's rarely full to capacity, even on weekdays, when getting a room elsewhere is tough. There's Internet access in the lobby.

Al. Korfantego 9. ✆ **32/258-82-81.** Fax 32/259-75-26. www.hotel-katowice.com.pl. 230 units. 270 zł double; rates discounted on weekends. AE, DC, MC, V. Parking (paid). **Amenities:** Restaurant; limited room service. *In room:* TV, hair dryer, Internet (free), minibar.

INEXPENSIVE

Etap ★ Etap hotels can be a life-saver. The budget arm of the same chain that runs Novotel invariably offers clean rooms at prices you could scarcely get in a private home. Yes, the rooms are tiny and amenities are few, but if you don't plan on spending much time in the room, what does it matter? For breakfast, there's a bare-bones paid buffet (30 zl) of coffee, cereal, and yogurt.

Al. Rozdzienskiego 18. ✆ **32/350-50-40.** Fax 32/255-55-01. www.accorhotels.com. 124 units. 140 zł double. AE, DC, MC, V. Parking (paid). *In room:* A/C, TV, Internet (free).

Where to Dine

Costa Coffee ★★ CAFE Keep this modern cafe chain in mind if you have to change trains in Katowice and have a couple hours to kill: It's just a short walk out of the train station for some excellent coffee, as well as good pre-made sandwiches and sweets like muffins and brownies (much better than the food you will find in the train station itself). There's also free Wi-Fi on the premises. It's an oasis in a city where "coffee" still usually means the instant variety.

Stawowa 8. ✆ **32/444-72-48.** www.costacoffee.pl. Coffee drinks & small sandwiches 7 zł–15 zł. AE, DC, M, V. Daily 9am–10pm.

Fantasmagoria ★★★ POLISH/INTERNATIONAL Easily the best restaurant in Katowice and possibly all of this part of Poland. The excellent and inventive home-style cooking takes inspiration from regional classics such as a delicious Ukrainian-style borsch and adds in a selection of grilled meats, including pork loin and lamb, that would feel more at home somewhere in the Middle East. The mixed beef and lamb kebabs, served with fresh-baked bread and baked potato, is a must-try. The restaurant is worth a trip out of your way.

Gliwicka 51. ✆ **32/253-00-59.** Main courses 20 zł–45 zł. AE, DC, M, V. Daily 1–11pm.

After Dark

As the leading city in Upper Silesia, Katowice has an active cultural life, with excellent classical concerts and a good experimental scene. The center of the action is the **Katowice Cultural Center** (pl. Sejmu Śląskiego 2; ✆ **32/251-79-25;** www.ck.art.pl). For popular music and visiting rock stars, don't forget the **Spodek** (see "Top Attractions," above). The tourist information office can let you know if anyone big is visiting while you are there. For opera, the **Silesian Opera (Opera Śląska)** in the nearby city of Bytom is one of the most celebrated houses in the country (Moniuszki 21/23, Bytom; ✆ **32/281-34-31;** www.opera-slaska.pl).

CAFES, PUBS & CLUBS

Not surprisingly, given the number of students here, there are tons of places to drink in Katowice. **Archibar** (Dyrekcyjna 9; ✆ **32/206-83-50;** www.archibar.pl) is an arty pub popular with the intellectual set. **2B3** (pl. Sejmu Śląskiego 2, enter from Henryka Sienkiewicza; ✆ **32/785-78-77;** www.2b3.com.pl) is exactly the opposite: a cheesy dance club that's popular with all ages, from 20s to 40s, with regular DJs and occasional live music acts.

CIESZYN

The southern border town of Cieszyn (pronounced *cheh-sheen*) is one of Silesia's oldest settlements. According to legend, it was founded in 810 by three brothers—Bolko, Leszko, and Cieszko—to celebrate their reunion. More likely, the city dates from around 1200, first emerging as a defense post along the traditional border between the Polish and Bohemian kingdoms, and then later developing into a trading center. Cieszyn served as the capital of the independent Duchy of Cieszyn from the end of the 13th century to the middle of the 17th century, before falling under the domination of the Habsburg Empire. Today, it's interesting for two reasons. One is that it's a nicely preserved medieval market town, with the original street plan intact, a handsome square, and—naturally—an impressive castle. The second is more geopolitical. In more modern times, Cieszyn proved to be a thorn in the side of Polish-Czechoslovak—later, Czech—relations. The town's roots are Polish, but the competing dynastic claims through the ages muddied the waters. At the end of World War I, Cieszyn was split down the middle along the Olza River, with one side going to newly independent Poland and the other side, known as Český Těšín, to the newly founded Czechoslovak state. The darkest moment arguably came ahead of World War II, in 1939. Just as Hitler was grabbing Czechoslovakia's German-speaking border regions, Poland forcibly annexed the Czech side of Cieszyn. At the end of the war, the original borders were restored, but the memory soured bilateral relations for decades. Now, with both countries in the European Union, all seems forgiven, and Cieszyn/Český Těšín has been officially declared an EU "Euroregion." Indeed, you're free to walk at will from one bank of the Olza to the other, enjoying the oddity of a town that is literally half-Polish and half-Czech.

Essentials

GETTING THERE

BY TRAIN Cieszyn has two train stations, but only the one on the Czech side of town, in Český Těšín, is of any practical use. Here, you'll find several decent trains to Prague (around 5 hr.), as well as trains to Slovakia and points east. The Cieszyn station on the Polish side has all but closed down, with most connections to Katowice and Kraków departing from Wisła, about 15km (9¼ miles) away. On the Czech side, the **station** is located in the center of town, across from the Piast Hotel, at Nádražní 1133 (✆ **420/840-112-113**). On the Polish side, Cieszyn's **train station PKP** is at Hajduka 10 (✆ **33/852-01-08**), about a 10-minute walk from the center.

BY BUS Cieszyn has excellent bus and minibus connections to Katowice and Kraków, with several departures daily to both cities. Expect to pay around 10 zł to Katowice and around 20 zł to Kraków. The bus station is just across the street from the train station at Korfantego 23 (✆ **33/852-02-79;** www.pkscieszyn.pl). Minibuses to Katowice and Kraków depart from a parking lot adjacent to Cieszyn's derelict train station.

BY CAR Cieszyn is located on the main north–south E75 highway and is well-signposted for miles around. It's a major road border crossing between Poland and the Czech Republic.

VISITOR INFORMATION

Cieszyn has two main tourist information centers, one on each side of the border. Both are useful for hotel and restaurant recommendations, planning outings, and figuring out transportation options, but each is much stronger on its respective part of town. Don't expect the Poles to have much info on the Czech side or vice-versa (in spite of the towns' shared EU "Euroregion" designation). On the Polish side, visit the **Cieszyn Information Center** (Rynek 1; ✆ **33/479-42-49;** www.cieszyn.pl). On the Czech side, try the **Český Těšín Regional Information Center** (Hlavní Třída 15; ✆ **420-558-711-866;** www.info.tesin.cz). There's also a tiny information center inside the castle complex on the Polish side (Zamkowa 3; ✆ **33/851-08-21;** www.cieszyn.pl). On our visit, the woman behind the desk could not speak English but had a few maps and brochures on the castle that she was happy to hand out.

GETTING AROUND

Cieszyn is a small city, and walking is the best way to get around. The center of the Polish side is the charming main square, the Rynek. From there, it's a short walk to the castle and then across the river to the Czech side. There is a modest city bus system, but you're not likely to use it. Taxis are around, but it's best to ask your hotel or restaurant to call one for you. **Halo Taxi** (✆ **33/852-19-19**) is a reliable company.

Top Attractions

Begin your exploration on the Polish side at the main square, the Rynek, the center of town life since the 14th century and where you'll find the tourist information office. Most of the buildings on the square date from the 19th century; several fires through the ages, including a devastating inferno in 1789, destroyed the original Gothic and Renaissance houses. From here, walk down the town's main drag, Głębocka, that leads past the town hall and the old market, the Stary Targ, to the castle and eventually to the **Most Przyjaźni/Most Družby (Friendship Bridge)** that connects the town's Polish and Czech sides. Once on the Czech side, you can meander along the Olza River or walk down Hlavní Třída to the second tourist information office. From Hlavní, make a left down Pražská to find the Nám. ČSA (ČSA Square) at the center of the Czech side and home to its own town hall.

Castle Hill (Góra Zamkowa) ★ The seat of power during the time of Duchy of Cieszyn and a site of human habitation since something like the 5th century A.D. In the 14th century, at the start of the duchy, a Gothic castle was built here. It was made over time and again through the ages as architectural fashions changed. The current appearance is neoclassical from the 19th century. Though the interior of the castle is not normally open to the public, there's a lovely garden here with a beautifully preserved Romanesque rotunda from the 11th century—one of Poland's earliest Christian churches (and duly recognized on the 20 zł bank note)—and a 14th-century Gothic tower that you can scramble up for views over the surrounding countryside.

Zamkowa 3. ✆ **33/851-08-21.** www.zamekcieszyn.pl. Tower 7 zł adults. Summer Tues–Sun 9am–5pm; winter Tues–Sun 10am–4pm.

The Museum of Cieszyn Silesia (Muzeum Śląska Cieszyńskiego) ★ This regional museum is loaded with historical curiosities from the period when Cieszyn was an independent duchy with its own coins and coats of arms, as well as household artifacts, old photos, and preserved interior pieces from the castle and the rotunda.

T. Regera 6. ✆ **33/851-29-33.** www.muzeumcieszyn.pl. 10 zł adults. Tues–Sun 10am–4pm.

Where to Stay & Dine

Since passport formalities no longer exist on the border, it doesn't matter which side of town you stay on. Most of the main tourist sights are on the Polish side, but the most useful railway station is on the Czech side. The pickings are slim when it comes to eating, but the hotel Liburnia (see below) has an excellent, informal pizza restaurant, and there are several cafes and small restaurants along the Rynek on the Polish side where you can grab a quick bite or drink.

Hotel Central ★ This is the nicer of the two main hotels in Český Těšín, on the Czech side of the border. This early-20th-century property has been renovated in a non-descript 1970s style but is nevertheless an excellent value and convenient to the train station (on the Czech side), if that's where you're arriving or departing. The Polish side is 10 minutes by foot across the bridge. Free parking and free in-room Wi-Fi help to make it a good budget pick. Note that you'll have to pay in Czech crowns.

Nádražní 10/16, Český Těšín. ✆ **420/558-713-113.** www.hotel-central.cz. 28 units. 990 Kč (about 160 zł) double. AE, DC, MC, V. Free parking. **Amenities:** Restaurant. *In room:* TV, Wi-Fi (free).

Hotel Piast This hotel is also on the Czech side, though not quite as pleasant as the nearby Hotel Central (see above). Judging from the handsome 1920s building, this must have been a great hotel in its day. Now, it's badly faded, with a sterile 1980s makeover, but still clean and with all the basic amenities you'd need for an overnight stay. The main dining room on the ground floor is an absolute photo-worthy time capsule of life in 1960s Czechoslovakia, with its worn carpets and long, heavy curtains, and yet buzzing with city life. Note that you'll have to pay in Czech crowns.

Nádražní 18, Český Těšín. ✆ **420/558-711-560.** www.hotelpiast.cz. 29 units. 850 Kč (about 140 zł) double. AE, DC, MC, V. **Amenities:** Restaurant. *In room:* TV, Internet (free).

Liburnia ★★ This modern hotel on the Polish side occupies a strange location behind a shopping plaza, but is just 5 minutes on foot from Cieszyn's bus station (look for the Kaufland Plaza). It's a cross between a business hotel and a boutique at prices you'd expect to pay at a pension. The stylish contemporary rooms come with card keys and individual climate-control settings. The mattresses are thick and comfortable; the cotton thread count in the sheets is well above the average at this price point. If you're driving, there's plenty of free parking out front. The in-house restaurant features Italian cooking, with a wood-fired pizza oven, and is one of the best places in town to eat.

Liburnia 10, Cieszyn. ✆ **33/852-05-31.** www.liburniahotel.pl. 30 units. 180 zł double. AE, DC, MC, V. Free parking. **Amenities:** Restaurant; limited room service. *In room:* A/C, TV, hair dryer, Internet (free), minibar.

Pod Merkurym ★★ POLISH You'll find excellent Polish food right on the Rynek on the Polish side of Cieszyn. The house specialty is pierogies, but here, they are served a little more imaginatively in a dressing of red pepper, sprouts, and corn (a nice change of pace). The setting is really cozy: an old-style cafe with dark-red walls and dark, wooden booths. There's good Czech Pilsener-Urquell beer on tap.

Rynek 9, Cieszyn. ✆ **33/857-74-07.** Main courses 15 zł–30 zł. No credit cards. Daily 10am–11pm.

7

KRAKÓW, ZAKOPANE & THE TATRA MOUNTAINS

by Mark Baker

Kraków, the capital of the Polish region of Małopolska, is one of the most beautiful cities in central Europe and a highlight of any visit to Poland. The city escaped significant damage during World War II, and its only serious regional rival for pure drop-dead beauty is the Czech capital, Prague. The size and formal perfection of its enormous central square, the Rynek Główny, is breathtaking, and the little lanes that fan off it in all directions ooze with charm. Kraków is one of those places you start plotting to move to nearly the moment you arrive. In addition to the Old Town, there's ancient Wawel Castle, home to Poland's earliest royal rulers and the country's capital until the end of the 16th century. The former Jewish ghetto of Kazimierz is also coming into its own, not just as a fascinating step back into the city's estimable Jewish past, but also as the emerging center of Kraków's booming nightlife.

Kraków's charms have always been known to Poles (and Kraków remains far and away the number-one domestic tourist destination), but now the word is spreading far and wide. The city is firmly, and justifiably, established on the main central European tourism axis that includes Vienna, Budapest, and Prague. All of this is good news for visitors. It means decent plane, rail, and bus connections from any point north, south, or west of the city. It also means that Kraków has some of the best restaurants and hotels in Poland and is fully accustomed to catering to the needs of visitors.

Outside of Kraków, several excursions merit a few hours or a full day of sightseeing. The most important of these is the former Nazi extermination camp at **Auschwitz-Birkenau** (in the town of Oświęcim, about 80km/50 miles west of the city). Also recommended is a trip to the unusual and unforgettable **Wieliczka Salt Mines.** If you've got the time and a penchant for modern architecture, check out the **Nowa Huta Steelworks** and the amazing post–World War II Socialist-Realist housing projects built around the mills.

To the south of Kraków, the High Tatra Mountains begin their rise toward the border with Slovakia. This is prime hiking and skiing country, centered on the main mountain resort of Zakopane. Dozens of hiking trails cover the hills south of town, with some of the most adventurous walks crossing the peaks and ending up in Slovakia. But Zakopane is more than just a hiking and ski resort. A hundred years ago, Poland's best young painters, poets, and architects decamped here in a bid to reinvent Polish culture. To this day, Zakopane retains a whiff of arty exclusivity.

The highlands around Zakopane and to the east of Kraków are less breathtaking but lovely in their own right. If you have extra time, check out the budding tourist town of **Tarnów**—"Little Kraków"—with its nicely preserved Renaissance town square and its own moving history of Polish and Jewish cultures living side by side for centuries, only to be destroyed by Nazi barbarism.

KRAKÓW

Kraków's precise origins are unclear, but the city first rose to prominence at the turn of the first millennium as a thriving market town. The enormous size of the Rynek attests to Kraków's early importance, even if the city's early history is more than a little bit cloudy.

As befitting any medieval metropolis, Kraków suffered the usual ups and downs related to religious strife, wars, natural disasters, plagues, and the occasional raid from Mongol hordes coming from the East. In the 13th century, the city was razed to the ground by Tatars sweeping in from Central Asia, but it was quickly rebuilt (and parts remain remarkably unchanged to this day). Kraków's heyday came arguably in the mid-14th century, when King Kazimierz the Great commissioned many of the city's finest buildings and established Jagiellonian University, the second university to be founded in central Europe after Prague's Charles University. For more than 5 centuries, Kraków served as the seat of the Polish kingdom (it only lost out to the usurper Warsaw in 1596 after a political union with Lithuania made the new Polish-Lithuanian kingdom so large that it became difficult for noblemen from the north to travel here).

Kraków began a long, slow decline around this time. Following the Polish partitions at the end of the 18th century, Kraków eventually fell under the domination of Austria-Hungary and was ruled from Vienna. It became the main city in the new Austrian province of Galicia, but had to share some of the administrative duties with the eastern city of Lwów (which must have been quite a climb-down for a former Polish capital!).

Viennese rule proved to be a boon in its own right. The Habsburgs were far more liberal in their views than either the Prussians or tsarist Russia (which ruled over the other parts of Poland), and the relative tolerance here fostered a Polish cultural renaissance that lasted well into the 20th century. Kraków was the base of the late-19th- and early-20th-century Młoda Polska (Young Poland) movement encompassing a revival of literature, art, and architecture (often likened to "Art Nouveau") that is fondly remembered to this day.

Kraków had traditionally been viewed as a haven for Jews ever since the 14th century, when King Kazimierz first opened Poland to Jewish settlement. The Kraków district named for the king, Kazimierz, began life as a separate Polish town but, through the centuries, slowly acquired the characteristics of a traditional Jewish quarter. By the 19th and early 20th centuries, Kazimierz was one of the leading

Jewish settlements in central Europe, lending Kraków a unique dimension as a center of both Catholic and Jewish scholarship.

World War II drastically altered the religious composition of the city and, for all intents and purposes, ended this Jewish cultural legacy. The Nazis made Kraków the nominal capital of their rump Polish state: the "General Gouvernement." The Nazi governor, and war criminal, Hans Frank, ruled brutally from atop Wawel Castle. One of the first Nazi atrocities was to arrest and eventually execute the Polish faculty of Jagiellonian University. Not long after the start of the war the Nazis expelled the Jews from Kazimierz, first forcing them into a confined ghetto space at Podgórze, about a half-mile south of Kazimierz across the river, and later deporting nearly all of them to death camps. (As an historical aside: Frank was prosecuted at the Nuremburg trials and executed in 1946.)

Kraków's architecture luckily escaped major destruction at the end of the war but fared poorly in the postwar decades under Poland's Communist leadership. The Communists never liked the city, probably because of its royal roots, and intellectual and Catholic pretensions. For whatever reason, they decided to place their biggest postwar industrial project, the enormous Nowa Huta Steelworks, just a couple of miles upwind from the Old Town. Many argue the intention was to win over the skeptical Kraków intellectuals to the Communist side, but the noise, dirt, and smoke from the mills, not surprisingly, had the opposite effect. The new workers were slow to embrace Communism, and during those wretched days of the 1970s, when a series of food price hikes galvanized workers around the country, the city was transformed into a hotbed of anti-Communist activism.

Kraków will be forever linked with its most famous favorite son, Pope John Paul II. The pope, Karol Woytyła, was born not far from Kraków, in the town of Wadowice, and rose up through the church hierarchy here, serving for many years as the archbishop of the Kraków diocese before being elevated to pope in 1978. If Gdańsk and the Solidarity trade union provided the industrial might of the anti-Communist movement, then Kraków and Pope John Paul II were the movement's spiritual heart. The pope's landmark trip to Poland in 1979, shortly after he was elected pontiff, ignited a long-dormant Polish spirit and united the country in opposition to the Soviet-imposed government.

Kraków's charms are multidimensional. In addition to the beautifully restored Old Town, complete with its fairytale castle, there's the former Jewish quarter of Kazimierz. If you've seen Steven Spielberg's Oscar-winning movie *Schindler's List,* you'll recognize some of the film locations as you walk around Kazimierz. For anyone unfamiliar with the film (or the book on which it was based, Thomas Keneally's *Schindler's List* [Simon & Schuster]), Oskar Schindler was a German industrialist who operated an enamel factory across the river from Kazimierz during World War II. By employing Jews from the nearby ghetto, he managed to spare the lives of around 1,100 people who otherwise would have gone to the death camps at Auschwitz. After years of neglect, Schindler's factory reopened in 2010, though this time around, as a museum of the city's history during the Second World War.

Essentials

GETTING THERE

BY PLANE **John Paul II International Airport** (✆ **12/295-58-00;** www.krakowairport.pl) is located in the suburb of Balice, about 16km (10 miles) west of the city center. The airport has two terminals, a larger international terminal and a

smaller domestic terminal at the back to handle flights within Poland. Most of the services, including rental-car outlets, ATMs, restaurants, and a branch of the city's tourist information office, are located at the international terminal. The best way to get into town from the airport is to take Polish Railways' **"Balice Express,"** regular train service to and from Kraków's main train station with regular departures on the half-hour. (The "express" part of the name must be some sort of inside joke at Polish Rail, since the train seems to chug along at about 32kmph/20 mph; still, it manages to make the journey in about 20 minutes.) The price is 8 zł each way (7 zł if purchased at a ticket machine). To reach the small station from where the express train departs, you need to take a blue shuttle bus that leaves from outside both terminals. **Kraków Shuttle** (**© 12/633-01-25;** www.krakowshuttle.com) offers reasonably priced door-to-door shuttle service from both Kraków and Katowice airports. The price from Kraków to in-town destinations is 70 zł total for up to four passengers. You can also take a taxi into town, but be sure to use only clearly marked cabs and refuse any offers of a ride you might get from individuals inside the terminal or just outside the door: These are likely to be scams. Expect to pay about 70 zł to 80 zł to destinations in the center.

BY TRAIN Kraków's main train station, the **Dwoczec Główny** (pl. Kolejowy 1; ✆ **12/393-15-80;** http://rozklad-pkp.pl) is a pleasant 15-minute walk from the center of the city. Kraków is well served by rail, and departures for Warsaw and other major cities are frequent. The rail distance from Warsaw is about 3 hours. Note that travel to popular international destinations like Prague sometimes requires a change of trains in Katowice.

BY BUS Kraków's **Central Bus Station** (Bosacka 18; ✆ **12/393-52-55;** www.rda.krakow.pl) is located just behind the main train station and is an easy walk or relatively cheap taxi ride to the center of town. Nearly all buses—international and domestic—use this station. This is also where buses to Zakopane and Oświęcim (Auschwitz) depart. The station has two levels, so make sure you know which level your bus is using. There's a bank of ticket windows, but often times, you'll simply buy your ticket from the bus driver.

BY CAR Kraków lies on the main east–west highway, the A4, running through southern Poland. It's nearly a straight 3- to 4-hour shot on mostly four-lane highway from the German border, through the cities of Wrocław and Katowice. You'll have to pay a toll (8 zł) covering the distance to and from Katowice, but for the speed and convenience (compared to other roads in Poland), it's a bargain. From other directions, including coming in from Warsaw to the north, you'll have to contend with much smaller roads and longer drive times. Once in Kraków, find a place to park the car (there's metered street parking) and leave it. The city's busy, tram-clogged streets are no fun to drive on.

VISITOR INFORMATION

The city of Kraków (www.krakow.pl) maintains a helpful network of tourist information offices around town conveniently located at main tourist junctures (look for "Info Kraków"). Here, you'll find rows of helpful flyers and brochures, including a very good one called *Three Days in Kraków.* They also dole out free maps and a wealth of suggestions, and can help find and book hotel rooms and excursions.

The main offices include the following. (***Note:*** Some offices have earlier closing hours from Oct–Apr.) At press time, an additional office was being planned near the river on Podzamcze below Wawel Castle, but was not yet open:

- **Town Hall Tower:** Main square; ✆ **12/433-73-10;** daily 9am–7pm
- **Św. Jana 2:** Old Town; ✆ **12/421-77-87;** daily 10am–6pm
- **John Paul II International Airport/Balice:** ✆ **12/285-53-41;** daily 9am–7pm
- **Szpitalna 25:** Old Town; ✆ **12/432-01-10;** daily 9am–7pm
- **Józefa 7:** Kazimierz; ✆ **12/422-04-71;** daily 9am–5pm

Confusingly, several private companies also maintain info booths around town that are designed to look like official information offices, complete with the "*i*" out front (the international tourist information symbol). While these offices usually also hand out free maps and can be helpful in a pinch, be forewarned that they're in fact private companies selling a range of tours and services.

CITY LAYOUT

Kraków's Old Town is relatively compact and comprised of the main square (Rynek Główny) and the streets that radiate from it in all directions (bordered by what remains of the medieval town walls and the circular park, the Planty). Most of the main tourist sites are situated within a 10- or 15-minute walk from the square.

The Wawel Castle district comprises a second major tourist destination and is a 15-minute walk south of the main square, following Grodzka Street.

The former Jewish ghetto of Kazimierz lies about a 25-minute walk south of the main square beyond the castle. To save time, it's possible to take a taxi from the Old Town to Kazimierz. Expect to pay about 15 zł. A number of trams also make the run between the two.

GETTING AROUND

ON FOOT Much of Kraków's Old Town is off-limits to private cars, so walking is often the only option. Distances are manageable.

BY TRAM Kraków is well served by a comprehensive tram network, and this is a quick and easy way to reach more far-flung destinations (such as Nowa Huta). Try to avoid tram travel at rush hour unless you enjoy getting pressed up against the doors like you're in the Tokyo subway. A standard ticket costs 2.50 zł (not valid for transfers) and can be bought at newspaper kiosks and ticketing machines located near tram stops. If you have to change trams or go from tram to bus, buy a 1-hour ticket for 3.10 zł. Validate your ticket on entering the tram and hold on to it until the end of the ride.

BY BUS Like trams, buses ply Kraków's streets from early morning until after 11pm or so, and are a vital part of the city's transit network. You probably won't need to use the buses unless your hotel is well outside the city center. A standard ticket (not valid for transfers) costs 2.50 zł and can be bought at newspaper kiosks around town. Validate your ticket on entering the bus and hold on to it until the end of the ride.

BY TAXI Taxis are a relatively cheap and dependable way of getting around. You can hail taxis directly on the street or at taxi stands around town. Dishonest drivers are rare but do crop up from time to time; to guarantee an honest driver, order a cab by telephone. Reliable firms include **Radio Taxi** (✆ **12/191-91**) and **Euro Taxi** (✆ **12/196-64**). The fare for a typical hop, such as from the Old Town to Kazimierz, will average about 15 zł. Fares rise by 50% at night.

BY BIKE Biking is popular, and there are now bike lanes scattered around town, including a nice run along the Vistula river to the village of Tyniec (14km/8¾ miles) and through the park, the Planty, that rings the main square. That said, unless you're an experienced cyclist, biking is a better bet for an hour or two of sightseeing, rather than as a practical means for getting around (cycling along the busy, tram-clogged roads is simply too dangerous). **Cruising Kraków** (Basztowa 17; ✆ **12/398-70-57** or 514/556-017; www.cruisingkrakow.com) offers fun and instructional 2-hour bike tours in season (May through September) in the afternoon and evening. They also rent bikes (starting at 30 zł a day) and conduct longer trips in summer.

BY GOLF CART Seeing the city via guided golf cart has become incredibly popular in recent years, and on some summer days, it seems there's an endless stream of carts parading around town. Golf-cart rides are undeniably cheesy but can be a lifesaver on hot days or if time is an issue. You'll find cart stands at popular tourist spots around town, including the main square, below Wawel Castle on Kanonicza, and on Szeroka in Kazimierz. Prices start around 80 zł per person for relatively short circuits around either the Old Town or Kazimierz. Longer tours, combining both areas, are more expensive. Audio headphones provide guided commentary in several languages.

The Bugler's Call

The most popular tourist attraction in Kraków isn't a church, building, or even a museum. It's actually a real-live bugler, who blows his bugle every day, every hour on the hour, from high atop St. Mary's Basilica (Kościół Mariacki; see below), just off the main square, the Rynek Główny. It's a strange sight and even a more surreal sound to hear the plaintive wail of the bugle call drift down into the modern square, which is usually filled with its own cacophony, from the clip-clop of horses' hooves to the murmur of the thousands strolling below or taking a drink at a square-side cafe. The tradition of the bugle call, or *hejnał* as it's known in Polish, goes back hundreds of years—to the 13th and 14th centuries—when Central European cities such as Kraków faced the ever-present threat of invasion by Tatar barbarians from the East. The buglers, the town's watchmen, would stand guard and alert the citizens of any threat of invasion. If you listen closely as Kraków's bugler plays, you'll hear him cut short his final note. Legend has it that in 1240, the sentry in the watchtower saw a band of Tatars approaching and began sounding the alarm. One of the invaders let fly an arrow that sliced the bugler in the throat midnote, and ever since, buglers have continued to make an abrupt ending in his memory. (Judging from the height and size of the window, that Tatar must have been an excellent shot!) To hear the bugler today, find an unobstructed view to St. Mary's close to the top of the hour. The bugler begins just after the clock chimes the hour. You'll see him lift his window, and if it's a sunny day, you'll probably catch a glint of sunshine off the bugle. When he's done, it's customary for you to wave—a gesture of thanks for keeping Kraków safe from the barbarians. If you'd like to see the bugler up close, in summer, it's possible to climb the 239 steps to the top of the tower. If you time your climb right, you might even get to see the bugler in action.

BY HORSE-DRAWN CARRIAGE Far more romantic than the tram and classier than a golf cart are the beautiful carriages that line up along the main square in Kraków's Old Town. Negotiate prices and routes individually with the driver, but expect to pay around 100 zł for 30 minutes (not including tip). Most drivers can manage some English.

Top Attractions

A sensible plan for sightseeing in Kraków is to divide the city into three basic areas: the Old Town, including the Rynek Główny; the Wawel Castle compound (with its many rooms and museums); and Jewish Kraków, including the former Jewish quarter of Kazimierz and the wartime Jewish ghetto of Podgórze farther south. Ideally, leave a day devoted to each. If you're pressed for time, you could conceivably link the Old Town and Wawel in one day, while leaving Kazimierz and a possible day trip to the Wieliczka Salt Mine for the next.

THE OLD TOWN & THE RYNEK GŁÓWNY

Kraków's Old Town is a pedestrian's paradise, and you could (and should) spend hours wandering the back alleys, arcades, and cellars, jammed with every manner of pub, club, cafe, and restaurant. It's hard to imagine a more attractive town core. It's a powerful argument for historical preservation and the value of vital urban centers.

Top Attractions

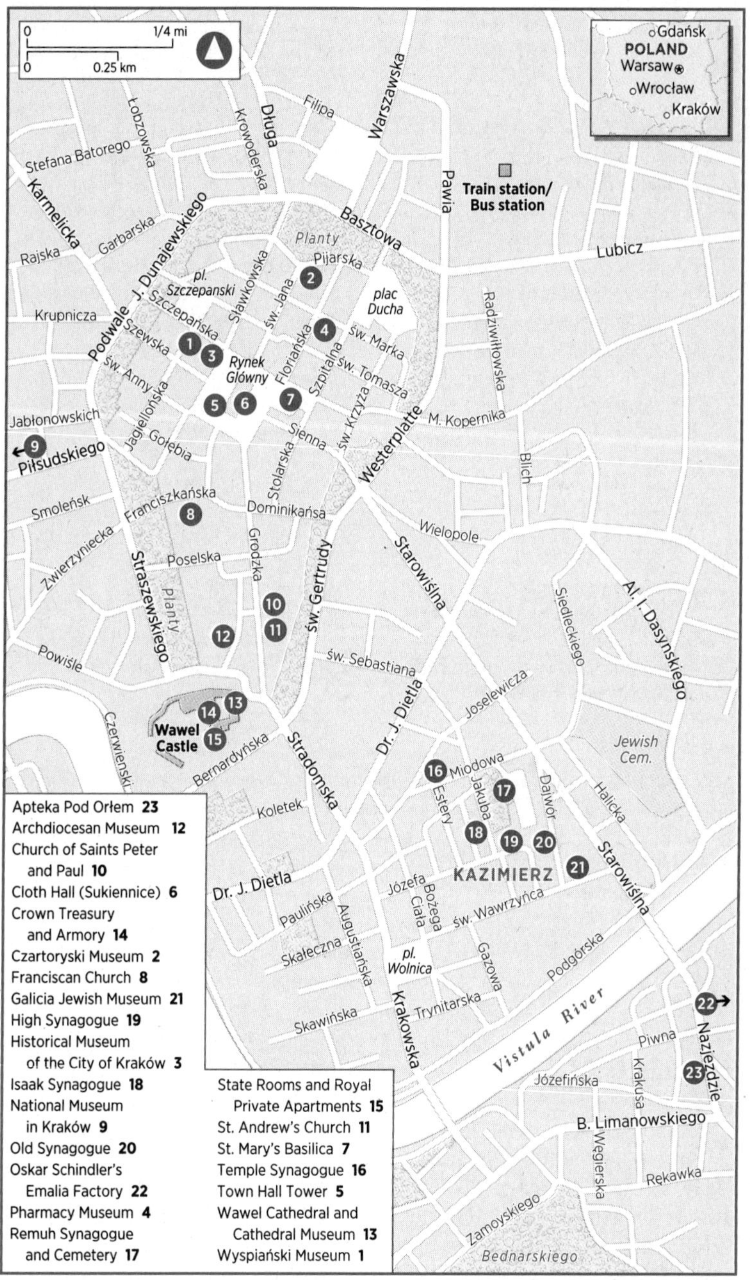

The **Rynek Główny,** by all accounts, is a remarkable public space. Measuring some 200m (656 ft.) square and ringed by stately buildings, it creates a natural arena for public performances of all stripes. The square is bordered on all sides by wonderfully restored noblemen's houses, many of which go back nearly 800 years, though they've been remodeled and refurbished throughout the centuries, depending on the style of the day.

The most striking building on the square is the beautiful Gothic cathedral of **St. Mary's**—its uneven towers evoking for Poles the very essence of the city. You can go inside to see an intricately carved wooden altar from the 15th century. Be sure to stop here at some point precisely on the hour to hear a lone bugler play from the open window of the highest tower (see "The Bugler's Call," above).

At the center of the square is the **Cloth Hall** (Sukiennice), which dates from the 14th century and served as the stalls of the town's original merchants. The original Cloth Hall burned down in the 16th century, and what you see today is a mostly Renaissance building, with neo-Gothic flourishes added in the 19th century (the exterior was being spruced-up and a given a fresh coat of paint at press time). Today, it's still filled with marketers, hawking good-value Polish souvenirs to throngs of visitors.

Just near the Cloth Hall stands the enormous **Town Hall Tower.** It's the last surviving piece of Kraków's original town hall, which was demolished in the early 19th century in an apparent bid to clean up the square. Today, the tower houses a branch of the tourist information office, and you can climb to the top for a view over the Old Town.

Streets and alleys lead off the square in all directions. Of these the most important are **Floriańska** and **Grodzka,** both part of the famed Royal Route of Polish kings. Floriańska leads to the Floriańska Gate, dating back to the start of the 14th century. The gate was once the main entryway to the Old Town and part of the original medieval fortification system. Grodzka flows out of the square at the square's southern end and leads to ancient Wawel Castle.

Archdiocesan Museum ★ This is essential viewing for fans of the late Pope John Paul II. John Paul lived here as the archbishop of the Kraków diocese until his elevation to pope in 1978. Today, the museum has largely been given over to his legacy, with a fine collection of gifts presented to the pope by heads of state from around the world. There's also a nice collection of sacral paintings and sculpture dating from the 13th century.

Kanonicza 19/21. ✆ **12/421-89-63.** 5 zł adults; guided tours 60 zł. Tues–Fri 10am–4pm; Sat & Sun 10am–3pm.

Church of Saints Peter and Paul (Kościół Św. Piotra i Pawla) ★★ One of the most evocative of Kraków's many churches, chiefly because of the statues of the 12 disciples lining the front entrance. It's said that the Jesuits spent so much money building the front and the facade that they ran out of money to finish the rest of the building (which, if you look behind the facade, you'll see is constructed from ordinary brick). The interior is less impressive, though still worth a peek in. One of the highlights is a model of Foucault's Pendulum, which demonstrates the rotation of the Earth. It's also a great spot for church concerts.

Grodzka 52a. ✆ **12/422-65-73.** Daily 7am–8pm.

Cloth Hall (Sukiennice) ★★ In the Middle Ages, town squares such as the Rynek Główny were built to support commerce. Kraków's Cloth Hall, which occupies a valuable chunk of real estate in the middle of the square, harkens back to this original purpose. The first stalls on this site date from before the 14th century. The ancient Cloth Hall burned down in a fire in the 16th century and was replaced by the current Renaissance building. Today, the Sukiennice plays the invaluable role of providing one-stop shopping for all those souvenirs you'll need to buy for the folks back home. The Polish crafts on display here, including carved wooden boxes, chess sets, lace, linens, and (naturally) amber are all of good quality and priced competitively with other shops around town. At press time, Cloth Hall was undergoing renovation, but the stalls were still open for business. Excavation work was also continuing on tunnels below the Cloth Hall with the plan to eventually offer guided tours to the public. These may be operational by the time you read this.

Rynek Główny 1/3. No phone. Stalls daily 10am–8pm.

Czartoryski Museum (Muzeum Książąt Czartorzyskich) ★★ The Czartoryski family members were gifted art collectors, and this collection is one of the finest in central Europe. (Note that the museum closed in January 2010 for a long-term renovation and may not be ready to reopen in 2011. Call ahead to check.) The museum holds at least two certifiable masterpieces of world art: Leonardo da Vinci's *Lady with an Ermine* and Rembrandt's *Landscape with the Good Samaritan.* A third work, Raphael's *Portrait of a Young Man,* was stolen by the Nazis during World War II and never recovered. An empty frame hangs in the museum awaiting the painting's return.

Św. Jana 19. ✆ **12/422-55-66.** www.muzeum-czartoryskich.krakow.pl. 10 zł adults; Thurs free admission. Tues, Thurs & Sun 10am–3:30pm; Wed, Fri & Sat 10am–6pm. Closed Mon.

Franciscan Church (Kościół Franciszkanow) ★ Another must-visit for fans of the late Pope John Paul II, who used to greet the faithful from the window across the street from this church when he was bishop of Kraków. On news of the Pope's death in 2005, this entire area was filled with mourners and candles. Inside the church, the paintings of flowers and stars on the ceiling, as well as the stained glass window over the entrance, are the work of Polish Art Nouveau master Stanisław Wyspiański.

Pl. Wszystkich Świętych 5. ✆ **12/422-53-76.** Daily 10am–4pm. No visits allowed during mass.

Historical Museum of the City of Kraków (Historia Muzeum Historyczne Miasta Krakowa) ★ This museum is worth a look for two reasons: the excellent overview of Kraków's development though the ages and for the building itself, the Palac Krzysztofory, a 17th-century Renaissance *palais,* built from Italian designs and complete with an arcaded Tuscan courtyard. In addition to the standard exhibits, the Fontana room hosts classical concerts, and in December, the museum holds a popular display of handmade nativity scenes in the days leading up to Christmas.

Rynek Glówny 35. ✆ **12/619-23-00.** www.mhk.pl. 8 zł adults. Wed–Fri 10am–5:30pm; Sat & Sun 10am–3pm.

National Museum in Kraków (Muzeum Narodowe w Krakowie) ★ With the Czartoryski museum closed for long-term renovation, the collection at the National is indisputably Kraków's best exposition of fine art. This is particularly true for the top floor, which is given over to an eye-catching collection of 20th-century modern and contemporary pieces. The rest of the museum can be perused fairly quickly and comprises peasant and applied art, weaponry, and crafts.

Al. 3 Maja 1. ✆ **12/295-55-00.** www.muzeum.krakow.pl. 8 zł adults. Wed–Sat 10am–6pm; Sun 10am–4pm. Closed Mon & Tues.

Pharmacy Museum (Muzeum Farmacji) ★★ This is one of the biggest and best old-style pharmacy museums in this part of the world, with fascinating exhibits of potions and leeches and concoctions that show just how far modern medicine has come. Just getting a peek inside this beautiful 15th-century house is almost worth the price of admission itself.

Floriańska 25. ✆ **12/421-92-79.** www.muzeumfarmacji.pl. 7 zł adults. Tues noon–6:30pm; Wed–Sun 10am–2:30pm.

St. Andrew's Church (Kościół Św. Andrzeja) It's hard to imagine a more perfect foil to the attention-grabbing Church of Saints Peter and Paul next door. This humble, handsome church dates from the 11th century and has been part of the city's history for some 900 years. Allegedly, it was the only church to survive the Tatar onslaught of 1241. The church's simple Romanesque exterior is a tonic to the eyes. The interior, on the other hand, borders on the jarring, remodeled in baroque style in the 18th century.

Grodzka 56. ✆ **12/422-16-12.** Daily 7:30am–5pm.

St. Mary's Basilica (Bazylika Mariacka) ★★★ The original church was destroyed in the Tatar raids of the 13th century, and rebuilding began relatively soon after. The hushed interior makes for essential viewing. The elaborately carved 15th-century wooden altarpiece, by the master carver Veit Stoss, is the immediate crowd-pleaser. The altar, carved from lime wood, measures some 11×13m (36×43 ft.) and is the biggest of its kind in Europe. The faces on the carvings are intended to depict biblical figures, but—as was the fashion of the day—Stoss used ordinary townspeople as models. The interior is impressive, but the highlight of the church is not on the inside, it's the forlorn trumpeter in the high tower, playing his hourly dirge to the defenders of Kraków from the Tatar hordes, in order that the people below know the correct time. Note that visitors are not permitted in the Basilica before 11:30am.

Rynek Glówny 4. ✆ **12/422-55-18.** www.mariacki.com. 6 zł adults. Mon–Sat 11:30am–6pm; Sun 2–6pm. No visits allowed during mass.

Town Hall Tower (Wieża Ratuszowa) ★ Kraków's forlorn-looking Town Hall Tower, part of the much larger Town Hall (Ratusz) that was pulled down by the Austrians in 1820, houses a branch of the tourist information office, so you'll likely end up here, even if you're not interested in climbing to the top for views over the square and out to Wawel Castle in the distance. The tower dates from 1316, though it was destroyed, remodeled, and repaired countless times through the centuries. In the 19th century, when Kraków came under the domination of the Habsburgs, the Town Hall was pulled down as part of an effort to tidy up the square. The tower was spared that fate by an apparent change of heart.

Rynek Główny 1. ✆ **12/619-23-18.** www.mhk.pl. May–Oct daily 10:30am–6pm. Closed Nov–Apr.

Wyspiański Museum ★ Fans of Polish art will have heard of Stanisław Wyspiański, one of the originators of a turn-of-the-20th-century art movement known as Młoda Polska (Young Poland). The Młoda Polska movement, based largely here in Kraków and in Zakopane, reinvigorated Polish culture in the years before World War I. You'll note parallels between Wyspiański's paintings and drawings, and the Art Nouveau movements in Paris and Brussels, and Jugendstil in Vienna.

Szczepańska 11. ✆ **12/292-81-83.** www.muzeum.krakow.pl. 8 zł adults. Wed–Sat 10am–6pm; Sun 10am–4pm.

WAWEL CASTLE

Wawel Castle (www.wawel.krakow.pl) is Poland's pride and joy. With Warsaw having been flattened by the Nazis, this ancient castle and former capital, rising 45m (148 ft.) above the Vistula, has become something of a symbol of the survival of the Polish nation. Understandably, for non-Poles, Wawel has less significance, but it's still a handsome castle in its own right and worth an extended visit.

The original castle dates from around the 10th century, when the area was first chosen as the seat of Polish kings. For more than 5 centuries, the castle stood as the home of Polish royalty. The original castle was built in Romanesque style and subsequently remodeled over the centuries, depending on the architectural fashions of the day. What you see today is a mix of Romanesque, Gothic, Renaissance, and baroque.

The castle fell into disrepair after the Polish capital was moved to Warsaw at the end of the 16th century, but its darkest days came during World War II, when it was occupied by Hans Frank, the Nazi governor of the wartime rump Polish state, and came to symbolize the humiliation of the Polish nation. On the plus side, the castle escaped serious damage during the war and, despite languishing under the Communist government, has now made a remarkable comeback, looking as beautiful and impressive as ever.

Aside from the castle, the complex comprises the **Royal Cathedral,** including the **Royal Tombs** and the **Cathedral Museum;** the **State Rooms,** with their impressive collection of tapestries; the **Royal Private Apartments;** and the **Crown Treasury and Armory.** (There are several other attractions, but these are the highlights.) It's a lot to see, and the tourist office will recommend putting in a whole day. But this is likely to be too much time if your knowledge of Polish history leaves something to be desired or castles aren't really your thing. Two to three hours, depending on the crowds, is usually enough to see the main castle attractions and the cathedral complex.

The grounds are open to the public free of charge, but entry to the individual sites, including the Cathedral and Royal Crypts, Royal Private Apartments, and the Crown Treasury and Armory, requires queuing at the castle visitor center and buying separate tickets for each. During the high season in mid-summer, the number of visitors is restricted, so you're best off calling ahead to the main ticket office (✆ **12/422-16-97;** www.wawel.krakow.pl) a day in advance to reserve tickets. Individual guides are also available if you're particularly interested in one or more of the attractions and want more in-depth knowledge. Contact the **Guide Office** (Biuro Przewodnickie; (✆ **12/429-33-36;** www.przewodnicy.krakow.pl) to ask about availability and prices. Guides are priced by attraction and start at around 70 zł for one attraction to up to 230 zł for five.

Wawel Cathedral and Cathedral Museum (Katedra Wawelska) ★★★ This is the spiritual home of the Polish state, testifying to the strong historical link between the Polish royalty and the Catholic Church. There's been a church here since around 1000 A.D., and the present, mostly Gothic, church dates from around the mid-14th century. The chapels here and the Royal Tombs below hold the remains of all but four of Poland's 45 rulers (King Kazimierz the Great's tomb is in red marble to the right of the main altar), as well as a clutch of national heroes, including Polish and U.S. Revolutionary War hero Tadeusz Kościuszko and Polish romantic poet Adam Mickiewicz. The most recent addition came in 2010, with the untimely death of Polish President Lech Kazcyński. Admission includes the tombs and the climb to the top of the Zygmunt Bell, which dates from the early 16th century. The bell is rung only occasionally to mark highly significant moments, such as the death of Pope John Paul II in 2005. Audio headphones are available for a nominal fee and, while the text is long and laborious, the headsets do make it much easier to negotiate the main sights.

Wawel Hill. ✆ **12/429-33-27.** www.katedra-wawelska.pl. Cathedral: free admission. Cathedral museum & Royal Tombs: 12 zł adults; audio headphones 7 zł. Mon–Sat 9am–4pm; Sun 12:30–4pm.

State Rooms and Royal Private Apartments ★ The highlight of a visit to the State Rooms are the 136 Flemish tapestries from the 16th century commissioned by King Sigismund August. The rooms hold vast collections of paintings, sketches, frescoes, and period furnishings. One of the more memorable rooms, on the top floor, is the Deputies' Hall, complete with the king's throne and a wooden ceiling carved with the likenesses of Kraków residents of the time. The splendor continues in the Royal Private Apartments (separate admission), with more tapestries and Renaissance decorations, as well as paintings by Titian, Raphael, and Botticelli.

Wawel Hill. ✆ **12/422-51-55.** www.wawel.krakow.pl. State Rooms: 17 zł adults; Royal Private Apartments: 24 zł adults. Tues–Sat 9:30am–5pm; Sun 11am–6pm.

Crown Treasury and Armory ★★ Exhibitions here include what's left of the Polish royal jewels, including the Szczerbiec, the ancient coronation sword. There's also an impressive show of medieval fighting instruments, including swords and full complements of knights' armor.

Wawel Hill. ✆ **12/422-51-55.** www.wawel.krakow.pl. 17 zł adults; Mon free admission. Mon 9:30am–1pm; Tues–Fri 9:30am–5pm; Sat & Sun 11am–6pm.

KAZIMIERZ, PODGÓRZE & JEWISH KRAKÓW

Kazimierz, the former Jewish quarter, is an absolute must that defies easy description. It's a tumbled-down, decrepit former ghetto, filled with the haunting artifacts of a culture that was brutally uprooted and destroyed a generation ago. It also happens to be Kraków's coolest nightclub district, filled with cafes, cocktail bars, and trendy eateries that would not be out of place in New York's SoHo or East Village. The juxtaposition is enlivening and jarring at the same time. To their credit, Kraków city authorities have resisted (at least, for the time being) the temptation to clean up the area to make it more presentable to visitors. Don't expect an easy, tourist-friendly experience. It's dirty, down at the heel, and at the same time thoroughly engaging.

Kazimierz began life as a Polish city in the 14th century, but starting from around 1500 onward, it took on an increasingly Jewish character as Jews first decided to live here, and then were forced to by edict. The original Jewish ghetto incorporated the northern half of modern-day Kazimierz, bounded by a stone wall along today's Józefa Street. In the 19th century, the Jews won the right of abode, and the walls were eventually torn down. Many elected to stay in Kazimierz, and the 19th century through World War I and the start of World War II is regarded as the quarter's heyday.

The Nazi invasion in 1939 put an end to centuries of Jewish life here. The Nazis first imposed a series of harsh measures on Jewish life, and then, in 1941, forcibly expelled the residents across the river to the newly constructed ghetto at Podgórze. By 1943, with the liquidation of the Podgórze ghetto, nearly all of Kazimierz's prewar Jewish population of 60,000 had been killed or died of starvation or exhaustion.

There's no prescribed plan for visiting the former Jewish quarter. The natural point of departure is the central **Plac Nowy,** once the quarter's main market and now given over to a depressing combination of fruit and flea market (no doubt with real fleas). The **Tourist Information Center** maintains an office at Józefa 7 (✆ **12/422-04-71;**

daily 9am–5pm), and can provide maps and information. Look, too, for signposted routes marked *"Trasa zabytków żydowskych,"* which include all the major Jewish sites. Visit the synagogues individually; each costs from 5 zł to 9 zł to enter, with prices for children and seniors about 60% of the basic adult admission fee. Don't expect to find gorgeous interiors; it's fortunate enough that these buildings are still standing.

After you've toured the major sites, don't overlook the **Galicia Jewish Museum** on Dajwór Street, just beyond the main ghetto area. Also check out the **New Cemetery (Nowy Cmentarz)** at the far end of Miodowa Street (Miodowa 55; Sun–Fri 9am–5pm); you have to walk below a railroad underpass to get to it. This became the main Jewish cemetery in the 19th century, and the thousands of headstones are silent testimony to the former size of this community.

Note: When entering all synagogues, men should cover their heads and women their shoulders.

High Synagogue (Synagoga Wysoka) ★ An only partially restored synagogue dating from the late 1500s, the name refers to the prayer hall, which was traditionally situated on the second floor above street level. Even if you don't choose to go in, check out the ground floor bookshop, which has the city's best collection of books on Judaica, Jewish history, and the Holocaust (see "Shopping," below). There's also an excellent collection of music CDs with traditional Jewish and klezmer music. A real treat.

Józefa 38. ✆ **12/430-68-89.** www.austeria.eu. 9 zł adults. Sun–Fri 9am–7pm.

Galicia Jewish Museum (Żydowskiego Muzeum Galicja) ★★ This often-overlooked museum, in a far corner of Kazimierz, is almost a must-see. The main exhibition features contemporary and often very beautiful photographs of important Jewish sites throughout southern Poland taken by the late British photographer Chris Schwarz. Schwarz and a colleague spent 12 years traveling throughout Poland using photography as a way of trying to preserve the country's rapidly disappearing Jewish heritage. The effect works beautifully. So much of the experience of visiting Poland is running across sites very much like the ones in these pictures and trying to piece together the histories behind them. The lesson here, sadly, seems to be that nearly every place has a tragic story to tell. There's also an excellent on-site bookshop, with books on Jewish history in Kazimierz and the Holocaust.

Dajwór 18. ✆ **12/421-68-42.** www.galiciajewishmuseum.org. 15 zł adults. Daily 10am–6pm.

Isaak Synagogue ★ Even though it was badly damaged during Nazi occupation, this is still considered the most beautiful synagogue structure in Kazimierz. Dating from 1664, it has been only partially restored but still sometimes holds exhibitions on Jewish life in Kazimierz.

Kupa 16. ✆ **12/430-55-77.** 5 zł adults. Sun–Fri 9am–7pm.

Old Synagogue (Stara Synagoga) ★ This stern-looking Renaissance building dating from the 15th century (and the recipient of an architectural makeover a century later) is the oldest surviving Jewish structure in the country. Today, it's home to a rather dry permanent exhibition on Jewish traditions and rituals, as well as a more interesting set of drawings and photos of Jewish life in Kazimierz.

Szeroka 24. ✆ **12/422-09-62.** www.mhk.pl. 8 zł adults. Tues–Sun 9am–5pm; Mon 10am–2pm.

Remuh Synagogue and Cemetery (Synagoga i Cmentarz Remuh) ★★ This synagogue dates from the middle of the 16th century and is still in active use. You can walk through the cemetery, which was used until 1800, when the New Cemetery was opened, and contains some of the country's oldest surviving tombstones.

Szeroka 40. ✆ **12/429-57-35.** www.krakow.jewish.org.pl. 5 zł adults. Sun–Fri 9am–6pm.

Temple Synagogue ★ The 19th century, when this progressive synagogue was built, was a period of great experimentation in Jewish architecture. This synagogue's exterior reflects the influence of Sephardic Jews. The interior has been partly restored, making it the most attractive inside of any of Kazimierz's surviving synagogues.

Miodowa 24. ✆ **12/429-57-35.** www.krakow.jewish.org.pl. 5 zł adults. Sun–Fri 10am–6pm.

PODGÓRZE

South of Kazimierz, across the Vistula River, is the wartime Jewish ghetto of Podgórze. It was here, at today's **Plac Bohaterów Getta,** where thousands of the city's Jews were forcibly moved and incarcerated in March 1941. Much of the area has since been rebuilt, and walking the modern street plan today, you'll be hard-pressed to imagine what it must have been like for thousands of Jews to be pent up here with only the prospect of eventually being sent to the camps at Auschwitz or, more nearby, Płaszów. The ghetto was eventually razed in 1943 and the inhabitants murdered. Look for the **Apteka Pod Orłem** on the Plac Bohaterów Getta, which today houses a small but fascinating museum on the history of the ghetto.

This part of Kraków is sometimes called "Schindler's Kraków" (see "Schindler's Kraków," below) since the enamel factory where German industrialist **Oskar Schindler** employed his Jewish workforce is a 10- to 15-minute walk away (follow Lipowa St., which leads away from the Plac Bohaterów Getta). The factory has recently been spruced up and now houses a museum to the history of Kraków during World War II.

Apteka Pod Orłem (Pharmacy Under the Eagle) ★★ You'll find a riveting collection of photographs and documents from life in the Podgórze ghetto here, from its inception in 1941 to its eventual liquidation 2 years later. During the war, the pharmacy was operated by a Pole, Tadeusz Pankiewicz, who provided medicine to Jews and helped at least some to escape. The exhibition here includes two excellent films. The first, an American documentary from the 1930s, shows typical Jewish life in Kazimierz. The second, a haunting, silent film taken by the Germans, shows the deportation process itself in 1941, as Jewish families are forced to move their belongings across the river amid hopes for a new life (but as we, the viewers, know, resulted in a certain death).

Plac Bohaterów Getta 18. ✆ **12/656-56-25.** www.mhk.pl. 6 zł adults; Mon free admission. Mon 10am–2pm; Tues–Sun 9:30am–4pm.

Oskar Schindler's Emalia Factory ★★ As this book went to press, Kraków finally saw the long-awaited and much-anticipated reopening of Oskar Schindler's former enamel factory, reincarnated here as an interactive museum on Kraków's sad history during World War II. Exhibitions explore Schindler himself, the tragedy of Kazimierz and the Podgórze ghetto, as well as broader injustices, such as the Nazi occupation of Wawel Castle and the murder by the Nazis of Polish professors at Jagiellonian University. Much of the presentation is modeled on Warsaw's highly

Schindler's Kraków

The tragic story of Poland's Jews and of life in the Nazi wartime ghettos has inspired no fewer than two Oscar-winning movies: Roman Polański's *The Pianist* (2002), set in Warsaw's wartime ghetto, and the possibly even bigger Steven Spielberg's *Schindler's List* (1993), starring Liam Neeson, Ben Kingsley, and Ralph Fiennes. The film won seven Oscars, including Best Picture and Best Director. The film was based on the novel *Schindler's List* (Simon & Schuster), by Thomas Keneally, and recounts the true story of German industrialist Oskar Schindler, who comes to Kraków at the start of World War II to make his fortune selling war goods to the German army. Though Schindler is a member of the Nazi party, he slowly comes to recognize the evil nature of the destruction of the Jewish community. By arguing to the Nazi hierarchy that he needs his Jewish workers to continue output for the German war effort, Schindler eventually manages to save some 1,100 Jewish people from certain death at Auschwitz. Much of the filming was done on location at various points around Kazimierz and Schindler's former enamel factory in Podgórze across the river, as well as at the former Płaszów labor camp and Auschwitz itself. If you've recently watched the movie, you'll recognize several shots as you walk through Kazimierz. The best-known location is the still highly evocative courtyard running between Józefa and Meiselsa streets (now home to several cafes and restaurants). Most travel agencies offer full-length tours of "Schindler's Kraków" (see "Customized Tours," below). The movie was not without criticisms, chief among them that Spielberg managed to diminish the inherently evil nature of Nazism by portraying Nazis merely as crazies and lunatics. Others said he commercialized the atrocities or had managed somehow to exaggerate Schindler's goodness. Be that as it may, the movie continues to rise in the eyes of film critics. The American Film Institute ranked it 8th on its list of 100 Best American Films.

successful Museum to the Warsaw Uprising (see p. 86), meaning you can expect lots of audio and video, as well as an abundance of helpful signs in English.

Lipowa 4. ✆ **12/257-10-17.** www.mhk.pl. 15 zł adults; Mon free admission. Mon 10am–2pm; Tues–Sun 10am–6pm. Closed first Mon of the month.

NOWA HUTA

In the 1950s, the Communist authorities decided to try to win over the hearts and minds of skeptical Cracovians by building this model Socialist community, just a tram ride away from the Rynek Główny. They built an enormous steel mill (*nowa huta* means "new mill"), as well as rows of carefully constructed workers' houses, shops, and recreational facilities for what was conceived of as the city of the future. It didn't quite work out as planned: Kraków intellectuals were never impressed by having a steel mill so nearby, and the workers never really cottoned to the Communist cause. But Nowa Huta is still standing and, in its own way, looks better than ever. Any fan of urban design or anyone with a penchant for Communist history will enjoy a couple hours of walking around, admiring the buildings, the broad avenues, and the parks and squares. There's even a small museum here, the **Museum of the History of Nowa Huta,** to tell the story. The structures have held up remarkably well, and indeed, the area looks better now than it ever has. Part of the reason for this is that the mills are no longer running at anywhere near capacity, so the air is cleaner. And, ironically, capitalism has added a touch of badly needed prosperity, meaning the residents now have a little extra money to maintain the buildings. Still, there's something undeniably sad, too; this grandiose project in social engineering has been reduced to little more than a curiosity (though more than 100,000 people still call Nowa Huta home). The shops that line the magnificent boulevards—once conceived to sell everything a typical family would need (even if the shops rarely had anything worth buying)—look forlorn; some are empty. You'll also search in vain for a decent restaurant, so plan on eating back in Kraków. The easiest way to reach Nowa Huta is to take tram no. 4 or 15 from the train station about 20 minutes to the stop "Plac Centralny," or tram no. 22 from Starowiślna near Kazimierz. From here, it's a short walk to the main square, renamed to honor former U.S. President Ronald Reagan. If you'd like a more in-depth tour, **Crazy Guides** (see "Customized Tours," below) offers guided visits to Nowa Huta, including travel in a Communist-era Trabant car, for about 120 zł per person.

Museum of the History of Nowa Huta ★ A must for fans of urban design or readers of trendy design magazines such as *Wallpaper* or *Dwell*. Others may want to skip it. The museum itself occupies a typical housing block built in 1958 and contains the history of the Nowa Huta quarter in documents, designs, and photos.

Os. Słoneczne 16. ✆ **12/425-97-55.** www.mhk.pl. 5 zł adults. Tues–Sat 9am–4pm.

Customized Tours

Several private companies offer walking and bus tours of the city, as well as themed tours, such as Jewish Kraków or Communist Kraków, and longer excursions to Zakopane, the Wieliczka Salt Mines, and Auschwitz-Birkenau, among other possibilities. The city's tourist information offices are filled with brochures, and the staff can advise on which ones might suit your timetable and budget. **Cracow City Tours** (Floriańska 44 and pl. Matejki 2; ✆ **12/421-13-33;** www.cracowcitytours.pl) offers possibly the fullest range of options, including, among others, a John Paul II tour, a *Schindler's List* tour, and a combined trip to Auschwitz-Birkenau and the Wieliczka Salt Mine in 1 day. They also offer longer excursions to Częstochowa and Zakopane, and a river-rafting trip on the Dunajec River. **SeeKrakow** (Floriańska 6 and Grodzka 59; ✆ **12/397-36-24;** www.seekrakow.com) offers tours to both Auschwitz-Birkenau and the Wieliczka Salt Mines. Both tours start at around 100 zł per person and include all expenses. They also offer a series of walking tours of Kraków, starting at 79 zł per person. **Kraków Travel/Marco der Pole** (Kanonicza 15; ✆ **12/430-21-17;** www.krakow-travel.com) is another good company for city walking tours. They offer at least two on most days: one focusing on the Old Town and the other on Jewish Kraków. Both cost around 50 zł per person. **Crazy Guides** (Krakusow 1a/31; ✆ **500/091-200;** www.crazyguides.com) specializes in highly popular Communist theme tours and offers both a "Communism" and "Communism Deluxe" tour, among others. Prices start at around 130 zł a person and include lunch.

Shopping

The main shopping areas are around the Rynek Główny in the Old Town, the Royal Route leading to Wawel Castle, and the former Jewish quarter of Kazimierz. While Warsaw may be better for high fashion and Gdańsk better for amber, there's no shortage of things to buy in Kraków. Traditional gifts include carved wooden boxes and chess sets, lace, traditional Polish clothing, vodka, chocolates, and yes, amber.

ART & ANTIQUES

Kraków is crammed with art, antiques, and junk shops. Most of the better stores are concentrated in the Old Town along the streets that radiate from the main square, especially Św. Jana. Poke your nose in at the ancient books, maps, and old postcards at **Stefan Kamiński** (Św. Jana 3; ✆ **12/422-39-65**). Sławkowska Street also has a nice grouping of art and antiques stores. **Atest** (Sławkowska 14; ✆ **12/421-95-19**) is one of the best. For some unusual modern Polish painting and sculpture, stop by **Galeria AG** (Dominikański 2; ✆ **12/429-51-78;** www.galeriaag.art.pl).

Kazimierz has emerged as a second shopping mecca; here, the emphasis understandably is on Judaica, but the little streets are filled with shops selling everything from trendy art and design to out-and-out junk. **Antyki Józefa** (Kupa 3; ✆ **12/422-01-27**) is typical for Kazimierz, an antique store offering both genuine antiques and junk, but it's not always easy to tell one from the other.

BOOKS, PRINTS & MAPS

For English-language books, Kraków is blessed with at least two treasures. The first is undeniably **Massolit Books** (Felicjanek 4; ✆ **12/432-41-50;** www.massolit.com), easily one of the best new and used English bookshops in Europe. Massolit is especially strong on Polish authors in translation but has thousands of titles under all conceivable categories (plus a very cute cafe and a quiet, contemplative ambience highly conducive to reading and thinking). The other is **Austeria** in Kazimierz (Józefa 38; ✆ **12/430-68-89**), next to the High Synagogue. Here you'll find dozens of titles on Judaica, Polish history, and the Holocaust, as well as some incredibly beautiful photographs, posters, CDs, and reproductions of old maps. **Empik** (Rynek Główny 5; ✆ **12/429-41-62;** www.empik.com) is a kind of Polish version of Borders or Barnes and Noble, with huge shelves filled with (mostly Polish) books, but also a good selection of magazines (including some English titles), CDs, and DVDs. **Cracow Poster Gallery** (Stolarska 8/10; ✆ **12/421-26-40;** www.cracowpostergallery.com) is one-stop shopping for vintage film and exhibition posters, an art form Poles are known for around the world.

GOURMET FOOD & VODKA

Kraków is a good place to scout out exclusive bottles of Polish vodka. Two stores stand out: **Szambelan** (Gołębia 2; ✆ **12/628-70-93;** www.szambelan.com.pl) and **F. H. Herbert** (Grodzka 59; no phone). Szambelan is best known for its exotic bottle shapes, but both stores carry a nice range of the best straight and flavored vodkas, as well as an excellent selection of wines and other beverages. **Krakowski Kredens** (Grodzka 7; ✆ **12/423-81-59;** www.krakowskikredens.pl) is a relative newcomer in the food segment, offering beautifully wrapped and packaged jams, jellies, teas, fruit syrups, and chocolates, as well as a huge deli case of mouthwatering sausages and cheeses. Come here to grab a gift food set or a picnic lunch. **Ciasteczka z Krakowa** (Św. Tomasza 21; ✆ **12/423-22-27**) specializes in homemade cookies, cakes, and chocolates, all wrapped up in fancy boxes. No discussion of Polish food shops would be complete without mentioning **Wawel Chocolates** (Rynek Główny 33; ✆ **12/423-12-47;** www.wawel-sklep.com.pl), where mouth-watering pralines, fruit-filled chocolates, and nuts are sold by the gram and packaged in cute little boxes.

SHOPPING CENTERS

Galeria Kazimierz (Podgórska 34; © **12/433-01-01;** www.galeriakazimierz.pl) is an upscale shopping mall within easy walking distance of the Plac Nowy in Kazimierz. It boasts more than 130 boutiques, shops, stores, and cafes of all kinds. Handy if you need to pick up something you forgot at home.

TRADITIONAL HANDICRAFTS & JEWELRY

For classic Polish souvenirs, including handicrafts, woodcarving, and (naturally) amber, first try the stalls at the **Cloth Hall (Sukiennice)** in the middle of the Rynek Główny. Hidden among the "Poland" T-shirts and mass-produced icons, you'll find some beautifully carved wood and amber chess sets, as well as locally produced cloth, lace, and leather goods. **Galeria Ora** (Św. Anny 3/1a; © **12/426-89-20;** www.galeria-ora.com) is a cut above the average amber place, with a group of young jewelry designers working with more contemporary settings. For amber, amber, and more amber, check out **Boruni** (www.boruni.pl), with shops in the Sukiennice (© **12/430-24-01**), at Kanonicza 22 (© **12/422-36-96**), and Grodzka 60 (© **12/428-50-86**), for high-quality, eye-catching stones in contemporary and traditional settings.

Where to Stay

Kraków has some beautiful hotels, and if you've got the cash and you want to splurge, you can do so in real style. Most of the stunning properties are located in the Old Town, along the streets running off the main square or tucked in a quiet park location off the Planty. A second cluster of decent places to stay is in Kazimierz. You won't find the 5-star luxury class here like in the Old Town, but there are a number of nice 3- and 4-star properties that are, on balance, a little cheaper and quieter than their Old Town counterparts. As for location, both are excellent. An Old Town property puts you just a few steps away from the restaurants and cafes around the square, as well as Kraków's main museums and sites. On the other hand, if you're into bars, clubs, and trendy restaurants, then Kazimierz is where you want to be. Either way, the distances between the two are not great, just a 15-minute walk or short cab ride.

Rates are generally highest between April and October, as well as over the Christmas and New Year holidays. Room prices drop by 20% or more from November through March (except during the holidays). The prices below are for a standard double room (twin beds) in high season (outside of the Christmas and New Year holiday season).

VERY EXPENSIVE

Amadeus ★ A fully modern hotel that is working hard—and succeeding—at recreating an authentic 18th-century feel. For the room interiors, think Colonial Williamsburg, with intricately carved white woodworking for the beds and nightstands, chandeliers, and floor-to-ceiling floral print drapes. Mozart could drop by and actually feel quite at home. The service is top-notch, and the location, just a few feet off the main square, is ideal. A perfect choice if you want a hotel that will stick in your mind as long as Kraków's main square will.

Mikołajska 20. © **12/429-60-70.** Fax 12/429-60-62. www.hotel-amadeus.pl. 22 units. 650 zł double. AE, DC, MC, V. **Amenities:** Restaurant; fitness club; limited room service; sauna. *In room:* A/C, TV, hair dryer, Internet (free), minibar.

Copernicus ★★★ Owned by the local Likus group (which also runs the Monopol in Wrocław), this is the best of the boutique-size properties—and possibly of all the hotels—in town. You'll be charmed immediately by the enormous Renaissance atrium

Where to Stay

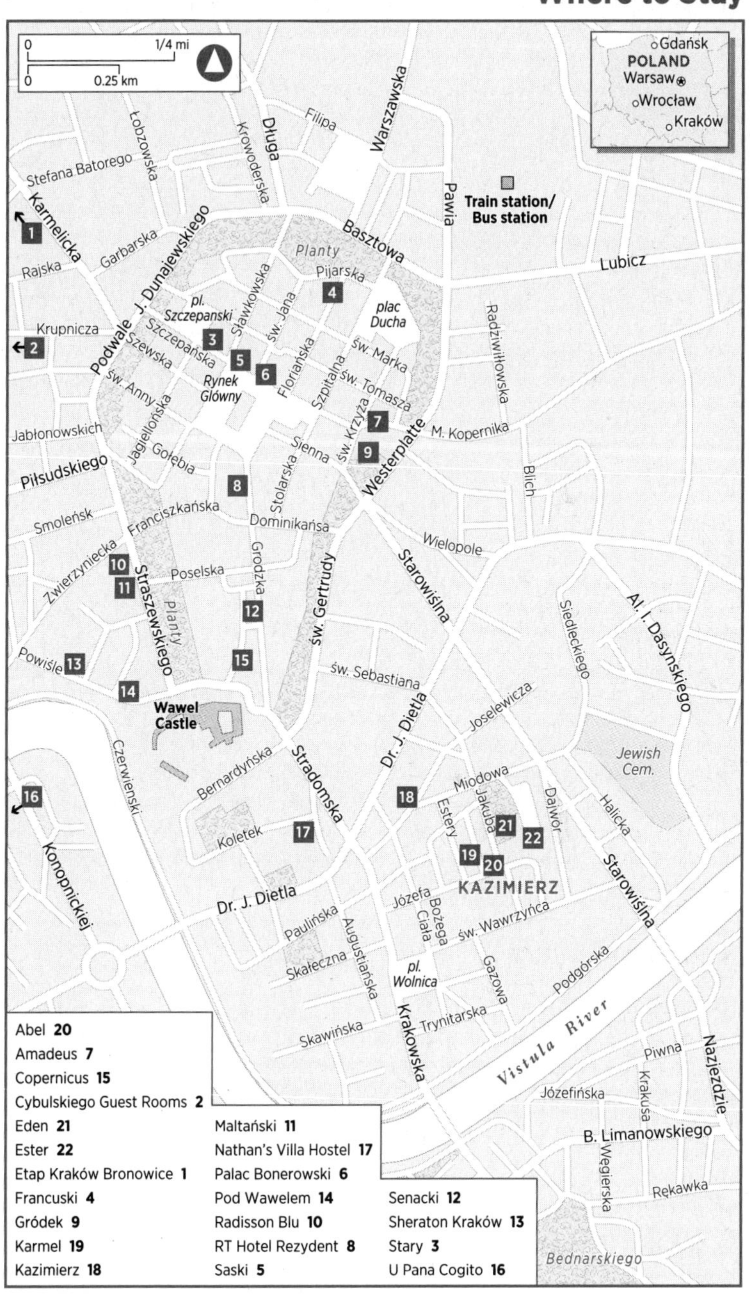

shooting to the ceiling and the period detailing from the 16th century that extends throughout the hotel and to the wood-beamed ceilings in the rooms on the first and second floors. A fresco dating from the year 1500, the *Four Fathers of the Church,* covers the wall in room no. 101.

Kanonicza 16. ✆ **12/424-34-00.** Fax 12/424-34-05. www.hotel.com.pl. 29 units. 900 zł double. AE, DC, MC, V. **Amenities:** Restaurant; indoor pool; room service; sauna. *In room:* A/C, TV, hair dryer, Internet, minibar.

Gródek ★★ This is a good choice if your taste runs to more traditional furnishings such as frilly bedspreads, thick carpets, and patterned drapes. The setting couldn't be more romantic, in a beautifully restored 16th-century town house in a quiet spot of the Old Town near a Dominican convent. There's an excellent in-house spa, and a restaurant—serving upscale international entrees such as cinnamon-marinated duck breast and curry-flavored lamb chops—rounds out the charm. It's slightly cheaper than the competition, making it a relatively good value in this category.

Na Gródku 4. ✆ **12/431-90-30.** Fax 12/378-93-15. www.donimirski.com. 23 units. 650 zł double. AE, DC, MC, V. **Amenities:** Restaurant; room service; sauna; spa. *In room:* A/C, TV, hair dryer, Internet, minibar.

Palac Bonerowski ★★★ Kraków's entry in the 5-star category is a jaw-dropper: a sensitively restored 13th-century town house just off the main square. Many period elements, including some original stonework and carvings, have been preserved in the spacious rooms. The furnishings are tasteful and traditional, with cream-colored leather sofas and armchairs, and hardwood tables and chairs. The floors are polished parquet, accented with Oriental carpets. You can't miss the 15m-high (49-ft.) crystal chandelier running down the main staircase.

Św. Jana 1. ✆ **12/374-13-00.** Fax 12/374-13-05. www.palacbonerowski.pl. 8 units. 800 zł double. AE, DC, MC, V. **Amenities:** 2 restaurants; 24-hr. room service. *In room:* A/C, TV, hair dryer, Internet, minibar.

Radisson Blu ★★ This is an excellent business-class hotel from a top-notch international chain. The location is ideal, just a short walk from the Old Town. The rooms are spacious and offer standard business amenities like trouser presses, coffee-makers, and free Wi-Fi. Harmony rooms are slightly more expensive; they are larger, have a "feng shui" design layout, and include high-end Nespresso coffee-makers. Probably not the first choice for leisure travelers, but an excellent selection if you're traveling on business or someone else is footing the bill.

Straszewskiego 17. ✆ **12/618-88-88.** Fax 12/618-88-89. www.radissonblu.com. 196 units. 800 zł double. AE, DC, MC, V. **Amenities:** 2 restaurants; concierge; executive-level rooms; health club; 24-hr. room service; sauna. *In room:* A/C, TV, fax, hair dryer, minibar, Wi-Fi (free).

Sheraton Kraków ★★ This is a relatively recent addition to the high-end corporate market, but is already setting standards as arguably the best business hotel in the city. Everything is conceived with comfort and convenience in mind, all the way down to the high-tech fitness center's special Cracow massages ("ideal after long sightseeing, travel, or work"). Unlike many Sheratons around the world, this one is actually in a good location for sightseeing, close to the river and within an easy walk of the Old Town or Wawel Castle. Ask for a room with a view toward the Wawel. The main in-house restaurant is excellent; the head chef also cooks for the Polish national soccer team.

Powiśle 7. ✆ **12/662-10-00.** Fax 12/662-11-00. www.sheraton.com/krakow. 232 units. 750 zł double. AE, DC, MC, V. Parking (100 zł/night). **Amenities:** 3 restaurants; concierge; executive-level rooms; health club; 24-hr. room service; sauna. *In room:* A/C, TV, fax, hair dryer, Internet, minibar.

Stary ★★★ This eye-catching, up-market renovation of a former *palais,* just off the Rynek Główny, comes complete with silk fabrics, exotic hardwoods, and high-quality marble. Some of the rooms have maintained their period details, showing off the building's original frescoes; others have a brushed-steel contemporary look that's right out of New York's East Village. Ask to see several and choose your mood. Luscious amenities include two indoor pools and a salt cave.

Szczepańska 5. ✆ **12/384-08-08.** Fax 12/384-08-09. www.hotel.com.pl. 53 units. 900 zł double. AE, DC, MC, V. **Amenities:** Restaurant; 2 indoor pools; room service; sauna. *In room:* A/C, TV, hair dryer, Internet, minibar.

EXPENSIVE

Ester ★ One of a handful of 4-star hotels in Kazimierz, the Ester is probably the nicest overall property in the former Jewish quarter. The hotel was renovated a couple years ago, and the rooms have an understated, white-linen feel synonymous with a good boutique property. The hotel's Wi-Fi access extends to the public areas and onto the outdoor terrace (so even if you're not staying here, you can bring your laptop and surreptitiously check your e-mail). The location, at the heart of the former ghetto, is just a short walk away from the synagogues and major sights.

Szeroka 20. ✆ **12/429-11-88.** Fax 12/429-12-33. www.hotel-ester.krakow.pl. 32 units. 500 zł double. AE, DC, MC, V. **Amenities:** Restaurant; limited room service; spa; Wi-Fi (free). *In room:* A/C, TV, hair dryer, Internet, minibar.

Francuski ★ This lovely Art Nouveau–style hotel dates from 1912 and is perched just beside St. Florian's Gate, near the traditional royal entryway to the Old Town. The rooms are on the small side but nicely appointed in a mix of contemporary and period furnishings. The romantic setting makes this a popular honeymoon hotel for Polish newlyweds. You may need to contact the hotel directly to book, since the hotel's Orbis-run website is a disaster to try to negotiate.

Pijarska 13. ✆ **12/627-37-77.** Fax 12/627-37-00. www.orbis.pl or www.accorhotels.com. 42 units. 450 zł double. MC, V. *In room:* A/C (in some), TV, hair dryer, Internet, minibar.

Maltański ★★ This beautifully renovated boutique with a crisp-linens-and-fresh-flowers kind of feel is under the same management as the similar but more expensive Gródek (see above). The location is excellent, within easy walking distance of both the Wawel Castle and the Rynek. The rooms are small but beautifully outfitted in a traditional Laura Ashley look.

Straszewskiego 14. ✆ **12/431-00-10.** Fax 12/378-93-12. www.donimirski.com. 16 units. 490 zł double. AE, DC, MC, V. **Amenities:** Restaurant; room service. *In room:* A/C, TV, hair dryer, Internet, minibar.

Pod Wawelem ★★ One of a number of newer boutique-style hotels that offer unfussy yet stylish rooms at a decent price, given the location. It's a short walk from here to Wawel Castle and the river, and about a 10-minute walk from the main square. Be sure to request a room with a view of the Wawel. The rooms are outfitted in a high-quality minimalist style, with cheery light-colored walls and dark woods. In-room amenities include free Wi-Fi.

Na Groblach 22. ✆ **12/426-26-26.** Fax 12/422-33-99. www.hotelpodwawelem.pl. 47 units. 450 zł double. AE, DC, MC, V. **Amenities:** Restaurant; room service; sauna. *In room:* A/C, TV, hair dryer, minibar, Wi-Fi (free).

RT Hotel Rezydent ★ Not quite the upscale boutique hotel that this place markets itself as, it's a nice choice nevertheless, given the absolutely top-notch location just off the main square and on the Royal Route that leads to Wawel and beyond. The rooms are relatively small but with sturdy, stylishly modern furniture and hardwood floors. Big discounts are available if you book online.

Grodzka 9. ✆ **12/429-54-10.** Fax 12/429-55-76. www.rezydent.krakow.pl. 59 units. 380 zł double. AE, DC, MC, V. **Amenities:** Restaurant. *In room:* A/C (in some), TV, hair dryer, Internet, minibar.

Senacki ★★ This is another sensitive restoration of an older town house. This popular hotel sports an excellent location, between the Wawel Castle and the Old Town along the former coronation route, and tastefully decorated rooms, many with views over the Old Town.

Grodzka 51. ✆ **12/422-76-86.** Fax 12/422-79-34. www.senacki.pl. 20 units. 500 zł double. AE, DC, MC, V. **Amenities:** Restaurant. *In room:* A/C (in some), TV, Internet.

MODERATE

Eden ★ This is a good second choice in Kazimierz at this price level if you can't get in at the Karmel (see below). It's similar in many ways, and well maintained and quiet, but not quite as immediately charming. The rooms are modestly furnished and on the plain side, more functional than inspiring. Uniquely, the Eden has a "salt grotto" spa in the basement. The idea is for you to sit in the special saline air for 45 minutes to reduce stress and heal a multitude of ills, ranging from asthma to tonsillitis to acne. Once you've cured whatever ails you, head around the corner to the local pub called (not kidding) "Ye Olde Goat."

Ciemna 15. ✆ **12/430-65-65.** Fax 12/430-67-67. www.hoteleden.pl. 25 units. 320 zł double. AE, DC, MC, V. **Amenities:** Restaurant; room service; spa. *In room:* A/C, TV, hair dryer, Internet, minibar.

Karmel ★★★ Karmel is the most charming and inviting of Kazimierz's hotels and pensions. Maybe it's the quiet location in a forgotten spot in the former ghetto, or the flowers hanging off the house windows, or the cute Italian restaurant on the ground floor. Something about the hotel says home. Splurge on a "comfort" room, with a big double bed and a couple of sofas in the room.

Kupa 15. ✆ **12/430-67-00.** Fax 12/430-67-26. www.karmel.com.pl. 12 units. 298 zł standard double; 398 zł "comfort" double. AE, DC, MC, V. **Amenities:** Restaurant; room service. *In room:* A/C, TV, hair dryer, Internet, minibar.

Kazimierz This is probably the most popular hotel in Kraków's former Jewish quarter, but not necessarily the best. The plain lobby and public areas are redeemed somewhat by a beautiful, enclosed inner courtyard. The rooms, too, are nothing special, but are clean and comfortable. The location is superb, near the entrance to the former Jewish quarter and also not far from Wawel Castle and the Old Town. They sometimes lower the rates on weekends, so ask when you book. If there are no free rooms in the building, the hotel has also runs a nearby annex on the same street.

Miodowa 16. ✆ **12/421-66-29.** Fax 12/422-28-84. www.hk.com.pl. 39 units. 360 zł double. AE, DC, MC, V. **Amenities:** Restaurant; room service. *In room:* A/C (in some), TV, hair dryer, Internet, minibar.

Saski ★ Kraków residents might laugh at this hotel being labeled a "find" since it's one of the best-known hotels in the city, right off the main square. But what many don't realize is that it's at least 100 zł a night less than other hotels in its class and location (especially if you go for a double with a shared bath). So, if you're looking for a glorious old hotel with a tiled-floor lobby and chandeliers, and don't want to shell out major cash, this is your place. Ask to see several rooms, since they're all different—some are quite modern and border on the plain, while others are in high period style with quaint, old-fashioned beds and tables.

Sławkowska 3. ✆ **12/421-42-22.** Fax 12/421-48-30. www.hotel-saski.com.pl. 20 units. 280 zł double w/ shared bathroom; 390 zł double. AE, DC, MC, V. **Amenities:** Restaurant; room service. *In room:* A/C (in some), TV, hair dryer, Internet, minibar.

INEXPENSIVE

Abel ★ There are lots of good reasons to stay in Kazimierz. Admittedly, the location is not as beautiful as the Old Town, but Kazimierz is cheaper and somehow feels closer to what makes Kraków tick these days, with all the clubs, restaurants, and party spots popping up. This small, plain hotel is in the heart of the former Jewish quarter. Don't expect much at this price point other than a clean bed and a private bath. There's no in-room Internet.

Józefa 30. ✆ **12/411-87-36.** Fax 12/411-94-90. www.hotelabel.pl. 15 units. 230 zł double. AE, DC, MC, V. *In room:* TV.

Cybulskiego Guest Rooms ★★ Not a hotel per se, this is a series of efficiency apartments with private showers and little kitchens that offers more privacy than a hostel. The rooms are clean and have good Wi-Fi access. The location is just outside the center, about a 10- to 15-minute walk to the central square. A big plus is the laundry service for about 25 zł per load, a life-saver in laundromat-deprived Poland.

Cybulskiego 6. ✆ **12/423-05-32.** www.freerooms.pl. 14 units. 140 zł standard double; 160 zł double w/ kitchen. AE, DC, MC, V. *In room:* TV, fridge, kitchen (in some), Wi-Fi (free).

Etap Kraków Bronowice ★ Something Kraków sorely needed: a big, budget hotel with clean beds at a fair price and without unnecessary amenities you're unlikely to use on a short stay that only pad the bill. The major drawback is location, about 5km (3 miles) from the center of town. (Though if you're traveling by car, it's convenient to both the A4 freeway to Wrocław and the E77 to Warsaw.) There's limited Wi-Fi access in the lobby and breakfast room.

Armii Krajowej 11a. ✆ **12/626-11-45.** Fax 12/626-20-60. www.orbis.pl. 120 units. 140 zł double; breakfast 19 zł. AE, DC, MC, V. **Amenities:** Restaurant; Wi-Fi (in lobby & breakfast room, free). *In room:* A/C, TV.

Nathan's Villa Hostel ★ The American owner of this well-run and highly regarded hostel just across from Wawel Castle says his aim is to combine the social aspects of a hostel with the amenities you'd expect from a hotel. And at this price, he definitely gets it right. In addition to the standard 8- and 10-bed rooms typical for a hostel, Nathan's rents out private doubles. In summer, most of the guests are backpackers, but during the rest of the year, the hostel fills up with people of all age groups looking to save money while not sacrificing on location or cleanliness. Perks include free laundry, an Internet room, and a DVD movie room for rainy days.

Św. Agnieszki 1. ✆ **12/422-35-45.** www.nathansvilla.com. 20 units. 60 zł dorm bed; 180 zł double. MC, V. **Amenities:** Bar. *In room*: no phones.

U Pana Cogito ★★ If you don't mind walking, this renovated villa complex, about 15 minutes by foot from the city center, represents real value. The modern rooms, done up in neutral beige and gold, have all the personality of a standard Holiday Inn, but they're clean and quiet, with nicely done bathrooms and unexpected touches at this price point like air-conditioning in the rooms and full Internet access (both Wi-Fi and LAN connections).

Bałuckiego 6. ✆ **12/269-72-00.** Fax 12/269-72-02. www.pcogito.pl. 14 units. 250 zł double. AE, DC, MC, V. **Amenities:** Parking (free), restaurant. *In room:* A/C, TV, hair dryer, minibar, Wi-Fi (free).

Where to Dine

Most of the fancier and more established restaurants are in the Old Town on the main square or along the streets running off the square, particularly to the south. The newer, trendier, and sometimes better places are located in Kazimierz. One area in the former ghetto to look is along Plac Nowy; the other dining cluster, including most of the Jewish-themed restaurants, is along Szeroka. Except for the very pricey places in the Old Town, dress is mostly casual. That's particularly true of the Kazimierz locales, which cater to a largely student and young professional crowd. Note that though many restaurants will claim to stay open until 11pm or "until the last guest," on slow nights kitchens often start closing down at 10pm. Go early to avoid disappointment.

VERY EXPENSIVE

Cyrano de Bergerac ★★ FRENCH It's such a pleasure to taste Polish food with a French twist when it's done this well. That means staples like game, pork, and duck, but with a nuance. The duck, for example, isn't served with apple or cranberry, but caramelized peach and cardamom, instead. The pork knuckle is candied in honey—the glazing giving it a light barbecue flavor. The exposed brick interior is stunning, with candlelight and white linens on the tables. The service is polished but can be slow on busy nights. Beware the prices on wines. Dress for this one and reserve in advance.

Sławkowska 26. ✆ **12/411-72-88.** Reservations recommended. Main courses 40 zł–90 zł. AE, DC, MC, V. Mon–Sat noon–midnight.

Edo Sushi Bar ★★ JAPANESE One of the best sushi restaurants in central Europe is on a quiet corner in Kazimierz. The hushed, spare, modern decor puts the emphasis firmly on the food. Very fresh *nigiri* sushi and some creative *maki* rolls keep the crowds happy. Ask the guys behind the sushi bar what looks good and settle in for a great meal.

Bożego Ciała 3. ✆ **12/422-24-24.** Main courses 40 zł–60 zł. AE, DC, MC, V. Daily noon–11pm.

Wierzynek ★ POLISH This is less a restaurant and more a revered institution on par with Wawel Castle and the Old Town Tower. This esteemed eatery has played host to visiting dignitaries, celebs, and heads of state since way back in 1364, when owner Mikołaj Wierzynek threw a banquet in honor of the marriage between Holy Roman Emperor Charles IV and the granddaughter of Polish King Kazimierz the Great. The cuisine is an imaginative take on traditional Polish cooking, with the emphasis on treats such as wild boar, quail, and venison. This one is worth reserving in advance and dressing up for.

Rynek Główny 15. ✆ **12/424-96-00.** Reservations recommended. Main courses 40 zł–90 zł. AE, DC, MC, V. Daily noon–11pm.

EXPENSIVE

Chimera ★★ POLISH Really two restaurants in one: First, it's an expensive but delicious Polish restaurant with old-style recipes centered on lamb, goose, and game. Then there's a cheaper salad bar that's a better value and extremely popular around lunchtime, with about 40 different salads and lots of vegetarian offerings.

Św. Anny 3. ✆ **12/292-12-12.** Reservations recommended. Main courses 40 zł–60 zł; salad bar (large plate) 16 zł. AE, DC, MC, V. Daily noon–11pm.

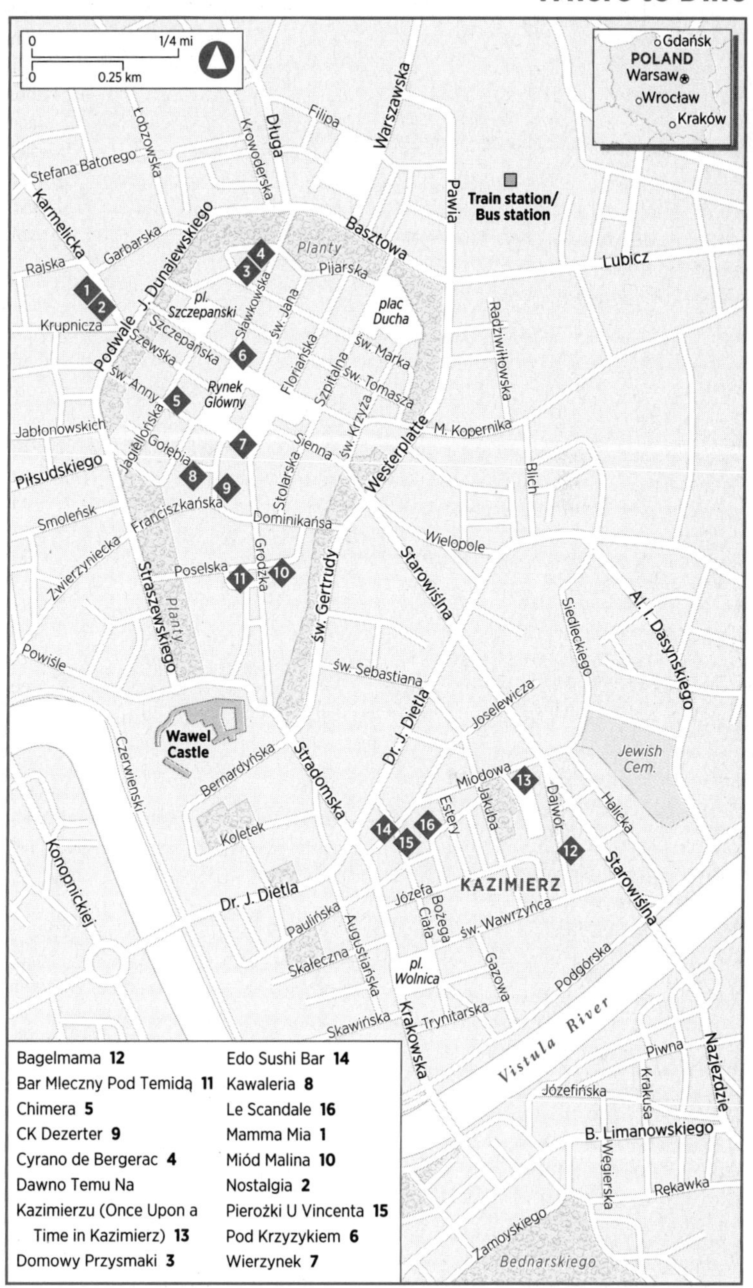
0
1/4 mi
0
0.25 km
Gdańsk
POLAND
Warsaw
Wrocław
Kraków
Train station/
Bus station
Filipa
Warszawska
Długa
Krowoderska
Łobzowska
Stefana Batorego
Karmelicka
Pawia
Basztowa
Lubicz
Garbarska
Rajska
Podwale J. Dunajewskiego
Planty
Pijarska
plac
Ducha
pl.
Szczepanski
Sławkowska
św. Jana
Krupnicza
Szczepańska
Szewska
Radziwiłłowska
św. Marka
Floriańska
Szpitalna
św. Tomasza
św. Anny
Rynek
Główny
Jabłonowskich
Jagiellońska
Gołębia
Sienna
św. Krzyża
Westerplatte
M. Kopernika
Piłsudskiego
Blich
Franciszkańska
Stolarska
Smoleńsk
Dominikańska
Wielopole
Zwierzyniecka
Straszewskiego
Poselska
Grodzka
św. Gertrudy
Starowiślna
Siedleckiego
Al. I. Dasynskiego
Powiśle
św. Sebastiana
Dr. J. Dietla
Joselewicza
Wawel
Castle
Czerwienski
Bernardyńska
Stradomska
Jewish
Cem.
Miodowa
Jakuba
Estery
Dajwór
Halicka
Koletek
Konopnickiej
KAZIMIERZ
Józefa
Bożego
Ciała
św. Wawrzyńca
Paulińska
Augustiańska
Skałeczna
pl.
Wolnica
Gazowa
Podgórska
Skawińska
Trynitarska
Krakowska
Vistula River
Piwna
Krakusa
Nadjezdzie
Józefińska
B. Limanowskiego
Węgierska
Rękawka
Zamoyskiego
Bednarskiego
Bagelmama 12
Bar Mleczny Pod Temidą 11
Chimera 5
CK Dezerter 9
Cyrano de Bergerac 4
Dawno Temu Na Kazimierzu (Once Upon a Time in Kazimierz) 13
Domowy Przysmaki 3
Edo Sushi Bar 14
Kawaleria 8
Le Scandale 16
Mamma Mia 1
Miód Malina 10
Nostalgia 2
Pierożki U Vincenta 15
Pod Krzyzykiem 6
Wierzynek 7

Dawno Temu Na Kazimierzu (Once Upon a Time in Kazimierz) ★★ JEWISH Finally, the kind of toned-down, less-kitschy Jewish restaurant that Kazimierz has long been waiting for: It's relaxed and intimate, with the inevitable knick-knacks and "homespun" interior, but this time creating a warming—not distracting (as with the other restaurants in the area)—effect. The food is great: Especially recommended is the roast duck with cherries.

Szeroka 1. ✆ **12/421-21-17.** Main courses 30 zł–45 zł. AE, DC, MC, V. Daily 11am–10pm.

Kawaleria ★ POLISH Similar to Chimera (see above) in terms of the menu and presentation. The wild boar gammon is the highlight, served in a cranberry sauce with cabbage and chickpeas. The surroundings are impeccable, and the location is just a short walk from the Rynek.

Gołębia 4. ✆ **12/430-24-32.** Reservations recommended. Main courses 40 zł–60 zł. AE, DC, MC, V. Daily noon–11pm.

Miód Malina ★★★ POLISH Plan to have at least one of your meals here, a Michelin-award-winning restaurant that nevertheless manages to keep prices relatively affordable. The cuisine could be described as "Polish-Italian," though the menu features a strong list of traditional Polish specialties, as well as mains like duck and lamb. The interior is colorful, and the attitude is casual. An excellent spot for a relaxed lunch or special dinner. Book in advance.

Grodzka 40. ✆ **12/430-04-11.** Reservations recommended. Main courses 30 zł–49 zł. AE, DC, MC, V. Daily noon–11pm.

Nostalgia ★★ POLISH A meal here is like dining in the country home of a well-to-do friend—warm and inviting, yet still refined and special. The atmosphere extends to the cooking, as well: Polish staples such as pierogi, pork, and game, but well turned out and served on fine china. This is a perfect balance between something like Cyrano de Bergerac (see above) and CK Dezerter (see below): the attention to detail of the former, but with the more relaxed feel and prices of the latter. Reserve in advance to be on the safe side.

Karmelicka 10. ✆ **12/425-42-60.** Reservations recommended. Main courses 25 zł–45 zł. AE, DC, MC, V. Daily noon–11pm.

Pod Krzyżykiem ★★ POLISH The chefs at this award-winning restaurant take traditional Polish cooking and give it a little tweak to good effect. The three-course lunch menu at 40 zł is particularly good value. The schnitzel, served with potato salad and berries, comes highly recommended. The funky interior is literally "surreal"—you'll have to see for yourself.

Rynek Glówny 39. ✆ **12/433-70-10.** Main courses 40 zł–60 zł. AE, DC, MC, V. Daily noon–11pm.

MODERATE

CK Dezerter POLISH This cozy, family-style tavern serves well-prepared traditional local cooking in a warm setting down a side street off the Rynek Główny. It's perfect if you've just arrived and want a hassle-free, decent meal and don't want to stray too far from the hotel. The only possible drawback is that it's popular with guidebooks (like this one), so while you'll probably find many Poles on the night you're here, you may also wind up next to a table of guests from your own hometown.

Bracka 6. ✆ **12/422-79-31.** Main courses 20 zł–30 zł. AE, DC, MC, V. Daily 10am–10pm.

Le Scandale ★ INTERNATIONAL This great breakfast or light-lunch spot is right on Plac Nowy in Kazimierz. Decent bagels, eggs, and coffee are served, starting at 8am. On weekends, arrive early to snag one of the highly coveted square-side tables, perfect for people-watching while sipping your espresso. The lunch and dinner menu is heavy on international munchies, simple pastas, and sandwiches, but also does well with steaks and seafood. Be aware that the restaurant morphs into a boisterous club after about 8pm.

Plac Nowy 9. ✆ **12/430-68-55.** Main courses 15 zł–30 zł. AE, DC, MC, V. Daily 9am–11pm.

Mamma Mia ★★ ITALIAN The truly excellent wood-fired pizzas and a full range of pasta dishes feature the freshest ingredients. The refined space, not far from the main square, is perfect for business or pleasure, dressy or casual. It has an excellent wine selection, too.

Karmelicka 14. ✆ **12/430-04-92.** Main courses 15 zł–30 zł. AE, DC, MC, V. Daily noon–11pm.

INEXPENSIVE

Bagelmama ★★ JEWISH/AMERICAN Kraków's premiere purveyor of lox and bagels, as well as other bagel-based sandwiches and hearty salads, has found a new, larger and brighter space on an up-and-coming street just below the Old Synagogue in Kazimierz. Great for breakfast or lunch.

Dajwór 10. ✆ **12/346-16-46.** Main courses 15 zł–20 zł. No credit cards. Mon–Sat 9am–9pm; Sun 9am–7pm.

Bar Mleczny Pod Temidą ★ POLISH Every visitor to Poland eventually has to have a "milk bar" experience, and this is one of Kraków's best—and certainly its most tourist-friendly. A milk bar—the "milk" refers to the fact that no alcohol is served—has no direct American or Western European equivalent. *Cafeteria* sounds too sterile and *greasy spoon*, well, too greasy. But that's the idea: heaping steam tables of mostly meatless Polish specialties you line up for and point to. Not bad tasting and good value.

Grodzka 43. ✆ **12/422-08-74.** Main courses 12 zł–18 zł. No credit cards. Daily 9am–8pm.

Domowy Przysmaki ★ POLISH This informal self-service lunch counter has excellent pierogi and other lighter Polish fare, including very good soups. This is the perfect spot for a filling, cheap lunch or early dinner in the Old Town.

Sławkowska 24a. ✆ **12/422-57-51.** Main courses 8 zł–15 zł. No credit cards. Open 10am–9pm.

Pierożki U Vincenta ★★ POLISH This tiny and inviting pierogi joint in Kazimierz serves every style of pierogi imaginable. The house version "Vincent" is stuffed with minced meat and spicy lentils, and served with fried onions and bits of bacon. Other concoctions include couscous pierogi and "Górale" (highlander) pierogi stuffed with sheep's cheese. Try them with a cup of homemade beet broth.

Bożego Ciała 12. ✆ **0501/747-407.** Main courses 10 zł–15 zł. No credit cards. Sun–Thurs noon–9pm; Fri & Sat noon–10pm.

CAFES

There is no shortage of cafes in Kraków catering to all tastes and budgets. You'll find the greatest concentration along the streets that radiate off the main square and around Plac Nowy in Kazimierz. In nice weather, the entire Rynek Główny is transformed into a giant cafe.

Camera Café ★ CAFE A laid-back, student-y cafe just off the Rynek Główny, with silent movies projected on the walls (hence the name). The specialty here is chocolate-based drinks, but they also serve excellent coffee, the standard offering of soft drinks, and salads and light meals.

Wiślna 5. ✆ **601/190-381.** Drinks 7 zł–10 zł. No credit cards. Daily 9am–midnight.

Dym ★★ CAFE A dark, relaxing space given over to arty and intellectual types. The name means "smoke," and indeed, this is the place to come if you want to have a cigarette with your coffee or beer (and possibly a place to avoid if you don't).

Św Tomasza 13. ✆ **12/429-66-61**. Drinks 5 zł–8 zł. No credit cards. Daily 10am–midnight.

Jama Michalika CAFE In the early 20th century, this cafe used to be the epicenter of all things cool in Kraków and a major meeting point for the Młoda Polska crowd. Alas, those days are long gone, and now, it's largely given over to tourists. The incredible Art Nouveau interior and the evocative period paintings are definitely worth a look. Beware, though, the unfriendly cloakroom attendants (coat and hat check mandatory). The service is legendarily unfriendly, and you may have to wrestle a waiter to the ground to take your order.

Floriańska 45. ✆ **12/422-15-61.** Main courses 12 zł–27 zł. AE, DC, MC, V. Daily 9am–midnight.

Les Couleurs/Kolory ★★ CAFE During the day, this Kazimierz locale is an innocent French-themed cafe, complete with good espresso drinks and arty French posters on the wall. In the evening, it morphs into a crowded bar for an after-dinner beer or cocktail. Just boisterous enough to feel lively, but quiet enough to hear yourself think.

Estery 10. ✆ **12/429-42-70.** Drinks 5 zł–8 zł. Mon–Fri 7am–2am; Sat & Sun 9am–2am.

Mleczarnia ★★ CAFE This quiet, intimate, candlelit bar/cafe is perfect for deep conversation or a low-key group outing. In summer, sit out in the garden across the street. Highly recommended.

Meiselsa 20. ✆ **12/421-85-32.** Drinks 5 zł–8 zł. Sun–Thurs 9am–2am; Fri & Sat 9am–3am.

Noworolski ★ CAFE The lovingly restored Art Nouveau interior recalls Kraków's elegant past. The perfect spot for a leisurely coffee and cake.

Rynek Główny 1. ✆ **12/422-47-71.** Main courses 15 zł–30 zł. AE, DC, MC, V. Daily 9am–midnight.

After Dark

THE PERFORMING ARTS

Kraków is the cultural hub of southern Poland and, as such, supports an active program of live theater, dance, classical music, and opera. The **Cultural Information Center** (Św. Jana 2; ✆ **12/421-77-87**) is the first stop to find out what's on and to see if tickets are available. The friendly staff can help guide you to the best events. The center for classical music is the **Philharmonic Hall** (Zwierzyniecka 1; ✆ **12/422-94-77;** www.filharmonia.krakow.pl; box office Tues–Sat noon–7pm). The city supports several opera companies, including the very good **Opera Krakowska** (Lubicz 48; ✆ **12/296-61-00;** www.opera.krakow.pl). Tickets are available for purchase online or at the theater box office and run anywhere from 30 zł to 100 zł per performance.

BARS, PUBS & CLUBS

For drinking, dancing, and clubbing, both the Old Town and Kazimierz are natural areas to start a night crawl. The Old Town caters more to tourists and students from nearby Jagiellonian University; in Kazimierz, the scene is more diverse and a little older, with young professionals, artists, and hipsters of all sorts attracted to some of the best clubs in central Europe.

Alchemia One of the original bars/clubs to lead the Kazimierz Renaissance in the late 1990s when the former Jewish quarter morphed from a forgotten corner of Kraków to its current "party amid the past" feel. The old furniture, faded photos, and frayed carpets set a design trend that's still going strong. It's no longer the bar of the moment but still a great place to get a feel for what Kazimierz is all about. Estery 5. ✆ **12/421-22-00.** Daily 10am–4am.

Łódź Kaliska This transplant from the industrial megalopolis of Łódź doubles as both a rowdy college bar and a somewhat more laid-back establishment suitable for a beer and an intellectual discussion. Weekends sometimes bring live music; nearly every night finds the place packed. Floriańska 15. ✆ **12/422-70-42.** Daily 6pm–5am.

Ministerstwo One of Kraków's best venues for DJs and house music. The action starts late and runs until dawn. Good location, just off the Main Square. Szpitalna 1. ✆ **12/429-67-90.** www.klubministerstwo.pl. Daily 5pm–5am.

Nic Nowego We hesitated before including this modern Irish-themed bar since it's so popular with tourists and is in every other guidebook. But if you're looking for a visitor-friendly place where English is spoken and the menu looks comforting and familiar, you could do far worse. In addition to decent cocktails and conversation, you'll find a nice array of burgers and sandwiches on the munchie menu. Breakfast is served daily, and the scrambled eggs and coffee here are probably a lot better than what your hotel or pension has planned for you. Św. Krzyża 15. ✆ **12/421-61-88.** Mon–Fri 7am–3am; Sat & Sun 10am–3am.

Pauza You'll have to look around a bit for this moody little cocktail bar, which now numbers among the coolest drinking spots in the city, despite few clues that it's even there. Order at the bar and head for the chill-out lounge in the back. Floriańska 18/3. ✆ **12/422-48-66.** www.pauza.pl. Daily noon–midnight.

Rdza This is another contender for best dance club in the Old Town. Choose something fashionable to wear in order to make it past the guys at the door, and then enjoy the trance, dance, and mood tunes served up by some of the best Polish and imported DJs on offer. Attracts an early-20s-to-30s crowd. Bracka 3/5. ✆ **60/039-55-41.** Thurs–Sat 9pm–4am.

AROUND KRAKÓW: THE WIELICZKA SALT MINE

Believe it or not, a visit to an abandoned salt mine is far and away the most popular daytrip from Kraków. Of course, the Wieliczka Salt Mine (Kopalnia Soli Wieliczka), located in the suburb of Wieliczka about 16km (10 miles) from Kraków, is no ordinary salt mine. It's listed as a UNESCO World Heritage Site and draws something like a million people a year. The main attraction is not the salt itself, but rather what a number of talented miners and artisans through the ages have managed to do with it, carving out amazingly ornate chambers, cathedrals, and statues. A visit here takes about 3 hours, and you'll want to leave a good half-day for it. Many travel agencies offer Wieliczka tour packages, complete with transportation and a guide. This is a good hassle-free way to do it; alternatively, Wieliczka is an easy 20-minute drive from Kraków and also easily reachable by minibus or train. Several tour operators also offer combined Wieliczka–Auschwitz tours, presumably for people who have only one day and want to do it all. Resist the temptation to do this. It's far too physically and psychologically ambitious. If you've got only a day for the environs of Kraków, you're better off choosing one or the other.

Essentials

GETTING THERE

BY TRAIN Wieliczka is easily reached by regular train service from Kraków's main station, the Dworzec Główny (pl. Kolejowy 1; ✆ **12/393-11-11;** www.pkp.krakow.pl). Departures average around one an hour. The journey from Kraków to the station Wieliczka Rynek takes about 25 minutes.

BY BUS/MINIBUS The quickest way by bus is to grab one of the minibuses that depart for Wieliczka every few minutes from bus stops near the main train station and at stops on Pawia and Dietla streets (at the corner of Dietla St. and Starowiślna). Tell the driver where you want to go and purchase tickets from him or her. In Wieliczka, leave the bus at the corner of Dembowskiego and Daniłowicza streets. Alternatively, take bus no. 304 that leaves from the Krakowska Galeria shopping center close to the train station.

BY CAR It takes about 20 minutes to drive to the suburb of Wieliczka from the center of Kraków in light traffic. Follow route E40 in the direction of Tarnów and turn right following signs to Wieliczka. Direction signs will guide you to parking lots around the mine.

Top Attraction

Wieliczka Salt Mine (Kopalnia Soli Wieliczka) ★★★ ☺ Salt has been mined here for around 1,000 years, and the oldest shafts date from the 13th century. In the Middle Ages, salt was a highly sought-after commodity, and much of the splendor of Kraków was financed by the white powder mined here. Commercial mining has since been abandoned, and the only salt extracted here now is sold to visitors. The tour takes about 2 hours and begins with a long descent into the mine on foot. The tour takes you down about 130m (427 ft.), but the mine itself is much deeper, going to a depth of some 300m (984 ft.). The highlights of the tour include hundreds of statues sculpted by the miners over the years, as well as underground lakes and incredibly ornate chambers and chapels, the most impressive of these being the Chapel of St. Kinga. Visits are by guided tour only. Polish-language tours run throughout the day; English-language tours are less frequent but still often enough (at least, in summer) that you won't have to wait very long (the last English tour is at 6pm). In winter, English-language tours are provided hourly from 9am to 5pm. Be sure to pack a sweater since it's cool down there, and wear comfortable shoes for climbing stairs. Claustrophobics should obviously think twice, but mild cases shouldn't have any problem, since the chapels and tunnels are large and well ventilated.

Daniłowicza 10 (Wieliczka). ✆ **12/278-73-02.** www.kopalnia.pl. 65 zł adults (w/English-language guided tour); 181 zł families. Mid-Apr to mid-Oct daily 7:30am–7:30pm; mid-Oct to mid-Apr Tues–Sun 8am–5pm.

Outdoor Activities

IN & AROUND KRAKÓW

WALKING/HIKING A great walk in the green that will take a good hour at a leisurely pace is simply to stroll the length of the Planty, making a full circle around Kraków's Old Town. There are plenty of benches to take a break and people-watch. For more adventurous outings in the wild, try **Las Wolski (Wolski Woods),** a forested area west of the city center between the street Królowej Jadwigi and the Vistula River. There are around half a dozen walking trails here, as well as cycling paths. Here, you'll find the **Kraków Zoo** ☺ (Kasa Oszczędności Miasta Krakowa 14; ✆ **12/425-35-51;** www.zoo-krakow.pl; 15 zł adults, 8 zł children; spring–fall daily 9am–5pm, winter daily 9am–3pm), with its impressive collection of exotic animals, including a rare herd of pygmy hippos. It's also home to the **Piłsudski Mound,** an artificial hill built to commemorate Poland's interwar leader Józef Piłsudski. If memorial mounds are your thing, Kraków's most interesting mound stands about 4km (2½ miles) from the city center and makes for a restorative jaunt out of the center. The **Kościuszko Mound (Kopiec Kościuszki),** honoring Polish war hero (and American Revolutionary War hero) Tadeusz Kościuszko, was built in the 1820s and has recently been restored. You can walk to the top of the mound for good views over the city and countryside.

CYCLING Biking is becoming increasingly popular, and the Tourist Information Office has free bike maps (*Mapa Szlakow Rowerowych Krakowa;* in Polish only) showing the best runs, including several bike trails along the Vistula River and through the park, the Planty, that rings the main square. One of the most popular daytrips follows the Vistula to the west about 14km (8¾ miles) to the village of Tyniec. That said, given the city's heavy traffic, for novices, biking is a better bet for an hour or two of sightseeing, rather than as a practical means for getting around. **"Cruising Kraków"** bike tours (ul. Basztowa 17; ✆ **514/556-017;** www.cruisingkrakow.com) offers fun and instructional 2-hour city bike tours in summer in the afternoons and evenings. They also rent bikes and conduct longer trips, including a trip to Tyniec.

GOLF **The Royal Kraków Golf & Country Club** (Ochmanów 124; ✆ **12/281-91-70;** www.krakowgolf.pl), in the village of Ochmanów, between Wieliczka and Niepołomice, is 18km (11 miles) from Kraków's city center and advertises itself as the city's nearest golf course. It has 9 holes and plans eventually to add another 9 holes. Greens fees start at 95 zł on weekdays and 110 zł on weekends.

SWIMMING **The Kraków Aqua Park (Park Wodny)** ☺ (Dobrego Pasterza 126; ✆ **12/616-31-90;** www.parkwodny.pl; 40 zł adults, 32 zł children; family discounts available; daily 8am–10pm) is Poland's biggest water park, with a giant indoor pool and huge water slides, as well as a sauna and spa. It's a great outing for kids in hot or cold weather, especially when the thought of yet another crowded museum brings howls of protest.

TENNIS The best place for tennis relatively close to town is the **Eskada Sports and Recreational Center** (Szuwarowa 1; ✆ **12/262-76-47**). Phone ahead to reserve courts a day in advance.

SPECTATOR SPORTS Football (soccer) is far and away Poland's biggest spectator sport, and Kraków is home to one of the country's biggest clubs: **Wisła Kraków** (stadium: ul. Reymonta 22; www.wisla.krakow.pl). Wisła traditionally challenges for the top of the first division, and taking in a match can be a real treat—especially if the opponent is archrival Legia Warszawa from Warsaw. Consult the website for game times. Buy tickets at the stadium at the sector B ticket window or at all ticket offices on game days 2 hours before game times. You'll need to show a photo ID to buy a ticket. You can get to the stadium on public transportation (trams 15 or 18; stop: "Reymana").

AUSCHWITZ-BIRKENAU (OŚWIĘCIM)

A trip to Kraków provides an excellent opportunity to visit the former Nazi concentration and extermination camps at Auschwitz (*Oświęcim* in Polish) and Birkenau. The camps lie about 80km (50 miles) to the west of the city and can be visited in an easy daytrip. Getting there is relatively straightforward. There are regular train and minibus services that make the journey in about 90 minutes. Additionally, several tourist agencies run coach tours; these usually include transportation from Kraków's main square and an English-language guide once you've arrived at the camps (see "Customized Tours," on p. 136). If you're not completely up on your WWII history, this is one place where taking a guided tour makes sense to get the most out of the experience.

Getting there may be easy, but taking in the experience is anything but. Auschwitz-Birkenau was Nazi Germany's most notorious death camp and has come to be seen as a symbol of the Holocaust itself. The exhibits are in turn shocking and profoundly depressing. At the end of the day, as you're slogging through the immense open fields at Birkenau, where hundreds of thousands of Jews, as well as Poles, POWs, and political prisoners of many nationalities, were held before meeting their ends in gas chambers just yards away, you'll find yourself wallowing in a mix of despair and disgust. Kraków's colorful square, filled with people laughing over their coffees, seems a million miles away.

At the same time, there are powerful reasons for coming here, including bearing witness to this epic human tragedy. Alongside the exhibits of yards of human hair of the victims or empty canisters of Zyklon-B gas that was used as the killing agent, you'll also see rows and rows of photographs of those who died here and learn part of the story of where they came from, how they got here, and what they went through. It's no exaggeration to say this is likely to be the most moving experience you'll have in Poland, and the impressions you form here will last a lifetime. That said, Auschwitz is no place for children. If you're traveling with children younger than 14 or so, it's best to skip the camps altogether.

Essentials

GETTING THERE

Getting to Auschwitz from either Kraków or Katowice is easy. From Kraków, several operators run guided tours in English to the camps (see "Customized Tours," earlier in this chapter), and trains and minibuses make the 90-minute trip several times a day. The Kraków tourist information offices can supply complete information and even book seats on the tours.

BY TRAIN Trains to Oświęcim (Auschwitz) leave from Kraków's main station and deposit you at Oświęcim station, which lies about 15 minutes by foot to the Auschwitz museum entrance. From Katowice, there are four trains daily, but be sure to check departure times. The journey takes about an hour.

BY BUS Minibuses leave from and return to Kraków's main bus terminal, situated just behind the train station. The buses have the advantage of dropping you off at the front entrance to the Auschwitz museum. Buses cost about 18 zł per person round-trip.

BY CAR From Kraków, it's an easy 90-minute drive. Find the main A4 highway in the direction of Katowice. Turn south at the Czarnów exit and follow the signs first to Oświęcim and, once in town, to "Auschwitz Museum." From Katowice, the drive takes around 45 minutes. There's plenty of paid parking near the museum. At the entrance, parking attendants will guide you to a free spot.

VISITOR INFORMATION

There's a small book kiosk inside the main entrance to the Auschwitz museum where you can buy booklets and maps to self-guide your way through the camps. Otherwise, there's not much on-site provision for visitors. It's best to stock up on info at one of Kraków's tourist information centers. The **Austeria** bookstore (Józefa 38; ✆ **12/430-68-89**) in Kazimierz, next to the High Synagogue, is an excellent source of information and books on Auschwitz and the Holocaust.

GETTING AROUND

The two main camps, Auschwitz and Birkenau, are about 2.5km (1½ miles) apart. It takes about 30 minutes to walk from one to the other. Alternatively, the museum runs free shuttle buses between the two camps. The timetable is posted at the stop outside the main entrance; the buses run about once an hour in both directions (less frequently in winter). A cab ride between the two camps will cost you about 15 zł.

Top Attractions

Auschwitz-Birkenau State Museum (Auschwitz-Birkenau Concentration Camp) ★★★ Whatever you've read or heard about the Nazi death camps, nothing is likely to prepare you for the shock of seeing them in person. Auschwitz is the best known of the two, though it's at Birkenau, south of Auschwitz, where you really see and feel the sheer scale of the atrocities. The precise number of deaths at the camps is unclear, but well over a million people were systematically killed in the gas chambers, or were hanged or shot or died of disease or exhaustion. Most of the victims were Jews, brought here from 1941 to 1944 from all around Europe, stuffed into rail cattle cars. In addition to Jews, thousands of POWs, including many Poles, Russians, and Gypsies (Roma), were exterminated here, too.

Most visitors start their exploration of the camps at Auschwitz, the first of three main concentration/extermination camps built in the area. (The third, Monowitz, was situated in a suburb of Oświęcim; it was abandoned after the war, and now all that's left is an open field. This is the camp where acclaimed writer Primo Levi, author of *Survival in Auschwitz* [Orion Press], was held.)

Auschwitz got its start in 1940, when the Germans requisitioned a former Polish garrison town, Oświęcim, for the purpose of establishing a prisoner-of-war camp. The first groups of detainees included Polish political prisoners and Russian POWs. Conditions were appalling, and in the first year alone, nearly all of the several thousand Russian POWs died of exhaustion and malnutrition. It was only later—in 1942, after the Germans decided on a policy of exterminating Europe's Jewish population—that Auschwitz became primarily a death camp for Europe's Jewry.

Admission to the Auschwitz museum is free, and you're allowed to roam the camp grounds at will, taking in the atrocities at your own pace. (If you're not employing a guide, be sure to pick up a copy of the *Auschwitz-Birkenau Guidebook* for 4 zł, available at the small kiosk at the museum entrance. This booklet contains short explanations of the main sites and maps of the camps.) On entering the museum, you'll first have the chance to see a horrific 15-minute film of the liberation of the camp by the Soviet soldiers in early 1945. The film is offered in several languages, with English showings once every 90 minutes or so (if you miss a showing, you can always come back to see it later). After that, you walk through the camp gates—passing below Auschwitz's infamous motto Arbeit Macht Frei (loosely translated as: Through Work, Freedom). Once inside, the buildings and barracks are given over to various exhibitions and displays.

Don't miss the exhibition at Block No. 4, "On Extermination." It's here where you'll see photos and descriptions of the system of rail transports, the brutal "selection" process to determine which of the new arrivals would go straight to the gas chambers and which would get a temporary reprieve to work, as well as the mechanics of the gas chambers. You'll also see actual canisters of the Zyklon-B gas used, and, in one particularly gruesome window display, yards and yards of human hair used to make rugs and textiles. Block No. 11 is called the "Death Block"; it's where prisoners were flogged and executed. Other blocks house national exhibitions, with particularly moving presentations from Poland, Hungary, and the Czech and Slovak republics (Block 16).

Birkenau, also known as Auschwitz II, lies about 2.5km (1½ miles) to the south. It's larger, more open, and even (if possible) more ghastly than Auschwitz. It's here where most of the mass gas-chamber exterminations took place at one of the four gas chambers located at the back of the camp. To get to Birkenau, take a free shuttle bus situated not far from the main entrance. You can also walk (about 20 minutes) or take a taxi (around 10 zł–15 zł, but agree on a price in advance).

Birkenau appears almost untouched from how it looked in 1945. Your first sight of the camp will be of the main gate, the "Gate of Death." The trains ran through this entryway. The passengers were unloaded onto the platforms, where they were examined by Nazi SS doctors and their belongings confiscated. About 30% were chosen to work in the camp and the rest—mainly women and children—were sent directly to the gas chambers, just a short walk away. The scale is overwhelming—prisoner blocks laid out as far as the eye can see. There are no films here and few resources for visitors (including no public restrooms). Instead, set aside an hour or so to walk around the camp to take it in. Don't miss the remains of the gas chambers situated toward the back of the camp, just to the right of the memorial to the Holocaust victims. The Germans themselves attempted to destroy the gas chambers at the end of 1944 and early 1945 to cover up their crimes once it was apparent the war could not be won. Now, little remains of them (but enough to get the general, gruesome idea). You can return to the main Auschwitz museum by foot, shuttle bus, or taxi, and from Auschwitz back to Kraków by bus or train.

Panstwowe Muzeum Auschwitz-Birkenau. ✆ **033/843-20-22.** www.auschwitz.org.pl. Free admission; groups of 10 or more required to rent an audio headphone (4 zł each), guided tours in English 39 zł per person. Open June–Aug 8am–7pm, May & Sept 8am–6pm, Apr & Oct 8am–5pm, Mar & Nov 8am–4pm, Dec–Feb 8am–3pm; Guided tours in English at 10, 11am, & 1 pm.

Auschwitz Jewish Center ★ This small museum and cultural center, located in the heart of Oświęcim town just off the central *rynek,* is certainly worth an hour or two to contemplate Jewish life in Oświęcim before the Holocaust put a sudden and brutal end to it. Prior to World War II, Oświęcim was a largely Jewish town, with Jews making up around half the population and having a preponderant influence on the town's affairs. The small permanent collection here documents Jewish life from the 16th century up until the Nazis torched the town's Great Synagogue in November 1939. Only a handful of the town's 7,000 Jews survived the war, many tragically perishing in crematoria located only a couple of miles from their homes.

Pl. Ks. Jana Skarbka 5. ✆ **033/844-70-02.** www.ajcf.org. 6 zł adults. Nov–Feb 8:30am–6pm; Mar–Oct 8:30am–8pm.

Where to Stay & Dine

In deference to the victims of the camp and because of efforts to limit the commercialization of Auschwitz, there are few places to eat or stay within easy walking distance of the main museum. There's a small, substandard canteen just to the right of the main entrance where you can get soup and sausages. Across the street, near one of the main parking areas, is a small strip of generic fast-food outlets that serve hamburgers, sandwiches, salads, and pizza that will do in a pinch. For something better, you'll have to drive, walk, or take a taxi.

Hotel Galicja ★★ Only a small percentage of visitors to Auschwitz choose to stay the night. This cheerful, reconverted 3-star villa, about 4km (2½ miles) from the Auschwitz state museum, is easily the best option in town. The rooms are plain, but the facilities are spotless and the reception desk helpful and friendly. There's secure parking in front of the building. The Galicja is also arguably the best place to eat in town. Two in-house restaurants, one serving traditional Polish food and the other pizza and pastas, are much better than anything near the museum.

Dąbrowskiego 119. ✆ **33/843-61-15.** Fax 33/843-61-16. www.hotelgalicja.com. 32 units. 220 zł double. AE, DC, MC, V. **Amenities:** 2 restaurants; room service. *In room:* A/C (in some), TV, Internet (free).

ZAKOPANE & THE TATRA NATIONAL PARK

Zakopane (pronounced *zah-koh-pah-neh*), in the foothills of the High Tatra Mountains, is Poland's leading mountain resort. It's absolutely mobbed during the winter ski season, so advance preparations are in order if you're coming from late December through March. The summer hiking season is also busy, especially in August, when the town hosts an annual folklore festival, though it's not quite as overrun as in winter. During the rest of the year, it's possible to sense some of the beauty and rustic charm that first began drawing artists and holidaymakers here in the 19th century.

Zakopane plays a role in Poland's literary and cultural history that may be unprecedented as far as mountain resorts go. In the late 19th and early 20th centuries, members of Poland's intellectual elite decamped here in a bid no less ambitious than to reinvent, or at least reinterpret, Polish culture. Many of the country's leading young writers, poets, painters, and architects gathered here and found something uniquely Polish in the unspoiled nature and solid mountain cottages of simple people.

The two world wars and the decades of Communism that followed put an end to the Zakopane art colony, but some of that special, funky feeling remains. Certainly, the huge wooden 19th-century houses here—known throughout Poland as the "Zakopane style"—are some of the most beautiful you'll see anywhere. And in and among the trees and the gardens—and away from the crowds—you can still find traces of a uniquely Polish resort that feels very much of a different age.

Zakopane has three main "seasons." The most important is over Christmas and New Year's, when it can feel like half of Poland has descended for a week-long after-Christmas party. Hotel reservations are nearly impossible to get, and rates are jacked up to the stratosphere. If you feel like this might be for you, be sure to reserve months in advance. Ski season runs from January through March and can be almost as crowded as Christmas. Summer walking season starts in June and runs through mid-September. Hotel rates are still high, but the crowds are less oppressive. The best time to come to have the mountains to yourself is in May or October. The air can be chilly, but the paths are blissfully free of tour groups. Bear in mind, though, that the trails on the highest elevations, including the trails that run across the mountain to Slovakia, are closed from November to mid-June.

Essentials

GETTING THERE

BY TRAIN Zakopane's tiny train station **Zakopane PKP** (Chramcówki 35; ✆ **18/201-50-31**) is centrally located but practically useless. Most visitors come here from Kraków, and the bus is simply much quicker.

BY BUS Several bus companies make the 2-hour trip from Kraków's main bus station to Zakopane's main station, **Zakopane PKS** (Nowotarska 24; ✆ **18/201-46-03** [information]), at near-hourly intervals throughout the day. One of the leading bus companies for trips to Zakopane is **Szwagropol** (ul. Kościuszki 19a; ✆ **18/201-71-23;** www.szwagropol.eu). It offers 18 departures daily to and from Kraków. Tickets are 18 zł each way. You can buy tickets at the station window or directly from the driver.

BY CAR It takes about 2 hours to drive the 100km (62 miles) from Kraków. It's mostly a straight shot south, following signs first to Nowy Targ and then Zakopane. Be sure to watch weather conditions. It can be sunny and warm in Kraków but completely snow-covered in Zakopane, so be sure to have winter tires and antifreeze.

GETTING AROUND

Central Zakopane is fairly compact and partly closed to car traffic, so walking is the only option for getting around. The town itself, though, spreads out a couple miles in both directions, so if you're staying outside the center (and don't have a car), you'll have to rely on taxis or local buses to get around. The main taxi stand is conveniently located just outside the main bus and train terminals. Bikes are another option in summer, but ask at the Tourist Information Office, since rental agencies change from season to season.

TOURIST INFORMATION

You will be surprised by the sheer number of private tourist agencies offering everything from information to accommodation, lift tickets, and day trips. Zakopane's small **Tourist Information Center** (**Centrum Informacji Turystycznej;** Kościuszki 17; ✆ **18/201-22-11;** www.promocja.zakopane.pl) can help with general orientation questions and provide maps, but that's about it. A private agency, **Zwyrtozłka,** two doors down toward town (Kościuszki 15; ✆ **18/201-52-12**), maintains a list of rooms. Both agencies can help arrange day trips, including excursions to Slovakia, as well as sell lift passes and advise on things like ski and bike rental.

Top Attractions

Krupówki merits about an hour's stroll, end to end. Toward the northern end of Krupówki (downhill), follow Kościeliska to the left for a couple of blocks to see two of the town's most interesting sites. One is a tiny wooden church, the **Church of St. Clement;** the other is the adjoining **cemetery,** with some of the most ornately carved wooden headstones you're likely ever to see. Look especially for the highly stylized totem pole that marks the grave of Stanisław Witkiewicz (see below), the architect who first set off the local craze for all things wooden.

Museum of Zakopane Style (Muzeum Stylu Zakopańskiego) ★★ Just beyond the wooden church and cemetery is the Villa Koliba, home to a small museum dedicated to the Zakopane style of wooden homes and a tribute to the work of Polish architect Stanisław Witkiewicz. The villa dates from 1894 and was the first to be built in this style, roughly Poland's equivalent of the "Arts and Crafts" movement in the U.S. and Britain. One of the draws here is simply the chance to walk around one of these big old houses, but there are also plenty of interesting examples of ornately carved furniture and accessories. Upstairs, there's a small gallery of the freaky and fascinating 1920s society portraits by Witkiewicz's son, Witkacy. He was portraitist of choice for Poland's Lost Generation.

Kościeliska 18. ✆ **18/201-36-02.** www.muzeumtatrzanskie.com.pl. Admission 6 zł adults. A Wed–Sat 9am–5pm; Sun 9am–3pm.

Tatra Museum (Muzeum Tatrzańskie) ☺ This museum is a bit of a disappointment. There's not much information in English, so you're not likely to get much out of this exhibition of the personalities and events that have shaped Zakopane and the Tatras down through the ages. Still, there are some interesting displays of folk architecture and costumes on the ground floor. Children will like the stuffed animals on the second floor.

Krupówki 10. ✆ **18/201-52-01.** www.muzeumtatrzanskie.com.pl. Admission 7 zł. Wed–Sat 9am–5pm; Sun 9am–3pm.

Exploring the High Tatras

The real joy of any fair-weather visit to the Tatras is the chance to get out into the mountains. Even though Zakopane can get pretty crowded, it doesn't take long to put the throng behind you. One good out-and-back hike of about 4 hours of moderate to heavy exertion and some awesome views begins from just behind the Hotel Belvedere, about 2km (1¼ miles) from the center. Begin by following the yellow-marked path that cuts through the Biała Valley (Dolina Białego). After about a 90-minute ascent, turn onto the black trail, following the signs for Stążyska Polana, and returning to Zakopane via the red trail along the Stążyska Valley. The walk will leave you about 3km (1¾ miles) from the center. Be sure to take along plenty of water, some snacks, sunscreen, boots or walking shoes, and rain gear (you never know what kind of weather you're going to get). A less-demanding walk, and one that is very popular with the masses, follows the red-marked trail to Morskie Oko, the largest of the Alpine lakes, in the far southern corner of Poland's share of the High Tatras. Many travel agencies in town offer packages that include transportation to the trail head to the east of Zakopane, but once you get off the bus, you'll have to walk or take a horse-drawn cart the 9km (5½ miles) uphill to the lake.

Outdoor Activities

HIKING Zakopane has plenty of hikes for walkers of all abilities and fitness levels. Many of the trails lead off just a short distance from the center of town. The trails are clearly marked, and good hiking maps are available from the tourist information office or shops around town that specialize in hiking equipment. Keep in mind that these are mountains and treat them accordingly: Get an early start, pack plenty of water and sunscreen, and start heading down the mountain at the first sign of an afternoon thunderstorm. For more ambitious climbs, guides are available from the **Polish Association of Mountain Guides** (Polskie Stowarzyszenie Przewodników Wysokogórskich; Droga na Wierch 4; www.pspw.pl in Polish only). On the website, you'll find a list of guides, with a photo and a telephone number for each. Individual guides start at daily rates of around 800 zł for one person and 900 zł for two. You can also sign up for one of the guided walking tours or extreme hiking tours offered by **Zakopane Tours** (www.zakopane-tours.com).

CYCLING Not surprisingly, in recent years, Zakopane has become increasingly popular with mountain bikers, and a network of cycling trails now complements the hiking trails. Biking is also a good way to get around in nice weather, since the resort is spread out and walking from place to place can take a lot of time. Check in with one of the tourist information offices for rental information and to buy a cycling map.

SKIING In winter, the most popular hill for skiing is Kasprowy Wierch (1,987m/6,519 ft.); several slopes of all difficulty levels start here. The cable-car operator **Polskie Koleje Linowe** has an excellent website (✆ **18/201-45-10;** www.pkl.pl) listing prices and timetables for lifts and cable cars, and also for the funicular to another popular destination, Gubałkowa. To reach it, take a bus from Zakopane to Kuźnice, and then go by cable car to the peak. The **Harenda** ski area (Harenda 63; ✆ **18/202-56-80;** www.harendazakopane.pl) is small but has several lifts and a snow park for boarding. **Nosal** (Balzera 30; ✆ **18/206-27-00;** www.nosal.pl) is another popular ski area, with ski rentals and a highly recommended ski school for beginners.

RAFTING ☺ Zakopane is a good base for rafting the Dunajec River, which runs through a gorge in the Pieniny mountains east of the Tatras along the border with Slovakia. Dunajec is about 60km (37 miles) from Zakopane and the drive/bus ride takes around an hour. Rafting season runs from April through October, and on a sunny afternoon this can be a fabulous day out, especially for kids. It's less whitewater rafting and more of a slow, gentle float down the river on group rafts manned by Górale mountain men kitted out in their traditional folk garb. The boating center on the Polish side is at Sromowce Kąty. For information, contact the main organizer, the unpronounceable **Polskie Stowarzyszenie Flisaków Pienińskich-Biuro Spływu** (✆ **18/262-97-21;** www.flisacy.com.pl). Prices start around 50 zł per person. Alternatively, the **Info-Tour** travel agency (Kościeliska 11b; ✆ **18/206-42-64**) is one of several agencies in Zakopane that can arrange rafting trips, including transportation, for about 120 zł a person.

Where to Stay

Hotel rates in Zakopane are high, and this is one town in Poland where you may want seriously to consider staying in a pension or private room. These abound. If you arrive in town early, simply walk around and inquire where you see signs saying Wolny

Pokoje or Noclegi. Or try **Info-Tour** (Kościeliska 11b; ✆ **18/206-42-64;** www.info-tour.zakopane.pl), which can help book private rooms and pensions. Expect to pay about 60-80 zł a person for a private room. Hotel and room rates rise considerably in the week between Christmas and New Year's. Aside from that, January, February, and August are the busiest times of the year, and pre-booking is essential. The rates below are for summer and winter season, outside of the Christmas and New Year period.

VERY EXPENSIVE

Hotel Belvedere ★★ This 1920s-era mountain resort is one of the classiest places to stay in Zakopane. The "Jazz Age" ambience is updated with extras like a Roman spa and a game room, as well as a bowling alley and other more modern pursuits. The in-house restaurant is top notch. The real advantage is the hotel's location, just where the mountains start, about 2km (1¼ miles) outside the center. That makes it a 10- to 15-minute walk down to Krupówki but means you can also escape the masses and enjoy the mountains if you want. One of the nicest hiking trails along the Biała river valley starts just above the hotel's doors. Discounted room rates are frequently available on the hotel's website.

Droga do Białego 3. ✆ **18/202-02-11.** Fax 18/202-12-50. www.belvederehotel.pl. 174 units. 600 zł double. AE, DC, MC, V. **Amenities:** Restaurant; bike rental; concierge; indoor pool; room service; spa. *In room:* A/C, TV, hair dryer, Internet (free), minibar.

Hotel Litwor ★ A luxury hotel occupying a handsome mountain chalet that admittedly looks a little out of place in the middle of busy Krupówki Street. When it opened in 1999, the hotel claimed to be the first 4-star hotel in this part of Poland. Certainly it's still one of the best in town, but the Belvedere offers more of a feeling of exclusivity, and the Grand Hotel Stamary is arguably smarter than both. The rooms are well-proportioned and furnished in contemporary browns and blues. Ask for one with a view to the mountains. Wi-Fi access is available throughout the hotel.

Krupówki 40. ✆ **18/202-02-55.** Fax 18/202-42-05. www.litwor.pl. 57 units. 600 zł double. AE, DC, MC, V. **Amenities:** Restaurant; bike rental; concierge; fitness room; indoor pool; limited room service; spa. *In room:* A/C, TV, hair dryer, minibar.

EXPENSIVE

Grand Hotel Stamary ★★★ This beautifully restored turn-of-the-century manor hotel quickly whisks you away to the stylish 1920s and '30s with its elegant lobby and cocktail bar, and wide corridors with dark-wood flooring. The period detailing extends to the rooms, furnished in browns and golds. The location is superb, just a short walk toward the center from the bus terminal. The main pedestrian street, Krupówki, is about 183m (600 ft.) down the street—near enough to be convenient but far enough to be away from the commotion. The spa has an indoor pool and Jacuzzi.

Kościuszki 19. ✆ **18/202-45-10.** Fax 18/202-45-19. www.stamary.pl. 53 units. 580 zł double. AE, DC, MC, V. **Amenities:** Restaurant; fitness center; indoor pool; spa. *In room:* A/C, TV, hair dryer, Internet, minibar.

Hotel Villa Marilor ★★ Occupying a sprawling cream-colored villa just across the street from the Grand Hotel Stamary, this is another contender for "nicest place to stay in Zakopane." Peace and quiet is what they're offering here, and once you step onto the beautiful grounds, you won't hear a sound. Everything feels refined, from the chandeliers and marble-topped desks in the lobby to the nicely sized rooms, furnished in late–19th-century style. The hotel offers special rooms for people with disabilities. Wi-Fi access is available throughout the hotel and in the garden. Room rates are discounted for stays of longer than 4 nights.

Kościuszki 18. ✆ **18/200-06-70.** Fax 18/206-44-10. www.hotelmarilor.com. 35 units. 580 zł double. AE, DC, MC, V. **Amenities:** Restaurant; concierge; fitness center; room service; spa; outdoor tennis court; Wi-Fi (free). *In room:* A/C, TV, hair dryer, Internet, minibar.

MODERATE

Hotel Gromada ★ This utilitarian, 1960s-era high-rise offers amenities like a spa and fitness room at rates about half those of the competition. The rooms are boxy, but clean and comfortable. Ask for a room away from the busy street. The location is central, just a couple steps off Krupówki. It tends to fill up fast, so book in advance. The reception says the hotel is due for a makeover, so some of the facilities may be updated by the time you arrive.

Zaruskiego 2. ✆ **18/201-50-11.** Fax 18/201-53-30. 55 units. 230 zł double. AE, DC, MC, V. **Amenities:** Restaurant; fitness room; sauna (w/salt grotto). *In room:* TV, hair dryer.

Sabala ★★ This traditional inn—dating from the end of the 19th century and built from hefty wooden logs—is a nice trade-off between the upper end (and practically unaffordable) luxury hotels in town and a pension. The wood-beamed rooms are plainly furnished but have the solid feel of a mountain chalet. The beds are big and comfortable, covered with thick wool comforters. There's a decent restaurant downstairs, and the location is good both for accessing the slopes and hitting Krupówki's shops and bars.

Krupówki 11. ✆ **18/201-50-92.** Fax 18/201-50-93. www.sabala.zakopane.pl. 51 units. Winter ski season 420 zł double; off-season 350 zł double. AE, DC, MC, V. **Amenities:** Restaurant. *In room:* TV, hair dryer, Internet.

INEXPENSIVE

Pensjonat Szarotka ★★ This small, eccentric 1930s villa feels more in harmony with Zakopane's artistic past. The pension is not far from the Belvedere, about 2km (1¼ miles) out of the center of town, and close to the Biała valley hiking trail. The squeaky stairways, the cozy little reading room with a fireplace, and the evocative black-and-white photos on the wall will remind you of your grandmother's house. The lovely 1930s breakfast nook is a real treat. On the downside, the rooms are tiny and crammed together (how did they carve 17 rooms out of this house?). Still, for the money, the atmosphere, and the location, it can't be beat.

Male Zywczańskie 16a. ✆ **18/206-40-50.** Fax 18/201-48-02. www.szarotka.pl. 17 units. 180 zł double. No credit cards. **Amenities:** Restaurant. *In room:* TV.

Where to Dine

Zakopane has no shortage of places to eat, but it could certainly use a few more *good* places to eat. Most restaurants are decked out in wood, with carved wooden tables and animal skins and wrought iron everything-but-the-kitchen-sink affixed to the walls. The servers are made up to look like mountain folk, and you might even get a folk band to accompany your meal. This is all great, but in practice, it often means that little attention is paid to the food. Most of the restaurants are situated in the center, on or near Krupówki.

VERY EXPENSIVE

Mała Szwajcaria ★★ SWISS The mountain setting is a good fit for the fondues, savory crepes, and other hearty Swiss dishes offered here at this high-end chalet restaurant. Main courses like grilled lamb chops and roast veal with mushrooms provide a welcome change of pace from the bland Polish cooking served at most Zakopane restaurants. And the tasteful interior—with flowers and white linens—is a world away from the Disney World–esque kitsch of "traditional" taverns that have sprung up all over town in the past couple of years.

Zamoyskiego 11. ✆ **18/210-20-76.** Main courses 30 zł -40 zł. No credit cards. Daily 11am-10pm.

EXPENSIVE

Kolorowe ★ POLISH Similar in attitude but perhaps slightly quieter and more civilized than several nearby faux-rustic grill houses, the highlights here are the pork and sausage shish kebabs cooked on the grill, accompanied with live music and waitresses in full peasant regalia. They also offer pizza and other dishes, but that's more of an afterthought. Stick with the grilled meats and enjoy.

Krupówki 26. ✆ **18/150-55.** Main courses 30 zł -40 zł. No credit cards. Daily 11am-10pm.

MODERATE

Kalina ★★ POLISH The quietest and altogether most pleasant of the Polish-style restaurants on Krupówki is certainly worth seeking out. Here, the folklore element is low-key. You won't always find live music, but as compensation, you'll get a cook who pays more attention to what's on the plate and some alternatives to grilled pork, like decent pierogi and roast duck. The interior is done up in traditional cottage style, meaning intricately carved woodworking, wood-beamed ceilings, and a nice warm fire.

Krupówki 46. ✆ **18/201-26-50.** Main courses 25 zł -30 zł. No credit cards. Daily 11am-10pm.

Pstrąg Górski ★★ SEAFOOD This popular little spot just off the main drag specializes in grilled river fish, especially—as the name suggests—trout *(pstrąg)*. It's a good choice for a nice lunch or a light early meal. In addition to fish dishes, they also have a full range of grilled meats. In summer, eat on the covered terrace overlooking the throngs on Krupówki.

Krupówki 6a. ✆ **18/206-41-63.** Main courses 25 zł -30 zł. AE, DC, MC, V. Daily 11am-10pm.

Soprano ★ ITALIAN If you're not in the mood for grilled meats and traditional food, you can still find pretty decent pizza around. Arguably the best is served here at Soprano, which offers the standard combinations, but also has healthier options, like broccoli and fresh spinach toppings. Sit out on the terrace and enjoy the view, or have a quieter, candlelit pizza in the back.

Krupówki 49. ✆ **18/201-54-43.** Main courses 25 zł-30 zł. No credit cards. Daily 11am-10pm.

INEXPENSIVE

Pizza Dominium ITALIAN Not as good as Soprano, but cheaper and quicker, Dominium is a popular and successful Polish pizza chain going head-to-head with titans like Pizza Hut. The locals have the advantage with thick-crust pizza and fresh ingredients. There's another branch at 2,000m (6,562 ft.) on the peak at Kasprowy Wierch, if you happen to end up there.

Krupówki 51. ✆ **18/540-89-98.** Main courses 20 zł-5 zł. No credit cards. Daily 11am-10pm.

Shopping

Krupówki is jammed wall-to-wall with souvenir shops, gold and silver dealers, and outdoor outfitters, all competing for your attention with a jumble of cafes, restaurants, pizza joints, and refreshment stands. Just about everything you might need, you'll find along this busy 5 or 6 blocks. Most of the gift and souvenir stores peddle in the same sorts of imported, mass-produced junk—wooden toys, T-shirts, hats and scarves, and mock traditional clothing—that sadly have little connection to Zakopane. For something more authentic, try looking in at **Cepelia,** with two locations on Krupówki (nos. 2 and 48; ✆ **18/201-50-48**). Here, you'll find locally produced carved wooden boxes, animal pelts, leather goods, and the odd knickknack or two. **Art Gallery Yam** (Krupówki 63; ✆ **18/206-69-84**) is about as funky as it gets in Zakopane. Check out the rotating exhibitions of contemporary Polish painters, some riveting modern Tatra landscapes, and other works that draw on the absurdist visual style of Polish art in the 1970s and '80s.

One souvenir you won't be able to miss are those little rounds of sheep's milk cheese, ***oscypek,*** that you see everywhere around town. The recipe apparently goes back some 500 years. The salty cheese goes great with beer.

After Dark

Café Piano Just next to Art Gallery Yam, the cafe draws on its neighbors artistic funkiness for its laid-back, hipster feel. Though it's just down a small alley from the Krupówki throng, it's a world away in attitude. Krupówki 63 (in the little alleyway). No phone. Daily 4pm–midnight.

Paparazzi This local outlet of a regional chain of cocktail bar/nightclubs occupies a beautiful creek-side location and is *the* after-hours spot in town for a cold beer or glass of wine. It also offers passable versions of global dishes like chicken burritos and Caesar salads. Ul. Gen. Galicy 8. ✆ **18/206-32-51.** Daily noon–1am.

TARNÓW

If you're not planning on traveling onward to Zamość (see p. 181), the town of Tarnów (pronounced *tar-nohv*), about 80km (50 miles) east of Kraków, is probably your best opportunity to see a well-preserved example of Renaissance town planning as practiced in the 16th century. Borrowing from the Classical period, the idea behind Renaissance town design was to achieve balance and harmony through symmetry. In Tarnów's case, that resulted in an oval-shaped Old Town, with the Rynek and Town Hall (Ratusz) at the center, and main arteries radiating from there. Each part of town was given over to a specific purpose, and the core surrounded by walls and fortifications.

Tarnów is not as well preserved as Zamość. Part of the town walls were pulled down over the years and insensitive new buildings intrude on the overall effect, but enough of the older structures, including the dominant Town Hall, remain to lend a strong impression to how life was lived in the late Middle Ages.

Tarnów is also a significant stop on Jewish heritage tours. In 1939, at the outbreak of World War II, the town's Jewish population was around 25,000, making it the fourth-largest concentration of Jews in this part of Poland, after towns like Kraków, Lublin, and Lwów. Here, as nearly everywhere else, during the war, the town's Jewish population was subjected to draconian and humiliating rules, mass killings, confinement in tightly guarded ghettoes, and finally deportations to extermination camps. There are few, if any, Jews left today, but the streets to the immediate east of the Rynek, including *Żidowska* (Jewish St.), appear little changed from the old times and still recall something of former Jewish life here.

Tarnów makes a convenient overnight stop, with good transport connections to both Kraków and Lublin. Hotel and restaurant facilities are not yet up to the highest Polish standards; but city fathers are looking to attract more visitors, and the future is certain to bring further improvements. The countryside here is especially pretty, and if you have your own wheels, it's worth heading out to the village of the Lipnica Murowana to see the UNESCO-listed St. Leonard's church.

Essentials

GETTING THERE

BY TRAIN Polish rail, PKP (✆ **14/194-36**; www.pkp.pl), operates several trains daily between Kraków's Główny station and Tarnów. The journey takes about 60 to 90 minutes, depending on the type of train. Several trains from Tarnów to Kraków continue onward to Katowice (3 hr.) and to Wrocław (6 hr.). Tarnów's rail station is about a 15-minute walk from the center on Krakowska. A taxi from here to the center will cost about 10 zł.

BY BUS Tarnów's bus station (Krakowska; ✆ **703/300-140**) is next to the train station and is about a 15-minute walk into town (or a 10 zł taxi ride). Service is good to Kraków and surrounding cities and towns.

BY CAR Tarnów is located 80km (50 miles) to the east of Kraków along the E40 international route. Figure on about 45–60 minutes behind the wheel.

GETTING AROUND

Tarnów is small, and much of the center of the city is closed to car traffic. This makes walking the only option; it also means it's almost impossible to get around in a car. If you're traveling with your own wheels, try to get as close to the center as you can, and then park the car at the first free space you see. Though you probably won't need it, public transportation is good and buses (2.30 zł) can get you around town quickly.

VISITOR INFORMATION

Tarnów's **Tourist Information Office** (Rynek 7; ✆ **14/688-90-90;** www.go-tarnow.com; Mon–Fri 8am–6pm, Sat 9am–5pm) routinely places near the top in the annual "Best Tourist Office in Poland" competition, and it's easy to see why. The staff is young, enthusiastic, and English-speaking. They have more free info on Tarnów, including a great walking map, than you'd likely need for a week's stay. What's more, they stay open until 8pm, rent bikes, and even offer cut-rate, decent accommodation in rooms located above the office (see "Where to Stay," below).

Top Attractions

Before setting off on a walking tour, pick up a handy map of the **Old Town** (Plan Starego Miasto) at the Tourist Information Office (see "Visitor Information," above). The map outlines several interesting walking tours, including the **Renaissance Trail** and **Tarnów's Jewish Trail** (look too for pamphlets in English that describe the sights along the trails). A good place to begin your exploration is naturally the main square, the Rynek. The square was first laid out in the 14th century when Tarnów acquired its town rights but was redesigned in the 16th century in Renaissance style as Tarnów reached the height of its economic and political power. The handsome **Town Hall** has been a symbol of the city for centuries since it was built at the start of the 15th century. It was closed to visitors for reconstruction at press time and was set to reopen sometime in 2011. While you're here, check at the house at

Rynek 20/21, now home to the **Tarnów Regional Museum** and considered the most attractive Renaissance town house on the square. The **Cathedral,** still in use, is a couple of minutes' walk northwest of the Rynek. It was originally built in Gothic style in the 14th century but was given a neo-Gothic makeover in the 19th century. Nearby is the highly recommended **Diocese Museum,** holding the original altar removed from the UNESCO-listed St. Leonard's church from nearby Lipnica Murowana.

The former Jewish part of the city is situated to the east of the Rynek, bounded by the present streets of Żydowska and Wekslarska. The area is still a ghetto of sorts, today housing part of the city's impoverished Roma community instead of Jews. The houses, with their narrow courtyards, still evoke the feel of the ancient Jewish quarter, and here and there you can still pick out Jewish inscriptions on the houses. Opposite Żydowska 11, look for the still-standing *bimah,* the podium from which the Torah was read and the only surviving piece of the former **"Old Synagogue"** that was burned to the ground by the Nazis on the anniversary of Kristallnacht on November 9, 1939. The former Nazi-imposed Jewish ghetto, where Jews were forced to live during the war, is situated farther to the north and east of here. Little remains of this ghetto today, but the gray, depressed housing stock still imparts a lingering sadness. The **Jewish Cemetery** (Cmentarz Żydowski) is about 15 minutes by foot northeast of the Rynek along Szpitalna and is one of the best-preserved of its kind in Poland. The several thousand graves, in varying states of repair and disrepair, are sadly all that remain of Tarnów's once-thriving Jewish community.

Tarnów Regional Museum This sleepy regional museum is worth a look inside chiefly because it occupies the most architecturally valuable building on the square, a Renaissance town house from the 16th century. The museum occasionally holds blockbuster exhibits such as the recent "Memories Saved from Fire," the story in words, pictures, and original documentation of the destruction of Tarnów's Jewry during the World War II (see "Memories Saved from Fire," below).

Rynek 20/21. ✆ **14/621-21-49.** www.muzeum.tarnow.pl. 2 zł adults. Tues–Sun 9am–4pm.

Ethnographic Museum (Muzeum Etnograficzne) ★★ This attractive museum houses a fascinating permanent exhibition of the history and culture of Europe's Roma (Gypsy) population. The exhibit traces the emergence of the Roma from parts of modern-day India some 1,000 years ago to their arrival in Europe and subsequent (mostly tragic) history, including the large-scale destruction of the Roma population by the Nazis during World War II. Outside is a colorful collection of Roma wagons.

Krakowska 10. ✆ **14/622-06-25.** www.muzeum.tarnow.pl. 5 zł adults. Tues 10am–5pm; Wed–Sat 9am–3pm; Sun 10am–2pm.

Diocesan Museum ★ This museum is the oldest of its kind in Poland, dating from 1888, and has an impressive collection of Gothic religious paintings and sculpture from the Middle Ages. The museum's most impressive holding is the original altar from the UNESCO-listed 15th-century St. Leonard's church from the nearby village of Lipnica Murowana. The altar was brought here to protect it from damage. The building that houses the museum, the Mikołajowsky House, dates from 1524 and is considered one of Tarnów's most beautiful Renaissance town houses.

Pl. Katedralny 6. ✆ **14/621-99-93.** www.muzeum.diecezja.tarnow.pl. Free admission. Tues–Sat 10am–noon & 1–3pm; Sun 9am–noon & 1–2pm.

"Memories Saved from Fire"

Tarnów is relatively rare in being one of a handful of Polish cities, including Kraków and Łódź, to actively embrace its Jewish past and begin to put the pieces together of what happened here under the Nazi occupation. A big part of that effort was a European Union–sponsored exhibition at the Tarnów Regional Museum in 2008–09 entitled "Memories Saved from Fire." The show attempted to tell the story in pictures and words, including original Nazi documentation, of the rounding up and eventual destruction of Tarnów's prewar Jewish population of 25,000.

The "Memories Saved from Fire" exhibition has unfortunately closed, but the text and photos are still available on the Web at www.msff.eu and are well worth taking a look at before or after your walk around town.

Outdoor Activities

The tourist information office can offer advice on hiking and cycling options around town, and even rent bikes. Around 20 hiking and biking trails fan out through the pretty countryside in all directions. There are also more than a dozen horseback-riding centers in the vicinity. Several offer riding lessons and group outings, including sledding in winter. For a kind of throwback Wild West experience, try the **Roleski Ranch** (✆ **0602/753-148;** www.roleskiranch.com.pl) in Stare Żukowice, about 15km (9¼ miles) north of Tarnów. They even have modest guest rooms if you'd like to spend the night.

Where to Stay

If Tarnów is ever hoping to break into big-time tourism, it could use a few more nice lodging options. For the moment, you'll have to content yourself with the properties below.

Euro Hotel U Janu ★ This hotel has a great location, right on the Rynek, with a beautiful and historic cafe-restaurant on the ground floor, and it still sports some Renaissance detailing from the 16th century. Check out the intricate doorway that links the bar and cafe. Unfortunately, much of the actual hotel part is a bit of a letdown, with only ordinary rooms and little in the way of service or amenities. The deluxe suites are nicer than the basic rooms and feature wooden floors, period beds, and views out over the Rynek. Still, the price is right for the location—and it's not that much of a step down from the much more expensive Bristol.

Rynek 14. ✆ **14/626-05-64.** www.hotelujana.pl. 11 units. 230 zł double; 330 zł suite. AE, MC, V. **Amenities:** Restaurant. *In room:* TV, Internet (free).

Hotel Bristol Tarnów's only 4-star hotel is crying out for a makeover. The 19th-century neoclassical building, on a main artery leading to the city's central square, is handsome, but the interior tends toward the gaudy. The overstuffed rooms are decorated in a heavy 1970s style—pink leather sofas and giant beds—that feels unintentionally retro. And the price tag for all this is somewhat inflated, reflecting the lack of quality accommodation in town. That said, it's clean, well run, and close to the center. All the rooms have Internet access, and there's plenty of free parking around (a relative luxury in Tarnów's Old Town).

Krakowska 9. ✆ **14/621-22-79.** http://hotelbristol.com.pl. 15 units. 320 zł double. AE, MC, V. **Amenities:** Restaurant; room service. *In room:* A/C, TV, hair dryer, Internet, minibar.

Tourist Information Office ★ Unusual for a Polish city, the tourist information office runs an informal lodging outfit, renting out the rooms above the office at some of the cheapest rates you'll find in the whole country. Don't expect luxury; rooms are modestly furnished with a bed and desk, but all are clean and have attached baths. Given the lack of a blockbuster hotel in town, this might just be the place to hunker down for a night and take it easy on the wallet. Although the tourist office claims the rooms have Wi-Fi, the signal doesn't reach very far.

Rynek 7. ✆ **14/688-90-90.** www.go-tarnow.com. 10 units. 100 zł double. AE, MC, V. *In room:* TV, Internet.

Willa Krzyska ★★ This well-maintained, refurbished former mansion is easily the city's most comfortable lodging option and one of the nicest small hotels in this part of Poland. During the week, most of the clients are businessmen, but the big backyard garden and green setting make it a good choice for families with children or anyone on a minor splurge. The rooms are smartly furnished, with warm yellow walls and big comfortable beds with thick cotton linens. The location is not ideal if you're not traveling by car, but bus no. 6 can take you from the center almost to the hotel's doors. The walk to the Old Town will take about 20 minutes. Free on-site parking and a reliable Internet connection are two big selling points. The in-house restaurant offers very good continental cooking, featuring steaks, chops and seafood. In summer, you can dine outdoors.

Krzyska 52b. ✆ **14/620-11-34.** www.willakrzyska.pl. 8 units. 240 zł double. AE, MC, V. **Amenities:** Restaurant. *In room:* A/C, TV, Internet.

Where to Dine

In warm weather, the Rynek, Tarnów's central square, morphs into one giant restaurant-cafe, with dozens of places offering a similar mix of coffee, drinks, beer, and light food. For more substantial fare, the choices are narrower. One of the best restaurants in town is at the Willa Krzyska hotel (see above).

Tatrzańska ★★ POLISH Excellent traditional Polish cooking in a refined setting that works both for a group night out or a quiet dinner for two. Main courses are inventive and well prepared. Our favorite is the potato pancake served with chicken in a sauce of mushrooms, peas, and carrots. The menu also has loads of creative salads, making this a good choice for a light meal. Finish off with a piece of fresh apple strudel served with ice cream and drizzled with chocolate.

Krakowska 1. ✆ **12/622-46-36.** Main courses 20 zł–40 zł. AE, DC, MC, V. Daily 9am–10pm.

LUBLIN & SOUTHEASTERN POLAND

by Mark Baker

8

Southeastern Poland is an enigma to most visitors to Poland. Lacking an international "must-see" on the order of a Kraków or a Gdańsk, most visitors from outside of Poland choose to give it a miss. And maybe that's the best reason of all to come. The region's hub, the city of Lublin, has a delightful Old Town that, while not quite on par with Kraków's main square, is nevertheless much more manageable and far less crowded. Lublin has a fascinating history at the confluence of Polish, Jewish, and Russian civilizations and maintains a lively cultural life, fueled by the presence of several universities and thousands of students.

Away from the big city, the smaller tourist towns of Zamość and Kazimierz Dolny have always been popular with Poles and are only now beginning to attract outside visitors. The former is a nearly perfectly preserved example of Renaissance town planning. It's undergone a thorough facelift in the past few years and is a great spot to relax for a day or two. Kazimierz Dolny, astride the Vistula River, is one of those artsy towns that draws legions of gallery owners and antique shoppers, and wouldn't be out of place in upstate New York or Vermont. It's a laid-back weekend spot for stressed-out Varsovians and Lubliners to hike and bike, browse the galleries, and just hang out. In summer, the town maintains an active cultural calendar; don't be surprised if you run into a klezmer music festival or something similar while you're here. Chełm, an easy day trip from Lublin, is best known for its underground chalk mines, which you can tour and that make for an interesting diversion (especially for kids).

Travelers with a special interest in Jewish heritage will want to spend extra time in Lublin, which was once called the "Jerusalem of the Polish kingdom." World War II and the Nazi occupation put an effective end to Jewish life there, but city authorities are making an effort to reclaim at least part of that heritage and have laid out a walking tour of the major Jewish sights.

In Poland, you're never far from World War II, and eastern Poland was brutally affected. Just outside of Lublin stands the former Majdanek concentration camp that was once planned by the Nazis to be the biggest such holding camp in all of Europe. South of Lublin, the Bełżec extermination camp was where the Nazis fine-tuned their "Final Solution." Both are now state museums.

LUBLIN

Poland's eastern metropolis of Lublin (pronounced *loo-blin*) is a surprisingly likable big city. There aren't many traditional tourist sites here, and not many foreign tourists either, but that's part of the charm. After visiting tourism behemoths like Kraków or Gdańsk—or even after spending time in the hustle and bustle of Warsaw—Lublin feels much more relaxed and "real." It's a decent place to plan an overnight stop, with a number of excellent hotels and restaurants, and enough evening activities like concerts and clubs to keep you occupied. During the day, be sure to take in the city's lovely and partially restored historic core, with two of the original town gates still standing.

Lublin traces its history back about 800 years, when it was an eastern outpost for the Polish kingdom to guard against invasions from Tatar and Mongol hordes. The town grew greatly in importance with the union between the Polish and Lithuanian kingdoms at the end of the 14th century and the formal union of 1569 (see "It Happened Here: Poland & Lithuania Form Early European 'Union,'" below). Before the union, Lublin had been a frontier town on the eastern fringe of the Polish kingdom, but the link-up with Lithuania placed the city directly between the then-Polish capital, Kraków, and the Lithuanian capital, Vilnius. Lublin suddenly found itself at the center of a country stretching from the Baltic to the Black seas.

The city thrived into the 17th century as an important commercial and legal hub, and was the seat of Poland's royal tribunal; but, as elsewhere in Poland, the countless wars took their toll. Lublin was sacked at least half a dozen times, by Muscovites, Swedes, Cossacks, and others. The Polish partitions at the end of the 18th century brought more confusion to Lublin. The town first found itself on the Austrian side of the border, then a few years later, it was attached to the Duchy of Warsaw, and then, ultimately—for most of the 19th century—it was ruled by tsarist Russia. The 19th century, however, brought industrialization and a measure of prosperity back to the city, and at the end of World War I, when Polish independence was fully restored, Lublin served for a short time as the country's capital. World War II, though, brought renewed disaster. Lublin had traditionally been an important city for Jews and for Jewish scholarship—its prewar population of 100,000 was more than one-third Jewish—but the Nazis destroyed this civilization in just a few short years. Polish Jews here were first herded into a restricted ghetto just off the Old Town, and then deported to the nearby concentration camp at Majdanek (see "Around Lublin: The Majdanek Concentration Camp," later in this chapter); many met their deaths at the exterminations centers at Sobibór and Bełżec. The Nazis even made Lublin the wartime seat of "Operation Reinhard," their covert plan to exterminate the Jewish population of German-occupied Poland.

After the war and with the shifting of Poland's borders westward, Lublin again found itself on the frontier, but this time with the Soviet Union. Thousands of Poles fled here from the east, and the city's population soared to its current 380,000. The Communist period was a mixed bag; Lublin acquired important industries, but the city suffered under insensitive planning and reconstruction. The city's historic core, the Old Town, was largely left to rot. Even today, Lublin's many charms are arguably blighted by a sea of Communist-era housing blocks. During the post-Communist period, the city authorities have tried to restore something of the city's noble past. The

Old Town is undergoing extensive long-term renovation, leaving elegantly restored Renaissance palaces still standing, in many cases, next to fallen-down, abandoned ruins.

Essentials

GETTING THERE

BY PLANE Lublin does not have an international airport, but plans are afoot to build one at Świdnik, not far from the city. That facility, however, is expected to be finished only by 2012 at the earliest. For the time being, the best air route into Lublin is to fly into Warsaw's Fryderyk Chopin airport (see p. 65), and then take a train or bus to Lublin (about 3–4 hr.).

BY TRAIN Lublin is fully integrated into Poland's national rail network, and trains are a good option for travel to Warsaw (3 hr.) and Kraków (5 hr.). The train is also convenient for going to regional spots such as Chełm (1 hr.) and Puławy (45 min.). There's even daily international service to the Ukrainian capital, Kiev (14 hr.). The **train station** (PKP, Gazowa 4; ✆ **81/194-36;** www.pkp.com.pl) is situated in a depressed part of town, about a 20-minute walk to the city center. A better bet to go

It Happened Here: Poland & Lithuania Form Early European "Union"

When Poland joined the European Union in 2004, it was seen as a tremendous "first" in the country's history, but maybe it was a really only a "second." It was here in Lublin, all the way back in 1569, that Poland and Lithuania agreed to fuse their considerable domains into a united entity that in many ways bears an uncanny resemblance to today's EU. From the original document: *"The Kingdom of Poland and the Grand Duchy of Lithuania are now one, inseparable and indistinguishable body, but also an indistinguishable, yet one, common republic which has coalesced into one people out of two states and nations."* As with the EU, the two agreed in principle to honor one authority, follow a single foreign policy, and adopt a common currency. At the same time, as with the EU, both retained separate treasuries, armies, and courts. The result portends both good and bad for today's EU. The union brought both kingdoms considerable prosperity and power—but only for a time. It eventually proved unworkable and left both at the mercy of more powerful neighbors.

from the station to the center is to take a taxi to the Brama Krakowska (Kraków Gate) at the entry to the Old Town (about 11 zł) or take public bus no. 13. Bus no. 28 is a direct connection from the station to the State Museum of Majdanek (see "Around Lublin: The Majdanek Concentration Camp," below).

BY BUS Unlike the layout in many Polish cities, Lublin's main **bus station** (PKS; Aleja Tysiąclecia 6; ✆ **81/747-66-49;** www.pks.lublin.pl) is not located next to the train station, but much closer to the Old Town, about a 5-minute walk from the center of town. You'll find regular connections here to Warsaw, Kraków, Katowice, Zakopane, Łódź, Zamość, and other cities. Several private companies also run buses and minibuses between Lublin and smaller regional cities such as Chełm, Puławy, and Kazimierz Dolny.

BY CAR Lublin is easily reachable by car. The drive to Warsaw is about 170km (106 miles) and takes between 2 and 3 hours, depending on traffic. From Kraków, expect a busy 4-hour drive along mostly two-lane highway. Lublin itself can be tricky to negotiate by car. Have a good map ready once you near the city and be careful not to miss your exit on the highway.

VISITOR INFORMATION

Lublin's helpful **Tourist Information Office** (Jezuicka 1/3; ✆ **81/532-44-12;** www.um.lublin.eu or www.loit.lublin.pl) is located just inside the main gate, the Brama Krakowska, to the Old Town. In addition to providing city and regional maps and other information, there's also a small gift shop for buying postcards, T-shirts, and souvenirs.

CITY LAYOUT

Lublin is a sprawling city, ringed by major highways, but most of the main attractions are located in a relatively compact area of the Old Town (Stare Miasto) and central city (Śródmieście), connected by a long central boulevard called Krakowskie Przedmieście. Part of Krakowskie Przedmieście is a pedestrian zone.

Getting Around

Lublin has an excellent public transportation system consisting of buses and trolley buses, but unless you're staying outside the center, you probably won't need them much. A car will be useless for getting around, since the Old Town and a major portion of the main street, Krakowskie Przedmieście, are off limits to autos.

ON FOOT Once in the center, you'll find walking the easiest way of getting around. Elsewhere, you'll want to use public buses or taxis.

BY BUS/TROLLEY BUS Lublin's public transportation (Miejskie Przedsiębiorstwo Komunikacji/MPK; ✆ **81/525-32-46;** www.mpk.lublin.pl) is cheap and efficient. Buses are a good way of getting to the train and bus stations, as well as out to the State Museum of Majdanek (bus no. 23, trolleybuses no. 156 and 158) and the Open Air Village Museum (bus nos. 5, 18, and 20). Buy tickets (2.40 zł) from newsagents or directly from drivers.

BY TAXI Taxis are useful for reaching outlying hotels as well as for getting from the center of Lublin out to Majdanek. You can hail them from the street, but watch out for rogue drivers and always make sure the driver turns on the meter. There are several reliable cab companies, including **Dwójki** (✆ **81/196-62**) and **Mercedes** (✆ **81/196-63**).

BY BIKE Traffic is relatively heavy, and bike-rental places are few and far between (ask at the tourist information center). But there are a few designated bike lanes in Lublin. The ride out to Majdanek (about 5km/3 miles) is fairly pleasant if you stick to the sidewalks, and once you're at the sprawling concentration camp, you'll be happy you brought your own two wheels.

Top Attractions

Lublin's historic core is tiny, and you can hit the major attractions in about 2 to 3 hours of walking at a leisurely pace. Begin your exploration at the ancient entryway into the city, the **Kraków Gate** (Brama Krakowska), a perfect Gothic-era photo op that's welcomed visitors here since the middle of the 14th century. The gate houses a museum on the city's history (entry is on the right before you walk through the gate). After you pass through the gate, on the first street on your right, you'll find the city's helpful **Tourist Information Office.** Keep walking down this street, Jezuicka, and you'll arrive at the **Trinitarian Tower,** the tallest structure in the city and site of the Archdiocese of Lublin's small Museum of Religious Art. At the center of the Old Town, you'll find the former market square, the **Rynek,** dominated by the **Old Town Hall** (Stary Ratusz). It's now used mainly for weddings and concerts, but the building has a grand tradition going back to the 16th century, when it housed Poland's tribunal, the royal court of appeals. From here, it's best just to amble around and admire the mix of burghers' houses from the Gothic and Renaissance periods. The Old Town is in the middle of a long-overdue renovation, and part of Lublin's charm is seeing virtual ruins standing side by side with sumptuously restored Renaissance palaces. Be sure to stop by the **Dominican Church and Monastery** to admire the church interior; off to the right, in a small chapel, is a well-known painting depicting Lublin's skyline in the late Middle Ages. Exit the Old Town by way of a second preserved medieval gate, the **Grodzka Gate,** which leads to Zamkowa Street and the **castle** (*zamek*). This was sometimes referred to as the "Jewish Gate" because it once led to the city's enormous Jewish quarter that sprawled over a huge area from here to the

It Happened Here: Jewish Lublin

It's no accident that Lublin bears two nicknames that attest to its once-important status among Jews. The first is "Jewish Oxford," referring to a respected yeshiva that was built here in 1515. The second is the "Jerusalem of the Polish Kingdom," a reference to the vitality of the city's Jewish community until the start of World War II. The history of Jews in Lublin goes back to at least 1316, when Jewish merchants settled in the city to take advantage of Lublin's trade position with Russia. Over the centuries, the community flourished. As hard as it is to imagine now, the vast area surrounding the castle was filled with the warren of tiny streets of the Jewish quarter. By the start of World War II, the Jewish community numbered nearly 40,000 out of a total city population of around 100,000. Sadly, little of this remains today. At the start of World War II, the Nazis forced the city's Jews into a tightly restricted ghetto area comprising part of the traditional Jewish quarter and a small adjoining piece of land bordered by today's Kowalska and Lubartowska streets. Much of the old Jewish quarter was razed. Eventually, the residents were sent to concentration camps at Bełżec, Sobibór, and Lublin's own Majdanek (see "Around Lublin: The Majdanek Concentration Camp," below). To add insult to injury, the Nazis made Lublin the headquarters of Operation Reinhard, the code name for its plan to murder the Jewish population of German-occupied Poland. After the war, many of the city's remaining Jews fled to newly formed Israel or the United States, and Lublin's Jewish community dropped to just a handful. Now, city authorities are trying to reclaim some of this history and have created a **Heritage Trail of the Lublin Jews.** To get the most out of the trail, first pick up a copy of the excellent pamphlet "Landmarks and Traces of Jewish Culture in Lublin" at the tourist information center. The trail begins in the Old Town and goes down through the Grodzka Gate into the former Jewish quarter and beyond. Don't miss the fascinating prewar Lublin scale model of the Old Town and Jewish quarter at the **Grodzka Gate Theatre NN Centre** (Grodzka 21; ✆ **81/532-58-67;** www.tnn.lublin.pl).

castle and in a wide swathe around the castle. The Nazis razed this neighborhood to the ground, and insensitive postwar planning led to what you see now: a big parking lot and a poorly maintained park. The castle is worth a peek inside. It was once a huge fortress built by King Kazimierz the Great to protect the kingdom's eastern flank from Tatar invasion. It was later partly destroyed and rebuilt in the 19th century as a prison. It houses the **Lublin Museum** and the **Chapel of the Holy Trinity.** At this point, you're free to follow your own interests, either exploring what little remains of the former Jewish quarter or heading back to the Old Town for a meal or a drink.

Dominican Church and Monastery ★ The Dominican order came to Lublin in the 13th century, and this church is considered the city's finest example of sacral art. Much of the church was destroyed by fire in 1575, and the original Gothic architecture was lost. What you see today is the Renaissance church that was built in its place. The highlights include the first chapel to the right, which holds a famous painting of the Lublin skyline, and the Firlej Chapel, with its lavish dome and 17th-century wall ornaments.

Złota 9. ✆ **81/532-89-80.** Free admission. Daily 9am–4pm.

Lublin Castle & Chapel of the Holy Trinity ★★ The castle is home to a rather dry museum on Lublin and Polish history, and a more interesting Gothic Chapel of the Holy Trinity. The chapel dates from the 14th century, and the Byzantine frescoes are the work of a team of Ruthenian painters from 1418. The castle played an important role in Lublin's history. It was the second home of Polish kings during the union with Lithuania, when they would make their trek from Kraków to Vilnius. It was here, too, that the Polish-Lithuanian Union (see "It Happened Here: Poland & Lithuania Form Early European 'Union,'" above) was signed in 1569. Look for the painting *The Union of Lublin* by the 19th-century master Jan Matejko that depicts the event. The castle was rebuilt in the 19th century in the current neo-Gothic style and served as a prison both under the Tsarist occupation and then later under the Nazis during World War II.

Zamkowa 9. ✆ **81/532-50-01.** www.zamek-lublin.pl. Museum & chapel: 6.50 zł adults, 4.50 zł children. Museum: Wed–Sat 9am–4pm, Sun 9am–5pm; chapel: daily 9am–4pm.

Lublin Village Open Air Museum (Skansen) ★★ Poland's open-air museums are always a treat, and this one is one of the best in the region. This museum has some 50 historic buildings, ranging from a Greek-Catholic church removed from Tarnoszyn to an 18th-century manor house from Żyrzyn. It's fun just to stroll the gardens and take in the range of architectural styles in Poland over the years.

Warszawska 96. ✆ **81/533-85-13.** www.skansen.lublin.pl. 8 zł adults, 4 zł children; English-speaking guide 90 zł. Apr–Oct daily 10am–5pm; Nov-Mar, call ahead to book a visit.

Museum of Lublin History ★ This small museum is dedicated to the history of the city. Non-Polish-speakers are likely to find the photographs of how the city has changed from the late 19th century to the 1960s to be the most interesting part. You can also climb to the top of the gate for a beautiful panorama of the Old Town.

Lokietka 3 (at the Krakowska Gate). ✆ **81/532-60-01.** www.zamek-lublin.pl. 5 zł adults; 2.50 zł children. Tues–Sun 10am–4pm.

Trinitarian Tower and Museum of Religious Art ★ The tower dominates Lublin's skyline and is visible for miles around. The good news is that the tower is open to the public and affords great views in all directions; the bad news is that it's a pretty good hike up at least several dozen rickety wooden stairs. The small museum consists of religious paintings and icons, wooden carvings, and statues. They're fascinating in their own right, but the commentary is only in Polish.

Pl. Katedralny. ✆ **81/743-64-33.** www.kuria.lublin.pl/muzeum. 7 zł adults; 5 zł children. Tues–Sun 10am–5pm.

Customized Tours

Lublin Tours (✆ **503/503-206;** www.explorelublin.pl), run by Sławomir Nowodworski, operates a series of English-language tours of Lublin and the surrounding region, including trips to Kazimierz Dolny, Zamość, and Bełżec. One of the most popular offerings is a 3- to 4-hour walking tour tracing Lublin's Jewish heritage; the price is around 200 zł per tour. **Antur** (✆ **502/097-263;** www.antur.eu) guide Maciej Zbarachewicz offers personalized tours of Lublin, as well as excursions to Majdanek and Bełżec, among others. A 4-hour tour of Lublin starts at around 270 zł per tour, while a full day out and back to Bełżec will run about 300 zł, including transportation.

Around Lublin: The Majdanek Concentration Camp

The former Nazi concentration camp of **Majdanek** ★★ (Droga Męczenników Majdanka 67; ✆ **81/710-28-33**; www.majdanek.pl; free admission; Tues–Sun Apr–Oct 9am–6pm, Nov–Mar 9am–4pm) is not as well known as Auschwitz-Birkenau, but Majdanek's sheer size and the fact that several crematoria here survived the war (those at Auschwitz were mostly destroyed) are compelling reasons to visit.

The camp is located about 5km (3 miles) from the center of Lublin and is easily reachable by public transportation (bus no. 23 or trolley bus no. 156 or 158; buy tickets, 2.40 zł, from newspaper kiosks or directly from the driver), taxi, or bike. Majdanek was originally conceived as a labor camp to hold up to 50,000 workers to help the Germans realize their resettlement aims for eastern Poland, but the plans were constantly revised upward. In the end, at least 150,000 people were eventually held here at some time and 80,000 perished, mostly Jews from across Europe, but there were also sizable numbers of Polish and Russian POWs and others. The single most horrific day at Majdanek came on November 3, 1943, when as many as 18,000 prisoners were killed in a single day.

The camp was liberated by the Soviet Red Army on July 22–23, 1944. The Red Army assault came unexpectedly and quickly, and the Germans didn't have enough time to destroy the crematoria and other pieces of evidence. In this respect, it's perhaps the best-preserved of the former Nazi concentration camps.

The camp layout itself can be a little confusing for first-time visitors. The highlights include two enormous stone monuments by Victor Tolkin built in 1969 to commemorate the 25th anniversary of the camp's liberation. One stands near the entrance to the camp and the other—in the shape of an enormous urn—is at the back. It's a mausoleum filled with the ashes of thousands of victims. Visitors are free to wander around from here visiting the barracks, some filled with exhibitions. Guided tours are available in English for 20 zł per person.

The Majdanek museum continues to carry out historical research, and in late 2005, a group of Majdanek survivors returned to the camp to help archeologists find dozens of personal objects—such as watches and rings—that had been buried by the inmates so the Germans would not get them. Amazingly, after some 60 years, the returnees were able to locate the buried objects within a few minutes.

Shopping

Lublin is blessed with an enormous shopping center, the **Lublin Plaza** (Lipowa 13; ✆ **81/536-22-03;** www.lublinplaza.pl), just off of the main street, Krakowskie Przedmieście, which is a real advantage if you've forgotten something at home. The mall houses dozens of shops, restaurants, and a multiplex cinema in case you get a rainy day. The Old Town is filled with galleries and gift and antique shops that are fun to browse.

Where to Stay

Lublin has some excellent hotels, including a glamorous makeover of a former bank building, the **Grand Hotel Lublinianka** (see below), and a new boutique, the

Vanilla (see below), that offers cutting-edge interiors and a location just off Krakowskie Przedmieście, a minute's walk from the Old Town.

VERY EXPENSIVE

Grand Hotel Lublinianka ★★ The current top address in Lublin has hosted the princess of Thailand and the band Morcheeba, among other notable guests. The handsome neoclassical building was once home to a bank, and the property still exudes money and luxury. The lobby is the prettiest among Lublin's hotels, with a baby grand piano and a turn-of-the-century cafe with gorgeous marble floors that's perfect to laze around in. The rooms are done in a classical style with high ceilings, chandeliers, and muted gold and beige interiors. There are a Turkish bath and Finnish sauna on the premises.

Krakowskie Przedmieście 56. ✆ **81/446-61-00.** Fax 81/446-62-00. www.lublinianka.com. 72 units. 600 zł double. AE, DC, MC, V. Parking (paid). **Amenities:** Restaurant; concierge; exercise room; room service; sauna. *In room:* A/C, TV, hair dryer, Internet (free), minibar.

Hotel Europa ★ This beautiful hotel right on Krakowskie Przedmieście on the approach to the Old Town (a 5-minute walk away) dates from 1867, and a strong sense of history pervades the place even now. The lobby is small but tidy, with high ceilings and a kind of Colonial-era feel. The rooms are nicely proportioned; some of the more expensive ones come with period furnishings and antiques. Room 104 is a gorgeous double with a nice view over the adjoining park. The guest roll reads like a Who's Who of Polish society, including the noted Polish travel writer Ryszard Kapuściński and former President Aleksander Kwaśniewski.

Krakowskie Przedmieście 29. ✆ **81/535-03-03.** Fax 81/535-03-04. www.hoteleuropa.com.pl. 73 units. 420 zł double. AE, DC, MC, V. Parking (paid). **Amenities:** Restaurant; room service. *In room:* A/C, TV, hair dryer, Internet, minibar.

EXPENSIVE

Hotel Victoria A modern high-rise that lacks character but is a solid choice for a business trip, with decent business amenities such as conference facilities and a large parking area. The rooms are small and plainly decorated; but the bathrooms are modern, and the facilities are generally of high quality. The near-central location is fine, but better suited to car travelers. The walk to the Old Town is about 10 to 15 minutes.

Narutowicza 58/60. ✆ **81/532-70-11.** Fax 81/532-90-26. www.hotel.victoria.lublin.pl. 120 units. 300 zł double. AE, DC, MC, V. Parking (paid). **Amenities:** Restaurant; exercise room; room service; sauna. *In room:* A/C, TV, hair dryer, Internet, minibar.

Hotel Vanilla ★★★ This bold, contemporary boutique hotel is a stone's throw from the Old Town on an inviting corner just off Krakowskie Przedmieście. The rooms are done up in jaw-dropping color schemes of bold reds, yellows, and oranges; the minimalist furnishings mesh perfectly with the strong colors. The bathrooms are a study in Japanese-style minimalism, while the corridors are plastered with bright-orange faux brickwork. It sounds outrageous—and it is—but it works. This is one hotel you're not likely to forget. The English-speaking receptionist is more than happy to help guests. The hotel's terrace cafe is Lublin's favorite spot for an ice cream sundae.

Krakowskie Przedmieście 12. ✆ **81/536-67-20.** Fax 81/536-67-21. www.vanilla-hotel.pl. 18 units. 350 zł double. AE, DC, MC, V. Parking (paid). **Amenities:** Restaurant; exercise room; room service; sauna. *In room:* A/C, TV, hair dryer, Internet, minibar.

MODERATE

Hotel Campanile ★★ This local representative of the upper-middle-market French hotel chain strikes a good balance between comfort and price. Don't expect lots of character—these are basically business hotels, but the rooms are nicely appointed, clean, and have goodies like air conditioning and free in-room Internet. The buffet breakfast is the best in town. The location, however, is less than ideal—the Old Town is a 15- to 20-minute walk—but the value for the money more than makes up for it. It's a good choice if you're arriving by car, since the hotel entrance is just off one of the main access roads, and there are even a few free parking spots out front.

Lubomelska 14. ✆ **81/531-84-00.** Fax 81/531-84-01. www.campanile.com.pl. 81 units. 249 zł double. AE, DC, MC, V. Parking. **Amenities:** Restaurant; exercise room; limited room service. *In room:* A/C, TV, hair dryer, Internet (free), minibar.

Waksman ★★ This small pension just at the edge of the Old Town near the former Jewish quarter is a perfect choice if you want a stay with a more personal touch. All the rooms are decorated with stylish, period-piece furniture and have polished wood floors, big timber beds, and antique desks. Each room is accented in a different color, with red reserved for the honeymoon suite (which features a big waterbed). The suite, with a separate lounge area and a castle view, is a steal at this price.

Grodzka 19. ✆ **81/532-54-54.** Fax 81/534-75-53. www.waksman.pl. 7 units. 220 zł double; 300 zł suite. AE, DC, MC, V. **Amenities:** Limited room service. *In room:* TV, hair dryer, Internet, minibar.

INEXPENSIVE

Lublin This is a standard Communist-era high-rise, situated about a 20-minute walk out of town, but it's a good value for the money, with clean rooms and decent service. It's pretty bare-bones, with the narrow twin beds that all hotels of this era seem to come with, but it's adequate for a night or two. It's particularly convenient if you're arriving by car or train, since it's on one of the main roads into town and is within walking distance of the train station. Ask for a room away from the road to cut down on noise.

Podzamcze 7. ✆ **81/747-44-07.** Fax 81/444-42-40. www.hotel-lublin.pl. 90 units. 190 zł double. AE, DC, MC, V. Parking. **Amenities:** Restaurant. *In room:* TV, Internet.

Where to Dine

Most of the restaurants are clustered along Krakowskie Przedmieście on the approach to the Old Town or in the Old Town itself, particularly on sloping Grodzka Street. Many of these places seem to specialize in the same mix of pizzas and sandwiches, and, with a few exceptions (see below), they are fairly ordinary. In summer, it's best to show up a little early on a nice evening (6–7pm) to maximize your chances of snagging one of the highly coveted outdoor tables.

VERY EXPENSIVE

Kobi ★★★ JAPANESE This is one of the top sushi restaurants in Poland and certainly the best in this part of the country. The *maki* rolls are a specialty, with innovative fillings like avocado and salmon; and tuna, butterfish, and leek standing alongside the usual offerings. The interior is warmer than the standard Japanese restaurant, but the service is still on the starchy side. Reserve in advance since this place fills up.

Kościuszki 10. ✆ **81/443-36-66.** Reservations suggested. Main courses 50 zł–70 zł. AE, DC, MC, V. Mon–Sat noon–11pm; Sun 1–10pm.

EXPENSIVE

Mandragora ★★★ JEWISH Definitely plan to have a meal at this highly atmospheric Jewish restaurant just off the Rynek. The interior is homey and warm with lace tablecloths and candles. As with any Jewish restaurant in Poland, the walls are plastered with old photos and mementos of the city's, and country's, Jewish past. What distinguishes this place is the quality of the food. Delicious appetizers include hummus served with pita bread, as well as more common Polish fare like herring served in an apple-cream sauce. For the main course, go with the grilled lamb chops with rosemary potatoes and sautéed mushrooms. There are kosher Israeli wines on offer, and a klezmer band plays some evenings.

Rynek 9. ✆ **81/536-20-20.** Main courses 30 zł–45 zł. AE, DC, MC, V. Daily noon–10pm.

Oregano Cafe ★★ ITALIAN/INTERNATIONAL This charming cafe-restaurant specializes in Mediterranean cuisine from Italy, Greece, and other sunny locales. Appetizers include a hearty tomato-basil soup that may even merit a rave mention on your postcard home. Main courses include an inviting mix of salads, pasta dishes, and inventive meat-based dishes such as short ribs cooked in a soy, anise, and ginger sauce. The interior is intimate and candle-lit, and ideal for a special night out.

Kościuszki 7. ✆ **81/442-55-30.** Main courses 30 zł–40 zł. AE, DC, MC, V. Daily noon–11pm.

MODERATE

U Szewca Irish Pub ★★ PIZZA/IRISH This pub is a Lublin institution and not a bad effort at all in recreating a piece of Dublin in eastern Poland. As you might expect with an Irish pub, the interior is all dark woods and carpeted floors, with walls festooned floor to ceiling with kitschy photos, old ads, and vintage signs. The food runs the gamut from salads and pizzas to fairly authentic Irish pub fare such as stews and fish and chips. It's phenomenally popular and a good choice for either a meal or just a drink.

Grodzka 18. ✆ **81/532-82-84.** Main courses 20 zł–35 zł. AE, DC, MC, V. Sun–Thurs 11am–midnight; Fri & Sat 11am–2am.

Złoty Osioł ★ POLISH This excellent, atmospheric Polish pub serves homemade potato pancakes, *bigos* (hunter's stew), pierogi, and more refined dishes like duck, all washed down with very good Żywiec beer. Although it's a pub, on most nights, the atmosphere is hushed enough to have a good conversation.

Grodzka 5a. ✆ **81/532-90-42.** Main courses 25 zł –40 zł. AE, DC, MC, V. Mon–Sat noon–11pm; Sun 1–10pm.

INEXPENSIVE

Pub Samarta PIZZA This is one of a number of generic pizza-pubs along Grodzka in the Old Town that draws crowds looking for cheap, filling food, lots of beer, and great open-air seating just off the main square. The thick-crust pizza actually isn't bad; one is more than enough to share between two people.

Grodzka 16/3. ✆ **81/534-63-89.** Main courses 15 zł–25 zł. No credit cards. Mon–Sat noon–1am; Sun 1–11pm.

After Dark

THE PERFORMING ARTS

Lublin is home to one of the country's finest orchestras, the **Lublin Philharmonic Orchestra** (Filharmonia Lubelska im. H. Wieniawskiego; Marii Sklodowskiej-Curie 5; ✆ **81/531-51-12** box office; www.filharmonialubelska.pl). Consult the tourist information office to see what's playing while you're in town. The office or your hotel can help arrange tickets, or visit the theater box office (Tues–Thurs noon–5pm, Fri 1–7pm). Tickets are also available at the theater an hour before the performance starts.

CAFES, PUBS & CLUBS

As the sun sets, do like everyone else in Lublin and head for the Old Town. The long pedestrian walkway Krakowskie Przedmieście is filled with clubs and late-night cafes. One of the most popular rock clubs in town is **Koyot** (Krakowskie Przedmieście 26; ✆ **81/743-67-35**), complete with sweaty crowds and pulsating dance music. For more traditional pubs and beer drinking, most of the action is on Grodzka in the Old Town. In addition to Samarta, the U Szewca Irish Pub, and Złoty Osioł (see "Where to Dine," above), check out **Legenda** (Grodzka 1; ✆ **81/532-53-72**) and at least half a dozen other joints offering a similar mix of beer and conversation.

CHEŁM

Lublin makes a good base to explore the nether reaches of southeastern Poland and the borderlands with Ukraine. One of the best day trips, especially if you're traveling with kids, is to the city of Chełm (pronounced *khelm*), about 60km (37 miles) east of Lublin.

The main attraction here is an abandoned underground chalk mine, part of which has been opened to the public. With the help of a guide, you can explore around 2km (1¼ miles) of the mine's length. The trip is in turns chilling (quite literally since the underground temperature is a constant 48°F/9°C) and fascinating, as the mine snakes below the town and you learn how chalk was mined here over the centuries.

Chełm itself has a long history, lying at the historic crossroads of Polish, Jewish, and Russian cultures. Up until World War II, around half the city's population was Jewish. Indeed, Chełm has traditionally played an outsized role in Jewish humor, with the city's residents usually cast in the role of the "country bumpkin." Not that long ago on the Borscht Belt, a comedian starting a joke with: "There once was this rabbi from Chełm…" was enough to bring down the house.

Today, regrettably, little of this once-vibrant Jewish culture remains. The Nazis cleared the town of its Jews, and the few who survived the horrors chose to make their lives elsewhere. Recent history has been a little kinder to Chełm. The opening of the border with Ukraine has brought some economic energy to the city, and the historic center has been spruced up. In addition to the chalk mine, the city's small Old Town is a pleasant stroll and the impressive hilltop monastery is worth the slog to the top. This hill saw an early Slav settlement as long as 900 years ago.

Essentials

GETTING THERE

BY CAR From Lublin, follow E372 south, bearing east on Poland route 12, following the signs to Chełm.

BY BUS At least three buses daily connect the city to Lublin. At least one bus daily makes the run to Zamość. Expect a ride of about an hour for each city and a fare of about 20 zł. The bus station **Chełm PKS** is close to the center at Lwowska 20 (✆ **82/564-28-04**).

BY TRAIN Frequent daily trains make the run to and from Lublin in a little more than an hour. Fares are about 20 zł each way. The train station **Chełm PKP** is located at Kolejowa 89 (✆ **82/194-36**).

VISITOR INFORMATION

Chełm's helpful tourist information office (Lubelska 63; ✆ **82/565-36-67;** www.itchelm.pl) is on the main street, Lubelska, which runs through the center of the Old Town. The entrance to the chalk mine is a 3-minute walk from the tourist office. The office has free walking maps of the city, as well as a few scattered brochures available in English on Chełm's history and attractions.

CITY LAYOUT

Chełm is a relatively small city with a compact Old Town. The entrance to the Chalk Mine and the tourist information office are within a couple of blocks of each other on the main avenue, Lubelska, in the center of town. As it passes through the center, Lubelska slopes upward, culminating in a peaceful park and hilltop monastery.

Getting Around

ON FOOT Chełm has a tiny Old Town area, and nearly anything you might want to see or do is within easy walking distance.

BY TAXI Try local operator **Radio Taxi MPT** (✆ **82/191-91**).

Top Attraction

Old Chalk Mine (Chełmskie Podziemia Kredowe) ★ ☺ White chalk had been mined here commercially since the Middle Ages before it was halted toward the end of the 19th century after the extensive shafts posed a danger to city residents. These days, most of the tunnels have been blocked off except for a 2km (1¼-mile) stretch that's open to visitors. Truth be told, there's not much to see down here; the thrill is exploring the passages below the Old Town, taking in the vastness of the mine, and enjoying the unadorned beauty of the smooth, white walls. Touring the mine is possible only with a guided tour (tours leave three times daily at 11am, 1, and 4pm) and last around 45 minutes. Most tours are in Polish, though it may be possible to arrange for an English-speaking guide through the Chełm tourist information office. Be sure to bring a sweater or jacket, since the underground temperature remains a chilly 48°F (9°C) year-round.

Lubelska 55a. ✆ **82/565-25-30.** www.itchelm.pl. 10 zł adults; 7 zł students & seniors. Ticket office: Mon–Fri 9am–5pm, Sat & Sun 10am–4pm.

Where to Stay & Dine

Hotel Kamena This grim, Communist-era affair nevertheless offers clean rooms and is just 10 minutes' walk from the entrance to the chalk mine. The hotel is undergoing a long-term renovation, and the rooms on the fourth and fifth floors, so far, are the nicest. Two categories of doubles are available—standard and deluxe—but there's little difference between the two except for newer carpets in the latter. Ask to see one of each before deciding. There's free parking out front.

Armii Krajowej 50. ✆ **82/565-64-01.** www.hotelkamena.pl. 63 units. 140 zł standard double; 180 zł deluxe double. AE, DC, MC, V. Free parking. **Amenities:** Restaurant. *In room:* TV, Internet (free).

Gęsia Szyja ★★ POLISH This hole-in-the-wall cellar restaurant just may serve southeastern Poland's best food. The menu is available only in Polish, but settle back and let the English-speaking waiter guide you through the choices. An excellent traditional appetizer is the herring served in a cream sauce with apples and chopped onion. For the main course, try to the *golonka* (pork knee), served with a basket of bread, and mustard and horseradish on the side. The meat literally falls off the bone. Easily worth a trip to Chełm on its own.

Lubelska 27. ✆ **82/565-23-21.** Main courses 25 zł–40 zł. AE, DC, MC, V. Mon–Sat 11am–11pm; Sun noon–10pm.

BEŁŻEC

Unless you have particular knowledge of the Holocaust, you may not know this obscure town and rail junction about 100km (62 miles) south of Lublin. Yet it was here that the Nazis first launched their "Operation Reinhard," the code name of their plan for the mass extermination the Jewish population of the Generalgouvernement, the name the Germans gave to Nazi-occupied Poland. Bełżec (pronounced *bayo-zhets*) was chosen because it was small and little known, yet not far from major Jewish populations in the cities of Lublin and Lwów.

The Nazis used Bełżec to refine the techniques of mass killing that would later be applied at other death camps, including the use of poison gas in gas chambers and forcing the Jewish prisoners themselves to carry out much of the work, including burying and later burning the bodies.

Bełżec operated from March 1942 until the end of that year. In the relatively short period of 8 months, some 450,000 people were put to their deaths here. The process was horrific and sickening. Unlike as with other camps, such as Majdanek or Auschwitz-Birkenau, there was no elaborate system of selections and work routines, and no chance of survival. Instead, victims would arrive by train at one part of the camp and then be forced through a small tunnel to gas chambers at another part within the span of a few hours. Initially, the bodies were buried in mass graves, but by late 1942, the decomposition process became so bad that the bodies had to be dug up again and burned on enormous pyres.

Bełżec was dismantled by the Nazis in 1943, and much of the killing apparatus was destroyed to hide the evidence of what went on. Throughout much of the postwar period, Bełżec remained simply a fenced-off mass grave. With growing interest in the Holocaust in the post-Communist period, however, officials later built a monument with a small visitor center and permanent exhibition to tell the story of what happened here.

Essentials

GETTING THERE

Bełżec is a small town and is not easy to get to without a car. If you're traveling from Lublin, the public transportation options are few and far between. In summer, there are some sporadic bus connections, but these dry up out of season. The best bet is to hire a tour guide from Lublin (see "Customized Tours," earlier in this chapter), or make your way to Zamość by bus and then connect to an onward bus to Bełżec from there.

BY CAR Bełżec lies about 100km (62miles) south of Lublin and is an easy 90-minute drive. Once in Bełżec, follow the signs to the Bełżec Memorial. There is ample paid parking out front for 5 zł per car.

BY TRAIN Currently, there are no direct train connections to Bełżec from either Lublin or Zamość. If you take a train from elsewhere, the camp is about a 5-minute walk from the station.

BY BUS In summer, a few buses make the run between Lublin's main bus station and Bełżec. Check the Lublin bus website (www.pks.lublin.pl) for an updated schedule. The trip takes around 3 hours and costs about 20 zł. From Zamość, several buses daily cover the distance in about 45 minutes and cost 10 zł.

Visitor Information

There's a small **visitor information center** (✆ **84/665-25-10**) at the entrance with a permanent photography exhibition, as well as restrooms and a small bookshop.

Top Attraction

Museum and Memorial Site at Bełżec ★★ A visit to Bełżec comprises two parts: the large monument that covers the entire former area of the camp and the small museum with a permanent photographic exhibition and explanatory materials. The monument itself is understated and deeply moving, simply a field of charred rocks to symbolize the scorched earth of the funeral pyres. A small tunnel runs through the middle, representing the "tube" the victims had to walk through from the trains directly to the gas chambers.

Ul. Ofiar Obozu 4; ✆ **84/665-25-10.** www.belzec.org.pl. Free admission; guided tours in English available for groups of 10 or fewer for 50 zł/tour. Daily May–Oct 9am–6pm and Nov–Apr 9am–4pm.

ZAMOŚĆ

The UNESCO-protected city of Zamość ★ (pronounced *zah-mohsch*) is a fascinating curiosity: It's a totally planned community from the 16th century and, as such, an almost completely intact example of Renaissance town planning. Call it Poland's first-ever mixed-use real estate development, with shops, offices, and housing all positioned for maximum efficiency and aesthetic beauty.

Zamość was the dream of Jan Zamoyski, a wealthy Polish nobleman who wanted to establish the family's seat and a regional center of culture and commerce. Zamoyski hired a noted Renaissance town designer, Italian architect Bernardo Morando, to design, in essence, a perfect town from scratch. Morando modeled the town on a hexagon, 600m (21,969 ft.) long and 400m (1,312 ft.) wide. The market square and town hall were situated at the center, with two lesser squares—Solny (Salt) and Wodny (Water)—positioned on the sides. Major axes were cut through the square at right angles, and the side streets were laid out in a grid. The hexagon was surrounded on all sides by high walls with seven bastions and a moat, turning Zamość, effectively, into a fortress town.

Much of this has survived to this day, including the impressive town hall, part of the walls and fortification system, and a good proportion of the houses. Indeed, it's a pleasure to stroll across the wide expanse of the Rynek and marvel at how well it all still works more than 400 years later. Zamość was besieged time and again over the centuries—first by the Cossacks, and then in turn by the Swedes, Saxons, and Russians—but the fortress managed to hold. The Zamoyski family lasted until the 19th century, when under the Russian occupation, the family was finally forced to exchange its town holdings for land.

During World War II, Zamość was first occupied by Soviet soldiers, and then brutally by the Nazis, who even considered renaming the town "Himmlerstadt" after SS Chief Heinrich Himmler. In the years before World War II, Zamość was a thriving center of Jewish culture, and the town's synagogue still stands, even though most of Zamość's Jews perished in the Holocaust.

Today, Zamość is a rebuilding regional center of around 70,000 people. Because of its unique architecture and lively cultural calendar, including a festival of flowers in May and an international folk festival in summer, the town remains a popular weekend spot, with several good hotels and some excellent restaurants. That said, Zamość is really at its best on a sunny summer day, when the Rynek's cafes are filled to brimming and there's a band playing on an impromptu stage on the main square. Outside of the main summer season, the town, and its huge square, can feel a little empty.

Essentials

GETTING THERE

BY TRAIN Zamość's **train station** (Szczebrzeska 11; ✆ **84/194-36**) has infrequent connections to both Kraków and onward to Warsaw. Figure on about 5 hours' travel time to Kraków and longer to Warsaw.

BY BUS Several buses and minibuses make the trip to and from Lublin daily; from there, you can easily make onward train and bus connections. There are also several daily buses from here to the former Nazi extermination camp at Bełżec (see above). Contact **Dworzec PKS** (Hrubieszowska 1; ✆ **84/638-49-86**).

BY CAR Zamość is an easy 80km (50 mile) drive from Lublin. Figure on about 60 to 90 minutes behind the wheel at a leisurely pace.

TOURIST INFORMATION

Zamość has an ambitious **Tourist Information Center** (Rynek 13; ✆ **84/639-22-92;** www.zamosc.pl or www.zoit.zamosc.pl) located on the ground floor of the Town Hall on the Rynek. It's a great source for town and regional hiking and biking maps, as well as postcards, picture books, and souvenirs from Zamość. The staff can book rooms and will help sort out transportation options. It also offers guided tours of the city starting at 80 zł for a standard 2½-hour tour. The Zamość city website (www.zamosc.pl) has an excellent list of the most architecturally significant houses on the square and an explanation of each.

GETTING AROUND

Zamość is compact; once you've arrived at the historic core, you can walk easily from place to place.

Top Attractions

Begin your exploration of Zamość at the center of Morando's 16th-century vision, the **Rynek Wielki (Great Square).** In keeping with the Renaissance ideal of perfect proportions, the square measures exactly 100m (328 ft.) across from top to bottom and side to side. Not surprisingly, this is the center of the action in Zamość and the site of numerous performances and cultural activities throughout the year, particularly in summer. The Rynek is dominated by the enormous **Town Hall (Ratusz),** which was purposefully placed off-center. The building still follows Morando's original design, though it was remodeled several times over the centuries (and was under scaffolding once again at press time). The sweeping fan-shaped double stairway was added later, in the 18th century. Many of the buildings that line the square have retained their original Renaissance arcades. The most noteworthy houses are the one at no. 25, where Morando himself once lived, and the colorful series of houses that start to the right of the town hall, known collectively as the Armenian houses both for their ornate appearance and the fact that a wealthy Armenian merchant built the house known as **"Under the Angel"** in 1632–34. The houses are now home to the **Zamojskie Museum.**

Follow Grodzka west across Akademicka to find the **Zamoyski Palace,** the family's former residence. While the palace was certainly fabulous in its time, it's a bit of a disappointment today. In 1809, the palace ceased to be the seat of Zamość's founders and was later sold to the state for use as an army hospital. Today, it houses regional administrative offices (and is closed to the public). The **cathedral** just across the street is more impressive and dates from the 16th century. You're free to walk around inside; the Zamoyski family are buried in the crypts below. You can also climb to the top of the balcony for a view of the Old Town and to see the old belfry. Also worth checking out are the two surviving town gates: The **Old Lubelska Gate,** which stands to the north of the Zamoyski Palace and has been walled since 1604, and the **Old Lwowska Gate,** toward the eastern end of Grodzka. This was once the town's main entryway from the east and was designed by Morando himself. The former Jewish quarter of Zamość ran north and east of the Rynek. There's little left today of this community that once numbered several thousand, though the city's grand Synagogue survived World War II and is now undergoing renovation.

Zamojskie Museum ★★ A visit to the museum is a nice way to sneak a peek inside the ornate Armenian houses, but it's also worth a stop for exhibits on the town's history, including a fascinating scale model of how Zamość looked around 1700, as well as exhibits on folk costumes and crafts.

Ormiańska 30. ✆ **84/638-64-94.** http://muzeum-zamojskie.pl. 6 zł adults; Wed free admission. Tues–Sun 9am–5pm.

The Arsenal Museum of Weapons ★ A tribute to Zamość's role as a fortress town and of interest primarily to fans of military history. On the ground floor, there is a permanent exhibition of 17th-century weaponry, firearms, and cannons, and an exhibition presenting the history of Zamość fortress, including a model of the town. The building itself was designed by Bernardo Morando in the 1580s.

Zamkowa 2. ✆ **84/638-40-76.** http://muzeum-zamojskie.pl. 6 zł adults; Wed free admission. Tues–Sun 9am–5pm.

The Rotunda Museum of Martyrdom ★★ It's well worth the short walk south from the historic core to visit the Rotunda, a 19th-century military bastion once used to store gunpowder and ammo that earned a sinister reputation during World War II, when the Nazis used it as a prison and interrogation center. Around 8,000 people were executed here, and their bodies were burned. The graveyard surrounding the building contains the ashes of more than 45,000 people.

Męczenników Rotundy. ✆ **84/638-64-94.** http://muzeum-zamojskie.pl. 6 zł adults. Tues–Sun 9am–5pm.

Zamość Synagogue Zamość's impressive Renaissance synagogue dates from the early 17th century and must have been quite a palace in its heyday. The synagogue somehow managed to survive World War II (the Nazis turned it into a workshop), and later, it was used as a public library.

Zamenhofa 9. ✆ **608/409-055.** http://fodz.pl.

Where to Stay

Artis ★★ This comfortable, upscale hotel occupies a suburban villa in a green area about 4km (2½ miles) north of Zamość's historic center. The location is inconvenient if you're traveling by bus or train, but appealing if you have a car and are looking for something quiet away from the city. The beautiful gardens include a pond and children's playground set in a grove of old-growth trees. The rooms are furnished in contemporary style but are on the plain side. Bathrooms have been updated, and everything is spotlessly clean.

Sitaniec 1. ✆ **84/616-62-62.** Fax 84/616-62-62. www.hotelartis.com. 28 units. Weekdays 298 zł double; weekends 268 zł double. AE, DC, MC, V. Parking (paid). **Amenities:** Restaurant; fitness club; room service. *In room:* A/C, TV, hair dryer, Internet (free), minibar.

Orbis Hotel Zamojski ★ This is widely considered the best address in town, both for its Rynek location, next to the Town Hall, and the highly regarded restaurant, though the Senator (see below) feels more cozy and exclusive. The reception desk is located under a handsome atrium created by linking three 16th-century town houses. The rooms are on the plain side, but the amenities are the best around. Several rooms are outfitted for people with disabilities.

Kołłątaja 2/4/6. ✆ **84/639-25-16.** Fax 84/639-25-16. www.orbis.pl. 45 units. 285 zł double. AE, DC, MC, V. Parking. **Amenities:** 2 restaurants; fitness club; room service; spa. *In room:* A/C, TV, hair dryer, Internet, minibar.

Renesans ★ The cheapest of Zamość's downtown hotels, the Renesans provides decent value for the money. You won't be bowled over by the 1960s-era building, which sticks out like a sore thumb amid Zamość's Renaissance architecture, or the 1970s chunky furniture in the rooms. But you will definitely appreciate the location (just a block from the main square) and niceties like a better-than-average buffet breakfast included and free parking.

Grecka 6. ✆ **84/639-20-01.** Fax 84/677-59-32. www.hotelrenesans.pl. 25 units. 200 zł double. AE, DC, MC, V. Free parking. **Amenities:** Restaurant; room service. *In room:* TV, Internet.

Senator ★★ This romantic hideaway is stuffed to the gills with antiques and period details that lend a homey, rather than a cluttered, feel. The rooms are well-proportioned and not nearly as festooned with mementos as the public areas. The reception-desk staff is friendly and helpful, and the included buffet-style breakfast is a cut above the normal fare with imaginative cheeses and smoked fish, among other relative rarities. Alas, there's no breakfast coffee, aside from Nescafe instant. If you're coming by car, the hotel has a few free parking spaces.

Rynek Solny 4. ✆ **84/638-76-10.** Fax 84/638-76-13. www.senatorhotel.pl. 34 units. 248 zł double. AE, DC, MC, V. Free parking. **Amenities:** Restaurant; room service. *In room:* A/C (in some), TV, hair dryer, Internet, minibar.

Where to Dine

For eating and drinking, your first port of call should be the Rynek, which is filled with cafes, pubs, and pizza joints that differ from each other chiefly in name only. In nice weather, this is the place to be: Sit at an open-air table and sip a cappuccino—or, as many Poles do, a beer sweetened with raspberry juice.

Muzealna ★★ POLISH This handsome and memorable restaurant is set in three brick Renaissance cellars that look amazingly like the backdrop to a 16th-century royal banquet. The traditional Polish cooking is superb. Try the herring appetizer made with wonderfully fresh fish stacked with fresh cut onions. Main courses include a very tender Wiener schnitzel served with an egg on top (don't knock it till you've tried it!). There's terrace seating along the Rynek in nice weather.

Ormiańska 30. ✆ **84/638-73-00.** Main courses 25 zł–40 zł. AE, DC, M, V. Daily 10am–11pm.

Bohema ★★ POLISH/PIZZA This warm and inviting cellar restaurant along the Rynek serves both traditional Polish dishes and a full menu of pizzas. The pizza toppings include the usual mix of ham, mushroom, and cheese, as well as more inventive toppings like chicken, beef, and kielbasa. Bohema does double duty as a club on weekends; it can get crowded on Friday and Saturday nights after 9pm.

Staszica 29. ✆ **84/638-14-14.** Main courses 25 zł–40 zł. AE, DC, M, V. Daily 11am–11pm.

Verona ★ ITALIAN Part cafe, part stylish pizzeria, the Verona does a good job at both. The espresso drinks here are some of the best in town, and in summer, you can sit on the terrace overlooking the Rynek. The pizza is very good and a nice alternative to the constant stream of pierogi.

Rynek Wielki 5. ✆ **84/638-90-31.** Main courses 20 zł–30 zł. AE, DC, M, V. Daily 11am–midnight.

KAZIMIERZ DOLNY

The charming riverside town of Kazimierz Dolny (pronounced *kah-zeh-meerzh dohl'-nee*) is Poland's version of an artsy weekend getaway, complete with a clutch of art and antique shops (some of possibly questionable artistic merit), the Polish version of aging hippies, and a lively festival calendar that features a lively folk festival in June and an increasingly popular klezmer music festival in August. Most of the week, it's relatively quiet, but come Friday afternoon, cars bearing license plates from as far away as Warsaw and Lublin stream into town for a relaxing weekend of hiking, gallery-hopping, and even boating on the Vistula. It's a lovely spot and certainly worth a detour if you're traveling in this part of Poland and looking for a place to chill out before tackling another city. There are a couple of good hotels, including one of the most beautiful pensions in this part of the country, plus a smattering of good restaurants. There are enough traditional sights to keep you occupied for at least a day, and some great hikes if—just this one time—you're not up for seeing another castle.

Essentials

GETTING THERE

Kazimierz Dolny is a little off the beaten track, but with some advance planning, it's not that hard to get to. There's regular bus and minibus services that make the 2-hour trip from Lublin several times a day; there are also decent daily bus and minibus connections to Warsaw (3 hr.). There's no train station in Kazimierz Dolny, but the neighboring town of Puławy has excellent train connections from Warsaw and Lublin, and you can connect to Kazimierz Dolny via local bus (nos. 12 and 14). By car, it's an easy 2-hour drive from Lublin. Once in Kazimierz Dolny, follow the signs to the center. The center of town is closed to motor vehicles, but there are plenty of paid parking lots where you can leave the car.

GETTING AROUND

Walking is really the only option to see the town center, which is small and clustered around a compact town square, the Rynek. Walk or take a taxi to more far-flung destinations. In summer, you can rent bikes, though the terrain is hilly, and cycling can be challenging. Check with the tourist information office (see below) for rental agencies.

VISITOR INFORMATION

Kazimierz Dolny's small tourist information office, **PTTK Biuro Obsługi Ruchu Turystycznego** (Rynek 27; ✆ **81/881-00-46;** www.kazimierzdolny.pl; Mon–Fri 8am–4pm, Sat and Sun 10am–2:30pm), is situated in the center of town on a corner of the main square. The English-speaking staff will help you sort out hotel and restaurant choices, as well as transportation options. They also stock lots of brochures and several good maps, including a free hiking and biking map of the area called "Kazimierz Dolny i okolice."

Top Attractions

Part of the appeal of a resort like Kazimierz Dolny is that the traditional tourist sights are definitely optional. It's perfectly fine just to stroll around the Rynek and go for a walk along one of the trails or out by the river.

Celej's House (Muzeum Kamienica Celejowska) ★ This is the town's general history museum, with everything you ever wanted to know about Kazimierz Dolny, starting from the 8th century. It comprises exhibits on archaeology, history, and especially painting from the late 19th and early 20th centuries. Highlights include the town's important role in Polish visual arts.

Senatorska 11/13. ✆ **81/881-01-04.** www.muzeumnadwislanskie.pl. 7 zł adults. May–Oct Tues–Sun 9am–5pm; Nov–Apr Tues–Sun 9am–4pm.

Janowiec Castle (Muzeum Zamek w Janowcu) ★★ It's worth the hike up here to see this partially restored 16th-century castle. The original building fell into ruins in the 19th century, and a rehab is now slowly bringing the castle back to life. The controversial restoration involves leaving part of the castle as a ruin and using bright colors to enhance the architecture. The castle houses a Museum of Royal Interiors. The surrounding park is home to an open-air architecture museum.

Lubelska 20, Janowiec. ✆ **81/881-52-28.** www.muzeumnadwislanskie.pl. 12 zł adults. May–Oct Tues–Sun 10am–5pm; Nov–Apr Tues–Sun 10am–4pm.

Museum of Goldsmithery (Muzeum Sztuki Złotniczej) ★ This rich collection of decorative and religious objects has been crafted through the centuries from gold and other precious metals, including a valuable gold chalice from the 15th century.

Zamkowa 2. ✆ **81/881-00-80.** www.muzeumnadwislanskie.pl. 7 zł adults. May–Oct Tues–Sun 9am–5pm; Nov–Apr Tues–Sun 9am–4pm.

Outdoor Activities

HIKING Kazimierz Dolny is a walker's paradise. The tourist information office has put together four comfortable day walks, suitable for families, that leave from the center. One of the most popular follows the Vistula south to the village of Józefów. Pick up the free map "Kazimierz Dolny i okolice" at the tourist information office.

CYCLING The same tourist map used for hiking also shows some great cycling trails that start out from the center and head out into the surrounding hills. Since rental places change by the season, check with the tourist office for where to get bikes and which routes are suited to your fitness level and interests. The terrain away from the river gets hilly fast, but most of the cycling trails are only moderately difficult and follow little-used country roads.

BOATING One of the most popular pastimes in this river town is a cruise up and down the Vistula on big party boats that hold up to 200 people. To find the port, follow Nadwiślańska out of town and take a right once you get to the river. Contact **Rejsy po Wiśle** (✆ **81/881-01-35;** www.rejsystatkiem.com.pl) for details.

Where to Stay

Kazimierz Dolny is a classic weekend-getaway destination, so be sure to book ahead if you're arriving on a weekend since rooms tend to fill up. At other times, you're probably safe just showing up, but you still may not get the room you want. Hotels usually cut rates during the week to fill beds. There are several hotels within easy walking distance of the central square, but some of the nicer resort-type places are situated away from town and may require a cab or car ride.

Agharta Pensjonat ★ This pretty and comfortable pension was built over an ethnic art gallery in a charming villa dating from the 1920s. The location is just a few minutes from the Rynek. The rooms reflect the good taste of the gallery below, with hardwood floors and eye-catching furnishings and fabrics from around the world. Don't expect much in the way of service, though.

Krakowska 2. ✆ **81/882-04-21.** www.agharta.com.pl. 5 units. 220 zł double. AE, DC, MC, V. Parking (paid). **Amenities:** Restaurant. *In room:* TV.

Dom Architekta The "House of Architects" occupies an attractive Renaissance town house right on the Rynek, making the location ideal. Unfortunately, the rooms are something of a letdown: plainly furnished in the kind of sterile style reminiscent of Communist-era hotels. The substandard breakfast completes the picture (so it's probably best to avoid the full-board pricing option) but, still, not a bad overall choice given the reasonable price and location.

Rynek 20. ✆ **81/883-55-44.** Fax 81/883-55-02. www.dom-architekta.pl. 37 units. 215 zł double; 280 zł double w/meals. AE, DC, MC, V. Parking. **Amenities:** Restaurant. *In room:* TV.

Hotel Król Kazimierz ★★ This is, by far, the most impressive big hotel in town and definitely the place to come if you're looking for a full-service hotel. Amenities include two bars, a big restaurant, and a beautiful indoor pool and spa. The rooms are bright and have the new feel of an upscale chain. The suites are built into a 17th-century granary behind the hotel and are fabulous (and priced accordingly), with oversized bathtubs and big canopy beds. The location is a little bit away from the action, on the left as you enter Kazimierz Dolny, about 2km (1¼ miles) from the Rynek.

Puławska 86. ✆ **81/880-99-99.** Fax 81/880-98-98. www.krolkazimierz.pl. 115 units. 650 zł double; 1,000 zł suite. AE, DC, MC, V. Parking. **Amenities:** Restaurant; 2 bars; indoor pool; room service; spa. *In room:* A/C, TV, hair dryer, Internet (free), minibar.

Villa Bohema ★ Exclusive retreat in a hillside villa about a 10-minute walk from town. The tiled lobby is gorgeous, as is the formal dining room on the ground floor. The rooms have a country feel, with big beds and floral-print wallpaper. The property attracts a well-heeled, young-professional clientele who come for the good food, the indoor pool, and the pleasant, family friendly atmosphere.

Malachowskiego 12. ✆ **81/881-07-56.** www.villabohema.pl. 12 units. 360 zł double. AE, DC, MC, V. Parking. **Amenities:** Restaurant; indoor pool; room service; spa. *In room:* A/C, TV, hair dryer, Internet, minibar.

Vincent Pensjonat ★★★ This enchanting family-run pension is about 5 minutes from the center along Krakowska. Everything is done in white, from the walls, floors, and lobby furniture to the pebbles that line the walk to the front door. The rooms are traditional, with lovely period details such as ornately carved wooden wardrobes and old-fashioned bathtubs from the 1920s. The most inviting room is number 1, but all the rooms have personality. Relax in the adjoining garden on a sunny afternoon.

Krakowska 11. ✆ **81/881-08-76.** www.pensjonatvincent.pl. 11 units. 280 zł double. AE, DC, MC, V. Parking. **Amenities:** Restaurant. *In room:* TV, hair dryer, Internet, minibar.

Where to Dine

Knajpa U Fryzjera ★★ POLISH/JEWISH This unique Jewish-themed tavern restaurant serves old-fashioned cooking with a kosher twist. This is the place to come for chicken liver with onions, baked peppers stuffed with lamb, stuffed veal, brisket, and other home-style delights. In nice weather, plan to sit on the terrace in the back and relax over a very filling meal and several beers.

Witkiewicza 2. ✆ **81/881-04-26.** Main courses 30 zł–40 zł. AE, DC, MC, V. Daily 9:30am–midnight.

Pod Wietrzna Góra ★★ POLISH This cozy little Polish restaurant is situated in a pension of the same name about 100m (328 ft.) from the main square. Sit down outside on the terrace in warm weather. The menu features simple Polish dishes done very well, including an exquisitely prepared roast duck with apples and roast pork served in plum sauce. Open early for breakfast.

Krakowska 1. ✆ **81/881-06-40.** Main courses 20 zł–30 zł. AE, DC, MC, V. Daily 9am–10pm.

Cafe Rynkowa CAFE This is not necessarily the best place for a substantial meal, but it's a great spot right on the Rynek for a light snack, cup of coffee, or glass of beer. Excellent espresso drinks are served in a kind of artsy space, with walls covered with paintings by local artists. There's a little Internet room next door, with computers for checking e-mail.

Rynek 7. ✆ **81/881-00-12.** Snacks & coffee drinks 10 zł–15 zł. No credit cards. Daily 10am–10pm.

WROCŁAW & LOWER SILESIA

by Mark Baker

The southwestern province of Lower Silesia (Dolny Śląsk in Polish) and its capital Wrocław are often overlooked by travelers who are focused on more traditional Polish tourist destinations such as Kraków. That's a pity. Wrocław is an engaging, cosmopolitan city with one of the country's largest and liveliest central squares and a compelling story of destruction and rebirth that rivals even Warsaw or Gdańsk. The rolling Silesian countryside, filled with farms and forests, is picture-perfect. To the south, along the border with the Czech Republic, the highlands give way to actual mountains: the Karkonosze range. Here, you'll find some of the country's best skiing and hiking, plus a burgeoning mountain-biking culture in the warmer months.

In many ways, Lower Silesia is the least traditionally "Polish" of the country's main regions. While Poles have been present here for more than 1,000 years, a complicated succession through the centuries saw Silesia go from Polish rule to Bohemian, and then Austrian, Prussian, and most recently, German. Indeed, Lower Silesia reverted back to Polish hands only following the destruction of Nazi Germany in World War II.

This historical version of musical chairs has lent a fascinating architectural and cultural overlay to the region, with castles that date back to the traditional Polish and Bohemian dynasties overlooking villages that a scant generation or two ago were part of Germany.

In addition to Wrocław and the Karkonosze range, don't miss the spectacular wooden churches of Jawor and Świdnica, both on UNESCO's list of World Heritage Sites, as well as the enormous Książ Castle at Wałbrzych near Wrocław.

The charming district capital of Jelenia Góra makes a good base for exploring the Karkonosze and border lands with the Czech Republic. More adventurous travelers will want to spend time in Kłodzko, a largely forgotten Polish region that extends like a dagger deep into the territory of the modern-day Czech Republic and where the Polish, Bohemian, and German cultural mosaic is still keenly felt.

WROCŁAW

Wrocław (pronounced *vrot-swahv*), the capital of Lower Silesia, is a surprisingly likable big city. Although it was extensively damaged during World War II and stagnated under Communism, it's bounced back in a big way. Part of the reason is its western location not far from the German border, which makes it easily accessible to the prosperous German day-trippers who pour over the border for a coffee and strudel. It's also drawn outside investment, particularly from the Japanese, who are eager to reach the rich markets of Western Europe while producing in still-low-wage Poland.

The heart of the city is a beautifully restored central square, the **Rynek,** and the playfully colorful baroque and Renaissance houses that line the square on all sides. On a warm summer's evening, the square comes to life as what seems like the entire city descends for a glass of beer or a cup of coffee. Most of this area lay in ruins in 1945, when the Germans held out for months against an intense Russian barrage. But all that seems forgotten now. Only the presence of several battle-scarred red-brick Gothic churches evokes a sense of the scale of the destruction.

Wrocław was founded some 1,000 years ago by Slavs, but its population had become increasingly Germanized through the centuries. Until the end of World War II, Wrocław was known as the German city of Breslau. The city came under Polish control with the defeat of Nazi Germany and the shifting of Poland's borders hundreds of kilometers to the West. The surviving Germans were driven out of the city, and Wrocław was repopulated by Poles—many coming from the east of the country, particularly the city of Lwów, which came under Soviet domination after the war (and is now part of Ukraine).

In spite of the border change and population shift, the city retains a Germanic feel, especially in the Rynek and the wonderfully atmospheric streets of the Old Town. Be sure to spend time, as well, along the Odra River, which passes just to the north of the Rynek, and the peaceful **Ostrów Tumski,** the "Cathedral Island," which is home to the city's leading religious sites.

Essentials

GETTING THERE

BY AIR **Nicolaus Copernicus Airport** (Skarżyńskiego 36; ✆ **71/358-13-81;** www.airport.wroclaw.pl) is a decent-sized airport with flights throughout Europe, including to London's Luton and Stansted airports. The airport is about 14km (8¾ miles) northwest of the city center. To get to town, take bus 406, which will drop you just behind the train station (see below). The trip costs 2.40 zł. Leave about 40 minutes for the journey (more during rush hour). Taxis to and from the airport cost about 60 zł.

BY TRAIN At press time, Wrocław's main train station, **Główny** (Piłsudskiego 105; ✆ **71/717-16-74;** www.pkp.pl), was undergoing a thorough multiyear renovation. The station was still operating, but entry was possible only through a confusing warren of tunnels. Leave extra time before departures to find your platform. The station is a tourist site in its own right: a spooky-looking multi-turreted castle dating from the 19th century. It's about a 15-minute walk to town from the station, or you can take a taxi (around 8 zł). Wrocław is well served by rail, and connections to major Polish cities are frequent, though the bus is usually a quicker bet for getting to Warsaw.

Lower Silesia

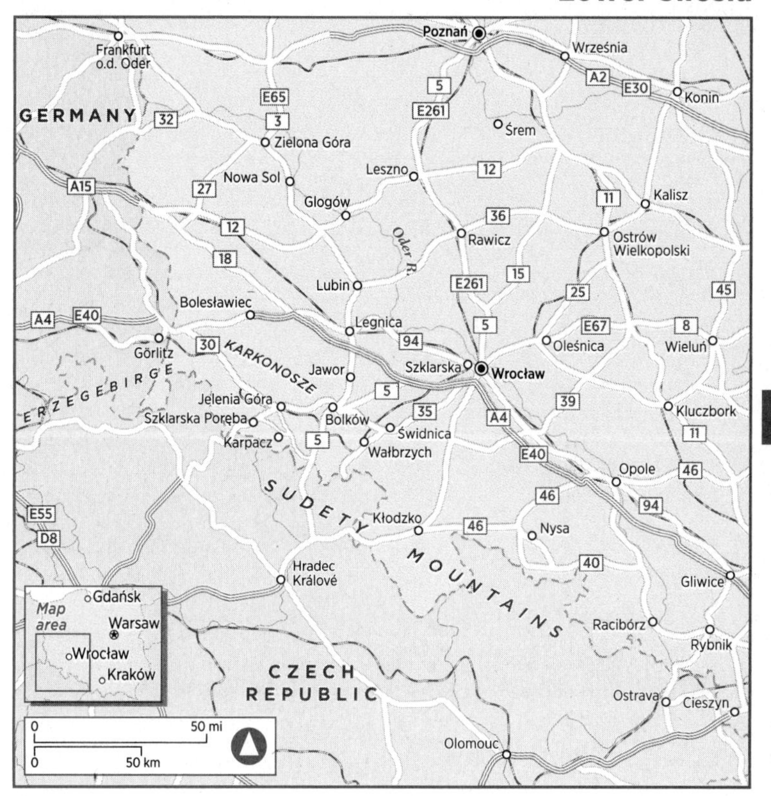

BY BUS The main bus station, **Dworzec Centralny PKS** (Sucha 1/11; ✆ **300/ 300-122**), is a giant Quonset hut of a building situated just behind the main train station, making it convenient for connections between bus and train. To get to the center, walk about 15 minutes or take a taxi (around 8 zł). The layout is a little confusing, but there's a large timetable (departures in yellow) in the main information hall. There's also a helpful information booth where you can get information on departure options. Long-haul buses run to and from Warsaw, Łódź, and Katowice, among other cities. Wrocław is a regional transportation hub, and frequent buses serve the main destinations listed in this chapter, including Kłodzko, Świdnica, and Jelenia Góra.

BY CAR Wrocław lies on the main four-lane highway (A4) linking the German border with Kraków, so getting here from Germany or Kraków is easy. The stretch from Kraków to Katowice will cost a toll of 8 zł, but it's well worth the money because of the time you save. Once in Wrocław, finding a parking spot may prove a challenge. Public metered parking costs 3 zł per hour in the immediate center and 2.10 zł per hour in other areas. Buy tickets from special machines in parking areas and display your ticket inside the car on the dashboard.

THE "battle FOR BRESLAU"

There's a kind of macabre competition among cities in Poland as to which one suffered the most during World War II and the epic battles between the Russians and Germans fought largely on Polish soil. Certainly Warsaw—which was 85% destroyed in the war—could win the prize, and Gdańsk was flattened, too, but Wrocław, or more precisely "Breslau," could also make a strong case. In 1944, as the war was turning decisively against the Germans, Adolf Hitler declared Breslau to be a fortress city and ordered that it be defended at all costs. By February 1945, the advancing Red Army had reached the city's outskirts and began an assault that was to last nearly 3 months, until the end of the war in May. The Germans had leveled much of the center of the city to build an airstrip to fly in supplies, but Ukrainian and Russian units surrounding the city successively knocked down the buildings, street by street, through a mix of artillery and mortars, and simply setting whole blocks on fire. The Nazis capitulated on May 6, just a day before Germany's total surrender. Casualty figures vary, but some German sources say more than 150,000 civilians died in the fighting. In the aftermath of the war, the surviving Germans were expelled to the German heartland, leaving just 3,000 Germans from a prewar population of around 700,000. The city was eventually repopulated by Poles brought in from the east, from territories ceded to the Soviet Union after the war, including from the former Polish (now Ukrainian) city of Lwów. Don't be surprised by the many restaurants around town offering "Ukrainian" cooking and specialties from eastern Poland—it's the real deal. The postwar population resettlement created an irony that persists to this day: Poland's westernmost metropolis is still in many ways its most "eastern" city.

VISITOR INFORMATION

Wrocław's helpful tourist information center is situated on the Rynek (Rynek 14; ✆ **71/344-31-11;** www.wroclaw-info.pl; spring–fall daily 9am–9pm, winter daily 9am–8pm). In addition to handing out maps and selling postcards, the staff can help arrange tours of the city, book hotel and restaurant reservations, sort out bus and train tickets, and even rent bikes. Another recommendable source of information, especially on cultural events, is **Wrocław-Info Souvenirs** (Sukiennice 12; ✆ **71/342-01-85;** www.wroclaw-info.pl; daily 9am–8pm), just opposite the information office by the Ratusz. A good source of general information is the free publication *The Visitor,* updated every 2 months, or the very helpful *Wrocław, In Your Pocket,* often given out free at hotel reception desks.

CITY LAYOUT

Wrocław is a sprawling city with roads and commerce spreading out in all directions. Most of the main sights, however, are located in the compact center around the enormous main square, the Rynek. Another clutch of main sights is situated on the Ostrów Tumski, across the Odra River and northwest of the city center, about a 10- to 15-minute walk from the Rynek.

GETTING AROUND

Car travel is limited in the immediate city center, so you'll find yourself doing a lot of walking. For journeys outside the center, there's a huge network of trams and buses.

Driving is pointless since traffic is usually heavy and you probably won't be able to park close to where you want to go anyway.

ON FOOT The center is compact and easy to manage on foot.

BY TRAM/BUS Outside of the Old Town, tram and bus lines are extensive. Tickets cost 2.40 zł for regular service and 2.80 zł for night buses, and are available from vending machines around town or newspaper kiosks. Validate your ticket on entering the vehicle and hold on to it for the duration of the ride.

BY TAXI Taxis are useful for getting to and from the airport, train station, and bus station, but you probably won't need them for anything else. Dishonest drivers have sometimes been a problem. Never get into an unlicensed taxi and use reputable firms. **MPT Radio Taxi** (✆ **71/191-91**) and **Lux** (✆ **71/196-23**) are two of the best.

BY BIKE The city is relatively flat, and bikes are generally exempt from basic traffic prohibitions like driving along pedestrian roads and on one-way streets, but the appeal of bike travel is limited by busy roads and a lack of dedicated bike trails. The main tourist information office on the Rynek (see above) rents bikes.

Exploring Wrocław

Wrocław's main attractions can be seen in a few hours of leisurely strolling. The natural place to start is the enormous central square, the **Rynek,** dominated (and that really is the right word, in this case) by the Town Hall, the **Ratusz,** in the middle. The Rynek is lined with some of the most cheerful baroque and Renaissance facades to grace a Polish town square. On the northwest corner of the square is the foreboding Gothic red-brick **St. Elizabeth Church** (Kościół Św. Elżbiety), Wrocław's most impressive building, and still pockmarked here and there by bullet holes from the siege of Breslau at the end of World War II. You can climb the tower, but keep in mind that it's over 90m (295 ft.) high and is pretty strenuous. To the east of the Rynek is another evocative and beautiful church, the **Church of Mary Magdalene** (Kościół Św. Marii Magdaleny). Just next to the Rynek, past the Tourist Information Office, is the smaller **Plac Solny,** the former salt market that's now given over to an enormous flower market. The side streets that lead off the square in all directions merit at least a couple hours of ambling. North of the Rynek, and along the Odra River, is the university district, where you'll find some of the city's best nightspots. To the northwest of the Rynek, around Kiełbaśnicza, is Wrocław's arty district—formed amid some weathered but pretty blocks of buildings that survived the onslaught of World War II.

From the university district, follow the Odra River to the right over a series of small, picturesque islands to the peaceful, restorative **Ostrów Tumski,** home to the city's main cathedral and the spiritual heart of Wrocław. It's perfect for a picnic and a few hours of contemplative strolling.

Town Hall (Ratusz) ★★ One of Poland's largest and most awe-inspiring town halls, it was originally built in the late 13th century but has been added to and renovated time and again over the centuries. Surprisingly, it survived World War II and now lends an immense amount of character to the town square. It has lost its administrative function and now serves a mostly decorative role—a place to situate a huge tower and hang an astronomical clock. The city museum inside is worth a quick peek, but more to see the inside of the building than to peruse the exhibits at length. After you've toured the building, have a meal and a cold one at one of the city's best beer halls, conveniently located in the Town Hall basement.

Rynek. ✆ **71/347-16-93.** www.mmw.pl. 10 zł adults; 7 zł children. Wed–Sun 11am–5pm.

Panorama of the Battle of Racławice (Panorama Racławicka) ★ This enormous 140m-long (459-ft.) "panorama" painting dates from the late 19th century and depicts the battle of Racławice, when Polish forces led by national hero Tadeusz Kościuszko defeated the Russian army on April 4, 1794. The battle came at a time when Poland faced threats from the east, west, and south, and aroused hopes that Poland might survive as a nation. Those hopes proved short-lived. A few months later, in November 1794, the Polish uprising was crushed, and Poland was later divided among Prussia, Russia, and Austria in the infamous Polish partition. The painting itself, executed while Poland was still partitioned, was a bold national statement at the time and still evokes strong national sentiment. In the years following World War II, the painting was hidden from view in case its anti-Russian sentiments offended Poland's Soviet overlords. With the rise of Solidarity in the 1980s, the painting was finally again made available to the general public in 1985.

Purkyniego 11. ✆ **71/344-23-44.** www.panoramaraclawicka.pl. 20 zł adults; 15 zł children. Tues–Sun 9am–5pm.

National Museum (Muzeum Narodowe) A vast collection of Polish art through the ages, combining the holdings of both the cities of Wrocław and Lwów, is on display here. The museum is very strong on medieval and religious painting, and sculpture from both eastern and western Poland. That said, unless you're particularly interested in Polish religious art or have some specific historical knowledge, you're unlikely to get much from the detailed holdings here. The National Museum is located near the Panorama Racławicka (see above), and you can use the same ticket for entry to both.

Pl. Powstańców Warszawy 5. ✆ **71/372-51-50.** www.mnwr.art.pl. 15 zł adults, 10 zł children; Sat free admission. Wed–Sun 10am–4pm.

Ostrów Tumski (Cathedral Island) ★★ The name is slightly misleading since it's not an island at all, but it does lie on the opposite side of the Odra River from the Rynek. This is the spiritual heart of the city and where Wrocław was founded around 1,000 years ago. Today, it's home to several churches, including the main Cathedral of St. John the Baptist, as well as the city's Botanical Gardens and a lovely clutch of timeless lanes and handsome buildings. Be sure to allow at least a couple hours to take it all in. The cathedral is worth a special look, with its 16th-century altarpiece, giant organ, and tower with gorgeous views over the city. The church dates from the middle of the 13th century but was nearly totally destroyed in World War II, and much of what you see today is a careful reconstruction of the original.

Katedra Św. Jana Chrzciciela (Cathedral of St. John the Baptist): Pl. Katedralny 18. ✆ **71/322-25-74.** www.katedra.archidiecezja.wroc.pl. Free admission. Mon–Sat 10am–4pm; Sun 2–4pm. No visits during mass.

CUSTOMIZED TOURS

Aga Tours (✆ **508/212-412;** www.agatours.pl) offers fun guided tours in a modified golf cart that holds up to five people. The most popular tours include "Wrocław by Night" and a combined tour that takes in both the Old Town and Cathedral Island. Both take a little over an hour, and prices start at around 130 zł per tour for a maximum of five people. **Eko-Tur** (✆ **663/222-660;** www.ekotur.wroclaw.pl) offers a similar range of tours and prices. Both companies can be booked directly by phone or through your hotel or the tourist information center.

Shopping

The Rynek and the streets that radiate from it are packed with little curio shops, antique dealers, and art galleries. For a pleasant ramble, try the little street **Stare Jatki,** which runs off of Kiełbaśnicza, just a couple of minutes' walk down from the Rynek. This strip used to house the city's butcher stalls, but today, it's home to numerous art galleries, studios, and little cafes where the shop clerks idle away the quiet hours.

Where to Stay

Hotel prices have been rising in recent years in step with rising standards for accommodation. You can beat the high costs by planning your visit on a weekend, when rates are cut by as much as 50%. There's a good cluster of hotels along Kiełbaśnicza, in the northern part of the Old Town near the university. Most hotels offer paid parking starting at around 30 zł a night.

VERY EXPENSIVE

Best Western Prima This is a clean and well-managed hotel, but it feels overpriced given some of the newer properties in town. The staff training is evident from the first encounter with the helpful reception desk. The rooms are upscale middle-market, and feel like a well-furnished suburban home with carpeting and floral prints. The hotel restaurant is an excellent choice if you don't feel like venturing out, with a surprisingly adventurous menu featuring a halibut salad, venison ragout, and stewed duck leg with red currant sauce.

Kiełbaśnicza 16/19. ✆ **71/782-55-55.** Fax 71/342-67-32. www.bestwestern-prima.pl. 79 units. 500 zł double. AE, DC, MC, V. **Amenities:** Restaurant; exercise room; limited room service; sauna. *In room:* A/C, TV, hair dryer, Internet, minibar.

Monopol ★★★ This landmark hotel, 5 minutes' walk from the Rynek, reopened in 2009 after a 2-year renovation that left the lobby sporting more marble than a Tuscan cathedral. The hotel dates from the late 19th century, with Art Nouveau flourishes on the exterior, but the designers opted instead for a starker contemporary look inside with brushed stainless steel, exposed concrete, and wide open baths. The contrast is stunning. The deluxe doubles are bigger than the standard, and the apartments are enormous. There's a rooftop terrace for a romantic after-dinner drink, and a spa, pool, salt cave, and fitness center in the basement. There's also an in-house wine shop and Italian deli. Infamous guests include Marlene Dietrich, who apparently favored room 108, and Pablo Picasso, who attended an international peace conference here in 1948. If price is no object, you can't do better anywhere else in town or perhaps in all of Poland.

H. Modrzejewskiej 2. ✆ **71/772-37-77.** Fax 71/772-37-78. www.monopolwroclaw.hotel.com.pl. 121 units. 550 zł standard double; 650 zł deluxe double; 750 zł–2,000 zł suite. AE, DC, MC, V. Parking (paid). **Amenities:** Restaurant; concierge; exercise room; pool; room service; sauna. *In room:* A/C, TV, hair dryer, Internet (free), minibar.

Scandic ★ A former Holiday Inn with all you would expect from a chain that focuses on high-end corporate travel. The rooms are on the small side and without any of the high-style touches of the Monopol, but they're well laid out, with large working spaces and nice touches like coffeemakers in the room. It's a good 10- to 15-minute walk to the Rynek, though the location is ideal if you are arriving by train or bus—just 5 minutes on foot from both. The friendly, English-speaking reception desk functions like an informal tourist information office. Be forewarned that parking costs a steep 65 zł a night, though there's cheaper metered parking on the street behind the hotel.

Piłsudskiego 49/57. ✆ **71/787-00-00.** Fax 71/787-00-01. www.scandichotels.com. 164 units. 400 zł double. AE, DC, MC, V. Parking 65 zł. **Amenities:** Restaurant; concierge; executive-level rooms; exercise room; room service; sauna. *In room:* A/C, TV, hair dryer, Internet, minibar.

EXPENSIVE

Art Hotel ★ Occupying two renovated burghers' houses in Wrocław's art (and hotel) quarter, this funky, bright-orange property is a welcome alternative to the chains. The reception area is sleek and cool, and each guest room has been furnished individually in an eclectic mix of modern and traditional. The restaurant gets high marks from local critics. It's popular, so make sure to book in advance.

Kiełbaśnicza 20. ✆ **71/787-71-00.** Fax 71/342-39-29. www.arthotel.pl. 77 units. Weekdays 500 zł double; weekends 320 zł double. AE, DC, MC, V. **Amenities:** Restaurant; exercise room; room service. *In room:* A/C, TV, hair dryer, Internet, minibar.

Hotel Patio ★★ This is another renovated burgher's house on Kiełbaśnicza, but slightly cheaper than its rivals. The Patio is every bit as inviting as the Art and Best Western Prima hotels, but what's absent here are a fitness room, a sauna, and air conditioning. The rooms, done in fresh colors, light woods, and whites, are even a notch more inviting than the competition.

Kiełbaśnicza 24/25. ✆ **71/375-04-00.** Fax 71/343-91-49. www.hotelpatio.pl. 49 units. 360 zł double. AE, DC, MC, V. **Amenities:** Restaurant; limited room service. *In room:* TV, hair dryer, Internet, minibar.

Qubus Hotel ★★ This smallish and smart hotel just a short walk from the Rynek caters mainly to business people. Qubus is a growing chain of high-quality hotels, and this one competes head-to-head with the Scandic and Best Western Prima, but gets an extra nod for its swimming pool and a more modern feel. Note that rooms are heavily discounted if you book on the Internet and reserve at least 7 days in advance. Rates fall another 25% on weekends.

Św. Marii Magdaleny 2. ✆ **71/797-98-00.** Fax 71/341-09-20. www.qubushotel.com. 83 units. 400 zł double. AE, DC, MC, V. **Amenities:** Restaurant; indoor pool; limited room service; sauna. *In room:* A/C, TV, hair dryer, Internet, minibar.

MODERATE

Dom Jana Pawła II ★★ This excellent-value hotel was purpose-built to welcome Pope John Paul II on his second visit to the city and is near the Cathedral of St. John the Baptist on tranquil Ostrów Tumski. A kind of hushed holiness surrounds the hotel and greets you the moment you enter the quiet lobby. This is not a good choice if you're in town to drink and carouse; on the other hand, you won't find a cleaner or better-maintained hotel around. Ask for one of the rooms overlooking the cathedral or the botanical gardens.

Św. Idziego 2. ✆ **71/327-14-00.** Fax 71/327-14-00. www.hotel-jp2.pl. 60 units. 390 zł double. AE, DC, MC, V. **Amenities:** Restaurants; concierge; room service. *In room:* A/C, TV, Internet, minibar.

Hotel Zaułek ★ A decent in-town choice given the excellent location and low price, the hotel is run by a foundation for the University of Wrocław and does double-duty hosting visiting professors and university guests. From the outside, the hotel looks like an aging housing complex, but inside, it's neat, clean, and quiet. The rooms are modestly furnished but perfect for a short stay, and there's free Wi-Fi throughout the hotel.

Garbary 11. ✆ **71/341-00-46.** Fax 71/375-29-47. www.hotel.uni.wroc.pl. 12 units. 290 zł double. AE, DC, MC, V. **Amenities:** Restaurant; Wi-Fi (free). *In room:* TV, hair dryer, minibar.

INEXPENSIVE

Avantgarde This is an acceptable budget alternative if the Centrum (see below) is booked up. This is a classic hostel, with cast-metal bunk beds and shared bathrooms. Nevertheless, it's secure, the service is friendly, and the rooms are clean. There are few amenities and no breakfast, but there's a computer terminal on the ground floor to check e-mail and complimentary Wi-Fi throughout. The walk to the Rynek is about 15 minutes. There's free parking at the hostel door if you're traveling by car.

Kościuszki 55. ✆ **71/341-07-48.** www.avantgardehostel.pl. 20 units. 120 zł double. AE, DC, MC, V. Free parking. **Amenities:** Wi-Fi (free).

Centrum ★ This property is highly recommended if you're on a budget and show up in town on a weekday without a reservation. Technically a hostel, the Centrum also offers private singles and doubles of average to high quality at excellent prices. There's not much in the way of amenities here, but expect clean rooms and hardwood floors in a bright, shiny space. The central location is a 5-minute walk from the Rynek.

Św. Mikołaja 16/17. ✆ **71/793-08-70.** Fax 71/793-08-70. www.centrumhostel.pl. 22 units. 120 zł double. AE, DC, MC, V.

Where to Dine

The Rynek is lined with restaurants, cafes, beer gardens, and bars from corner to corner. Most restaurants post their menus out front, so peruse the square and see what you're hungry for.

VERY EXPENSIVE

Sakana Sushi Bar ★★ JAPANESE At this standout sushi bar, you sit on stools around a counter, and little boats of delicacies float by. You select the ones that fit your appetite (or your wallet). Each plate has a different color and price; white is the cheapest (starting at around 15 zł), and prices head steeply north from there. Three plates make for a filling meal—if you choose carefully, you can stay on a budget, but what's the fun of that when the food is this good?

Odrzańska 17/1a. ✆ **71/343-37-10.** Main courses (three plates) 60 zł–80 zł. AE, DC, MC, V. Mon–Sat noon–11pm; Sun 1–10pm.

EXPENSIVE

Akropolis ★★ GREEK This elegant Greek restaurant on the Rynek makes a great choice either for a long, quality lunch or a romantic dinner for two. All the salads, appetizers, and meat and fish dishes (including grilled or fried calamari) you'd expect at a Greek restaurant, with everything fresh and prepared with care. Reserve a table outside on the square in nice weather.

Rynek 16. ✆ **71/343-14-13.** Main courses 30 zł–50 zł. AE, DC, MC, V. Daily noon–11:30pm.

Karczma Lwówska ★ POLISH/UKRAINIAN This is named for the former Polish, now Ukrainian, city from where many current Wrocław residents originally hail. The menu here features many hard-to-find specialties from eastern Poland, including *gołąbki kresówki,* peppers stuffed with spiced minced meat and mushrooms. Dine on the terrace in summer or in the evocative, tavern-style interior in winter. Book ahead, especially on a warm summer evening, when the terrace fills to brimming.

Rynek 4. ✆ **71/343-98-87.** Reservations recommended. Main courses 23 zł–45 zł. AE, DC, MC, V. Daily 11am–midnight.

MODERATE

Abrams' Tower ★★ MEXICAN/ASIAN "Where the East Meets the West" is the motto of this unique restaurant occupying a formerly abandoned bastion in one of Wrocław's medieval town walls in the neighborhood just behind the city market (Hala Targowa). The menu is a smorgasbord of hard-to-find items in Poland, including the city's best Mexican food and Asian-inspired dishes like Thai fish cakes, satay, and prawn tempura in a soy-ginger sauce. Dining is on three levels: the top floor, with a mix of tables and trendy Moroccan-style floor pillows, is the most popular. There's an extensive wine list and a small shop that sells wines.

Kraińskiego 14. ✆ **71/725-66-52.** Main courses 20 zł–50 zł. AE, DC, MC, V. Tues–Fri noon–midnight; Sat 6pm–2am; Sun 4pm–midnight.

Novocaina ★ ITALIAN This trendy entry and club on the Rynek promises only the freshest ingredients, and the Italian-influenced menu mostly delivers. The pizzas are cooked in a traditional cherry-wood-fired oven and come out just right. The high points are the salads and sandwiches, making this a good lunchtime pick and popular with Wrocław's young professional crowd. Very good coffee and free Wi-Fi are two more reasons to visit.

Rynek 13. ✆ **71/343-69-15.** Main courses 25 zł–40 zł. AE, DC, MC, V. Daily 9am–11pm.

Piwnica Świdnicka ★★ POLISH Few city halls in Europe have a giant beer garden in their basement, and few beer gardens anywhere offer food of this quality. Local specialties, such as beef roulade served with beet purée, are some of the best you'll taste, and the atmosphere—either on the terrace in summer or down in the vast cellar in winter—is festive and memorable. There's great beer here, too. Note that service slows down significantly on crowded evenings.

Rynek-Ratusz 1. ✆ **71/369-95-10.** Main courses 23 zł–45 zł. AE, DC, MC, V. Daily 11am–11pm.

INEXPENSIVE

Rodeo Drive ☺ TEX-MEX One of the better chain restaurants to emerge in Poland in the last few years, this one features "Texas-style" steaks, ribs, and burgers. Ordinarily, we'd hesitate before recommending a burger joint in a city that has as many good restaurants as Wrocław, but places like this can be a lifesaver if you're traveling with kids who are starting to tire of pierogies and cabbage. While the burgers are good, the Black Angus steaks are even better and reasonably priced. There's a large no-smoking area in the upstairs dining room.

Rynek 28. ✆ **71/343-96-09.** Main courses 20 zł–35 zł. AE, DC, MC, V. Daily 11am–11pm.

After Dark

THE PERFORMING ARTS

Wrocław is renowned for its theater, which has been long regarded as some of the most daring and experimental in the country. For non–Polish speakers, though, this is likely to be of little interest. The Tourist Information Office at the Rynek is a good source of information on more accessible performances of classical music and opera. The **Wrocław Philharmonic** (Piłsudskiego 19; ✆ **71/342-24-59** box office; www.filharmonia.wroclaw.pl) is a good bet for an excellent concert during the cultural season from September to May. The **Wrocław Opera** (Świdnicka 35; ✆ **71/344-57-79** box office; www.opera.wroclaw.pl) is one of the country's leading companies.

CAFES, PUBS & CLUBS

For culture of the lower-brow sort, Wrocław is a great drinking and partying town. Its festive spirit, not surprisingly, is bolstered by the presence of thousands of college students. The university area has more than its fair share of beer gardens, cafes, and cocktail bars. For a good pub crawl, try Ruska and Kuźnicza streets that lead off from the Rynek. The Plac Solny is also lined with drinking spots, and the Rynek itself is a major draw. What appear to be normal restaurants and cafes during the day transform into everything from rowdy beer halls to ultra-chill dance clubs after sunset.

Czeski Film ★★ This popular pub is a personal favorite and a great spot to get a good beer. While we enjoy the lively atmosphere, we particularly like the name, which translates as "Czech film," a Polish expression that means loosely, "I have no idea what's going on," or, as we might say in English, "It's all Greek to me." Kiełbaśnicza 2. ✆ **71/342-25-49.** Mon–Thurs 9am–midnight; Fri & Sat 9am–2am.

Graciarnia ★★ In spite of its unpromising location and doorway, this is a great spot if you're looking for a quiet beer or drink a little bit away from the action. A self-described "chill zone" features antique furniture, a laid-back clientele, and very friendly servers. K. Wielkiego 39. ✆ **71/795-66-88.** Mon–Fri noon–2am; Sat 5pm–2am; Sun 5pm–midnight.

AROUND WROCŁAW: KSIĄŻ CASTLE, ŚWIDNICA & JAWOR

The most popular day trips from Wrocław include the massive Książ (pronounced *kshawnzh*) Castle, near Wałbrzych, about 75km (47 miles) southwest of Wrocław, and the two remarkable 17th-century wooden "Peace" churches at Świdnica (pronounced *shveed'-neet-sah;* 60km/37 miles from Wrocław) and Jawor (pronounced *yah'-vor;* 80km/50 miles from Wrocław). If you have your own wheels, it's easy to combine the three sites in one day, setting off first for Świdnica from Wrocław, then continuing on to Wałbrzych and Książ, and then heading north to Jawor before looping back to Wrocław. It's also possible, but slower, to go by public transportation, taking the bus or train to Wałbrzych, then the bus to Świdnica, and then continuing by bus or train to Jawor. Alternatively, several Wrocław tour operators offer day bus trips with guides. If you've got a couple of days, Książ Castle has several beautiful hotels near it and is a great overnight choice. Świdnica is also worth an extra day and has at least two decent hotels. Jawor is smaller, but it's possible to put in there for the night, too.

Essentials

GETTING THERE

BY CAR Książ Castle is easily accessible from Wrocław by car, following signs to Wałbrzych along Polish Route 35 (you'll see the entrance to the castle just before you reach the center of town). Conveniently, the route takes you near Świdnica, meaning it's easy to plan a stopover at the Peace Church there. There's ample parking (4 zł/hr.) at Książ Castle, and if you've booked a room at one of the hotels there, you're permitted to drive practically up to the castle gates. To reach more remote Jawor from Wrocław, follow the A4 highway to Legnica and turn south on E65 when you see signs to Jawor. From Wałbrzych, drive along Route 35 in the direction of Świdnica, following signs first to Strzegom and from there to Jawor.

BY TRAIN Regional train travel has been curtailed a bit in recent years. You can reach Wałbrzych by train from Wrocław, but you're better off taking the bus for other destinations. From the Wałbrzych train station, use local bus connections (city bus no. 8) to get to Książ Castle. From Świdnica, it's possible to take the train to Jawor (about 1 hr.) or to Kłodzko (about 2 hr.). From the Świdnica train station, walk or take a taxi to the Peace Church.

BY BUS Wałbrzych, Świdnica, and Jawor are all on regular bus routes. To reach Książ Castle, take Wałbrzych city bus no. 8, which takes you to the castle gate, or take a taxi from the bus station.

VISITOR INFORMATION

Książ Castle has a small tourist information office just as you enter the castle compound in the lobby of the Książ Castle Hotel (Piastów Śląskich 1; ✆ **74/664-38-90;** www.ksiaz.walbrzych.pl). Don't expect much in the way of service or English, but they do carry a few brochures and maps. In Świdnica, the main tourist information office is conveniently located on the central square (Wewnętrzna 2 [Rynek]; ✆ **74/852-02-90;** www.um.swidnica.pl). Look for the brochure *Świdnica, Tradition of the Market,* which has a small map and a good list of sights and accommodation options. Jawor also has a small but helpful tourist information office on the main square (Rynek 3; ✆ **76/870-33-71;** www.gci.dja.pl). The English-speaking staff is eager to recommend hotels and restaurants, and help sort out transportation options.

Top Attractions

Książ Castle (Fuerstenstein Castle) ★★ Reputedly the largest castle in Lower Silesia, the 400-room Książ Castle was originally laid out in the 13th century by members of the early Polish nobility. It's been refurbished and rebuilt several times through the centuries, resulting in today's baroque-Renaissance-rococo-neoclassical mishmash. From 1509 to 1940, the castle was owned by the Hochberg family, and its most famous resident—at least, to English-speaking readers—is Winston Churchill's aunt, Princess Daisy Hochberg, who lived here from 1891 to 1923 and then again in the tempestuous years at the start of World War II, from 1938 to 1940. During the latter half of World War II, the castle was seconded by the Nazis, who dug huge tunnels in the ground below. It's never been fully revealed what the Nazis were up to, but theories include preparing the castle as a residence for Adolf Hitler or simply clearing space to build an underground munitions factory.

After the war, the occupying Soviet Army requisitioned the castle and, according to the Poles, stayed a suspiciously long time; perhaps trying to figure out what the Germans wanted to do here. After the Russians left, the castle languished unoccupied. Now, it's making a comeback as one of the most popular tourist sites in these parts and also as a conference and party venue.

There are two possibilities for seeing the interior: one is to take a guided tour (offered only in Polish), the other is to tour the castle on your own. The former includes a visit to the underground Nazi-era tunnels, while the latter unfortunately does not. Before embarking on the individual tour, be sure to stop in at the antique store on the ground floor to buy a little booklet in English on the castle. The guided tour lasts about 70 minutes. (English tours are available, but must be booked in advance and are conducted only for groups of 15 or more.)

Piastów Slaskich 1. ✆ **74/664-38-50.** www.ksiaz.walbrzych.pl. 14 zł adults; guided tour 20 zł. Apr–Sept Mon–Fri 10am–5pm, Sat & Sun 10am–6pm; Oct–Mar Tues–Fri 10am–3pm, Sat & Sun 10am–4pm.

"Peace" Churches of Świdnica and Jawor ★★ The spectacular 17th-century wooden "Peace" churches of Świdnica and Jawor are both listed as UNESCO World Heritage Sites and have provisions for English-speaking visitors (written information and an English audio tape they will play in the church on request) that are often frustratingly lacking at other tourist destinations in Poland. The "Peace" in the names refers to the Peace of Westphalia of 1648 that ended the Europe-wide Thirty Years War. Though the war finished inconclusively, this part of Europe fell under the domination of the staunchly Catholic Habsburg Empire, ruled from Vienna. Local Lutherans sought the protection of the King of Sweden for the right to build three Lutheran churches in the area (a third church at Głogów later burned to the ground). The Habsburgs relented but stipulated that the churches could be built only under very difficult circumstances: They had to be constructed completely from wood without the use of iron nails, located outside the town walls, and completed within a calendar year. That the churches were finished at all was a miracle; that they turned out so beautifully is fitting testimony to the faith of the believers. The Świdnica church, which can hold up to 7,000, is the largest wooden church in Europe, but both structures are amazing in terms of their size, the engineering skills that went into their construction, and their enduring beauty.

Świdnica Peace Church: Pl. Pokoju 6; ✆ **74/852-28-14;** www.kosciolpokoju.pl; 8 zł adults; Apr–Oct Mon–Sat 9am–5pm, Sun noon–5pm; open Nov–Mar by appointment only. Jawor Peace Church: Park Pokoju 2; ✆ **76/870-32-73;** www.luteranie.pl; 8 zł adults; Apr–Oct Mon–Sat 10am–3pm & 4–5pm, Sun 3–5pm; open Nov–Mar by appointment only.

Where to Stay

The three hotels in the immediate vicinity of Książ Castle are some of the nicest properties in this part of Poland. The problem with staying here, though, is that the castle is a bit remote, and once you've toured the buildings and walked the grounds, there's not much else to do. In nearby Świdnica, there are two good hotels, and the city is big enough to offer some diversions in the evening. Jawor has one decent hotel and a small town center worth about an hour of exploration. If you're traveling by car, the Hotel Bolków, 15km (9¼ miles) south of Jawor, offers cheap rates and one of the best restaurants in southwestern Poland.

KSIĄZ CASTLE/WAŁBRZYCH

Hotel Książ This is not as luxurious inside as the brochures might indicate. The rooms are a bit spare and, compared to the two other hotels here, not as good value-for-money. Nevertheless, this is a comfortable night's stay, with a very good in-house restaurant and just a short walk away from the main castle entrance.

Piastów Slaskich 1. ✆ **74/664-38-90.** Fax 74/664-38-92. www.ksiaz.walbrzych.pl. 20 units. 240 zł double. AE, DC, MC, V. Parking (fpaid). **Amenities:** Restaurant; room service. *In room:* A/C, TV, Internet, minibar.

Hotel Przy Oślej Bramie ★★ 🎁 The most romantic of the three hotels within the castle complex, the property comprises several remodeled guesthouses, including part of the old castle bastion walls, that have been hewn together to pleasing effect. Ask to see several rooms, since they are all a little different. Some are done out in period furnishings, and a few have retained the original arched ceilings. The little garden terrace is the perfect spot for an afternoon coffee or tea.

Piastów Slaskich 1. ✆ **74/664-92-70.** Fax 74/664-92-71. www.mirjan.pl. 27 units. 250 zł double. AE, DC, MC, V. Parking (paid). **Amenities:** Restaurant; room service. *In room:* TV, hair dryer, Internet, minibar.

Hotel Zamkowy ★★ Another beautifully renovated former castle outbuilding, this has been given the royal touch with stunning red carpet and contemporary room decor that looks both restrained and luxurious at the same time. Everything is spotless, and the hotel is one of the few wheelchair-accessible properties around. The Zamkowy offers special horseback riding weekends that take advantage of the former castle stables just up the street.

Piastów Slaskich 1. ✆ **74/665-41-44.** Fax 74/665-41-44. www.hotelzamkowy.pl. 25 units. 275 zł double. AE, DC, MC, V. Parking (paid). **Amenities:** Restaurant; exercise room; room service. *In room:* A/C, TV, hair dryer, Internet, minibar.

SWIDNICA

Park Hotel ★★ This nicely reconstructed 19th-century villa is on a park about 5 minutes' walk from the train station, 10 minutes from the town center, and about 15 minutes from the Świdnica Peace Church. The rooms are furnished in early-Modern period style, and the bathrooms are big and spotless, though the beds could use just a bit more padding. Take a look at the suites if you're in the mood for a splurge; Room no. 3 is a corner with a delightful canopy bed and a rack rate not much higher than a standard room. The friendly reception desk will sometimes cut deals on slow nights. The very good restaurant downstairs seals the deal.

Pionierów 20. ✆ **74/853-77-22.** Fax 74/853-70-98. www.park-hotel.com.pl. 23 units. 230 zł double. AE, DC, MC, V. Parking (paid). **Amenities:** Restaurant; room service. *In room:* A/C, TV, hair dryer, Internet, minibar.

Piast-Roman Hotel A comfortable in-town option. The location, on a side street off the main square, is closer to the action than the Park, but the rooms are colder and not as homey. Wi-Fi is available on some floors; if this is important to you, be sure to ask. The restaurant comes highly recommended by the locals for its decent Polish and international dishes in a town that has relatively few good places to eat. You can walk to the Peace Church from here in about 10 minutes.

Kotlarska 11. ✆ **74/852-13-93.** www.hotel-piast-roman.pl. 23 units. 220 zł double. AE, DC, MC, V. Parking (paid). **Amenities:** Restaurant; room service. *In room:* TV, Internet, minibar, Wi-Fi (in some, free).

JAWOR

Bolków Hotel ★ This small, family-run hotel about 15km (9¼ miles) south of Jawor in the town of Bolków is a good value and perfectly fine for a night. The rooms are tiny and no-frills, but the reconstructed roadside villa, which uses old black-and-white photos to evoke a 1920s feel, is a nice change of pace from characterless modern hotels. The hotel offers free Wi-Fi, but the connection is often fickle. Because of the location, this hotel is really an option only if you are traveling by car.

Sienkiewicza 17. ✆ **75/741-39-95.** Fax 75/741-39-96. www.hotel-bolkow.pl. 23 units. 140 zł double; breakfast 15 zł. AE, MC, V. Parking. **Amenities:** Restaurant. *In room:* TV, Wi-Fi (free).

Hotel Jawor ★ Head and shoulders above anything else in town, this modern hotel makes a perfect overnight stop and is popular with both tourists and traveling businessmen. The rooms are done up in a contemporary style and are clean and comfortable. The restaurant is one of just a handful of reasonable dining options in town, and there's a little cafe off the lobby that serves the only drinkable coffee for miles. The central location is an easy 10-minute walk to the town square and the Jawor Peace Church.

Staszica 10. ✆ **76/871-06-24.** Fax 76/871-15-46. www.hoteljawor.com.pl. 23 units. 220 zł double. AE, DC, MC, V. Parking (paid). **Amenities:** Restaurant; room service. *In room:* TV, Internet, minibar.

Where to Dine

Decent dining options are few and far between in these parts. At Książ Castle, try the restaurant at the Hotel Książ (see above) or the informal terrace grill that offers sausages and beer in the summer (follow the signs for "Grill" from the main castle entrance). If you're stuck in Jawor without a car, the restaurant at the Hotel Jawor (see above) will do in a pinch.

ŚWIDNICA

Park Hotel Restaurant ★ POLISH/CONTINENTAL The best restaurant in town, the menu here runs the gamut from traditional Polish specialties such as *żurek* and pierogi to international pasta dishes, grilled salmon, and lots of meat and chicken entrees. There are also excellent salads and friendly service. Most nights, you can just show up at the door, but book ahead on weekends.

Pionierów 20. ✆ **74/853-77-22.** Reservations accepted. Main courses 25 zł–45 zł. AE, DC, MC, V. Daily noon–11pm.

JAWOR

Bolków Hotel Restaurant ★★ POLISH/CONTINENTAL For one of the best meals on offer in this part of Poland, head to the restaurant at the Bolków Hotel. Specializing in home cooking done well, the menu includes big plates of roast meats served with mounds of mashed potatoes, and local specialties such as roast veal and fresh grilled trout. The desserts are homemade, and the throwback atmosphere is fun and inviting.

Sienkiewicza 17. ✆ **75/741-39-95.** Main courses 20 zł–50 zł. DC, MC, V. Daily 10am–11pm.

Restauracja Ratuszowa ★★ POLISH Jawor is busy sprucing up its central square, and this romantic candlelit spot next to the main entrance to town hall provides the right setting to enjoy it. The menu is in Polish only, but items like pork medallions, steak, and goulash are easy enough to make out. The helpful English-speaking staff can advise on what looks good in the kitchen that day. The wine list is impressive. The hushed interior makes for a perfect night out for two.

Rynek 1. ✆ **76/870-21-31.** Main courses 25 zł–40 zł. DC, MC, V. Daily 11am–10pm.

JELENIA GÓRA & KARKONOSZE NATIONAL PARK

To the south, the rolling hills of Silesia give way to a chain of low-rise mountains that run southeast and define the border between Poland and the Czech Republic. Nearly the entire area, including the Czech side of the border, is a protected national park (Karkonosze National Park in Polish; Krkonoše National Park in Czech). The origin of the word "Karkonosze" is not known, but in German and English, the range is often referred to as the "Giant" mountains. This rather overstates the case. The highest peaks are in the 1,600m (5,249-ft.) range. Nevertheless, the mountains and the national park make for a perfect low-stress stopover for hiking or biking in summer and skiing in winter. The region's major city, Jelenia Góra (pronounced *ye-len'-ee-ah gu'-rah*), has a beautifully preserved town square and is worth at least a few hours of poking around. With good transportation connections, as well as decent hotels and restaurants, it makes a fine base for exploring the national park. Alternatively, if you're coming specifically to ski or hike, you'll probably want to stay within the boundaries of the national park itself at one of the main resorts of Karpacz (pronounced *kar'-pahch*) or Szklarska Poręba (pronounced *sklar'-skah por-en'-ba*).

Essentials

GETTING THERE

BY TRAIN Jelenia Góra is the main transportation center for this part of Lower Silesia and has decent rail connections with Wrocław (3–4 hr.) and neighboring towns.

BY BUS Buses link Jelenia Góra to cities across southern Poland, and buses are generally a quicker option than trains for reaching regional cities. Frequent buses link Jelenia Góra to the mountain resorts of Karpacz and Szklarska Poręba. Figure on around 8 zł each way. Note that going from Karpacz to Szklarska Poręba and vice versa is not as easy on public transportation. Inquire at the helpful tourist information office in either town to figure out the best transportation option.

BY CAR Jelenia Góra lies on the E65 highway, linking this part of Poland with the Czech city of Liberec. It's an easy 90-minute drive from Wrocław and about an hour from Liberec. Szklarska Poręba is on the same highway, just 10km (6½ miles) from the Czech border. Karpacz is more remote. To find it, follow Poland Route 367 south out of Jelenia Góra about 10km (6¼ miles). Figure on about 15 minutes for the journey.

TOURIST INFORMATION

The **Jelenia Góra Tourist and Cultural Information Center** (Bankowa 27; ✆ **75/767-69-25;** www.jeleniagora.pl) is exceptionally helpful and offers maps and good advice for exploring the nearby Karkonosze National Park. The English-speaking staff can help arrange transportation, find a room, or recommend a good place to eat. There are several tourist information offices within the Karkonosze National Park. Main branches are at **Szklarska Poręba** (Jedności Narodowej 1a; ✆ **75/754-77-40;** www.szklarskaporeba.pl) and **Karpacz** (Konstytucji 3 Maja 25; ✆ **75/761-97-16;** www.karpacz.pl). In Karpacz, in addition to the tourist information office, just down the street (in the direction of the town center), you'll find an outdoor electronic kiosk open 24/7, showing which hotels and pensions have free rooms. The Szklarska Poręba branch carries a free cycling map and doles out information on bike and ski rentals.

GETTING AROUND

Regular bus and minibus service connects Jelenia Góra with the mountain resorts of Karpacz and Szklarska Poręba; public transportation, however, between Karpacz and Szklarska Poręba is not as frequent. Most visitors come by car. Figure on about 20 minutes of driving from Jelenia Góra to each of the resorts, and about 40 minutes to drive from Karpacz to Szklarska Poręba.

Top Attractions

JELENIA GÓRA

This is the largest town in the vicinity of the Karkonosze Mountains and is a good jumping-off spot for exploring the mountains and Karkonosze National Park because of its decent lodging and dining options. The town's history goes back some 900 years. The focal point is an impressive medieval square, the Plac Ratuszowy, surrounded by baroque- and rococo-facaded burghers' houses and with the town hall, the Ratusz, in the middle. There's not much in the way of traditional sightseeing options, though the burghers' houses deserve closer inspection. In the town's heyday, these were occupied by the wealthiest citizens, and many are still marked with the signs of the traditional guilds. Today, the intact baroque arcades serve mainly to shield the customers of the many cafes and pubs that line the square. If you get a rainy day or have a few hours to spend in town, walk about 500m (1,640 ft.) south of the square to the Karkonosze Regional Museum, a good primer on the park's history and natural bounty.

Muzeum Karkonoskie (Karkonosze Museum) This presents a pleasant if slightly dull presentation of the history of the Karkonosze region, as well as this part of Lower Silesia, including examples of traditional folk architecture and crafts, as well as some atmospheric old photos of what was once certainly a golden age in these parts. Display information is in Polish and German only.

Jana Matejki 28. ✆ **75/752-34-65.** www.muzeumkarkonoskie.pl. 7 zł adults; 4 zł children. Tues–Fri 9am–3:30pm; Sat & Sun 9am–4:30pm.

KARKONOSZE NATIONAL PARK/KARPACZ/ SZKLARSKA PORĘBA

Most visitors to Karkonosze National Park choose to base themselves at one of the mountain resorts of Karpacz and Szklarska Poręba, where the best hotels, restaurants, and tourist information offices are located. In truth, there's not much difference between the two. Karpacz is a little smaller and more remote than Szklarska Poręba, lying farther from a main highway. On the down side, the ski facilities here are slightly inferior, and in summer, the mountain-biking infrastructure is not as built up as in Szklarska Poręba. Either resort is fine if you're just passing through for a couple of days to go walking in the mountains. Aside from the beautiful nature, along with hiking, biking, and skiing, there's not much here in the way of traditional tourist sites. If you get a rainy day, both resort centers are suitably picturesque and filled with little souvenir shops and diversions. Karpacz has two modest tourist attractions: A sports museum and a transplanted Norwegian church that's certainly worth seeking out.

Muzeum Sportu i Turystyki w Karpaczu (Museum of Sports and Tourism in Karpacz) The main exhibitions here focus on the history of the Giant Mountains. Exhibits start from the early 12th century, when the first Polish armies slogged through here, paving new routes to Bohemia, and also include a history of sports in the mountains, particularly sledding and skiing in the 19th century.

Kopernika 2. ✆ **75/761-96-52.** www.muzeumsportu.dolnyslask.pl. 5 zł adults; 3 zł seniors, students & children. Tues–Sun 9am–5pm.

Wang Church ★★ Probably the last thing you'd expect to find in the Giant Mountains of Poland is a 12th-century Norwegian church. This wooden beauty was transplanted here from Norway's Vang valley in 1842 by Prussian King Frederick William IV to serve as a place of worship for the local Lutheran community. It's one of just a handful of old Viking churches to survive anywhere in the world and is an excellent example of Old Nordic sacral architecture. It's located about 4km (2½ miles) outside of the main center of Karpacz in Karpacz Górny. To get there, you can hike (about an hour), take a bus, take a taxi (about 10 zł from Karpacz), or drive.

Na Śnieżkę 8. ✆ **75/752-82-92.** www.wang.com.pl. 5 zł adults; 4 zł seniors, students & children. Mon–Sat 10am–6pm; Sun 11:30am–6pm.

Outdoor Activities

Biking, hiking, and skiing are the three most popular sporting activities here, but there are lots of other more adventurous pursuits, such as bouldering, mountain climbing, and gliding, that have become more popular in recent years. As operators change by the year, the best advice is to ask at the tourist information office to see what's available during the time of your visit.

BIKING In the last decade or so, Szklarska Poręba has evolved into the mountain biking capital of southern Poland. Around 20 numbered trails of more than 400km (249 miles) in total length, catering to all skill levels, fan out from the town in all directions. Some of the trails are all-day affairs running 40 to 60km (25–37 miles) in length, while others are shorter and oriented toward recreational cyclists or families with children. Pick up the free cycling map *Rowerowa Kraina* from the tourist information office. They can also advise you on the best routes and bike rentals. In Szklarska Poręba, bike rental outfits are located at Wzg. Paderewskiego 5 (✆ **75/717-20-74**) and at Jednosci Narodowej 15 (✆ **888/721-883**). Rentals start at around 10 zł per hour and around 40 zł for all day.

HIKING Most visitors come here for the opportunity to walk in the mountains. Karkonosze National Park is crisscrossed by hundreds of miles of marked trails, and that number is effectively doubled if you count the trails on the Czech side. Note that you can freely walk across the border without having to show a passport, but it's always a good idea to carry it with you in the rare event you are stopped. Trails on both sides of the border follow an informal color guide, with the most popular and rewarding walks marked in red, and the hierarchy moving down to blue, green, and yellow. Both Karpacz and Szklarska Poręba are excellent hiking bases. The first port of call should be the tourist information office for advice on routes and maps. A popular day-long slog in summer is to the peak at Śnieżka, the highest point in the range at 1,602m (5,256 ft.) above sea level.

SKIING Both Szklarska Poręba and Karpacz have excellent facilities for downhill and cross-country skiing. In downhill skiing, Szklarska Poręba gets the nod both for the number and quality of its slopes, as well as having the country's longest continuous run at around 4.5km (2.8 miles). The Masyw Szrenicy and the Łabski Szczyt region form the largest ski center, with five separate slopes and a joint length of about 20km (12 miles). Contact Ski Arena Szrenica (Turystyczna 25a; ✆ **75/717-21-18;** www.sudetylift.com.pl) for details. In Karpacz, the center of the action is the Śnieżka Ski Complex (Turystyczna 4; ✆ **75/761-86-19;** www.kopa.com.pl). One of Karpacz's main lifts is located right in the middle of town.

Where to Stay

JELENIA GÓRA

Hotel Jelonek ★ The most pleasant of several choices directly in the city center, this small family-run hotel occupies an 18th-century town house on a pedestrian promenade just a 5-minute walk to the main square and 15 minutes by foot from the bus station. The rooms are simply furnished, but are warm and inviting, with traditional wood furniture and hardwood floors. Only some rooms have an Internet connection. There's parking behind the hotel on Mostowa.

1-go Maja 5. ✆ **75/764-6541.** Fax 75/752-3794. www.hoteljelonek.pl. 12 units. 220 zł double. AE, DC, MC, V. Parking. **Amenities:** Restaurant. *In room:* TV, Internet (in some), minibar.

Hotel Mercure ★ This chain hotel about 2km (1¼ miles) outside of the center lacks charm but compensates with a complete set of hotel amenities, plus comfortable rooms and upscale bedding and bathrooms. The large lobby has a cafe, as well as several little souvenir shops. The rooms are boxy and a little sterile, but have everything you need for a couple days' stay. The walk to the center will take about 15 minutes, but if you're arriving by bus or train with luggage, it's better to take a taxi (about 10 zł from the center). Rates offered on the hotel's website are often significantly lower than the rack rates.

Sudecka 63. ✆ **75/754-91-48.** Fax 75/752-62-66. www.mercure.com. 190 units. 300 zł double. AE, DC, MC, V. Parking. **Amenities:** Restaurant; concierge; exercise room; room service. *In room:* A/C, TV, hair dryer, Internet, minibar.

Pałac Paulinum ★★ This elegant, secluded 19th-century *palais* was originally home to a Silesian textile baron and is now a stunningly renovated luxury hotel—but without the luxury price tag. The refined public areas are done out in parquets with ornately carved wall panels and impressive chandeliers. Rooms feature period furnishings but differ greatly in size, from tiny to gargantuan. Ask for an upgrade on a slow night. There are several restaurants on the premises, as well as a full-service spa with salt grotto, a winter garden, and a billiards room. You will have to take a taxi (about 10 zł–15 zł) from the center.

Nowowiejska 62. ✆ **75/649-44-00.** Fax 75/649-44-03. www.paulinum.pl. 29 units. 320 zł double. AE, DC, MC, V. Parking. **Amenities:** Restaurant; concierge; exercise room; room service; sauna; spa. *In room:* A/C, TV, hair dryer, Internet, minibar.

KARPACZ

Relaks ★ This decent modern mountain chalet makes up what it lacks in traditional charm with big clean rooms, great service, and one of the best hotel-based spas in Karpacz. All the rooms are nonsmoking, and some of the higher-floor doubles have a small attached kitchen. If you're traveling by car, a big perk is free guarded parking. There's also a small fleet of high-quality Trek bikes on hand for guests to use. It's outside the center by a couple of kilometers, so you'll have to walk (15 minutes) or take a taxi from town. It discounts rates on weekends.

Obrońców Pokoju 4. ✆ **75/648-06-50.** Fax 75/648-06-53. www.hotel-relaks.pl. 40 units. 260 zł double. AE, DC, MC, V. Parking. **Amenities:** Restaurant; exercise room; room service; sauna; spa. *In room:* TV, hair dryer, Internet, minibar.

Rezydencja ★★ This delightfully restored 350-year-old villa, just a short walk from town, is one of the most charming hotels in Karpacz. Most of the rooms are generously-sized apartments, with a bedroom and separate sitting room. The furnishings are modern, but the colors are warm and inviting. The in-house restaurant is arguably the best in town, and a small fitness room is a comfortable place to unwind after a long day of biking or skiing.

Parkowa 6. ✆ **75/761-80-20.** Fax 75/761-95-13. www.hotelrezydencja.pl. 14 units. 270 zł double. AE, DC, MC, V. Parking. **Amenities:** Restaurant; exercise room; room service; sauna. *In room:* A/C, TV, hair dryer, Internet, minibar.

SZKLARSKA PORĘBA

Hotel Szrenica ★ Not nearly as spiffy as the Szrenicowy Dwór (below), but much more relaxed and family-oriented. The decor is mid-century modern, a kind of throwback 1960s look, with ranch-style architecture, flagstone on the walls, and bright colors in the rooms and public areas. The rooms themselves are clean and quiet, done out in a more contemporary look, some with flat-screen TVs. The reception desk is plugged into all of the leisure possibilities in town and can advise on biking and skiing in season. There's also a whirlpool and sauna on hand to relax in when you come back.

Turystyczna 29. ✆ **75/717-35-99**. www.hotelszrenica.pl. 50 units. 260 zł double. AE, DC, MC, V. Parking. **Amenities:** Restaurant; exercise room; whirlpool; sauna. *In room:* TV, hair dryer, Internet.

Szrenicowy Dwór ★★ If you're looking to splurge a bit on truly memorable accommodation, try a night or two here at the Szrenicowy Manor House Hotel, situated in a giant villa that rises castle-like on a bluff over the town center. There's plenty of period touches here to recapture some of the 19th-century atmosphere, such as the Biedermeier furnishings in some of the rooms (ask to see a few rooms before choosing), though the hotel keeps at least one foot in the 21st century with LCD flat-screen TVs and Wi-Fi in the rooms. There's a small fitness room and a playground for the kids. To find the hotel, head to the center where the river runs under the road and just look up.

Wzg. Paderewskiego 12. ✆ **75/717-34-61.** www.szrenicowydwor.pl. 34 units. 300 zł double. AE, DC, MC, V. Parking. **Amenities:** Restaurant; exercise room; sauna. *In room:* TV, hair dryer, minibar, Wi-Fi (free).

Where to Dine

JELENIA GÓRA

Bistrot 26 ★★ FRENCH/POLISH The high-quality French cooking at this tiny eatery on the main square comes as a pleasant surprise in a middling burgh like Jelenia Góra. Traditional French fare like snails and frog legs support imaginative main courses such as pork roulade wrapped around pâté and served with a duo of blue cheese and creamy pesto sauces. Friendly, English-speaking service and a spot on the terrace on a warm evening round out the city's only must-dine experience.

Pl. Ratuszowy 26. ✆ **508/821-067.** Main courses 30 zł–50 zł. AE, DC, M, V. Daily noon–10pm.

Kawiarnia Naleśnikarnia ★ POLISH Excellent Italian espressos and other coffee beverages are on offer here, as well as their signature enormous sweet pancakes (crêpes) filled with nuts and chocolate, and small items like sandwiches. Early opening hours make for a convenient breakfast stop of a coffee and pancake. If all the chairs are full, try Memories of Africa next door at Pl. Ratuszowy 4, another very good square-side coffee joint.

Pl. Ratuszowy 2. ✆ **75/647-54-44.** Main courses 10 zł–20 zł. No credit cards. Daily 9am–7pm.

Sorrento ★ ITALIAN This upscale Italian eatery just behind the Town Hall on the main square serves big salads, good homemade soups, and pizza. Decent pasta offerings include tagliatelle with wild mushrooms and an unusual, but delicious, spaghetti with tuna and spinach.

Pl. Ratuszowy 15/17. ✆ **75/752-59-28.** Main courses 20 zł–30 zł. AE, DC, M, V. Daily 11am–10pm.

SZKLARSKA PORĘBA/KARPACZ

Both towns are stuffed with little dining places and pizza joints. In Karpacz, in summer, there's a big open-air eatery in the center of town that serves heaping platefuls of *bigos* (hunter's stew) and grilled sausage. Most of the hotels have good restaurants, including the highly recommended Hotel Rezydencja in Karpacz.

Alfredo ★★ POLISH This unassuming cafe serves excellent home-style cooking, including pierogi, kielbasa (sausages), and the ever-popular potato pancake–goulash combo, as well as fresh-caught fried trout served with garlic butter and fries.

Finish up with an espresso and a slice of homemade apricot cheesecake. From the outside, it doesn't look like much, but it's one of the best and easiest meals around.

1 Maja 15 (Szklarska Poręba). ✆ **508/673-701.** Main courses 20 zł–30 zł. No credit cards. Daily 11am–10pm.

Metafora/Klub Jazgot ★★ POLISH/CONTINENTAL Most restaurants in town cater to undemanding groups of skiers and day-trippers, and standards are not very high. This ambitious combination of ground-floor restaurant and basement jazz pub is different. It's clear from the slick service and beautiful presentation that they really care about the food. The traditional pork cutlet served with beets and mashed potatoes is superb. Be sure to book well in advance in ski season and on weekends. Worth a special trip. Klub Jazgot is a popular pub and a good place to head for an after-dinner drink.

Objazdowa 1 (Szklarska Poręba). ✆ **75/717-36-89.** www.jazgot.pl. Reservations accepted. Main courses 25 zł–35 zł. AE, DC, M, V. Daily noon–11pm.

Oberża u Hochoła POLISH This is exactly what you'd expect at a mountain resort: A loud, fun, rustic tavern with plenty of traditional Polish food and lots of beer to wash it all down. Eat outside in nice weather.

1 Maja 11 (Szklarska Poręba). ✆ **75/717-34-30.** Main courses 20 zł–30 zł. AE, DC, M, V. Daily noon–11pm.

KŁODZKO

South and east of the Karkonosze range lies a sparsely populated region of woods and hills that extends southward deep into the territory of the modern-day Czech Republic. The Kłodzko region (www.powiat.klodzko.pl) was one of the first parts of Silesia to be settled by Slavs in the years before 1000 A.D. During the early centuries of its existence, Kłodzko (pronounced *kwahdz-koh*) was part of the Bohemian crown lands and ruled from Prague. Even today, the statue-lined main pedestrian bridge in the capital city bears a noticeable resemblance to Charles Bridge in Prague. When the Habsburgs assumed control of Bohemia in the 16th century, they got the Kłodzko region as well, only to lose it to Prussia in the 18th century. Later, Kłodzko became part of Germany, and then, after World War II, it fell back into Polish hands. Today, while Kłodzko is unmistakably Polish, here and there, you'll still find traces of the Prussian and Czech presence. The Polish spoken here is laced with traces of Czech, and in the countryside, much of the rural architecture has a Prussian or Germanic feel. Kłodzko is best explored by car since trains are scarce and bus timetables can be tricky to negotiate. The main sights include the beautifully preserved Prussian fortress town of Kłodzko and the pleasant spa town of Kudowa-Zdrój, with an eerie bone church, which merits a diversion. Nature is another draw here, unspoiled and wilder the farther south you go toward the Sudety mountains and the popular hiking base of Międzygórze.

Essentials

GETTING THERE

Kłodzko city is served by both regular train and bus service from Wrocław and other large cities. The bus station is particularly convenient, across the road from the statue-lined stone bridge that leads to the center of town. By car, from Wrocław, Kłodzko is a straight shot south down the E67 highway about 120km (75 miles). The drive is about 2 hours. Kłodzko is about 40km (25 miles) from the Czech border and is an easy drive to the Czech regional city of Hradec Králové. Prague lies 180km (112 miles) to the southwest. The drive takes about 3 hours.

GETTING AROUND

Make Kłodzko your base, and use buses or your own car to get around the Kłodzko region. Regular buses connect Kłodzko with the towns of Kudowa-Zdrój and Międzygórze. The Kłodzko tourist information office can advise on transportation. Within Kłodzko city, walking is the only option. The city is small, and 10 minutes on foot will get you anywhere you want to go.

TOURIST INFORMATION

Kłodzko's Tourist Information Office is situated on the main square (Plac Bolesława Chrobrego 1; ✆ **74/865-89-70**). Don't expect much in the way of help; but it's a useful stop to check on trains and buses, and see what's going on in town. The Tourist Information Office in Międzygórze (Wojska Polskiego 2; ✆ **74/813-51-95**) is a good starting point for hiking maps and suggestions on trails.

Top Attractions

Begin your exploration of Kłodzko by crossing the city's miniature version of Prague's Charles Bridge, a small Gothic stone crossing topped with baroque statuary. The bridge leads into the town's outsized central square, Plac Bolesława Chrobrego, which houses the Town Hall, the Ratusz, and the tourist information office. Continue walking to the city's main attraction, the enormous Prussian fortress, with its high-tower vantage point and fascinating warren of underground tunnels. Church lovers will also want to peek in to the Parish Church of Our Lady NMP, with its stern Gothic façade hiding an elaborate Baroque interior.

Kłodzko Fortress ★★ ☺ The Kłodzko hill has played an important strategic role for centuries, straddling the traditional borderland first between the Polish and Bohemian kingdoms, and then later Prussia and Austria. There's been a fortress of one kind or another here for around 1,000 years. The present massive structure dates from the middle of the 18th century, when the Prussians defeated the Austrians and embarked on a massive rebuilding project using prisoners of war as laborers. Early on, Napoleon shattered the fortress's illusion of invincibility by capturing it in 1807. During World War II, the Nazis used the fortress to hold political prisoners. Today, it is the region's leading tourist attraction, both for its tower with commanding views over Kłodzko's hinterland and its labyrinth of underground tunnels once used for troop mustering, hiding, and escape, if necessary. The tunnels can be seen by guided tour only. Be sure to bring a jacket, even in summer, as it can get quite cold down there. To find the entrance to the fortress, head to the top of the main square and walk left on Czeska Street.

Grodzisko 1. ✆ **74/867-34-68.** Fortress only: 7 zł adults, 5 zł children; fortress & tunnels: 14 zł adults, 10 zł children. Summer Tues–Sun 9am–7pm; winter Tues–Sun 9am–4pm.

Chapel of Skulls ★ A "bone-chilling" spectacle awaits at a small church and cemetery just north of the spa town of Kudowa-Zdrój (35km/22 miles west of Kłodzko) in the village of Czermna. If you've already been to the Czech Republic, chances are you've seen the well-known ossuary (bone church) in Kutná Hora. If not, you have a real treat here: an entire chapel decorated with the skeletal remains of some 3,000 victims of the Thirty Years' War, and other conflicts and epidemics to have hit this area over the centuries. Ghoulish and fascinating in equal measure, it may not be suitable for children. To find the chapel, head to Kudowa-Zdrój and follow the signs to "Kaplica Czaszek" about 2km (1¼ miles) out of the spa center.

Moniuszki 8. ✆ **605/540-927.** 4 zł adults. Tues–Sun 10am–4:30pm (closes earlier in winter).

Where to Stay & Dine

Kłodzko city is not exactly bursting with five-star lodging opportunities. The city has two modestly priced hotels, both of which will do in a pinch for a night or two. Both, luckily, have excellent in-house restaurants; this is one destination where there's no good reason not to eat at the hotel.

Casa D'Oro ★ Kłodzko's nicest hotel is this modest inn on a relatively quiet corner close to the central square and above a decent Polish/Italian restaurant of the same name. The rooms are nicely furnished with big beds and cherry-wood furniture. The location is excellent, practically next door to Kłodzko's famed mini–"Charles Bridge." There's free parking nearby and free in-room Wi-Fi.

Grottgera 7. ✆ **74/867-02-16.** Fax 74/867-02-17. www.casadoro.pl. 11 units. 180 zł double. AE, MC, V. Free parking. **Amenities:** Restaurant; room service. *In room:* TV, hair dryer, Wi-Fi (free).

Hotel Korona ★ This roadside "motel," tucked away behind a gas station about 180m (591 ft.) outside the center, looks like something you might see on the side of an American highway. The rooms are small and sparsely furnished with twin beds and a writing table, but are clean, relatively quiet, and acceptable for a short stay. There's free Wi-Fi, but ask to make sure the signal will stretch to your room. The high point is the restaurant, decorated in a faux-rustic style, with a nice terrace in summer and a wood-burning fireplace in winter. It's worth a stop, even if you're not staying here. The big salads are especially recommended.

Noworudzka 1. ✆ **74/867-37-37.** Fax 74/867-07-73. www.hotel-korona.pl. 20 units. 160 zł double. AE, MC, V. Parking. **Amenities:** Restaurant. *In room:* TV, Wi-Fi (free).

CENTRAL & NORTHWEST POLAND

by Kit F. Chung

The central and northwestern region is the new Poland, awaiting your discovery. "New" it is, but only in the sense of tourism exposure. It is, in fact, a very old historical hotspot. The Polish state was founded here in the Middle Ages. Within the region, Gniezno and Poznań's Cathedral Island are the main contenders vying for the title of the cradle of Catholic Poland. In this distinct landscape of historical rubble, churches, castles, and palaces, you'll also find the impressive Iron Age settlement of Biskupin.

Poznań is the place to start your exploration of the region. The city is unfairly brushed off as a stopover to get your business done as you hurry off elsewhere. That would be a mistake. The charming Old Market Square pulses with life force. The historical buildings and esoteric museums reflect the locals' pride in their history and identity. Moving in the northeasterly direction, you'll come to Toruń, the birthplace of Copernicus and the Gothic center of the country. Take the time to meander among the red-brick towers and churches that survived the ages, then pause to munch on the gingerbread culture.

Outside of Poznań and Toruń, the attractions are more spread out. It's easiest to see the area by car. To manage with just public transportation, you'll need to plan carefully.

POZNAŃ

Poznań, the capital of Wielkopolska (Greater Poland) and a bustling city of 600,000 people, is known mostly for its numerous annual trade fairs. Its tourism potentials are (mistakenly) underrated, hence during weekends, you don't have to jostle with crowds, reservations aren't required in most restaurants, and hotel rooms are available at reduced rates. The city works well as a base for exploring the Piast Route and is a vibrant business and academic hub.

Poznań has a history of prosperity that's directly attributable to its position along the main transportation routes and astride the Warta River. A fortified settlement has been located here as far back as the 9th century.

It was a key settlement of the Piast Dynasty, which ruled Poland from the 10th to the 14th centuries. During the Prussian occupation, when the town was known as Posen, it became one of the region's leading industrial centers, a position it retains to this day. Poznań's prosperity is evident in the sheer size of the square and in the many handsome buildings that stretch out along it in all directions. The Old Market Square has been the city's cultural and commercial center for centuries. Although much of it, and the city proper, were destroyed in World War II, many of the buildings you see today are faithful reconstructions of the originals. Currently, as the city prepares to host matches during the Euro Cup 2012 Football Championship, more accommodation and food options have sprung up.

Essentials

GETTING THERE

BY PLANE Poznań's **Lawica International Airport** (Bukowska 285; ✆ **61/849-23-43;** www.airport-poznan.com.pl) is 5km (3 miles) west of the city center. It has grown in importance and has direct flights not only to Polish cities, but also to a number of major European cities. Express bus line "L," regular bus no. 59, and night bus no. 242 take about 30 minutes to get to Poznań's central train station.

Worker's First Stand

In 1956, Poznań was the home of anti-Communist riots, the first-ever show of resistance in Poland against the Communist authorities. Tens of thousands of workers took to the streets to demand better working conditions and higher pay. The strikes turned violent, and the government responded by deploying soldiers and tanks. In all, some 76 civilians and eight soldiers died in the fighting. The unrest was a major embarrassment throughout Central and Eastern Europe, and pierced the veil of Communist Poland as a workers' state. The June 1956 Monument (pl. Mickiewicza), comprising of two towering metal crosses, was unveiled in 1981 to commemorate the uprising.

BY TRAIN Poznań lies on one of Europe's main east–west train lines, stretching from Paris and Berlin to Warsaw and Moscow. The **train station** (Dworcowa 1; ✆ **197-57**) is 2km (1¼ miles) from the town center. It's a 15-minute walk, or a short tram or bus ride, to the center.

BY BUS Poznań lies on major national and international bus routes. The **PKS bus station** (Dworzec Autobusowy; Towarowa 17/19; ✆ **61/664-25-00;** www.pks.poznan.pl) is near the train station.

BY CAR Poznań is on the main Berlin–Warsaw Highway E30. The tolled highway is a dream to drive on, but make sure to set aside about 30 zł for tolls. Unfortunately, the road is not yet upgraded all the way to Warsaw. On the stretch from Warsaw to Łódź (122km/76 miles), you'll still have to drive the old (but free) highway. From Warsaw (325km/202 miles), the journey takes about 4 hours.

VISITOR INFORMATION

The city's main **Tourist Information Center** (Stary Rynek 59/60; ✆ **61/852-61-56;** www.poznan.pl) is open in season (May to mid-Oct) weekdays from 9am to 8pm, Saturday from 10am to 8pm, and Sunday from 10am to 6pm. Off season, the open hours are Monday through Friday from 10am to 7pm, Saturday 10am to 5pm. It's conveniently located on the Old Market Square and is a good place to pick up walking itineraries, maps, and advice on rooms. Pick up a copy of *Poznań, In Your Pocket* (5 zł), which has coverage of the city. The Polish *IKS* magazine (3.90 zł) has its cultural events listing in English. Another information point is the **City Information Center** (Ratajczaka 44; ✆ **61/851-96-45;** www.cim.poznan.pl), which is good on cultural activities and sells concert tickets. They are open weekdays 10am to 7pm and Saturday 10am to 5pm. If you hire a guide, it's best to incorporate the Parish Church, Cathedral Island, and Zamek in your tour. This will take 3 to 4 hours. Contact the Tourist Information Center on the Stary Rynek 3 days in advance to book a guide. The prices are 190 zł for 2 hours, 260 zł for 3 hours, and 320 zł for 4 hours.

GETTING AROUND

Most of the attractions can be covered on foot. Poznań has an efficient public transportation system of buses and trams. Tickets can be bought at Ruch kiosks (or nearly anywhere they sell newspapers and tobacco) and cost 3 zł for rides of 30 minutes. There are also day and weekly passes priced at 12 zł and 32 zł, respectively. You can also consider getting the **City Card** (Poznańska Karta Miejska) at the tourist information center. It's a package of access to public transport and discounts at selected museums, hotels, and restaurants. It comes in 1-day (30 zł), 2-day (40 zł), and 3-day (45 zł) formats. The city is gradually ceding more road space to bike lanes. Bicycles can be rented from **Malta Bike** (Jana Pawła II; ✆ **510/316-118;** www.maltabike.pl) and from some of the hostels in the center.

Top Attractions

Naturally, any exploration must start at the Old Market Square (Stary Rynek), a lively spot filled with color, people, and a range of performance art from early morning to late at night. Poznań's unofficial nickname could well be the "Museum City," for you trip on museums everywhere. Some notable ones are the **Model of Former Poznań** (Ludgardy; ✆ **61/855-14-35;** www.makieta.poznan.pl), which has a meticulous miniature model of medieval Poznań and gives an audio narration of the city's history, and the **Musical Instruments Museum** (Stary Rynek 45; ✆ **61/852-08-57**). ***Note:*** Most museums have free admission on Saturdays.

Cathedral of Saints Peter and Paul (Katedra Św. Piotra i Pawła) ★ History is palpable on the peaceful and quiet Cathedral Island (Ostrów Tumski). Excavations revealed the presence of a church on this site for more than a millennium. It is believed that Mieszko I (father of Poland's first crowned king, Bolesław the Brave) was baptized here in the 10th century. The crypt holds the rubble of the baptism bowl. Architectural tinkering and rebuilding through the years, and the 1945 fire in the cathedral, have greatly altered its appearance, giving it the current ensemble of everything from pre-Romanesque to Gothic, baroque, and classicist. Eclecticism is also seen in the naves and chapels. The most eye-catching features are the frescos, dating from 1616, depicting the 12 apostles; the 19th-century Golden Chapel, with unabashedly brazen Byzantine designs; the crypt containing the remains of Mieszko and Bolesław the Brave; and the four Vischers bronze plaques that were looted by the Nazis, recovered by the Russians, and returned to the cathedral in 1990.

The cathedral has no guide service. If you want a guide, make arrangements at the city's tourist center. To cover the crypt and the major artifacts, it's about 1½ hours.

Ostrów Tumski 17. ✆ **61/852-96-42.** www.katedra.archpoznan.org.pl. Free admission. Mon–Sat 9am–6pm; Sun 1:15–6pm. Tram: 4, 8 & 17 to Ostrów Tumski stop. On foot: Take Wielka St. east to Chwaliszewo St.; at the end of Chwaliszewo St., turn right toward the Bolesława Chrobrego bridge & use the underpass to get to the Cathedral Island.

Citadel Park (Park Cytadela) ★ Located in the north of the Old Town, the sprawling park started life as a Prussian fortress in 1828. Badly damaged in 1945, it now serves locals as a site for recreational and cultural pastimes. Visitors also come to reflect on the past at the numerous graveyards in the park's southern section, including the **Commonwealth Cemetery for Allied Soldiers** perished in World War II. The park is dotted with monuments: from a towering Socialist-Realism column in honor of the Red Army to a more recently installed and still controversial "The Unrecognized," a cluster of over 100 headless, larger-than-life cast-iron bodies. The park is also the site of the **Museum of Weapons** and the **Museum of the Poznań Army.**

Al. Armii Poznań. No phone. Free admission. Daily dawn–dusk. Tram: 4 to Za Cytadelą.

Emperor's Castle (Zamek) ★ Built in the early 20th century, during the days when Poznań was a German outpost known as Posen, the castle once served as a residence of Kaiser Wilhelm II. In the late 1930s, the interior was refurbished as quarters for Adolf Hitler. Within the walls of this imposing neo-Romanesque building, Polish cryptologists worked to decode the Enigma Machine, the main secret-code generator used by the Germans. Their work contributed to the Allies' victory in War World II. In the clock tower, you can walk into the rooms done in the Third Reich style and look out of the balcony that was intended for the Fuhrer to inspect military parades. As the castle is still seen as a symbol of foreign domination (a fate shared by Warsaw's Palace of Culture), locals are ambivalent toward it. After World War II, there were talks of demolishing it, but pragmatism for office space kept it standing. Today, it houses the **Castle Culture Center (Centrum Kultury Zamek),** which hosts exhibitions, theater performances, and concerts, and screens films. A quick visit will take no more than 30 minutes. You can use the exhibitions as an excuse to see the castle's interior, notably the golden mosaic ceiling on the clock tower's ground floor. However, the Kaiser's marble throne can be seen only with a guide on Wednesdays at 6pm.

Św. Marcin 80/82. ✆ **61/646-52-00.** www.zamek.poznan.pl. Free admission for most exhibitions; Kaiser's throne 7 zł adults. Mon–Fri 11am–7pm; Sat & Sun 11am–5pm.

Lech Brewery Visitor Center ★ Even bearing in mind this is a PR exercise for the brewery, it's still a fascinating insight into a plant that produces an average of 1.3 million bottles, 1 million cans, and 2,000 beer kegs daily. The bubbly guides walk you through the factory, filling your head with production ingredients, stages, and numbers. The bottling and canning process is the most interesting, for kids and adults alike. The tour takes 2 hours, including a quiz, but you can squeeze out of the Q&A and head straight to the pub to fill up on complimentary beer. (See "Gniezno," later in this chapter, to learn who Lech was.) Call a day ahead to book the tour.

Szwajcarska 11. ✆ **61/878-74-60.** www.zwiedzaniebrowaru.pl. Free admission. Mon & Wed 10am–8:30pm; Tues & Thurs–Sat 10am–2pm. Bus: no. 81 from Rondo Rataje to the M1 shopping mall (the brewery is opposite M1).

National Museum: Paintings and Sculpture Gallery ★★ This is one of Poland's top galleries and a great place to get acquainted with key Polish artists and their works. It's also notable for having had a Monet snatched from its premises in 2000. Start your visit in the Polish Baroque Room, which holds an extensive collection of "coffin portraits," hexagonal and octagonal-edged portraits that are the relics of funeral practices from the 17th and 18th centuries. Jan Matejko's sketch *Stańczyk* (the Court Jester) is one of the images Poles instantly recognize. From the Młoda Polska (Young Polish) movement of the late 19th to early 20th centuries, Jacek Malczewski's *Vicious Circle* is an enthralling study of brightness against darkness. Stanisław Wyspiański's pastels of his slumbering children, Mietek and Staś, are endearing. In the Interwar collection, see the portraits by Stanisław Ignacy Witkiewicz, who jotted on the corners of some canvases the drugs, nicotine, caffeine, and alcohol he ingested prior to unleashing his imagination on the fantasy works.

Marcinkowskiego 9. ✆ **61/852-59-69.** www.mnp.art.pl. 12 zł adults; 8 zł seniors, children & students; Sat free admission. English-speaking guides 80 zł (call ahead). Tues & Thurs 10am–6pm; Wed 9am–5pm; Fri & Sat 10am–5pm; Sun 10am–3pm.

Old Town Hall (Ratusz) ★ Originally dating from the 14th century, the building was extensively renovated in the 16th century in Renaissance style by the Italian architect Giovanni Quadro. Much of the structure was destroyed in World War II, and little of the original walls remain. The best example of what survived is the early Gothic cellars, which today house the **Historical Museum of Poznań.** The museum is worth a visit if you're curious about Poznań's development from the 10th century on. Entry to the museum leads to the rich interior of the building itself. At noon, join locals, school kids, and tourists in craning your neck at the clock outside the Town Hall to see two **mechanical goats** butt heads. There are several myths as to how and why these two animals locked horns; the most popular is that they were drawing the townspeople's attention to a fire and thus saved the town from burning down. Pop around to the back of the building to see another symbol of the city: the **Statue of Bamberka,** a petite sculpture of a peasant in folk costume, shouldering two pails. The Bambers are ethnic Germans who settled in this region in the 18th century and assimilated into the local community.

Stary Rynek 1. © **61/856-81-93.** www.mnp.art.pl. 7 zł adults; 5 zł seniors, students & children; Sat free admission. Guided tours (for groups of 10–25) 80 zł. Mid-June to mid-Aug Tues–Thurs 11am–5pm (off season Tues–Thurs 9am–3pm), Fri noon–9pm, Sat & Sun 11am–6pm.

Parish Church (Kościół Św. Stanisława) ★★ Built between 1651 and 1732, this beguiling baroque church used ingenious methods to create the illusion of grandeur at reduced cost. For example, even though the church seems to be adorned with a generous deployment of marble, all the fluted columns and pedestals are actually made from marble-toned stucco. The columns were also designed to make you think the nave is longer than its 40m (131 ft.). The facade uses larger statues on the first tier and significantly diminutive figures on the second tier to generate an illusion of imposing heights. Further intrigue can be found in the 19th-century piped organ, built by Friedrich Ladegast, one of the finest craftsmen of his time. Its construction was partially financed by an anonymous lady in black: Whenever the organ undergoes conservation work, her ghost is said to be sighted. (Her last visit was in 2002.) To fully appreciate the church, time your visit with a free organ concert. You can feel the chords reverberating on the pews as you take in both the unique architecture and the works depicting the lives of St. Stanisław and Mary Magdalene, the church's patron saints. At press time, plans were underway to open up to the public the attic and the tunnels in the cellar, some of which reportedly lead to the Town Hall.

Gołębia, at the Świętoławska crossing. Free admission. Daily 6am–7:30pm. Concerts July & Aug Mon–Sat 12:15pm; off season, check at the Tourist Information Office.

OUTDOOR ACTIVITIES

SPECTATOR SPORTS The Lech Poznań Football Club (www.lechpoznan.pl) enjoys a large fan base. In view of hosting the preliminary matches of the Euro Cup 2012 Football Championship, the club's home stadium, Stadion Miejski (Bułgarska 5/7; © 602/312-412), has been expanded and upgraded. Cultural events are also held there. Match tickets can be bought at the stadium or from sports shop in the center, such as Tifo (Piekary 10; © 61/855-22-05; www.tifo.pl).

OUTSIDE POZNAN

Kórnik and **Rogalin,** both 20km (12 miles) south of Poznań and 12km (7½ miles) apart from each other, visited together make for a good day out. The 14th-century neo-Gothic **Kórnik Castle** (Zamkowa 5, Kórnik; © **61/817-00-81;** www.bkpan.poznan.pl) survived World War II and has many intriguing curios assembled by its former masters. The **Rogalin Palace ★** (Arciszewszkiego 2, Rogalin; © **61/813-80-30**), an impressive late-baroque to early-classicism palace, was the seat of the Raczyński clan, a politically influential noble family. It was recently given a thorough spruce-up. Within the palace are works by the noted Polish painter Jan Matejko. The on-site restaurant, **Dwa Pokoje z Kuchnią ★** (© **61/898-17-47**), is a homey spot

Huff and Puff

Michael Palin did it. In his 2006–07 jaunt through New Europe, the travel show host (and Monty Python comedian) veered west to Poznań to hop on the steam-engine train that chugs regularly from Poznań to Wolsztyn. The Wolsztyn Experience (www.thewolsztynexperience.org) allows train enthusiasts to learn to drive a steam-engine train on a regular service line with commuters on board (about 600 zł).

that serves sweet and savory pancakes (crêpes). At the nearby park are the **Oaks of Rogalin ★**, three great oak trees that are more than a thousand years old (and look very much like they're on their last legs). They are named Lech, Czech, and Rus, after the legendary brothers and founding fathers of Poland, the Czech Republic, and Russia. Public buses from Poznań serve both Kórnik and Rogalin.

SHOPPING

Souvenirs of Poznań available from stalls in the Old Market Square include crafts depicting the pair of hotheaded goats and the *bamberka* (see "Old Town Hall," above).

Antique Market at Stara Rzeźnia ★★ Located in the compound of a disused abattoir, this market has esoteric collector items ranging from old LPs to obsolete but still functioning amplifiers. The indoor stalls have a huge stockpile of tableware, including prewar samovars (with their original user manuals in German), silver cutlery, and ceramic sauceboats and tureens. It is open on weekends from 8am to 2pm. Garbary 101 (entrance from Północna St.). ✆ **61/852-11-26.** www.gielda.poznan.pl. Tram: 4, 8 & 17.

Where to Stay

Poznań's accommodation rates are reasonable—except when a trade fair comes to town and hotels unabashedly jack up their prices by 30% to 40%. The summer months are fairly safe, but the rest of the year sees a trade fair at least once a month (check www.mtp.pl for the trade fair schedule). Since business travelers fill the hotels, come on weekends—when many places offer reduced rates.

VERY EXPENSIVE

IBB Andersia ★★ Located in the first nine floors of a glass-fronted office tower, IBB Andersia makes no bones about being targeted at business travelers. But it's situated next to the Stary Browar shopping mall and linked by a pedestrian street to the Old Town, so leisure travelers can very well enjoy the luxuries aimed at the expense-account set. The minimalistic but plush rooms in shades of brown are well designed for dependable comfort. The bathrooms are finished in granite and have heated floors. In some cases, only glass panels separate the bathroom from the bedroom.

Plac Andersa 3. ✆ **61/667-80-00.** Fax 61/667-80-01. www.andersiahotel.pl. 171 units. Weekdays 530 zł double; weekends 430 zł double. AE, DC, MC, V. Underground parking 50 zł. **Amenities:** Restaurant; bar; concierge; indoor pool; room service; spa center. *In room:* A/C, plasma TV, hair dryer, minibar, Wi-Fi (free).

Sheraton Poznań Hotel ★★ Everything in this hotel opposite the Trade Fair center still feels brand-spanking-new, even though it's been open several years. Spacious rooms have dark wood furnishings and luxurious granite bathrooms. The Qube

Bar on the ground floor stirs up some of the best drinks in town and it's always lively at the Somewhere Else Restaurant, where guests gather for live music or sports on the widescreen. The top-notch staff here goes beyond the perfunctory call of duty to make guests feel spoiled.

Bukowska 3/9. ✆ **61/655-20-00.** Fax 61/655-20-01. www.sheraton.pl. 300 zł–1,000 zł double. AE, DC, MC, V. Basement parking 80 zł. **Amenities:** 2 restaurants; pub; lounge; concierge; gym; indoor pool w/ city view; room service; sauna. *In room:* A/C, TV, hair dryer, minibar, Wi-Fi.

EXPENSIVE & MODERATE

Brovaria ★ For the money, it's probably the best bed (with a view) in town. Occupying three tastefully renovated town houses on the Stary Rynek, the hotel's location is ideal. Both single and double rooms are reasonably spacious. Furnishings, mostly brooding black-lacquered wood, fall somewhere between 1930s "modern" and contemporary. The carpet looks slightly worn, but the white ceramic bathrooms are fresh and recently renovated. Rooms facing the Market Square command a higher price; those on the third floor are quieter.

Stary Rynek 73/74. ✆ **61/858-68-68.** Fax 61/858-68-69. www.brovaria.pl. 21 units. 290 zł double; 330 zł double w/view. AE, DC, MC, V. Public parking. **Amenities:** Restaurant (see p. 221); bar; limited room service. *In room:* A/C, TV, hair dryer, Wi-Fi (free).

Don Prestige Residence ★ "Feel at home" is their tag line, and you could very well feel just that in these apartments. Although it's a central location, they don't skimp on space. The bedrooms and living area are separated, so those whipping up a meal in the kitchen would not bother the snoozing ones. The property went through a name change, but the management is just as competent, and the fixtures still look like they were just put in as a luxury show apartment. The only down side is the building is wedged between two busy streets, and trams screech to a halt at a nearby stop.

Św. Marcin 2. ✆ **61/859-05-90.** Fax 61/859-05-91. www.donprestige.com. 40 units. Weekdays 400 zł double; weekends 260 zł double. MC, V. Underground parking 50 zł. *In room:* A/C, TV, fully equipped kitchen, Wi-Fi (free).

Garden Boutique Hotel ★ Most of the rooms here, though exquisitely opulent, are fairly similar to the luxury hotel chain's take on conservative and chic elegance. However, the suite with a rotund bathtub right next to the bed, plus staff that address you as "Sir" or "Madame" will surely make fun post-holiday talking points. The front door is a breath away from the Old Market Square. And the breakfast in a bright, French-inspired rustic cafe is a welcomed change from the buffets in hotel chains.

Wroniecka 24. ✆ **61/223-66-35.** www.gardenhotel.pl. 18 units. Weekdays 320 zł double, 470 zł suite; weekends 245 zł double, 370 zł suite. DC, MC, V. **Amenities:** Restaurant; cafe; lounge. *In room:* A/C, TV, hair dryer, Wi-Fi (free).

NH Poznań ★★ "Sleek, chic, and modern" are the words that spring to mind when you see the rooms of this centrally located hotel. And when you come in contact with the staff, you'd choose words like "well trained, professional, and eager to help" to describe them. It's hard to find fault with anything, except the narrow tunnel leading to the parking space that puts your driving skills to test.

Św. Marcin 67. ✆ **61/624-88-00.** Fax 61/624-88-01. www.nh-hotels.com. 93 units. Weekdays 296 zł–636 zł double; weekends 256 zł double. AE, DC, M, V. Parking 60 zł. **Amenities:** Restaurant; gym; spa. *In room:* A/C, TV, hair dryer, Internet, minibar.

Royal ★ The location is excellent, situated between the railway station and the Old Town. The hotel is tucked in a little courtyard away from the street, making it very quiet. The Royal has a distinguished pedigree, dating from the turn of the 20th century, and was the first hotel in the city to open for business following World War II. The rooms are stylish, with floral-print spreads and high-quality woods throughout. The guest book at reception bears evidence of high customer satisfaction.

Św. Marcin 71. ✆ **61/858-23-00.** Fax 61/858-23-06. www.hotel-royal.com.pl. 31 units. Weekdays 420 zł double; weekends 294 zł double. AE, M, V. Free parking. **Amenities:** Restaurant; concierge; limited room service. *In room:* TV, Wi-Fi (free).

Rzymski ★ Despite this hotel's dated appearance, the rooms here are in good condition, the staff is friendly and competent, and the location, just 500m (1,640 ft.) from the Old Market Square, is great. This 150-year-old hotel has gone through several name and role changes during its long history, and during World War II, German soldiers even camped here. The high-ceilinged rooms are spacious and comfortable, but note that the many renovations have resulted in varying bathroom fixtures. Rooms looking out to Marcinkowskiego Street are drenched in morning sun, but their occupants have to contend with the rumbles of passing trams and cars; rooms at the back have no views but are quiet.

Marcinkowskiego 22. ✆ **61/852-81-21.** Fax 61/852-89-83. www.hotelrzymski.pl. 87 units. Weekdays 310 zł double; weekends 250 zł double. AE, DC, MC, V. **Amenities:** 2 restaurants; bar; Wi-Fi (in lobby; free). *In room:* TV.

Stare Miasto ★★ This is a relatively new hotel and a great choice for the price; rates are lower than you might expect for the quality because of the hotel's location in a slightly dodgy but still safe neighborhood, about a 10-minute walk from the Stary Rynek. The rooms are on the small side but nicely furnished in a contemporary style. The doubles are not uniformly furnished, so ask to see a couple of different styles before choosing. The breakfast buffet is in a spacious sun-lit room.

Rybaki 36. ✆ **61/663-62-42.** www.hotelstaremiasto.pl. 23 units. Weekdays 340 zł double; weekends 225 zł double. MC, V. Free parking. **Amenities:** Bar; breakfast room; Wi-Fi (free). *In room:* A/C (in some), TV, Internet.

INEXPENSIVE

Hostel 8 This newly open hostel is located just off the pedestrian street that links the Stary Browar Mall to the Old Town. The dorms don't have the institutional pinewood bunk beds, but sturdy metal ones that were salvaged from a military base in the former East Germany. The bathroom fixtures are modern, while the private rooms are spacious and uncluttered. Music fans can chat with the English-speaking owner about the best live acts in town.

Długa 43. ✆ **61/842-77-90.** Fax 61/842-77-91. www.hostel8.com. 6 units. 50 zł dorm bed; 110 zł double w/shared bathroom; 130 zł double. AE, M, V. *In room:* Internet (free).

Hostel Cameleon ★★ Hostel is a bit of a misnomer since the Cameleon feels more like a boutique B&B. The entrance is on a respectable street just off the Old Market Square, and not from the dingy side lanes. The LV Monogram leather chest in the reception is a hint that style and quality reign in this establishment. The private rooms sport knitted pillowcases and cast-iron beds. In their showpiece room, the bathtub next to the bed is a feature that delights the guests. But even if you're using the common showers, you'll find them smelling fresh. On both floors, there's an above-par kitchen that invites you to linger.

Potato Heads!

Folks here are more potato-obsessed than the rest of the country. *Pyry* means potatoes in Poznań's dialect. It is also an affectionate nickname for the locals.

Świętosławska 12. ✆ **61/639-30-41.** www.hostel-cameleon.com. 23 units. 50 zł–65 zł dorm bed; 155 zł double w/shared bathroom; 190 zł–230 zł double. DC, M, V. **Amenities:** Bike rental. *In room:* Wi-Fi (free).

IBIS The IBIS chain is always a safe choice since it sticks to a clean, plain, comfortable layout. The T-shirted staff here is as up-to-par as any of the designer-uniformed crew in up-market hotels. And actually, it isn't as far from the Old Market Square as it looks on the map, plus there's a tram stop at the doorstep to whisk you to the attractions in a blink.

Kazimierza Wielkiego 23. ✆ **61/858-44-00.** www.accorhotels.com. 146 units. Weekdays 259 zł double; weekends 179 zł double. MC, V. Parking 30 zł. **Amenities:** Restaurant. *In room:* A/C, TV, Wi-Fi (free).

Where to Dine

Food central is definitely around the Old Town Square. Away from Old Town, **Zagroda Bamberska** (Kościelna 43; ✆ **61/843-41-14**) offers regional cuisine and is worthy of attention. If you want to try Poznań's version of *dans le noir* (eating in the dark), make a reservation at the **Dark Restaurant** (Garbary 48; ✆ **61/852-91-70;** www.darkrestaurant.pl).

VERY EXPENSIVE

Bażanciarnia ★★ POLISH This is the northwestern outpost of Magda Gessler, one of Poland's top restaurateurs. Expect floral and candle-lit giddiness, and a menu replete with game and new Polish cuisine twists. The competent staff makes this restaurant one of the brightest stars in the Gessler series. *Bażanciarnia* means an aviary for pheasants, but the house specialty is beef drizzled with a lip-smacking mushroom sauce. The *czernina* (duck blood soup) is both sour and mildly sweet from the addition of dried fruit, and very good. As for the desserts, pick any; you can't go wrong. The wine selection is an extensive coverage of Old and New World, some costing an arm and a leg. Before you leave, check out the fixtures in the washrooms.

Stary Rynek 94. ✆ **61/855-33-58.** www.bazanciarnia.pl. Reservations recommended. Main courses 54 zł–290 zł. AE, DC, MC, V. Daily noon–11pm.

Piano Bar Restaurant & Cafe ★★ ITALIAN Don't dismiss this just because it's in a mall. The elegant, cosmopolitan setting with a dash of neo-'60s might not say "Italy," but pasta and fish are their forte. The local beautiful people are willing to pay a premium for the steaks, while business people on a mission to impress their clients are assured by the top-class service for a glitch-free chow down.

Półwiejska 42 (Stary Browar Mall). ✆ **61/859-65-70.** www.pianobar.poznan.pl. Main courses 16 zł–149 zł. AE, DC, MC, V. Mon–Sat noon–11pm; Sun noon–8pm.

EXPENSIVE & MODERATE

Brovaria ★★★ EUROPEAN At one of the hippest spots in town, beer-sloshing is the key activity of the evening. The house-brewed beer (you'll see the copper tanks at the far end), which is hoppier and tangier than the traditional Polish beer, comes in both a standard pilsner and a recommendable honey-flavored lager. The menu is a balance of inventive international dishes and Polish standards with a view toward

No Bloody Way

Don't miss the opportunity to try ***czernina,*** a soup made from duck's blood and bits of offal. Once upon a time (when kings ruled the land), if the parents in aristocratic households were to reject the proposal for their daughter's hand in marriage, they would dole out *czernina* to the unsuccessful suitor before sending him on his way. Such a scene was enacted in the epic poem "Pan Tadeusz" written by Polish poet Adam Mickiewicz. Apparently, saying no with *czernina* is still practiced in the countryside. The best place for *czernina* (and roast duck)—without having to propose to someone—is at **Hacjenda ★** (Morasko 38; ✆ 61/812-52-78; www.hacjenda.poznan.pl), located in the northern suburbs of Poznań. Reservations recommended on weekends.

presentation and use of fresh ingredients. The cheerful atmosphere, friendly staff, prime location on the Stary Rynek, and fair prices explain its popularity with both trendy locals and visitors alike.

Stary Rynek 73/74. ✆ **61/858-68-68.** www.brovaria.pl. Main courses 19 zł–56 zł. AE, DC, MC, V. Daily 11am–1am.

Figaro ★ ITALIAN The opulent, open-space dining room, where the tables are lined with wine glasses and the waiters wear starched white aprons, might suggest that this is a splurge option. However, on closer look, the short menu, with an emphasis on seafood, is fairly priced, especially since Figaro is considered to have the best Italian food in town. If pasta and fish don't appeal, try the Argentinean steak.

Ogrodowa 17. ✆ **61/852-08-16.** Main courses 24 zł–75 zł. AE, MC, V. Mon–Sat 1–11pm; Sun 1–5pm.

Mykonos ★ GREEK On weekends, Mykonos has to turn away guests with no reservations. A plate of complimentary, fresh-made tapenade on toast kicks off the meal. Highlights of the menu include *halumi* with spinach and the seafood pilaf. To round things out, there's Greek coffee, wine, and music to go with the deliciously caramelized walnut baklava. Service sometimes slips up slightly as waitresses strive to keep pace.

Plac Wolności 14. ✆ **61/853-34-36.** www.tawerna-mykonos.com.pl. Reservations recommended weekends. Main courses 33 zł–49 zł. AE, DC, MC, V. Mon–Fri 11am–11pm; Sat & Sun noon–11pm.

Pod Koziołkami ★★ POLISH As you pass the grill station, note the trophies won by the chefs for their grilled meats and potato dishes in various regional and European culinary showdowns. The regional duck specialty is accompanied by a mushroom sauce that outshines the poultry, while the *pyzy* (steamed bun) is crisscrossed with a delectable cranberry sauce. The cellar walls are the original Gothic bricks, and during restoration, the owner referred to old photos and paintings as authenticity aids. **Kredens,** run by the same folks, is on the ground floor. It serves inexpensive, homemade Polish classics where 20 zł will buy you more pierogi than you can handle in 2 weeks.

Stary Rynek 95. ✆ **61/851-78-68.** www.podkoziolkami.pl. Main courses 14 zł–78 zł. DC, MC, V. Sun–Thurs 1–10pm; Fri & Sat 1–11pm.

INEXPENSIVE

Avanti ★★ ITALIAN Avanti shows that you can eat well and inexpensively on the Old Market Square. It looks like a McDonald's outlet doing pasta instead of burgers. Tidiness, cleanliness, and paper roses trailing the pastel-toned wall lend a homey atmosphere. Students, grandparents and their grandkids, and office workers queue for spaghetti, lasagna, and risotto in Styrofoam plates and bowls, and salads in plastic beakers. Spaghetti comes in size S, M, and L.

Stary Rynek 76. ✆ **61/852-32-85.** www.avanti.poznan.pl. Main courses 3.90 zł–16 zł. No credit cards. Mon–Thurs 9am–midnight; Fri & Sat 9am–1am; Sun 11am–midnight.

Mammamija INTERNATIONAL Similar to Avanti in prices but with a menu extending to burritos, tortellini, salads, Polish staples, and snacks such as *zapiekanki*, Polish-style pizza. Like Avanti, it is popular with students and also has the self-service and seating-at-bar-table concept. There's a second outlet on Św Marcin 12 (✆ **61/665-85-08**).

Półwiejska 41. ✆ **61/852-42-66.** www.mammamija.pl. Main courses 3.50 zł–15 zł. No credit cards. Mon–Thurs 10am–9pm; Fri & Sat 10am–midnight; Sun 11am–10pm.

Pod Arkadami POLISH Poznań's most authentic milk bar is still using crockery with vintage insignia; quite an impressive act since many of its peers have replaced the chipped ceramics with new, characterless plates and bowls. Get a student in the queue to help you with deciphering the menu. After the main course, you can pop over to the cafe section for squares of cakes that are sold by weight. And they even have real coffee. ***Note:*** A routine practice in Poznań's milk bars is the nominal fee for using the plastic cutlery.

Pl. Ratajskiego 10. ✆ **61/852-22-98.** Main courses 2.50 zł–10 zł. No credit cards. Mon–Fri 8am–7pm; Sat 9am–6pm; Sun 11am–6pm.

CAFES

Żydowska Street in the Old Town is the cafe mile. In good weather, the loveliest cloistered garden to escape to is **Cocorico Café ★★** (Świętosławska 9; ✆ **61/852-95-29**). Sweets lovers vouch for the classic apple pies, cheesecakes, and cherry tarts. In winter, the indoor pub-like space can get smoky. Next door is **Weranda Caffe** (Świętosławska 10; ✆ **61/853-25-87;** www.zielonaweranda.pl). It also has a lovely

Saintly Buns

Rogale Święto Marcińskie **is a croissant-shaped sweet bread with a poppy-seed and dried-fruit filling and a nut-encrusted glazed exterior. Having qualified for the EU's Protected Designation of Origin label, the sweet bread is in the rarefied company of items made only in a particular geographic region, such as Parma ham and champagne. The buns are for sale all year, but the most festive time to eat them is on Saint Martin's Day (Nov 11), when residents reportedly wolf down 300 tons' worth. Find them in the Old Town at Cukiernia Grüszecki (Stary Rynek 50; ✆ 61/826-81-07) or in an alleyway off Św Marcin at the no-frills "since 1958" Pracownia Cukiernia Słodki Kącik ★ (Św Marcin 26; ✆ 61/852-06-34).**

patio out back. The delicious walnut meringue with a creamy mascarpone filling could feed two. The wait staff is young and sometimes inattentive and petulant. The sister outlet is **Zielona Weranda** (Paderewskiego 7; ✆ **61/851-32-90**).

After Dark

PERFORMING ARTS

The **Zamek Cultural Center** (Św. Marcin 80/82; ✆ **61/646-52-60;** www.zamek.poznan.pl) is the first stop for information on happenings in Poznań. The ticket office is open from Tuesday to Sunday 11am to 7pm. Event tickets can also be bought at the **City Information Center/CIM** (Ratajczaka 44; ✆ **61/851-96-45;** www.cim.poznan.pl). **Teatr Wielki** (Fredry 9; ✆ **61/659-02-80;** www.opera.poznan.pl) is the place for operas. The **Polski Teatr Tańca** (Kozia 4; ✆ **61/852-42-41;** www.ptt-poznan.pl) hosts Polish and international troupes at various venues around town, including Teatr Wielki. Tickets can be purchased at their website, the CIM, or Teatr Wielki. The **Poznań Philharmonic** (**Filharmonia Poznańska;** Św. Marcin 81; ✆ **61/852-47-08;** www.filharmoniapoznanska.pl) hosts Polish and international musicians. The box office is open daily 1 to 5pm.

PUBS & CLUBS

The Old Town isn't one to go to bed early; most of the drinking and dancing establishments can be found here. One in four patrons is a student, which means beer is good business in this town. On the side streets of the Old Town Square, the drinks get cheaper, so poke around **Woźna Street** for value deals. **Warta** (Świętosławska 12; ✆ **61/851-51-17**), a cavernous bar, is where the eponymous beer company filmed its commercial. The basement fills with hundreds of revelers when they hold concerts. The dress-to-impress types converge at the **SQ Klub Muzyczny** (Półwiejska 42; ✆ **61/859-65-78**; www.sqklub.pl) for the drum and bass tunes, international DJs, and live gigs. More dancing room is found at **Cute** (Wielka 27/29; ✆ **61/851-91-37;** www.cuteklub.pl), one of the city's best-known venues for house, techno, trance, and just plain dance music. **Blue Note Jazz Club ★★** (Kościuszki 76/78; ✆ **61/657-07-77;** www.bluenote.poznan.pl) is a reputable venue with top-notch live jazz by leading Polish and international musicians. However, it also plays teenybopper tunes. To hang out with local fans of "intelligent techno," **Café Mięsna** (Garbary 62, entrance from Mostowa; ✆ **663/374-654;** www.myspace.com/cafemiesna) is the place to be.

GNIEZNO

Gniezno is generally regarded as the first capital of Poland, though there are contentions from other places. Gniezno's story dates back to the legend of Lech, the founder of Poland. It's said that he came across a white eagle guarding her nest *(gniazdo)* and decided to settle there, naming it Gniezno and adopting the white eagle as his emblem (which today is still the symbol of Poland). From recorded history, Gniezno's importance came about as the coronation site of Poland's first king, Bolesław the Brave. The capital has moved on, but Gniezno has not turned into a sleepy town propped up by school excursions. The cobblestoned Old Town has brightly painted early-19th-century tenement houses, sunshine-filled beer gardens, and side streets filled with quaint, time-warped shops. It is an easy day trip from Poznań.

Essentials

GETTING THERE

Gniezno is 286km (178 miles) to the east of Warsaw and 50km (31 miles) to the northeast of Poznań.

BY CAR From Poznań, take Road 5. If you're coming from Warsaw, take E30, exit at Września, then turn north on Road 15. Figure on 4 hours' driving time from Warsaw and 1 hour from Poznań.

BY TRAIN Trains run regularly from Poznań to Gniezno's train station (Dworcowa 15; ✆ **197-57**). Tickets cost about 20 zł, and the journey time is 45 minutes. The Town Square is a 10-minute walk in the northwest direction.

BY BUS Frequent bus service is available from Poznań's PKS bus station to Gniezno's bus station (Dworcowa 15; ✆ **61/428-26-53**).

VISITOR INFORMATION

Gniezno Tourist Information Center (Rynek 14; ✆ **61/428-41-00;** www.szlakpiastowski.com.pl) is open from April to September weekdays from 8am to 6pm, Saturdays from 9am to 3pm, and Sundays from 10am to 2pm. Off-season, it's open on weekdays only from 8am to 4pm. It is an excellent place for maps, English-language resources, and hotel and restaurant listings. They can advise on the Piast Route beyond Gniezno. To book English-speaking tour guides, call 2 days in advance. It's 140 zł for 2 hours; that covers the cathedral and the two museums. Another tourist information point is the **PTTK office** (Łaskiego 10; ✆ **61/426-36-60**).

Top Attractions

Gniezno Cathedral ★ The original cathedral was built by Mieszko I before 977 A.D. If the present cathedral looks newer than that to you, it's because centuries of fires and invasions took their toll, and the building was reconstructed in the 14th century. Baroque chapels and steeples were added over the years. Most visitors make a beeline to see the 12th-century Romanesque bronze doors, regarded as the finest example of their kind in Poland. The 18-panel doors are diminutive in stature but glorious in bas-relief, depicting the life of St. Adalbert. You could easily spend 30 minutes studying the key moments leading to his death in the hands of pagans during his mission to evangelize Northern Poland. His remains lie in the silver sarcophagus

Model Behavior

If you're interested in folk culture, head to the **Wielkopolska Ethnographic Park ★** (Dziekanowice 32, Lednogóra; ✆ **61/427-50-40;** www.lednicamuzeum.pl), an open-air park 18km (11 miles) to the west of Gniezno. It has 50 life-sized models of historical folk architecture from the last 250 years. The pieces, from all over the country, include farmsteads of rich peasants, a potter, windmills, a chapel, a cemetery, and a manor house. It's a fair bit of walking, so wear comfortable shoes. It's closed on Mondays. To get there by bus, take any of the buses to Poznań or Pobiedziska, and alight at Komorowo. The park is a 5-minute walk away. By car, take Road no. 5 toward Poznań.

in the cathedral's nave. Outside the cathedral is the statue of Bolesław the Brave, the first Polish king crowned here, in 1025. Four subsequent kings had their coronations here before the capital moved to Kraków. The rather kitschy portraits of these royals are hung above the portal opposite the bronze doors.

Łaskiego 9. ✆ **61/426-19-09** (office) or 602/708-231 (guides). Cathedral: free admission. Doors of Gniezno: 4 zł adults; required guide 10 zł/group (no guide service on Sun). Cathedral: May–Sept Mon–Sat 9–11:45am, daily 1–5pm; Oct–Apr daily 9am–4pm. Viewing tower: daily 9:30am–5:30pm.

Where to Stay & Dine

Tumska and Chrobrego are the main streets in the Old Town. They are flanked by restaurants and beer terraces where refreshments are of high standard and come at a much lower price than those in comparable establishments in Poznań.

Adalbertus You can't get nearer to the cathedral than this. This hotel is part of the Pietrak Hotel (see below) chain, but it feels cozier here than at its big brother's on Chrobrego Street. The exterior retains the charm of the monastery the property used to be, but the interior has had all its monastic character renovated out of it. Nevertheless, the pokey rooms are nicely furnished, and the cramped bathrooms are clean. There are two restaurants, one Polish, which has value-priced two-course set lunches; the other serves Italian fare.

Tumska 7A. ✆ **61/426-13-60.** www.pietrak.pl. 24 units. 190 zł double. DC, MC, V. Parking 15 zł. **Amenities:** 2 restaurants; Wi-Fi (free). *In room:* TV.

Atelier ★★ Opened in early 2010, this new neighbor of the Adalbertus started off as a restaurant-cum-cafe before converting the upper floors into sleeping quarters. The rooms, done in country style with contemporary big-city accents, stand out from most of the competitors in town, which favor a formal, regal look. A broad range of food, from pizza to chicken *tikka masala,* can be had in the front patio with a view of the cathedral or in the cloistered back garden.

Tumska 5. ✆ **61/424-85-50.** Fax 61/424-85-30. www.hotelatelier.pl. 30 units. 240 zł double. MC, V. Parking 30 zł. **Amenities:** Restaurant; cafe. *In room:* TV, Wi-Fi (free).

Nest ★ A 5-minute walk from the main pedestrian street brings you to this red-brick, single-storey complex. Newly converted from military barracks, the spacious rooms have the style and comfort of mid-range hotel chains. The area is behind offices and in the midst of potholed parking lots. Scenic it isn't—but it's safe, and there's free guarded parking. Another freebie is an hour of bowling on the premises.

Sobieskiego 20. ✆ **61/423-80-00.** Fax 61/423-80-02. www.hotelnest.pl. 12 units. 190 zł double. DC, MC, V. Free parking. **Amenities:** Restaurant. *In room:* A/C, TV, Wi-Fi (free).

Pietrak ★ The location is ideal, along the main street of the Old Town, which is lined with lively pubs and restaurants. The single and double rooms are similar in size and have green carpets, brown lacquered furniture, and fussy curtains. The hotel has hosted many key political figures, so the staff is fine-tuned to the art of hospitality. The restaurant has seen diners such as the former German Chancellor Helmut Kohl, and serves European fare with a selection of vegetarian options.

Chrobrego 3. ✆ **61/426-14-97.** www.pietrak.pl. 54 units. 210 zł double; 380 zł suite. DC, MC, V. Parking 15 zł. **Amenities:** 3 restaurants; bar; gym; Jacuzzi; room service. *In room:* A/C (in suite); TV, hair dryer, minibar, Wi-Fi (free).

BISKUPIN

Dubbed the "Polish Pompeii," Biskupin is the only known Iron Age settlement in Poland. It is also one of the most engaging attractions on the Piast Route. Though it is not connected to the Piast Dynasty, it is regarded as a key fragment in piecing together the origins of the country. The site was discovered by accident in 1933 by a teacher on a school excursion to Lake Biskupieńskie. Wooden stakes sticking out of the lake caught his eye. Excavations revealed a network of well-preserved wooden foundations and defensive ramparts, and evidence indicates it was a fortified settlement of the Lusatian clan dating from around 550 B.C.

The present-day settlement you see is an impressive mockup of an Iron Age village. As the site is in the middle of nowhere, careful consideration has been given to make this a satisfying and complete afternoon out. There is a museum to give context to the place and, in season, daily demonstrations of pottery, archery, fire working with flint stone, and pony and leisure-boat rides. The archeological festivals in September showcase earlier civilizations—from not just Europe, but also around the world, so don't be surprised to see a samurai gaiting by.

Biskupin can be stringed along with Gniezno as a day trip from Poznań.

Essentials

GETTING THERE

BY BUS From Gniezno, regular buses run to Żnin (10km/6¼ miles to the north of Biskupin) and Gąsawa (2km/1¼ miles to the south of Biskupin). The journey is about an hour. From either Żnin or Gąsawa, you catch a bus or the train to Biskupin. The bus service runs regularly on weekdays. Should you miss your bus at Gąsawa, the 2km (1¼ miles) to Biskupin is manageable on foot.

BY TRAIN The narrow-gauge railway (✆ **52/302-04-92**) runs from Żnin to Gąsawa and stops right in front of the reserve. From mid-April to August, the trains run from 9am to 3pm every 1½ hours. There is an additional run at 4pm during the archaeological festival in September. The journey takes 40 minutes from Żnin and 25 minutes from Gąsawa. Tickets, bought from the train driver, are 10 zł one-way and 18 zł round-trip.

BY CAR From Poznań, it takes 1½ hours. Leave the city on Road 5, turning north at Gniezno. As you approach Gąsawa, you will see signs for the reserve.

VISITOR INFORMATION

Guides and demonstrations of pottery-making and flint-stone fire-working have to be booked in advance by calling ✆ **52/302-50-55.** English-speaking guides cost 100 zł for 1½ hours. The ticket office sells a good map of the Piast Route by Bik (7 zł).

At the reserve's parking lot, several outdoor stalls serve snacks and meals. Across the road, **Karczma Biskupińska** (Biskupin 6; ✆ **52/302-50-14;** www.karczma-biskupinska.pl) offers a similar spread but with indoor seating. They also have basic accommodations, priced at 100 zł for a double.

Top Attraction

Archaeological Reserve (Rezerwat Archeologiczny) ★ ☺ On the way to the centerpiece Iron Age Village, you'll pass the museum, which has a small but well-designed exhibition of artifacts and models depicting life in the area some 2,700 years ago. Press on to the village at the northern edge of the park by the lake, and follow the "tour direction" (Kierunek Zwiedzania) boards to see the palisades and rampart fortifications, thatched roofs, wood-beam floors, and wicket doors of the settlement. In this compound, you'll find demos of pottery and other aspects of Iron Age life, all enacted by enthusiastic and educated staff sporting coarse robes. If you haven't made reservations for the demos, keep an eye out for school groups and just piggyback on their demo sessions (they will be in Polish, but you don't need to understand the talk to appreciate the crafts). It takes no more than an hour to cover the grounds. The kids might want to have a go at the pony rides or a trip on the leisure boat to nowhere. Although it opens at 8am, the settlement is in full swing only at about 10am. It's an outdoor museum, so April through September is the best time to visit.

Biskupin 17. ✆ **52/302-50-25.** www.biskupin.pl. 8 zł adults; 6 zł seniors, students & children. Summer daily 8am–6pm; winter daily 8am–dusk.

TORUŃ

Toruń is a picturesque university town with at least three things in its favor. First, it has an unrivaled stock of Gothic buildings. Unlike many Polish towns its size, Toruń escaped major damage in World War II. The Old Town joined UNESCO's World Heritage Site list in 1997. Now, gearing up in the bid to be the European City of Culture in 2016, Toruń's theme is *Gotyk na Dotyk* (literally, "Touch Gothic"). Beneath the baroque, Renaissance, and classical facades are the medieval Gothic red bricks. Second, this is the birthplace of "the man who stopped the Earth and moved the Sun," Nicolaus Copernicus. Third, it had knights. Not the Templar, but the no-less-formidable Teutonic Order (see "Malbork," p. 262), a German religious order that was originally invited by Polish kings to secure the area, but later turned on its hosts and amassed its own empire. Tensions between the Knights and Toruń residents ran high, culminating in a siege in 1454, when the citizens stormed the Knights' castle just outside the Old Town and effectively ended the Knights' domination of the city.

You can make a whirlwind tour of the town in a couple of hours, but that would be a shame. Toruń is ideal for a slow and easy weekend. Be sure to stroll along the river (Bulwar Filadelfijski) for a spectacular view of the town walls that is especially pretty at night. And stop by the ruins of the former castle of the Teutonic Knights (at the crossing of Przedzamcze and Bulwar Filadelfijski).

Essentials

GETTING THERE

Toruń lies on major bus and rail links, with frequent daily service to major cities.

BY CAR From Warsaw (200km/124 miles), take Road E77 and switch to A10 in Płońsk. From Gdańsk (207km/129 miles), take E75. From Poznań (150km/93 miles), it's E261 followed by A10 at Bydgoszcz. Figure on 2 to 3 hours' driving time from any of these starting points. You'll find parking along the river on Bulwar Filadelfijski.

BY TRAIN Trains arrive at **Toruń Główny** (Kujawska 1; ✆ **197-57;** www.intercity.pkp.pl) in the south of the city, across the Vistula river. Take bus no. 22 or 27 to get to town.

BY BUS The **PKS bus station** (Dąbrowskiego 8/24; ✆ **703/303-333;** www.veolia-transport.torun.pl) is about 5 minutes to the east of the Old Town.

VISITOR INFORMATION

The **Toruń Tourist Information Center** (Rynek Staromiejski 25; ✆ **56/621-09-31;** www.it.torun.pl) is centrally located in the Old Town Square and staffed by friendly English speakers. There is a free Internet terminal here, as well. The center is open on Monday from 9am to 4pm, Tuesday through Friday from 9am to 6pm, and Saturday from 9am to 4pm. From May to August, it's also open on Sundays from 10am to 1pm. You can get **audio guides** (10 zł per 4 hr. or 15 zł for a full day) here, or download the audio files from their website. If you prefer a "live" guide, they'll direct you to private tourist agencies. The rate is about 170 zł for 2 hours. For quirky holiday photos, hire the guides from **Copernicana** (Kopernika 35/37; ✆ **56/622-30-02;** www.copernicana.pl), who are dressed up as medieval townsmen and women, Copernicus, and Teutonic Knights. The rates are 265 zł for 2 hours and 365 zł for 3 hours. Call a day in advance to book.

Top Attractions

The charm of Torun's Old and New towns is that they feel like a living Gothic theme park. There are innumerable statues and minor museums for you to make pit stops at. It's one of the best Old Towns to explore with kids since it's quite compact.

Cathedral of St. John the Baptist & St. John the Evangelist (Katedra Świętego Janów) ★★ The construction of the cathedral that dominates Toruń's skyline started in the 1260s and took 200 years to complete. The star attraction is the **Tuba Dei,** the oldest medieval bell in Poland, cast in 1530. It's also one of the 11 historic bells in Toruń that survived looting and recasting into weaponry. In the past, Tuba Dei's peal heralded the arrival of popes and Polish kings. A twirl up the claustrophobic spiral stairway gets you a view of the bell and the added bonus of postcard views of the Old Town Square and the river. The cathedral's 15th-century clock has a single hand, referred to as ***Digitus Dei*** (God's Finger). The ongoing renovation work in the chapel is expected to be completed by 2012.

Żeglarska 16. ✆ **605/858-471.** Cathedral: 3 zł adults, 2 zł seniors & children; tower: 6 zł adults, 4 zł seniors & children. Apr–Oct Mon–Sat 9am–5pm, Sun 1–5pm; Nov–Mar by appointment only.

You Made the Earth Move under My Feet?

Nicolaus Copernicus, or Mikołaj Kopernik in Polish, is Toruń's most famous son and the precursor of the archetype Renaissance man. During his lifetime, he served not only as a priest, but also as a physician, classical scholar, jurist (church law), governor, military leader, diplomat, and economist. However, he is first and foremost remembered for *De Revolutionibus Orbium Coelestium (On the Revolutions of the Heavenly Spheres),* in which he presented his theories of the Earth revolving around the Sun. The Church initially viewed it as blasphemy. Copernicus died shortly after *De Revolutionibus* was published, though he probably never saw it in print. His work paved the way for a series of astronomical breakthroughs in the 16th and 17th centuries, including the work of Galileo, Tycho Brahe, and Sir Isaac Newton. Learn more at the House of Copernicus (Dom Mikołaja Kopernika; Kopernika 15/17; ✆ 56/622-70-38; www.muzeum.torun.pl), which has some of the oldest editions of *De Revolutionibus.*

Hands On

Make your own decorative gingerbread at the Gingerbread Museum (Muzeum Piernika) [kids] (Rabiańska 9; ✆ 56/663-66-17; www.muzeumpiernika.pl). In a hall emulating a 16th-century abode, the cheerful English-speaking crew here gets you to chant an oath to keep the secrets of gingerbread crafts before allowing you to play dough. Sessions start every hour on the hour, with a minimum group size of 5. The House of Copernicus (see "You Made the Earth Move under My Feet?" above) also has a similar program.

Old Town Hall (Ratusz Staromiejski) ★ This 14th-century red-brick Gothic building, dotted with 365 windows and crowned with four pinnacles, is one of the most captivating Town Halls in the country. It started life as a site for trading stalls. The Renaissance turrets were added later. Inside, there's the town museum, where you'll find an impressive collection of stained glass, gingerbread molds and other crafts through the ages, and paintings of former prominent residents. It's worth panting up the 42m (138-ft.) tower for a view of the city and across the river.

Rynek Staromiejski 1. ✆ **56/660-56-21.** www.muzeum.torun.pl. Museum: 10 zł adults, 6 zł, seniors, students & children; Wed free admission. Tower: 10 zł adults; 6 zł seniors & children. Museum: May–Sept Tues–Sun 10am–6pm, Oct–Apr Tues–Sun 10am–4pm; tower: May–Sept daily 10am–8pm, Oct–Apr daily 10am–5pm.

Shopping

Synonymous with Toruń is *piernik* (gingerbread). The decorative ones with motifs such as *kareta* (horse-carriage), *katarzyna* (indented rectangles), and burgher houses are tooth-breakers. They are meant as keepsakes. The edible ones are soft and filled with preserves, such as plum, and icing-glazed or chocolate-coated. One supplier, **Kopernik** (Rynek Staromiejski 6; ✆ **56/622-88-32**), overruns the town. At **Pierniczek** (Żeglarska 25; ✆ **56/621-05-61**), you can buy the goods by weight. **Emporium** ★★ (Piekary 28; ✆ **56/657-61-08**) is best for a variety of souvenirs. The presents are bundled up with a wax seal imprinted with the emblem of Toruń. They also have bike rentals for 5 zł an hour.

Where to Stay

Toruń has a wide range of rooms. Those in heritage buildings in the Old Town are charming, but may not have elevators and may require you to negotiate steep staircases.

VERY EXPENSIVE

Bulwar ★★ Open in early 2009, the hotel is a successful marriage of a restored 19th-century Prussian military barracks and 21st-century cosmopolitan swank. Though it has the exclusive club-like ambience from lobby and bar to the rooms, the well-trained and courteous staff does not bat an eyelid when you show up dressed down. At the restaurant's patio, you can laze on Kartell chairs to take in the river view.

Bulwar Filadelfijski 18. ✆ **56/623-94-00.** Fax 56/623-94-01. www.hotelbulwar.pl. 98 units. 435 zł double. AE, DC, MC, V. Underground parking 30 zł. **Amenities:** Restaurant; bar. *In room:* A/C, TV, hair dryer, minibar, Wi-Fi (free).

Hotel 1231 ★ Next door to the ruins of the Teutonic Knights castle is this attractive, new boutique hotel, remodeled from a 13th-century mill. As opposed to the majority of rooms in town dressed up in period style, 1231 offers the look and feel of a high-end global hotel. One side of the building looks out to a public football pitch, and it can get noisy. If so, escape to the inviting patio, which has part of an old city tower-gate on its grounds. Staff here, though friendly, is not as polished as Bulwar's.

Przedzamze 6. ✆ **56/619-09-10.** Fax 56/619-09-11. www.hotelesolaris.pl. 23 units. 360 zł double. AE, DC, MC, V. Parking 30 zł. **Amenities:** Restaurant; bar. *In room:* A/C, TV, hair dryer, minibar, Wi-Fi (free).

EXPENSIVE & MODERATE

Gotyk This hotel's location, opposite the Hotel Petite Fleur, is superb. Rooms are fashioned in dark classical tones. Compared to Petite Fleur, the rooms are much bigger, but the quality of the furnishings is lower and the atmosphere is more casual; they do, however, have parking and elevators here, which the Fleur doesn't. The hotel also has four higher-standard rooms in a building across the street.

Piekary 20. ✆ **56/658-40-00.** Fax 56/658-40-01. www.hotel-gotyk.com.pl. 42 units. 270 zł–320 zł double. AE, DC, MC, V. Limited street parking 25 zł. **Amenities:** 2 restaurants; bar. *In room:* A/C (in some), Wi-Fi (free).

Heban The hotel occupies two renovated town houses in the section between the Old and New towns. One building, much more atmospheric, dates from the 17th century, and the other, across the street, from the 19th century. The latter is pitched at business clients. Ask for room number 3 in the older building: It's a picture-perfect double with hardwood floors and wood-beamed ceilings.

Małe Garbary 7. ✆ **56/652-15-55.** Fax 56/652-16-65. www.hotel-heban.com.pl. 20 units. 300 zł double. AE, DC, MC, V. **Amenities:** Restaurant; bar. *In room:* TV, fridge, Wi-Fi (free).

Mercure Helios Toruń Part of the Orbis hotel chain, this has all the reliable comforts of a mid-sized hotel such as ample parking, which some of the boutique hotels in the Old Town lack. Located 700m (2,297 ft.) from the Old Town, it's an easy walk to the sights. The rooms are not soulful, but clean and cheerful with pictures of Copernicus's Helios system.

Kraszewskiego 1/3. ✆ **56/619-65-50.** Fax 56/622-19-54. www.orbis.pl/our-hotels/mercure. 110 units. 350 zł double. AE, DC, MC, V. Parking 50 zł. **Amenities:** Restaurant; bar; concierge; gym. *In room:* A/C, paid TV (59 zł), hair dryer, minibar, Internet (free).

Petite Fleur Located in the Old Town, this boutique hotel occupies two stunningly renovated Renaissance burghers' houses. The rooms, some with wood-beamed ceilings and exposed red-brick alcoves, are cozy and tastefully adorned with floral paintings. Steep stairs lead to the rooms. Mind where the corridor light switches are; otherwise, you'll be groping in the dark. The so-called "guesthouse rooms" are in another building on the same street (no. 28). If you stay at the guesthouse, you must walk to the hotel for your breakfast.

Piekary 25. ✆ **56/621-51-00.** Fax 56/621-51-20. www.petitefleur.pl. 16 units. Guesthouse 190 zł double; hotel 270 zł double. AE, DC, MC, V. **Amenities:** Restaurant; hair dryer. *In room:* A/C (in some), TV, Wi-Fi (free).

Retman Also in the Old Town, this is a clean, quiet, family-run inn. Rooms are on the small side, but scrubbed clean and have agreeable dark wood finishings. The buffet breakfast, where they usually throw in something seasonal, gets raves but also rants.

Rabiańska 15. ✆ **56/657-44-60.** Fax 56/657-44-61. www.hotelretman.pl. 29 units. Weekdays 250 zł double; weekends 200 zł double. AE, DC, MC, V. **Amenities:** Restaurant; pub. *In room:* TV, Wi-Fi (free).

Spichrz ★★ Located by the Bridge Gate in the Old Town, the hotel occupies a restored Swedish granary built in 1719. Don't be put off by the modern lobby; the rooms retain the original building details including wooden columns, ceiling beams, and granary windows. Rooms are small to medium in size, with modern bathrooms. Some look out to the Vistula River. The restaurant's forte is meat and more meat.

Mostowa 1. ✆ **56/657-11-40.** Fax 56/657-11-44. www.spichrz.pl. 19 units. 290 zł double. AE, DC, MC, V. Parking 20 zł. **Amenities:** Restaurant. *In room:* A/C (in apt), TV, hair dryer, minibar, Wi-Fi (free).

INEXPENSIVE

B&B Hotel ★ Bare minimum but not low quality is the winning strategy of the B&B Hotels chain. This one in Toruń was open in July 2010, so it's sparkling from top to toe. The chirpy crew at the front desk treats you like you're in a five-star establishment. The only glitch is getting the hang of using the key-code for opening the doors. Its location is just outside the eastern end of the Old Town.

Szumana 8. ✆ **56/561-81-00.** Fax 56/621-81-01. www.hotelbb.pl. 93 units. 129 zł double. AE, MC, V. Basement parking 20 zł. **Amenities:** Breakfast room. *In room:* A/C, TV, Wi-Fi (free).

Green Hostel ★ This hostel could qualify as a minimalistic boutique hostel since it's furnished by the owners who are backpackers with a taste for stylish designs and an emphasis on cleanliness. You also get solid, comfortable beds with quality linen. It's housed in the Old Town, so it also comes with steep stairs.

Małe Garbary 10. ✆ **56/561-40-00**. www.greenhostel.eu. 13 units. 180 zł quad; 100 zł double w/shared bathroom. AE, MC, DC, V. **Amenities:** Breakfast room; Wi-Fi (free). *In room:* TV, fan.

Where to Dine

Toruń is a great place to escape from hotel dining and slip into places with great ambience and reasonable prices. And remember to save your ice cream allowance for **Lenkiewicz** (Wielkie Garbary 14; ✆ **56/622-56-35**).

Bar Miś POLISH This is a milk bar fashioned after a Polish cult movie of the same name, which parodied life during the Communist era. The hay "bear" at the window is an icon from the movie. So are the aluminum bowl screwed to the bar counter and the two spoons chained together. A whack of chunky, sausage-laden *bigos* (hunter's stew) is only 4 zł; pierogi and pork chops are also popular. Return your plate to the service hatch when you're done.

Stary Rynek 8. ✆ **56/622-35-59.** Main courses 4 zł–12 zł. No credit cards. Mon–Fri 9am–6pm; Sat 10am–3pm.

Leniwa ★★ POLISH Delicious scents reel you in to this IKEA-country-style space. *Leniwa* is a typical Polish starchy staple and it also means "lazy." But the genial folks here are anything but lazy in making some of the best pierogi ever. Sample the various types of sweet and savory dumplings at bargain-basement prices. Locals tuck in here, so be prepared to wait for your freshly made orders.

Ślusarska 5. ✆ **56/477-54-03.** www.leniwa.pl. Pierogi 9 zł–13 zł. No credit cards. Daily 11am–9pm.

Manekin ★ PANCAKE Manekin gets rave reviews from pancake (crêpe) fans. The square packages, made from wheat or buckwheat flour, are padded with sweet or savory fillings. The chicken, bean, and onion combo, topped with spicy tomato sauce, is filling without going overboard. For the sweet tooth, the simple apple with cinnamon is a winner. In summer, you can eat on the terrace overlooking the Old Town Square.

Rynek Staromiejski 16. ✆ **56/621-05-04.** Pancakes 7.50 zł–13 zł. AE, MC, V. Sun–Thurs 10am–11pm; Fri & Sat 10am–midnight.

Oberża ★ POLISH At this self-service buffet, you compose your own plate of one meat, one salad, and one starch, choosing from a tempting range of Polish staples. It's definitely better value than the state-sponsored milk bars. What's more, you eat off sturdy plates with proper cutlery in a rustic-style hall.

Rabiańska 9. ✆ **669/100-400.** Set meals 13 zł. AE, MC, V. Sun–Thurs 11am–10pm; Fri & Sat noon–1am; Sun 11am–9pm.

Róże i Zen ★★ POLISH From the street, you wouldn't know that this cafe and restaurant hides a secret garden sheltered by trees and cloistered by old walls. The homey-feeling inside showcases an eclectic array of antiques. There's sophisticated home cooking, featuring chanterelle quiche and buckwheat *blini* with caviar. Many come especially for the house-made cheesecake and tarts. On weekends, a guitarist strums away, enticing you to linger.

Podmurna 18. ✆ **56/621-05-21.** Main courses 17 zł–55 zł. No credit cards. Sun–Thurs 11am–10pm; Fri & Sat 11am–11pm.

After Dark

New life surfaces in the Old and New towns after sunset. **Piwnica Pod Aniołem** (Rynek Staromiejski 1; ✆ **56/622-70-39;** www.myspace.com/piwnicapodaniolem), one of the most famous clubs in Toruń, hosts concerts, as well as photography and art exhibits. Located in the Town Hall's cellar, it oozes pungent clouds of nicotine. Running a similar show is **Toruńska Piwnica Artystyczna** ★ (Łazienna 30; ✆ **56/658-11-22;** www.tpart.pl). **Tantra** (Ślusarska 5; ✆ **601/682-701**) breaks from the Gothic spirit to ply you with Tibetan and Nepalese vibes.

11 GDAŃSK & THE BALTIC COAST

by Kit F. Chung

Gdańsk and the Baltic Coast don't have to do much to attract visitors; they come without bidding. The region is a treasure trove of historical gems, and the backdrop of sandy beaches is never far away. An affluent Baltic port for centuries, Gdańsk has an enchantingly rich architectural heritage that lends itself to endless discoveries. Then there's the jolting experience of walking on Westerplatte, the spot where the first shots of World War II were fired. As the birthplace of the Solidarity movement, the city also makes you aware of how far Poland has come since the anti-Communist struggle in the 1980s. But it's not all about reflecting on the past. As Gdańsk gets ready for the Euro Cup 2012 football championship, new venues and rejuvenation programs are creating more cultural options. Moreover, Gdańsk, Sopot, and Gdynia form the Tri-City (Trójmiasto), a coastal trio with beach life, affordable restaurants, first-rate accommodation, and cosmopolitan nightlife.

Don't leave the region without making a stop at Malbork Castle, the largest brick fortress in the world and the medieval stronghold of the Teutonic Knights. If your appetite for Middle Ages matters is still unsated after your visit, there are still other smaller Gothic castles to choose from in the vicinity.

For winding down, options abound. Within the Tri-City, you can ramble on the white-sand beaches of Sopot. A quick boat cruise lands you on endless stretches of pristine shores and the sleepy fishing villages of the Hel Peninsula, the nation's summertime playground by the Baltic Sea. Mingle with the locals on the slow, sandy lanes or get an adrenaline rush from deep-sea fishing or diving excursions to World War II shipwrecks. Idyllic seashore living can be also found in Łeba. From Łeba, you're a just a hop away from the famous "moving dunes" of Słowiński National Park. Another form of slowing down is on the Elbląg-Ostróda Canal. The canal, singled out by Poles as one of the nation's Seven Wonders, is the only one of its kind in Europe, where waterways are linked with rail tracks giving you the sensation of a boat cruise and a San Francisco cable-car ride packaged into one.

Though the region is most popular in summer, the autumn hues are spectacular, and in winter, snow-white beaches reward hardy souls with breathtaking sights. Speaking of hardy, a note on keeping warm: Even in summer, sea gusts dip the mercury, especially after sunset. So be sure to pack some warm layers with you.

GDAŃSK

Gdańsk is a sensory blast. If you were expecting a dingy Baltic seaport, perhaps reinforced by that foggy, black-and-white TV footage of Lech Wałęsa and the embattled Solidarity dockworkers, you are in for a pleasant surprise. Modern-day Gdańsk is a beautiful seaside town, with a lovingly restored Old City. The city was severely damaged in World War II, with the Russians and Allied bombers effectively finishing up where the Germans left off. But Gdańsk is luckier than many Polish cities in that the reconstruction after the war was commendably sensitive. And, unlike the reconstruction of Warsaw's Old Town (which mostly benefits tourists), Gdańsk's newly built Old City feels thoroughly authentic and lived-in by the locals. In this vibrant atmosphere, it's easy to forget that the first shots of World War II were fired here—and that this is also where history took another sharp turn when the shipyard's dockworkers, led by Lech Wałęsa, brought down the Communist government. You can still see the

Changes of the Guard in a Nutshell

Even for Poland, Gdańsk has a particularly twisted past, with convoluted shifts of power. The city rose to prominence in the 16th and 17th centuries as one of the most vital towns of the Hanseatic League, a grouping of prosperous river and seaport cities that controlled much of the trade in the North and Baltic seas. Due to its wealth, Gdańsk was hotly contested between German and Polish interests, though it managed to retain its status as a semi-autonomous city-state. After the Polish partition at the end of the 18th century, the city fell under Prussian rule and became firmly identified as "Danzig," its German moniker. Following Germany's defeat in World War I, the city's status became one of the thorniest issues facing the drafters of the Treaty of Versailles. They opted to create what they called the "Free City of Danzig"—neither German nor Polish—alongside a Polish-ruled strip of land that would effectively cut off mainland Germany from its East Prussian hinterland. Hitler was able to exploit very effectively the existence of this Polish "corridor" as part of his argument that the Treaty of Versailles was highly unfair to Germany. He even chose the port of Gdańsk to launch his war on Poland on September 1, 1939, when German gunboats fired on the Polish garrison at Westerplatte.

During the Communist period, Gdańsk was in the public's eye as the home of the Lenin Shipyards and the Solidarity Trade Union. It was here, now known as the Gdańsk shipyards, where intense negotiations in August 1980 between Solidarity, led by a youngish Lech Wałęsa, and the government resulted in the August Treaty, an official recognition of the first independent trade union in Communist Central and Eastern Europe. The government later reneged on the agreement and imposed martial law, but Gdańsk continued as a hotbed of labor unrest and strikes. Roundtable talks in the late 1980s saw the government agreeing to a power-sharing arrangement that in 1989 led to the first semi-free election and a nationwide political triumph for Solidarity. The events here eventually triggered the toppling of Communist regimes in Poland and throughout Eastern Europe.

shipyards, about a 15-minute walk north of the Old City, and visit an inspirational museum, the **Roads to Freedom,** that details the tense moments of the 1980s. From May to October, the calendar is jam-packed with festivals, including the 3-week long St. Dominic's Fair held in August.

Essentials

GETTING THERE

BY PLANE **Lech Wałęsa International Airport** (Słowackiego 200; ✆ **58/348-11-63;** www.airport.gdansk.pl) is the main airport in northeastern Poland, and it has good direct domestic and international routes. Flights take off from here to major European cities including London (Luton and Stansted), Berlin, and several Scandinavian cities. It's served by, among others, LOT, SAS, and WizzAir. The airport is about 10km (6¼ miles) west of the city. Bus B is the economy option to get to town. It runs twice hourly during daylight hours to Gdańsk Główny (the central train station). Bus N3 is the night bus to the main railway station and the Wrzeszcz railway station. The trip costs 3 zł. Leave about 40 minutes for the journey (more during rush hour). The **Airport Bus** (✆ **58/554-93-93** or 515/181-161; www.airportbus.com.pl), located outside the arrivals hall, takes you straight to Hevelius Hotel, a 15-minute walk from the Old City. It costs 9.90 zł, and you must pre-book your ride. The Gdańsk Shuttle (✆ **12/633-01-25** or 506/175-495) costs 79 zł for up to four people and must be pre-booked, as well. A taxi from the airport to Gdańsk costs about 50 zł, to Sopot about 60 zł, and to Gdynia 90 zł. The taxi company recommended by the airport authorities is **City Plus Neptune** (✆ **196-86** or 58/511-15-55; www.cph.gda.pl).

BY TRAIN For most arrivals, **Gdańsk Główny** train station (Podwale Grodzkie 1; ✆ **194-36;** www.pkp.pl), to the southwest of the Old City, is the first port of call. The Old Town is a 5-minute walk; use the underpass to cross the highway. Gdańsk is well served by railroad, and departures to Warsaw and other major cities are frequent. Local trains to Sopot and Gdynia also depart from here.

BY BUS The main bus station, **Dworzec PKS** (3 Maja 12; ✆ **58/302-15-32;** www.pks.gdansk.pl), is located next to the train station. As Poland's Baltic hub, the city is a primary destination for domestic and international bus lines.

BY CAR The roads to Gdańsk are improving, but traffic nightmares are frequent. The major, and seemingly permanent, road work has badly tied up routes coming from all directions, so leave plenty of travel time. The main roads running south are the E75 to Toruń and E77 to Warsaw. The E28 is the main route to the west toward Germany. Coming from the west, it skirts Gdańsk as it heads south. The E28 is planned to be a major four-lane north–south artery. Once you arrive in the city, brace yourself for hour-long jams during the morning and evening rush hours. The drive from Warsaw may take anywhere from 4 to 5 hours.

BY BOAT It is possible to arrive in Gdańsk by ferry from Sweden. **Polferries** (www.polferries.pl) offers regular service between the Swedish port of Nynäshamm (60km/37 miles south of Stockholm) and **Gdańsk's Nowy Port** (Przemysłowa 1; ✆ **58/343-00-78**), which is 7km (4¼ miles) south of the city. From the train station, there aren't any convenient bus or tram connections to the ferry terminals. Taxi rides should cost around 30 zł. The ferries depart from Sweden every second or third day at 6pm and arrive at noon the following day. Returns from Gdańsk follow the same schedule. **Stena Line** (www.stenaline.pl) runs a similar service from the southern

Swedish city of Karlskrona (500km/311 miles south of Stockholm) to Gdynia's passenger ferry port. In summer, the ferries make the 10-hour journey twice daily at 9am and 9pm.

VISITOR INFORMATION

The main tourist information office, the **PTTK office** (Długa 45; ✆ **58/301-91-51;** www.pttk-gdansk.pl), is conveniently located in the heart of the Główne Miasto, opposite the Neptune Fountain. This office is overstretched in the summer. They offer services like making hotel reservations or booking tickets to the philharmonic and opera. To hire a city guide, you need to call in advance. The price is 80 zł to 160 zł per person, depending on the group size, for a 2½ hour walking tour. Pick up a copy of the *Gdańsk, Stare Miasto* map, a large-format, easy-to-read guide to all the major sights in the center of town. Also, look for the free brochures *The Best of Gdańsk* and *The Royal Route;* both are comprehensive, self-guided walking tours in English. The office sells copies of *Gdańsk, In Your Pocket* (5 zł), which has an excellent overview of the city, including sections on Sopot, Gdynia, and Malbork. For more extensive exploration, the Copernicus Tri-City map with public transport routes is a good buy. The **GTO Gdańsk Tourist Information Center** (Długi Targ 28/29; ✆ **58/301-43-55**; www.gdansk4u.pl), run by the city authorities, has a similar stock of material but tends to be less crowded. It is open June to August daily from 8:30am to 6:30pm and the rest of the year daily from 9am to 5pm. They sell the **Gdańsk Tourist Card** (see "Getting Around," below) and rent audio guides (www.audioguide.com.pl) with humorous narrations for 12 zł per 4-hour usage.

CITY LAYOUT

Unlike other Polish cities, the heart of Gdańsk is technically not called the "Old Town" (Stare Miasto). There is a **Stare Miasto,** but it lies just to the north of the main center, the **Główne Miasto** (Main Town). The Główne Miasto is where you'll find the main pedestrian walks, **ul. Długa** (Long St.), **Długi Targ** (the Long Market), and interesting side streets. Then comes **Długie Pobrzeże,** a major pedestrian walkway along the **Motława Canal.** Stare Miasto is about a 15-minute walk north, and it is here you'll find the **Gdańsk shipyards** and the **Solidarity memorial,** and the **Roads to Freedom** exhibit. To the south of Główne Miasto is **Stare Przedmieście** (Old Suburbs). Farther to the north, in the direction of Sopot, lies the unlovely **Nowy Port,** as well as the serene suburbs of **Wrzeszcz** and **Oliwa.** The former is home to many of the city's more affordable hotels and pensions. The **Tri-City** (Trójmiasto) refers to the trio of Gdańsk, Sopot, and Gdynia. The heart of **Sopot** is about 6km (3¾ miles) to the north of Gdańsk city center. **Gdynia** is about 15km (9¼ miles) to the north.

GETTING AROUND

Walking is the most enjoyable mode to see the city's historical sites. To get to Sopot, Gdynia, or farther afield, use the city's good network of public transportation or ferry services targeted at tourists. If you plan to use the trams and buses (run by ZTM) and the SKM commuter trains throughout the Tri-City, you can get a day ticket (18 zł). The newly launched **Gdańsk Tourist Card** (www.gdansk4u.pl) packages together access to the city's public transportation and discounts at selected museums, restaurants, and hotels. They're sold at the GTO offices and are available in 24-hour (35 zł) or 72-hour (65 zł) formats.

ON FOOT Much of central Gdańsk, including ul. Długa and the walkway along the Motława Canal, is closed to motor vehicles. The center is compact and easy to manage on foot.

BY TRAM Gdańsk has an efficient network of **trams** (✆ **58/341-00-21;** www.ztm.gda.pl) that whisk you from the center of the city to the suburbs of Wrzeszcz and Oliwa in a few minutes. Note that trams do not run to Sopot and Gdynia. Tickets cost 3 zł for a 15-minute ride; a day ticket costs 9 zł. Buy tickets at Ruch kiosks, newspapers counters, and from the ticket machines.

BY BUS City **buses** (www.ztm.gda.pl) are useful for getting to some of the suburbs. Bus nos. 117, 122, and 143 go to Sopot, while bus no. 171 gets you to Gdynia. Ticketing is the same as for the trams.

BY SKM COMMUTER TRAIN The **SKM** (Szybka Kolej Miejska; ✆ **58/721-21-70;** www.skm.pkp.pl), nicknamed **Kolejka,** is a quick and reliable local "urban train" service, linking the main stopovers of the Tri-City. The SKM runs at about 10-minute intervals from 5am to 7pm through the Tri-City. Get tickets in any of the main stations or from the ticket vending machines located on the platforms. (***Note:*** Ticket machines are prone to breaking down. You can also buy the tickets from the conductor at the front of the train.) Validate your tickets before boarding. From Gdańsk, it takes about 20 minutes and a 4-zł ticket to reach Sopot, and 30 minutes and a 4.50-zł ticket to Gdynia.

BY TAXI Taxis are a good way to get to your hotel from the bus or train stations, but you won't need to use them much once you've sorted out the public transportation system. Figure on about 25 zł for rides in town.

BY BOAT It's fun and relaxing to hitch a boat from Gdańsk to several local and regional destinations, such as Westerplatte and Gdynia. The service is run by **Żegluga Gdańska** (Długie Pobrzeże; ✆ **58/301-49-26;** www.zegluga.pl). The main ferry landing and ticket office is near the Green Gate, at the intersection of the Długi Targ and the Motława Canal. In the summer months, the **ferry trams** (*tramwaj wodny;* Nabrzeże Motławy; ✆ **58/309-13-23;** www.ztm.gda.pl) go to Sopot and the Hel Peninsula. Note that the ferry trams offer daily service June through August. Tickets, sold at Targ Rybny 6, cost 10 zł to Sopot and 18 zł to Hel.

BY BIKE Gdańsk is navigable by bicycle, and several new bike lanes now connect the center with the suburbs of Wrzeszcz and beyond, toward Sopot. That said, the network is spotty, and there are plenty of places where you'll still have to contend with stairways, sidewalks, heavy traffic, and Polish drivers unaccustomed to cyclists. The rental of choice is **Rowerownia** (Fieldorfa 11/3; ✆ **58/320-61-69;** www.rowerownia.gda.pl), which also issues sturdy locks.

Top Attractions

Central Gdańsk is one of the most pleasantly walkable cities in central Europe. Equip yourself with a copy of *Gdańsk, The Royal Route,* a complimentary pamphlet from the tourist information office, for details about the notable Renaissance houses along the route. Gdańsk also has stunning bird's-eye views. Aside from the towers in St. Mary's Church and the Town Hall, the **Archaeological Museum** (Mariacka 25/26; ✆ **58/322-21-00**) also has a viewing tower.

Amber Museum ★ This is a must for all fans of the ossified pine resin that continues to make Gdańsk prosper. On six floors of exhibits, located inside the medieval

Torture Tower, you'll learn everything you'll ever need to know about amber, including how it's mined and processed, what it looks like under a microscope, and how it was used through the ages, not just as jewelry, but in art and medicine. If you're thinking of buying some amber while in Gdańsk, stop here first for an educational primer. One part of the exhibition is given over to fake amber and how to identify the genuine stuff. Mind the steep stairs.

Targ Węglowy 26. ✆ **58/301-47-33.** www.mhmg.pl. 10 zł adults, 5 zł children & seniors; Mon free admission. Mon 11am–3pm; Tues–Sat 10am–6pm; Sun 11am–6pm.

Artus Court (Dwór Artusa) ★ One of the most impressive houses in the city was reopened to the public after extensive renovation. The Court, so named after King Arthur (though he had nothing to do with this place), was founded as a meeting place for the town's wealthiest traders and leading dignitaries. The house dates from the 14th century but was remodeled several times, including once in the 19th century when it was given its neo-Gothic look to be in vogue with the prevailing trends. The exterior was demolished in World War II, but many of the interior pieces had been removed beforehand and survived the fighting. In the main hall, the over 10m-tall (33-ft.) Renaissance furnace dates from mid–16th century. It has 520 tiles, many of which have embossed faces of townspeople. Slip through the back door to find the small yard with samples of Gothic stone portals.

Długi Targ 43/44. ✆ **58/767-91-83.** www.mhmg.pl. 10 zł adults, 5 zł children & seniors; Mon free admission. Mon 11am–3pm; Tues–Sat 10am–6pm; Sun 11am–6pm.

Central Maritime Museum (Centralne Muzeum Morskie) The best of four separate museums that highlight Gdańsk's history as a port city, here, you'll find an excellent A-to-Z compendium on Polish maritime history, from the turn of the first millennium to modern times. Some of the finest exhibits are the detailed models of ships, lots of old weaponry, and the oil paintings of old boats. The museum is housed in three Renaissance-era granaries.

Ołowianka 9/13. ✆ **58/310-86-11.** www.cmm.pl. 8 zł adults; 5 zł children & seniors. Aug–June Tues–Sun 10am–4pm; July Tues–Sun 10am–6pm.

Long Waterfront (Długie Pobrzeże) As you turn off Długi Targ Street, you come to the Motława Canal waterfront, a touristy but nevertheless delightful promenade of restaurants, cafes, amber boutiques, and souvenir shops. Street buskers add to the outdoor merriment. Just beyond the **Gate of the Holy Spirit** (Brama Św. Ducha) is another Gdańsk landmark, the **Crane** (**Żuraw;** Szeroka 67/68; ✆ **58/301-53-11;** www.cmm.pl). Built mid–15th century, it was once the biggest crane in medieval Europe. It is no longer operational, but up until the mid–19th century, it was used to unload cargo as heavy as 4 tons.

Długie Pobrzeże.

Monument to the Fallen Shipyard Workers This gigantic steel monument, some 40m (131 ft.) high, was built in 1980 to commemorate the 44 people who died during the bloody anti-Communist riots of 1970. Its construction was one of the demands put forward by the striking workers in August 1980. The design is replete with symbolism. The crosses depict resurrection and victory, while the anchors nailed on the crosses represent the "crucifixion" of hope. The structure emerges from broken concrete to denote the idea of defeating Communism. From the monument's center, "roads" spiral outward—showing that the idea would spread around the world.

Plac Solidarnośći.

Roads to Freedom Exhibition (Drogi do Wolnośći) ★★★ This proves an inspiring, sobering, and thorough history lesson of the anti-Communist struggle in Poland. By the entrance to the underground exhibition, you see an example of a military tank that was a common and menacing sight during the riots on Gdańsk's streets. The mock-up of a typical empty grocery store in the late 1970s, grainy news reels, interactive displays, and documentary films keenly capture the atmosphere of the times. The multilingual exhibition walks you through the riots in 1970 that tore the country apart, to the rise of the Solidarity trade union later that decade, and finally to the historic agreement, the August Accords. The Solidarity movement was the first independent trade union to be recognized in the Eastern Bloc. It eventually paved the way for the first semi-free election in 1989 and finally the toppling of Communist regimes in Poland and throughout Eastern Europe. The exhibition also acquaints you with Lech Wałęsa, the key figure behind Solidarity who went on to be the President of Poland and win the Nobel Peace Prize in 1983.

Wały Piastowskie 24. ✆ **58/308-44-28.** www.fcs.org.pl. 6 zł adults, 4 zł children & seniors; Wed 2 zł adults, children & seniors. Tues–Sun 10am–6pm.

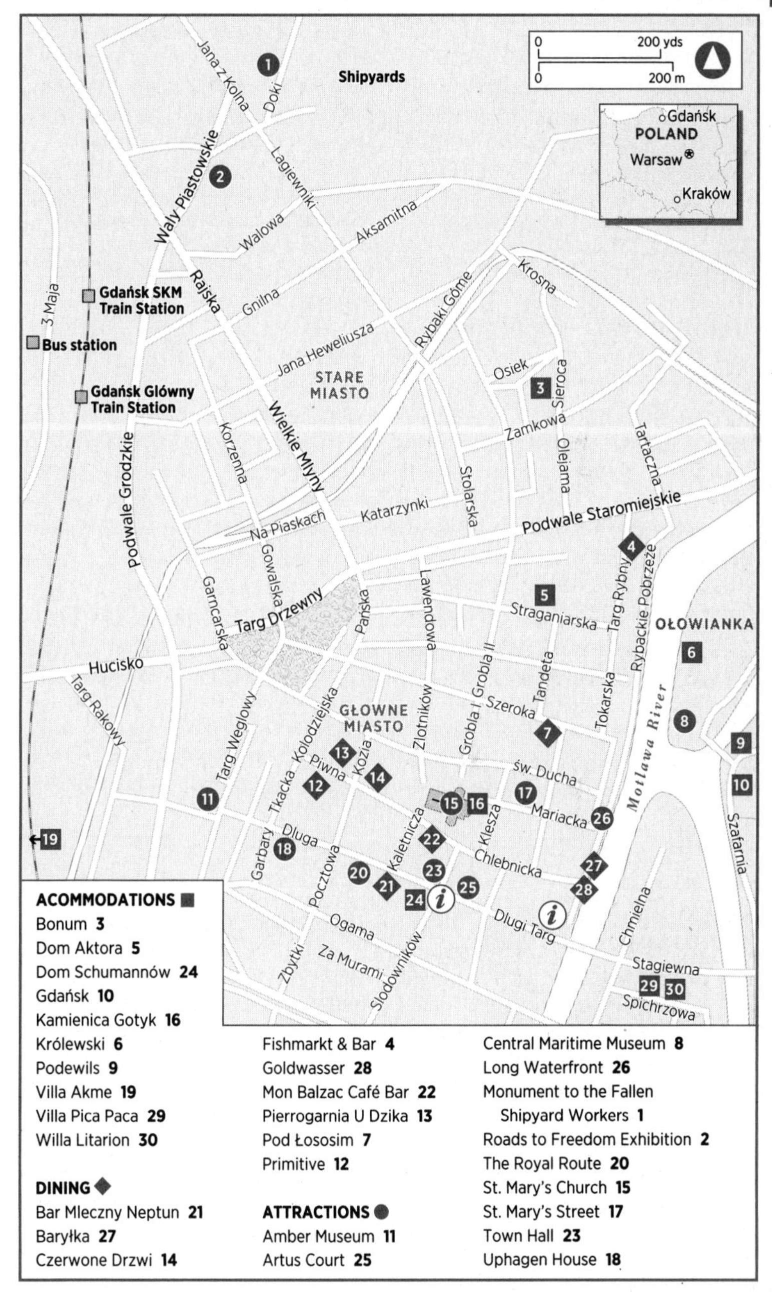
0 200 yds
0 200 m
Gdańsk
POLAND
Warsaw
Kraków
Shipyards
Jana z Kolna
Doki
Łagiewniki
Wały Piastowskie
Walowa
Aksamitna
Rajska
Gnilna
3 Maja
Gdańsk SKM Train Station
Bus station
Gdańsk Glówny Train Station
Jana Heweliusza
STARE MIASTO
Rybaki Górne
Krosna
Osiek
Sieroca
Zamkowa
Olejarna
Tartaczna
Korzenna
Wielkie Młyny
Podwale Grodzkie
Stolarska
Na Piaskach
Katarzynki
Podwale Staromiejskie
Gowalska
Garncarska
Targ Drzewny
Lawendowa
Pańska
Straganiarska
Targ Rybny
Rybackie Pobrzeże
OŁOWIANKA
Hucisko
Targ Rakowy
Targ Weglowy
Kołodziejska
GŁOWNE MIASTO
Złotników
Grobla I
Grobla II
Tandeta
Szeroka
Tokarska
Motława River
Piwna
Kozia
Tkacka
Św. Ducha
Mariacka
Szafarnia
Garbary
Długa
Pocztowa
Kaletnicza
Klesza
Chlebnicka
Ogarna
Zbytki
Za Murami
Słodowników
Długi Targ
Chmielna
Stągiewna
Spichrzowa
ACOMMODATIONS
Bonum 3
Dom Aktora 5
Dom Schumannów 24
Gdańsk 10
Kamienica Gotyk 16
Królewski 6
Podewils 9
Villa Akme 19
Villa Pica Paca 29
Willa Litarion 30
DINING
Bar Mleczny Neptun 21
Baryłka 27
Czerwone Drzwi 14
Fishmarkt & Bar 4
Goldwasser 28
Mon Balzac Café Bar 22
Pierrogarnia U Dzika 13
Pod Łososim 7
Primitive 12
ATTRACTIONS
Amber Museum 11
Artus Court 25
Central Maritime Museum 8
Long Waterfront 26
Monument to the Fallen Shipyard Workers 1
Roads to Freedom Exhibition 2
The Royal Route 20
St. Mary's Church 15
St. Mary's Street 17
Town Hall 23
Uphagen House 18

A Subjective Bus Line ★★★

The former Gdańsk Shipyard, the roots of the Solidarity movement, is open to the public only May to September. You gain passage via the twice-daily (11am and 2pm) "Subjective Bus Line," which is guided by shipyard workers who share their interpretations of historical events (hence the "subjective" nature of the ride). The bus takes off from the shipyard entrance near the Monument to the Fallen Shipyard Workers (see above). It makes several stops in the compound, including Wałesa's workshop, the dockyard, and the Wyspa Art Institute. The narrations are in Polish only, so you'll need to bring a translator. Plans to regenerate the shipyard may kick in anytime, resulting in the discontinuation of the tour. But no one knows when "anytime" is, so call the organizers at Wyspa Art Institute (✆ 58/320-44-46; www.wyspa.art.pl) for updates and ticket prices.

The Royal Route: The Long Street and Long Market (Długa and Długi Targ) ★★ You couldn't ask for a more strikingly beautiful and colorful main street than Długa and Długi Targ, the thoroughfare of the Main Town (Główne Miasto). As you walk its length, from the **Golden Gate** at the western end to the magnificent **Green Gate** at the eastern end, bear in mind that nearly everything you see was rebuilt after World War II. The bas-reliefs and colorful frescos on the burgher houses and gabled town houses will keep your eyes darting about. Musicians and street performers are out in force; no sooner is one violinist out of earshot than another string quartet fills the air with Vivaldi's *Four Seasons*. An iconic landmark is the **Neptune Fountain,** for the god of the sea, which dates from 1549. Legend has it that this was the source of Goldwasser, vodka with gold flakes. Behind the fountain is **Artus Court** (see above), while at the corner is the **Town Hall** (see below). The **Green Gate,** erected in the 1560s, was originally meant to house visiting royalty. Now, it functions as an exhibition space and the office of the former President of Poland and Solidarity leader Lech Wałęsa.

Długa & Długi Targ.

St. Mary's Church (Bazylika Mariacka) ★★ This enormous red-brick church is the largest of its kind in the world. Its nave and 31 chapels can hold more than 20,000 people. The church endeared itself to the people of Gdańsk in the years after the imposition of martial law in 1981, when members of the Solidarity trade union took shelter here. The sheer size of the church is just as impressive from the inside as it is from the outside. During World War II, it was severely damaged. Most of the walls were painted over in white, but some frescoes can be found behind the altar. Note the 500-year-old astronomical clock, dating from 1464, an oddity for a medieval Catholic establishment: It not only tells time, but also gives the phases of moon and shows the position of the sun and the moon in relation to the zodiac signs. There is a theater of figures at the top tier, which rotates at the hour. Also note the series of Ten Commandments paintings: The left side depicts the lives of commandment-abiding believers; the right side depicts the waywards. Climb the 402 steps to the top of the tower for an unparalleled view of Gdańsk.

Podkramarska 5. ✆ **58/301-39-82.** www.bazylikamariacka.pl. 4 zł adults; 2 zł children & seniors. Mon-Sat 9am-5pm; Sun 1-5pm.

St. Mary's Street (ul. Mariacka) ★★★ You can easily while away an afternoon on this cobblestone lane, drifting from one amber jewelry boutique to the next, stopping at arts and crafts stands (see "Shopping," later in this chapter), and in between, resting your feet in any of the enticing cafes while you take in the masonry details of the 17th-century burgher houses. The street was severely damaged in World War II and beautifully reconstructed after the war.

Mariacka.

Town Hall ★★ This is easily one of the country's finest town halls. The original building dates from the 14th century, but it was badly damaged during World War II, and what you see today is a meticulous reconstruction. Check out the Red Room (Sala Czerwona), which lives up to its name with a blushing color scheme and sumptuous furniture, ornate ceilings, and wall paintings. The centerpiece is a painting entitled *The Glorification of the Unity of Gdańsk with Poland*. For a contrasting experience, walk through the historical museum here, noting the black-and-white photographs of Gdańsk in 1945 and its near total destruction in the war.

Długa 46/47. ✆ **58/767-91-00.** 10 zł adults, 5 zł children & seniors; Mid-June to Sept Mon free admission, Oct to mid-June Tues free admission. Mon 11am–3pm; Tues–Sat 10am–6pm; Sun 11am–6pm. Closed Mon Oct to mid-June.

Uphagen House (Dom Uphagena) ★ The three floors of this museum, named after its original owner, give you a picture of how well-to-do merchants in 18th century Gdańsk worked, played, dined, and slept. The property, like much else in the Old City, was destroyed in World War II. Pictures made by German conservators before the war were used in reinstating the rococo details. From the vestibule, a high-ceiling front hall, you walk up to the upper levels to see the function-specific chambers, such as the Chinese-style tearoom, smoking room, and dining room.

Długa 12. ✆ **58/301-23-71.** www.mhmg.pl. 10 zł adults, 5 zł children & seniors; Mon free admission. Mon 11am–3pm; Tues–Sat 10am–6pm; Sun 11am–6pm.

Westerplatte ★★ World War II began here. On September 1, 1939, the German gunboat *Schleswig-Holstein* first fired on a small garrison of about 180 Polish troops on the wind-swept Westerplatte Peninsula. The Poles lead by Major Henryk Sucharski, though severely outnumbered, held out valiantly, repelling 3,000 German soldiers for 7 days. The badly damaged guardhouse and barracks are left pretty much as they were after the battle. The **Guard House No. 1 Museum (Wartownia Nr. 1)** outlines the events of those first few days of the war and includes a model of *Schleswig-Holstein* and photos of the capitulation. In the southwest of the peninsula, the 23m (75-ft.) **Statue to the Defenders of Westerplatte** is the focal point for World War II commemoration ceremonies.

Sucharskiego 1. ✆ **58/343-69-72.** www.mhmg.pl. Museum 3 zł adults. May–Oct Tues–Sun 9am–4pm. Bus: 106 from Podwale Przedmiejskie St. Boats from Motława: See "Getting Around," earlier in this chapter.

OUTSIDE THE GDANSK OLD CITY

Monumental Paintings in Zaspa ★★ This is believed to be the only "gallery" in the world of outdoor murals painted on the walls of a residential estate. Zaspa is a sprawling 1970s housing project constructed on a disused airfield, and it was the former home of Lech Wałesa. The grey, Communist-era tower blocks got a splash of colors in 1997 when the first mural was commissioned for Gdańsk's millennium celebration. Zaspa now has more than 40 works, each measuring 15 or 30m (49 or 98 ft.) in height, scattered all over the estate. Painted by local and foreign artists, all the murals have historically relevant themes, such a pixel portrait of Lech Wałesa and a Bollywood-like movie poster of Pope John Paul II and Wałesa. At present, there are no maps marking the sites of the murals. Most of them are along Pilotów and Dywizjonu 303 streets. Szymon Wróblewski, the Polish-speaking curator, has an office in Plama, an artists' workshop in Zaspa. He'll show you around if he has time.

Pilotów 11. © **58/557-42-47.** www.miejskieznakikultury.pl. Free admission. SKM: Gdańsk-Zaspa.

Oliwa Cathedral (Katedra Oliwska) ★ The cathedral's centerpiece is its organ, which has an impressive 7,896 pipes and 110 registers, allowing it the dynamic range to produce rousing renditions of Beethoven's masterpieces, the chirping of birds, the humming of human voices, or the rippling of water. Johann Wuff constructed the organ, which has an oval stained glass in the middle and is flanked by cherubs and trumpet-wielding angels, from 1755 to 1780. At the time, it was the largest instrument of its kind in Europe. The imposing three-nave vaulted basilica started life as a wooden structure in the 12th century. Since its expansion in 1224, it has had its share of fires and plunders through the ages by Prussians, Teutonic Knights, the Swedish invasion, and World War II. Time your visit with the free organ concerts. During the 20-minute concerts, the main entrance is closed, but you can gain access via the side entrance.

Biskupa Edmunda Nowickiego 5. © **58/552-47-65.** Free admission (donations welcomed); concerts 4.50 zł adults. Mon–Fri 9am–5pm, Sat 9am–3pm, Sun 2–5pm; concerts summer begin every hour Mon–Sat noon, Sun 3pm. SKM: Gdańsk-Oliwa. Tram: 6, 8 & 12.

OUTSIDE THE TRI-CITY

Stutthof (Sztutowo) Death Camp ★ Often labeled as the "forgotten camp," Stutthof was the first concentration camp built outside of Germany by the Nazis. Constructed in September 1939, it was also the last camp to be liberated by the Allies in May 1945. Out of the 110,000 Jews and others held here, an estimated 70% were killed by lethal injections, firing squads, hanging, or gas chamber. The barracks and crematoria, the "hospital," the "holocaust stake" (a memorial on the site of an excavated mass grave), and the exhibits in the museum give you an unnervingly vivid and harrowing picture of the atrocious and inhumane conditions the inmates here endured. ***Note:*** Children 13 and under are not admitted. On-site, there is a shortage of English information. The guided tours in English cost 140 zł per group (up to 40 people) and must be confirmed in advance via e-mail (stutthof@stutthof.pl). The tour takes 1½ to 2 hours.

Muzealna 6, Sztutowo. © **55/247-83-53.** www.stutthof.pl. Free admission (donations welcomed). May–Sept daily 8am–6pm; Oct–Apr daily 8am–3pm. Stutthof lies 55km (34 miles) to the east of Gdańsk. From the main bus station, buses to Sztutowo (in the direction of Krynica Morska) take 1½ hr. By car, journey time is 1 hr.

CUSTOMIZED TOURS

Joytrip.pl ★★ (Fieldorfa 11/3; © **58/320-61-69;** www.joytrip.pl) has energetic guides who will take you around the Tri-City on foot, bike, kayak, motorboat, or any other means of transportation of your choice. While you bounce on bikes along the cobblestone lanes of the Old City (or off the beaten tracks), the guides pump you full of facts on history, art, and culture. After a short break, they are ready to party with you in bars and clubs. They'll tailor the ride to your fancies, going to Malbork if that's what you have in mind. The cost, naturally, depends on the package. It's roughly 450 zł for 4 hours and 650 zł for 8 hours.

Where to Stay

VERY EXPENSIVE

Hotel Gdańsk ★ This property is considered the lucky one, having survived the war while the surrounding buildings didn't make it. Now, this canal-side 18th century granary is one of the newest luxury hotels in the Old City. The restoration work retains the exposed wood beams and the characteristic granary windows. Though the mood leans on the side of conservative elegance, some rooms have worked in the sexy concept of sliding windows between the bathroom and the bed. You'll want a room that looks out to the Motława Canal, and not the modern office development at the back. The hotel's microbrewery (see "After Dark," later in this chapter) has made its restaurant one of the liveliest after-work watering holes in town.

Szafarnia 9. ✆ **58/300-17-17.** Fax 58/300-17-18. www.hotelgdansk.com.pl. 48 units. 590 zł double. AE, MC, V. Parking 30 zł. **Amenities:** Restaurant; bar; room service. *In room:* A/C, TV, hair dryer, minibar, Wi-Fi (free).

Podewils ★★★ This relatively small, old-fashioned villa across the river from the town center is widely billed as the city's finest boutique hotel. Be sure to ask for a city view, not one that looks out onto the side road. Each room is meticulously decorated with fine antiques but still retains a cozy, personal touch. The old-school (in the positive sense) staff will see to your every whim. Don't pass up the chance to have a meal or a glass of wine on the terrace overlooking the canal and the Old Town.

Szafarnia 2. ✆ **58/300-95-60.** Fax 58/300-95-70. www.podewils.pl. 10 units. Apr–Oct 160€ double. Nov–Mar 86€–130€ double. AE, DC, MC, V. Free parking. **Amenities:** Restaurant; room service; Turkish & Finnish saunas. *In room:* A/C, TV, hair dryer, minibar, Wi-Fi (free).

EXPENSIVE

Bonum Hotel ★ It's located in a part of town that looks a bit beat up, but you're a stone's throw from the attractions. This five-story hotel is made up of two adjoining structures: an 18th-century town house and a newer neighbor. The exposed brick walls show off the building's origins. The plush rooms are modern yet homey, employing a combination of light blonde and dark woods. You can hear St. Bridget's church bells tolling. That, plus its proximity to the old Gdańsk post office, adds to your sense of being right in the heart of history. What's more, the service and its restaurant have improved under a new management.

Sieroca 3. ✆ **58/304-78-10.** Fax 58/304-78-11. www.hotelbonum.pl. 32 units. 374 zł double. AE, DC, MC, V. Free parking. **Amenities:** Restaurant; babysitting; room service. *In room:* TV, hair dryer, Wi-Fi (free).

Królewski ★★ This sleek, modern hotel is in a tastefully remodeled former granary just across the canal from Gdańsk's town center. If you can get it, ask for room no. 310, a corner double with drop-dead stunning views of the riverside and all of Gdańsk's spires and gables. All the rooms are tastefully modern, some with hardwood floors and bathtubs. The restaurant and breakfast room look out over the river through a round little window like you're on a cruise.

Ołowianka 1. ✆ **58/326-11-11.** Fax 58/326-11-10. www.hotelkrolewski.pl. 30 units. May to mid-Oct 470 zł double; Mid-Oct to Feb 370 zł double; Mar & Apr 380 zł double. AE, DC, MC, V. **Amenities:** Restaurant; bar; room service. *In room:* TV, hair dryer, minibar, Wi-Fi (free).

Villan Pica Paca ★ While the rooms here are named after a variety of classy and brainy folks, like Grace Kelly and Albert Einstein, the style in each room isn't wildly different. All rooms are minimalistic and accented with selected designer pieces; some bathrooms have lime-green rubber showerheads. On the second floor, there is a pretty, secluded garden in the back. The less-than-attractive front street doesn't stop the beautiful people from checking into this boutique hotel.

Spichrzowa 20. ✆ **58/320-20-70.** Fax 58/320-88-50. www.picapaca.com. 15 units. May–Sept 110€ double; Oct–Apr 90€ double. AE, MC, V. Parking 8€. **Amenities**: Bar. *In room*: TV, Internet, minibar.

MODERATE

Dom Aktora ★ Located in the Old Town and a short walk to the Motława Canal, this warm and homey setup has basic but clean rooms and apartments in a variety of shapes and sizes. In a charming way, the property is reminiscent of humble abodes during the Communist period. The apartments, which can hold two to four occupants, come with fully equipped kitchens. Proximity to a nearby farmers' market makes Dom Aktora a good self-catering option. Breakfast is a generous spread of homemade pâté, pierogi, and cakes. A helpful English-speaking manager mans the front desk.

Straganiarska 55/56. ✆ **58/301-59-01**. www.domaktora.pl. 12 units. June–Sept 360 zł double, 410 zł–590 zł apt; Apr, May, Oct & Nov 280 zł double, 480 zł apt; Dec–Mar 240 zł double, 450 zł apt. AE, MC, V. Free parking. **Amenities:** Lounge. *In room:* TV, fan, fridge, kitchen (in apt), Wi-Fi (free).

Kamienica Gotyk ★★★ Ordinarily, you'd part with a fortune for the location in Gdańsk's oldest house (1541) on its loveliest street, so get organized and book early to take advantage of the great rates and setting of this petite B&B. The stone stairs are flanked by original Gothic portals, and the Gothic details continue indoors, where arched doorframes usher you into the small but brightly furnished rooms. The windows are thoughtfully equipped with blackout blinds. Breakfast on the petite patio in the shadows of St. Mary's church adds to the sense of history.

Mariacka 1. ✆ **58/301-85-67.** www.gotykhouse.eu. 7 units. May–Sept 310 zł double; Oct–Dec 250 zł double; Jan–Apr 220 zł double. MC, V. **Amenities:** Breakfast room. *In room:* TV, Wi-Fi (free).

Willa Litarion A newcomer on a street that is fast becoming the accommodation mile, the hotel exterior looks deceptively like it can't be bothered. But you'll be surprised by the high standards within, where each room and bathroom is unique. And the helpful front desk is anything but indifferent. Although the hotel is opposite an empty lot, it has an in-town location, just across the bridge from the Green Gate and the delights of Długa Street.

Spichrzowa 18. ✆ **58/320-25-53.** Fax 58/320-25-63. www.litarion.pl. 13 units. Apr–Sept 330 zł double; Oct–Mar 290 zł double. AE, DC, MC, V. Underground parking 20 zł. **Amenities:** Breakfast room. *In room:* TV, minibar, Wi-fi (free).

INEXPENSIVE

Dom Schumannów ★ Perched above the main tourist information office, the rooms here are right in the heart of the Royal Route. For a view of the thoroughfare, however, you've got to put up with the high decibels. The quarters facing the courtyard in the back are quiet and cozy. The small rooms provide just enough space to stretch but are definitely atmospheric with period furniture, velvet cushions, and bright, puffy bed covers. ***Note:*** There are no elevators, and some rooms are without curtains. Breakfast is in a cafe a few doors away.

Długa 45. ✆ **58/301-52-72.** Fax 58/301-91-51. www.domschumannow.pl. Apr–Sept 285 zł double; Oct–Mar 230 zł double. AE, DC, MC, V. *In room:* TV, Wi-fi (free).

Villa Akme ★ This three-story pension is very clean and well-run; the rooms are basic but a good value in Gdańsk's overpriced hotel market. It's outside the city center, but the English-speaking staff will direct you to a nearby tramline that will whisk you to the attractions within 10 minutes.

Drwęcka 1. ✆ **58/302-40-21.** Fax 58/300-09-24. www.akme.gda.pl. 19 units. July & Aug 260 zł double; Sept–June 240 zł double. AE, MC, V. Free parking. *In room*: TV, Wi-Fi (free).

Where to Dine

Most of the places in the Główne Miasto, though in a tourist zone, offer good value and quality food. If you want a change of scene, look into the laid-back options in Sopot, which cater to the residents and beachcombers.

VERY EXPENSIVE

Pod Łososiem EUROPEAN Every city in Poland has an establishment with a track record of feeding visiting royalty and dignitaries, and Pod Łososiem is Gdańsk's. Expect renditions of high-end European fare served in a grandiose baroque-style dining room. The menu has an emphasis on seafood, but the roast duck is also quite good. It's reportedly the original source of Goldwasser vodka, so round out your meal with a shot of the gold flakes–imbued liquor.

Szeroka 52/54. ✆ **58/301-76-52.** www.podlososiem.com.pl. Reservations required. Main courses 40 zł–70 zł. AE, DC, MC, V. Daily noon–11pm.

Restauracja Villa Uphagena ★ POLISH Located in the suburbs of Wrzeszcz, this grand manor house is for special occasions. The high-ceilinged, opulent rooms drip with chandeliers and are lavished with period furniture and tables decked out with whiter-than-white linen. There are five dining rooms; for a party of two, the Crystal Room and the Orangery are the coziest. Start off with steak *tartare*—or, if you've had *barszcz* (beet soup) elsewhere and wondered what the fuss is about, try it here. The wild boar roulade is tender and flavorful. Top it off with the traditional apple pie.

Jana Uphagena 23, Gdańsk Wrzeszcz. ✆ **58/345-83-72.** www.villauphagena.pl. Main courses 32 zł–69 zł. AE, DC, MC, V. Daily noon–10pm.

EXPENSIVE & MODERATE

Baryłka ★★ POLISH You can break bread here without the pomp and circumstance that ooze out from many of the restaurants in this neighborhood. The duck is roasted and given a regional slant with a mead sauce. Another highlight is the fried eel with chanterelle sauce. If neither appeals, the sheer enthusiasm of the waiter will convince you to try one of his favorites.

Długie Pobrzeże 24. ✆ **58/301-49-38.** www.barylka.pl. Main courses 17 zł–49 zł. AE, MC, V. Daily 10am–midnight.

Czerwone Drzwi ★★ INTERNATIONAL This restaurant's concise menu consistently wins praise from the locals. Behind the "red door" (as the name translates), you'll find an inviting compact, chimney-like space filled with eclectic antiques and an equally mishmash selection of paintings. There's the traditional pasta and pierogi, but the excellent veal with Gorgonzola sauce and house-made minidumplings best represent the strong suits of the house. End your meal with *pascha,* a supremely sweet dessert made from farmer's cheese and lots of raisins.

Piwna 52/53. ✆ **58/301-57-64.** www.reddoor.gd.pl. Main courses 18 zł–65 zł. AE, MC, V. Daily noon–10pm.

Fishmarkt Restaurant & Bar SEAFOOD The name means fish market, and it's one of the best places for fish in town, both grilled and fried. It's located in the northern end of Motława Canal walkway, so its terrace has a good view of the Baltic

Philharmonic. Inside, it's homey lightwood furniture and tables covered with blue-checkered cloths. The menu is regularly updated; recommended dishes include the grilled salmon and the whitefish pierogi.

Targ Rybny 6C. ✆ **59/320-90-11.** www.targrybny.pl. Main courses 20 zł–125 zł. MC, V. Daily 11am–midnight.

Goldwasser ★ INTERNATIONAL This local institution is well worth a splurge, both for the food and the unbeatable riverside location. Slip into one of the dining booths in this brazenly embellished scarlet space. The fresh fish dishes come highly recommended, as do the house-made pierogi. The excellent service leaves guests in high spirits. In summer, sit out on the terrace. In winter, warm yourself up in the cozy tavern-like surroundings.

Długie Pobrzeże 22. ✆ **58/301-88-78.** www.goldwasser.pl. Main courses 26 zł–78 zł. MC, V. Daily 10am–11pm.

Mon Balzac Café Bar ★ EUROPEAN Despite the cafe-bar tag, Mon Balzac dishes out proper meals like chicken with spinach and mozzarella, and cheese fondue. The interior has a sophisticated look that combines exposed brick walls with leather bench seats. On weekends, drop by for the live music.

Piwna 36/39. ✆ **58/682-25-25.** www.monbalzac.pl. Main courses 15 zł–39 zł. MC, V. Daily 10am–1am.

Pierogarnia U Dzika ★★ POLISH *Pierogarnia* are restaurants specializing in pierogi. Once dismissed as dowdy, they're now all the rage, as you no doubt have noticed. This one, centrally located, is better than most and a good place to sample the ubiquitous doughy dumplings and, naturally, a glass of beer to wash them down. The interior is 1980s–'90s Polish chic, with taxidermy to justify the "*dzik*" (wild boar) in the name. The menu includes both the usual fillings, like ground beef and cabbage, plus a few inventive variations including pierogi "Wileński"—a rarity these days—stuffed with buckwheat and bacon. Servings are 10 pieces per plate, enough for a full meal and then some.

Piwna 59/60. ✆ **58/305-26-76.** www.pierogarniaudzika.com. Main courses 15 zł–31 zł. AE, DC, MC, V. Daily 11am–10pm.

Primitive ☺ INTERNATIONAL You'll either be tickled or put off by the play-on-names on the menu here, such as Neandertalian Potato and Brontosaurus Steak. Look past the cheesy caveman theme, and you'll find well-executed meat dishes, mostly grilled, but some pan-fried or stewed. The portions assume the modern man has the same carnivorous consumption capacity as a Stone Age man.

Piwna 3/4. ✆ **58/305-41-20.** www.primitive.pl. Main courses 19 zł–50 zł. AE, MC, V. Daily noon–midnight.

INEXPENSIVE

Bar Mleczny Neptun POLISH If you haven't checked off the "milk bar" experience yet, here's a decent one to try out. There are few budget eateries that are as brightly lit by natural light as this one or located at as prestigious an address. The queue moves faster than you'd think. When it's your turn, choose your main course, sides, and sauces, collect the food, and then pay. When in doubt, go for *kotlet schabowy* (meat cutlet; but take care, some are embedded with splinters of bone), pierogi, or *bigos* (hunter's stew). Food is sold out pretty quickly to students and retirees, so get there around noon to have the best selection. In moving with the times, the eatery now has free Wi-Fi, but it's still operating in Polish only.

Długa 33/34. ✆ **58/301-49-88.** www.barneptun.pl. Main courses 3.50 zł–13 zł. No credit cards. Mon–Fri 7:30am–6pm; Sat & Sun 10am–5pm.

Get "Stoned"

After a tour of the Amber Museum, you'll know amber is not just for dressing up, but did you know that you could drink it, too? Steeping fruits, nuts, and spices in vodka to make *nalewka* is a very homey Polish pastime. But even for *nalewka*-savvy Poles, immersing amber granules in vodka comes as a novelty. Don't go dunking your funky pendants into alcohol; you need the unpolished pebbles, which you can find in stalls along the Motława Canal or Mariacka Street. Brama Mariacka (Mariacka 25/26; ✆ 668/163-303) sells them in packets or bottles at 7 zł. Add 50g (1¾ oz.) of amber into 0.5L (17 oz.) of pure vodka and leave in a dark place for 10 days for the resin to dissolve. It's reportedly good as a rub on temples to alleviate headaches. Or add to tea as a warmer on chilly days.

Shopping

For centuries, the center of the Baltic amber trade was Gdańsk, and it's still *the* place to get amber accessories and other amber crafts. You'll find no shortage of amber dealers in town. The biggest concentration is on the main street of **Długa** and along the prettier but just as crowded **Mariacka.** While the majority of the dealers are reputable, amber fakes abound, so it's caveat emptor. The Amber Museum is a good place to learn how to detect the real McCoy. If you haven't time for the museum, **Bernstein ★** (Długi Targ 22/23; ✆ **58/305-15-97;** www.bernstein-ninard.com), a third-generation jeweler, can give you a quick demo on recognizing the genuine article. (***Note:*** Real amber floats in salt water, while the fakes simply sink.) **Galeria S&A ★** (Mariacka 36; ✆ **58/305-22-80;** www.s-a.pl) is one of three shops on Mariacka Street with a certification from *Societas Svccinorvm in Polonia* (the International Amber Association). It also has an outlet on the ground floor of the Amber Museum.

Another 100% Gdańsk take-away is **Goldwasser vodka.** While the sweetish taste is not everyone's glass of tipple, who could pass up flakes of gold in their cocktail? You can buy a gift box at the Goldwasser restaurant (see "Where to Dine," above). **Kashubian folk art** (Kashubian is an ethnic minority group) in the form of embroidered linen is also a unique regional gift. You'll find them on Mariacka Street or at **Galeria Sztuki Kaszubskiej** (Św. Ducha 48; ✆ **503/005-978;** www.gskart.pl). **Benedicte** (Garbary 5; ✆ **58/305-69-03;** www.benedicite.pl) is good for tea, honey, and fruit preserves made by Benedictine monks in Poland and other Central European countries. **Hala Targowa ★★** (Plac Dominkański 1; ✆ **58/346-31-33;** www.halatargowa.pl) is a traditional fresh produce and household goods market frequented by locals. From Monday to Saturday starting at 9am, you can pick up seasonal fruits, cheese, sausages, and pierogi for picnics.

After Dark

THE PERFORMING ARTS

Most of the serious culture here revolves around two venues: the **Fryderyk Chopin Baltic Philharmonic** (Ołowianka 1; ✆ **58/320-62-62;** www.filharmonia.gda.pl) and the **State Baltic Opera** (al. Zwycięstwa 15; ✆ **58/763-49-12;** www.operabaltycka.pl). The Philharmonic's main home base is the stunningly restored site right across the Motława canal in the center of the Old City. You can buy tickets at the Motława box office (✆ **58/763-49-06**) or at the performance venue up to 4 hours before the show. The Opera maintains a lively program in season, with visiting and local companies. You can buy tickets online or at the box office during office hours, Tuesday to Friday from noon to 7pm and Saturday from 2 to 7pm.

From May to October, there's a constant stream of music and performing arts festivals in the Tri-City. Get the current schedule from http://rozrywka.trojmiasto.pl or www.gdansk4u.pl.

CAFES, PUBS & CLUBS

Most night owls make a beeline for Sopot after sunset, but the nightlife in Gdańsk isn't lackluster, especially in the recent years. It's worked (and partied) hard in shedding its image as a venue suitable only for teens and students.

Brovarnia ★★ The microbrewery of Hotel Gdańsk has shifted the nighttime life force to this previously quiet part of town. Lager, dark, and wheat beer flow from the taps. The indoor has a no-smoking policy that does not extend to the patio with a quayside view. Szafarnia 9. ✆ **58/320-19-70.** www.brovarnia.pl.

Café Absinthe At this fun and highly recommended bar, the emphasis is definitely on drinking, though not necessarily absinthe. It's all DJs and dancing-on-tables from Thursday to Saturday. Św Ducha 2. ✆ **58/320-37-84.** www.cafeabsinthe.pl.

Cico "Come in and Chill Out" is what the moniker stands for. And folks of all ages seem to do just that, livening up the modern chill-out space until late, especially on weekends when live music gets underway. Piwna 28/30. ✆ **58/305-04-55.**

La Dolce Vita ★★ Café Absinthe's crowds often migrate to its sibling, a club cum lounge bar, where live concerts and dancing can be found. Chlebnicka 2. ✆ **058/304-78-87.**

Tekstylia ★ This new cafe-bistro is thriving on a local clientele that favors contemporary settings to the yester-century milieu of the Royal Route. Szeroka 121/122. ✆ **58/304-77-63.**

SOPOT & GDYNIA

Sopot and Gdynia are the duo that makes up the other two cities of the Tri-City area. Neither can outmatch Gdańsk's historical sites, but each has its own distinct appeal.

Sopot's blend of small-town charm and cosmopolitan chic give it a special spot in the hearts of Poles. The century-old villas, embellished with turrets and crowned with cupolas, contribute to a beguiling, fairytale-like atmosphere. In 1823, Jean Georges Haffner, a doctor in Napoleon's army, introduced the idea of reaping the health benefits of sea-bathing in the waters of Sopot, and subsequently elevated the town into a fashionable seaside resort of the moneyed classes. This was the kind of place where, in order to properly summer, you had to be somebody. During the Communist period, the resort lost some of its sheen; the idea of decadent seaside frolicking didn't chime with the reigning ideological aesthetic. Since 1989, however, Sopot has mounted a comeback, cashing in on its former glamour while affirming its identity as Poland's top summer party town. During the day, its waterfront attracts sun, sea, and sand lovers. After dark, party animals flock to the most happening clubs in the Tri-City. In July and August, the visitor density surges up; late spring and early autumn are the best time to enjoy Sopot without jostling for hotel rooms or beach space.

While Sopot has obvious appeal, Gdynia, the most northerly of the Tri-City set, is an acquired taste and often skipped by tourists. You, too, could do the same unless you have time to spare. It is a concrete mass that started life as a quiet fishing village. In the early 20th century, the Treaty of Versailles created the Free City of Gdańsk and thrust Gdynia into the newly reformed Polish State. It became Poland's access point to the sea and, in May 1921, the development started to convert it into a modern port. Today, it is a port city with all the trappings of a seaside town.

Essentials

GETTING THERE

Sopot and Gdynia share the same transport network as Gdańsk. See Gdańsk's "Getting There" and "Getting Around," earlier in this chapter.

VISITOR INFORMATION

The **Sopot Tourist Office** (Dworcowa 4; ✆ **58/550-37-83;** www.sopot.pl) is opposite the train station. From June to mid-September, it's open weekdays from 9am to 7pm, and weekends from 10am to 6pm. The rest of the year, it's open Monday through Saturday from 10am to 6pm. The attentive staff can help you with booking rooms and hand out complimentary maps. As for Gdynia, from May to September, the handiest place to go is the **Baltic Point of Tourist Information** (Molo Południowe; ✆ **58/620-77-11;** www.gdynia.pl), located at the eastern tip of Skwer Kościuszki. It's open weekdays from 9am to 6pm, on Saturdays from 10am to 5pm, and on Sundays from 10am to 4pm. If you're arriving by SKM, pop by the tourist information booth at the railway station for a map.

Top Attractions

SOPOT

Life centers on the pedestrian **Bohaterów Monte Cassino Street** (nicknamed "Monciak"), the main axis of trendy cafes, clubs, and restaurants. You'll see the much-photographed **Crooked House** (Bohaterów Monte Cassino 53; ✆ **58/555-51-23**), though it's not much to write home about. At the end of Monciak, you'll come to a 5km (3-mile) stretch of sandy beach and the **Pier (Molo) ★★**. Built in 1928, and stretching 515m (1,690 ft.) into the Gulf of Gdańsk, it is the longest wooden pier along the Baltic coast. Strolling on the pier is a Sopot de rigueur and a certifiable must-do for the romantically inclined. In summer, you'll find opera singers crooning tunes from Sopot's heyday in the 1930s and old-timer sailors selling tickets for peeping into binoculars. To the north of the beach is another stunning landmark of Sopot: the **Grand Hotel** (see "Where to Stay," below). Once you have had enough of the

Catch of the Day

Fish lovers, make your way to **Przystań Rybacka w Sopocie** (Wojska Polskiego 7, Sopot), next to Bar Przystań, on the beach. At about 7:30am, from Monday to Saturday, fishermen return from the sea with freshly caught, still-flipping flounder, cod, salmon, and turbot. Join the early birds to buy the best of the Baltic Sea, and then cajole your hotel kitchen into cooking it up for your lunch. In the same building, from 8am to 6pm, there's flavor-packed smoked fish from Hel Peninsula for sale.

sun and sand, you can escape to the greens and shades of the hilly **Opera Park** (**Opera Leśna;** Moniuszki 12). The annual **International Sopot Festival** (www.sopotfestival.onet.pl) is held every August.

GDYNIA

Most of the tourist attractions are by the **Southern Pier (Molo Południowe)** waterfront. The destroyer ***Błyskawica*** ★ (✆ **58/626-36-58;** www.navy.mw.mil.pl) is moored here and a must-see for fans of maritime history. Upon news of imminent invasion by the Germans in 1939, the vessel was dispatched to join the Allied naval forces. Retired from active service, it became the only Polish ship to receive the Golden Cross of Military Virtue in 1987. Chirpy, uniformed mariners conduct you through the engine rooms and the on-board museum. The tour is in Polish, but English information booklets are available for sale at the ticket booth. A quick tour of the ship will take about 30 minutes, but you might spend more time queuing, as this is a popular attraction. On the opposite side of the Southern Pier is the **Oceanographic Museum & Aquarium (Muzeum Oceanograficzne i Akwarium)** ☺ (Al. Jana Pawła II 1; ✆ **58/732-66-01;** www.akwarium.gdynia.pl). A state-of-the-art facility it's not, but it has some rare specimens such as Chinese water dragons and snapping turtles to make a less-than-an-hour visit enjoyable.

Outdoor Activities

IN & AROUND THE TRI-CITY

BEACHES Come fair weather, the beaches and waters of Sopot and Gdynia are inundated by throngs of sun worshippers. Both locations have changing rooms and shower facilities. **Gdańsk-Orłowo** has a beach and a pier that's smaller than Sopot's but still quite charming. But if you've got a day to spare and the sun is shining, why not go for something a little more remote? The sandy stretches of the **Hel Peninsula** (see p. 256) make a fun and relaxing change of pace.

BANANA BOATS On the pier in Sopot, youth sporting the vests of the **Water Taxi Company** (✆ **502/334-534**) will entice you to strap on a lifejacket and get bounced about in a motor boat on the Gulf of Gdańsk. It's 20 zł for 15 minutes of adrenalin rush.

CATAMARAN & WINDSURFING The **Sopot Sailing Club** (Hestii 3; ✆ **58/555-72-00;** www.skz.sopot.pl) is about a 20-minute walk from the pier. The club houses a few facilities. For windsurfing equipment rentals, the **Sopot Surf Centrum** (✆ **55/555-72-22;** ssc122@wp.pl) hires out the complete set of equipment for 30 zł per hour. They also offer individual and group lessons. **Navigo** (✆ **503/114-384;** www.katamaran.sopot.pl), located in the third hangar on the left side of the entrance, is where the catamaran people are. Call ahead; the site can be deserted when the crew is out on the waters conducting the courses. If you're here for the watersports, the **guest rooms at the Sopot Sailing Club (Hotel-Pokoje Gościnne Sopocki Klub Żeglarski)** ★ (Hestii 3; ✆ **58/555-72-03;** www.skz.sopot.pl) are clean and spacious, and equipped with basic kitchenettes. Some rooms can take up to eight people. Prices are 180 zł to 230 zł for double rooms.

CYCLING An easy and tranquil 10km (6¼-mile) bike lane skirts the beaches from Sopot to the northern Gdańsk suburbs. **Rowerownia** (Fieldorfa 11/3, Gdańsk; ✆ **58/320-61-69;** www.rowerownia.gda.pl) has a fleet of comfy bikes for 40 zł per day. They deliver and pick up the bikes at an addition charge of 60 zł or more, depending on the location.

DEEP-SEA FISHING At the price of 400 zł per hour, the **Water Taxi Company**—the same folks doing the banana boat tumbles—can take up to six people angling in the Gdańsk Bay. Call 2 days in advance to book.

DIVING **Ticada Centrum Nurkowania** (Wiśniewskiego 26, Gdynia; ✆ **58/629-48-46;** www.ticada.pl) offers diving excursions to more than 10 shipwrecks in the Bay of Gdańsk. Excursions are from 50 zł. You can also consider the options in Hel Peninsula (see below).

GOLF There are several golfing facilities in and around the Tri-City. The handiest is **Golf Park Gdynia** (Spółdzielcza 1, Gdynia; ✆ **58/721-24-24;** www.golfpark gdynia.pl), an outdoor driving range that also has an indoor simulator. Farther afield, as you head north of the Tri-City and then turn west at Reda, you'll come to the **Sierra Golf Club** (Pętkowice, Wejherowo; ✆ **58/778-49-00;** www.sierragolf.pl). The greens fee for the 18-hole course is 190 zł on weekdays, 250 zł on weekends and holidays. The club is 52km (32 miles) from Gdańsk. The **Postołowo Golf Club** (Postołowo, Ełganowo; ✆ **58/683-71-00;** www.golf.com.pl), 26km (16 miles) south of Gdańsk, is a spectacular 18-hole golf course. Expect to negotiate waters along the challenging courses, nestled in the midst of the greenery of the Kashubian Lakeland. The club is open year-round daily from 8am to sunset.

SPECTATOR SPORTS Gdańsk's brand new **PGE Arena** stadium (Długi Targ 39/40; ✆ **58/526-81-09;** www.euro.gdansk.pl), built for the Euro Cup 2012 football championship, is scheduled to be up and running in 2011. The venue will be also be used for concerts and cultural events.

Where to Stay

Sopot has a range of choice accommodation. Even if you're spending most of the day in Gdańsk, stay here if you want to be close to the beach and clubs. Gdynia, on the other hand, is short on well-located good lodgings. Some hotels ratchet up their prices during the August Sopot Festival. One global chain here is the **Sheraton Hotel** (Powstańców Warszawy 10; ✆ **58/767-10-00;** www.sheraton.pl/sopot). It's a neighbor of the Grand Hotel; over the last 2 years, the expansion of its spa and restaurant wings have invaded much of the real estate by the Molo pier.

WHERE TO STAY IN SOPOT

Very Expensive

Grand Hotel Sopot by Sofitel ★★ Built in 1927, this stunning seafront hotel with a neo-baroque facade is one of the most instantly recognizable landmarks in the country. Check into a sea-facing room for a taste of where the Polish rich and famous play. It's also the hotel of choice for visiting heads of states when the government wants to show off the "Best of Poland." The building was spruced up in 2006 but retained many of its original fixtures. Orchids adorn the sleek, modern rooms with fish-bone parquet floors; suites are furnished with period pieces. In the French garden, the sea breeze caresses you while the vested staff is at your beck and call, ferrying you nibbles and cocktails.

Powstańców Warszawy 12/14. ✆ **58/520-60-00.** Fax 58/520-60-99. www.sofitel.com. 127 units. 1,000 zł-1,300 zł double. AE, DC, MC, V. Parking 60 zł. **Amenities:** Restaurant; concierge; gym; Jacuzzi; indoor pool w/water massage; room service; sauna; Wi-Fi. *In room:* A/C, TV, hair dryer, Internet, minibar.

Moderate & Inexpensive

Lalala Arthotel ★★ You wouldn't expect a street lined with warehouses and car workshops to yield such a fantastically creative boutique hotel. Photographers and artists applied their skills at interior decorating, resulting in rooms for various moods, such as the dreamy white (no. 7) and the chirpy orange sakura (no. 1600). If you're not wild about ravens and bats, then avoid dramatic no. 44, created by a comic artist. The service level has not been spoiled by press attention from design and food magazines. Its restaurant is also gaining recognition. It's one stop by SKM to Sopot's center or a brisk 15-minute walk.

Rzemiślnicza 42. ✆ **792/840-293. www.lalala.lu/** 7 units. May–Sept 260 zł–290 zł double; Oct–Apr 220 zł–260 zł double. DC, MC, V. Street parking (free). SKM: Sopot Wyścigi. **Amenities:** Restaurant; wine bar. *In room:* Hair dryer, Wi-Fi (free).

Plac Rybaków Inn Despite its proximity to the beach, this new family-run guesthouse doesn't charge an arm and a leg. It's near the famous Bar Przystań (see "Where to Dine in Sopot," below) but out-of-the-way enough to be quiet. The brick-exterior is attractive, and the rooms, though clean, are plain. A simple breakfast is included. A downside is hunting for a spot to park along the narrow lanes.

Plac Ryabków 11. ✆ **58/551-65-78.** www.placrybakowinn.pl. 6 units. 200 zł double. Rates include breakfast. AE, MC, V. Street parking (free). **Amenities:** Wi-Fi (free). *In room:* TV, Internet (free).

Willa Zacisze This excellent self-catering option is in a restored town house located within a quick dash to the beach. You sleep on modern roll-out sofa beds. The cleanliness and staff friendliness are outstanding for accommodations in this price bracket. So, not surprisingly, rooms are booked out months ahead.

Grunwaldzka 22A. ✆ **58/551-78-68.** Fax 58/551-78-68. zacisze.sopot@wp.pl. 11 units. 260 zł double. MC, V. Free parking. *In room:* TV, fully-equipped kitchenette, Wi-Fi (free).

Where to Dine in Sopot

EXPENSIVE & MODERATE

Bar Przystań ★★ FISH A veteran on the beachfront, this fish-fry is neither posh nor ramshackle. Join the queue at "Receiving Order" to place your order from an array of freshly caught items, ranging from eel to shark to tuna; there's also pickled and marinated herring galore. You'll be issued a number—when your turn is up, pay and collect some plastic utensils, along with your catch served up on a cardboard plate. The wait can be agonizingly long on busy days.

Wojska Polskiego 11. ✆ **58/555-06-61.** www.barprzystan.pl. Fish 4 zł–9 zł per 100g. AE, DC, MC, V. Daily 11am–11pm.

Cyrano et Roxane ★ FRENCH Head west on Monciak from the pier; as you come up from the railway underpass, you'll suddenly slip into less congested terrain and this cozy wine bar–cum–bistro. The owners, a French husband and Polish wife team, are more than happy to talk *terroir.* They have 50 different labels from Southern France regions. Nibbles include foie gras, and heartier sustenance comes in the form of duck confit. Conversations are intermittently drowned out by the rumblings of trains chugging by.

Bohaterów Monte Cassino 11. ✆ **660/759-594.** www.cyrano-roxane.com. Main courses 29 zł–57 zł; wine 12 zł–16 zł per glass. MC, V. Daily 1–10pm.

Rucola ★ INTERNATIONAL Stashed in the basement of the Museum of Sopot, Rucola is a charming place favored by the residents for semi-formal meals. The interior resembles the den of a compulsive souvenir collector, plastered with bric-a-brac from India, Mexico, and elsewhere. The food is somewhat eclectic, too: anything from *tagine* to Malaysian seafood. On a warm afternoon, enjoy a coffee in the garden by the shadows of the lovely villa that houses the museum.

Poniatowskiego 8. ✆ **58/551-50-46.** Main courses 17 zł–49 zł. AE, DC, MC, V. Daily 1–10pm.

Tawerna Rybaki ★★ ☺ FISH Although overshadowed by neighboring Bar Przystań (see above), the fish here is just as fresh. In fact, some swear that it's better. What's more, it isn't self-service. There are also kids meals like fish fingers, while grown ups can go for the Fisherman's Special platter consisting of cod, trout, and salmon in green pepper sauce. Satisfaction is assured.

Wojska Polskiego 26. ✆ **58/551-47-74.** www.tawernarybaki.pl. Main courses 20 zł–39 zł. AE, MC, V. Daily noon–10pm.

INEXPENSIVE

Bar Bursztynowy ★ POLISH You'll get a more authentic milk bar experience at Sopot's equivalent to Gdańsk's Bar Neptun. For a start, there's less tourist traffic here. Aside from the new lime-green chairs, everything else, from the patterned metal screen separating the service hatch and seating section to the colors and typeface on the windows, are all Communist-retro. Point at one of the sample dishes on display should the language be an obstacle for you.

Grunwaldzka 88. ✆ **58/551-44-34.** Main courses 6 zł–10 zł. No credit cards. Daily 9am–5pm.

After Dark in Sopot

CONCERTS

On summer weekends, **Opera Park** (**Opera Leśna;** Moniuszki 12) hosts regular outdoor concerts, including the annual **International Sopot Festival** (www.sopot festival.onet.pl) in August, which draws the likes of Tracy Chapman. At press time, the park's amphitheatre was undergoing renovation. Until it's completed, events are relocated to other venues, such as the horse-riding ring at **Hipodrom** (Polna 1). Contact the tourist office for event schedules.

CAFES, PUBS & CLUBS

Come Friday and Saturday nights, most of the cafes, pubs, and clubs on Bohaterów Monte Cassino Street keep their doors open till dawn. There's a velvet rope in some clubs, so be sure to gloss up and come with a clubbing attitude to get past the doormen.

Café Ferber Considered a snobby spot by some, this is where flashy locals and visitors rub elbows. The interior has great blown-up black-and-white pictures of Sopot's heyday as a seaside resort, while the huge windows let you people-watch the passers-by on the street. Bohaterów Monte Cassino 48. ✆ **58/551-45-81.**

Mandarynka ★ It's still a much-talked-about name, though some claim it's a shadow of its former self. If you've been clubbing in Warsaw, you'll find this place similar to the Platinum Club, but a few notches less haughty. Bema 6. ✆ **58/550-45-63.** www.mandarynka.pl.

Monte Vino ★ It's not far from the Molo, so it's right in middle of tourist traffic. However, regulars are locals who appreciate a wine bar that also supplies filling meals like pastas. Bohaterów Monte Cassino 11. ✆ **660/759-594.**

Papryka ★★ Have a thoroughly enjoyable night out at a relatively laid-back bar and nightclub, where nearly everything—from the leather sofas to the walls—is bathed in warm, red hues. Great DJs and usually just quiet enough to converse under the music. Grunwaldzka 11. ✆ **58/551-74-76.** www.klubpapryka.pl.

Sfinks ★ This detached building, in the park to the north of the Grand Hotel, is frequented by young, creative sorts for art openings, techno music, and gigs by international DJs. Mamuszki 1. ✆ 501/856-153. www.sfinks700.com.

Spatif ★★ One of the oldest players in the nightlife scene, it still churns out some of the best cocktails in town and thus has a loyal following, despite the hazardously steep flight of stairs leading up to it. On weekends, sardines in tins have more breathing space than the patrons here. Bohaterów Monte Cassino 54. ✆ **58/550-26-83.**

THE HEL PENINSULA

The Hel Peninsula, to the northeast of the Tri-City, is a pencil-thin strip of land that juts out into the Baltic Sea. This picturesque stretch of windswept, sandy beaches and pine forests is saturated with local holidaymakers in the summer months. Although the resort villages have the usual trappings of kitschy amber shops and fish-fry shacks, the peninsula retains a throwback-to-yesteryear charm. So much so, you can almost see a sepia glazing around you.

Aside from beachcombers, the area also reels in health-conscious vacationers who come here for its microclimate of salubrious iodine-rich air. It is a place to wind down, but the peninsula also has a reputation for high-speed pastimes. The Puck Bay is very shallow, making it a natural wading pool for beginner windsurfers; even 200m (656 ft.) from the shore, the water comes up only to your waist. However, daredevils take to these waters, too. The winds pick up enough gusto for old hands to get adrenaline kicks from kite surfing.

Before the area became a holiday zone, it was a Polish naval base. The navy has moved out, but what remains in the surrounding waters are over 1,500 shipwrecks, mostly casualties of World War II, attracting divers to dip in for viewing.

From end to end, the peninsula measures 34km (21 miles). At the northwestern tip, where the strip of land joins (or, rather, leaves) the mainland, is the fishing port of Władysławowo (pronounced *va-di-swa-vo'-vo*). And at land's end, so to speak, is Hel, another fishing port. In between Władysławowo and Hel are the small villages of Kuźnica, Jastarnia, Chałupy, and Jurata. All of them are tourist hubs. From the Tri-City, Hel is a popular destination for a day of kicking about in the sand. In summer, if you plan to stay overnight or do any watersports, book at least 2 months ahead. Off season, the special deals in the spa hotels are the reason to come.

Essentials

GETTING THERE

For day-trippers, the sea route to Hel is the most laid-back choice. If you're traveling by train or bus, you can get off at Władysławowo or any of the resort villages en route to Hel.

BY BOAT **Ferry trams** (*tramwaj wodny;* www.ztm.gda.pl/ferry.html) to Hel depart from Gdańsk (Motława Canal), Sopot (at the pier), and Gdynia (Nabrzeże Pomorskie; ✆ **669/441-202;** www.zkmgdynia.pl), and take about 30 minutes to 1 hour. From June to August, the ferry tram runs daily. Tickets are sold at the booths near the ferry landing. The one-way ticket from Gdańsk costs 18 zł; from Sopot, it's 16 zł; and from Gdynia, it's 12 zł.

BY TRAIN Regular trains to the peninsula leave from the Tri-City's train stations. The journey takes 1½ to 2 hours.

BY BUS There is minibus service from the northern side of Gdynia's bus station. The buses leave when they are filled up.

BY CAR From the Tri-City, take the E28 to Reda. Turn onto Road 216 and head for Władysławowo. It should take 2 hours to reach Hel. It's an enjoyable drive, passing by little towns, but keep in mind that the traffic can be a drag.

TOURIST INFORMATION

You can find tourist information points along the villages on the peninsula. In Hel, the **Tourist Information Point** (Marina Helska Port Rybacki; ✆ **58/675-10-10;** www.gohel.pl) is near the ferry landing. It operates year-round daily from 8am to 4pm. The English-speaking staff can assist with finding rooms and has public transportation schedules.

GETTING AROUND

At Hel's train station, electric-car operators mill around for customers. Prices are negotiable. Buses and trains run the length of the peninsula. In summer, there are five daily buses running from Hel to Władysławowo; cost is 8 zł one-way. ***Note:*** The main road can get quite congested around midday.

Top Attractions

Since it's easy to get to, most visitors eventually end up at the **Fokarium** (Morska 2; ✆ **58/675-08-36;** www.fokarium.com), a sanctuary for Baltic grey seals. The visitors' section is small, and you'll be done in about 10 minutes. Outside the village, the **Museum of Coastal Defence (Muzeum Obrony Wybrzeża) ★★** (Helska 16; ✆ **58/675-74-88;** www.helmuzeum.pl) is surprisingly entertaining and well worth catching a taxi to get to. The museum is located in the German-built *Schleswig-Holstein* artillery gun emplacement. Aside from the displays of weapons, medical equipment, and German mess kits, it also documents the Polish Navy's courageous effort in defending the peninsula for 32 days before falling into enemy hands at the beginning of World War II. The museum is open daily July through August 9am to 7pm, and admission is 6 zł; off-season hours are available on the website.

Outdoor Activities

BEACHES Parts of the peninsula are so narrow, especially between Chałupy and Kuźnica, you could be caressed by the breeze from the Baltic Sea, then cut through pine woods and be facing Puck Bay on the other shore of the peninsula in just 5 minutes. In all of the villages, you will find signs and pathways leading to beaches.

DEEP-SEA FISHING In the villages, you'll find outfitters taking tourists out for cod fishing in the Baltic Sea. **Marian Wiśniewski** (Kliprów 1, Chłapowo, Władysławowo; ✆ **604/992-298;** www.neptun.intermedia.net.pl) is a merry, white-bearded sailor who runs such an operation year-round. He charges 150 zł per person. If you're on your own, he'll slip you in with a group. The vessel leaves Port Władysławowo at 7am and returns 8 to 9 hours later. There's coffee, tea, and hot sausages on board. Marian doesn't speak English, but there's usually no communication problem once you're sailing away. **Waldermar Popowski ★** (see "Diving," below) offers a similar deal for 120 zł per person.

DIVING The chirpy **Waldermar Popowski ★** from **Baza Nurkowa Hel** (Kuracyjna 1, Hel; ✆ **604/294-009;** www.nurek.org), has a basic grip on English and will take you to any shipwrecks of your choice, having identified about 1,700 underwater wreckages on his charts. Fees start from 50 zł for a 1-hour dive at the closest-to-shore shipwreck.

WINDSURFING, KITE SURFING & CATAMARAN SAILING Watersports lovers converge on Puck Bay from mid-June to the end of August. **BO Sport ★★** (Chałupy 3; ✆ **58/674-37-42;** www.bosport.pl) has group and individual courses for all levels. A 2-day course starts at 200 zł. They also rent wetsuits and equipment. Although they claim to have English-speaking instructors, the command of the English language varies from one instructor to another. Pitch a tent on the campsite or let BO Sport set you up at Arka Hotel in Jastrzebia Góra 10km (6¼ miles) away, but they don't provide transfers between Arka and Chałupy. **Orka Surfstation** (Droga Helska, Chałupy; ✆ **601/620-361;** www.obozy-windsurfingowe.pl) rents windsurfing gear and catamarans.

Where to Stay & Dine

Most of the sleeping options here are in pensions and private rooms. These are usually rented out to vacationing families for weeks at a time, and they are unlikely to accept guests for 1 or 2 nights during the summer. Camping sites also line the beaches. During peak season, some of them resemble congested refugee camps. The official website of Hel (www.gohel.pl) has listings of rooms, chalets, and villas for rent. While Hel is fun for daytime window-shopping and eating out, rooms at the other resorts have better access to the beaches.

Dining wise, there are a plethora of fish restaurants and salad bars. **Maszoperia ★** (Wiejska 110; ✆ **58/675-02-97;** www.maszoperia.net) has excellent cod in garlic sauce. Meals accompanied by Italian, Georgian, and Hungarian wines can be had at the family-run **Restauracja Winiarnia** (Wojska Polskiego 31, Jurata; ✆ **58/675-27-92;** www.winiarniajurata.pl).

Chałupy 3 ★ This beachside campsite, on the side of Puck Bay, is popular with surfers, and BO Sport surfing school runs its courses here. You pitch your tent among families and young backpackers. The on-site **Surf Tawerna** eatery serves grilled meats and fish, plus some Polish staples, and is very popular with campers and day visitors. It has both indoor and alfresco seating. In the evenings, surfers and backpackers congregate at the tavern to lap up beer and rowdy music.

Pole Namiotowe Nr. 3, Chałupy. ✆ **58/674-12-75.** www.chalupy3.pl. 15 zł adults; 12 zł 2-person tent; 14 zł larger-than-2-person tent. DC, MC, V. **Amenities:** Restaurant; watersports equipment rental; Wi-Fi.

Jantar Hotel The mere mention of this name sends chills down the spines of some folks. The 22-hectare (54-acre) complex is a holiday facility for the army, but it's also open to civilians. This is a true example (as opposed to the mockups in Berlin) of a Communist-era resort. The fixtures, from the carpet to the dining area, and the service mentality provide for an undiluted pre-Solidarity cultural experience. The basic rooms are faultlessly clean. Other perks include a private pier on the shore of Puck Bay and a dining room with a sea view.

Wojska Polskiego, Jurata. ✆ **58/675-42-03.** Fax 58/675-42-62. www.wzwjantar.pl. 196 units. July & Aug 200 zł double; June, Aug 31 to Sept 13 & Dec 19 to Jan 2 160 zł double; Jan 3 to Apr 24 120 zł double; Apr 25 to May 140 zł double. Half- & full-board packages available. MC, V. **Amenities:** Restaurant; gym; sauna; tennis courts; kayak rental. *In room:* TV, minibar.

Hotel Bryza The Baltic Sea view, a sandy beach right at the doorstep, and a whole gamut of bells and whistles like an indoor pool, spa, and good restaurant mean this hotel fills up quickly in summers, despite the price tag. The rooms are adequate, though not finished with top-quality material. However, the staff's helpfulness is commendable.

Międzymorze 2, Jurata. ✆ **58/675-51-00.** Fax 58/675-54-80. www.bryza.pl. 90 units. Apr to June 24 & Sept to mid-Oct 500 zł double, 750 zł suite; June 25 to Aug 890 zł double, 1500 zł suite; mid-Oct to Mar 350 zł double, 500 zł suite. AE, DC, MC, V. **Amenities:** Restaurant; beach bar (in summer); cafe; bike rental; gym; indoor & outdoor pools; spa center; tennis court. *In room:* A/C (in suites), TV, Wi-Fi (free).

Pensjonat Birna While Hotel Bryza's strategy is "more is more," this privately-owned guesthouse has the opposite approach. It provides clean, comfy rooms but not much more, except the ready-to-help mother-and-son team. It's the perfect fit for those intending to spend the day out and about. The beaches, shops, and restaurants are close at hand. The rooms have basic tableware for snacking on the individual balconies that face the street or woods.

Wojska Polskiego 55, Jurata. ✆ **58/675-24-65.** www.birna.com.pl. 24 units. July & Aug 280 zł double; off season 180 zł double. AE, DC, MC, V. Free parking. *In room:* TV, fridge, Wi-Fi (free).

After Dark

PUBS & BEACH BARS

Follow the surfers, and you'll find them at the watersports-cum-camping sites that transform into tropical-style beach bars and dance floors after sunset. Aside from the **Surf Tawerna** (see "Where to Stay & Dine," above), you can get up-close to the hyperactive mobs at **Solar** (Chałupy 4; ✆ **58/674-20-91;** www.solar-windsurfing.pl).

ŁEBA & SŁOWIŃSKI NATIONAL PARK

Just 2 hours to the northwest of the Tri-City is a laid-back world of Polish-style seaside vacationing. Łeba (*pronounced where'-ba*), a sleepy, quaint fishing village with miles of sandy beaches, is one of the much-loved Baltic-shore sanctuaries valued for its clean air and clear waters. The village is also the entry point to Słowiński National Park, on the UNESCO's list of protected biospheres and famed for its "moving dunes."

Łeba and the sand dunes can be done as a day trip from the Tri-City. Or, like the Poles, you could stay for a night (or 14) for low-key repose by the Baltic Sea.

Essentials

GETTING THERE

From the Tri-City, take the SKM to Lębork. From Lębork, buses run by **Boguś** (✆ **59/728-23-00;** www.przewozy.info.pl) and **Tredetrans** (✆ **59/863-19-09**) leave for Łeba every 15 minutes and cost 6 zł per person. They drop you on pl. Dworcowy, just around the corner from the tourist information office. Total journey time is about 2 hours. If you're driving, follow the E28 highway in the direction of Słupsk, bearing right at Lębork. Journey time is about 1½ hours.

GETTING AROUND

The village is manageable on foot, and Słowiński National Park is a 2km (1¼-mile) walk. There are bikes for rent outside the tourist information office. Bike rental company **Ciułałła** (on a yard opposite Sienkiewicza 4; ✆ **696/042-119**) charges 4 zł per hour or 20 zł per day. They also rent bicycles with child-seats and children's bicycles. From May to September, **EKO-Tour Melex** (✆ **59/866-11-55** or 601/664-183) runs trams to the park entrance for 5 zł per person. They speak Polish only; get the staff at the tourist information office to reserve for you.

TOURIST INFORMATION

Stowarzyszenie Lokalna Organizacja Turystyczna Łeba (11 Listopada 5A; ✆ **59/866-25-65**; www.lotleba.pl) is the local tourist office. In July and August, it's open weekdays 8am to 8pm, Saturdays 8am to 6pm, and Sundays 10am to 4pm. Off season, it's open weekdays only from 8am to 4pm. Aside from providing the usual local maps, the helpful English-speaking staff also offers advice on rooms and directions to the park. Pick up the complimentary *Walking Through Łeba* for other attractions if you are spending more time here. A good Web resource for the area is **www.slowinskipn.pl.**

GETTING AWAY

In summer, there are two to three buses leaving Łeba for Lębork every hour until 8pm. Get the current schedule from the tourist information office or at www.przewozy.info.pl. If you take an early train out of the Tri-City and spend 4 to 5 hours here, you will still make the connection back to the Tri-City.

Top Attraction

Słowiński National Park ★ This remarkable landscape of wetlands and giant sand dunes, butted up against the Baltic Sea, is unique enough to be included on UNESCO's list of protected biospheres. The highlights here are the park's two lakes and the enormous, shifting sand dunes that rise to a height of 40m (131 ft.).

The park has something for everyone. The protected wetlands make it a great spot for birders. The area is on the spring and autumn migratory paths of a vast number of bird species, making it a paradise for ornithologists keen to see sea eagles, eagle owls, mergansers, and auks. World War II history buffs will be interested to hear how the Nazis used the unique sandy landscape as a training ground for Rommel's Afrika Korps. The Germans also conducted early experiments in rocketry here. About 3.5km (2¼ miles) from the park entrance is the Rocket Launchpad Museum (Muzeum Wyrzutnia Rakiet), where you'll find an early and eerie-looking launch pad. And, of course, there's the amazing giant dunes themselves, stretching for a length of about 5km (3 miles). The dunes migrate up to 10m (33 ft.) every year. Plodding up the shifting sands with sea wind gusting is somewhat arduous, but you're rewarded with a mind-jolting "I can't be in Poland" vista.

All in all, there's a lot of walking involved, so have good shoes. If you're pressed for time, at the park's entrance, there are bikes for rent (10 zł/hr.): Pedaling will get you to the dunes in about 15 minutes. Those preferring to save foot power for scaling the sand dunes can take the electric-power trolley (15 zł one-way). If you fast-track your visit, you can be done in an hour, but most visitors stay for around 3 hours. It can get blustery, even in summer, so bring a light jacket.

✆ **59/811-72-04**. www.slowinskipn.pl. Park: 4 zł adults, 2 zł children & seniors; Rocket Launchpad Museum: 14 zł adults, 10 zł children & seniors. May–Sept daily 7am–8pm; Oct–Apr 8am–4pm. The park entrance is 2km (1¼ miles) to the east of Łeba in the hamlet of Rąbka; leave Łeba via ul. Turystyczna.

Outdoor Activities

DEEP-SEA FISHING Along the canal, numerous boats take visitors out to the Baltic Sea for cod fishing throughout the year. The boats depart at 5am and remain at sea for about 8 hours. **Marcel** (Lzbica 15A; ✆ **502/481-907;** hotel_golabek@post.pl) has boats that hold 8 to 24 people, with a minimum group size of two; the price is 140 zł per person. Fishing equipment is provided. Food on board, naturally, is the catch of the day. For weekdays, booking a few days ahead will suffice. But for weekends, he's booked up 2 months in advance. The English-speaking staff at Hotel Gołąbek (see "Where to Stay & Dine," below) can assist with the booking.

RIDING INTO THE SUNSET If you've ever dreamed of horseback riding into the sunset on a Baltic Sea beach, here's your chance to live the fantasy. On the sandy shores of Łeba, the stables at **Gospodarstwo i Stadnina Koni Maciukiewicz ★★** (Św Huberta 4, Nowęcin; ✆ **59/866-18-74;** www.nowecin.com.pl) organize rides that leave for the beach—about 4km (2½ miles) away—each evening at 6 or 7pm. Once at the shore, you gallop away with cool wind in your hair, feeling the steeds' glee as they chase the receding waves. Call a day in advance to book. The warm and friendly proprietors speak Polish, Russian, and German (but no English). The price is 90 zł for 2 hours. In season (late June to Aug), the minimum group size is four; off season, it can be as few as two. Wear comfortable riding pants and boots; the stable provides helmets. You should be at least proficient in trotting; they will give you a test ride at the stable to gauge your level of horsemanship. The stables are 3km (1¾ miles) to the south of Łeba. If you're traveling by public transportation, in season, there are taxis in Łeba, or call **EKO-Tour Melex** (see "Getting Around," above). Off season, with prior notice, the staff from the stables can pick you up from Łeba. If you're looking to stay overnight, they have four good, value-priced standard rooms at 50 zł per person.

Where to Stay & Dine

Łeba is a resort town, so there are plenty of guest rooms (*pokoje gościnne*) and camping sites. **Camping Leśny No. 51** (Brzozowa 16A; ✆ **59/866-28-11;** www.camping51.pti.pl) is open from mid-April to mid-October. It also has double and triple rooms. **Pod Zegarem** (Kościuszki 92; ✆ **59/866-24-49;** www.podzegarem.pl), on the main street of Łeba, has good basic rooms, with amenities such as restaurant and sauna. A similar but slightly more expensive option is **Hotel Gołąbek** (Wybrzeże 10; ✆ **59/866-21-75;** www.hotel-golabek.leb.pl), located along the canal. ***Note:*** Most places will collect a "climate" tax of about 2 zł per person per day. For food, you'll find a multitude of fish and pizza eateries, delis, and bakeries on the canal embankment and along the main streets of Kościuszki and Nadmorska.

Hotel Neptun ★★ For some, this century-old villa on the shore of the Baltic Sea is a destination in itself. The building fell into disrepair after World War II; it's only in recent years that restoration work reinstated the belle époque ambience. Be sure to ask for a room with a sea view. Beyond the French windows, you'll see wind-twisted pine trees and seagulls gliding past. All rooms are in plush, modern-classical style. Rooms in the corner turrets are especially charming. It's worth splurging on the suites for the additional space. The house specialty at the Polish restaurant is a traditional roast duck with apples and cranberry sauce complemented by attentive but unobtrusive staff, and ocean views. In the morning, you'll wake up to the symphony of winds and waves. It's great for a romantic getaway or a restful break with the family.

Sosnowa 1. ✆ **59/866-14-32.** Fax 59/866-23-57. www.neptunhotel.pl. 32 units. Sept to June 355 zł-395 zł double, 570 zł-650 zł suite; July & Aug 500 zł-620 zł double, 980 zł- 1,180 zł suite. AE, DC, MC, V. Free parking. **Amenities:** Restaurant; bar; bikes; outdoor pool; sauna; tennis court. *In room:* TV, hair dryer, minibar, Wi-Fi (free).

MALBORK

Malbork's *pièce de résistance* is the jaw-dropping Teutonic Knights castle, the biggest brick castle in the world and a UNESCO World Heritage Site. The castle will effortlessly convert anyone into a devout fan of knights and Gothic grandeur. Malbork is only an hour's drive from Gdańsk, so it works perfectly as a day trip. Or you can time your visit with one of the numerous festivals held at the castle. The main ones are the July's **Siege of Malbork** (a reenactment of the 1410 Battle of Grünwald) and August's **Magic Malbork** (an impressive display of acrobatics and fireworks). You'll find schedule of events at www.visitmalbork.pl. Summer is the busiest period, but Malbork Castle makes an atmospheric sojourn into the medieval epoch any time of year.

Essential Information

GETTING THERE

Malbork is about 60km (37 miles) south of Gdańsk and 316km (196 miles) north of Warsaw.

BY TRAIN Malbork lies on the main Gdańsk–Warsaw rail line. Departures from both cities are frequent. The trains arrive on Dworcowa Street, which is about a 15-minute walk from the castle. Taxis to the castle cost around 15 zł.

BY CAR From Gdańsk, drive south along the E75 highway. Figure on about 45 minutes. From Warsaw, take the E77 and exit to Road 22 for Malbork. Journey time is about 4½ hours. There is paid parking on Piastowska Street, near the castle.

BY TAXI From Gdańsk, a taxi ride costs about 250 zł, depending on traffic conditions. You can use **City Taxi Plus Neptun** (✆ **196-86**).

TOURIST INFORMATION

The **Malbork Welcome Center** (Kościuszki 54; ✆ **55/647-47-47;** www.visitmalbork.pl) is open weekdays from 8am to 4pm. *The Living History* guide produced by the center includes a section on the minor attractions in town. If all you need is a map, any hotel will be able to give you one.

Top Attraction

Malbork Castle ★★★ If you have time for only one medieval castle, then this is it. Following the Knights' defeat in the early 15th century, the castle fell to the Polish kings, who used it as an occasional residence. After the Polish partition at the end of the 18th century, the Prussians took over Malbork and the castle, turning it into a military barracks. German control lasted until the end of World War II, when heavy fighting between Germans and Russians destroyed the town and left the castle in ruins. What you see today is the result of a long and steady restoration process that was completed only about a decade ago.

Allow 2 hours or more to give the brick and masonry complex at least a cursory once-over. History aside, the architectural details—from trefoils to cinquefoils, friezes, gables, and arches—are all very arresting. It's breathtaking, also in the literal

Knight Raiders

The Teutonic Order of the Hospital of St. Mary was founded in 1190 as a brotherhood to serve the sick. These warrior-monks took arms in the Crusades, fighting in the Holy Lands. However, upon sustaining a string of military defeats, they were forced to retreat to Europe. In 1226, Polish Duke Konrad of Mazovia enlisted the Knights to subdue pagan Prussians in the West. Around 1276, the Knights began construction of the Malbork Castle and named it Marienburg (the Fortress of Mary). The Knights were ruthless and highly disciplined, and eventually came to rival the Polish kings for control over the vital Baltic Sea trade, including the amber trade. Towns that came under the Knights' control included Toruń, Elbląg, and Kwidzyn. A century later, in 1410, Poles, along with Lithuanians and troops of other lands, joined forces to defeat the religious warriors at the epic Battle of Grünwald (also referred to as the "Battle of Tannenberg" in history books). This marked the beginning of the end of the Knights' dominion in northwestern Poland. In 1457, King Kazimierz Jagiełło forced the Knights to abandon the Malbork Castle and dispatched them to East Prussia. Today, the Teutonic Order still exists, but they are devoted to the peaceful endeavors of running schools and hospitals.

sense, to lose yourself in the corridors and spiral staircases. You enter the castle via a wooden drawbridge that takes you into the courtyard of the Middle Castle (Zamek Średni). The building to your left houses an impressive amber collection and medieval weaponry. Another drawbridge takes you to the High Castle (Zamek Wysoki). Here, you'll find the Knights' dormitory, kitchen, and refectory. The castle's main square tower gives you a grand view of the complex. Do budget time for rambling along the river to view the castle from the exterior. The tickets come with a Polish guide, but you can wander off on your own. You can pick up an English audio guide by the main entrance (37 zł). The museum sometimes closes for special events; call or check the website before heading out.

Starościńska 1. ✆ **55/647-09-78.** www.zamek.malbork.pl. 35 zł adults, 25 zł children & seniors; family & group tickets available. July & Aug guided tour in English 210 zł/group of 40. AE, DC, MC, V. Mid-Apr to mid-Sept daily 9am–7pm; Apr 1 to Apr 14 & Sept daily 10am–5pm; Oct–Mar daily 10am–3pm. Guided tours July & Aug 11am, 1:30 & 3:30pm.

Outside Malbork

If you've been bitten by the Gothic bug, there are a number of fortresses either built, or captured, by the Teutonic Knights in the vicinity of Malbork. The entire series is listed on www.zamkigotyckie.org.pl. However, in comparison with Malbork Castle, the other properties may come across as dwarfs. The castles in **Kwidzyn** ★ and **Gniew,** both about 40km (25 miles) southwest of Malbork, can be bundled in as a side trip. Both can be reached by public buses from Gdańsk or Malbork.

Formerly known as Marienwerder, Kwidzyn is unique for the side-by-side construction of a 14th-century castle and cathedral. Another interesting feature is the *gdanisko,* roughly translated as a sewage tower used for depositing waste into the river below (which has since changed course). The *gdanisko* is connected to the main castle via a bridge, and it's the longest of its kind in Europe. The complex, featuring original interiors, now houses the **Kwidzyn Museum** (Katedralna 1; ✆ **55/646-37-80;**

Sundowner

Cross the footbridge to get to the riverbank opposite the castle at day's end. The stunning vista of the sun setting over Malbork Castle, coupled with the inkblot reflections on the River Nogat, is an indelible memory.

www.zamek.kwidzyn.pl). The museum has a quirky habit of deviating from the stipulated opening hours, so call before you visit.

Visiting the **castle in Gniew** (Zamkowa 3; ✆ **58/535-35-33;** www.zamek-gniew.pl) only makes sense if it coincides with a festival. Gniew is known for its world-class reenactments of historical battles. The **European Festival of History** ★ (last weekend of July) covers power struggles from the medieval period to World War II, while **Vivat Vasa** (second weekend in Aug) focuses on a 17th-century tussle between the Polish and Swedish royals. At both events, you can expect meticulous attention to armory and retro hairdos, plus displays of horsemanship.

Where to Stay & Dine

Along the river and around the castle, there are plenty of eateries doling out grilled sausages, fish, and pancakes. On Kościuszki Street, between the castle and the railway station, pizzerias and a McDonald's can be found. Locals endorse the sweet breads of **Kawiarnia Niucka** bakery (Kościuszki 5; ✆ **55/273-48-36**). It's open from 8am Monday to Saturday, so it's great for the morning caffeine fix.

Gothic Café & Restaurant ★★ INTERNATIONAL Most restaurants with a prime location on the grounds of a major attraction are blasé. Not this one, though. The compact menu is whipped up by an ebullient New York–trained chef. His dishes are based on the original recipes and ingredients found in the castle's records but are dished out with 21st-century inspiration. One example of which is black chicken with beer pancakes. Culinary workshops are available with advanced booking. On sunny days, you can tuck into a meringue cheesecake on the secluded back patio. To dine here without buying a ticket to the castle, call the restaurant, and the staff will come to the entrance to let you in.

Starościńska 1. ✆ **783/464-828.** www.gothic.com.pl. Main courses 29 zł–49 zł. AE, MC, V. Apr–Dec daily 9am–9pm; Jan–Mar access by reservation only.

Grot Hotel ★★ Built in 2007 and located just off Kościuszki Street, Grot Hotel is a 10-minute walk from the castle. The rooms have pinstriped champagne wallpaper, a minimalistic design, and spotless bathrooms. Choose a room facing the back street; the other side looks out to the busy Road no. 22. Kościuszki is a shopping street, so delis, restaurants, and ATMs are close at hand. Its city-modern restaurant has reasonably priced continental cuisine.

Kościuszki 22D. ✆ **55/646-96-60.** Fax 55/646-96-70. www.grothotel.pl. 18 units. May to mid-Sept 289 zł double; mid-Sept to Apr 279 zł double. AE, MC, V. **Amenities:** Restaurant; bar. *In room:* TV, hair dryer, Wi-Fi (free).

Hotel Parkowy Malbork's Sports and Recreation Center has a campsite and a double-story building with simple, clean rooms. It's an easy 15-minute walk along the River Nogat to get to the castle. In summer, your fellow guests are children and youngsters in sports camps. But worry not about the noise; the hotel has a strict "silent night" policy. The grounds also have an eatery serving inexpensive snacks.

Parkowa 3. ✆ **55/272-24-13.** www.osir.malbork.pl. 20 units. May, June & Sept 160 zł double; July & Aug 140 zł double; Oct to Apr 120 zł double. AE, DC, MC, V. Free parking. *In room:* TV, Wi-Fi (free).

Hotel Zamek Housed in a heritage building that was the Teutonic Knights' former hospital, it's as near to the castle as you can get. During the Communist era, it was the grandest spot in town, but the old-fashioned brown sofas and heavy velvet curtains today feel a bit dark and dated. The rooms have small granary windows that either look out to the river or the car park. Beds are decked out with spotless sheets, and the marble-tiled bathrooms are well scrubbed. The staff doesn't let their limited English stop them from being helpful.

Starościńska 14. ✆ **55/272-84-00.** www.hotelprodus.pl. 42 units. May 16 to mid-Sept 300 zł–400 zł; Sept 16 to mid-May 200 zł–300 zł double. AE, MC, V. Parking 15 zł. **Amenities:** Restaurant; bar. *In room:* TV.

ELBLĄG

Elbląg (pronounced *air'-blong*) is the starting (or finishing, depending on the direction of your travel) point of a one-of-its-kind canal in Europe: its only counterpart in the world is the Morris Canal in New Jersey. Boat trips on the Elbląg–Ostróda Canal can be described as a calm float coupled with a San Francisco cable-car ride through lush nature, most of which is conservation area. The canal, an engineering marvel, has been singled out by Poles as one of the nation's Seven Wonders, alongside Kraków's Wawel Castle.

Founded in 1246 by the Teutonic Knights (see "Malbork," above), Elbląg itself is a humble affair. Though the Old Town has been skillfully restored, where the postwar houses blend harmoniously with the gables of burgher buildings, Elbląg is another example of Polish towns whose architectural gems were lost in World War II. Elbląg's proximity to Gdańsk makes it a good access point to the canal. In addition, the most interesting stretch is the first half of the canal, from Elbląg to Małdyty. Once you've had enough of pounding Gdańsk's cobblestone lanes, a leisure-boat ride on the canal is a welcome rest for weary feet.

Essentials

GETTING THERE

BY CAR From Gdańsk, take Road no. 77 followed by Road no. 22 into the Old Town. There's parking right by the Old Town on Rycerska Street. Within the Old Town, if you're early enough, there's parking around the church on Mostowa Street.

BY BUS OR TRAIN The bus and train stations are next to each other to the southwest of the Old Town. Regular PKS (www.pks.elblag.pl) buses run from Gdańsk and take about 90 minutes. Similarly, there are regular trains from Gdańsk that take about 75 minutes. To get to the Old Town, tram nos. 1, 2, and 4 drop you off at the crossing of pl. Słowiński and 1 Maja, at the edge of the Old Town.

VISITOR INFORMATION

There is a **tourist information point** (Brama Targowa; ✆ **55/611-08-20;** www.ielblag.pl) in the Market Gate in the north of the Old Town. From mid-June to September, it's open daily from 10am to 6pm. Off season, it's open weekdays only from 10am to 4pm. If all you need is information about boat rides on the canal, the operator of the leisure boats, **Żegluga Ostródzko-Elbląska** (Wodna 1B; ✆ **55/232-43-07;** www.zegluga.com.pl), is located in the Old Town along the canal.

Top Attraction

Elbląg-Ostróda Canal (Kanał Ostrodzko-Elblaski) ★ Have your binoculars ready as you sit back for a sedate boat ride through showpieces of nature and engineering. You'll journey through woods, swamps, and marshland where cormorants, grebes, gulls, graylag geese, and the occasional eagle wing by. You'll be stirred from your serene stupor when the boat reaches a slipway. A metal crate rises up from the water and scoops up the boat onto rail tracks on grassy slopes. Mind the weather forecast, since the best vantage points are from the deck seats. The booth seats below deck give you a "water-level" perspective. Bring your own snacks or buy from the nothing-to-write-home-about bistro on board. ***Note:*** This slow and easy journey is mainly about the peace and tranquility of watching flora and fauna. While this appeals to adults, it could drive active young kids 'round the bend.

The boats, run by **Żegluga Ostródzko-Elbląska** (see "Visitor Information," above), operate from May to September. At 8am, the boats depart from both Elbląg and Ostróda. The journey, from one end to the other, lasts 11 hours. If you're pressed for time, do the 5-hour Elbląg–Buczyniec ride, which covers the most interesting parts in terms of slipways. You must call at least a day in advance to book your tickets. At 7:30am on the day of the trip, pick up your tickets from the office. On busy days, as many as three boats, each with a capacity of 65 passengers, depart from Elbląg. When there are fewer than 20 passengers, the trip is cancelled. Although the canal is a major tourist attraction, the infrastructure for delivering passengers back to their starting points is spotty. If you are relying on public transportation, one option is to take the trip to Małdyty. Boats arrive here at 2:30pm; a 2:54pm train gets you back to Elbląg in 30 minutes. The Małdyty's train station is near the boat landing, but it's an uphill pant to the station. The boat company organizes buses (11 zł) from Buczyniec to Elbląg on an ad hoc basis; call a day or two earlier to find out if this service is on. Yet another option is to take the Buczyniec-Elbląg return boat journey. The risk here is the seats may be fully taken up by passengers coming from Ostróda.

Boarding at Bulwar Zygmunta. May–Sept Elbląg-Buczyniec 75 zł adults, 55 zł children & seniors; Elbląg-Małdyty 80 zł adults, 60 zł children & seniors; Elbląg-Ostróda 90 zł adults, 70 zł children & seniors. Elbląg-Buczyniec 8:20am–1:10pm & 8:40am–1:30pm; Elbląg-Małdyty 8am–2:30pm; Elbląg-Ostróda 8am–7pm.

Where to Stay & Dine

The Old Town has plenty of informal eateries. **Restauracja pod Kogutem ★** (Wigilijna 8/9; ✆ **55/641-28-82;** www.podkogutem.elblag.pl) is a small country-style spot with fairly priced and dependable Polish mainstays. More up-market is **Kuchnia Wędrowca** (Wigilijna 12; ✆ **55/611-00-22;** www.kuchniawedrowca.pl), but it has inexpensive lunchtime specials. Both places stir into action at around 11am daily. Early birds can flock to **Piekarnia Raszczyk** (1 Maja 2; ✆ **600/050-232**), a bakery that also dispenses coffee and tea. It opens at 7am from Monday to Saturday. Breakfast starting at 7am is available daily at **Pensjonat M.F.** (see below) for 22 zł.

Hotel Pod Lwem ★ The facade of this new hotel is an attractively restored brick town house. Inside, it's a contemporary blend of wood, leather, and metal. The street-facing, high-ceilinged rooms are well lit by natural light. In the bathrooms, you'll find a neat bundle of toiletries. And it has an Old Town location, to boot.

Kowalska 10. ✆ **55/641-31-00.** Fax 55/641-31-39. www.hotelpodlwem.pl. 35 units. 330 zł double. AE, DC, MC, V. **Amenities:** Breakfast room. *In room:* TV, Wi-Fi (free).

Pensjonat Boss ★ This efficiently run pension in the Old Town is around the corner from the boarding point for canal boats, a major draw for the large number of German-speaking guests. The town house was renovated and turned into a hotel in 1996. Expect rooms with light-color walls, brown furniture, clean bathrooms, and a friendly English-speaking crew. **Pensjonat M.F.** ★ (Św Ducha 26; ✆ **55/641-26-10;** www.pensjonatmf.pl), a similar operation, is a few doors away.

Św Ducha 30. ✆ **55/239-37-29.** Fax 55/239-37-28. www.pensjonatboss.pl. 13 units. May–Aug 200 zł–230 zł double; Sept–Apr 190 zł–200 zł double. AE, DC, MC, V. **Amenities:** Cafe. *In room:* TV, Wi-Fi (free).

12

NORTHEAST POLAND

by Kit F. Chung

Despite the unique look and feel of Northeast Poland, most international travelers neglect this region. However, should you choose to trek this way, your reward will be a satisfying sense of discovering the faces of Poland that are not commonly seen. Outdoor adventures, historical highlights, close encounters with wildlife, and cultural diversity are all part of the well-rounded package offered by Northeast Poland, whose borders touch Russia, Lithuania, and Belarus.

In the Northeast is the Mazurian and Suwałki lake districts, the "land of a thousand lakes," where retreating glaciers sculpted lakes and islets, rivers, undulating meadows, and woodlands. Vacationers flock here to blend sailing, kayaking, and cycling with rustic living. The top man-made attractions are the Wolf's Lair, the site of a 1944 assassination attempt on Hitler, and a series of Gothic castles.

Moving east and southeast, Prussian influence gives way to Eastern Orthodox churches. Białystok, the regional capital, changed hands from Poles to Prussians, Russians, and Lithuanians. Jews and Tatars also settled in these parts, and you'll find some remnants of their footprints in the vicinity of Białystok in forms of a 17th-century synagogue and two wooden mosques.

Further south is the Białowieża Forest, one of the last parcels of primeval forest in Europe and an area where European bison still roam freely.

Even if rumble and tumble in mud and puddles isn't your thing, the scenic drives, selection of atmospheric lodging, and good, inexpensive regional food still make the Northeast an ideal place to unwind.

In the major lakeside resort towns, room rates are higher due to their proximity to transportation terminals and other amenities. You'll find better value and more atmospheric rooms away from the main hubs. Some pensions and hotels, in addition to owning fleets of kayaks and bicycles, also throw in outings such as mushroom picking, horseback riding, and day trips to local sights or even guided tours to Poland's eastern neighbors. It's most convenient to navigate the terrain in a car, but with some planning, you can get by with the network of trains and buses.

Stork Options

A quarter of the world's white stork population roosts in Poland. Most of the 40,000 pairs have their base in Northeastern Poland. From May to September, you'll see stork families in nests perched on lamp posts, chimneys, and pillars, and on the roofs of farm houses, pensions, or run-down heritage buildings. The storks swoop overhead like ancient pterodactyls. If you're lucky, you'll see one returning to its nest with a fish or a writhing snake to feed the brood. Come September, as the flock gets set to migrate to Africa, the juveniles take to the air for test flights.

THE MAZURIAN LAKE DISTRICT

The Mazurian Lake District is a vast expanse of interconnected waterways that lie to the northeast of Warsaw. Lakes Śniardwy, Mamry, and Niegocin are famed for sailing, while Krutynia River has one of the most scenic lowland kayaking routes in Poland. Several organizers run multi-day sail, bicycle, and paddle (kayak) trips covering much of the region. For aqua adventurers, days can be spent out on lakes and rivers, and nights on boats or in simple bunks along the way. Cycling routes are often designed to fit in pit stops at the Wolf's Lair ★★ (the site of a 1944 attempt on Hitler's life) and a monastery in Wojnowo. Though it is now largely an outdoor sports center, during the medieval period, it was the roaming grounds of the Teutonic Knights (see "Malbork", p. 262). Some original Gothic outposts are now museums and hotels that you can work into your itinerary. Dotted with resort towns and agro-tourist farms, you can basically set up camp anywhere, depending on your raison d'état.

Giżycko and **Mikołajki,** only 35km (22 miles) apart, are the common entry points to the Mazurian Lake District. The former was founded by Teutonic Knights but severely damaged in World War II. In a strategic location on the northern shore of **Lake Niegocin,** it's the largest sailing center in the Mazurian Lakes, where folks come to hire yachts and load up on supplies. Mikołajki, dubbed the Mazurian Venice, is in the middle of watersports traffic between **Mamry** and **Śniardwy lakes,** the two biggest lakes in the region. It has a fair share of blinged-out holidaymakers. Both locations have scores of sailing, canoeing, and biking outfitters.

Essentials

GETTING THERE

Giżycko and **Mikołajki** are about 320km (199 miles) from Warsaw and 280km (174 miles) from Gdańsk. The duo is served by trains (www.pkp.pl) and buses. From Warsaw, trains to Giżycko and Mikołajki take about 6 hours. Buses are better options and faster, taking about 5 hours. By car, you leave Warsaw on E77, switching to Road no. 61 in the direction of Ostrołeka, followed by Road no. 63 at Łomża. The journey takes about 4 hours. From Gdańsk, it's also 4 hours on the road. You leave the city on Road E77, switching to Road no. 16. At Mrągowo, Road no. 59 goes to Giżycko, while Road no. 16 takes you to Mikołajki.

VISITOR INFORMATION

Giżycko's tourist information center (Wyzwolenia 2; ✆ **87/428-52-65;** www.gizycko.turystyka.pl) is centrally located. July and August it's open weekdays 9am to

6pm and weekends 10am to 4pm. For the rest of the year it's open on weekdays 8am to 4pm and Saturdays 10am to 2pm. The helpful staff speaks English. Aside from maps, you can pick up listings of campsites and hotels, yacht and bicycle rentals, plus suggested cycling and kayaking routes. Filling a similar function, but only from May to August, is **Mikołajki's tourist information center** (Pl. Wolności 3, Mikołajki; **✆ 87/421-68-50;** www.mikolajki.pl). In June, it opens daily from 10am to 8pm. At other times, it's the same open hours, but from Monday to Saturday only.

THE MAZURIAN TOWNS & VILLAGES IN BRIEF

Ruciane-Nida, the most southerly sizeable base, is the finishing point of the Krutynia River kayaking route. It is also a central point for cycling trips into the Mazurian Landscape Park and Piska Forest (Puszcza Piska). The most northerly lakeside town is **Węgorzewo.** Most of the villages with historical interests, such as **Olsztyn, Lidzbark Warmiński,** and **Święta Lipka,** are in the west. **Krutyń,** a main village along the **Krutynia River** kayaking route, is 23km (14 miles) to the south of Mikołajki.

GETTING AROUND

BY BUS & CAR Once you're in Giżycko or Mikołajki, you can get around in buses (www.pks.mragowo.pl). The bus terminal in Giżycko is to the south of the center. In Mikołajki, the bus station is next to the Protestant church on the west side of the town center. A fairly extensive network of roads crisscrosses the area. Some of the roads can be a squeeze when a milk tanker or harvester gets in the way.

BY TAXI For short trips, taxis can be a solution. The average taxi rate is about 1.50 zł to 3 zł per kilometer. If you take a taxi out of town, you pay the fare for the empty taxi returning to its base. **Radio Taxi 19621** (**✆ 196-21;** www.radiotaxi-gizycko.com) operates from Giżycko.

BY FERRY From mid-April to October, ferries run by **Żegluga Mazurska** (Wojska Polskiego 8, Giżycko; **✆ 87/428-53-32;** www.zeglugamazurska.com.pl) glide to Ruciane-Nida in the south and Węgorzewo in the north. These boats are a means of transportation, as well as enjoyable cruises to nowhere-and-back. Get timetables at the tourist information offices or from the boards at the departure jetties. A round trip from Giżycko to Mikołajki on Lake Śniardwy takes 3 hours. In Giżycko, the departure point is on **Kolejowa 8** (**✆ 87/428-25-78**), which is right by the canal's embankment. In Mikołajki, it's on **Pl. Wolności 15** (**✆ 87/421-61-02**), the embankment on the east side of the town.

Exploring the Area

Most visitors, largely made up of Poles and Germans, are here to enjoy nature and rural living while dabbling in sailing, fishing, kayaking, or cycling. There are plenty of cultural and historical attractions, but, truth be told, with the exception of the Wolf's Lair (see below), not many would travel some 300km (186 miles) just to see the minor Gothic castles or baroque churches. Having said that, however, if you incorporate these minor attractions along with outdoor activities, or string them together as part of a drive in the countryside, they complement each other well as cultural interludes. If you are spending more time here, get a copy of *Across the Land of Great Masurian Lakes,* by Stanisław Siemiński (20 zł; available in tourist information centers), which details the region's history, canals, forests, and wildlife.

Northeast Poland

Fans of church organs should keep an eye out for the May to September performances in Święta Lipka at the **Church of Our Lady** (Święta Lipka; ✆ **89/755-14-81;** www.swlipka.org.pl). You can combine it with a trip to the Wolf's Lair.

There are numerous Gothic castles in this neck of the woods. The full series are listed on www.zamkigotyckie.org.pl. However, after seeing Malbork Castle, the samples here can come across as disappointingly dwarfish. The strongest selling point for the **castle in Lidzbark Warmiński ★** is it's a well-preserved original, not reconstructed like most of the others. The town, 98km (61 miles) west of Giżycko, was captured by the Teutonic Knights in 1240. It became the command center of the Warmian Bishops (the religious and political leaders that depended on the Teutonic Knights for military protection), and the location where Copernicus drafted *De Revolutionibus Orbium Coelestium* (see "Toruń", p. 228). The interior houses the **Museum of Warmia** (Plac Zamkowy 1; ✆ **89/767-21-11;** www.muzeum.olsztyn.pl), which has filled the halls and chapels with medieval arts and paraphernalia related to Copernicus and the bishops. It's open from Tuesdays to Sundays from 9am to 4pm. To dig into the architectural details, it's worth getting a guide, but you will have to arrange it in advance since not much English is used here. At the time of publication, the castle has just started a renovation project, and part of the grounds is being converted into a hotel.

The **Old Believers Monastery** (**Klasztor Starowierców;** Wojnowo 76, Ukta; **© 87/425-70-30;** www.klasztor.com.pl) is mentioned in all the regional guides, but it's actually a very modest affair. It is mainly of interest to those tracing the roots of the Old Believers, a minority group that defied the reformations led by Patriarch Nikon for the Russian Orthodox Church in the mid–17th century. The last of the monastery's nuns passed away in 2006. The Orthodox chapel retains the golden religious icons, and behind the church, there is a small cemetery with three-bar crosses. If you're not driving, the best way to get here is by bike along the Green Route. Kayakers on the Krutynia Trail to Ukta can access the monastery by detouring to Lake Duś. A quick browse of the compound will take no more than 15 minutes. For a longer stay, literally, you can check into the rough and ready rooms (40 zł per person) above the chapel.

Wolf's Lair (Wilczy Szaniec) ★★ A visit to the Wolf's Lair will leave you mulling over how different the course of history could have been if this attempted assassination on Hitler were successful. The Wolf's Lair was once Hitler's eastern command base and comprises a large camp of reinforced-concrete bunkers, some with walls as thick as 8m (26 ft.). The top Nazi leadership, including Hitler and Hermann Goering, maintained their own personal bunkers. Additionally, there were bunkers for communication and troop commands, a train station, an airstrip, and even a casino bunker. Hitler was a frequent visitor to the Wolf's Lair from its initial construction in 1941 until 1944, when it was abandoned just ahead of the Russian advance as the war drew to a close. In January 1945, the Germans dynamited the bunkers to prevent them from falling into enemy hands. The remains are what you see today. The moss-covered bunkers have been preserved in their original "destroyed" state. You are free to walk along the marked paths among the jarring, jagged brick and concrete ruins sitting incongruously amid beautiful pine forests. With the exception of the multimedia film center, the more than 30 ruins are exposed to the elements.

Summer is the best time for unhurried explorations. In winter, the snow-clad view is also quite spectacular. It's worth hiring a guide to give context to the rubbles. Guides mill around the entrance, charging 50 zł for 1½ hours of narration; you can also contact Jadwiga Korowaj (**© 601/677-202;** jagoda10@poczta.onet.pl), who has been telling the Lair's tales for over 20 years, in advance. The site also has a basic hotel where a double room goes for 100 zł.

Gierłoż (8km/5 miles east of Kętrzyn). **© 89/752-44-29.** www.wolfsschanze.pl. 12 zł adults; 6 zł seniors & children. Daily 9am–sunset. From Giżycko, take the train or bus to Kętrzyn, then take one of several daily buses from Kętrzyn (about 15 min.); or take the Red Route cycling route.

Outdoor Activities

SAILING The beauty of sailing in the Mazurian Lake District is that the interconnecting waterways allow you the freedom to waltz from one lake to another. In summer, however, it gets congested around Giżycko and Mikołajki. Spend a day sailing from Mikołajki to **Okartowo** (in the east) and you escape to relative isolation. Be sure to moor at **Lake Tuchlin ★**, a bird sanctuary. Similarly, you have nature to yourself (more or less) once you pass the lock at Ruciane-Nida into **Lake Nidzkie ★**. Serene, too, is the southeasterly **Lake Roś ★**. You get there by passing the lock in Karwik and slipping into the 6km (3¾-mile) Jegliński Canal. The lakes

Hit and Missed

The details of Hitler's attempted assassination at the Wolf's Lair read like a spy thriller (and indeed, *Valkyrie* [2008], the movie starring Tom Cruise based on these events, is just that). In 1944, the would-be assassin, Claus Schenk von Stauffenberg, an officer of aristocratic bearing, had come to see the war as unwinnable. He and other like-minded officers believed that if Germany had any hope of avoiding total annihilation, Hitler had to be stopped. On July 20, 1944, von Stauffenberg was dispatched to the Wolf Lair's to brief the Fuehrer and other top Nazi leaders on troop levels in the Eastern Front. He arrived at the meeting with a time bomb stashed in his briefcase. Just before the meeting started, he placed the briefcase near Hitler, activated the bomb, and left the room. The resulting explosion killed four people, but not the target. One of the generals had moved the briefcase just before it exploded, unwittingly saving the Fuehrer's life. Von Stauffenberg flew back to Berlin believing the assassination attempt had succeeded. Once Hitler recovered from his minor injuries, he ordered von Stauffenberg's arrest; the officer was executed by firing squad later that night. In the ensuing witch hunt, some 5,000 people were executed.

reward you with parades of grey herons, cormorants and ospreys, and storks galore. On the banks, elk skirt by, belting out their mating tunes. You won't be bored by the bays and peninsulas of **Lake Dobskie ★★** (northwest of Giżycko). Here, you find the peculiar **Cormorant Island** (Wyspa Kormoranów), where trees cannot grow, and Gilma Island, which reportedly was the site of an ancient pagan temple. **Lakes Dargin** and **Śniardwy** can be challenging for novices.

The sailing season lasts from May to late January. To avoid rubbing helms with other enthusiasts, May to mid-June and after August are the best. But in July and August, the weather is sunnier, and in the evenings, you'll find merry beer-imbibing at all of the resort towns. To enjoy the lakes without the hassle of renting a boat, hop on a ferry (see "Getting Around," above). But if you want to command your own vessel, yacht rentals abound. Some pop up and fold up just as quickly. The www.mazury.info.pl portal has an updated list of rentals. It is advisable to browse through local sailing magazines such as ***Jachting*** (www.jachting.pl) or ***Żagle*** (www.zagle.com.pl), where you'll find many advertisements for outfitters. In July and August, advance reservations are a must. Locals sometimes book at two different outfitters and, on the day of the trip, check out the vessels before selecting one. ***Caution:*** When picking up a boat, look for any damages and report them before setting sail to avoid complications later.

One of the biggest marinas and outfitters is **Sailor** (Czartery Jachtów Sailor, Piękna Góra; ✆ **87/429-32-92;** www.sailor.com.pl) in Piękna Góra, situated just outside Giżycko. Another is **Tiga Yacht and Marina** (Sztynort 11; ✆ **87/427-51-79;** www.tigayacht.pl) in the lovely marina of Sztynort (northwest of Giżycko), complete with a derelict heritage manor house, restaurants, hotel, and campsites. **mJacht** (✆ **791/141-331;** www.mjacht.pl) has yachts scattered in marinas around the district. The friendly, English-speaking Daniel Żuchowski is ever ready to answer questions and make accommodation recommendations.

Note: If you don't have a sailor's license, the rental company will try to help you locate an English-speaking skipper. The going rate for skippers is about 200 zł to 250 zł per day, plus meals. Depending on the size of the boat, expect to place a deposit of 500 zł to 2,000 zł. The smallest boat for four could cost as little as 70 zł per day. On the other end of the scale, a luxury yacht for eight, fitted with creature comforts, can command 650 zł per day. Before setting out, check with your rental agency to obtain local emergency numbers, water safety information, and local sailing customs.

CANOEING & KAYAKING The **Krutynia River ★★** wins hands down as the loveliest lowland kayaking route in the country. The route starts in Sorkwity (35km/22 miles west of Mikołajki). The 102km (63 miles) will have you paddling from lake to lake via streams, moving east by zigzagging from north to south. Along the way, you pass the Mazurian Landscape Park. On the whole, it is rated as an easy route, but from Zgon to Krutyń, you paddle along Lake Mokre, a sizeable lake that requires care. If you're going solo or have kids in tow, a carefree and manageable route is from Krutyń to Ukta (about 4 hours). Most outfitters deliver both you and the equipment to the set-off point and then pick everyone up at any of the stopover or finishing points. The season begins in May and continues through October; July and August are the busiest.

For multi-day tours, there are various overnight options. Along the route, campsites run by **PTTK** (www.mazurypttk.pl) are located in Sorkwity, Bienki, Babięta, Krutyń, Zgon, and Kamień. The chalets cost about 25 zł per person. To pitch your own tents, the fee is 15 zł per person. If you don't care to rough it, look for outfitters like **Hotel Habenda** (Krutyń 42, Piecki; ✆ **89/742-12-18;** www.habenda.com), which will pack you out for the day and ferry you back to the hotel's comfort at day's end.

There are many outfitters in Krutyń, a one-main-street town. ***Note:*** There are no ATMs here—the nearest is in Piecki, 11km (6¾ miles) away—so make sure you have enough cash with you to cover rental, food, and accommodation expenses. As a guideline for rental costs, refer to **AS-Tours's** website ★★ (Krutyń 4, Piecki; ✆ **89/742-14-30** or 601/650-669; www.masuria-canoeing.com), which has been in the business for over 20 years.

CYCLING Nature-loving biking fiends could spend a week zigzagging the Lake District. Pick up the cycling routes from the tourist information office and a 1:50,000 map of *Wielkie Jeziora Mazurskie* by Tessa. For newcomers, a popular choice is the 60km (37-mile) Giżycko-to-Sztynort round-trip. Dismount at Sztynort to see the 300-year-old oak trees in the park of the derelict 16th-century palace of the Lehndorf family. Pressing on, it's storks galore. The historical **Red Route** takes you westward from Giżycko to the Wolf's Lair. You can push on westerly to **Kętrzyn** to see a mid–14th-century Teutonic castle. Puff on another 13km (8 miles) on Road no. 594, and you'll come to the celebrated baroque church in **Święta Lipka.**

Locals lug their bikes with them. Most hotels have bikes for rent for about 40 zł per day. For well-maintained wheels and the gear needed for longer trips, contact **Techmet TC ★** (Zwycięstwa 38, Piecki; ✆ **89/742-21-04** or 607/132-314; www.rowery-mazury.com). Their bikes go for 25 zł per day. There are no charges for delivery up to 20km (12 miles) from Piecki. Otherwise, it's 1 zł per kilometer. When you're done, they'll pick them up from anywhere you've landed. Ask for Monika; she speaks English.

HUNTING The wide expanse of woods and meadows is fertile ground for big- and small-game hunting. Most common are wild boar, deer, and birds. Hunting in Poland is strictly regulated. As such, it has the reputation as one of the top hunting grounds on the continent, attracting hunters from Scandinavian and other European countries. **Dzikie Mazury** (Wyszowate 44; ✆ **87/421-15-50** or 604/636-691; www.dzikiemazury.eu), 16km (10 miles) from Giżycko, is a licensed hunting office that organizes outings in the northeastern region. The autumn-to-winter season is from October to February, while the spring-to-summer season starts in May. Contact the office to sort out the paperwork for firearms and hunting permits prior to your arrival. The company is affiliated with **Hotel Myśliwski** (Wyszowate k/Giżycka 44, Miłki; ✆ **87/421-15-50;** www.hotelmysliwski.pl), which does full-board lodging for hunters.

ORGANIZED TOURS A great way to explore the region is to combine cycling and canoeing. **Kampio** ★ (Os. Wichrowe Wzgorze 22/143, Poznan; ✆ **61/223-27-94;** www.kampio.com.pl) specializes in stitching together scenic stretches and historical attractions. The 7- to 8-day packages (about 2,600 zł) are popular with German tourists. They also have self-guided packages.

Where to Stay & Dine

In Giżycko, the moderately priced **Hotel Cesarski** (Pl. Grunwaldzki 8; ✆ **87/428-15-14**; 250 zł double) is good for a night if you need a central location to get your bearings. It's newly renovated and a short walk from the tourist information center. If you want to stay in a castle, there are two to choose from. The 14th-century **Zamek Reszel** ★ (Podzamcze 3, Reszel; ✆ **89/755-01-09;** www.zamek-reszel.com; 280 zł double) was for 500 years the seat of bishops. It now has a Polish restaurant where the dishes are reasonably priced, and the rooms combine medieval ambience with contemporary creature comforts. A much bigger cousin is **Zamek Ryn** (Plac Wolności 2, Ryn; ✆ **87/429-70-00;** www.zamekryn.pl; 450 zł double). It doesn't feel as authentic as Zamek Reszel, but it has more amenities. Both places are about 20km (12 miles) from Giżycko.

AROUND GIŻYCKO

Old Mill Inn (Karczma Stary Młyn) ★ This heritage mill, dating from the turn of 20th century, fell into disrepair after World War II, but the current owner has lovingly restored it. There are four small rooms in the attic, and another four were added recently. Antique bed frames (two rooms have wrought-iron bedposts) stand on the pinewood floorboards. Throughout the petite, homey establishment, the emphasis is on bygone rustic life. The restaurant opens to the public late in the morning, which means if you spend the night, you have the whole place to yourselves for an unhurried breakfast of pancakes and scrambled eggs. Visitors come for the regional fare, such as *plińce,* a potato-and-pork patty drizzled with fresh mushroom sauce.

Upałty 2, Giżycko (10km/6¼ miles south of Giżycko). ✆ **87/429-27-18.** www.karczma-upalty.com. 8 units. July & Aug 170 zł double; May, June & Sept 140 zł double; Oct–Apr 120 zł double. AE, DC, MC, V. Free parking. Head south from Giżycko on Rd. no. 63; turn left about 8km (5 miles) from town onto Rd. no. 655, which leads to the inn. **Amenities:** Restaurant; Wi-Fi (free). *In room:* TV, no phone.

Pod Czarnym Łabędziem ★ Some say no trip to the Mazury is complete without a visit to this restaurant-inn-campsite-marina, situated on the southern bank of the picturesque Lake Niegocin. The 100-year-old stable, with whitewashed walls reinforced by exposed dark wood beams, has been converted into guest rooms and a restaurant. In the cottage-style rooms, you'll find pinewood headboards and creamy bedcovers. Request the rooms at the lake's end (as opposed to the road). The barn-style restaurant buzzes with the hustle and bustle of vacationers. Waitresses in blue folk-style pinafores deliver *dzyndzałki* (regional pierogi) and excellent house-brewed beers.

Rydzewo k/Giżycka. ✆ **87/421-12-52.** www.gospoda.pl. 17 units. 220 zł double. AE, DC, MC, V. Parking 10 zł. **Amenities:** Restaurant; bike rental. *In room:* TV, Wi-Fi (free).

AROUND MIKOŁAJKI

Potocki Gałkowo (Dwór Łowczego) ★★ Part of the same Mazurian conservation group as **Oberża Pod Psem** (see below), this is rustic simplicity and genteel sophistication rolled up into one. The owner, Alexander Potocki (of Polish aristocratic lineage), led the restoration work of the heritage buildings. Rooms (some with shared bathrooms) are found in three wood-and-brick cottages, all which feature vintage farm and riding paraphernalia. The restaurant is a busy operation all week from May to September. Off season, fans have to wait until the weekend. The compact menu has items that confound even those familiar with Polish cuisine. *Zsiadłe mleko z ziemniakami* (potatoes cooked in sour milk) is a peasant dish that's a rarity these days.

Gałkowo 46, Gałkowo (20km/12 miles south of Mikołajki). ✆ **87/425-70-73.** www.galkowo.pl. 20 units. 135 zł double. AE, MC, V. Free parking. **Amenities:** Restaurant; Wi-Fi (free).

Oberża Pod Psem ★★ You're assured of a taste of old Mazurian village life at this pension. The owners are ardent conservationists and champions of Mazurian folk culture. They salvaged the centenarian wooden buildings (some from other parts of the country) to set up a restaurant, an ethnographical museum, and rooms to let. The cottage, which sleeps six, has functioning traditional heaters and a kitchen. The double rooms are in the same rural vein, with incredible attention put on details such as door handles, locks, and hinges. However, you can still access the Internet in the garden, which blooms with hollyhocks and wildflowers. The informal homeyness extends to the restaurant, a magnet for foodies. *Wereszczaki* (pork braised in beetroot sauce) is a rare find anywhere in the country.

Kadzidłowo 1, Ukta (12km/7½ miles south of Mikołajki). ✆ **87/425-74-74** or 601/094-641. www.oberzapodpsem.com. 4 units. 120 zł double; 250 zł–450 zł cottage. No credit cards. Free parking. From Mikołajki, take Rd. no. 609 & turn right into a dirt road at the Kadzidłowo road sign. **Amenities:** Restaurant; sauna w/traditional stone heating. *In room:* Wi-Fi (free).

AUGUSTÓW & THE SUWAŁKI LAKE DISTRICT

Arriving from the Mazury to the Suwałki (Suwalszczyna) Lake District, you can't help but notice how much wilder the terrain seems. You are not wrong. This most northeasterly part of Poland, whose borders touch Russia, Lithuania, and Belarus, has the lowest population density in the country. Even for Poles, this is uncharted territory.

The Suwałki region boasts the most talked about kayaking routes. The Rospuda, Czarna Hańcza, and Biebrza rivers are linked by the Augustów Canal, resulting in over 100km (62 miles) of connected waterways. With the Schengen Zone agreement, you are free to wander into neighboring countries (except Russia) without a visa.

Augustów (pronounced *aw-goos'-stoof*) is a good stepping-off point into the region due to its strategic location amid lakes and parklands. Founded in 1550, the town lost most of its architectural beauty to battles ranging from the 17th-century Tatar invasion to World War II, when 70% of the town was reduced to rubble. The regional capital is Suwałki, 30km (19 miles) to the north of Augustów. But the main roads and railway reach Augustów first before trundling northward to Suwałki and beyond. To the north of Augustów is the Wigry National Park, while Biebrzański National Park spans the southern rims. In the east is the Augustów Forest, one of Poland's largest continuous woodlands. Augustów is the finishing line for the Rospuda and Czarna Hańcza water routes. Via the Augustów Canal, you can access the Biebrza River.

The tourism infrastructure here is not as extensive as in the Mazury, but many outfitters are based in and around Augustów.

Essentials

GETTING THERE

By car from Warsaw, Road no. 61 leads you to Augustów. It's about 260km (162 miles) and 4 hours on fairly good and very scenic roads. From Giżycko, it's a 108km (67-mile) journey. Road no. 16 takes you here in about 1½ hours. Daily trains (www.pkp.pl) and buses (www.pks.pl) leave from Warsaw and the towns in the Mazurian Lake District for Augustów. From Warsaw, the journey time for bus and rail is about 4½ hours. The **railway station** (Kolejowa 1; ✆ **194-36**) is 3km (1¾ miles) from the center. The **bus station** (Rynek Zygmunta Augusta 19; ✆ **87/643-36-49**) is in the town square.

VISITOR INFORMATION

The **tourist information center** (Rynek Zygmunta Augusta 44; ✆ **87/643-28-83;** www.augustow.pl) is in a modern building in the town square. In July and August, it operates Monday through Saturday from 8am to 8pm. The rest of the year, it's open weekdays only from 8am to 3pm. The earnest staff speaks passable English. Aside from maps and accommodation listings, they have bus schedules and current listings of bicycle, canoe, and kayak rentals; excursion organizers; and fishing information.

GETTING AROUND

Most of the kayak and bike rentals, and tour guides, set up shop on Nadrzeczna on the south side of River Netta and on Portowa and Zarzecze on the northern bank. To get beyond Augustów, you can arrange with your outfitter for transport; many are willing to collect you from Augustów. The **PKS** bus service (www.pks.suwalki.com.pl) serves the region.

Outdoor Activities

CANOEING & KAYAKING The paddling season is from May to September, peaking in July and August. The best time to paddle on the Biebrza River is in late spring. In the summer, the reeds shoot up and waterweeds clog the passage. To see the spring flooding on this river, you should aim for mid- to late April. Outfitters cater to one- and multi-day outings, delivering paddlers and equipment to the drop-off points. When you're done, call them, and they'll come to ferry you back to your campsite or hotel. Since you pay for the transportation (about 2 zł per km for up to eight people), it makes economic sense to select an outfitter that is located closer to your chosen trail. In July and August, it's advisable to call at least a day ahead to book. Rental prices range from 25 zł to 40 zł per day. For the Augustów Canal, have cash available for the locks, about 3 zł per vessel. Get the schedule of the locks' operating hours at the tourist information office. In Augustów, the **Augustów Canoe Center ★★** (✆ **501/274-244;** www.frontierpoland.com) not only will equip you, but also will load you up with tips and advice. Another outfitter with extensive

Rivers (and Canals) Run through It

The waterways are the perfect conduits for accessing the natural and man-made marvels of this area. The landscape varies from reed-filled marshlands to pine and coniferous hills. Connecting the 11 rivers and seven lakes is the **Augustów Canal (Kanał Augustowski),** a heritage canal dating from 1823, which is older than both the Suez and Panama canals. From Augustów, it stretches east to the Niemen River in Belarus—never reaching the Baltic Sea in Latvia, for work was interrupted by the November Uprising (1830–31). The 101km-long (63-mile) waterway is a hydraulic engineering marvel with lovely water locks along the way. Part of the fun of kayaking on the canal is to be huddled into the narrow lock channels, bobbing up or down as the water level rises or drops.

The **Rospuda River,** the second longest in the Suwałki region, is rated as an intermediate kayaking route and also is one of the loveliest. It takes 5 days to negotiate the route if you start at the village of Supienie (68km/42 miles northwest of Augustów). The **Czarna Hańcza River** (to the northeast of Augustów) has a section for experts and another for novices. From Lake Hańcza (the deepest lake in the country) to Lake Wigry is a 47km (29-mile) route of adrenaline-pumping steep drops. Beginners can kick off from the picturesque Lake Wigry and meander from marshland into the woods of Augustów Forest. Along the riverside settlements, local peddlers tempt you with *pączki* (donuts) and cold beer. The woody stretch from Frącki to Mikaszówka is considered the prettiest.

experience is **Szot** (Konwaliowa 2; ✆ **87/644-67-58;** www.szot.pl), which mainly deals with large Polish groups. **Łukowy Kąt ★** (Stary Folwark 44; ✆ **87/563-77-89** or 693/705-487; www.wigry.info) has its base at the Lake Wigry starting point of the Czarna Hańcza route. Bogdan Łukowscy, the amicable owner, says he speaks "easy" English.

CYCLING This is great cycling terrain because, even in the peak of summer, there aren't hordes of bicycles. There are plenty of well-marked routes, plus the Eurovelo (European cycle route) R11 crosses the region on its way from Athens to Oslo. The 1:85,000 laminated maps by ExpressMap are good resources. In general, the routes in Augustów Forest and Biebrza valley are flat tarmac, dirt, or sandy tracks. Farther afield in Wigry National Park and Suwałki Landscape Park, the undulating terrain means panting and puffing, followed by exhilarating freewheeling. Most kayak rentals have bikes for hire, too. Rent yours from the multitasking Andrew of the **Augustów Canoe Center** (see "Canoeing & Kayaking," above) or **Jan Wojtuszko** (Nadrzeczna 62A; ✆ **87/644-75-40;** www.sprzetwodny.prv.pl) for about 25 zł per day.

BOAT EXCURSIONS The leisure boats run by **Żegluga Augustowska** (29 Listopada 7; ✆ **87/643-28-81;** www.zeglugaaugustowska.pl) are a relaxing way to see the scenery along the lakes and canals. From May to September, the daily rounds start at about 9:30am. Tours last from 1 to 2 hours and cost 30 zł to 40 zł.

FISHING The Suwałki region is blessed with fish-rich clear waters. What makes it hassle-free for tourists is the consolidated information on where to fish and where to get your permits. The list of lakes for angling can be obtained at the tourist information office in Augustów or at the regional fishery office website (www.pzw.suwalki.com.

pl). Permits (20 zł per day) can be bought at the **post office** (Rynek Zygmunta Augusta 3; ✆ **87/643-32-33**) or at some fishing equipment shops, such as **J. Kamiński** (Mostowa 24; ✆ **87/644-75-85**). If you need gear, you'll find plenty of fishing equipment stores *(sklep wędkarstwo)*.

HORSE-RIDING The Augustów Forest is frequented by horse-riders throughout the year. Outings can be as short as an hour (30 zł) or multiple days (100 zł per day). **Ostoja ★** (Kalinowa 15; ✆ **513/004-470;** www.ostoja.augustow.pl) has an English-speaking owner who will saddle you up on Arabian steeds. The same family also runs a guesthouse; it's comfortable and fairly priced, but located by a busy road.

ICE SAILING Winter in this region is much more severe than the rest of the country, giving rise to ice-sailing *(bojery)* opportunities. The sport resembles windsurfing on ice, an extreme sport practiced in very few places on Earth. For it to happen, the surface of the frozen lake must be snow-free, a condition that is harder to come by in recent years. The best chance is in January and February. If you're tempted, get a Polish speaker to contact Jarek Ossowski of **Nord-Way** (Zarzecze 1; ✆ **608/504-974**) at the Schroniska Młodzieżowe for equipment and user instructions.

WILDLIFE-WATCHING Ornithologists from around the world flock to this region. The early spring flooding of the Biebrza River more or less coincides with the return of migratory birds when, in Augustów, cranes, storks, and graylag geese fill the sky. On the canals, there are goldeneye duck, mergansers, and marsh harriers. May is when the birds do their courtship song and dance. September, as the nomads get set to bolt for winter, is another great time for bird-gazing. The ultimate bird safari is in the marshlands of Biebrza National Park to the south of Augustów. **Augustów Canoe Center ★★** (see "Canoeing & Kayaking," above) has customized tours. So does Katarzyna Ramotowska of **Biebrza Eco-Travel ★★** (Kościuszki, Goniądz; ✆ **85/738-07-85;** www.biebrza.com), who specializes in the **Biebrzański National Park** (www.biebrza.org.pl) area. She also has special programs for kids.

Beyond Poland

From Augustów, tour operators offer single and multi-day bus trips into neighboring countries such as Estonia, Latvia, Lithuania, and Russia. With the exception of Russia, the countries are within the Schengen Zone, so there's no visa hassles. You can look into the options offered by **Ela-Travel** (Rynek Zygmunta Augusta 15/2; ✆ **87/643-55-00;** www.netta.pl/elatravel). If there's any language problem, Bart from Korona (see "Where to Dine," below) downstairs can assist.

Where to Stay

AUGUSTÓW

Logos ★ This uninspiring, squat building hides remarkably comfortable rooms where the walls are a cheerful orange and the cotton sheets are whiter than white. The sparkling-clean bathrooms have basic toiletries. The setup may remind you of Communist leftovers, but the service is helpful and warm.

29 Listopada 9. ✆ **87/643-20-21.** Fax 87/643-54-10. www.augustow-dn.pl. 48 units. 145 zł double. AE, DC, MC, V. Parking 15 zł. **Amenities:** Restaurant; bike rental; spa. *In room:* TV, Wi-fi (free).

Szuflada Café & Bar Conveniently located on a side street of the main square, this new hotel has tastefully furnished, minimalistic modern rooms with squeaky-clean bathrooms. Bedcovers, chairs, and carpets are coordinated in shades of brown.

There are no elevators, but the friendly staff will help you with your luggage up the stairs. At the cafe, you can tuck in to the 16 types of pancakes; the best is the mushroom.

Ks Skorupki 2c. ✆ **87/644-63-15.** Fax 87/643-11-65. www.szuflada.augustow.pl. 7 units. May–Sept 170 zł double; Oct–Apr 140 zł double. AE, MC, V. Parking 5 zł. **Amenities:** Cafe; bar. *In room:* A/C (in some), TV, Wi-Fi (free).

OUTSIDE AUGUSTÓW

Dom Pracy Twórczej ★ Constructed on a breathtaking and dreamy hilltop in the wilderness of the Wigry Peninsula, this complex is a former Camaldolese monastery dating from 1694. Even though it doesn't have 5-star trimmings, you'll still get more than monastic simplicity here with homey furnishings reminiscent of house-proud Polish grannies. The *erem* (hermitages used by monks for contemplation) have private gardens and shared bathrooms on the lower level. **Dom Wigierski Restaurant** snatched the top place in a regional culinary showdown for its baked carp with berry sauce. On summer days, busloads of tourist come to visit the church, crypt, and the Papal Apartment, where Pope John Paul II resided in 1999. But at dusk, when a sublime serene peace pervades the peninsula, you'll have the place all to yourself.

Stary Folwark. ✆ **87/563-70-00.** www.wigry.org. 43 units. May–Aug 150 zł double w/shared bathroom, 170 zł double; Sept-Apr 120 zł double w/shared bathroom, 140 zł double. MC, V. Free parking. On Road no. 653 from Suwalki to Sejny; do not turn into Stary Folwark, instead keep going & turn right at Ryżówka (about 3km/1¾ miles from Stary Folwark). ***Note:*** Reception desk closes at 9pm. **Amenities:** Restaurant; Wi-Fi (in restaurant, free). *In room:* TV, no phone.

Gościniec Jaczno (Jaczno Lodge) ★★★ This cluster of stone-and-timber houses, on a peninsula in the Suwałki Landscape Park, is hemmed in by woods and the pristine, aquamarine water of Lake Jaczno. Since this lodge is far from Augustów, it's for those who want to stay put and enjoy the surroundings. The owners are architects who have designed every space—from the rooms, to the lounge and bar, to the rose-bush– and fruit-tree–strewn garden—to be picture perfect. People-shy guests have many cozy nooks and crannies to escape to, both indoors and outdoors, including a secluded pier. There are no restaurants in the vicinity, so unless you have a car, you'll have to go full board. Neighboring farms supply the milk, cheese, and meat, and veggies and herbs come from the lodge's own patch. Try out the steep hiking and cycling routes nearby, or ask for directions to farmsteads where you can milk cows or buy cheese.

Jaczno 3, Jeleniewo. ✆ **87/568-35-90.** Fax 87/568-35-91. www.jaczno.pl. 15 units. 290 zł–330 zł double. Lunch 35 zł; dinner 25 zł. No credit cards. On Rd. 655 heading north, go past Jeleniewo toward Gulbieniszki, then turn left into Gulbieniszki & drive through the village of Udziejek (you'll pass Gościniec Drumlin on the way); at a Y-crossing, follow the signs for Jaczno on right to property. **Amenities:** Dining room; bikes; sauna; *bania* (Russian sauna). *In room:* TV, minibar, Wi-Fi (free).

Where to Dine

AUGUSTÓW

Albatros ★ POLISH A legend with over 60 years service to the community, the locals even have a song about the seven girls who worked there. The dining room is updated, but the set menus are the evergreen combo of fish or meat, veggie, and starch, to be washed down with *kompot* (a fruit drink). Guests put up with the "where is the waitress?" service because of the delicious food at bargain prices. On the ground level, the **Bartek** eatery is a self-service outlet with typical Polish fares at milk bar prices.

Mostowa 3. ✆ **87/643-21-23.** www.spolem.augustow.pl. Main courses 13 zł–17 zł. MC, V. Daily noon–6pm.

Local Specialties Decoded

Kindziuk is a type of deli meat made from chopped and seasoned sirloin cooked in a pig's stomach. *Kartacze* are chubby potato dumplings filled with meat or lentils. Potatoes are also transformed into *babka ziemniaczana* (potato terrine) and *kiszka ziemniaczana* (potato sausage). The indigenous fish are *sielawa* and *sieja*. For dessert, you'll see the pyramidal *sękacz* everywhere. The batter (whipped up from 40 eggs, 1kg/2¼ lb. flour, sugar, butter, lemon juice, and vanilla essence) is poured over a rotary spit and baked layer by layer, creating the characteristic rings while the dripping dough hardens into spiky stalactites.

Korona ★★ REGIONAL Although this basement restaurant doesn't score well for its modern pub decor, it makes up for it with genial service and good food. The menu features Polish classics, including a steak *tartare* that will delight raw-food fans. Bart, the merry English-speaking owner, recommends the Lithuanian *kibiny* (a pork pastry), which you eat with your hands.

Rynek Zygmunta Augusta 15/3. ✆ **87/643-44-00.** www.korona.augustow.pl. Main courses 9 zł–40 zł. AE, DC, MC, V. Daily noon–10pm.

Ogródek Pod Jabłoniami ★★ 🎁 REGIONAL "The Apple Garden" (as the name translates) blossomed from a seasonal alfresco eatery into an all-weather and year-round establishment. It's the same yummy and fairly priced sustenance delivered by an English-speaking couple. Paweł rustles up pizzas and sautés the catch of the day, while Sylwia's mother upholds the traditional front with chanterelle soup and *kartacze*.

Rybacka 1. ✆ **516/025-606.** Main courses 10 zł–40 zł. No credit cards. Daily noon–10pm.

BIAŁYSTOK & ENVIRONS

Białystok (pronounced *byah-way'-stok*), the regional capital, has a history that dates back to the 15th century. In this part of the country, it will become obvious to you that Poland was once a multiethnic territory. The region served under various flags, from Polish to Prussian, Russian, and Lithuanian, and was at one time ceded to Belarus. While the rest of the country was also subjected to the winds of change, this area has managed to hang on to the tangible evidence, the most prevalent being the onion-domed Orthodox churches. Today, about one third of Białystok's residents are of the Orthodox faith, and the region has the largest Orthodox population in the country. It's common to see a Catholic cross and a three-bar cross standing side-by-side, bearing proof to the religious harmony. In Supraśl ★, the Church of Annunciation stands out for merging a prayer chamber and a defense fortress. Behind the church is the Museum of Icons ★ that gives excellent coverage of Orthodox religious icons.

Until 1939, about half of Białystok's population were Jewish. Many were involved in the textile industry in the region, and the factories operated until 1944, when the retreating Nazis burned them down. Like most places in Poland, the Jewish communities here never recovered from the war. Today, there are hardly any traces of their presence, except the 17th century synagogue in Tykocin ★.

Tatars, whose lineage is traced back to the Mongol empire of Genghis Khan, settled in the region in the 17th century under the patronage of King Jan III Sobieski, who rewarded them with lands for their vital role in the Battle of Vienna (1683). The majority of the Tatars' descendants are in present-day Belarus, while those in Poland have assimilated into local communities. The Tatar Route tracks through their former settlements. Only two Tatar wooden mosques are left. One is in Kruszyniany ★, and the other is in Bohoniki.

While Białystok's blend of classical attractions, like an Old Town, interspersed with Communist-era structures does yield unexpectedly enjoyable explorations, you don't need to budget much time for the city itself. Instead, use it as your base and allocate time for visiting the points of interest outside the city.

Essentials

GETTING THERE & AROUND

BY CAR Well-paved roads take you to Białystok, 193km (120 miles) northeast of Warsaw, in under 3 hours. Kruszyniany, Supraśł, and Tykocin are all within 30 to 58km (19–36 miles) from Białystok.

BY TRAIN & BUS Białystok is the main transportation hub in the area. There are daily trains to Białystok **train station** (Kolejowa 9; ✆ **194-36**) from Warsaw and other major towns. From Białystok **bus station** (Bohaterów Monte Cassino 10; ✆ **193-16;** www.pks.bialystok.pl), hourly buses run to Supraśl and Tykocin. Both destinations take under an hour. The service to Supraśl presses on to Kruszyniany three times a day. Travel time from Białystok is about 1½ hours.

VISITOR INFORMATION

Białystok has an impressively well-run **tourist information center** (Malmeda 6; ✆ **85/732-68-31;** www.podlaskieit.pl). It is also the regional information headquarters, so they also have information on the attractions outside Białystok. The office is open weekdays from 8am to 5pm. Another **tourist information point** (Kolejowa 9/10; ✆ **85/673-35-75**) is at the railway station; it's open weekdays 8am to 8pm.

Top Attractions

BIAŁYSTOK

Unlike a typical *rynek* (market square), the handsomely restored **Rynek Kościuszki** isn't a square but an elongated triangle. To the south of the Rynek, you'll find the city's landmark: the baroque-style **Branicki Palace** ★ (Kilińskiego 1), built for Count Jan Klemens Branicki in 1726 with the aim of outshining the Wilanów Palace in Warsaw. Nazis wrecked the building, and it was reconstructed after the war. The modernized interior is now a medical academy, but the surrounding manicured gardens are good for photo opportunities. Also a casualty of the Nazis was the **Great Synagogue** (Suraska 3A), burned down in 1941 with an estimated 2,000 Jews trapped inside. A monument, in the skeletal shape of a dome, stands in its place. You'll find it behind the BGŻ Bank. To see the other historical sites and monuments, pick up *A Stroll in Białystok* from the Tourist Information office.

Church of the Holy Spirit ★ The largest Orthodox Church in Poland was built in 1982, and it has a delightfully unconventional, modern design. Its one central dome flanked by four smaller ones resembles a rising flame from afar. At press time, a new tower was being constructed. The doors are closed except during prayer services. On weekdays, they are held at 8:30am in the smaller basement level prayer room. You can ask to be taken up to the main prayer room to see golden icons and frescoes. On Sunday, there are three services (8:15, 10am, and 5pm) in the main hall. To view the interior at other times, contact the office in advance.

Antoniuk Fabryczy 13. ✆ **85/653-28-54.** www.orthodox.bialystok.pl. Free admission. Church office Mon–Fri 8–11am & 3–5pm. Bus: 5 from Lipowa St.

KRUSZYNIANY

Mosque and Cemetery ★ The oldest mosque in Poland is a late–18th-century wooden building hidden behind a patch of trees. It bears a striking similarity to small wooden Orthodox churches because carpenters of Orthodox faith built it for the Tatars. During Prince Charles' 2010 official visit to Poland, he visited this mosque. You are to remove your shoes before stepping into the carpeted prayer room. In itself, the chamber doesn't tell you much, so let mosque guide Dżemil Gembick fill you in. About 200m (656 ft.) behind the mosque is a *mizar* (Muslim cemetery) where the oldest tombstone dates from 1699.

Kruszyniany. ✆ **502/543-871.** kruszyniany@op.pl. 4 zł adults. May–Aug daily 9am–7pm; Sept–Apr call ahead.

SUPRAŚL

Orthodox Monastery ★★ The main attractions in town are in the Monastery compound, located to the north of Supraśl's town center. Founded in the early 16th century, the monks here had substantial influence in the religious life within and beyond Białystok's borders. It hasn't always been smooth sailing for the monks, though: In 1915, as the German army closed in, the monks escaped to Russia, taking with them precious religious objects, including the Supraśl Icon of Mother of God. After World War II, the buildings were taken over by postwar authorities. Monastic life was finally reinstated in the 1980s. The monastery now conducts regular prayer services, summoning believers to worship with church bells that don't exactly chime but chant, in an upbeat manner. Listening to the "call to prayer" is an unforgettable experience.

Klasztorna 1. www.orthodox.bialystok.pl/en/suprasl.htm. Free admission. Tues–Fri 10am–3pm & 4–5pm; Sat 10:30am–3pm & 4–5pm; Sun 2–5pm Services Mon–Sat 5:30pm, Sunday 9:45am.

Church of the Annunciation ★ Built in the early 16th century, the church is a unique specimen of a fortified temple that merges Byzantine and Gothic architectural styles. The main cornice is lined with orifices that were used as rifle ranges, while the prayer chamber was richly decorated with icons and frescoes. In 1944, retreating Nazis demolished the church. What you see now was rebuilt in 1984, but the interior walls are still plaster-bare. You can see the 16th-century post-Byzantine frescos, salvaged from two pillars in the rubble, and a model of the original interior in the Museum of Icons (see below).

Klasztorna 1. ✆ **85/713-37-80.** Free admission (donations accepted). Tues–Fri 10am–3pm & 4–5pm; Sat 10:30am–3pm & 4–5pm; Sun 2–5pm.

Museum of Icons ★★ The strength of this museum is not so much in its extensive collections of Eastern Orthodox icons in Poland, although they are impressive, but in the way it has laid out the 350 exhibits to give you a multi-sensory experience and insight into Orthodox religious art and history. Icons are religious works of art that are an integral part of daily prayers. Eighty percent of the samples here were confiscated from smugglers trying to take them across Poland's eastern borders. The works are segregated into nine thematic rooms; the oldest piece dates from the mid-16th century, but 90% are from the 18th to 19th centuries. Most icons were painted on wood, but there are also elaborate metal crosses and simpler metal pendants found in the Traveler's Icon room. Some halls have audio-inputs of liturgical chants or church bells; in the last room, which exhibits the 16th-century post-Byzantine murals, a roar of collapsing brick and mortar is played to demonstrate 1944 bombing (see Church of the Annunciation, above). Guided tour lasts about an hour; book the English-language tours in advance.

Klasztorna 1. ✆ **85/718-35-06.** www.muzeum.bialystok.pl/suprasl. 10 zł adults, 5 zł seniors & children; English guides 40 zł. May–Sept Tues–Sun noon–7pm; Oct–Apr Tues–Sun 10am–5pm.

TYKOCIN

From the 16th to 17th centuries, Tykocin was one of the most influential Jewish communities outside Kraków. In August 1941, 2,500 Jewish men, women, and children, 50% of Tykocin's population, were marched to the nearby Łupochowo forest and murdered by the Nazis. The victims were buried in mass graves. In the Jewish Quarter, the baroque-style synagogue, built in 1642, miraculously survived the war. Today, it is one of the oldest and finest examples of Polish Orthodox synagogues. Visitors tracing Jewish history tend to combine Tykocin with a visit to Treblinka (see p. 91) on the same day.

Museum of Jewish Culture ★★ Religious services where conducted in this 17th-century synagogue until the Nazis plundered it. The building made it through the war by serving as a warehouse, and it continued to be used for storage after the war. It became a museum in 1977 after extensive restoration works. The frescos on the walls are original and were recovered from beneath layers of white paint during the 1970s. They depict decorative Hebrew text from the Holy Scripture and the names of donors. The focal points of the main hall are the *bima* (a raised platform for holding prayer services) and the Holy Ark (used for storing Torah scriptures). The adjacent room has a small display of black-and-white photos and objects belonging to Tykocin Jews. For English-speaking guides, call in advance.

Kozia 2. ✆ **85/718-16-13.** www.muzeum.bialystok.pl/tykocin. 10 zł adults; 5 zł seniors & children. Tues–Sun 10am–5pm.

Where to Stay

BIAŁYSTOK

Branicki ★★ It's named after the region's top nobility family, and the Branicki would be proud of this hotel, not only for supplying posh rooms and quality toiletries, but also for deploying a highly professional staff. The central location is an additional plus. Breakfast here is something special, too.

Zamenhofa 25. ✆ **85/665-25-00.** Fax 85/665-25-01. www.hotelbranicki.com. 32 units. 370 zł double. AE, DC, MC, V. Parking 30 zł. **Amenities:** Restaurant; room service. *In room:* TV, hair dryer, Internet (free), minibar.

Gołębiewski ☺ The hotel is an ugly tower block, the receptionist is haughty, and the lobby is tacky. So, you'd be surprised to find tastefully furnished rooms. It's a bit further from the center than Hotel Cristal, which is in same price bracket, but Gołębiewski's newly renovated bathrooms are far superior. The huge pool with slides and three types of Jacuzzi should please the kids.

Pałacowa 7. ✆ **85/678-25-00.** Fax 85/678-25-00. www.golebiewski.pl. 218 units. 300 zł double. AE, MC, V. Parking 20 zł. **Amenities:** Restaurant; bar; pool. *In room:* TV, Internet (free).

Villa Tradycja ★★ It's not quite traditional, but it's elegant in a modern, minimalistic way from the bedrooms to the bathrooms, and it's manned by a genial team. A leisurely 10-minute walk will get you to the center of town. If you feel like a swim, there's a public pool opposite the villa.

Włókiennicza 5. ✆ **85/652-65-20.** Fax 85/744-88-33. www.villatradycja.pl. 28 units. 260 zł double. AE, MC, V. Parking 15 zł. **Amenities:** Restaurant; bar. *In room:* A/C, TV, hair dryer, Internet (free), minibar.

OUTSIDE BIAŁYSTOK

Villa Regent This new pension next to the synagogue is a welcome respite from rough and ready guestrooms in the villages. The rooms are spacious and have comfortable, modern furnishing. You'll find a good standard bathroom behind the wooden double-paneled door. The restaurant plays host to communions and wedding parties, giving you a glimpse of contemporary Polish culture.

Sokołowska 3, Tykocin. ✆ **502/332-886.** 8 units. 150 zł double. MC, V. Free parking. **Amenities:** Restaurant; canoe rental. *In room:* TV, Wi-Fi (free).

Where to Dine

BIAŁYSTOK

You can eat very well here without straining your budget. **Podlasie** (Rynek Kościuszki 15; ✆ **85/742-25-04;** www.spolem.bialystok.pl) is Białystok's traditional milk bar, complete with authentic metal trays and chrome furniture.

Astoria ★ POLISH Astoria is something of a food empire that has been around since time immemorial. In the older building is an elegant, tablecloth dining room where high-end dishes include chicken with spinach and cheese. Locals favor the adjacent self-service newer annex diner, which doles out items based on the recipes of a Polish celebrity chef. Finally, you can choose from a selection of desserts, most of them are under 10 zł, in their third-floor cafe that has a balcony with a view of the Rynek.

Sienkiewicza 4. ✆ **85/665-21-50.** www.astoriacentrum.pl. Main courses 27 zł–62 zł. DC, MC, V. Mon–Fri 1–10pm; Sat 1pm–2am; Sun noon–10pm.

Hort-Café POLISH Hort-Cafés were born during Communism. Most of them have died out with the introduction of capitalism, but this one does a brisk trade. The cottage-cheese pancakes and salads are constantly refreshed with new batches. They offer more than what you can see in the buffet, like pizzas. Place your order at the cashier, and when it's ready, they'll call out your number over the loudspeaker.

M. C. Skłodowskiej 15. ✆ **85/744-70-34.** www.hort-cafe.pl. Main courses 2 zł–10 zł. No credit cards. Daily 8am–8:30pm.

OUTSIDE BIAŁYSTOK

Tatarska Jurta ★★ TATAR You can fill up here on Tatar cuisine made by Tatar descendants. "Fill up" because the portion size could keep a warrior going for days. Even those familiar with the regional cuisine will find new bites like *bielusz* (bread filled with turkey and pumpkin). They recently applied for an EU local specialty tag for their *pierekaczewnik* (a meat-filled pastry).

Kruszyniany 58. ✆ **85/749-40-52.** www.kruszyniany.pl. Main courses 15 zł–18 zł. No credit cards. Daily 11am–6pm.

Tejsza POLISH/JEWISH The curator of the Museum of Jewish Culture endorses this genial, rustic-style eatery near the synagogue. In Yiddish, *tejsza* means "goat," which was revered by local Jews as a symbol of luck and prosperity. The food isn't kosher, but it's a treat for those partial to sweet and sour tastes, such as *cymes* (beef goulash with carrots, nuts, and honey), and liver or fish in raisin and honey sauces. An unsweetened dish is the very memorable *kreplech* (meat dumplings).

Kozia 2, Tykocin. ✆ **85/718-77-50.** http://tejsza.restauracja.w.interia.pl. Main courses 15 zł–30 zł. No credit cards. Daily 10am–7pm.

BIAŁOWIEŻA

Białowieża (pronounced *byah-wo-vie'-za*), 2km (1¼ miles) from the Belarusian border, is synonymous with the European bison. Hunted to near-extinction by soldiers during World War II, the European bison has made a comeback in the sanctuary of the Białowieża National Park (BNP). Though the park covers a modest 105 sq. km (41sq. miles), it is one of Europe's last remaining parcels of primeval forest and, since 1979, has been on the UNESCO list of World Natural Heritage Sites. In addition to bison, the park shelters populations of deer, lynx, black storks, beaver, and wolf, as well as hundreds of species of birds and a staggering variety of trees, fungi, mushroom, and insects. So, no surprise—it's inundated by scientists from around the world.

However, flora and fauna aren't the only highlights. History has also left its marks on the landscape. The Białowieża Forest used to be the hunting grounds of Polish kings, Lithuanian princes, and Russian tsars. Once you make it this far to the eastern frontier, you'll naturally be drawn to the ethnic diversity left by Russians, Lithuanians, Belarusians, and Ukrainians, whose faiths range among Catholic, Orthodox, Protestant, and Adventism. Cycling in the woodlands is a great way to discover the onion-dome churches *(cierkiew)*, three-bar papal-cross cemeteries, 18th-century wooden architecture, and other historical sites in the vicinity. And with all these attractions, the tourism infrastructure here is well developed; there are even a couple of hotels that are destinations unto themselves.

Essentials

GETTING THERE

BY CAR From Warsaw, take Road E77 in the direction of Białystok. At Zambrów, turn southeast onto Road no. 66; it leads you to Hajnówka. From there, Road no. 689 takes you into the village of Białowieża. The distance from Warsaw is 258km (160 miles), and it should take about 3½ hours of drive time.

BY TRAIN & BUS There are daily trains from Warsaw's Central Station to Hajnówka. Depending on service, the journey time is about 4½ hours. **PKS** buses, outside the Hajnówka train station, depart for Białowieża up to eight times a day. There is also **Oktobus** (✆ **606/740-849;** www.oktobus.pl), a private bus company, with five daily services to Białowieża. The pickup point is also outside the railway station, near the church. The bus journey is about 30 minutes, and tickets are 5 zł. Alight after Hotel Żubrówka, near the PTTK office.

VISITOR INFORMATION

It would be ideal to make a pit stop at Hajnówka's **Białowieża Forest Regional Tourist Office** (3 Maja 45, Hajnówka; ✆ **85/682-43-81;** www.powiat.hajnowka.pl). They are open year-round Monday through Friday from 9am to 5pm and Saturday from 9am to 2pm. The information stock here is extensive, covering attractions such as the Orthodox churches in the area. And they hand out good maps with cycling routes, which you don't get for free in Białowieża. The **PTTK tourist agency**

(Kolejowa 17; ✆ **85/681-22-95;** www.pttk.bialowieza.pl) in Białowieża is good for hiring guides and arranging for bikes, rickshaws, and horse-drawn carts. In July and August, it's open daily 8am to 6pm; off-season, daily 8am to 4pm.

GETTING AROUND

Cycling is a popular mode for getting around during the warmer months. There are plenty of bike rentals for about 7 zł per hour or 30 zł per day. You'll also find that most accommodations have their own stash of bikes. In season, bicycle rickshaws (✆ **505/044-742**) take visitors to the Bison Reserve and other points of interest. The rides are 50 zł for two passengers. Horse-drawn carriages fit four but are meant for recreational rides, not as transportation. Any tourist agency and most lodgings can arrange this for you at around 140 zł for 2 hours.

Top Attractions

Your first stop will probably be the **Palace Park** (**Park Pałacowy;** Park Pałacowy 5; ✆ **85/681-29-01;** www.bpn.com.pl). The oldest building in the grounds was constructed in 1890 for Russian royalty. The site was originally the hunting grounds of Polish kings. There is no admission charge, and you can wander 'round the English-style lawns. The **Natural History Museum** (Park Pałacowy; ✆ **85/681-22-75**), which has an interesting coverage of the ecosystem and the history of the area, is also located here. You'll immediately notice the "juvenile" 250-year-old oak trees in front of the museum. To see older oaks, take the 3km (1.9-mile) yellow trail from the PTTK office to the **Royal Oaks (Dęby Królewskie)** ★. These magnificent specimens have clocked more than 400 years under their bark. Outside the eastern park entrance, you'll find the double-domed late–19th-century **St. Nicholas Orthodox Church** (Sportowa 9; ✆ **85/621-25-00;** www.bialowieza.cerkiew.pl). Church services are on weekends only (Saturday 5pm; Sunday 10am and 5pm). At other times, you'll have to call the office in advance in order to see the colorful icons within. With the exception of the **Strictly Protected Area** (SPA; see below), the rest of Białowieża National Park can be accessed with or without a guide.

European Bison Reserve (Rezerwat Pokazowy Zwierząt) ★ ☺ A ranch-style zoo showcasing a small but engaging selection of animals, namely the crowd-pulling European bison, from fully grown to young ones. Not to be missed are the tarpans, a species related to the extinct Eurasian wild horse that looks like something that has just stepped out of the Ice Age. Another oddity is zubron, the result of crossing European bison with domestic cattle. If you drag your feet, it will take an hour to see everything, including the lynx, elk, wild boar, wolves, stags, and roe deer.

3km (1¾ miles) west of the Palace Park. ✆ **85/681-23-98.** 6 zł adults; 3 zł seniors & children. May–Sept daily 9am–5pm; Oct–Apr Tues–Sun 8am–4pm. Follow the green or yellow trails from the PTTK office.

Number Crunching

The park area has about 500 European bison. An adult male can weigh up to 900kg (1,984 lb.); a female, 640kg (1,411 lb.). They may look like lumbering giants, but they are agile enough to clock 40kmph (25 mph) when charging.

Strictly Protected Area (SPA; Obszar Ochrony Ścisłej) ★★ The SPA is the oldest section of the park. A characteristic that distinguishes primeval parks from managed parks is that, for the former, no human intervention is permitted. So you'll find many dead trees left fallen (or standing) where they are. The name, along with the fact that you can access it only with a licensed guide, might lead you to think that this is a zone teeming with big game. The guides will tell you, "The problem with animals is, they move." You'll see birdlife, but mainly what you get is a fun stroll on muddy trails and wooden walkways among ancient foliage accompanied by an entertaining, fact-filled commentary on the park's origin, and animal and plant life. They'll point out fungus like dead man's fingers (which you might have dismissed as "something black and moldy") and tree trunks pockmarked by eight species of woodpeckers.

The routine tour is 7km (4¼ miles) and 3 hours long. You spend about 30 minutes getting to the SPA entrance. There's an option to get there by horse-drawn cart (140 zł per cart). The SPA is best in the morning when there is more animal activity. You can book a guide at any of the tourist offices or at the Natural History Museum, where you also purchase admission tickets to the SPA. If you book your guide at the museum, they can pool visitors together to split the guide's cost. No advanced booking is needed, but do call ahead to reserve a tour with Mateusz Szymura ★ (✆ **601/450-035;** bialowieza@tlen.pl), a particularly enjoyable guide at the BNP.

Park Pałacowy. ✆ **85/681-28-98.** www.bpn.com.pl. 6 zł adults; English-speaking guides 165 zł per group of 20. Daily dawn–dusk. Closed during storms or flooding.

Outdoor Activities

IN & AROUND BIAŁOWIEŻA

EUROPEAN BISON SIGHTING Although the image of the bison is slapped on every brochure and water, beer, and vodka bottle to promote the area, don't expect to encounter a bison lurking behind every tree. You are assured of seeing them in the Bison Reserve (see above). Sighting those living in the wild requires some luck and effort. ***Note:*** Bison are on the Red List of Endangered Species. As such, the BNP forbids activities that distress these animals, such as trailing them. Dogs are not allowed. Read the BNP's advisory on the do's and don'ts, and should you cross paths with a bison or a herd, keep your distance and do not startle them. You don't want tons of muscle charging at you.

To see the free-range bison, the BNP's recommendation is to go in winter, at dawn or dusk, to the public feeding stations. A shortage of vegetation in the forest brings the bison out to these hay huts, which are accessible to the public. There are observation platforms by the three feeding posts to the north of Białowieża at **Kosy Most, Czoło** (near Stare Masiewo village), and **Babia Góra.** At any time of the year, the general advice from licensed guides is to go for a walk and try your luck. The yellow trail to Topiło, the red trail to Narewka, and the green trail (also called the Wolves' Trail) are tracks with reportedly higher probability of bison sighting. ***Note:*** Park regulations require you to stay on the marked trails. You shouldn't be overly discouraged about your chances. The locals are blasé about the bison, claiming that the animals often graze at the perimeters of their homesteads (between the villages of Narewka and Siemianówka).

CYCLING Cycling routes crisscross the villages around Białowieża and are great for getting acquainted with the rich ethnic character of the region. Pick up the English-language *Bicycle Routes in the Region of the Białowieża Forest* (available in Hajnówka's Tourist Information Office). The most interesting is the **Land of Open Shutters** (16km/10 miles from Narew to Puchły) route, which takes you past Orthodox churches, cemeteries with three-bar papal crosses, and 19th-century wooden cottages with ornate wood cravings.

WALKING There are plenty of flat and relatively easy walking routes that you can pick up at the PTTK office. A popular track to get a feel of the primeval forest is the 4km (2.5-mile) **Bison's Rib (Żebra Żubra),** which is dotted with information boards about the plants. The green 11km (6.8-mile) **Wolves' Trail ★** takes you to the Hwoźna Protected Area, which has a similar feel to the SPA.

Where to Stay & Dine

The village has no shortage of guest rooms *(pokoje gościnne),* especially along Waszkiewicza Street. In summer, even the most expensive rooms get snapped up. **Siciliana** (Waszkiewicza 22; ✆ **85/681-25-54**) is a friendly, family-run pizzeria if you want a break from regional specialties, and it's easy on the pockets.

BIAŁOWIEŻA

Best Western Hotel Żubrówka ★★ This four-star number recently expanded its repertoire to include a spa center and a well-designed indoor pool. In the rooms, you'll find tasteful reproduction of mahogany-colored period furniture, complete with shiny brocade bed covers. Its location next door to the PTTK office is ideal, but there is no view to speak of. They make up for that, however, with an ultra-luxurious breakfast (40 zł).

Olgi Gabiec 6. ✆ **85/681-23-03.** Fax 85/681-25-70. www.hotel-zubrowka.pl. 112 units. 420 zł double. AE, DC, MC, V. Parking 29 zł. **Amenities:** Restaurant; cafe; bike rental; indoor pool; spa center. *In room:* Fan, TV, hair dryer, minibar, Wi-Fi (free).

CEM Guest House (CEM Pokoje Gościnne) The park takes good care of the visiting scientists and researchers by putting them up in very clean and respectable rooms that are stashed inside the same complex that houses the Palace Park's museum. The non-scientific communities are welcome to check in, too.

Park Pałacowy 11. ✆ **85/682-97-29.** http://bpn.com.pl. 44 units. 120 zł double. AE, MC, V. Free parking. Car entrance from Zastawa St. **Amenities:** Restaurant; bike rental; sauna.

Hotel & Restauracja Carska ★★ A must for fans of unique hotels, this property is an old railway station constructed for Nicholas II, the last tsar of Russia. The station's waiting room has been converted into an upscale restaurant that is now a gourmand destination. The traditional regional dishes, like *solianka* (a Russian soup) and oatmeal cake (a regional Christmas Eve dessert), can be had at the tables on the platforms by the disused rail tracks. Two duplex suites have been fitted into a water tower, with beds on one level and a spiral staircase up to the luxurious bathroom. There is a ground-floor room in a separate chalet. Though this is the cheapest room, it may just be the most comfortable since you don't have to negotiate any stairs. The adjacent *bania* (Russian sauna), complete with an outdoor wooden barrel tub, is easily the most refined in the region.

Stacja Towarowa 4. ✆ **85/681-21-19** or 602-243-228. www.restauracjacarska.pl. 3 units. 280 zł double; 380 zł–550 zł suite. MC, V. Free parking. **Amenities:** Restaurant; bike rental; *bania* (Russian sauna). *In room:* TV, minibar.

Wejmutka ★ It's the new kid in the neighborhood, but it's giving the competition a run for its money. The rooms are adorned in a folk theme, but not in an overwhelmingly manner. You'll find the bathrooms spotless. Guests can mingle by the fireplace or socialize with the house dogs and cats in the back garden.

Kolejowa 1A. ✆ **85/681-21-17.** www.wejmutka.pl. 20 units. 160 zł double. AE, MC, V. Free parking. **Amenities:** Breakfast room. *In room:* Wi-Fi (free).

AROUND BIAŁOWIEŻA

Pensjonat Sioło Budy ★★ This homestead is for those who want a taste of rural living without forsaking clean toilets and hot showers. Rooms feature wood or cast-iron bedposts, agrarian tools, and a smattering of Russian knick-knacks, such as birch vodka bottles. The "settlement" captures the cultural heritage of the area as intended by the owners, who are folk-history enthusiasts. **Karczma Osocznika,** a barn-style restaurant with long tables and benches for communal feasting, offers deliciously executed regional dishes such as Russian *solanka* soup, bison *bigos* (stew), regional *hałuszki* (a baked potato dish), and *marcinek* layered cream cakes. The prices? Similar to Warsaw's mid-level restaurants. But sipping Obolon, an unfiltered Ukrainian beer, by the campfire while an accordionist playing Belarusian music serenades under a star-speckled sky? Priceless.

Budy 41 (9km/5½ miles west of Białowieża). ✆ **85/681-29-78.** www.siolobudy.pl. 10 units. 198 zł double. No credit cards. Free parking. From Białowieża's PTTK office, take the road toward Narewka. **Amenities:** Restaurant. *In room:* Minibar.

APPENDIX A: FAST FACTS & USEFUL WEBSITES

FAST FACTS: POLAND

American Express The office (Chłodna 51; (✆ **22/581-51-00**) is open weekdays 9am to 7pm and Saturday 10am to 3pm.

Area Codes Poland's country code is 48 (011-48 from the U.S.). Area codes for major cities include: Warsaw (22), Kraków (12), Gdańsk (58), Wrocław (71), Łódź (42), and Lublin (81).

ATMs/Cashpoints See "Money & Costs," p. 38.

Automobile Organizations The Polish Motoring Association (Polski Związek Motorowy/PZM; Kazimierzowska 66; ✆ **22/849-93-61;** www.pzm.pl) is Poland's main automobile club. It promotes road safety, publishes maps, and conducts driving lessons. For visitors, the most useful service is its 24-hour nationwide emergency breakdown hotline: ✆ **9637.**

Business Hours Stores and offices are generally open weekdays 9am to 6pm. Banks are open weekdays 9am to 4pm. Many stores have limited Saturday hours, usually 9am to noon. Large shopping centers and malls are open 7 days a week from 10am until at least 8pm. Museums and other tourist attractions are often closed on Mondays.

Drinking Laws The legal age for buying and consuming alcohol is 18, though ID checks are not common. Alcoholic beverages are widely available and can be bought just about anywhere, including convenience stores, tourist shops, grocery stores, and naturally, in shops specializing in liquor. Though alcohol is easy to get, police take a dim view of public drunkenness, and fines for a night in the drunk tank are steep. The legal blood alcohol limit for driving is 0.02%—approximately one beer. Spot alcohol checks are frequent.

Driving Rules See "Getting There & Getting Around," p. 34.

Electricity Polish outlets follow the continental norm (220V, 50Hz) with two round plugs. Most appliances that run on 110V will require a transformer.

Embassies & Consulates All foreign embassies are located in the capital, Warsaw, though some countries maintain consulates in Kraków and other large cities.

The **United States Embassy** is located at Ujazdowskie 29/31 (✆ **22/625-14-01;** http://poland.usembassy.gov). There's also a **U.S. consulate** in Kraków (Stolarska 9; ✆ **12/424-51-83;** http://krakow.usconsulate.gov).

The **embassy of Australia** is situated on the third floor of the Nautilus building (Nowogrodzka 11; ✆ **22/521-34-44;** www.poland.embassy.gov.au).

The **embassy of Canada** is at ul. Jana Matejki 1/5 (✆ **22/584-31-00;** www.canadainternational.gc.ca).

The **embassy of Ireland** is at Mysia 5 (✆ **22/849-66-33;** www.embassyofireland.pl).

The **embassy of the United Kingdom** is at Kawalerii 12 (✆ **22/311-00-00;** www.ukinpoland.fco.gov.uk).

Emergencies In an emergency, dial the following numbers: **Police** ✆ **997, Fire** ✆ **998, Ambulance** ✆ **999, Road Assistance** ✆ **981** or ✆ 9637 (Polish motoring association/PZM). The general emergency number if using a cell phone is ✆ **112.**

Gasoline (Petrol) Unleaded gasoline, *benzyna,* is widely available; a green-marked tank with "95" is regular octane and "98" is high-test. Most stations are self-serve, but occasionally, you'll still find a gas attendant. He'll fill up your tank and wash your windows, and expect a złoty or two as a tip. Gasoline is sold by the liter, with one U.S. gallon equal to about 3.8 liters. At press time, a liter of gas costs about 4.40 zł.

Holidays Poland observes the following holidays: January 1 (New Year's Day); Easter Sunday and Monday; May 1 (State Holiday); May 3 (Constitution Day); Corpus Christi (ninth Thurs following Easter Sun); August 15 (Assumption); November 1 (All Saints' Day); November 11 (Independence Day); and December 25 and 26 (Christmas). Offices, banks, museums, and many stores are closed on holidays, though some larger stores and restaurants remain open.

Hospitals Medical standards in Poland are generally acceptable, and if something should happen during your trip, you can be confident that you will receive adequate care. In terms of private medical facilities, in Warsaw, the **LIM Medical Center** is centrally located in the Marriott complex and staffs a full range of English-speaking doctors and specialists (Al. Jerozolimskie 65/79; ✆ **22/458-70-00;** www.cmlim.pl). For dentists, the **Austria-Dent-Centre** (Żelazna 54; ✆ **22/654-21-16;** www.austriadent.pl) is highly recommended.

Hotlines The Polish national tourist organization and the police operate a special tourist hotline (✆ **800/200-300**) in season from May through September for visitors to check safety conditions and report dangerous situations. The hotline is available in English, German, and Russian.

Insurance **Medical Insurance** Foreign citizens are obliged to pay for any medical services they receive in Poland, so it's worth checking whether your home health insurance will cover you while you are abroad and, if not, how to supplement your insurance. Insurance providers offer a wide range of policies that are cost-effective and valuable for travelers.

Canadians should check with their provincial health plan offices or contact **Health Canada** (✆ **866/225-0709;** www.hc-sc.gc.ca) to find out the extent of their coverage and what documentation and receipts they must take home in case they are treated abroad.

Travelers from the U.K. should carry their **European Health Insurance Card (EHIC),** which replaced the E111 form as proof of entitlement to free/reduced cost medical treatment abroad (✆ **845/605-0707,** or 44/191-212-7500 from abroad; www.ehic.org.uk). Note, however, that the EHIC covers only "necessary medical treatment," and for repatriation costs, lost money, baggage, or trip cancellation, travel insurance from a reputable company should always be sought (www.travelinsuranceweb.com).

Travel Insurance The cost of travel insurance varies widely, depending on the destination, the cost and length of your trip, your age and health, and the type of trip you're taking, but expect to pay between 5% and 8% of the vacation itself. You can get estimates from various providers through InsureMyTrip.com. Enter your trip cost and dates, your age, and other information for prices from more than a dozen companies.

U.K. citizens and their families who make more than one trip abroad per year may find an annual travel insurance policy works out cheaper. Check www.moneysupermarket.com, which compares prices across a wide range of providers for single- and multi-trip policies.

Most big travel agents offer their own insurance and will probably try to sell you their package when you book a holiday. Think before you sign. Britain's Consumers' Association recommends that you insist on seeing the policy and reading the fine print before buying travel insurance. The Association of British Insurers (✆ **020/7600-3333;** www.abi.org.uk) gives advice by phone and publishes *Holiday Insurance,* a free guide to policy provisions and prices. You might also shop around for better deals: Try Columbus Direct (✆ **0870/033-9988;** www.columbusdirect.net).

Trip Cancellation Insurance Trip-cancellation insurance will help retrieve your money if you have to back out of a trip or depart early, or if your travel supplier goes bankrupt. Trip cancellation traditionally covers such events as sickness, natural disasters, and State Department advisories. The latest news in trip-cancellation insurance is the availability of expanded hurricane coverage and the "any-reason" cancellation coverage—which costs more but covers cancellations made for any reason. You won't get back 100% of your prepaid trip cost, but you'll be refunded a substantial portion. **TravelSafe** (✆ **800/523-8020;** www.travelsafe.com) offers both types of coverage. Expedia also offers any-reason cancellation coverage for its air/hotel packages. For details, contact one of the following recommended insurers: **Access America** (✆ **800/284-8300;** www.accessamerica.com); **Travel Guard International** (✆ **800/826-4919;** www.travelguard.com); **Travel Insured International** (✆ **800/243-3174;** www.travelinsured.com); and **Travelex Insurance Services** (✆ **800/228-9792;** www.travelex-insurance.com).

Internet Access Internet cafes are ubiquitous throughout Warsaw, Kraków, and other large cities. Internet cafes generally charge around 6 zł per hour of Internet use. Many hotels now set aside at least one public computer for guests to use. Nearly all hotels these days offer some type of in-room Internet access, either via LAN connection or wireless, and a growing number of cafes offer wireless Internet, though connections can be spotty.

Legal Aid The police are authorized to collect fines on the spot for minor infractions, such as speeding. It's usually futile to try to argue your case, and you're best advised simply to pay the fine and move on. For more serious crimes, there are few legal resources at your disposal. Contact your local embassy or consulate immediately.

Lost & Found Be sure to alert all of your credit card companies the minute you discover your wallet has been lost or stolen, and file a report at the nearest police precinct. Your credit card company or insurer may require a police report number or record of the loss. Most credit card companies have an emergency toll-free number to call if your card is lost or stolen; they may be able to wire you a cash advance immediately or deliver an emergency credit card in a day or two. In Poland, to report a lost or stolen Visa, call ✆ **800/111-15-69;** MasterCard, call ✆ **800/111-12-11.** To report a lost Amex card, call ✆ **22/581-51-00** during business hours.

If you need emergency cash over the weekend when all banks and American Express offices are closed, you can have money wired to you via Western Union (www.westernunion.com), which maintains offices throughout Poland.

Mail Postal rates vary by weight, and it's always safest to have letters weighed at the post office in order to ensure the proper postage. The rate for mailing a postcard or light letter abroad will run about 4 zł. The postal service is generally reliable, but don't trust it for highly valuable packages or letters that simply must arrive. For that, use FedEx, DHL, or another trackable delivery service.

Measurements Poland uses the metric system. See the chart on the inside front cover of this book for details on converting metric measurements to nonmetric equivalents.

Medical Conditions Be sure to bring along extra quantities of any prescription medications you will need on your trip. Poland's pharmacies are well stocked, but the pharmacist may not recognize your doctor's prescription. Also, know the generic term for the drug (e.g. acetaminophen for Tylenol) since brand names can differ in different countries.

Newspapers & Magazines You'll find newspapers and magazines widely available at kiosks in city centers and at train and bus stations, though most kiosks stock only Polish titles. English newspapers and magazines usually available include the *International Herald Tribune,* the *Wall Street Journal, The Economist, The Financial Times,* and *The Guardian.* In terms of local English publications, Warsaw has a few, including the weekly *Warsaw Voice* and the monthly *Warsaw Insider. The Warsaw Business Journal* is a weekly publication on market news. *New Poland Express* is a weekly electronic publication; you can subscribe to at www.newpolandexpress.pl. Also, keep an eye out for regular editions of the irreverent *Poland In Your Pocket* city guides for Warsaw, Kraków, Gdańsk, Łódź, Katowice, and Wrocław. You can usually find them at tourist information offices or in lobbies of large hotels.

Passports The websites listed provide downloadable passport applications, as well as the current fees for processing applications. For an up-to-date, country-by-country listing of passport requirements around the world, go to the "International Travel" tab of the U.S. State Department at http://travel.state.gov. Allow plenty of time before your trip to apply for a passport; processing normally takes 4 to 6 weeks (3 weeks for expedited service) but can take longer during busy periods (especially spring). And keep in mind that if you need a passport in a hurry, you'll pay a higher processing fee.

For Residents of Australia You can pick up an application from your local post office or any branch of Passports Australia, but you must schedule an interview at the passport office to present your application materials. Call the **Australian Passport Information Service** (✆ **131-232**), or visit the government website (www.passports.gov.au).

For Residents of Canada Passport applications are available at travel agencies throughout Canada or from the central **Passport Office** (Department of Foreign Affairs and International Trade, Alberta, ON K1A 0G3; ✆ **800/567-6868;** www.ppt.gc.ca). ***Note:*** Canadian children who travel must have their own passport.

For Residents of Ireland You can apply for a 10-year passport at the **Passport Office** (Setanta Centre, Molesworth Street, Dublin 2; ✆ **01/671-1633;** www.foreignaffairs.gov.ie). Those under age 18 and over 65 must apply for a 3-year passport. You can also apply at 1A South Mall, Cork (✆ **21/494-4700**) or at most main post offices.

For Residents of New Zealand You can pick up a passport application at any New Zealand Passports Office or download it from their website. Contact the **Passports Office** in New Zealand (✆ **0800/225-050** or 04/474-8100) or log on to www.dia.govt.nz.

For Residents of the United Kingdom To pick up an application for a standard 10-year passport (5-yr. passport for children under 16), visit your nearest passport office, major post office, or travel agency, or contact the **United Kingdom Passport Service** (✆ **0300/222-0000**) or search its website at www.ips.gov.uk.

Police The police emergency number is ✆ **997.** If calling from a mobile phone, dial ✆ **112.**

Smoking Smoking rates tend to be higher in Poland than in the U.S., though increasingly, cafes and restaurants are setting aside more tables for nonsmokers. Many hotels are now completely smoke-free, and almost all hotels offer nonsmoking rooms or rooms that are on totally nonsmoking floors. Be sure to request this in advance.

Taxes All taxes, including a 22% value added tax levied on most goods and excise duties on tobacco, alcohol, and gasoline, are already calculated in the purchase price. Buyers with permanent residency outside the European Union are entitled to reclaim VAT on purchases above 200 zł, provided the goods are permanently taken out of the EU within 3 months from the date of purchase. Look for shops with "Tax Free Shopping" in the window for details.

Telephones Poland's country code is 48. To dial Poland from abroad, dial the international access code (for example, 011 in the U.S.), plus 48, and then the local Poland area code (minus the zero). The area code for Warsaw is 22. To call long distance within Poland, dial the area code, plus the number. To dial abroad from Poland, dial 00 and then the country code and area code to where you are calling. A call to the U.S. or Canada would begin 00-1.

Telegraph, Telex & Fax You'll find Western Union outlets throughout Poland for wiring money or to have it wired to you quickly, but this service can cost as much as 15% to 20% of the amount sent.

Most hotels have fax machines available for guest use (be sure to ask about the charge to use it).

Time Poland is in the Central European Time zone (CET), 1 hour ahead of GMT and 6 hours ahead of the eastern United States. Daylight Saving Time is in effect from early spring until late autumn. Daylight Saving Time moves the clock 1 hour ahead of Standard Time.

Tipping In restaurants, round up the bill by 10% to reward good service. Bellhops, taxi drivers, and tour guides will also expect a small amount in return for services rendered. Around 5 zł to 10 zł is usually enough under any circumstances.

Toilets Public toilets are a relative rarity, so you'll find yourself seeking out nearby restaurants or hotels, and asking to use the facilities. This is usually not a problem. Some establishments will charge 1 zł for the privilege. Service stations and other places often have toilets available for free or a nominal fee. Some public toilets still use the older symbols to designate men's and women's facilities: men are upside-down triangles; women are circles.

Useful Phone Numbers U.S. Dept. of State Travel Advisory: ✆ **202/647-5225** (in the U.S.; manned 24 hr.). U.S. Passport Agency: ✆ **202/647-0518** (in the U.S.). Poland Traveler's Hotline: ✆ **800/200-300.**

Visas Visitors from the U.S., Canada, the U.K., Australia, and New Zealand do not require visas for stays under 90 days. Nationals of other countries should consult the Polish Ministry of Foreign Affairs (general and visa information; www.msz.gov.pl) or contact the Polish embassy in their home country.

Water Tap water is generally safe, but you may think twice about drinking from taps in older buildings with rusty pipes. If you're concerned, let the water run a few seconds before drinking. Bottled water is cheap and widely available.

AIRLINE WEBSITES

Air France
www.airfrance.com

Alitalia
www.alitalia.com

American Airlines
www.aa.com

Austrian Airlines
www.aua.com

British Airways
www.britishairways.com

Continental Airlines
www.continental.com

CSA Czech Airlines
www.czechairlines.com

Delta Air Lines/Northwest Airlines
www.delta.com

Finnair
www.finnair.com

LOT
www.lot.com

Lufthansa
www.lufthansa.com

Qantas Airways
www.qantas.com

Swiss International Air Lines
www.swiss.com

United Airlines
www.united.com

US Airways
www.usairways.com

BUDGET AIRLINES

Air Berlin
www.airberlin.com

BMI Baby
www.bmibaby.com

easyJet
www.easyjet.com

Germanwings
www.germanwings.com

Jet2.com
www.jet2.com

Ryanair
www.ryanair.com

WizzAir
www.wizzair.com

APPENDIX B: USEFUL TERMS & PHRASES

BASIC VOCABULARY

There are a fair number of English speakers around, and nearly all hotels, tourist offices, and restaurants will be able to manage some English.

ENGLISH–POLISH PHRASES

English	Polish	Pronunciation
Hello/Good day	**Dzień dobry**	Djeen *doh*-bree
Yes	**Tak**	Tahk
No	**Nie**	Nee-yeh
Hi! or Bye! (informal)	**Cześć!**	Chesh-ch
Good evening	**Dobry wieczór**	*Doh*-bree *vyeh*-choor
Goodbye	**Do widzenia**	*Doh* vee-*djen*-ya
Good night	**Dobranoc**	Doh-*brah*-nohts
Thank you	**Dziękuję**	Djem-*koo*-yeh
Excuse me/Sorry	**Przepraszam**	Pshe-*pra*-sham
Please/you're welcome	**Proszę**	*Proh*-sheh
How are you? (informal)	**Jak się masz?**	*Yahk* sheh mahsh?
How are you? (formal)	**Jak się pan (to a man)/ pani (to a woman) ma?**	*Yahk* sheh pahn/pah-nee mah?
Fine	**Dobrze**	Dohb-zheh
Do you speak English?	**Czy pan/pani mówi po angielsku?**	Chee pahn/pah-nee *moo*-vee poh ahng-*yel*-skoo?
I don't understand	**Nie rozumiem**	Ne-yeh roh-*zoom*-yem
How much is it?	**Ile kosztuje?**	Eel-eh kosh-*too*-yeh?
Menu	**Menu**	Men-yoo
The bill, please	**Poproszę o rachunek**	*Proh*-sheh oh *rahk*-oo-nek
Cheers!	**Na zdrowie**	Nah-*zdroh*-vyeh
Bon appétit!	**Smacznego**	Smahch-*neh*-go
Where is . . . ?	**Gdzie jest . . . ?**	Gjye yest. .?
the station	**dworzec**	*Dvoh*-zhets
a hotel	**hotel**	*Hoe*-tel
a restaurant	**restauracja**	Res-to-*ra*-tia
the toilet	**toaleta**	Toy-*le*-ta

B

English	Polish	Pronunciation
Do you have . . . ?	**Czy jest. .?**	Chee yest . . . ?
When?	**Kiedy?**	*Kye*-day
What?	**Co?**	Tso
Today	**Dziś/Dzisiaj**	Jeesh/*jee*-shay
Tomorrow	**Jutro**	*Yoo*-tro
Yesterday	**Wczoraj**	*Fcho*-ray
Good	**Dobry**	*Doh*-bree
Bad	**Niedobry**	Nee-yeh *dob*-bree
More	**Więcej**	*vyen*-tsay
Less	**Mniej**	*Mer*-nyey

DAYS & MONTHS

Poniedziałek (po-nye-*jya*-wek) Monday
Wtorek (*fto*-rek) Tuesday
Środa (*shro*-da) Wednesday
Czwartek (*chfar*-tek) Thursday
Piątek (*pyon*-tek) Friday
Sobota (So-*bo*-ta) Saturday
Niedziela (nye-*jye*-la) Sunday

Styczeń (*sti*-chen) January
Luty (*loo*-ti) February
Marzec (*ma*-zhets) March
Kwiecień (*kfye*-chen) April
Maj (mai) May
Czerwiec (*cher*-vyets) June
Lipiec (*lee*-pyets) July
Sierpień (*sher*-pyen) August
Wrzesień (*vzhe*-shen) September
Październik (pazh-*jyer*-neek) October
Listopad (lees-*to*-pat) November
Grudzień (*groo*-jyen) December

Rano (*ra*-no) In the morning
Po południu (po po-*wood*-nyoo) In the afternoon
Wieczorem (vye-*cho*-rem) In the evening

GENERAL

Apteka Pharmacy
Brama Gate
Cmentarz Cemetery
Cukiernia Cake shop
Dolina Valley
Dom House
Droga Road
Dwór Country manor
Dworzec Station
Główny Main, as in *Dworzec Główny* (Main Station)
Góra/Góry Mountain/mountains
Granica Border
Jaskinia Cave
Jezioro Lake
Kantor Currency exchange office
Katedra Cathedral
Kawiarnia Cafe
Kemping Camping
Kino Cinema
Klasztor Monastery
Kościół Church
Księgarnia Bookshops
Miasto Town
Most Bridge
Ogród Garden
Piekarnia Bakery
Plaża Beach
Poczta Post Office
Pogotowie Emergency
Pokój Room
Policja Police
Prom Ferry
Przystanek Bus stop
Ratusz Town hall
Restauracja Restaurant

Rynek Market/town square
Skansen Open-air museum
Stary Old, as in *Stary Miasto* (Old Town)
Teatr Theater
Ulica Street. Abbreviated to ul.
Wieża Tower
Zajazd Inn
Zamek Castle
Zdrój Spa

NUMBERS

1 **Jeden** (*ye*-den)
2 **Dwa** (dvah)
3 **Trzy** (tshi)
4 **Cztery** (*chte*-ri)
5 **Pięć** (pyench)
6 **Sześć** (sheshch)
7 **Siedem** (*she*-dem)
8 **Osiem** (*oh*-shem)
9 **Dziewięć** (*jye*-vyench)
10 **Dziesięć** (*jye*-shench)
11 **Jedenaście** (ye-den-*nash*-che)
12 **Dwanaście** (dva-*nash*-che)
15 **Piętnaście** (pyent-*nash*-che)
20 **Dwadzieścia** (dva-*jyesh*-cha)
30 **Trzydzieści** (tshi-*jyesh*-chee)
50 **Pięćdziesiąt** (pyen-*jye*-shont)
100 **Sto** (sto)
1,000 **Tysiąc** (*tee*-shonts)

SIGNS

Ciągnąć/Pchać Push/Pull
Dla panów/Męski Men
Dla pań/Damski Women
Kasa Ticket office, cashier
Nieczynny Closed, out of order
Nie dotykać Do not touch
Nie palić No smoking
Otwarty/Zamknięty Open/Closed
Toalety Toilets
Uwaga Caution
Wejście/Wyjścia Entrance/Exit
Wolny Vacant
Występ wzbroniony No entrance
Zajęty Occupied

MENU TERMS

GENERAL TERMS

Filiżanka Cup
Gotowany Boiled
Grill/z rusztu Grilled
Łyżka Spoon
Marynowany Pickled
Mielone Minced
Nadziewany Stuffed/Filled
Nóż Knife
Pieczeń Roast
Słodki Sweet
Słony Salty
Surowy Raw
Świeży Fresh
Talerz Plate
Wędzony Smoked
Widelec Fork

BASIC FOODS

Bułka Rolls
Chleb Bread
Cukier Sugar
Drób Poultry
Frytki French fries/Chips
Grzyby Mushroom
Jajko Eggs
Jarzyny/warzywa Vegetables
Kanapka Sandwich
Kiełbasa Sausage
Makaron Noodles, pasta
Masło Butter
Ocet Vinegar
Olej Oil
Orzechy Nuts
Owoce Fruits
Pieprz Pepper
Ryby Fish
Ryż Rice
Ser Cheese

Śmietana Cream
Sól Salt
Surówka Salad
Szaszłyk Shish kebab
Twaróg Cottage cheese
Zupa Soup

BEVERAGES

Gorąca czekolada Hot chocolate
Herbata Tea
Kawa Coffee
Biała White
Czarna Black
Miód pitny Mead
Mleko Milk
Piwo Beer
Sok Juice
Sok jabłkowy Apple juice
Sok pomarańczowy Orange juice
Wino Wine
Białe White
Czerwone Red
Słodkie Sweet
Wytrane Dry
Woda Water
Gazowana Sparkling
Niegazowana Still
Mineralna Mineral
Wódka Vodka

CAKES & DESSERTS

Budyń Milk pudding
Ciastko Cake/slice of cake
Ciasto drożdżowe Sweet yeast bread
Czekolada Chocolate
Lody Ice cream
Makowiec Poppyseed cake
Pączki Donuts
Sernik Cheesecake
Szarlotka Polish-style apple pie
Tort Layered cream cake

FISH, MEAT & POULTRY

Baranina Mutton
Bażant Pheasant
Boczek Bacon
Cielęcina Veal
Dorada Sea bass
Dorsz Cod
Dziczyzna Game
Dzik Wild boar
Gęś Geese
Golonka Leg of pork
Indyk Turkey
Jagnięcina Lamb
Kaczka Duck
Karp Carp
Kotlet schabowy Breaded pork cutlet
Kurczak Chicken
Łosoś Salmon
Makrela Mackerel
Pasztet Pâté
Polędwica Tenderloin
Pstrąg Trout
Sarnina Venison
Śledź Herring
Szynka Ham
Wątróbka Liver
Węgorz Eel
Wieprzowina Pork
Wołowina Beef
Zając Hare
Żeberka Ribs

FRUITS, GRAINS, NUTS & VEGETABLES

Buraczki Beetroot
Cebula Onion
Cytryna Lemon
Czarne porzeczki Blackcurrant
Czereśnie Wild cherries
Czosnek Garlic
Fasola Beans
Groch Lentils
Gruszka Pears
Grzyby Mushrooms
Jabłko Apple
Kalafior Cauliflower
Kapusta Cabbage
Kapusta kiszona Sauerkraut

Kasza Gryczana Buckwheat
Kurki Chanterelle
Maliny Raspberries
Migdały Almonds
Morele Apricots
Ogórek Cucumber
Orzechy włoskie Walnuts
Pieczarki Button mushroom
Pomarańcze Orange
Pomidor Tomato
Śliwka Plum
Szparagi Asparagus
Truskawki Strawberries
Winogrona Grapes
Wiśnia Cherries
Ziemniaki Potatoes

MEALS

Śniadanie Breakfast
Obiad Lunch
Kolacja Dinner
Na miesjcu Eating on premises (as opposed to take away)
Na wynos Take away

MENU GLOSSARY

Barszcz or barszcz czerwony A clear broth made from beetroot, sometimes comes with pasta pieces.
Barszcz ukraiński White borscht.
Bigos Hunter's stew made from pickled cabbage, sausage, and sometimes game meat.
Bryndza A soft cheese made from sheep's milk.
Chłodnik A summer cold soup; pink, creamy, and made from young beets.
Ćwikła z chrzanem A slightly sharp condiment made from beetroot and horseradish served with meats and cold cuts.
Gołąbki Cabbage leaves stuffed with a mixture of rice, minced meat, and sometimes mushroom. A Polish version of the Greek *dolma.*
Grochówka Bean soup, sometimes served with sausage.
Jajecznica Scrambled eggs.
Kajmak A thick and sweet light brown mixture made from milk and sugar. It is often added to cakes, tarts, and *mazurek.*
Kapuśniak A very sour pickled cabbage soup.
Kartoflanka Potato soup.
Kawa po turecku Poland's rendition of Turkish-style coffee where coffee grounds are added to a glass and hot water is poured directly on top.
Kisiel A jelly-like dessert made from milk and corn or potato starch.
Knedle A steamed bread bun. The sweet version is stuffed with prunes (*z sliwkami*).
Kompot A syrupy drink made from boiled fruit.
Kopytka A kind of potato dumpling that is similar to gnocchi.
Kotlet Schabowy A breaded pork cutlet that is a national staple.
Krupnik A clear soup made from barley, it often comes with boiled vegetables and chunks of meat.
Leniwe pierogi Similar to *kopytka* but made with cottage cheese, usually a dessert.
Makowiec A sweet poppy seed roll, usually a Christmas and Easter treat but available year-round.
Mazurek A dessert for Easter, but available year-round. The shortcrust pastry is topped with *kajmak* or chocolate and decorated with dried fruit.

Mizeria A salad of thinly sliced cucumbers dressed with cream and dill.

Naleśniki z serem Pancakes filled with cottage cheese.

Nalewka Vodka infused with fruits, nuts, spices, or herbs.

Oscypek Smoked cheese from the Tatry region, usually made from a combination of sheep's and cow's milk.

Pierogi Dumplings, usually filled with minced meat, cabbage, and mushroom. Sweet versions are stuffed with seasonal fruit such as strawberries (z *truskawkami*) and blueberries (z *jadodami*).

Pierogi "Ruskie" A savory *pierogi* stuffed with potato and cottage cheese and served with fried onions.

Pyzy Steamed bread bun.

Racuchy Fruit fritters; the most traditional is made from apples.

Rosół A clear chicken broth.

Sztuka mięsa Literally, it means a piece of meat. It's normally boiled pork or beef, served plain with sauce.

Zrazy zawijane Beef roulade, normally filled with a mixture of vegetables, bacon, and mushrooms.

Żurek A sourish soup made from fermented rye. Often comes with potatoes and sausage.

Index

See also Accommodations and Restaurant indexes, below.

General Index

A

B

C

D

E

F

G

H

I

J

K

Accommodations

Restaurants